# BUSINESS ANALYTICS

## APPLICATIONS TO CONSUMER MARKETING

# BUSINESS ANALYTICS

## APPLICATIONS TO CONSUMER MARKETING

*Sandhya Kuruganti*

*Hindol Basu*

McGraw Hill Education (India) Private Limited

Published by McGraw Hill Education (India) Private Limited,
444/1, Sri Ekambara Naicker Industrial Estate, Alapakkam, Porur, Chennai 600116,
Tamil Nadu, India.

**Business Analytics: Applications to Consumer Marketing**



Third reprint 2020
**RLDLYYRYPDQAAC**



**ISBN (13 digits): 978-93-5134-159-8**
**ISBN (10 digits): 93-5134-159-3**

**04 05 06 07 08 RAJ 24 23 22 21 20**

Managing Director: *Lalit Singh*
General Manager—Production: *Rajender P Ghansela*
Manager—Production: *Reji Kumar*



Typeset at White Lotus Infotech Pvt. Ltd., Puducherry, and,
Printed and Bound in India at Rajkamal Electric Press, Plot No. 2, Phase – IV, Kundli,
Sonepat, Haryana.

Visit us at: www.mheducation.co.in ; (Toll free in India): **1800 103 5875**
Write to us at: info.india@mheducation.com

CIN: U80302TN2010PTC111532

*In loving memory of my father*
*Professor K. Krishnamurty*

*—Sandhya*

*To my little*
*Rupkatha*

*—Hindol*

# Preface

## Introduction to Business Analytics

Today we see an explosion of data around us, with an exponential increase in the volume, velocity and variety of data. Global data volume is expected to grow at a CAGR of 41 percent during 2009–2020 and is estimated to be 35 Zettabytes (ZB) by 2020[1]. As per market estimates there were close to 7 billion mobile phone subscribers in the world[2] in 2014, MasterCard and Visa processed a total of 97.1 billion transactions in 2013[3], and Wal-Mart handles more than 1 million customer transactions every hour[4]. Each of these statistics points to the staggering amount of information that gets generated every minute in the information economy. Today data is seen as an asset that provides competitive advantage and delivers superior returns. According to an Economist Intelligence survey[5], 9 out of 10 business leaders believe that data is now the fourth factor of production. Over half the senior leaders interviewed as part of the survey were of the opinion that management decisions based purely on intuition or experience are increasingly being regarded as suboptimal. Furthermore, 65 percent emphasized that more and more, management decisions are being based on "hard analytic information". This point is further corroborated by an extensive global study conducted by Accenture[6]. An important finding of this research is that one of the key success factors that make a company a high performance business and a market leader is the use of data and

---

[1] "The Next Big Thing", *Business Standard*, Print Edition, Dec 20, 2012.

[2] International Telecommunication Union, https://www.itu.int/en/ITU-D/Statistics/Documents/facts/ICTFactsFigures2014-e.pdf.

[3] As per annual reports of MasterCard and Visa, investor.mastercard.com/files/doc_financials/annual/2013-MasterCard-AR.PDF; http://investor.visa.com/files/doc_downloads/annual%20meeting/Visa%20Annual%20Report%20 2013%20final%20website.pdf.

[4] "Data, Data Everywhere", *The Economist*, Feb 25, 2010.

[5] "The Deciding Factor: Big Data & Decision-Making", A Global Survey and Report from *The Economist Intelligence Unit* commissioned by Capgemini, June 2012.

[6] "Analytics is the Key to Better Business Decisions", Q&A: Jeanne Harris, Senior Executive, Accenture's Institute for High Performance, *The Strategist – Business Standard*, Nov 8, 2010.

information for improved decision-making; this relationship was found to be true for 19 different industries in 35 different countries.

According to analytics visionary Professor Davenport, "business analytics" is defined as the broad use of data and quantitative analysis for decision making within organisations. Specifically, business analytics involves leveraging data for the purpose of drawing actionable insights and conclusions, and for predicting business outcomes. The application of business analytics for driving marketing strategies has delivered substantial incremental returns for companies and its shareholders across industries. Capital One, a leading financial services company that relies heavily on analytics, witnessed at least a 20 percent growth in earnings per share every year over its first decade, ever since it went public[7]. Sprint, a telecom operator realised more than USD 1 billion of value and USD 500 million in incremental revenue over five years, through analytically driven strategies. American Airlines was able to increase its revenue by more than USD 1 billion in the first three years, post the implementation of a dynamic pricing strategy. Proctor and Gamble used operations research methods to save the company USD 1.2 billion in inventory costs.

In the context of an emerging market, "The analytics market in India, which clocked revenues of about USD 1 billion in FY2014, is slated to more than double to reach USD 2.3 billion by 2018", according to the findings of a study launched at NASSCOM Big Data & Analytics Summit 2014.

## Introduction to Book

Over the last few decades, marketing professionals and academic experts have embraced the customer centric approach to marketing, whereby marketing is no more looked at as a set of isolated processes, but as a continuum of activities centered around the customer. The customer centric approach propels businesses to put the customer at the centre of marketing strategy and take a holistic view of the customer, while designing every component of the marketing strategy. Consequently, the book leverages the customer centric approach for illustrating the application of analytical approaches aimed at enhancing customer lifetime value.

The book navigates through the customer life cycle starting from initiation of the relationship with the customer, following through the phase of relationship deepening, and finally customer retention. Industries such as financial services and telecom receive wider attention in the book as the customer life cycle approach is being extensively used in these industries for formulating marketing strategies. Travel and entertainment, and retail are referenced in areas where these sectors have been early adopters of some key analytical initiatives.

[7] The financial results presented in this paragraph are referenced from the book by Davenport and Harris, *Competing on Analytics*.

While most organisations certainly value the potential benefits of an analytically driven business strategy, many face challenges in effectively turning information into actionable insights. From the perspective of a business manager, answers to questions such as: Why is analytics needed? How will the results be used? and What are the incremental financial benefits? are critical for the successful implementation of analytics. The experience of practitioners and academicians also suggests that business analytics is not always an exact science, as it involves the art of analysing data and synthesizing business knowledge and judgement with quantitative results. However, from a practitioner's perspective the technical details sometimes tend to receive more attention.

Academicians and practitioners have been looking at methodologies that could help them in making sense out of the huge mountain of data at their disposal. However, some of the important academic advancements in the area of analytics, which belong to the larger realm of decision sciences, are yet to be completely understood and adapted by industry.

The book is designed as a reference that links quantitative analysis to business applications in an easy-to-understand fashion, so as to address the strategic imperatives of analytics. The current work adopts an approach whereby the business objective is taken as the starting point in the exploration of an analytical strategy, and the quantitative analysis has been presented within the context of a business objective and not as stand-alone methodologies. Examples across financial services, insurance, telecom, retail, utilities, and airlines have been used to showcase the critical value of analytics for formulating marketing strategies. The book also attempts to leverage academic literature to illustrate the successful practice of evolving research in this area for business applications. The financial benefits resulting from the implementation of an analytical solution are presented through numerical examples from credible sources, wherever available.

## Organisation of the Book

The book has been organised along the customer life cycle and analytical strategies have been presented with reference to each stage of the customer life cycle. The customer life cycle starts with the acquisition of new customers, followed by strategies of enhancing value of existing customers through usage enhancement and cross-sell. It is also important that customers do not end or reduce the depth of their relationship with the firm and hence, managing attrition is yet another important aspect of customer life cycle management. Therefore, acquiring the right customer and managing existing customers are the two key levers of enhancing customer value.

*Acquisition:* The book begins by describing the application of analytics for designing new customer acquisition strategy. All analytical strategies hinge upon availability of the right data. However, data on prospects is much more limited compared to existing customers. Hence the chapter on acquisition provides an initial overview of the data sources available for designing a data driven acquisition strategy. The explanation of the common data sources is followed by methodologies of how these data sources are used for creating an acquisition strategy.

*Usage Management and Cross-Sell:* Following customer acquisition, the firm attempts to enhance customer value by deepening the relationship with existing customers. Two most common strategies for enhancing existing customer value are usage management and cross-sell. Post initiation of the relationship with the firm, customers start using the products and services of the firm. The pattern of usage generates a wealth of data that could be leveraged along with other customer information for designing optimal strategies for activation, usage and loyalty programs, and for identifying the right products to cross-sell to an existing customer. The chapters on usage management and cross-sell are focussed on using analytics for enhancing customer value.

*Retention Management:* While it is important to acquire the right customer and to ensure that the firm is able to derive the maximum value from an existing customer, it is also equally important that the customer does not terminate his/her relationship with the firm. The chapter on retention describes how data on existing customers can be best used for reducing voluntary attrition and increasing customer tenure.

*Pricing:* Firms use a variety of marketing tools to drive their marketing objectives, a combination of all these tools have been defined as the marketing mix. Broadly, marketing mix consists of four components namely Product, Price, Place (distribution) and Promotion or the 4Ps, as they are called in marketing parlance. Each of these components represents a multitude of marketing tools that can be leveraged by the marketer. Of these 4Ps, price is the most flexible marketing mix element. Price is one of the most visible elements of the marketing mix and the key determinant of buyer's choice. Price is also an important determinant of profitability for the firm. The chapter on pricing dwells upon the usage of analytics for determining the right price for both prospects and existing customers.

*Credit Bureau:* In the current economic environment, the sale of most products and services involve a credit extension to the customer. Effective information sharing between companies within and across industries has evolved as an effective mechanism for minimising credit and fraud risk. Credit bureau is one of the most important data sources, particularly for the consumer financial services industry. The chapter on credit bureau outlines the structure of credit bureau data and the use of the same for designing analytical strategies for customer acquisition and existing customer management.

*Quantitative Methods:* Quantitative methods are the building blocks of any analytical strategy. The chapter on quantitative methods outlines the frequently used quantitative techniques that are of importance for designing an analytical marketing strategy. While elaborating, care has been taken to ensure that the explanations are not "too technical". Application oriented examples have been used to illustrate the concepts and usage of each of these methodologies.

*Analytics Ecosystem:* It is critical for organisations to realise that analytics is not a standalone discipline. It needs an ecosystem to survive and deliver incremental business value. This fact becomes even more important because analytics is a much more recent addition to the list of disciplines that are critical to the organisation's success. The last chapter on analytics ecosystem describes the supporting processes and technologies that are needed for the successful implementation of analytics. Along with the many facilitators of an analytical strategy, the chapter also focuses on the data warehouse, which is the primary source of internal data.

## Target Audience

The primary aim of the book is to act as a bridge over the huge chasm that divides theory and practice. Practicing business managers and analysts would find this book useful for understanding how best they can harness the power of analytics for making better and more objective decisions in the area of marketing. The extensive references and illustrations of academic research in the book would allow analytics experts to adapt some of the already proven academic research into practice. Students of management and quantitative disciplines will find the book useful for obtaining a view of how business analytics is used in real life. The book would also facilitate the transition from academia to a corporate environment. Data warehousing and business intelligence professionals can expect to gain an understanding of how analytics can be embedded into their offerings. For the benefit of readers, the chapters have been written in such a manner that prior background in quantitative subjects such as mathematics or statistics is not a must to follow the book.

SANDHYA KURUGANTI
HINDOL BASU

Acknowledgements

The concept of this book germinated during our initial years of analytics team building and training responsibilities in the financial services industry. The idea was further encouraged by the absence of an applied analytics reference book to refer to. Since then, it has taken us several years to finally see our vision fructify into reality. Writing the book has indeed been an enriching experience and this endeavour would not have crossed the finish line without the cooperation of our colleagues, friends and families.

We are thankful for the valuable feedback on the manuscript shared by our colleagues. Our special thanks to Nirmalya Acharya, Arun Aggarwal, Nitin Agarwal, Firoz Anam, Ramanuj Bagchi, Anindya Chaudhuri, Nitin Jain, Sunandha Karthik, Suddha Sattwa Kundu, Subhankar Mukherjee, Amey Pathak, Sayan Sen, Rupesh Shetty, and Naga Prashanth Tumuluri. We are obliged to friends, Vasavi Ramachandran of Stanford University and Professor Madhu Kalimipalli of Wilfrid Laurier University, for helping us with academic references. Our thanks to Padmapriya Shetty for her valuable support on illustrations.

We are grateful to the editorial team at McGraw Hill Education for their patience and partnership. In particular, we would like to thank Mitadru Basu and Rita Sarkar for their cooperation.

We are deeply indebted to our families for their moral support during this long journey. Sandhya's father, who was also her mentor and role model, had been the inspiration for initiating the proposal relating to this manuscript. Sandhya wishes to convey her deepest gratitude to her mother for being a silent pillar of strength. She could not have endured the challenges of writing this book without the patient support and guidance of her husband Arvind and his extended family. Sandhya would also like to gratefully acknowledge her teachers and family friends for believing in her—Professors K.L. Krishna, V.N. Pandit and P. Venkatramaiah.

Hindol would like to thank his wife Anwesha for her constant involvement and encouragement, without which this book would not have seen the light of the day. Hindol would also like to thank his parents for their moral support. He is deeply indebted to his colleagues, seniors and team members for stimulating a plethora of exciting ideas, which have been the key building blocks for the book.

SANDHYA KURUGANTI
HINDOL BASU

# Contents

ONE

# Acquisition

## 1.1 Introduction

Competition in the current economic scenario has caused major changes in business strategies; product-centric or process-centric strategies of yesteryears have been replaced by customer-centric strategies where the customer is the key element of the value creation process. Today the valuation of a firm is driven largely by the volume and value of their customer base. Hence, creation, enhancement, and maintenance of customer value have come to be recognised as the cornerstone of enhancing firm valuation in the new economy.

Traditional marketing have been focussing on the volume of the customer base. Over time, firms have realised that every customer is not equally valuable for the firm. This has led most companies to follow a segment-driven strategy, whereby the focus has shifted to creating a relationship with the right customer who will provide the maximum value to the firm. Companies have also started to focus on customer lifetime value instead of a transactional approach.

As a parallel, development firms have also realised that every customer or prospect is different and hence, one-to-one marketing has become the norm of the day and has replaced the traditional "one-size-fits-all" strategy. The confluence of these two developments has resulted in the adoption of analytical and data-driven strategies that facilitate a deeper understanding of customer need and the intrinsic value of each customer.

Closely related to this customer-centric thinking is the idea of the customer life cycle. Marketers across industries have started to adopt the customer life cycle approach, whereby the focus is on effectively managing the entire customer life cycle and not look at marketing processes in isolation.

The customer life cycle starts with the acquisition of new customers, followed by strategies of enhancing value of existing customers through usage enhancement and cross-sell. This is represented in Fig. 1.1. It is also important that customers do not end or reduce the depth of their relationship with the firm. Hence managing attrition is yet another important aspect of customer life cycle management. Therefore, acquiring the right customer and managing existing customers are the two key levers of enhancing customer value. Acquisition feeds into the pool of existing customers, while due to attrition one constantly loses customers from the existing pool. Existing customer management strategies like usage enhancement and cross-sell are targeted at generating value from the pool of existing customers, while acquisition and retention strategies are aimed at creating and maintaining the customer pool.

Acquisition is the first step in the long-term relationship between the firm and the customer and hence, is critical in creating a long-term enduring and profitable buyer–seller relationship. In his article titled *The Loyalty Effect: A New Look at Lifetime Value* Arthur Hughes, one of the prominent thinkers in the area of customer value, uses the findings on customer loyalty by Frederick Reichheld to illustrate the importance of acquiring the right customer in order to drive loyalty. Hughes argues that though better service is important for enhancing customer retention, it is far more important to acquire the right customer so as to drive higher loyalty and retention. He provides a number of examples across credit

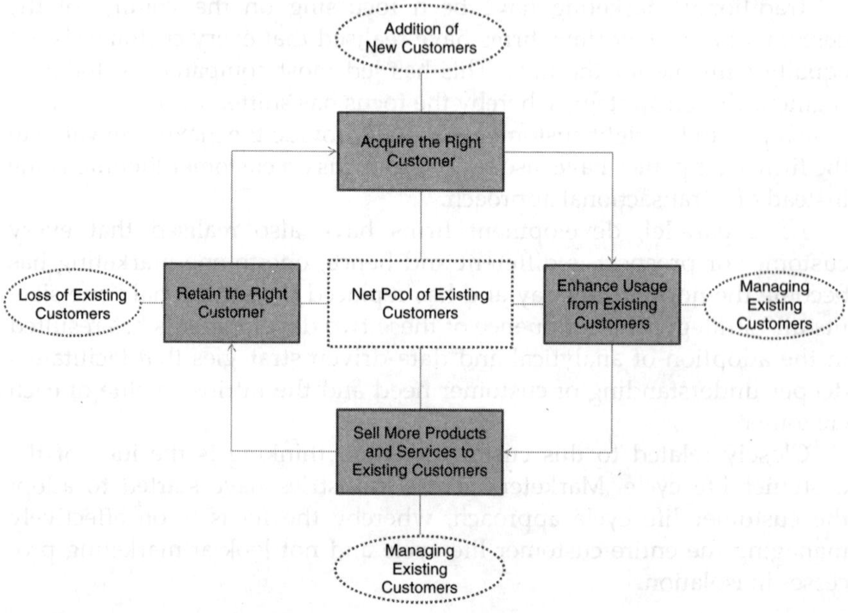


**Figure 1.1** Customer Life Cycle

cards, insurance, and automobile industries to illustrate the importance of acquiring the right customer for driving loyalty.

Data plays a crucial role in identifying the right prospects and targeting them with the right offer through the right channel. Some of the key data sources used for acquisition involve census data, geographic data, specialised lists, credit bureau data and market survey data. These data sources provide information about the prospect universe, which is used in conjunction with information about existing customers for making decisions on the right prospect, the right offer, the right price, and the right channel.

At this point, it is important to note that the dynamics of acquisition are slightly different for various types of industries based on the characteristics of revenue realisation and tenure of customer relationship. Industries like financial services, telecom and utility, are characterised by low purchase frequency; longer term relationship; absence of major revenue realisation at the time of purchase; presence of a regular revenue realisation post purchase and relatively higher switching costs. Hence, for companies in these industries, the cost of acquisition has to be borne up-front at the time of acquisition but the benefits flow through over a longer time span. Moreover, because of the longer tenure of customer relationship and the higher switching costs, the loss of a prospect to competitor signifies a huge lost opportunity.

On the other hand, industries like retail and consumer packaged goods are characterised by higher purchase frequency, low switching costs, entire revenue realisation at time of purchase and relative ease of winning back lost customers. Hence, these industries focus more on total sales and not necessarily on new customer acquisition, though new customer acquisition becomes critical in cases when companies belonging to these industries strive to penetrate new markets or launch new products.

The travel and entertainment industry is characterised by immediate perishability of their inventory. Hence, these industries focus more on yield management. Companies belonging to this industry strive to set the right price so as to maximise bookings and revenue. New customer acquisition in these industries is viewed as a component of yield management.

This chapter focuses more on industries like telecom and financial services where acquiring the right customer is more critical for creating a long-term profitable buyer–seller relationship. The pricing aspect of new customer acquisition will be dealt with in Chapter 5, "Price Management".

With a view of comparing the relative importance of acquisition and existing customer management strategies, it needs to be noted that though new customer acquisition is the primary driver of value creation, it is also well-known that acquiring a new customer is several times costlier than cross-selling to an existing one. The higher costs of acquisition compared to cross-sell can be attributed mostly to the availability of information. A company has a wealth of information about existing customers, which can be used to predict the chances of cross-sell. Whereas for prospects, very limited information is available and hence, prediction of their chances of becoming customers is less accurate. To add to the above, existing customers develop a loyalty towards the company, which makes cross-sell easier. Thus every company needs to adopt a balanced focus between new customer acquisition and existing customer management. The relative importance of the two strategies is driven primarily by the economy and the industry in which the company operates. Emerging economies like India and China have a large proportion of young population and are experiencing a steep growth in demand for various products and services. Hence, new customer acquisition is relatively more important in these economies. The developed economies in Western Europe, North America, and Japan, on the other hand, are experiencing a demographic shift towards older population and demand for most products in these markets have been flattening. Hence, companies in these economies have been focusing more on cross-sell and customer retention, so as to derive maximum value out of their existing customer base. In spite of these differences across emerging and developed economies, new customer acquisition is still a critical aspect of the marketing strategy for every company across the world.

The chapter starts with an overview of the components of a data-driven acquisition strategy. This is followed by an explanation of the common data sources that can be used by the marketer for identifying and targeting the right prospect. The explanation of the data sources is followed by methodologies of how these data sources are used for creating an acquisition strategy. Next, a section is dedicated to the use of geographic information system (GIS) along with prospect information for location planning of stores, branches or sales channels. This is followed by a section on print media testing, which is of critical importance to acquisition. Acquisition like all other business processes needs to be managed keeping in view profitability and cost constraints. Hence, a profit & loss (P&L) example from acquisition has been discussed.

## 1.2 Components of the Acquisition Strategy

Acquisition being one of the most important elements of the sales and marketing strategy calls for a well-thought-out strategy for maximising the short- and long-term impact of each marketing and sales dollar spent on new customer acquisition. An acquisition strategy closely reflects the traditional marketing paradigm, wherein the marketer identifies the addressable universe, performs a segmentation of the prospect universe, creates a targeting strategy for each of the segments, and finally prioritises among the segments. Once the segments are prioritised, the marketer then needs to determine the right price, the right offer and the right channel for each segment. Figure 1.2 illustrates the broad steps in designing an acquisition strategy.

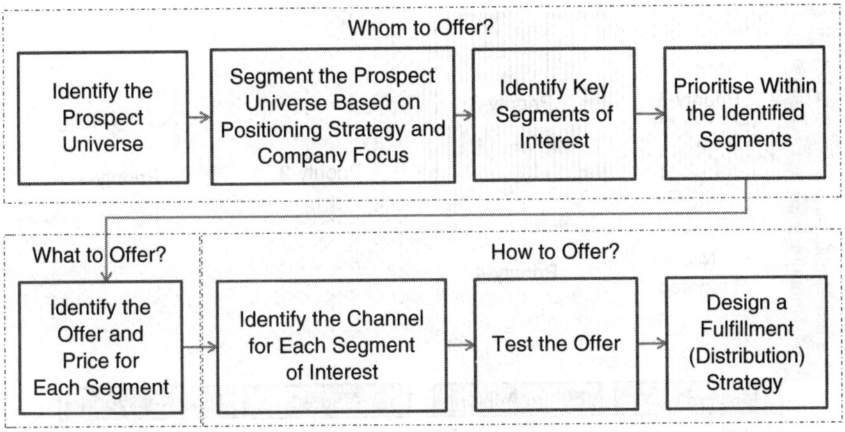


**Figure 1.2** Components of the Acquisition Strategy

Prospect universe identification involves identification of the entire universe of prospects that can be addressed by the firm. The boundaries of the prospect universe are created by the broad level business strategy of the firm. For example, some of the brands like the Fasttrack brand of watches, eye wear, and leather items are focused on the younger population; hence, their prospect universe is limited to the younger population. Sometime the prospect universe is limited by the geographic reach of the distribution channels used by the company. For example, a bank branch normally defines a branch trade area; prospects that live outside the branch trade area are not considered part of the prospect universe for the particular branch.

A particular segment within the prospect universe represents a homogeneous group of prospects that are similar with respect to characteristics, which are important for driving response and future profitability. On the other hand, a particular segment is very different from all other segments in terms of these characteristics. The common jargon among analysts state that "the segments should have minimum variation within the segments and maximum variation between the segments". Hence, a particular segment is usually treated with the same offer through the same channel.

It is important to have the right data for segmenting the prospect universe. In case no data is available, the company collects data through market research and proprietary surveys or uses business judgement to segment the prospect universe. Figure 1.3 is an example of segmentation used by a bank to segment its prospect universe.

As illustrated in Fig. 1.3, affluence and channel preference have been used as the segmentation criteria. The identified segments are homogeneous with respect to these criteria and are quite different when compared to any other segment. Furthermore, the financial needs of all prospects within a segment will be very similar and they can be served through similar channels. A real-life segmentation of individuals (based on data

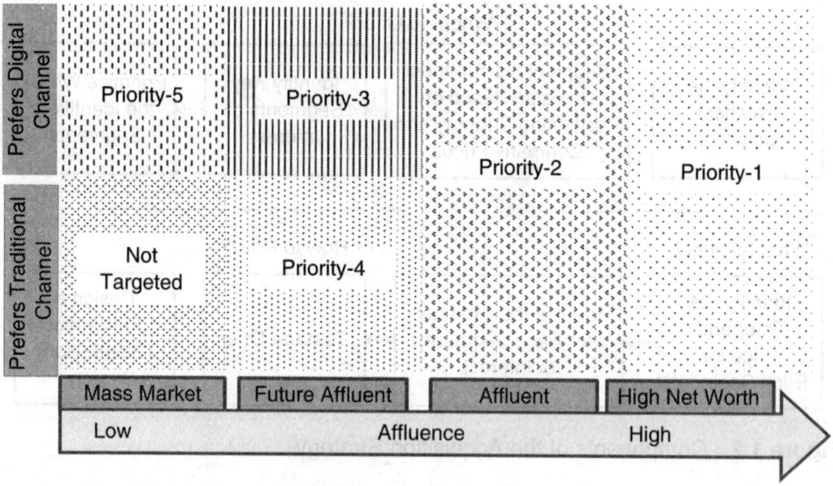


**Figure 1.3** Segmentation of Individual Prospects

availability) will include additional characteristics about the attitude, cultural factors, reading habits, entertainment preference, etc. These factors are called psychographics; along with these psychographic characteristics, the segmentation for individuals will also include geographic location and their attitude to financial services. Some of these will be discussed in greater detail in later sections.

As stated in Fig. 1.3, closely related to segmentation is the idea of prioritisation. Once the entire prospect universe is broken down into homogeneous segments, the marketer needs to find out which of these segments are more important given the company's overall business strategy. For a bank which wants to focus on premium customers, the high net worth segment will have the highest priority.

Once the segments are identified and prioritised, the next step involves designing the right offer for each segment. The offer design is based mostly on the need of the segment and company-specific profitability goals and budget constraints. Offer design will not be extensively discussed in this chapter. Post offer design, the right channel needs to be identified for the segment. As illustrated in Fig. 1.3, the segments of individual customers who prefer traditional channels need to be serviced through the branch network, whereas the segments that are comfortable with digital media may be reached using the Internet channel. The segment comfortable with digital media can be encouraged to fill in the application online, upload a scanned copy of the required documents and engage in an interactive Internet chat with the representative to clarify questions regarding account opening.

Another part of the acquisition strategy involves testing. Testing is important at every stage of the acquisition strategy. The segmentation, offer design and channel selection that was made by the marketer might have been performed using the right data and the right tools. However, they may not work in real life. For example, it is possible that some customers are comfortable using the digital channel for day-to-day account usage but prefer a human interaction while initiating the relationship with the bank. In addition, the bank may also realize that during a face-to-face interaction, bank employees are more effective at cross-selling other products (like insurance and credit cards) to the prospect. Hence, testing is important to validate the hypothesis made by the marketer. A detailed discussion on testing methodology has been provided in Chapter 8. This chapter will focus only on print media testing.

Once testing confirms the hypothesis of the marketer, it is important to design and implement the distribution and fulfilment processes, that should be able to support the acquisition strategy. The design of the distribution processes varies widely across industries and has been kept outside the purview of this chapter.

## 1.3 Data Sources for Supporting Acquisition Strategy

Data is the key building block for creating a data-driven acquisition strategy. Acquiring detailed quality data about prospects is possibly the biggest challenge in building a data-driven acquisition strategy. As already stated, companies tend to have very rich data about their own customers. However, they need to procure data about prospects from external sources. Usually prospect data tends to be less richer and costlier as compared to internal data. Companies in data-rich markets like the United States and western Europe have access to far richer prospect data compared to developing economies, where very limited prospect data is available. In some cases, where the desired prospect data is not available, companies use proprietary market research surveys to collect the required prospect data. However, such surveys can only be conducted for small samples and the results have to extrapolated for a wider population, with some amount of approximation. This section provides an overview of the common data sources, which can be used for obtaining prospect data. Table 1.1 provides a summary of key data sources used for acquisition.

Companies also obtain data about new customers while acquiring them. Most of these data is obtained through the application form, which newly acquired customers fill in. These data items are not part of the data sources that will be discussed in this section, because these data items can only be obtained post-acquisition and are not of any use in identifying or targeting prospects. However, these data can be used for building rules and models to identify the type of prospects who have the highest likelihood of responding to an offer.

**Table 1.1** Key Data Sources

| Data Source | Key Elements | Usage in Customer Acquisition |
|---|---|---|
| Census data | Demographic, economic, employment data at an aggregated level | Understanding overall market potential and the potential of geographic areas |
| Public records data | Key events like marriage, divorce, property registration, birth etc. | Identify key events in the life of a prospect, which can be used as a trigger for acquisition |
| Mailing lists and commercially available data sources | Available at a prospect level. Lists provide information on psychographic and behavioural elements along with contact information | Identify, segment, prioritise, and target individual prospects |
| Geographic data | Geographic information at a street, collection of street, zip or city level | Potential of a geographic area from a distribution perspective |
| Credit bureau data | Credit profile of prospect | Mostly used for credit checks in cases where a lending decision is involved. Also used for pre-screen acquisition. |
| Data on business entities (e.g., D&B data) | Data on business entities like industry type, revenue, employee size etc. | Identify, segment, prioritise, and target business entities |

### *1.3.1 Census Data*

Census provides the most reliable data on demographics. In most countries, the starting point of a census is the list of housing units collected from the previous census. This section will discuss the content of the census in an advanced market (taking the United States as an example) and in an emerging market (taking India as an example).

In the United States, most housing units are mailed census forms, which they need to fill up and return by mail. Follow-up visits are conducted for housing units, which do not respond. One out of six randomly selected household receives a long questionnaire requesting a broad set of demographic data, whereas the rest receive a short one. The content of the short questionnaire is as follows:

- Population information
  - Name, relationship to householder
  - Sex, age, date of birth, race, origin
- Housing information
  - Number of people in the household
  - Telephone number
  - House ownership status

Table 1.2 compares the census information available in the United States and in India. The content of the United States census data has been taken from *Small Area and Business Demography* by Stanley K. Smith and Peter A. Morrison. The contents of the Indian census data has been taken from the Government of India website http://www.censusindia.gov.in/default.aspx.

As is evident from a comparable analysis of the data captured in the United States census and the India census, the breadth of the data captured is similar across the two countries. However, because of the wide difference in the demographic and socio-economic panorama of the country, the Indian census data seems to lack a lot of granular details, which are important for marketing purposes. For example, with regards to asset ownership, the census does not capture an indication of the type of vehicle ownership.

As stated earlier, census data is available for small geographic areas (zip or a collection of streets) and is never available at the household level. Usage of census data for marketing hinges on the belief, that birds of the same feather flock together, that is, people of similar types live in the same geographic area. However, that assumption may not always be true and people of very different socio-economic backgrounds can live in the same geographic area. This phenomenon is very evident in India, where people of very different socio-economic status and income, live in the same geographic area. The above is another aspect, which makes census data in India much less applicable for marketing purpose compared to census data in the United States. Section 1.5 illustrates the use of census data for developing an effective acquisition strategy.

### 1.3.2 Administrative Records

A major limitation of census data is that it is available every 10 years and hence, use of census data is tantamount to use of information that is quite dated. To tide over this problem and to add additional information, administrative records kept by the local and country administration can be utilized to augment census data. Most countries have a fair record of births, deaths, marriages, and divorces, though the data tends to be sparse for developing countries. The above can be used in conjunction with other administrative data like building permits, motor vehicle registration, etc. Data on motor vehicle registration has been found to be a very

**Table 1.2** Overview of Census Data (2001 Census)

| Type of Information | United States | India |
|---|---|---|
| Population information | • Marital status<br>• School enrolment<br>• Educational qualification<br>• Ethnicity<br>• Language spoken at home<br>• Place of birth<br>• Citizenship<br>• Year of entry in the country<br>• Place of residence five years age<br>• Disability status<br>• Whether living with grand children<br>• Military service<br>• Emplcyment status<br>• Employment history<br>• Place of work<br>• Transportation to work<br>• Occupation<br>• Industry<br>• Income | • Name, age, gender<br>• Relationship to head of the household<br>• Marital status, age at marriage<br>• Religion<br>• Whether belonging to scheduled caste or scheduled tribe<br>• Mother tongue, languages known<br>• Literacy, highest educational level, whether attending educational institution<br>• Whether physically or mentally disabled<br>• Working status–main worker, marginal worker, non-worker<br>• Economic activity if working–cultivator, agricultural labourer, worker in household industry, other worker<br>• Occupation of the person<br>• Nature of industry<br>• Class of worker–employer, employee, single worker, family worker<br>• Migration characteristics<br>  ◦ Birth place<br>  ◦ Place of current residence<br>  ◦ At the time of migration was the place of last residence rural or urban<br>  ◦ Reason for migration<br>  ◦ Duration of stay since migration<br>• Fertility particulars for ever married women |
| Housing information | • Type of housing unit<br>• Year built<br>• Length of residence | • Household number<br>• Use of house<br>• Material of roof, wall, and floor |

(*Continued*)

**Table 1.2** Overview of Census Data (2001 Census) (*Continued*)

| Type of Information | United States | India |
|---|---|---|
| | • Number of rooms<br>• Number of bedrooms<br>• Plumbing facilities<br>• Kitchen facilities<br>• Telephone in unit<br>• Type of heating fuel used<br>• Number of motor vehicles<br>• Size of parking lot<br>• Presence of home business<br>• Annual cost of utilities<br>• Monthly rent or mortgage payment<br>• Presence of second mortgage<br>• Real estate taxes<br>• Property insurance<br>• Value of property | • Condition of the house<br>• Number of people living in the house<br>• Ownership of the house<br>• Number of married couple living<br>• Number of rooms and bedrooms<br>• Drinking water source and type<br>• Source of lighting<br>• Sanitation details<br>• Kitchen details and fuel usage<br>• Ownership of assets like radio, television, telephone, bicycle, scooter, motorcycle, car, jeep, van etc.<br>• Whether members avail banking services<br>• For household engaged in cultivation<br>  ◦ Total area under cultivation<br>  ◦ Net area of irrigated land<br>  ◦ Tenure status of land under cultivation |

good source of information for consumer marketing because the type of car purchased by an individual is indicative of a host of income and psychographic variables. The use of administrative records suffers from two important limitations: *first* is the lack of quality and up-to-date data and the *second* is the unavailability of this data for small geographical units. Most administrative records are maintained at a state or province level and hence, drilling down into smaller geographic units like neighbourhoods and zip codes is mostly not possible.

### *1.3.3 Publicly Available Surveys*

In addition to the census data, many other public surveys are available in many countries. These surveys are conducted by the government for estimating various socio-economic indicators that serve as inputs for policy formulation. However, surveys (as opposed to census) cover a sample of specific population groups and is mostly undertaken at a country or province level and hence, survey data at times is only indicative and suffers from small sample size problems when used for smaller geographic units.

### 1.3.4 Proprietary Data Sources

Up to this point, the discussion on data sources has mainly focused on publicly available data sources like census, administrative records, and public surveys. These data sources are available mostly with government agencies and can be obtained for analysis by paying a stipulated fee. However, there are two important limitations of using public data sources for prospect identification. The *first* limitation is that in most cases, public data sources are available in a summarised format (e.g., summarised by zip code, parish, election ward, etc.). Hence, a deeper drill down into individual households is mostly not possible. The *second* limitation of publicly available data is the richness of the data source. Though census data in developed markets have been used extensively for creating prospect maps for various products and services, public data sources are mostly collected for the government's planning purpose and hence, does not cover important demographic and psychographic dimensions, which are needed by a marketer.

To tide over the limitations of using public data, marketers rely on proprietary data sources to identify, prioritise and target the desired prospect segment. In the parlance of direct marketing, proprietary data are called "lists". This section will focus on the types of available lists and their applicability. Following are the major types of lists commonly available in most markets:

- **Consumer lists,** which are lists of a company's customers
- **Response lists,** which are compiled by using the consumer's response to earlier direct marketing campaigns
- **Compiled lists,** which are created by combining various other lists
- **Survey lists,** which are created by conducting proprietary surveys

Consumer lists (sometimes also called house lists) are the most easily available lists and consist of the lists of consumers who have purchased certain products and services including products like magazine subscription and services like club membership. Owing to data confidentiality issues, there is a limitation on the extensive use of these lists. Consumer lists in the United States are classified into groups based on psychographic dimensions. Some of the key types of house lists in the United States include Boating and Yachting, Art and Antiques, Brides, Crafts Hobbies and Models, Gift Buyers, Home Computers and Software, Dogs and Pets, Consumer Electronics and Video Games, Gardening (at home), Fashions, Business Leaders, etc. These list types have been taken from the popular book on direct marketing by Edward Nash. A similar orderly classification of lists is lacking in most emerging markets though similar lists are used by marketers for direct marketing campaigns. For example, club membership lists are widely available in the Indian market and are used to target affluent prospects.

Response lists are lists of consumers who have responded to a direct marketing campaign in the past. The key aspect of these lists is that it clearly demonstrates the willingness of the consumer to respond to direct marketing media. Response lists rarely exist in emerging markets like India.

Survey lists comprise of surveys conducted by various agencies and companies on a sample list of households or consumers. Most surveys include responses to capture a consumer's psychographic profile and intentions to purchase certain types of products and services.

Compiled lists consist of lists created by drawing information from multiple sources and because of their very nature, have a wider breadth of information compared to any other lists. The advantage of using compiled list is the ability of performing better segmentation based on individual characteristics and area characteristics. A single list is seldom used in isolation because the richness of information provided by a single list is very limited. Information from multiple lists is compiled together and is combined with geographic information to create the prospect database for segmentation and targeting.

### 1.3.5 Commercially Available Databases

In developed markets like the United States, a number of commercially available databases, such as the ones offered by Donnelly Marketing, R.L. Polk, National Demographics and Lifestyle, InfoBase, etc., provide household level information. These databases provide information on demographic profile of the household (e.g., age, estimated income, occupation, spouse details, marital status, number of children, etc.), socio-economic information (e.g., estimated asset value, credit card holding and some lifestyle attributes). However, these databases do not have data directly related to a specific product or channel preference. To tide over this limitation, companies conduct surveys to seek specific information from a small stratified random sample. The results are then extrapolated for a bigger population. The paper titled *New Customer Acquisition: Prospecting Models and the Use of Commercially Available External Data,* by Thomas et al. is an example. In this paper, the authors have used a survey conducted on 2,500 individuals to extrapolate the results on the population of 170 million individuals and 80 million households. The methodology used by the authors involves asking respondents questions on the metric of interest, for example, whether the respondent has ever responded to direct mail or whether the respondent has ever purchased anything online. Next the characteristics of the respondents are appended from the commercial database. These characteristics are used as profiling variables to understand, which type of respondents are most likely to respond to a direct mailer or are most likely to purchase anything online. Once the profiling rules are established, they are applied on the overall database to select prospects who have a higher propensity to respond to a direct mailer or who have a higher propensity of purchasing anything online. A logistic regression or CHAID analysis is used to create the profiling rules. For a detailed understanding of logistic regression or CHAID (Chi Square Automatic Interaction Detection), the reader can refer to Chapter 7, "Quantitative Methods".

### 1.3.6 Market Research and Primary Survey Data

In many cases, one may not have access to any source of prospect data and hence, would have to conduct primary surveys for data collection. However as pointed out earlier, most primary surveys are limited to a small sample of representative prospects. But, on the other hand, one can ask very detailed and specific questions to the respondents of a survey, so as to obtain very detailed information. Even in cases where detailed prospect data is available, companies often use market research as a tool to obtain detailed information about attitudes and preferences of prospects. Market research is also used for a deeper understanding of existing customers.

Broadly market research is divided into qualitative and quantitative research. Qualitative market research is used to understand the needs and preferences of the prospects from a subjective perspective. Qualitative market research focuses more on the attitudes, feelings, and motivations of the buyer. The researcher needs to use his or her judgement to interpret the qualitative data rather than using quantitative tools for making inference. Quantitative market research, on the other hand, focuses on making data-driven statistical inference about the choices and preferences revealed by prospects. Typically qualitative market research tends to be based on smaller samples, while quantitative research is based on relatively larger samples.

One important type of quantitative research is based on panel data or syndicated data. Market research companies recruit a panel of consumers who are required tabulate their day-to-day purchase behaviour. This detailed purchase behaviour is used to measure various aspects of their choices and preferences. The panel is created as a stratified sample of various consumers type based on their age, socio-economic status and other factors. The panel data can also be used for estimating changes in market share of key brands. The type of panel described above is referred to as consumer panel. Market research companies also create a panel of various types of stores to monitor the types and quantities of various products sold. This data is mostly recorded at a stock keeping unit (SKU) level. A stock keeping unit is a unique product or item for sale in a store. For example, the same brand of detergent might be available in 1Kg and 2Kg packs; each of these two are considered separate SKUs. Scanner data, which is provided by companies like AC Neilson and IRI, is another key source of data. These companies scan every single purchase at a select set of retail outlets and provide data on the items purchased at an SKU level. They also provide information on coupons and various other promotions. This data is a very valuable source of information for all consumer packaged goods companies, which may use this information for fine-tuning their marketing mix. A third important type of panel data involves data on television viewing. AC Neilson, for example, has a television audience measurement system, which monitors the type of TV channels viewed by a panel of selected households. For this purpose, a special device is installed in the television of all the households in the panel and it monitors the TV viewing pattern.

Typically these three types of market research data are used for a wide range of marketing applications. Some of the common uses of market research are as follows:

- Market measurement (market characteristics, market size, market potential, market share, forecasting market growth)
- Competitive analysis
- Pricing analysis (understanding price elasticity, understanding the value of key product features)
- New product/concept testing (testing product features, price points)
- Advertisement or brand awareness (aided and unaided brand and ad recall)
- Customer satisfaction analysis
- Mystery shopping (to understand service quality, channel effectiveness)
- Attitude and preference study
- Media effectiveness evaluation

Market research is not only used in cases where limited prospect information is available, it is also used to obtain richer information, which can be overlaid on existing data. Market research data may also be used for testing some of the hypothesis that are created based on other analysis. A detailed discussion of market research techniques is beyond the scope of the book and the interested reader can refer to specialised texts for more information.

### 1.3.7 Data Sources for B2B Marketing

In contrast to consumer marketing, business-to-business marketing needs to rely on a very different set of information for prospect identification. In most cases, it is relatively easy to identify information sources for identifying the universe of prospects in the B2B scenario. However, the major difficulty for B2B marketing revolves around identifying the decision maker for various types of purchases. In most markets, business entities are categorised based on some form of industry code (standard industry classification or SIC code). The industry code is designed in such a manner that each incremental digit provides a further level of detail. For example, in the United States, industry codes are divided into 20 divisions (e.g., agricultural, mining, construction, etc.). All codes starting with 31, 32 and 33 belong to manufacturing. For example, within manufacturing code, 335911 represents storage battery manufacturing. One can refer to http://www.ehso.com/naics.php for further details. The site also provides a mapping of the new codes with the older versions. Most countries follow a similar structure for creating industry codes. With regards to B2B data, industry type is by far the most important information. In addition to industry type, the following data elements are important from a B2B perspective:

- **Firmographic data or the firm related data:** Just as demographic data provides information about an individual, similarly information about the company is often termed as firmographic information. Typical firmographic information include employee size, address of main office, number of locations, number of years in business, type of company (e.g., public limited, privately held), number of directors, whether it is a multi-national company, etc.
- **Financial data:** These involve data on financial performances like annual sales, annual profit, fixed asset, liabilities, etc. In most countries, financial data of un-listed companies and small proprietorship companies tends to be sparse and inaccurate.
- **Trade data:** Trade data involves data on how a company pays its creditors including suppliers, banks, etc. Trade data is one of the most difficult to obtain and is provided by specialised information providers like Dun&Bradstreet. D&B's trade programme is a unique method of collating payment data from a host of commercial entities. Please refer to https://tradexchange.dnb.com/trade/ for more information on D&B's trade programme. Using the trade data, D&B calculates a Paydex score, which is an indication of how promptly a commercial entity pays its dues. Table 1.3 provides an interpretation of the Paydex score. The website listed in the table provides additional details on the Paydex score. At this point, it is important to mention that the Paydex score is available in a limited set of markets particularly, the United States and European markets. In emerging countries like India, the Paydex programme has been launched recently and it will take some time before Paydex information can be used for targeting. Table 1.3 provides a description of the PAYDEX scores.
- **Credit data:** Credit data refers to the credit history of the commercial entity vis-à-vis credit taken from banks and financial institutions. In case of small proprietorship companies, the credit data of its proprietor is also an important dimension.

**Table 1.3** D&B PAYDEX Score

| D&B PAYDEX Score | Payment Habit |
|---|---|
| 100 | Anticipate |
| 90 | Discount |
| 80 | Prompt |
| 70 | 15 days beyond terms |
| 60 | 22 days beyond terms |
| 50 | 30 days beyond terms |
| 40 | 60 days beyond terms |
| 30 | 90 days beyond terms |
| 20 | 120 days beyond terms |
| UN | Unavailable |

*Source:* http://www.dnb.com/us/customer_service/paydex_tables.html

- **Public records:** Public records are an important source of information for commercial entities; public records include data on number of suits filed against the company, the value of suit filed, number of favourable and unfavourable judgements in the past, amount of money paid as compensation or settlement, number of liens, etc. Bankruptcy filing is also an important information, and details of the bankruptcy filing provide data on other commercial entities, which can also be affected. In countries where public records data is not easily available, companies normally share a negative list among them. The negative lists consist of companies involved in fraud, financial crime, etc.
- **Contact data:** Contact data pertain to the contact information of the company and of key decision makers therein
- **Standard Industry Code (SIC):** Standard industry codes are used to identify the industry type for a commercial entity. The SIC codes are specific to a particular country and uses a hierarchical structure for grouping industry types. For example, in the United States, all SIC codes starting with 10 belong to the metals and mining industry. Out of these, the SIC code 1011 represents companies engaged in iron ore mining. The SIC code has been found to be a very important source of information for commercial entities.

D&B is one of the most comprehensive sources of data for commercial entities worldwide and the D-U-N-S number can be used as a global unique identifier for commercial entities across the globe.

### 1.3.8 Credit Bureau Data

Credit bureaus and credit registries have emerged as chief information aggregators for achieving seamless exchange of credit information, between companies involved in the lending business. Though these information aggregators have historically focused on the financial services industry, the scope and purview of their operations have been extended over time to cater to other industries as well. Today there are specialised credit bureaus for consumers and small businesses. In addition, there are specialised information aggregators for other industries such as insurance, telecom, utilities, etc. Details about credit bureau information and its usage will be covered in Chapter 6. At this point, it is important to mention that in cases where new customer acquisition also involves credit assessment, it is important to check the credit history of the prospect before approving him/her. In such cases, the credit bureau is used to obtain the credit information. In the some markets, financial services companies are allowed to use bureau information for selecting prospects for pre-approved credit offers. Hence, in such situations credit bureau information can be used for prospect identification and targeting as well. The section on pre-screen acquisition describes the acquisition process using credit bureau information.

### 1.3.9 Data Matching and Data Cleaning

The data sources described above are seldom used in isolation; multiple data sources need to be matched in order to harness the power of each of them. Hence, it is important to focus on methodologies of matching multiple lists. Various approaches can be used for matching multiple data sources and the details of the methodology depends upon the context and the peculiarities of the data sources involved. This section provides a view of the generic methodologies used for data matching and data cleaning.

Marketing lists seldom contain fields like national ID (e.g., social security number in the United States), hence data matching becomes a major challenge. However, in the United States and other developed markets, many of the commercially available data sources provide their own individual identification number that can be used as a primary key to match various data sources. Acxiom, one of the largest information aggregator, uses its proprietary ABLITEC methodology to create an ABLITEC ID for each individual and the ABLITEC ID can be used for matching individuals within multiple data sources. Similarly some of the other commercially available prospect lists provide their own individual or household ID for matching multiple data sources. However, in many cases one may not be fortunate enough to have any of these IDs. Moreover in emerging markets like India, China, etc. such IDs are not available in any commercially available prospect list. In the absence of any of these IDs, the next best alternative is the phone number. In lists containing phone numbers, one may use a match based on phone number, which should be sufficiently reliable. But phone numbers do change over time and the same individual can have a mobile number in one list and a home or office phone number in another list, thus making phone number matching a less reliable method. In many cases, a number of match criteria are used in unison to determine the strength of a match. Some typical examples of possible match criteria are as follows:

- **Criteria 1—name match:** If the name field of an incoming record (from any data source) has a perfect match with the name field of an existing record, then a score of 5 is awarded; if there is an imperfect but strong match then a score of 3 is awarded; if there is a loose match then a score of 1 is awarded to the name search path. The definition of strong and loose match is derived by using various text matching algorithms (like fuzzy matching), which are tuned or trained using data specific to a particular country.
- **Criteria 2—address match:** Similar to name, match points are awarded for perfect match, strong match and loose match. For example, 7 for perfect, 3 for strong, and 2 for loose. However, the effectiveness of address-based match becomes limited in a country like India where address information is not well-structured and where the younger population is extremely mobile.
- **Criteria 3—telephone number match:** Telephone numbers are an other key criteria for matching records; for each perfect match of telephone numbers points are awarded for the match. For example, if an incoming record has two telephone numbers and the existing record has three telephone numbers, then each telephone number match is awarded, say 4 points.
- **Criteria 4—demographic criteria match:** Demographic criteria such as gender, marital status, number of children, etc. are also used as match criteria. Scores are provided for exact match of one or all of the demographic details that are available. For example, a score of 2 for any two demographic criteria matching and a score of 1 for at least one matching.

At the end, a match score is awarded to a set of records and two records with more than a threshold match score are considered as the same record. Various algorithms are used for finding out the optimal score for each type of match and the threshold scores for defining a match. The details of these algorithms are beyond the scope of this book.

### 1.3.9.1 Data Cleaning

Usually lists from multiple sources are used for developing an acquisition strategy. A major issue in using these lists involves the accuracy of data contained in the list, particularly data pertaining to contact information. To tide over the problem of inaccurate data, every list must go through a list cleaning exercise so as to augment the information as much as possible. The first cleaning exercise involves internal de-duplication, whereby all indicative information about prospects included in the list is taken and matched with all internal databases so as to make sure that the prospect in the list is not an existing customer. In case information from multiple lists are compiled to create a compiled list, a similar matching exercise needs to be undertaken to merge multiple lists. Sometimes another objective of the matching process involves pulling in additional contact information for the prospect. This is particularly important when telemarketing is used as the channel for targeting the prospects.

The next step in the cleaning process involves removing improper address and telephone numbers. In some cases, the list information is matched with telephone directory information to update phone numbers. Another important aspect involves standardization of data fields. A field like date of birth may contain entries in multiple formats. For example, entries like "15th Nov 1978", "15/11/78", "11/78" may be present in the date of birth field. It is critical to standardize these entries into a common format. In some cases, lists may include multiple individuals from the same household, the marketer may consider removing these cases as well. Sometimes a particular individual may be targeted in multiple campaigns, which may give rise to irritation and negative image of the company. In order to prevent such negative consequences, the marketer can consider de-duplicating the list with the list of prospects targeted in the last few campaigns. The last step in checking through the list involves a pre-testing, wherein a small random sample of prospects is identified and tele-called to ascertain the veracity of the information provided in the list. In some cases such as credit cards, loans, etc. it is critical to match the list against any internal or external negative files, which can include cases of previous fraud, write-off, etc. In some countries, the credit bureau is used for this purpose; details of usage of credit bureau will be covered in Chapter 6. Similarly, if there are negative areas which have been identified by the company, the address information needs to be scanned so as to avoid targeting these prospects.

## 1.4 Prospect Universe Identification

The first stage of acquisition strategy development involves identifying the prospect universe which the company wants to target. Referring to the earlier example in Fig. 1.3, for individual consumers, it needs to be noted that, the bank may not want to target mass market prospects who prefer traditional (bank branch) channels. Hence, this segment will not even be part of the prospect universe on which any further analysis is to be carried out. The prospect universe definition is used as a limiting criterion for defining prospects, which the company aims to target. The definition of the prospect universe is closely related to the idea of acquiring the right customer. The segment of prospects who are excluded from the prospect universe represent those prospects who will not yield long-term value or who may have a very low chance of responding to the offer made by the company. The earlier example of mass market prospects who prefer traditional channels represent the prospect pool that may be un-profitable for the bank. On the other hand, if a credit card company wants to launch a new card which does not charge a foreign transaction fee, then it may not want to target people who have never made a trip abroad, because it may be assumed that these people are unlikely to respond to this offer. Thus, there are two possible dimensions of selecting a prospect universe: one being future profitability and the other being probability of responding to the offer. Based on these two dimensions, companies rely on multiple approaches for utilising every available data to identify the prospect market. Some of the common approaches used for this purpose are:

- **Subjective judgement** based segmentation of the market based on factors like economic indicators and demographic profiles
  - For example, any prospect having income or asset below a threshold or beyond a certain age bracket are not part of the prospect universe
- **Geographic location**
  - In many cases, the addressable universe of prospects is limited by the geographical reach of the distribution channel used. For example, prospects within a specific distance of a store or bank branch are only targeted by the specific store or bank branch.
- **Geo-demographic clustering**
  - Prospects having a certain geo-demographic profile can only be part of the addressable universe for certain products

In reality, a company seldom uses one of these approaches in isolation, a combination of several approaches is normally used.

## 1.5 Prospect Universe Segmentation

Segmentation of the prospect universe is a key success factor for any marketing initiative. Segmentation involves identifying similar groups or clusters within the prospect universe. For the purpose of marketing the term "similar" is defined as having similar needs and similar consumer behaviour. Two individuals who have very different demographic characteristics may be part of the same segment with respect to a particular type of product or service. For example, if a travel company wants to focus on low cost week-end adventure trips and treks, it may group all customers of a trekking magazine into one segment, irrespective of their income or marital status, because these people display similar needs while having very different demographic characteristics. However, the same company may want to segment the prospect universe based on income and family size while positioning tours to Disneyland and similar destinations. Traditionally, marketers tend to define segments in a unilateral context, expecting most prospects in a particular segment to be similar in terms of variables like family size, income, etc. In a statistical sense, this can be described as segmentation based on univariate characteristics, whereby one or a few variables are used to divide the prospect universe into segments. The advent of cluster analysis has brought a multivariate way of segmenting the prospect universe, whereby a cluster consists of individuals having similar needs as against individuals who are just similar vis-à-vis a few characteristics. Punj and Stewart in their work titled *Cluster Analysis in Marketing Research: Review and Suggestions for Application* have provided a comprehensive review of the techniques used in defining clusters in the marketing context. A brief description of the common techniques will be provided in this section.

This chapter will outline the basic tenets of geo-demographic clustering and will provide a view of the commercial clustering schemes that are available in the market. While most of these discussions are relevant for an advanced market, this chapter will also discuss ideas of implementing such a scheme for an emerging market.

In many cases companies attempt to profile existing customers and identify similar profiles among the prospect population. A look-alike model is used to score each prospect; the look-alike model attributes how closely the prospect resembles an existing customer. The closer a prospect looks like an existing customer, higher is the score of the look-alike model. The score of the look-alike can then be used as an important criterion for segmentation. However, in cases of limited data availability, the segmentation is purely based on business judgement.

## 1.5.1 Geo-demographic Segmentation

As already discussed, geo-demographic segmentation in most cases forms the basic building block for building any segmentation scheme. Geo-demographic segmentation is based on identifying demographically similar small geographical areas (zip code, election ward, parish, etc.). The basic theory behind geo-demographic segmentation rests in the old adage that "birds of a feather flock together". Charles Booth is regarded as the father of geo-demographic segmentation. Booth initiated his research with the objective of proving that poverty in London is not as widespread as reported. His study concluded that 30.7% of London's population lived below the poverty line. The information from Booth's survey was used to find out the socio-economic conditions of individuals; this information was then used to assign each street to a group, which is indicative of the socio-economic status of its residents. Some of the groups identified as part of Booth's research included very poor, mixed, comfortable, middle class, wealthy, etc. Some of the original works of Booth can be accessed in the online archives of the London School of Economics. The next landmark work in the area of geo-demographic classification was carried out by Park and Burgess. They developed an area classification of Chicago; the classification consisted of five concentric rings starting from the centre of the city, the transition zone, the working men's homes, the residential zone, and the commuter's zone. With the availability of machine readable census data in the United States and the United Kingdom, various companies started providing geo-demographic clustering systems to aid marketers with a profile of households and individuals living within a small geographical area. Census data forms the basic building block of any geo-demographic cluster system though data from other sources like survey data (lifestyle and other behavioural information) are also used. For example, the latest PRIZM cluster system for Canada uses the following types of data (http://www.pcensus.com):

- The 2001 census of Canada
- Proprietary enhanced dissemination area (a new geographical area level introduced in the 2001 census) level census data, including income estimates
- Proprietary spatial databases that relate to the urban–rural continuum
- Automotive ownership data from surveys
- Social values data from surveys
- Product preference and behavioural data from large established surveys by third parties such as the Print Measurement Bureau (PMB), BBM RTS—Canada, Environics Research, NADbank, Polk Canada, Canadian Financial Monitor (CFM), and Canadian Community Health Survey (CCHS)

The *PRIZM Canada marketers handbook* (2008) released by Environics Analytics provides a brief yet comprehensive note on the methodology of creating a geo-demographic cluster system. Two important aspects of the PRIZM Canada development methodology are important to note. The *first* is the selection of the smallest geographical unit to be used in the cluster system and the *second* is the judgemental criterion (over and above the statistical criteria) for selecting the final clusters. The cluster system uses dissemination area as the smallest geographical unit, each dissemination area has approximately 250 households and there are about 53,000 dissemination areas in Canada. Due to the unavailability of quality zip code level data, the analysis was limited to a dissemination area. However, the handbook points to research carried out in European markets, which suggest that the variance of geo-demographic data tends to become too high if areas smaller than a neighbourhood is used for building a cluster system.

Richard Webber, one of the pioneers in the field of geo-demographic segmentation, points out in his paper titled *Designing Geo-demographic Classifications to Meet Contemporary Business Needs*, that some of the geo-demographic variables are more valuable at the smaller geographic unit level, while others are more valuable at a higher level of aggregation. He points out that for the United Kingdom, characteristics like property are more valuable at a small geographic unit level while characteristics like employment are more valuable at a higher level of aggregation. In his paper, he also illustrates the usage of address in order to infer the housing type. For example, an address which contains numbers like "D24" suggests that the residence is an apartment while an address like "House No 15" suggests a single occupancy house. Similarly a house with a name containing the name or surname of the owner like "Agarwal Vila" suggests a high end single house owned by a very affluent owner.

With regards to the judgemental criteria for selecting the final segment, each segment must be intuitively appealing (sociologically, demographically, and from a marketing standpoint), reflect recent demographic changes, have an attitudinal and behavioural dimension as well, and should be neither too large nor to small. Table 1.4 provides a description of all the major geo-demographic cluster systems.

As evident from Table 1.4, various cluster systems attempt to capture the variability of the geo-demographic landscape from various dimensions. Each system uses income or financial condition as a primary criterion for rank ordering the segments. A discussion of all the cluster systems is beyond the scope of this chapter; however, a few cluster systems will be discussed in detail, so as to provide an outline of the way clusters are organised. The links to key websites provided in the table will aid the reader in knowing in detail about the other cluster systems. A discussion of the basic mosaic group is important because it is by far the most widely available (in terms of countries covered) clustering system. Table 1.5 from the Mosaic handbook illustrates the 10 basic mosaic groups for the United States and possible use in acquisition strategy. Each of these basic clusters is composed of a number of sub-clusters. The reader can refer to the Mosaic handbook for a detailed profile of each of these clusters (http://www.appliedgeographic.com/).

It is important to note that Table 1.5 is only of an indicative nature. Each geo-demographic cluster described here can be further broken down into a number of sub-clusters, which despite their similarity are quite different in terms of their composition. Hence, a specific combination of product proposition, pricing, and channel needs to be adopted for each of them. For example, the group "Upscale America" consists of the following sub-groups:

- Status-conscious consumers
- Affluent urban professionals
- Urban commuter families
- Solid suburban life
- Second-generation success
- Successful suburbia

**Table 1.4** Major Geo-demographic Classification Systems

| Cluster System | Developed by | Markets | Feature | Cluster Summary |
|---|---|---|---|---|
| ACRON | CACI Marketing Systems | United Kingdom | ACORN categorises all 1.9 million United Kingdom postcodes, which have been described using over 125 demographic statistics within England, Scotland, Wales, and Northern Ireland and 287 lifestyle variables | ACRON consists of 56 clusters, categorised into 17 categories which are further grouped into 5 broad groups.<br>ACRON also provides an ACRON financial classification map to categorise the United Kingdom market based on financial position of individuals. There are 49 financial clusters grouped into 11 groups (http://www.caci.co.uk/acorn/acornmap.asp) (http://www.caci.co.uk/acorn/whatis.asp) |
| Cluster PLUS 2000 | Strategic Mapping Inc. | United States | Census data and survey data on lifestyle | Introduced the concept of atomic clusters where each cluster consists of a very small number of households but is homogeneous enough. The current system consists of 450 atomic clusters |
| PRIZM | Nielsen Claritas | United States, Canada | Claritas is the pioneer of geo-demographic classification in the United States. Along with demographic data, Claritas uses financial survey, lifestyle survey, car ownership, media survey, health care behaviour survey, and other | PRIZM consists of 66 clusters for the United States and Canadian markets. These clusters are divided into 18 groups based on income. Claritas has also developed a clustering system called workplace PRIZM which |

(*Continued*)

**Table 1.4** Major Geo-demographic Classification Systems *(Continued)*

| Cluster System | Developed by | Markets | Feature | Cluster Summary |
|---|---|---|---|---|
| | | | company specific files like mutual fund ownership etc. In the new PRIZM released, claritas has used a new segmentation tool called multivariate divisive partitioning | ties an individual to his or her place of work (http://www.claritas.com/target-marketing/market-research-services/marketing-data/marketing-segmentation/prizm.jsp.) |
| P$YCLE | Nielsen Claritas | United States, Canada | P$YCLE is a segmentation system that evaluates consumers using demographic factors that have the greatest effect on their financial behaviour, such as income, age, presence of children, home ownership, and Claritas' proprietary measure of income producing assets | P$YCLE consists of 58 clusters, within 13 Lifestage groups, each with distinct usage patterns for financial products and services. (http://www.claritas.com/target-marketing/market-research-services/marketing-data/marketing-segmentation/psycle.jsp) |
| Personicx | Acxiom | United States, United Kingdom | Personicx uses 7 key dimensions for every household for creating the cluster system | Personicx has 70 clusters for the United States market and 52 clusters for the United Kingdom market. These clusters are ranked in order of net worth and income. Acxiom combines the cluster system with its cuting edge marketing data base INFOBASE for creating very powerful acquisition solutions (http://www.acxiom.com/personicx) (http://www.acxiom.co.uk/MarketingSolutions/Customer Information/SegmentationGISSolutions/PersonicxHousehold/index.html). |

(*Continued*)

**Table 1.4** Major Geo-demographic Classification Systems *(Continued)*

| Cluster System | Developed by | Markets | Feature | Cluster Summary |
|---|---|---|---|---|
| CAMEO | EuroDirect | United Kingdom | Built using census data, property valuation data, household tax data, individual share-holder and directorship data, consumer credit data, and residency data | The cluster system consists of 57 clusters, which are categorised into 10 major groups (http://www.eurodirect.co.uk/pages/cameo-uk) |
| MOSAIC | Experían | Australia, China (three provinces), Denmark, Finland, France, Germany, Greece, HongKong, New Zealand, Norway, Ireland, Spain, Sweden, United Kingdom, United States | Built using demographic data and proprietary household level data | The mosaic classification in each country consists of 10 major groups (in some countries additional groups are also present). The number of clusters in each group vary for each country. (http://www.appliedgeographic.com/Mosaic%20Global%20E-Handbook.pdf) |
| PSYTE | R.L Polk Company | United States, Canada, Australia, United Kingdom, France, Spain, Germany, China, Japan | Is most suited for the automotive industry. This cluster system combines Polk's extensive automotive data and buyer characteristics from its detailed consumer database with census demographics to classify neighborhood characteristics | The cluster system consists of 70 clusters. Polk also offers a cutting edge lead scoring solution for prioritising leads for an auto dealer or manufacturer (http://www.polk.com/) |
| VALS | Strategic Business Insights | United States, United Kingdom, Japan | Attempts to combine a consumer's demographic traits, psychological traits and a resource dimension. VALS uses proprietary psychometric technology to measure concepts that researchers have proved empirically correlate with consumer behaviour. | Consists of 8 basic cluster types namely Innovators, Thinkers, Believers, Achievers, Strivers, Experiencers, Makers, and Survivors |

**Table 1.5** Illustration of Basic Mosaic Groups

| Group Description | Group Characteristics from (http:// www. appliedgeographic.com/) | Possible Implications for Acquisition Strategy |
|---|---|---|
| Group A Affluent Suburbia | The wealthiest households in the nation. This group outranks all other mosaic types in terms of household income, home value, and educational achievement | This group is possibly the biggest market for selling investment and related services. A premium pricing startegy may work well with this group |
| Group B Upscale America | This group consists mostly of college-educated couples and families living in the metropolitan sprawl. Most of the adults work as executives and white-collar professionals, and their upscale incomes provide them with large homes and comfortable lifestyles. This group consists of avid internet users | Internet may be an important channel for selling products like financial services, insurance etc |
| Group C Small-town Contentment | This group consists mostly of middle-aged, upper-middle-class families living in small towns and satellite cities. As a group, they share moderate education and a mix of well-paying jobs in white-collar, blue-collar, and service professions. This group loves out door activities and are also active internet users | This group is possibly less likely to experiment with new concepts |
| Group D Blue-collar Backbone | This group features above-average proportions of both old and young residents. Most residents live in older outlying towns and cities, and work at blue-collar jobs in manufacturing, construction, and retail trades. These budget-conscious households shop at discount clothiers and department stores, and they have low rates for buying investments or insurance products. Traditional media is the best way of targeting this group | This is a segment for value for money offerings and a target market for traditional media like TV |

(*Continued*)

**Table 1.5** Illustration of Basic Mosaic Groups (*Continued*)

| Group Description | Group Characteristics from (http:// www. appliedgeographic.com/) | Possible Implications for Acquisition Strategy |
|---|---|---|
| Group E<br>American Diversity | This group consist of households with average education and middle-class incomes from blue-collar and service industry jobs. Many of the members are ageing singles and couples. They are more attuned to traditional media | This is a segment for value for money offering and a target market for traditional media like TV |
| Group F<br>Metro Fringe | Many of the group's households consist of young singles and couples who work at blue-collar and service industry jobs. They tend to live in older single-family homes, semi-detached houses and low-rise apartments. They shop mostly at discount retailers where they buy the latest fashion and tech gear at low prices. They tend to use the internet significantly | Though price sensitive this group is more likely to explore new products and concepts. This group will also respond to discount offers on the internet |
| Group G<br>Remote America | This group mostly consists of working-class couples and families. Members of this group tend to be employed in agriculture and blue-collar jobs that pay modest wages | A value for money offering using traditional channels is possibly optimal for this group |
| Group H<br>Aspiring Contemporaries | This group consists of relatively young people who live in new homes and apartments. They are the emerging affluents. They spend a lot of their discretionary income on the latest fashions and consumer electronics and are very Internet savvy. | Can be a key market for new gadgets |

(*Continued*)

**Table 1.5** Illustration of Basic Mosaic Groups *(Continued)*

| Group Description | Group Characteristics from (http:// www. appliedgeographic.com/) | Possible Implications for Acquisition Strategy |
|---|---|---|
| Group I<br>Rural Villages and Farms | This group maintains a tranquile lifestyle and visits big-box home improvement chains and watch how-to shows on TV | A value for money offering using traditional channels is possibly optimal for this group |
| Group J<br>Struggling Societies | This group tends to be disadvantaged and uneducated. They shop at discount clothiers and sporting goods stores for casual apparel and athletic shoes. This group relates a lot to ethnic-oriented media | A value for money offering often involving deep discounts using traditional channels is possibly optimal for this group. |
| Group K<br>Urban Essence | This is the least affluent group and consists of relatively young minorities living in older apartments. With their above-average household size, they make a strong market for children's toys and electronic gear, especially video games, dolls, and board games | Discount stores may deign specific bundling kind of offers for this group, as they are usually more price sensitive |
| Group L<br>Varying Lifestyles | This is an unconventional group. What they share is the singular experience of living in group quarters | |

A company may not focus on every sub-group, and it may have very different strategies for each of these sub-groups. The interested reader can refer to the Mosaic website for a complete description and relative size of each of the geo-demographic groups.

Most emerging markets do not have a cluster system that can be used by marketers. However, in most markets it is possible to develop a rough-cut geo-demographic classification using multiple lists and overlaying the same with various primary surveys. For example, in the Indian market, a broad classification based on socio-economic category (SEC) can be used to segment the desired market. The SEC classification is based on a combination of asset ownership and education. Table 1.6 provides an overview of the SEC classification system.

Mapping all the SECs with the geographic span of the country remains a challenge and hence, companies tend to depend a lot on feet on street sales model, whereby sales agents with deep knowledge of a particular locality are deployed to find a target population within a particular geography.

### *1.5.2 Developing a Segmentation Scheme*

This section focuses on the methodology of utilising all the prospect data sources and the geo-demographic classification system to build a customised segmentation to suit the marketing needs of the company. As stated earlier, census data is the most important data source for identifying and sizing the prospect universe. It provides an estimation of the addressable universe and also helps in identifying possible universe expansion opportunities. For example, a particular company may have a historical focus on big urban centres. However, the analysis of the census data may point out possible universe expansion opportunities into emerging urban centres. It must be noted that census data is available at a geographic unit level and so cannot be used directly for targeting individual households.

The analysis of census data starts with an estimation of the size of the universe along key dimensions of interest. Most often income, age, and socio-economic classification, are used for this purpose. Figure 1.4 depicts the analysis of census data along these key dimensions.

The dimensions depicted in Fig. 1.4 are some of the key dimensions for assessing the size of the addressable universe. For example, if a telecom company looks at the income pyramid as suggested in Fig. 1.4, it can clearly outline the size of the segments for its various products. The high income segment will be the target universe for high-end third generation mobile telecom products like extremely fast data connection, video calling, global positioning applications, etc. The mid-income group will be the target for second generation post-paid connections wherein "value for money" rate plan is a key customer need. The low-income population usually referred to as the "bottom of the pyramid" presents a challenge for most companies and it is critical to launch products that can serve

**Table 1.6** Socio-economic Classification (Urban) GRID

| Occupation | Illiterate | School Upto 4 Years/ Literate But No Formal Schooling | School Upto 5–9 Years | SSC/HSC | Some College But Not Graduate | Graduate/ Post Graduate/ General | Graduate/ Post Graduate/ Professional |
|---|---|---|---|---|---|---|---|
| Unskilled workers | E2 | E2 | E1 | D | D | D | D |
| Skilled workers | E2 | E1 | D | C | C | B2 | B2 |
| Petty traders | E2 | D | D | C | C | B2 | B2 |
| Shop Owners | D | D | C | B2 | B1 | A2 | A2 |
| **Business/Industrialist with number of employees** | | | | | | | |
| Business/Industrialist—no employees | D | C | B2 | B1 | A2 | A2 | A1 |
| Bus./Industrialist—1–9 employees | C | B2 | B2 | B1 | A2 | A1 | A1 |
| Bus./Industrialist—10+ employees | B1 | B1 | A2 | A2 | A1 | A1 | A1 |
| Self-employed professionals | D | D | D | B2 | B1 | A2 | A1 |
| Clerical/Salesmen | D | D | D | C | B2 | B1 | B1 |
| Supervisory level | D | D | C | C | B2 | B1 | A2 |
| Officers/Executives–Junior | C | C | C | B2 | B1 | A2 | A2 |
| Officers/Executives–Middle/Senior | B1 | B1 | B1 | B1 | A2 | A1 | A1 |

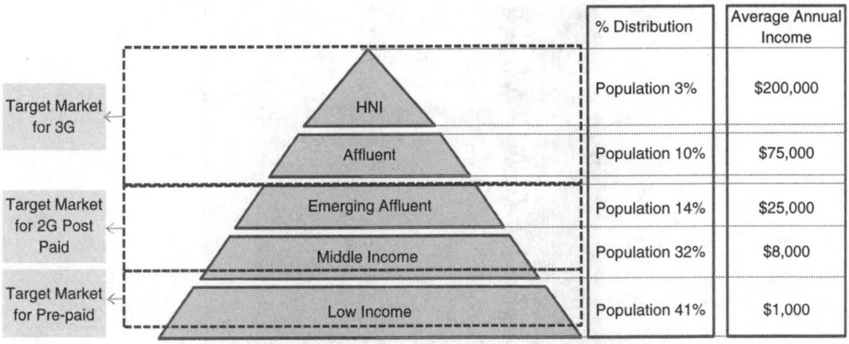


**Figure 1.4** Offer Design Based on Socio-economic Profiles

the need for this population, while delivering profits for the organisation. From a telecom perspective, a pre-paid offer with easy top-up may be the right product for this segment.

Another frequently used analysis involves an age–income grid, which is used in market size determination across a number of products and services. Table 1.7 depicts a typical age–income grid.

The grid depicts the product offers and customisation, which can be used to satisfy the need of each of these groups. For example, for the 18–35 years group a telecom company may provide an offer of free download of certain number of latest hit songs, which can be used as caller tunes as well. The age–income grid can also be used as a measure of risk for products like loans and credit cards. Usually it has been found that prospects with higher age and higher income present lower risk. It is important to note, the entire 18–35 years age population may be interested in downloading latest songs. However, the higher income groups within this age bracket may not be interested in the free download offer. Thus it is important to use both age and income for offer design. In markets where an extensive geo-demographic classification is available, it is possible to perform a more detailed analysis of each of these groups to gain a deeper understanding of the prospect universe.

In the absence of a geo-demographic classification of areas, it is imperative to segment key cities and towns based on macroeconomic and population indicators. Some of the key macroeconomic indicators include GDP and GDP growth rate of the city, average income, average savings, average value of homes and the like. Key population indicators include education level and percentage of population in various socio-economic brackets, etc. Figure 1.5 depicts a sample cluster diagram for classifying cities and towns. The sizes of the bubbles in the figure represent the size of the addressable universe within each of these categories.

Companies need to overlay their internal information and competitive information on the geographic classification to determine the strategy they may adopt in each of the cities and towns, which are of interest. Table 1.8 depicts the result of the overlay of internal and competitive information

**Table 1.7** Age–Income Grid

| | | Income | | | | | | |
|---|---|---|---|---|---|---|---|---|
| | | <$1,000 | $1,000–$8,000 | $8,000–$25,000 | $25,000–$75,000 | $75,000–$200,000 | >$200,000 | Total |
| Age | 18 years–25 years | 15.2% | 11.8% | 5.2% | 3.7% | 0.7% | 0.4% | 37% |
| | 25 years–35 years | 11.5% | 9.0% | 3.9% | 2.8% | 0.6% | 0.3% | 28% |
| | 35 years–45 years | 6.2% | 4.8% | 2.1% | 1.5% | 0.3% | 0.2% | 15% |
| | 45 years–60 years | 4.9% | 3.8% | 1.7% | 1.2% | 0.2% | 0.1% | 12% |
| | >60 years | 3.3% | 2.6% | 1.1% | 0.8% | 0.2% | 0.1% | 8% |
| | Total | 41% | 32% | 14% | 10% | 2% | 1% | |

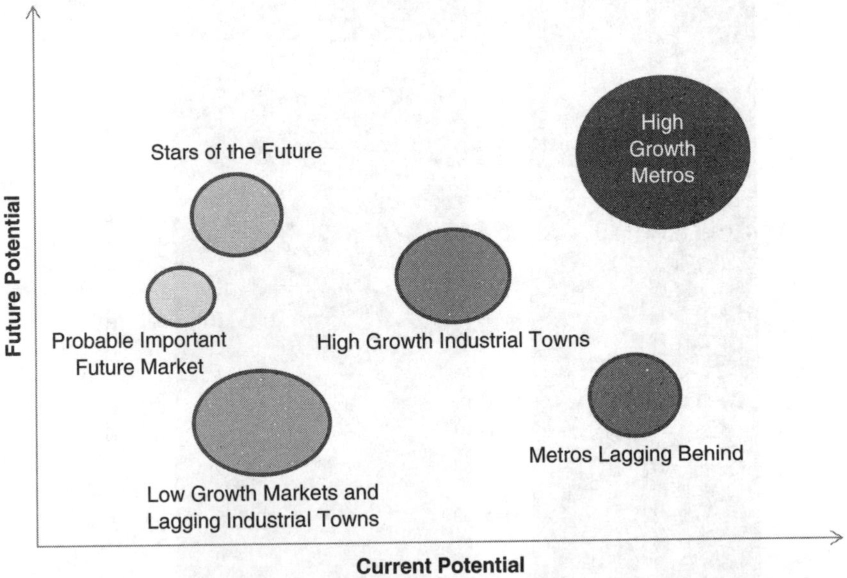


**Figure 1.5** Clustering Geographies Based on Current and Future Potential

on the geographic classification to determine the final targeting strategy. Usually a multivariate approach is used to combine multiple data fields for creating the segmentation scheme. For products like credit cards and loans, the level of risk within various segments is also an important consideration. A common approach titled "straw man analysis" is often used to create the profile of "the most desired prospect".

The factors used for the classification in Table 1.8 are as follows:

- **Macroeconomic characteristics**
  - Gross domestic product (GDP) of the city
  - GDP growth rate
  - Bank deposit volume
- **Population characteristics**
  - Percentage of population in affluent, high net worth (HNI), and emerging affluent category
  - Size of the population
- **Internal dimensions**
  - Size of the customer base
  - Customer satisfaction score for existing customers
  - Brand awareness in the city or town
  - Strength of the sales and distribution network
- **Competitive dimensions**
  - An index of competitive activity in the city or town

The above characteristics are used along with city classification clusters to determine the targeting strategy for the city. For example, some

**Table 1.8** Classification of Cities Based on Attractiveness

| City | Type | % HNI | % Affluent | % Emerging Affluent | % Current Customers | Average Customer Satisfaction Score | Brand Awareness | Strength of Sales Network | Competittive Activity | % of Total Population | Contribution to National GDP | % of Total Bank Deposits | Growth Rate | City Cluster Classification | Decision |
|---|---|---|---|---|---|---|---|---|---|---|---|---|---|---|---|
| C1 | Metro | 7.70 | 14.95 | 22.95 | 9.20 | 72 | High | High | High | 11.53 | 12.20% | 12.9 | High | | |
| C2 | Metro | 7.20 | 14.79 | 22.13 | 5.70 | 68 | High | High | High | 4.27 | 5.10% | 5.2 | High | High growth metros | Continue focus |
| C3 | Metro | 6.80 | 13.92 | 21.85 | 6.20 | 73 | High | High | High | 3.71 | 4.50% | 5.1 | Medium | | |
| C4 | Metro | 6.30 | 13.40 | 20.47 | 5.40 | 73 | High | High | High | 4.99 | 4.50% | 5.2 | High | | |
| C5 | Metro | 5.30 | 12.33 | 19.50 | 4.12 | 68 | High | Medium | High | 3.76 | 3.10% | 3.4 | Low | Metros lagging behind | Slightly deprioritize |
| C6 | Metro | 5.20 | 12.56 | 20.42 | 3.20 | 51 | Medium | Medium | High | 3.64 | 3.10% | 4.1 | Low | | |
| C7 | Emerging city | 4.10 | 11.11 | 18.70 | 3.00 | 54 | Medium | Medium | High | 3.06 | 2.10% | 3.0 | High | | |
| C8 | Emerging city | 3.93 | 11.43 | 19.02 | 2.89 | 52 | High | Medium | High | 2.64 | 2.40% | 2.7 | High | | |
| C9 | Emerging city | 3.76 | 10.78 | 18.59 | 0.50 | 41 | Low | Low | High | 3.15 | 2.70% | 3.3 | High | | |
| C10 | Emerging city | 3.56 | 10.68 | 18.64 | 1.10 | 37 | Medium | Low | High | 2.42 | 2.20% | 2.3 | High | Stars of the future | Increase marketing effort |
| C11 | Emerging city | 3.36 | 11.03 | 18.17 | 0.99 | 48 | Low | Low | Medium | 2.36 | 2.00% | 2.2 | High | | |
| C12 | Emerging city | 3.16 | 10.28 | 18.24 | 1.00 | 54 | Low | Low | Medium | 1.95 | 1.60% | 2.0 | High | | |
| C13 | Emerging city | 2.96 | 10.27 | 17.27 | 3.00 | 71 | Medium | Medium | High | 2.02 | 2.00% | 2.9 | High | | |
| C14 | Industrial centre | 3.20 | 10.96 | 18.64 | 2.83 | 68 | Medium | Medium | High | 2.96 | 2.20% | 2.3 | Medium | | |

(*Continued*)

**Table 1.8** Classification of Cities Based on Attractiveness *(Continued)*

| City | Type | % HNI | % Affluent | % Emerging Affluent | % Current Customers | Average Customer Satisfaction Score | Brand Awareness | Strength of Sales Network | Competitive Activity | % of Total Population | Contribution to National GDP | % of Total Bank Deposits | Growth Rate | City Cluster Classification | Decision |
|---|---|---|---|---|---|---|---|---|---|---|---|---|---|---|---|
| C15 | Industrial centre | 3.19 | 10.49 | 17.70 | 2.66 | 66 | Medium | Medium | Medium | 3.39 | 2.50% | 2.8 | Medium | High growth Industrial towns | Continue focus |
| C16 | Industrial centre | 3.50 | 10.91 | 18.25 | 2.49 | 54 | Medium | Medium | Medium | 2.17 | 1.60% | 2.5 | Medium | | |
| C17 | Industrial centre | 3.39 | 11.06 | 18.50 | 2.50 | 48 | Medium | Medium | Medium | 1.14 | 1.10% | 2.0 | High | | |
| C18 | Industrial centre | 2.12 | 9.40 | 16.99 | 2.36 | 44 | Medium | Medium | Medium | 2.84 | 2.30% | 3.1 | High | | |
| C19 | Industrial centre | 2.34 | 10.01 | 17.07 | 1.10 | 44 | Low | Low | Medium | 1.59 | 1.00% | 1.6 | Low | Lagging industrial | Do not focus |
| C20 | Industrial centre | 2.18 | 9.18 | 17.16 | 0.96 | 38 | Low | Low | Medium | 0.92 | 0.60% | 0.6 | Low | | |
| C21 | Industrial centre | 2.02 | 9.24 | 16.29 | 3.00 | 54 | Medium | Medium | Medium | 1.54 | 1.20% | 1.3 | Low | Low growth markets with high brand | Slightly deprioritise |
| C22 | Large district town | 3.06 | 10.41 | 18.28 | 2.86 | 67 | Medium | Medium | Medium | 1.00 | 1.00% | 2.0 | Low | | |
| C23 | Large district town | 3.20 | 10.41 | 18.41 | 2.72 | 61 | Medium | Medium | Low | 2.02 | 1.30% | 1.4 | Medium | | |
| C24 | Large district town | 3.08 | 10.79 | 18.21 | 0.20 | 68 | Low | Low | Low | 1.83 | 1.50% | 2.1 | Medium | Probate important future market | Increase marketing effort |
| C25 | Large district town | 2.96 | 10.46 | 18.07 | 0.30 | 71 | Low | Low | Low | 1.40 | 1.00% | 2.0 | Medium | | |
| C26 | Large district town | 2.84 | 10.07 | 17.31 | 0.60 | 66 | Low | Low | Low | 1.56 | 0.70% | 1.1 | Medium | | |

of the large district towns (C24, C25, and C26) that have relatively lower contribution to national GDP and are growing only at a medium pace can still be an important part of the acquisition strategy because of the low-competitive activity in these cities.

An analysis of the prospect universe based on census data can only be performed based on geographic area level. In order to segment the prospect universe at an individual or household level, the marketer needs to source other data at a prospect level. Figure 1.6 depicts an example of collating multiple data sources.

Once the data is matched across these multiple lists, it is possible to perform a detailed segmentation at an individual prospect level. Figure 1.7 depicts the results of the segmentation. It needs to be noted that the clusters depicted in Fig. 1.7 are built specifically for a particular company, whereas the geo-demographic clusters discussed earlier are generic clusters based on census data. The customized clusters can be utilized along with the generic geo-demographic clusters for developing the marketing strategy. At this point, the company can marry the city level targeting strategy with the prospect level targeting strategy to determine the strategy for each prospect cluster within each city.

## 1.6 Prioritisation

Marketing wisdom suggests that segmentation can best be harnessed if it is coupled with the right targeting or prioritisation strategy. One approach to prioritisation involves matching the targeting strategy with the needs of each of the segments. For example, if a luxury brand's targeting strategy entails only targeting the super-rich, then lifestyle and income segmentation is enough to identify the market pockets which need to be targeted. However, if the business of a company entails an intensive and costly sales process often involving targeted campaigns, then the company may further want to segregate the "eligible" set of prospects based on their propensity to buy. For the purpose of ascertaining the propensity among prospects, one may use a number of approaches including market research based approaches (both quantitative and qualitative) and statistical approaches using past data. Look-alike modelling is one of the most used statistical approaches for this purpose. Look-alike modelling involves looking at the present set of customers that a firm has and identifying similar customer profiles in the prospect base. Logistic regression can be used to develop such models. In case one does not have internal data, one can use lists of customers who have purchased similar products in the past. An important limitation of using look-alike modelling is the fact that the results are heavily dependent on past targeting strategy and sales process. For example, if in the past a firm has concentrated mostly on certain geographic regions, then a look-alike profile will always return prospects from that geographic region. Similarly, if the firm had a more

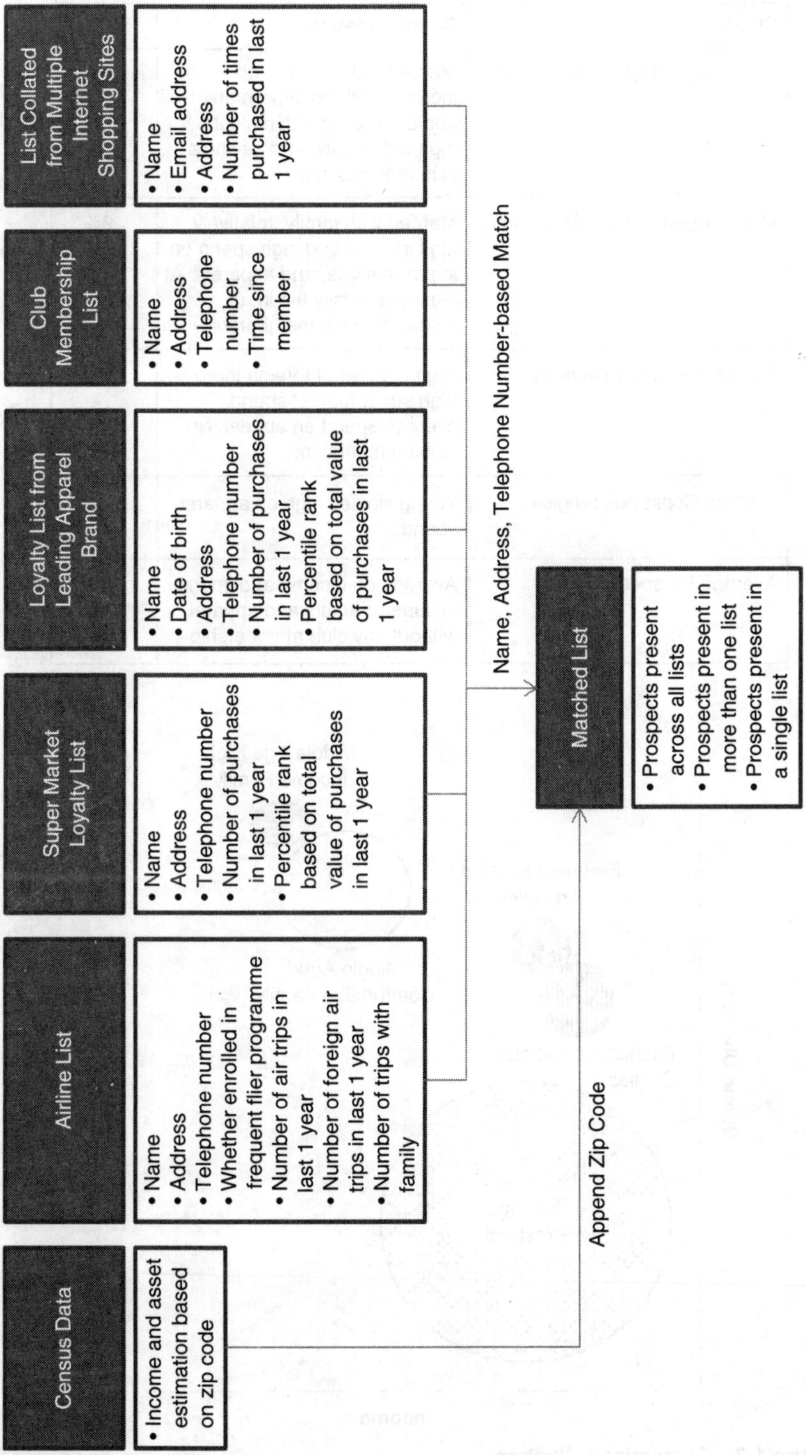


**Figure 1.6** Combining Multiple Data Sources

| Cluster | Characteristics | Size |
|---|---|---|
| Middle Aged High Income Family | Married with family, high income, high on supermarket and apparel spend, multiple trips with family, and having a club membership | 4% |
| Middle Aged Comfortable Family | Married with family, relatively high income and high spend on super markets, and apparels. At least one family trip in an airline. No club membership. | 9% |
| Frequent Foreign Traveller | High number of foreign trips, high super market spend, average spend on appeal. No club membership. | 7% |
| Fashion Conscious Singles | Young singles high on apparel spend | 10% |
| Average Prospect | Average on income and spend in super markets and apparel without any club membership | 70% |

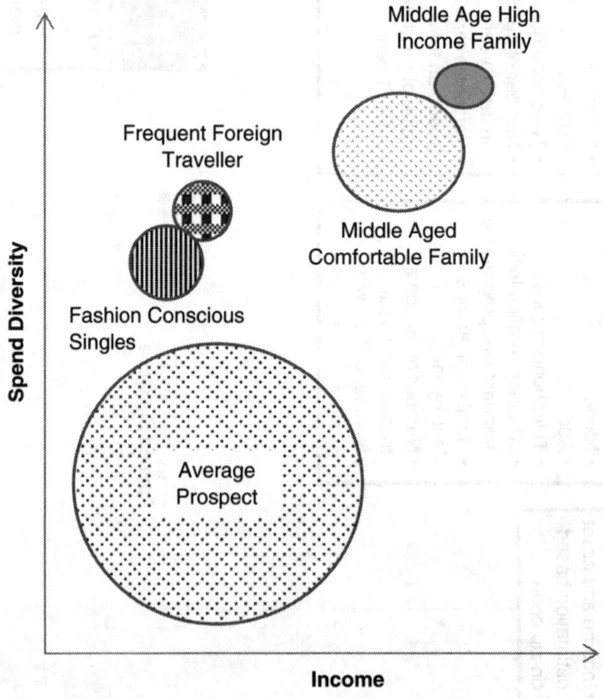


**Figure 1.7** Customized Clusters

productive sales manager in charge of a particular segment, then that will bias the results of the look-alike model in a similar manner. To tide over this problem, it is critical to conduct random testing so as to target a wide range of prospects as part of a test campaign. The test data can be used to obtain an unbiased sample, which can be used for model development. The geographic prioritization, described in Table 1.8 also acts as an important tool for identifying key markets where the company needs to focus its marketing efforts.

### *1.6.1 Prioritisation Example*

The prioritisation methodology discussed in the last section has been illustrated here with an example of a mobile telecom offer. The product involves an offer for a post-paid mobile connection using direct mailer and telecalling as key channels of communication. Prospect data is sourced from a number of lists and commercially available data sources like InfoBase. InfoBase is a commercially available data source, in the United States, which provides a large variety of information about prospects including their level of assets, financial sophistication, media usage, internet usage and the like. These data elements act as key predictors for predicting the chances of the prospect responding to a direct mail offer. For the direct mail channel, prospects can respond back to the offer by filling in the return mailer that is attached with the offer mailer or they can call a toll free number provided with the mailer or go to the website and enter the offer code. For the telecalling channel, prospects can respond to the offer during the call or can log into the website and enter the offer code provided by the tele-caller. As the offer involves a post-paid connection, there is a credit check, which happens after the prospect responds. Responders deemed too risky are rejected. The company uses a response model built out of a random mailing that have been carried out to select prospects that are most likely to respond. The offer has two variants, which are as follows:

- **Voice offer:** 200 minutes of free calling per month to anywhere in the country
- **Data offer:** Up to 2GB of download free per month

As pointed out, the company has performed tests on a random sample of prospects; within this randomly selected sample, one half is randomly selected for a voice offer and the other randomly selected for the data offer. Based on the results three models are built. Some of the key variables used in the models include prospect age, geo-demographic profile, indicator as to whether the person has moved to a new area, time the household has lived in the current address, whether the customer has purchased a phone or wireless product in the last 24 months, indicator if the customer is an active investor, home value, type of Internet connection, name of Internet provider, and the like.

#### 1.6.1.1 Model 1: Generic Response Model

This model predicts whether the prospect will at all respond to any offer. For the purpose of this model, the entire random sample, which was mailed, is used. Responders to the offer (irrespective of the offer type) are tagged as "1" and non-responders are tagged as "0". Further, logistic regression is used to build a model to separate the "1s" from the "0s". The model provides a score, which ranges between "0" to "1000" wherein a higher score indicates higher chance of responding to an offer (irrespective of the type). The model is validated in another campaign, where similar random mailing was carried out. The results of the model are depicted in Fig. 1.8.

The first column of the table shows the score range. The score ranges have been designed in such a way that each score range captures 5% of the population. The second column represents the cumulative population distribution. The first score range (1000–840) accounts for 5% of the population. The second score range (839–820) also accounts for 5% of the population. Together these two score ranges (1000–820) accounts for 10% of the population. All the score ranges together capture 100% of the population.

The third column represents the cumulative number of non-responders captured. As the number of non-responder is very high (99.44%), the cumulative percentage of non-responders is very similar to the cumulative percentage of the total population.

The fourth column represents the cumulative percentage of responders captured. The first score range captures 37.97% of the responders, the first two score ranges together captures 51.65% of responders and so on. It is important to note that if prospects would have been selected into 20 groups at random, then the first group would have captured only 5% of responders, the second group would have captured 10% of responders and so on. However, due to the model one can identify 37.97% of responders in the first group compared to 5%, which would have been the case for random selection. The graph alongside the table represents this effect. The dotted straight line represents the percentage of responders that would have been captured based on random selection and the solid curved line represents the responders that are captured by the model. A chart like this is called the gains chart. The last column represents the response rate of the particular group. The first group has the maximum response rate and the response rate keeps on decreasing as the score decreases. This is called the rank ordering property of the model.

The overall response rate for the campaign is 0.56%. However based on the model score (score more than 811) it is possible to identify the top 20% of the population in such a way that these 20% population accounts for 67.8% of the responders. The response rate of the top 20%

| Score Range | Cumulative Prospect Percent | Cumulative Non Responder Percent | Cumulative Responder Percent | Response Rate Percent | |
|---|---|---|---|---|---|
| 1000–840 | 5.00% | 5.11% | 37.97% | 4.20% | Represents the top 20% prospects based on the response score. This group captures 67.8% of the responders. This group has a response rate of 1.9% compared to the overall response rate of 0.56%. |
| 839–820 | 10.00% | 10.12% | 51.65% | 1.55% | |
| 819–816 | 15.00% | 15.16% | 61.30% | 1.08% | |
| 815–811 | 20.00% | 20.46% | 67.82% | 0.70% | |
| 810–806 | 25.00% | 25.04% | 72.44% | 0.57% | Represents the next 15% prospects based on the response score. This group has a response rate of 0.5%, which is similar to the overall response rate of 0.56%. |
| 805–802 | 30.00% | 30.31% | 76.85% | 0.47% | |
| 801–797 | 35.00% | 35.50% | 80.28% | 0.37% | |
| 796–793 | 40.00% | 40.59% | 83.12% | 0.32% | Represnts the bottom 65% prospects. This group has response rate of only 0.17% compared to the overall response rate of 0.56%. |
| 792–788 | 45.00% | 45.45% | 85.36% | 0.26% | |
| 787–782 | 50.00% | 50.17% | 87.48% | 0.25% | |
| 781–776 | 55.00% | 55.16% | 89.28% | 0.20% | |
| 775–770 | 60.00% | 60.71% | 90.94% | 0.17% | |
| 769–762 | 65.00% | 66.10% | 92.39% | 0.15% | |
| 761–754 | 70.00% | 70.43% | 93.56% | 0.15% | |
| 753–745 | 75.00% | 75.80% | 94.78% | 0.13% | |
| 744–735 | 80.00% | 80.58% | 95.90% | 0.13% | |
| 734–684 | 85.00% | 85.24% | 96.92% | 0.12% | |
| 683–587 | 90.00% | 90.39% | 97.91% | 0.11% | |
| 586–410 | 95.00% | 95.27% | 99.17% | 0.15% | |
| 409–0 | 100.00% | 100.00% | 100.00% | 0.10% | |
| Overall Response Rate: 0.56% | | | | | |

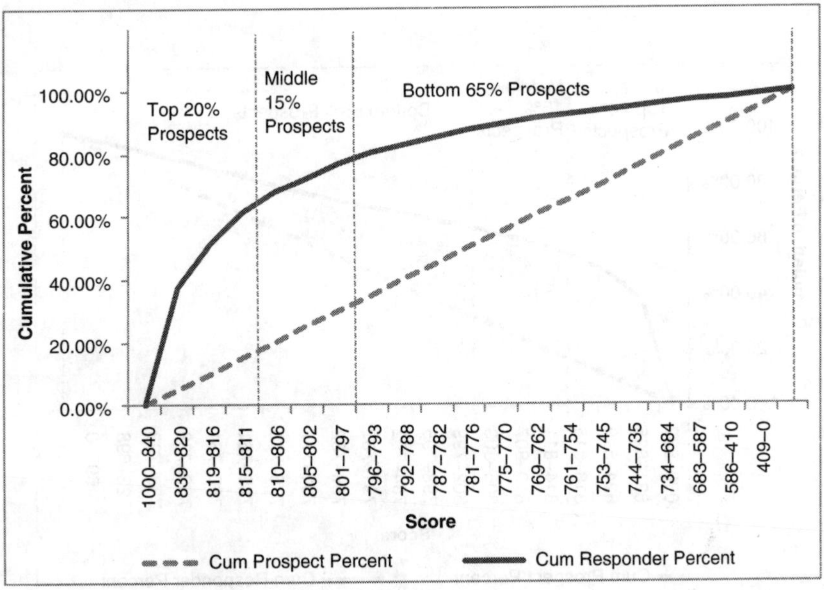


**Figure 1.8** Response Model – Lift Chart

population is 1.9%, compared to the overall response rate of 0.56%. The same information has been graphically depicted in the adjoining figure. Instead of using the response rate for identifying the cut-off score, one can also use Return On Investment (ROI) for determining the cutoff score.

### 1.6.1.2 Model 2: Response Model for Voice Offer

The second model is built on prospects that are targeted with the voice offer. The score for the voice offer model predicts the chances of the prospect responding to a voice offer.

### 1.6.1.3 Model 3: Response Model for Data Offer

The third model is built on prospects that are targeted with the data offer. The score for the data offer model predicts the chances of the prospect responding to a data offer. The results of these models can be analysed in a manner similar to Model 1 for overall response. Figure 1.9 depicts the gains chart for the two models. Based on the results of the models, the bottom 65% prospects as per the model 1 score are not targeted at all. Figure 1.10 below depicts the targeting strategy for prospects with high (more than 811) overall response score. Figure 1.11 depicts the targeting strategy for prospects with medium (811–797) overall response score.

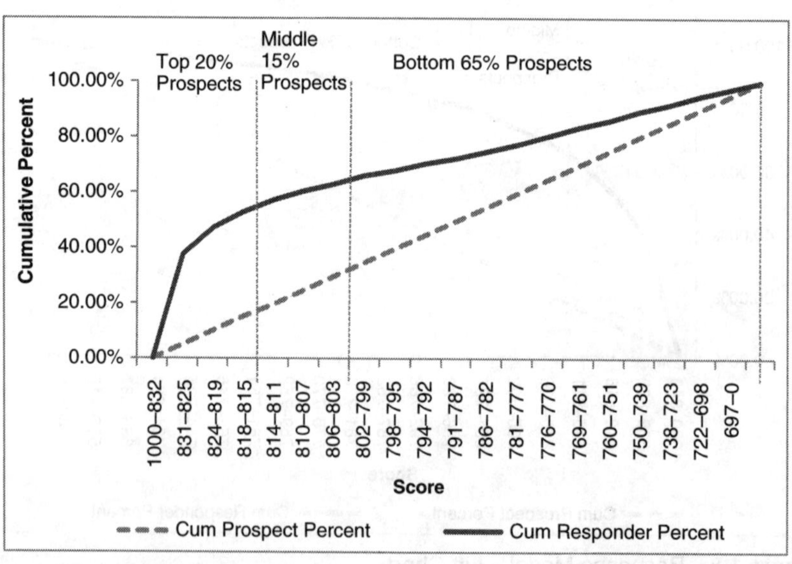


**Figure 1.9** Lift Chart for Model 2

(*Continued*)

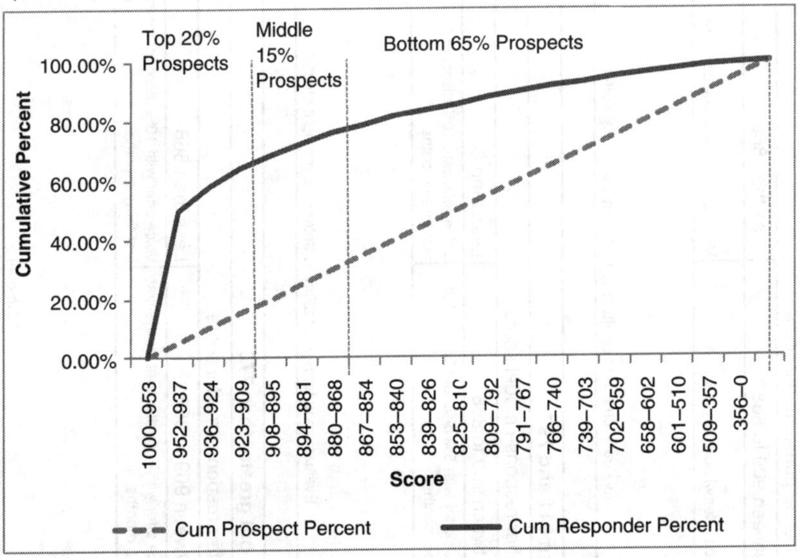


**Figure 1.9** Lift Chart for Model 3

## 1.7 Offer Design

The particular offer for each segment needs to be designed based on the profitability and response characteristic of the segment. Generally speaking, a more lucrative promotional offer increases the probability of response. However, a more lucrative offer may reduce profitability and might attract the wrong type of customer. Lewis et al. in their paper titled *Customer Acquisition Promotions and Customer Asset Value* point out that customers acquired through promotions tend to have lower repurchase rate and lower customer value compared to customers acquired without promotions. Hence, an offer design needs to consider the following criteria:

- Acquisition costs
- Offer cost
- Acquisition volume
- Short-term success metrics (like response rate, sales volume)
- Long-term profitability
- Type of customer acquired
- Long-term potential of acquired customers (potential of cross-selling other products, chances of attrition, potential of enhancing usage)

Table 1.9 depicts an offer grid, which compares multiple offers along these key dimensions.

| Generic Response Score Greater than 811 | | | | |
|---|---|---|---|---|
| | | Data offer response model score | | |
| | | Greater than 909 | Between 909 to 868 | Less than 868 |
| Voice Offer Response Model Score | Greater than 815 | Evaluate long-term profitability to determine the right offer | Voice offer without any discount | Voice offer without any discount |
| | Between 815 and 803 | Data offer without any discount | Evaluate long-term profitability to determine the right offer | |
| | Less than 803 | Data offer without any discount | | |

| Generic Response Score Between 811 and 797 | | | | |
|---|---|---|---|---|
| | | Data offer response model score | | |
| | | Greater than 909 | Between 909 to 868 | Less than 868 |
| Voice Offer Response Model Score | Greater than 815 | Evaluate long-term profitability to determine the right offer | Voice offer with 5% discount for the first three months | Voice offer with 10% discount for the first three months |
| | Between 815 and 803 | Data offer with 5% discount for the first three months | Evaluate long-term profitability to determine the right offer | |
| | Less than 803 | Data offer with 10% discount for the first three months | | |

| Generic Response Score Less than 797 but greater than 775 | | | | |
|---|---|---|---|---|
| | | Data offer response model score | | |
| | | Greater than 909 | Between 909 to 868 | Less than 868 |
| Voice Offer Response Model Score | Greater than 815 | Evaluate long-term profitability to determine the right offer | Voice offer with 10% discount for the first three months | Voice offer with 10% discount for the first three months |
| | Between 815 and 803 | Data offer with 10% discount for the first three months | No offer | |
| | Less than 803 | Data offer with 10% discount for the first three months | | |

**Figure 1.10** Offer Selection Based on Response Scores

**Table 1.9** Offer Comparison for Credit Card

| | Offer 1 | Offer 2 | Offer- 3 | Offer 4 | Offer 5 |
|---|---|---|---|---|---|
| **Key Driver/Offer** | The customer earns twice the reward points per dollar of purchase | The card comes loaded with 1000 (equivalent to 50 dollars) reward points which can be redeemed at select stores | All purchases made in the first six months will attract a lower interest rate | All gasoline purchase will earn twice the reward points and the customer will get a free one month subscription of an auto magazine along with the card | The customer can transfer his/her balance from another card and the transferred balance will enjoy a lower rate for 12 months |
| **Offer Cost** | Low | Medium | High | Medium | High |
| **Response Rate** | Low (as there is limited benefit to the customer right away, the benefits flow through over time) | Medium | Medium | Medium (provided the right prospects are targeted) | High |
| **Long-term Customer Engagement** | High (as the offer will drive long-term spend) | Low | Low | High (if the right set of prospects are targeted) | Low |
| **Type of Customer Acquired** | Less risky, high spending customer | Moderate risky customers seeking one time benefit | Higher risk high spending customers who think they cannot pay their dues fully in future | Less risky, high on fuel spend | High risk customers who have balances with other cards which they are not able to pay-off |
| **Long-term Profitability** | Medium as these customers might always pay their dues in full and hence, the issuer will not earn any interest | Low as they might switch over to competition easily | Medium as these customers might stop spending after six months. Also more of these customers might go delinquent in future | Medium as most of these customers might pay their dues in full | Medium as many of these customers might shift their balances to a different card after the 12 month low interest period is over. Also as these customers are more risky some of them will go delinquent |

At this point, it is important to note that the offers need to be tested before final roll out. A particular offer may have various components like discounts, promotional pricing for a limited period, etc. It is important for the marketer to find out the optimal combination of all these factors. A design of experiments approach needs to be utilised to test the individual and joint effect of all these factors. The interested reader can refer to Chapter 8 for an understanding of the usage of design of experiments for testing.

## 1.8 Direct Marketing Channels

Success of direct marketing is driven largely by the efficiency with which one can manage the channels used for direct marketing. Typically, the channels used are: direct mailers, telemarketing, sales agents, and Internet and email. In many cases, more than one channel is used or the same channel is used twice for reinforcing the offer. For example, it is a common practice to send a direct mailer to a large population and then follow it up with telemarketing for the sub population, which has a higher propensity of responding. In some cases, a primary direct mailer is supported by a remailing programme for reinforcing the offer. A detailed discussion on channels is also provided in Chapter 8; the interested reader can refer that for further details.

### *1.8.1 Direct Mailer*

Of all the direct marketing channels, direct mailer is the most used channel and accounts for most of the direct marketing in the developed markets. Cost per response (CPR) is possibly the most common benchmark for evaluating any direct mailer campaign. The metric takes on slightly different names in various industries. Its term varies as cost per lead, cost per subscriber, cost per click, etc. However it is always calculated as the total cost of the mailing programme divided by the response. Some of the cost heads in a direct mailer programme include:

- Cost of mailing list
- Cost of media buys (if the direct mailer is sent as an insert to a magazine or newspaper)
- Creative design cost, which involves the cost of designing
- Production cost
- Mailing cost
- Fulfilment costs (including shipping and processing)
- Cost of return

In most cases these cost elements are expressed as Cost Per Mailer or Cost Per Mailbase (CPM), which represents the cost for 1000 mailers. On top of these costs one will also incur an offer cost for each mailer sent. The offer cost consists of the cost of freebies and booklets that are sent along with the direct mailer to incentivise response. The return on investment (ROI) of a direct mailer campaign is calculated by netting the costs from the margin earned from the number of final conversions. Table 1.10 provides an example.

While designing a direct mailer one has to take into account every driver that is important for generating response. Some of the common drivers, which are critical for the success of a direct mailer, are:

- **Product feature:** The direct mailer must have a section dedicated to the product; its unique features, the benefits that it can provide to the buyer, etc. For example, an offer for a term insurance may state that the offer is "among the cheapest term plans today", alternatively it may state that, "you could save upto ₹2,000 per year" by investing in the insurance scheme. The second one is definitely a better offer as it clearly articulates the exact benefit of the offer.
- **Personalisation:** The direct mailer must have some reference to its recipient; this is an important advantage of direct marketing over and above top of line advertising, whereby careful segmentation can be employed to identify the correct message for each individual. For example, if a credit card company launches a direct mailer

**Table 1.10** ROI Calculation for a Direct Mailer Campaign

| | |
|---|---|
| Material CPM per thousand (including creative design and production) | ₹500 |
| Postage CPM per thousand | ₹100 |
| List CPM per thousand | ₹40 |
| Total CPM per thousand | ₹640 |
| Number of mail pieces | 50,000 |
| Promotion cost (Number of pieces * Total CPM per thousand)/1000 | ₹32,000 |
| Response rate (this indicates leads generated by the campaign) | 2% |
| Conversion rate (this indicates conversion of the leads generated) | 50% |
| Number of leads (Number of mail pieces * Response rate) | 1000 |
| Number of conversion (Number of mail pieces * Response rate* Conversion rate) | 500 |
| Cost of fulfilment (per unit) | ₹50 |
| Unit sales price | ₹300 |
| Revenue (Number of conversion * Unit sales price) | ₹150,000 |
| Gross margin | 45% |
| Margin (Gross margin * Revenue) | ₹67,500 |
| Total cost of fulfilment (Cost of fulfilment per unit * Number of conversion) | ₹25,000 |
| Net profit (Margin – Total cost of fulfilment – Promotion cost) | ₹10,500 |
| ROI of campaign (Net profit/Promotion cost) | 33% |

programme for its airline co-brand card then it can refer to a message like "For a frequent business traveller like you".

- **Involvement device:** Many direct mailers may include involvement devices that will make the recipient spend more time with the mailer. Common involvement devices include "scratch and win" offers, quizzes, inclusion of collectibles, etc.
- **Creative devices:** Direct mailers often utilize additional creative devices to enhance their appeal. Examples of common creative devices include print that looks like a handwritten note, a mailer that looks like a real check or currency note etc. Sometimes, small gift items like a pen or a key chain is also included with the direct mailer.
- **Convenience and immediacy of benefit:** Direct mailers need to emphasise the convenience that the offer provides. At the same time, it is important for a direct mailer to emphasise the need on the part of the recipient to act immediately. One important convenience aspect, which can be used very effectively, involves speed of fulfilment. Direct mailers sometime use expressions such as "the card will be delivered to you within 24 hours" or "please SMS your contact number and we will ensure that the product reaches you on the same day".
- **Credibility:** This is the last and possibly one of the most important aspects that needs to be taken into consideration. Today with the plethora of offers in the market the consumer tends to disbelief most offers suspecting that there are hidden cost elements not explicitly mentioned in the offer. Hence, every mailer needs to provide an exact cost which the responder will incur and also needs to reassure that there will be no other cost or overhead over and above what has been stated in the mail.

### *1.8.2 Telemarketing*

Telemarketing is a useful direct marketing channel but is definitely costlier than direct mailers. In most cases, telemarketing does provide high returns on investments. In the case of emerging markets where manpower costs are lower, the telemarketing channel generates significantly higher returns, compared to developed markets. In most developed markets, telemarketing is often used to reinforce a direct mailer. The biggest advantage of telemarketing involves opportunity of speaking and convincing the prospect. However, it is an intrusive media and might cause significant irritation to the prospect. The other advantage of telemarketing is the ability of capturing the feedback of the call. In most cases, callers are provided with a list of feedback that they can select. Some of the common feedbacks include:

- Not interested
- Offer is not attractive
- Not interested now

- Have recently made a similar purchase
- Dissatisfied with the company's products purchased in the past
- Dissatisfied with the particular product category
- Do not disturb
- Do not call again
- Call later

An analysis of the feedbacks can help marketers in fine-tuning marketing campaigns in future. It is important to note that in most countries there exists a "Do-Not-Call" registry, which contains telephone numbers of people who do not want to receive marketing calls. Such telephone numbers need to be removed from the calling list for any telemarketing campaign. Of late, the efficiency of telemarketing has been tremendously enhanced by the use of high volume automatic diallers that checks the validity of a phone number before dialling and makes necessary changes to the number based on recent changes in phone numbers of a particular region. These diallers also match the phone numbers with the telephone directory to ascertain their validity. Diallers also come with specialised queuing features, whereby high propensity prospects can be called at a time of the day when there is highest likelihood of response. In cases of call backs, the diallers can also schedule call backs based on the preferred time given by the prospect.

### 1.8.3 Internet and Email

The internet is increasingly becoming an important direct marketing channel. The biggest advantage of the Internet as a direct marketing channel is its flexibility and low cost. In case of the Internet, even top of line advertising in the form of banner ads and pop ups can be customised to work as a direct mailer. Based on a prospects click stream data in a given site the banner ads can be customised so as to achieve the maximum benefit of exposure. Also opt in mailings are an important direct marketing channel. In cases where prospects provide their contact information along with the permission of sending promotional mailers it works as a very powerful self selection tool for targeting. The email channel works in a manner very similar to the direct mailer; however, the use of web links in the email allows easy response and self-selection. Also in case of direct mailers, the company is never able to find out whether a prospect goes through the mail at all. However email allows the flow back of information so that the marketer is able to find out if the subject line of the email is effective enough to prompt the prospect to look through the content of the email.

### 1.8.4 Mobile Phone

The mobile phone as a channel has witnessed tremendous transformation over the years. Till a few years back, mobile was mostly used as a contact for telecalling and the SMS channel was used almost like the email channel. SMS, like email, is a low-cost channel and the prospect can immediately reply back to the SMS offer pretty much like email. However, the mobile channel has witnessed a huge transformation with the advent of smartphones and global positioning software (GPS). Companies today can create a number of exciting smartphone applications, games and contests, which attempts to engage the prospect and position the company's offers in a much more engaging manner. The advent of GPS has also provided companies the flexibility of location-based targeting. For example, a large apparel store can push it's latest offers to customers and prospects only when they are in and around the store. This makes the offer much more relevant and the prospect is able to walk in immediately to the store. Such targeted offers are expected to generate much higher response and return on investments. The use of GPS and smart phone applications have made it possible to provide more contextual offers to customers and prospects, thereby increasing probability of response.

### *1.8.5 Social Media*

The emergence of Internet-based social media has changed the way companies communicate with prospects or existing customers; it has also revolutionised the way customers and prospects communicate with each other. Social media is increasingly becoming an important element of the communication and acquisition channel for most companies. However, the consumer-to-consumer communication in the social media spheres is beyond the control of the company and hence, it creates an entirely new set of challenges for the marketer. Social media consists of various types of information sharing mechanisms; the key ones are:

- Social media networks like Facebook, Google Plus
- Specialised networking sites like LinkedIn
- Photograph and video sharing sites like Picasa, YouTube
- Various blog sites
- Company sponsored blog sites like Apple user community site
- Product review and price comparison sites like MouthShut.com

Figure 1.11 depicts the types of communication involved in social media. The framework is inspired by the paper titled *Social Media: The New Hybrid Element of the Promotion Mix* by Glynn Mangold and David Faulds.

Social media mainly facilitates three types of communication – consumer to firm, firm to consumer and consumer to consumer. The consumer-to-consumer communication is what makes social media most significant. Within the realm of social media, consumer-to-consumer communication may assume two forms: one is discussion and the other is broadcasting. Discussion happens when consumer groups or discussion forums are used to discuss several aspects of the product or services involved. Broadcasting

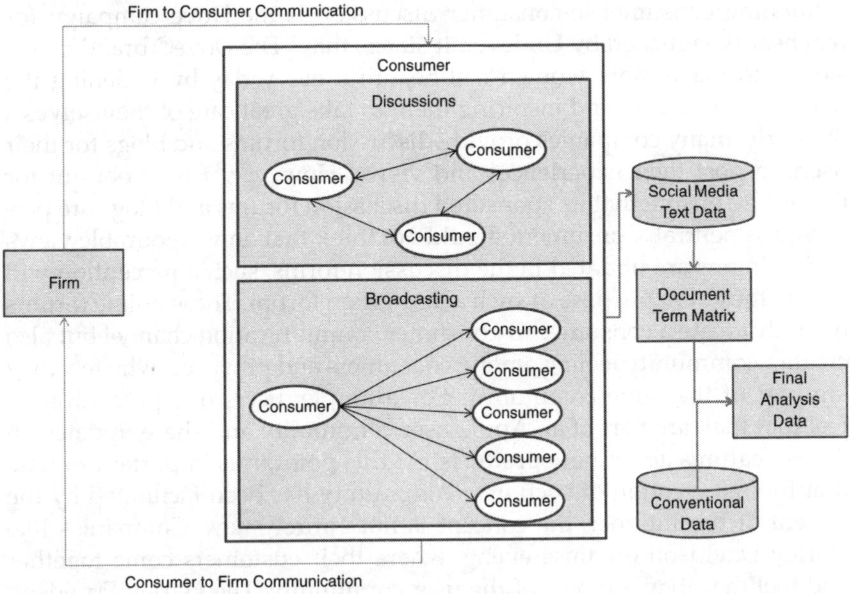


**Figure 1.11** Analyzing Social Media Data: An Overview

involves one consumer communicating his or her reaction about a product or a company to a large number of prospects or existing customers. The power of the Internet allows a consumer to broadcast his or her views to thousands or millions of other consumers using broadcasting tools like YouTube.

Another aspect of social media, which is important from an acquisition perspective, is the effectiveness of social media as a channel of acquisition. Even though the volume of customers acquired through social media might be small, these customers tend to have higher lifetime value, are more loyal and in turn bring in more new customers through referrals. As pointed out by Julian Villanueva et al. in their paper titled *The Impact of Marketing Induced vs. Word of Mouth Customer Acquisition on Customer Equity Growth*, customers acquired through word of mouth tend to have much higher long-term profitability. Another power of social media is the consumer-to-consumer communication. While consumers look at all marketing messages from the firm with some amount of scepticism, they are far more likely to believe in the testimonials and views shared by other consumers.

Hence, social media is fast becoming an important channel for acquisition. Subsequently companies need to provide consumers the right platform to share their views and to communicate with one another. However, it is important to ensure that the platform facilitates more "consumer to consumer" and "consumer to firm" communication and less of "firm to consumer" communications. A key example of an effective platform for facilitating consumer-to-consumer discussion is the Dove campaign for real beauty launched by Unilever. It states, that "The Dove® brand's mission is to make more women feel beautiful every day by widening the definition of beauty and inspiring them to take great care of themselves". Similarly, many companies provide discussion forums and blogs for their users to post their experiences and views. However, it is important for the firm to ensure that its sponsored discussion forums and blogs are perceived as neutral. Consumers should not think that only favourable views and opinions are updated in the discussion forms, such a perception will negate the entire purpose of such a discussion forum. These online forums not only create a consumer-to-consumer communication channel but also create a community feeling among consumers and prospects who feel they are part of the same community. For example, users of Apple strongly feel that they are part of an Apple user community and share updates on Apps, features about new products. At this point, it is important to note that though creation of such user community has been facilitated by the advent of the Internet, the concept is not entirely new. Companies like Harley Davidson organise events where their customers come together and feel that they are part of the user community. The Harley Davidson sponsored motor cycle rallies are typical examples of such communities in the offline space. The Internet has facilitated the creation of larger communities across geographical barriers.

From the acquisition perspective, companies can create discussion boards and online communities where interested prospects can interact with other prospects or existing customers about the product and service and thereby the company can engage prospects even before they become customers. This also provides an opportunity to use the opinion of satisfied existing customers for driving new acquisition. For example, real estate companies can create discussion forums for some of their upcoming big apartment complexes, whereby customers who have already purchased apartments in these complexes can share their views about the apartment and the quality of services provided by the builder. Furthermore, customers and prospects can share views about the facilities like schools and hospitals available in the vicinity of the upcoming apartment. According to an Accenture consumer survey (The Strategist, Business Standard, 13th August 2012), a third of the Indian consumers believe that positive comments posted on social media sites contribute to their consideration of buying a product or service. The proliferation of social media and it's impact on consumer decision making have made it an important channel for communication, new customer acquisition and existing customer management. Companies have started using social media data to enhance their understanding of prospects and customers.

Analyzing social media data involve analysis of huge volumes of unstructured text data. Such huge volumes of data is often referred to as "Big Data" by practitioners. The key aspect of social media data, that makes it different from other data sources is it's unstructured nature. Most conventional data sources consist of well defined data elements which can be analyzed and used as inputs in models and strategies. Unstructured data on the other hand, is devoid of such well defined structure. Hence, the unstructured data needs to be transformed to a more structured format before further analysis. For the purpose of transforming unstructured text data like face book posts, into structured data, one first needs to parse the text data through an algorithm that breaks it into individual words. Next, connecting words like "a", "an", "the", "then" etc. are removed. After removing connecting words, the rest of the words are grouped into logical word groups, for example, words like "prefer", "preferred", "preferable", "like" are grouped into a single category. Post creation of these categories, the data can be transformed into a "document term matrix". A "document term matrix" states the frequency of each word category in the text. For example, a document term matrix of 1000 face book posts will consist of 1000 rows, one row for each post and a number of columns, each enumerating the frequency of a particular word category. For instance, columns like frequency of "preferred category", "dislike category", "complain category", and so on. The document term matrix, is a structured data set, which can be added to other conventional data sources for further analysis.

Similar analysis is also used by product comparison sites and e-retailers for ranking products based on customer feedback. Customer feedbacks which, consists of a large number of negative word categories are classified as negative reviews. While feedbacks having high frequency of positive word categories are classified as positive feedbacks. In addition the frequency and intensity of a negative category is used for isolating a very negative feedback from a mildly negative feedback. It is possible to use similar analysis for mining customer complaints for identifying customers who are likely to attrite.

### *1.8.6 Direct Sales Agents*

In emerging markets, a lot of companies use direct sales agents for direct marketing of financial services, telecom, and other similar products. Though this channel can prove effective in generating significant acquisition volume, it suffers from a few major limitations. The first drawback is the chances of mis-selling or adverse selection as the sales agent is left with the sole responsibility of product positioning. There remains the risk that the sales agent may try to convince prospects with "false claims" or "exaggerated claims" about the product. Many a times the agent may also select the wrong prospect and convince him or her to buy the product, this in turn leads to customer dissonance and creates a negative image for the company in the long run. The second difficulty with this channel is that it is extremely person dependent. The company needs to invest heavily to train sales agents and in case of attrition, this poses a major challenge. In spite of these limitations, sales agents are an effective channel particularly because the face-to-face conversation with the prospect allows the sales agents to customise the offer and product feature communication to the maximum extent. Also for products like insurance policies, which are complex in nature, sales agents are able to provide the prospects with all the information they need for making a decision. Sometimes the prospect also likes to talk to a "human face" rather than typing information in a computer screen or speaking to a voice recording device. In cases where the fulfilment process is longer and complicated, the prospect wants a point of contact from the company whom he or she can call up if there are delays. Sales agents act as this point of contact and hence, are able to generate a lot of credibility for the company. Today a number of customer relationship management software provide a detailed functionality of managing direct sales agents. Many of these like salesforce.com are offered in the ASP (application service provider) mode, whereby field sales personnel are able to upload their leads and conversions online from the field and the same can be tracked, analysed, and reported in real time by the central acquisition team. New geographic information systems (GIS) also provide a lot of new tools for market sizing and understanding each zip code in greater detail.

### 1.8.6.1 Methodology for Evaluating Direct Sales Agents

Companies use a variety of measures for evaluating the performance of direct sales agents (DSAs). Some of the key metrics used for evaluating DSAs are similar to the metrics used for measuring the acquisition programme in general. Once a company is able to identify the top performing DSAs it needs to find out the drivers that drive performance. The key factors that drive DSA performance include:

- The incentive structure (the amount of incentive for volume and value of sales)
- Training and mentoring provided to the DSA
- The geography or prospect segment (defined as the territory) that has been assigned to the DSA
- Characteristics of the DSA such as education, past experience, communication skills, and the like

Determining the optimal incentive structure for DSAs is an important part of designing the channel strategy because the incentive provided to DSAs is possibly the most important factor that motivates them. In addition, as the DSA channel is the most expensive channel, one needs to design the right incentive so as to achieve desired results while keeping costs under control. The incentive structure needs to be designed keeping in mind the overall marketing and financial objectives of the company. In most cases, companies link incentives with volume of sales, value of sales, and future profitability of acquired customers. Most companies design a score card for DSAs based on these factors; however, such score cards should be simple and easy to communicate so that DSAs can understand it easily.

The other factor that governs DSA performance is the characteristics of the DSA such as education, experience, etc. The business manager can design a *criteria* consisting of these factors for evaluating candidates before recruiting them as sales agents. Similarly in order to drive the right financial outcome and product mix, the company needs to design an incentive structure that will prompt desired behaviour from DSAs. Table 1.11 depicts a sample incentive structure for DSAs selling investment products. As suggested in the table, the incentive is a function of two factors: the first is the ease of selling and the second is the revenue generated. As it can be seen from the table, the amount of incentive increases with an increase in difficulty of selling. Similarly, the amount of incentive also increases with an increase in expected revenue generation. Incorporation of ease of selling in the incentive structure ensures that DSAs also strive to sell the more difficult product. The exact incentive for each combination is determined based on the financial and product mix goals for the particular year. The incentive can be calculated as a function of difficulty and expected revenue generation. For example, one can develop an incentive function as follows: Incentive = A * Difficulty + B * Expected revenue; for instance difficulty ranges from 1 to 5, where 1 is least difficult and 5 is most difficult. The values of the coefficients, "A" and "B" can be determined based on past DSA performance data, the portfolio targets, and revenue goal of the organization.

## 1.9 Testing

Testing is one of the most important components of any campaign, be it for acquisition or portfolio management. This section will involve issues pertaining to testing in the context of acquisition programmes. The most significant aspect which distinguishes testing for acquisition programmes from testing for portfolio management or cross-sell is the way control groups are used. In case of acquisition programmes, use of "no mail" control groups is very limited. A "no mail" control group refers to the strategy of keeping aside a random sample of the target population and not making any offer to them and comparing their behaviour to the behaviour of the population that is subjected to a particular offer. Use of "no mail" control does not make sense in case of acquisition as one cannot expect to generate any reading from such a control group.

A testing strategy for acquisition attempts to test the offer, the price, the creative, the channel, and the criteria of prospect selection. Given the interplay of these factors, the number of unique combinations that needs to be tested becomes unmanageable and hence, practitioners resort to techniques like experimental design to reduce the number of combinations that need to be tested. The reader can refer to Chapter 8 for a detailed usage of experimental design for testing.

**Table 1.11** Sample Incentive Structure

| | Products | Savings Account | Credit Card | Fixed Deposit | Insurance | Mutual Fund | Equity Linked Investment | Pension Product | Private Equity Fund |
|---|---|---|---|---|---|---|---|---|---|
| | Level of difficulty in selling the product (in a scale of 1 to 5 where 1 denotes least difficult and 5 denotes most difficult) | 1 | 1 | 2 | 3 | 3 | 4 | 4 | 5 |
| Expected one year revenue | <$200 | $67 | $67 | $125 | $155 | $155 | $216 | $216 | $246 |
| | $200–$500 | $116 | $116 | $215 | $268 | $268 | $372 | $372 | $424 |
| | $500–$1200 | $175 | $175 | $326 | $405 | $405 | $563 | $563 | 642 |
| | $1200–$2000 | $240 | $240 | $447 | $555 | $555 | $772 | $772 | $880 |
| | >$2000 | $273 | $273 | $508 | $631 | $631 | $877 | $877 | $1,000 |

### 1.9.1 *Interpreting a Sample Test Result*

It is important to understand how one can interpret the test result for a sample. If a testing is performed on a sample of size "N" with a response rate "r" then a marketer will want to know the response rate, that he or she can expect if the same campaign is rolled out on a larger prospect universe.

For an analysis of the above, one can assume that the process of whether a particular prospect will respond to a campaign or not will follow a binomial distribution. A binomial distribution is one where the outcome of any process can take on either of two values. The most common binomial distribution is the tossing of a coin where the outcome may be either head or tail. If the sample size is large enough then a binomial distribution can be approximated by a normal distribution and one can use the property of the normal distribution to find out the expected response rate. Hence, if the campaign is run on a larger population then the response rate will have a mean of "r" and a standard deviation of Sqrt(r(1 – r)/N), which in turn implies that one can state with 95% confidence that the response rate will lie between r + 1.96 * sqrt(r(1 – r)/N) to r – 1.96 * sqrt(r(1 – r)/N). One can refer to the normal distribution table or can use the normdist function of Microsoft XL to obtain the above formula.

For example, a test run is performed on a sample of 1000 prospects and a response rate of 2% is obtained. In that case it is expected that the mean response rate of similar campaign will be 2% and standard deviation will be 0.4427% (this is obtained by sqrt (0.02 * 0.98/1000)). Hence, one can say with 95% confidence that if a full rollout is planned on the basis of this test, then one might expect a response rate between 2% + 1.96 * 0.4427, that is, 2.86% and 2% – 1.96 * 0.4427, that is, 1.132%. Table 1.12 provides a calculation of expected response rates for a series of sample size and test response rates.

### 1.9.2 *Print Media Testing*

The print media still remains an important advertising media and is a key element of any acquisition strategy. However, evaluating the returns from a print media campaign is sometimes difficult. Hence it is important to focus on methodologies for evaluating impact of print media campaigns.

Testing the effectiveness of an advertisement in the print media involves two components. The first component involves testing the effectiveness of the particular publication and the second component involves testing the effectiveness of the advertisement. In order to test the effectiveness of the publication, one can use only a portion of a particular magazine for placing an advertisement. Some magazines have regional publications and one can place an advertisement only in the circulation for a particular region. Some magazines allow the advertiser to buy a portion of the circulation across the board on a national

**Table 1.12** Expected Response Rates

| Sample Size | Response Rate | Standard Deviation | Standard Deviation Times 1.96 | Response Rate Range (High) | Response Rate Range (Low) |
|---|---|---|---|---|---|
| 1000 | 2.0% | 0.4427% | 0.8677% | 2.868% | 1.132% |
| 2500 | 2.0% | 0.2800% | 0.5488% | 2.549% | 1.451% |
| 3000 | 2.0% | 0.2556% | 0.5010% | 2.501% | 1.499% |
| 5000 | 2.0% | 0.1980% | 0.3881% | 2.388% | 1.612% |
| 7000 | 2.0% | 0.1673% | 0.3280% | 2.328% | 1.672% |
| 9000 | 2.0% | 0.1476% | 0.2892% | 2.289% | 1.711% |
| 10000 | 2.0% | 0.1400% | 0.2744% | 2.274% | 1.726% |
| 1000 | 1.5% | 0.3844% | 0.7534% | 2.253% | 0.747% |
| 2500 | 1.5% | 0.2431% | 0.4765% | 1.976% | 1.024% |
| 3000 | 1.5% | 0.2219% | 0.4350% | 1.935% | 1.065% |
| 5000 | 1.5% | 0.1719% | 0.3369% | 1.837% | 1.163% |
| 7000 | 1.5% | 0.1453% | 0.2848% | 1.785% | 1.215% |
| 9000 | 1.5% | 0.1281% | 0.2511% | 1.751% | 1.249% |
| 10000 | 1.5% | 0.1216% | 0.2382% | 1.738% | 1.262% |
| 1000 | 3.0% | 0.5394% | 1.0573% | 4.057% | 1.943% |
| 2500 | 3.0% | 0.3412% | 0.6687% | 3.669% | 2.331% |
| 3000 | 3.0% | 0.3114% | 0.6104% | 3.610% | 2.390% |
| 5000 | 3.0% | 0.2412% | 0.4728% | 3.473% | 2.527% |
| 7000 | 3.0% | 0.2039% | 0.3996% | 3.400% | 2.600% |
| 9000 | 3.0% | 0.1798% | 0.3524% | 3.352% | 2.648% |
| 10000 | 3.0% | 0.1706% | 0.3344% | 3.334% | 2.666% |

or international level. In order to test the effectiveness of the advertisement, one can either use a "split run" testing or a "flip flop" testing. Split run testing is by far the most effective way of testing a print advertisement. For running a "split run" testing two different versions of the same advertisement, each with a different identification number, are placed in the publication as a split insertion on the same date. This will ensure that exactly half of the publications will carry version one of the advertisement and the other half will carry the second version. Hence, the results of the split run test can be thought of as two advertisements run on a random sample of the publication. The way the advertisements are inserted ensures that the samples are absolutely random in every respect. In case a magazine is published regionally (e.g., a separate publication for western, eastern, northern, and southern regions), one can use each regional publication separately to run multiple split run advertisements. This will help in testing more than two versions of the advertisement. In case a magazine does not have the flexibility of running a split run campaign but has a separate regional publication for various regions, then one can use the region-1 publication for one version of the advertisement and the region-2 publication for the other version of the advertisement. This form of testing is called flip flop testing and is an approximation of a split run testing. The biggest shortcoming of this testing is that the two samples are not random and hence, there can be an inherent regional bias in the test results. Suitable business judgement or other test results need to be utilised to correct the bias.

## 1.10 Location Planning

While planning the location of a new store or a new bank branch, the marketer is faced with the question of selecting an optimal location so that the new store or the new branch is profitable. Today it is possible to harness very rich zip code level data and sophisticated geographic information systems (GIS) to make decisions not only about store location, but also about a host of other decisions that are of interest to marketers. This section will discuss the use of GIS primarily for location planning. However, the concepts can well be applied in other areas of marketing.

Before starting a discussion on the usage of geographic information for marketing purpose, it is important to clarify three important concepts: the first is the concept of the retail trade area, the second is retail gravity model and the third is the potential of an area.

### *1.10.1 Retail Trade Area*

Retail trade area of a store or a bank branch is defined as the geographic region from which a store or a bank branch draws most of its customers. The simplest way of defining the retail trade area involves use of ring-based estimates where a circular region of specified radius with the store as the centre is defined as the trade area for a store. The limitation of this approach is that it does not take into account natural or man-made barriers of movement, which can make access of the store more difficult for certain customers. For example, if on one side of a store there is a river or an industrial district then the trade area of the store will not be a circle but will be a polygon or a semicircle. Today, more complex GIS applications are available, which are able to model traffic flow, taking into account the road conditions, traffic conditions, congestion, time of the day, etc. These are used to create an approximate measure of travel time to the store from various locations. All locations, which are within a specified travel time, are included in the trade area for the store. This approach results in a polygon rather than a circle as the assigned trade area. To illustrate this further, all locations which are within say 30 minutes of drive time from a particular store will be part of the trade area for that store.

## 1.10.2 Retail Gravity Model

Retail gravity models are one of the most important analytical frameworks used by marketers for analysing spatial data. The Huff model is one of the most important retail gravity model most frequently used. The model was pioneered by Professor David L. Huff in 1963. As stated by Huff and M. McCallum, in one of the ESRI publications, the model is based on the idea that when one has to choose between several alternatives then the probability of choosing a particular alternative is proportional to the utility of the alternative compared to all other available alternatives. To explain this further, if one tries to quantify the utility of a store, then the utility will be directly proportional to the attractiveness of the store, and inversely proportional to the distance of the store from the consumer's residence. In this case, attractiveness can be a combination of several factors such as size, level of service, availability of ample parking space, etc. Similarly, distance can also consist of several factors like point-to-point distance or distance along principle drive way, traffic condition, road condition, etc. Hence, the utility of a store is defined as:

- **Utility of a particular store** = (Attractiveness of store)$^{A}$ (Distance of store)$^{-B}$

Probability of a consumer visiting a particular store is defined by:

- Utility of the particular store to the customer divided by the sum of utilities of all (N) stores in the vicinity hence, it can be written as:
- Pi (probability of the customer visiting the ith store) = [(Attractiveness of store i)$^{A}$ (Distance of store i)$^{-B}$]/$\sum_{k=1 \text{ to } N}$ [(Attractiveness of store k)$^{A}$ (Distance of store k)$^{-B}$]
- Intuitively, the parameter A can be thought of as the importance of attractiveness in getting customers to visit a store, while B can be thought of as the importance of distance in preventing customers from visiting the store. The interplay of these two factors determine the final likelihood of the customer to visit the store.

If a particular zip has three stores in its vicinity, then the probability of visiting any of the stores can be defined by using the Huff model. Now, it is important to define what geographical area may be termed as the vicinity of a particular zip code. For this purpose, one can define a drive time and all stores within that drive time to be candidate stores. Conversely, all zips within a particular drive time of a store to be candidate zips for that particular store. Based on the above, one can outline an area that will form the trade area for a store. The store will have to compete with all other stores within its trade area to attract prospective customers.

## 1.10.3 Potential of a Geographic Area

Along with the probability of a customer to visit a store, a marketer also wants to estimate the profitability of customers from a particular geography. For example, customers from a relatively distant affluent neighbourhood may have 30% probability of visiting a store, whereas customers from a relatively nearby middle income neighbourhood may have 50% probability of visiting the store. However, the affluent customer on an average may buy more costly items and hence, generate twice the revenue compared to the middle income customers. Hence, it is important to ascertain the revenue or profitability potential of a neighbourhood. For most purposes, the zip is the lowest level of geographic unit for which enough data is available. Hence, all these analysis are performed at a zip level. The potential of a particular geographic unit is a combination of multiple factors like average income of people within the zip, proportion of affluent people, proportion of young people, proportion of graduates, and the like. In addition to these generic data, companies can utilise their internal data to create other data elements for evaluating the potential of a zip. For example, if one considers a bank which has a large credit card base and wants to cross-sell investment products to it's credit card customers. The bank can develop a look-alike model to identify profiles of its credit card customers that looks like its investment customers. In this case, the proportion of credit card customers that look like investment customers can be used as an important measure of potential.

### 1.10.4 Methodology of Application of GIS or Spatial Analysis

Having defined the key concepts it is important to understand how all of these concepts can be used together to harness the power of geographic or spatial data. A hypothetical case study will be used to illustrate the concept. For this hypothetical example, Google maps have been used as the GIS.

If one considers a case, where a big retail chain is planning to open a new store in the Indian city of Bangalore. Bangalore is one of the big cities in India, and is known for its information technology and services industry. The city is experiencing a very high growth rate. However, the city experiences a lot of traffic congestion particularly in the peak hours. The retail chain already has a few stores in the city and is planning to open another new store. The store will be a large retail store, which will sell all items of everyday use along with home appliances, clothing, and toys. There are two locations that have been shortlisted, and the management has to decide the optimal location. The two prospective locations considered are as follows:

- Koramangla, a predominantly residential area near the centre of the city. It is a very well-known old neighbourhood with a large number of shopping malls in the vicinity. Along with professionals, a lot of self-employed people with high income live in this neighbourhood. This will be referred to as location-X.
- Whitefield, a residential district far away from the city centre. Whitefield is home to a lot of offices and residential apartments. Mostly professionals live in this area. This location will be referred to as location-Y.

If one defines an area, which is within a specified drive time from the proposed location of the new store, then that will help us in defining the stores, which will be competitors to the proposed store. If one defines a drive time of 45 minutes, then one can chart out the area that will be the trade area of the proposed new store. Figure 1.12 shows the location map for location-X, the trade area is shown by the dark line, which is drawn on the map.

There are two stores which are possible competitors to the new proposed store. These are marked in the map; the two existing stores will be referred to as store-1X and store-2X. Figure 1.13 depicts the location map for location-Y. For location-Y there is only one store in the vicinity, which will be a competitor to the new store. This will be referred to as store-1Y.

In both the maps, it is important to note that due to traffic congestion problems in the city, the trade area has been defined along the main roads that surround the area. Within the identified trade area, traffic congestion is expected to be minimal and hence, prospective customers should be able to reach the store within a drive time of 30–45 minutes. In case of location-Y, as it is in the outskirts of the city, the trade area identified is larger owing to lower traffic congestion and hence, the drive time is lower for this area compared to location-X, which is near the centre of the city.

Once the trade area of the store is identified, the next step involves listing the zip codes/streets which will be covered by the trade area. After defining the trade areas and the streets that are part of the trade areas, it

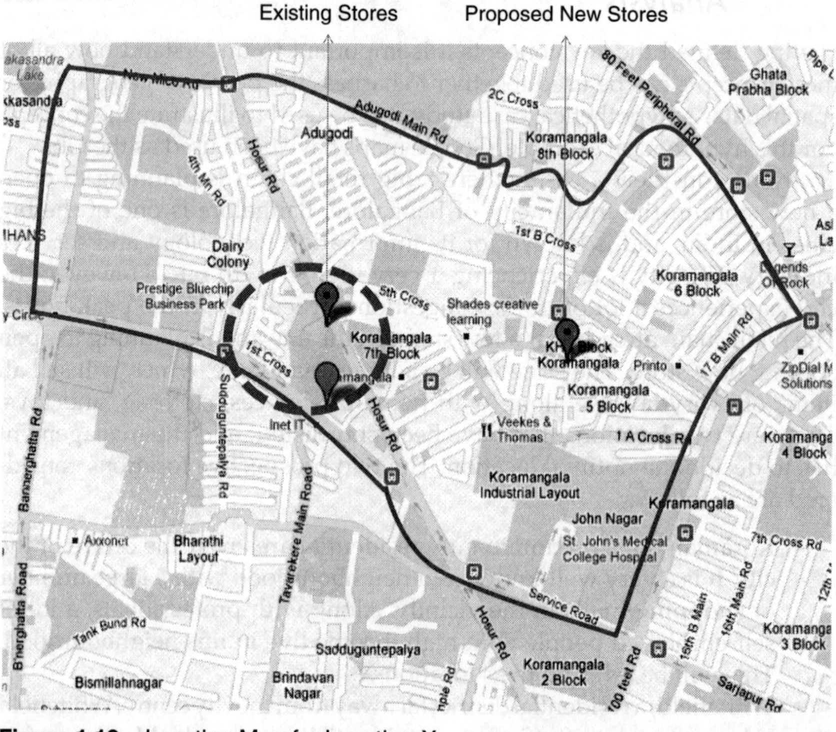


**Figure 1.12** Location Map for Location-X

**Figure 1.13** Location Map for Location-Y

is important to define the attractiveness, distance, and potential measures. Based on past data and business experience, these are defined as:

*Attractiveness* is function of

- Square foot area
- Number of sales person per square foot
- Measure of stock out
- Available number of brands
- Attractive promotions
- Attractive loyalty programme
- Availability of enough parking space

*Distance* is function of:

- Distance from store along the identified drive way
- Traffic congestion along primary route
- Average drive time during peak hours

*Potential* for the new store is defined as:

- Average size of population in a particular street
- Number of families where both the husband and wife are working
- Average income of people living in the street
- Number of people in the street who have ever shopped in other outlets of the particular retail chain
- Number of people in the street who have shopped more than once in the last 3 months in other outlets of the particular chain

- Number of people who hold a loyalty card of the particular retail chain and have demographic characteristics similar to the most profitable customers for the retail chain
- Expected future economic growth rate of the area

The potential of a particular geographic area is a combined index of all these factors. It is important to note that Google maps and Google earth can be used to calculate the shortest distance between two points only based on longitude and latitude. In order to incorporate other factors like traffic condition, etc., it is important to use other sophisticated GIS tools.

Once the attractiveness and distance parameters have been established, one can calculate the probability of prospects from each street visiting the store. The probability can be calculated as follows:

- **For location-X**
  - Probability of a prospects from a street visiting the new store = (Attractiveness of store new)$^A$ (Distance of new store)$^{-B}$/ [(Attractiveness of store new)$^A$ (Distance of new store)$^{-B}$ + (Attractiveness of store-1X)$^A$ (Distance of new store-1X)$^{-B}$ + (Attractiveness of store-2X)$^A$ (Distance of new store-2X)$^{-B}$]
- **For location-Y**
  - Probability of a prospects from a street visiting the new store = (Attractiveness of store new)$^A$ (Distance of new store)$^{-B}$/ [(Attractiveness of store new)$^A$ (Distance of new store)$^{-B}$ + (Attractiveness of store-1Y)$^A$ (Distance of new store-1Y)$^{-B}$]

In order to ascertain the exponent A and B in the above framework, one needs to conduct some sample surveys for individuals within each street. Based on the choices demonstrated in the survey, one will have to ascertain the A and B exponent. Otherwise A and B can be based upon business judgement also. After arriving at the A and B exponents, one needs to calculate the probability for every street within the marked trade area and group them into probability band. This will result in a table similar to the one shown in Table 1.13. The table provides the number of streets within a particular probability band.

Next, one needs to calculate the potential of each street. In this case, a measure of potential has been created. The measure is created as an index, which varies between 0 and 10, where 10 is the maximum potential. The potential of each street needs to be multiplied by the probability of prospects from each street visiting the store, to calculate the total potential of the proposed new store. The probability weighted potential is the final metric for accessing a particular location. This metric should be compared across the two candidate locations and the location with the highest probability weighted potential should be chosen. Table 1.14 depicts the final results. The probabilities in Table 1.14 have been obtained by applying the Huff model for each street within the retail trade area of a particular store. Next, the streets have been grouped based on the range of probabilities.

An analysis of the results suggests that location-Y has a larger number of streets within the trade area and the numbers of streets with higher probability are also more for location-Y compared to location-X. This is due to the fact that location-Y being in the outskirts has a larger trade area, which results in more number of streets within the trade area. *Secondly*, location-Y has only one competing store and hence the denominator in the Huff model is lower for location-Y. Because of this, location-Y has higher proportion of streets in the higher probability ranges. However, location-X has higher potential and hence, when we multiply the probability with the potential, location-X scores higher compared to location-Y. Based on the total potential measure, location-X will be chosen for the new store. However, another important factor in calculating potential is the future growth rate, which is a forecasted number and if business is of the opinion, that the forecasted growth of location-Y may be higher

**Table 1.13** Probability of Visiting a Particular Store

| | Location-X | | |
|---|---|---|---|
| **Probability** | **Average Probability** | **Number of Streets** | **Percentage of Streets** |
| 1–0.7 | 0.75 | 38 | 7 |
| 0.7–0.5 | 0.62 | 112 | 20 |
| 0.5–0.4 | 0.43 | 43 | 7 |
| 0.4–0.3 | 0.32 | 52 | 9 |
| 0.3–0.15 | 0.2 | 60 | 10 |
| 0.15–0.1 | 0.12 | 73 | 13 |
| 0.1–0.05 | 0.08 | 88 | 15 |
| Less than | 0.01 | 108 | 19 |
| | | 574 | 100 |
| | **Location-Y** | | |
| **Probability** | **Average Probability** | **Number of Streets** | **Percentage of Streets** |
| 1–0.7 | 0.73 | 80 | 10 |
| 0.7–0.5 | 0.58 | 186 | 24 |
| 0.5–0.4 | 0.44 | 50 | 6 |
| 0.4–0.3 | 0.31 | 73 | 9 |
| 0.3–0.15 | 0.2 | 76 | 10 |
| 0.15–0.1 | 0.11 | 94 | 12 |
| 0.1–0.05 | 0.07 | 112 | 14 |
| Less than | 0.02 | 110 | 14 |
| | | 781 | 100 |

**Table 1.14** Calculating Total Potential for a Location

| Probability Range | Location-X | | | | |
|---|---|---|---|---|---|
| | Average Probability | Number of Streets | Percentage of Streets | Average Potential | Total Potential (Average Probability * Number of Streets * Average Potential) |
| 1–.0.7 | 0.75 | 38 | 7 | 6.3 | 179.5 |
| 0.7–0.5 | 0.62 | 112 | 20 | 8.1 | 562.4 |
| 0.5–0.4 | 0.43 | 43 | 7 | 7.8 | 144.2 |
| 0.4–0.3 | 0.32 | 52 | 9 | 4.5 | 74.8 |
| 0.3–0.15 | 0.2 | 60 | 10 | 6.2 | 74.4 |
| 0.15–0.1 | 0.12 | 73 | 13 | 5.4 | 47.3 |
| 0.1–0.05 | 0.08 | 88 | 15 | 6.3 | 44.3 |
| Less than 0.05 | 0.01 | 108 | 19 | 2.1 | 2.2 |
| | | 574 | 100 | | 1129.4 |

| Probability Range | Location-Y | | | | |
|---|---|---|---|---|---|
| | Average Probability | Number of Streets | Percentage of Streets | Average Potential | Total Potential (Average Probability * Number of Streets * Average Potential) |
| 1–0.7 | 0.73 | 80 | 10 | 4.2 | 245.2 |
| 0.7–0.5 | 0.58 | 186 | 24 | 3.6 | 388.3 |
| 0.5–0.4 | 0.44 | 50 | 6 | 2.5 | 55 |
| 0.4–0.3 | 0.31 | 73 | 9 | 3.8 | 85.9 |
| 0.3–0.15 | 0.2 | 76 | 10 | 7.3 | 110.9 |
| 0.15–0.1 | 0.11 | 94 | 12 | 2.5 | 25.8 |
| 0.1–0.05 | 0.07 | 112 | 14 | 4.3 | 33.7 |
| Less than 0.05 | 0.02 | 110 | 14 | 1.6 | 3.5 |
| | | 781 | 100 | | 948.6 |

(because it is in the outskirts and hence, is expected to grow rapidly), then that may change the decision.

GIS applications, have immense potential in other areas as well. For example, a bank may want to set up point of sale kiosks in retail outlets for acquiring customers for small ticket personal loan or loans for financing purchase of consumer durables like television, washing machine, etc. Now, if there are a number of similar retail outlets in an area and the bank has limited sales agents, then it has to prioritise the retail outlets where it wants to set up kiosks. In this case, a similar analysis can be used. One important consideration is the fact that in this case, there is a risk associated with the sale of the loan because the customer may not pay back. From past experience, the bank knows that loss rates tend to be higher for certain zips or streets. The loss rate from each zip or street can be a negative factor for calculating potential. Similarly the bank may be having a large deposit base and developed a look-alike model between the deposit base and its small size loan base to identify deposit customers who are likely to take a small ticket size loan. This model can be applied to all deposit customers in the particular trade area, and the number of deposit customers who live in a particular zip and have high likelihood of accepting a small ticket size loan can be used as a positive factor while calculating potential. Hence, this can act as an input to a cross-sell strategy as well. Similar analysis can be utilized for determining where one will like to locate a new ATM (Automated Teller Machine), a bank or insurance branch or a service station.

### *1.10.5 Hurdles in Utilising the Retail Gravity Model*

Though the Huff model is a very appealing proposition there are some serious limitations involved in using this framework. The most important limitation lies in estimating the A and B, that is, the exponent of attractiveness and distance respectively. In order to estimate these exponents, one needs to have data on store traffic for the particular store in question and all competing stores in the vicinity. Usually most companies have good data regarding their own store traffic but have very limited or no data about traffic flow to competing stores. In such a case, one needs to rely on primary market surveys to estimate the exponents A and B. In some cases, business analysts use their own judgement to arrive at the A and B parameters. As already mentioned, the parameter A can be thought of as the importance of attractiveness in getting customers to visit a store, while B can be thought of as the importance of distance in preventing customers from visiting the store. The interplay of these two factors determines the final likelihood of the customer to visit the store.

For further details on analytical estimation of the exponents in the Huff model, the interested reader can refer to papers like Nakanishi et al. titled, *Simplified estimation of marketing models* or *Parameter Estimation for a Multiplicative Competitive Interaction Model—Least Squares Approach* published by the same set of authors.

## 1.11 Pre-screen Acquisition for Financial Services

In most developed markets, direct mailers are the primary channel for customer acquisition for credit cards. Sometimes a direct mailer channel is supported by telemarketing. To start with, a target prospect list is generated either by using available lists or by providing eligibility criteria to a credit bureau or another information company. There are strict legal restrictions on the use of a credit bureau for marketing. Usually credit card companies have two major types of acquisition programmes: pre-screened programmes and non-prescreened programmes. A pre-screened programme can use credit bureau data for selecting customers for mailings but the lender is liable to approve almost all the applications, which are generated out of a pre-screened programme.

Both the programmes involve mailing an offer for a particular type of credit product to the prospects. The customer can respond by mailing back the filled in application form that is provided along with the mail, or can use the offer code to fill up the application form online. The customer can also call up the lender and provide the application details along with the offer code. After receiving the application, the lender can either approve or decline the application based on data provided in the application and the customer's credit details in the credit bureau. The approval rate of a pre-screened programme is subject to strict legal and compliance checks and only cases, which have experienced a major worsening of the credit file in the bureau between the time of mailing and the time of application can be rejected. At this point, it is important to note that there are strict legal regulations on how credit bureau data can be used for a pre-screened mailing programme. The lender can create a set of criteria for selecting customers and send those to an independent entity. The independent entity, in turn runs those criteria on the credit bureau data and sends the list to another independent entity. The second independent entity, creates the actual mails (as per the creative format provided by the lender) and sends those mails out. The lender can only receive queries and applications from prospects. This process ensures that the concerned financial institution can never look into the entire credit bureau file but may run specific checks on the entire credit bureau file to create a list of prospects. Additionally, the financial institution is never able to know the exact list of prospects that have been mailed to. This ensures that a pre-screened mailing programme involves the use of credit bureau data only for credit screening before making an offer and not for creating marketing lists. In case the institution has a prospect list on which it wants to run a preapproved programme it can send the prospect list to an independent entity along with the eligibility criteria, which needs to be checked at the credit bureau. The independent entity will run the above checks and send the eligible cases to a mailing company for sending the direct mail. The institution can get the number of cases from the prospect list that got selected and mailed but will not have the list of prospects that got selected. Once the prospect responds back, then the institution gets their response and can process their credit application. In industry parlance, the credit check before sending out a pre-screened offer is called front-end credit check, whereas the credit check after receiving an application for credit is called back end credit check.

Pre-screened acquisition process exists only in the developed markets; emerging markets (even ones, which have a credit bureau) do not have the pre-screen acquisition process. In these cases, the direct mailer, telecalling or direct marketing (through direct sales agents) relies on marketing lists that are available. All credit checks need to be performed at the back end, that is, after the prospect has responded to the offer of credit. Hence, approval rate of newly sourced applications is an important monitoring criterion, which acts as a major driver for the success of an acquisition programme.

## 1.12 Acquisition Metrics

Companies use a variety of metrics for monitoring the acquisition process. In most cases companies use multiple sources for obtaining prospect information and multiple channels to target those prospects. Each unique combination of prospect source and channel is given a unique source code. Even within a particular channel if there are various sub channels, then each sub channel is given a unique source code. For example, if a company sources prospect information from two sources (e.g., referrals and marketing lists) and uses two call centres for telecalling these prospects then it should assign four unique source codes to uniquely identify a customer to its source of acquisition. Usually, all acquisition metrics are tracked at the source code level so as to assess the effectiveness of each channel and information source. For example, all acquisitions from a particular club membership list, through the direct mailer channel will bear the same source code.

The key metrics, which are usually used for tracking the acquisition process, can be divided into the following categories:

- **Volume metrics**
  - *Prospect sourcing metrics:* Number of prospects targeted by each source code
  - *Response metrics:* Response rate by each source code. Response rate is calculated as number of responders divided by number of prospects targeted.
- **Cost metrics**
  - *Cost per response:* Cost per response by each source code. Cost per response is calculated as total cost of the acquisition campaign divided by number of responders.
  - *Cost per contact:* Calculated mostly for telecalling channel. Cost per contact is calculated as total telecalling cost divided by number of contacts made.
  - *Cost per mail base/telecalling base:* Calculated as total cost of mailing or telecalling divided by the number of prospects in the mail or telecalling file
- **Value metrics**
  - *Quality of customer sourced:* Percentage of various types of customers sourced. For example, percentage of high net worth customers sourced.
  - *Value of sale:* Average value of sales per new customer. For example, average credit line for credit cards, average loan size for mortgage and personal loan, average annualised premium for insurance.

- For products like credit cards, loans, post-paid mobile connections, etc., which involve a lending decision there are some **additional metrics** that are usually tracked:
    - *Approval rate:* Approval rate by each source code. Approval rate is calculated as number of responders approved divided by number of responders.
    - *Rejection rate:* Rejection rate by reject reasons and source codes (the common reject reasons are bureau no hit, presence of delinquency or derogatory information in the bureau, low credit score, high debt, low income, too old or too young, etc.). Rejection rate is calculated as number of rejects divided by number of responders.
    - *Cost per approval:* Approval rate by each source code. Cost per approval is calculated as cost of the acquisition campaign divided by number of approved responders.
    - *Credit quality:* Credit quality is measured mostly by using a benchmark credit score. Credit quality is measured as percentage of acquired customers in various score ranges. The volume of sale such as credit limit or loan size is also measured at a score band level so as to find the riskiness of the lending, which has been made.

In some cases, geography is not part of the source codes. This is particularly true where only direct mailer and telecalling are used as channels. In these cases, all the above metrics are measured at a geographic level as well. Table 1.15 depicts the acquisition metrics for selling personal loan through a direct mailer channel.

**Table 1.15** Acquisition Metrics

| | | | |
|---|---|---|---|
| A | | Number of mailers sent | 535,000 |
| B | | Total cost (USD) | 1,250,000 |
| C | | Number of mailers delivered | 232,400 |
| D | | Number of responders | 8,230 |
| E | | Number of rejects | 5,513 |
| | E1 | Missing application information | 230 |
| | E2 | Age less than or more than threshold | 121 |
| | E3 | Improper documents | 173 |
| | E4 | Bureau no hit | 115 |
| | E5 | Suspected fraud | 23 |
| | E6 | Presence of derogatory information in the bureau | 143 |
| | E7 | Presence of delinquency in the last 12 months | 1,285 |
| | E8 | Score less than threshold | 1,024 |
| | E9 | Recently opened unsecured trade | 325 |

*(Continued)*

**Table 1.15** Acquisition Metrics (*Continued*)

| | | | |
|---|---|---|---|
| | E10 | Total outstanding balance across all trades too high | 375 |
| | E11 | Income too low | 245 |
| | E12 | Debt burden too high | 328 |
| | E13 | Fixed income to obligation ratio too low | 1,126 |
| F | | Approved (D-E) | 2,717 |
| G | | Total credit extended (USD) | 8,694,400 |
| Key metric | | Response rate (D/A) | 1.5% |
| | | Approval rate (F/D) | 33.0% |
| | | Cost per mailer (B/A) | 2.34 |
| | | Cost per contact (B/C) | 5.38 |
| | | Cost per response (B/D) | 151.88 |
| | | Cost per approval (B/F) | 460.07 |
| | | Average ticket size per approval (G/F) (USD) | 3,200 |

## 1.13 Acquisition Profit and Loss Framework

As discussed earlier, each acquisition programme needs to be tracked not only on the basis of the number of new customers acquired but also on the basis of overall profitability generated. While actual profitability is important for evaluating an acquisition campaign, it is also important to forecast profitability for a campaign before it is launched. Usually profitability is forecasted for a period of 12 to 18 months, because this has been found to be the typical time needed to recover the cost of acquisition for credit related products. The profitability forecast is used to arrive at a "go" or "no-go" decision for a campaign. The profitability framework for an acquisition programme has four key components:

- Acquisition costs, which are observed immediately after the acquisition campaign
- Revenue realisation, as stated earlier, the revenue from new customers accrue over a period of time
- Ongoing costs, which include maintenance, servicing, and other costs are also incurred for the next 18–24 months and the same needs to be factored in order to measure profitability
- For industries like credit card, loans, and insurance where there is a probability of making a huge credit loss or loss due to insurance claims. The probability of making such huge losses need to be factored in for estimating profitability of the newly acquired customers. It needs to be noted that, a waterfall analysis of the reject reasons need to be performed to identify the reason that is responsible for the maximum number of rejection.

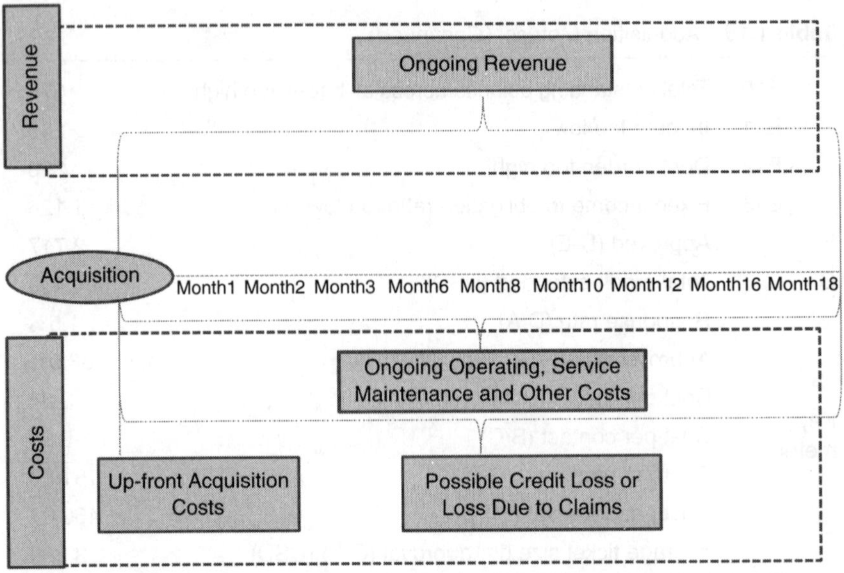


**Figure 1.14** Acquisition Revenue and Cost Framework

As stated earlier, a forecast of the revenue and cost items is essential in judging the expected profitability of the campaign. Revenue items need to be forecasted for a period of 18–24 months as this is the typical break even period for recovering acquisition costs.

Figure 1.14 depicts each of these components.

## 1.13.1 Acquisition Costs

Acquisition costs are easier to measure because they can be observed as soon as the campaign is executed. Table 1.16 depicts the short-term metrics and campaign cost for an acquisition campaign. The campaign is designed to target 70,000 prospects, out of which all will be sent a direct mailer. Out of the 70,000 prospects, 20,000 will be sent a single mail, 30,000 will be sent two mailers and 20,000 will be sent a mailer followed by a tele-call.

## 1.13.2 Revenue and Cost Forecast

The ongoing revenue and cost items need to be forecasted for a period of 18–24 months (sometimes even longer). For this purpose, the various revenue and cost components need to be separately forecasted. The reader can refer to Chapter 8 for an understanding of the revenue and cost drivers for banking (liabilities), credit card, and telecom. The methodology of forecasting these items have also been discussed in detail in Chapter 8.

Table 1.16 depicts the cost and revenue dynamics of a campaign. From the table it can be seen that the entire cost of the campaign is incurred on the campaign month (month-0). The revenue from customers acquired as part of

**Table 1.16 (a)** Campaign Profitability Calculation

**Assumptions**

Annual interest rate is 18%. Monthly interest rate is 1.5%

Cost of fund rate has been assumed as 0.3% per month

Interchange income is 1% of sales

Reward cost is $ 0.001 per dollar of sales made

A monthly discount rate of 0.2% has been used to discount future profits

For the sake of simplicity balance transfer or loan on cards have not been considered

Account maintenance cost is $1 per open account

| | | Month-0 (Campaign month) |
|---|---|---|
| Size of the campaign | Mail file size (total number of prospects) | 70,000 |
| | Number of prospects targeted through single mail – A | 20,000 |
| | Number of prospects targeted through single mail and re-mail – B | 30,000 |
| | Number of prospects targeted through single mail and telemarketing – C | 20,000 |
| Response Rate | Response rate for single mail – D | 0.66% |
| | Response rate for single mail and re-mail – E | 1.28% |
| | Response rate of single mail and telemarketing – F | 2.38% |
| Number of responders | Number of responder – G (A*D + B*E + C*F) | 992 |
| Campaign cost items | Cost of list processing each record – H | $0.07 |
| | Cost of each mail piece – I | $0.46 |
| | Cost of each telemarketing – J | $1.50 |
| | Cost of processing for each responder – K | $1.10 |
| | Cost of welcome kit – L | $6.00 |
| | Cost of reward for each responder – M | $8.00 |
| Total cost of campaign | Total cost of list processing – N (H*(A + B + C)) | $4,900 |
| | Total cost of contacting the prospect – O (A*I + 2*B*I + C*I + C*J) | $76,000 |
| | Total cost of fulfilment – P (G*K + G*L + G*M) | $14,979 |
| | Total cost of acquisition – Q (O + P) | $90,979 |
| Campaign Profitability | Cumulative discounted value of revenue net of cost – R | $102,509 |
| | Campaign profitability – S (R – Q) | $11,530 |
| | Return on Investment – T (R – Q)/Q | 13% |

**Table 1.16 (b)** Detailed Revenue and Cost Calculation

| | | Month Post Campaign | | | | | | | | | | | | | | | | | |
|---|---|---|---|---|---|---|---|---|---|---|---|---|---|---|---|---|---|---|---|
| | | 1 | 2 | 3 | 4 | 5 | 6 | 7 | 8 | 9 | 10 | 11 | 12 | 13 | 14 | 15 | 16 | 17 | 18 |
| Number of accounts | Number of inactive accounts – a | 763 | 725 | 580 | 529 | 469 | 400 | 319 | 300 | 280 | 260 | 239 | 134 | 137 | 144 | 150 | 159 | 168 | 176 |
| | Number of active accounts – b | 229 | 267 | 285 | 333 | 390 | 456 | 534 | 550 | 567 | 584 | 602 | 632 | 619 | 607 | 595 | 583 | 571 | 560 |
| | Number of closed accounts – c | – | | 127 | 130 | 133 | 136 | 139 | 142 | 145 | 148 | 151 | 226 | 236 | 241 | 247 | 250 | 253 | 256 |
| | Total number of accounts – d (a + b + c) | 992 | 992 | 992 | 992 | 992 | 992 | 992 | 992 | 992 | 992 | 992 | 992 | 992 | 992 | 992 | 992 | 992 | 992 |
| Revenue and cost drivers | Sales per open account – Sales | $270 | $360 | $452 | $738 | $886 | $1,274 | $1,749 | $1,786 | $1,809 | $1,832 | $1,855 | $1,879 | $1,903 | $1,927 | $1,951 | $1,976 | $1,979 | $1,982 |
| | Balance per open account – Balance | $128 | $284 | $382 | $451 | $797 | $1,147 | $1,574 | $1,607 | $1,644 | $2,011 | $2,862 | $4,073 | $5,389 | $6,641 | $8,122 | $8,392 | $8,671 | $8,959 |
| | Revolve rate | 4.28% | 8.33% | 9.12% | 12.73% | 13.59% | 15.27% | 18.61% | 19.25% | 22.67% | 23.72% | 25.41% | 26.00% | 28.91% | 30.66% | 32.82% | 33.17% | 34.21% | 34.21% |
| | Net credit loss as percentage of total balance – NCL | 0.00% | 0.00% | 0.00% | 0.00% | 0.01% | 0.02% | 0.02% | 0.02% | 0.03% | 0.05% | 0.08% | 0.13% | 0.13% | 0.15% | 0.17% | 0.21% | 0.22% | 0.22% |
| On-going revenue | Interest income – d (Balance * Revolve rate * Interest rate)* (a + b) | $82 | $352 | $452 | $742 | $1,396 | $2,248 | $3,748 | $3,945 | $4,735 | $6,039 | $9,174 | $12,167 | $17,667 | $22,937 | $29,789 | $30,982 | $32,882 | $33,836 |
| | Fee income – e | $0 | $0 | $172 | $177 | $182 | $188 | $194 | $200 | $206 | $213 | $220 | $1,327 | $224 | $224 | $228 | $228 | $233 | $233 |
| | Interchange income – f (Sales per open account) * (a + b)* Interchange rate, which is 1% | $268 | $357 | $391 | $636 | $761 | $1,091 | $1,492 | $1,518 | $1,532 | $1,546 | $1,560 | $1,439 | $1,439 | $1,447 | $1,453 | $1,466 | $1,462 | $1,459 |

*(Continued)*

**Table 1.16 (b)** Detailed Revenue and Cost Calculation (*Continued*)

| | | Month Post Campaign | | | | | | | | | | | | | | | | | |
|---|---|---|---|---|---|---|---|---|---|---|---|---|---|---|---|---|---|---|---|
| | | 1 | 2 | 3 | 4 | 5 | 6 | 7 | 8 | 9 | 10 | 11 | 12 | 13 | 14 | 15 | 16 | 17 | 18 |
| On-going costs | Cost of funds – g (Balance per open account * Cost of funds rate, which is 0.3% per month) * (a + b) | $254 | $563 | $661 | $778 | $1,370 | $1,963 | $2,685 | $2,733 | $2,785 | $3,395 | $4,814 | $6,240 | $8,148 | $9,975 | $12,102 | $12,454 | $12,816 | $13,188 |
| | Cost of rewards – h (Reward cost per dollar of sale, which is $0.001)*(Sales per open account) * (a + b) | $268 | $357 | $391 | $636 | $761 | $1,091 | $1,492 | $1,518 | $1,532 | $1,546 | $1,560 | $1,439 | $1,439 | $1,447 | $1,453 | $1,466 | $1,462 | $1,459 |
| | Account maintenance and operations cost – i | $992 | $992 | $865 | $862 | $859 | $856 | $853 | $850 | $847 | $844 | $841 | $766 | $756 | $751 | $745 | $742 | $739 | $736 |
| | Cost of credit loss – j (NCL * Balance per open account) * (a + b) | $0 | $0 | $0 | $0 | $82 | $147 | $201 | $260 | $362 | $764 | $1,950 | $3,900 | $5,215 | $7,232 | $10,408 | $13,201 | $14,225 | $14,638 |
| On-going profit | Revenue net of all costs – k (d + e + f – g – h – I – j) | –$1,164 | –$1,203 | –$902 | –$720 | –$651 | –$383 | $404 | $563 | $1,309 | $2,013 | $3,739 | $6,488 | $8,987 | $12,435 | $17,170 | $18,014 | $19,560 | $20,146 |
| Revenue net of cost | Discounted value of revenue net of cost – I | –$1,162 | –$1,199 | –$896 | –$714 | –$644 | –$378 | $398 | $554 | $1,286 | $1,974 | $3,658 | $6,334 | $8,757 | $12,092 | $16,663 | $17,447 | $18,907 | $19,434 |
| | Cumulative discounted value of revenue net of cost – R | | | | | | | | | | | | | | | | | | $102,509 |

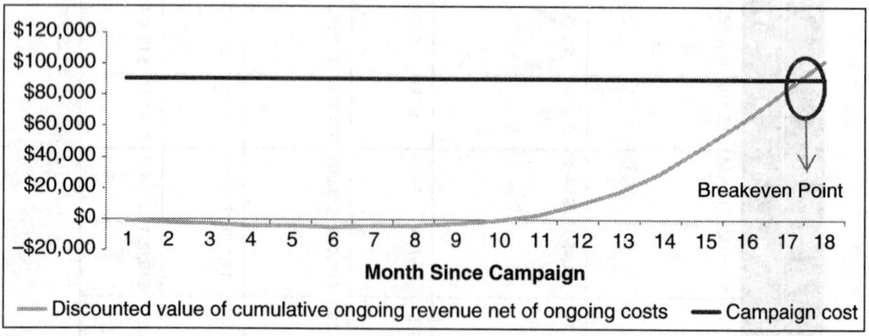


**Figure 1.15** Loss Rate Since Acquisition

the campaign, is realized over a longer time frame. The key ongoing revenue streams are: interest, interchange and fees. The key ongoing cost items are: cost of funds, reward cost, account maintenance cost and cost of credit loss. After acquisition, customers increase usage of their credit card over time, hence, the interest and interchange revenue also increases over time. It needs to be noted that fee income shows a spike on the 12th month post campaign. This is because an annual fee is levied on the 12th month post acquisition.

Credit losses are incurred on customers, who do not pay their dues. Credit losses from new customers will not be realized immediately after they are acquired. It normally takes some time for these losses to show up. In the parlance of risk managers, this effect is called maturation of the vintage and the loss trajectory from a cohort of customers who have been acquired as of a particular month and year are termed as the vintage curve.

The ongoing revenue net of ongoing costs are discounted back to the campaign month. The discounting is performed to take care of the fact that the revenue is realized in future, while campaign costs are realized immediately after the campaign. In this example a monthly discounting rate of 0.2% has been used for the purpose of discounting.

For forecasting the profitability of the campaign, one needs to forecast the future revenue and cost items. Forecasted future revenue and costs are discounted back to the campaign month so as to calculate the return on investment for the campaign. Figure 1.15 compares the up-front campaign costs with the discounted value of future revenue. It can be seen from the figure that the campaign achieves a break-even point only 17 months after the campaign.

TWO

# Usage Management

## 2.1 Introduction

Usage management has multiple facets. On the one hand, it involves influencing demand related customer behaviours of activation, spend, balance build, and loyalty. On the other hand, supply side factors of price and credit line need to be managed. Customer management programmes focussed on enhancing usage are formally practiced in retail, telecom, financial services, hospitality, and T&E. These programmes are key to delivering profitable growth in these sectors as usage management programmes have a direct correlation with customer lifetime value (CLV). In most of these sectors, the bulk of the revenue from a customer is realised not in the initial years of customer acquisition but during a period of on-going relationship. Hence, it is important to ensure that usage by the customer remains high during the entire period of the relationship.

Consumer spend has implications on economic momentum through demand generation. Understanding how firms can influence consumer spend behaviour using sales promotions and assessing their impact is essential. Household borrowing that has been rising, is an important contributor to revenue via portfolio outstanding balances of a lender. Balance build programmes using promotional or teaser interest rates are quick wins for banks to build balances and enhance wallet share in the short-term. These programmes are aimed at attracting more balances from customers through initiatives such as debt consolidation, balance transfer on credit card, loan on card, and conversion of large purchases into monthly instalments. Pricing and credit line are levers of portfolio profitability for lending institutions. Line management is a critical supply side parameter, to accelerate consumer demand for credit and function as a brake for curtailing credit loss[1]. Prior to the sub-prime

[1] As a reactive measure to double digit loss rates resulting from the sub-prime mortgage crisis, lenders had drastically cut down credit lines in *(Contd.)*

mortgage crisis, line management had gone through a paradigm shift, with a shift from risk-based to profitability-based strategies in advanced markets. This has been encouraged by fierce competition for wallet share and the multiple forms of credit line exposure (e.g., second card, personal loan) available to a lender.

Loyalty management has both qualitative (satisfaction and patronage) and quantitative (usage and tenure) dimensions. Furthermore, the relationship between loyalty, and profitability, satisfaction, and retention are important to evaluate as they are inter-linked. However, with price discounts becoming the order of the day, loyalty is at risk as shoppers look for the best deals. Hence, for the high investments in such programmes, whether loyalty schemes work is a debated topic in a competitive and commoditised loyalty market.

With regard to sectoral trends, the mobile telecom industry has been facing challenges of a declining voice revenue. Tariffs plans, bundling, and plan migration are some of the actions that telecom operators resort to, for managing minutes of usage (MOU), average revenue per user (ARPU), and average revenue per minute (ARPM). Sales promotions are widely practised by the retail sector, which comprises of a variety of short-term tactical promotional tools to generate an immediate market response. While scanner technology of the 1980s has encouraged the trend towards promotional discounts, consumer promotions constitute a significant part of the marketing mix budget of a retailer. In the loyalty space, the airline industry has been the leader with frequent flier programmes[2], followed by the retail, hospitality, and T&E sectors.

The chapter layout is as follows. Factors driving usage are highlighted followed by activation. Some of the key considerations of the activation section are identifying inactivity and its trends; isolating self-activators; deciding appropriate targeting and offer strategies; and evaluating the impact of these programmes. Spend management for retail emphasises on the role of sales promotions and the different quantitative models to evaluate its effectiveness. For the telecom sector, bundling and plan migration strategies are discussed. Discounting in the hospitality and airline sectors comes under the purview of yield management and therefore, will be reviewed in Chapter 5. The balance transfer programme for credit card is the focal point of the balance build section with price testing, segmentation, and targeting. While credit line management will be scoped out in this chapter, price management is discussed as a separate chapter. Of special interest specific to line management are the different

---

the US for even good-standing customers. Research has repeatedly shown that amount of available credit utilised remains highly predictive of the likelihood of future delinquency.

[2] The top three North American airlines-American, Delta, and United each makes close to $1 bilion in revenues from their loyalty programmes, according to Watterson et al. *The New Economics of Customer Loyalty Programs*, 2008.

analytical methods relating to decisions on credit exposure—how much and to whom, and in which form, using both risk-based and profitability-based approaches. Theoretical as well as the practical aspects of loyalty management are covered at the end of the chapter. Industry exemplars and evidence on whether loyalty schemes work are highlighted. Basic concepts of rewards are also discussed along with a P&L example of a retail loyalty programme.

Figure 2.1 depicts the multifarious aspect of usage management that provides an overview of the levers that the marketer can utilise for driving higher usage. A key point to note is that there are interdependencies among the multiple facets of usage management that will be highlighted during the course of the chapter.

## 2.2 Factors Affecting Usage

It is important to understand the factors that affect usage, so that programmes related to enhancing usage can be better understood. Some of these factors are:

- Acquisition strategy—Product proposition (price, rewards, value-added services), initial credit limit, bundling strategy, value proposition, channel of acquisition, target market, and alignment of product with customer profile/segment

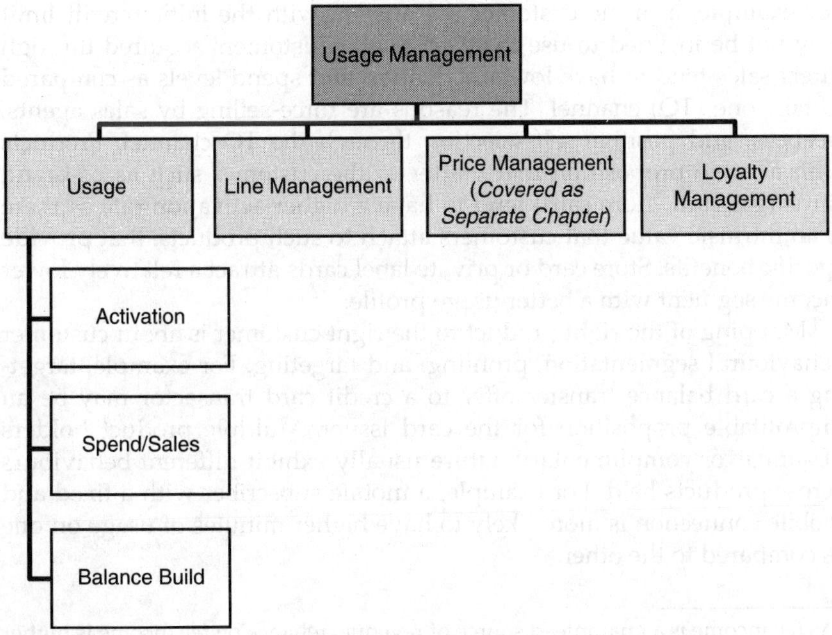


**Figure 2.1** Structure of Usage Management

- Single vs. multiple product holding
- Customer-portfolio management programmes relating to activation, sales and balance build, line increase/decrease policies, cross-selling and up-selling, loyalty, and retention management
- Servicing—customer product education, on-boarding customer experience, and overall customer service
- Competitive factors
- Macroeconomic environment
- Seasonality

For most of this section, credit card product has been used to illustrate the importance of usage management programmes. Usage management programmes for a cards portfolio are a significant component of the marketing budget for issuers. The combination of fixed and variable pricing components is an important strategy. Presence of a fee is likely to increase the activation rate while depressing response (product take-up) and this impact is likely to intensify with a higher fee amount. For an overdraft line linked to a customer's bank account, an activation fee is levied if the line is not used up during a specified period of time. This is done as a step to discourage non-usage of the credit facility and provide an alternate source of revenue for the financial institution[3]. The impact of pricing (rate, fee) will be discussed in the context of balance transfer programmes. The initial line assigned for credit cards affects activation, spend and balance build depending on various parameters such as line relative to competitor lines of the customer and credit worthiness of the customer. For example, a prime customer dissatisfied with the initial credit limit may not be inclined to use the card at all. Customers acquired through direct sales tend to have lower activation and spend levels as compared to take-one (TO) channel. The reasons are force-selling by sales agents, freebees, and positive self-selection through the TO channel. Products with a value proposition that matter to the customer such as co-brand cards (gas card, store card) tend to have a higher activation rate as there is an intrinsic value that customers attach to such products, that provide specific benefits. Store card or private label cards attract a relatively lower income segment with a better usage profile.

Mapping of the right product to the right customer is about customer behavioural segmentation, profiling, and targeting. For example, targeting a card balance transfer offer to a credit card transactor may be an unprofitable proposition for the card issuer. Multiple product holders of similar or complimentary nature usually exhibit different behaviours across products held. For example, a mobile subscriber with a fixed and mobile connection is more likely to have higher minutes of usage on one as compared to the other.

---

[3] As fee income is a guaranteed source of revenue, reliance on fee income is higher when other components, for example, net interest margin is compressed.

The role of customer management programmes in driving usage will be discussed in the relevant sections. The aggressiveness and timeliness of these programmes is essential to manage usage and can sometimes become a never ending circle. An offer of a loan on card or a balance transfer to a credit card customer is one way to ensure that credit line is used up. On the contrary, a customer who transfers balances from competition cards has a strong tendency to become sales inactive (stop purchasing or withdrawing cash on the credit card).

The reaction to competition in the form of wallet share programmes will be highlighted through the use of credit bureau information for line management in the financial services sector. The same analogy can also be used for telecom and retail, contingent on the availability of similar information for these sectors.

## 2.3 Activation

Activation is defined as the posting of an activity or transaction on the records of an account[4] belonging to a customer. For instance, an account is considered active in a given month if the customer uses the product or service at least once during this period. In reference to the telecom sector, TRAI (Telephone Regulatory Authority of India) defines an account as "active" for the month, if at least one outgoing call has been made in that month. For financial services, activation can be defined as a purchase or cash transaction (sales active) or payment of minimum due (statement active) on a credit card; a credit (non-interest) or debit (non-minimum balance fee) on a deposit account. Activation needs to be managed primarily in industries that provide a product or service on contractual terms, and which requires continuous engagement with the customer, as in financial services and telecom. However, the focus will be on financial services as most telecom service providers charge an activation fee. For example, if there is no usage (either incoming or outgoing call or SMS) in the first "x" days of account opening, it is identified as zero usage. Subsequently, the service may be suspended until the customer requests for reactivation.

Early activation programmes focus on the first activity on the product or service. Reactivation programmes involve activating an inactive account that was previously active. Both these programs are shown as Fig. 2.2. Self-activators or self-starters are customers who activate on their own without any intervention. Figure 2.2 is a generalisation and the cut-off for vintage or months on book (MOB) to distinguish early activation and reactivation varies across sectors.

[4] A customer can have multiple accounts of a product. For example, two mobile connections; a checking and savings account; classic and a premium credit card.

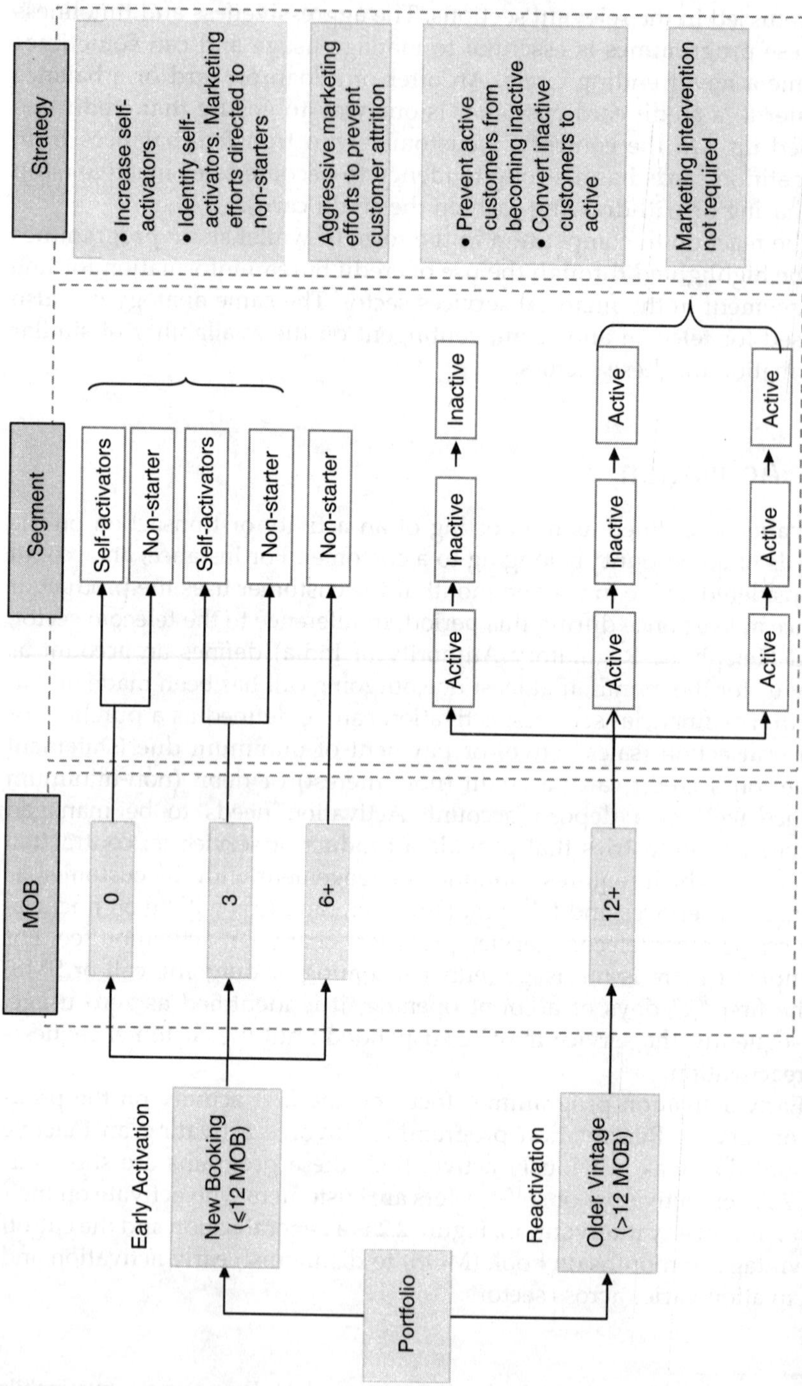


**Figure 2.2** Activation Strategy

### 2.3.1 Early Activation

The first activation signifies the initiation of usage of the product or service. Early activation programmes usually last for a duration ranging anywhere between 1 and 12 months on book (MOB). After this time frame, a customer is considered mature for further portfolio management actions. When a firm acquires a new account, it has very little insights on expected levels of activity, spend and balance behaviour. This phase related to early engagement is mostly focused on early activation, spend, and balance build-up. Managing the customer involvement with the product or service early on is important for a variety of reasons—building block of the customer–firm relationship, customer orientation to the product, and origination of customer lifetime value (CLV). One aspect of timing of activation is its relationship with voluntary attrition, which will be covered in Chapter 4. One important inference is that an account, which is active within the first quarter of account opening, is much more likely to complete an additional year as compared to delayed activators.

There are different approaches to early activation programmes and one such strategy is to scale up intervention based on the degree of inactivity, with aggressive and more costly programmes being put in place for the serial inactives. This point is also highlighted in Fig. 2.2. and Fig. 2.5. However, there is no hard and fast rule as the choice of activation offers will depend on a cost-benefit analysis of such offers. For example, an opposite strategy will be proposed for reactivation. The rationale is that it is tougher to convert inactives to actives with increasing duration of inactivity, due to weak response. Moreover, the resulting revenue post intervention may not be sufficient to justify the costs for a reactivation programme. In some cases, it has been observed that customers who initiate or enhance usage as a result of activation programmes fall back into dormancy, once the programme is withdrawn.

It is critical to have the right test and control set in place in order to measure the "stickiness" of early activation programmes. Campaigns and appropriate champion challenger schemes should be based on behavioural segments, to determine which offer works best for which type of customer. Different variants of activation offers should be tested as well. The example relating to a reactivation programme will show case a test-control scenario for impact measurement. Identifying self-activators is another area of attention to avoid wastage of resources on customers, who would have anyhow become active without any intervention. However, it can be a challenge to accurately predict potential self-activators due to data issues. Limited information available at the time of application may not able to explain this behaviour completely and transaction data is too nascent to be predictive. In addition, it is also difficult to obtain a sample that has not been touched by historical activation programmes, in order to capture the behaviour of "true" self-activators (without any programme intervention). Nonetheless, a brief write-up on identifying self-activators will be discussed shortly. Furthermore, response models can prove to be useful for selecting customers who are more likely to respond to a particular offer, thereby increasing the cost-effectiveness of activation campaigns.

#### 2.3.1.1 Early Activation: Financial Services

For a credit card, product features are used as stimuli for activation at the time of acquisition and during post-acquisition. As an example, features of a credit card are presented in Figs. 2.3 and 2.4. For a credit card product, inactivity takes the form of sales inactivity or statement inactivity. Sales inactivity is the absence of a purchase or cash transaction on the card account. Statement inactivity is more severe because there is absolutely no activity (sales or payment). The first activation strategy for credit cards is shown in Fig. 2.5. Similarly, for deposits and investments, balance build for a new account is more important to track than activation alone. For example, for a high net worth individual acquired as a premium investment customer, it is expected that the quantum of assets under management (AUM) will grow quickly and would reach the minimum threshold required for profitability. Balance build programmes are discussed in Section 2.5.

#### 2.3.1.2 Identifying Self-activators: Financial Services

The identification of self-activators involves predicting the probability that an account will activate during a specified time period from account opening date (e.g., 6 months) without any programme intervention. Application and credit bureau data can be used for this purpose.

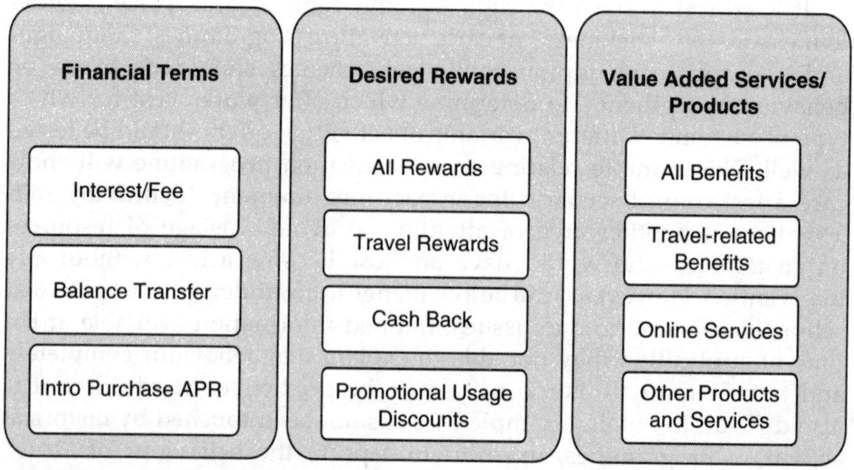


**Figure 2.3** Features of Credit Card

| Financial Terms | Desired Rewards | Value Added Services/Products |
|---|---|---|
| 2.90% APR for 6 months. After that APR will be a variable rate of 12.99%. No fee. | Earn 5000 bonus reward points for $600 in purchases within the first 3 months. Earn 3 × reward points when you shop at select supermarkets and drugstores. No expiration of reward points. | Road side assistance/extended warranty. |
| 0% Intro APR on balance transfers for 21 months. After that variable APR of 11.99%–20.99% based on credit worthiness. | Earn one mile for every dollar spent and double miles on travel on a specific airline. Earn 20,000 bonus miles after $600 in purchases with the first 4 months of card membership. | Check your first bag for free; concierge services/access to airport lounges. Access to exclusive events/ complimentary tickets. |
| % Intro APR on purchases for 15 months. After that variable APR of 16.99%. | Earn $100 cash back on $500 in first 3 months of card membership and full 1% thereafter. 5% cash back offer on $1500 spent at select categories in a quarter. | Bill pay, one bill, on-line tax payment facilities, spend tracking report. |
| | Flat 5% discount/10% discount at select stores with minimum purchase of $150; 2 consecutive nights, get 3rd night free at a specific hotel. | Insurance (credit, travel, health, life), add-on card, easy EMI for consumer durable, loan on card. |

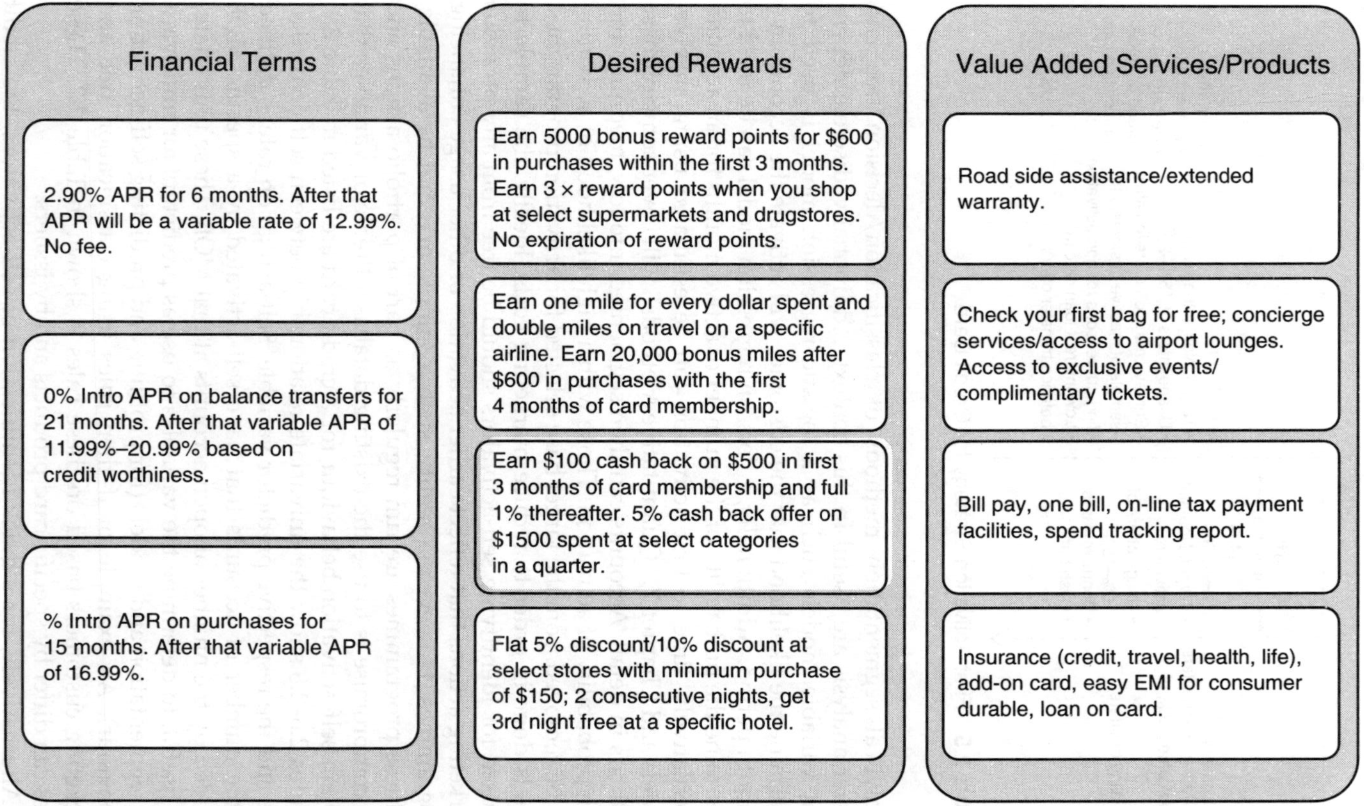

**Figure 2.4** Features of Credit Card: Examples

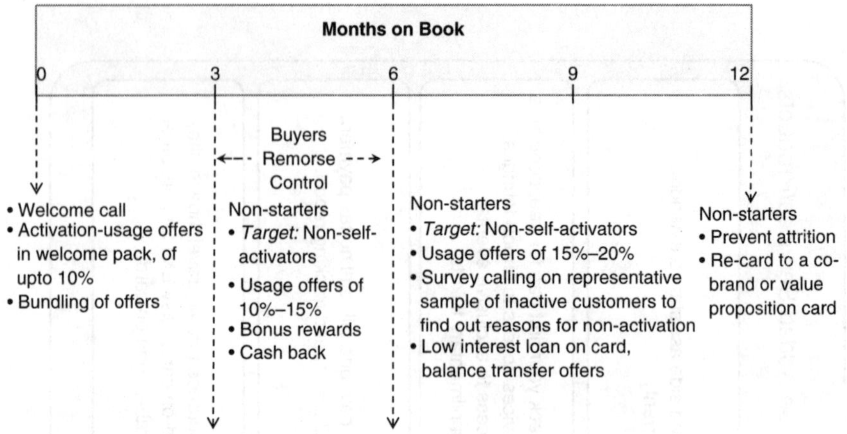


**Figure 2.5** First Activation Strategy for Credit Card

Analytical segmentation methods of classification/decision tree and cluster analysis are useful in this context. Additionally, discrete dependent variable models such as a logistic regression model is used to determine the likelihood that the customer will activate the account in a 6 month period. Additionally, a Poisson regression model can be used to determine the probability of the number of active months for an account. Alternatively, time to first activation can be estimated using survival models and Chapter 7, "Quantitative Methods" will cover some of these methods in detail. Accounts can then segmented into low, medium, and high probability of activation. Those with a high likelihood of activation can be removed from the target base selected for activation programmes. This is done in order to reduce marketing costs. Ideally, the sample to be used for identifying self-activators should be free from any previous marketing actions that reflect earlier activation or other usage enhancing programmes. However in reality, such a sample may not be available, as these programmes are run regularly as part of portfolio actions and the compromise is to use the existing database. Predictor variables that explain self-activation behaviour for a credit card are listed in Table 2.1. Figures 2.6–2.8 show the univariate relationship between self-activation rate and the respective predictor variable. Self-activation rate is defined as the number of accounts that have self-activated by a specific MOB divided by the number of open accounts at that MOB. These univariates are useful, to determine the variables to use as predictors for multivariate segmentation and models (for profiling and predicting self-activation behaviour). An example of if–then rules using classification tree and bucketing customers based on these rules is shown in Table 2.2. These rules can differ by specific card products and by issuers.

Alternatively, for a quick identification of self-activators, the credit bureau score measure of customer credit worthiness (based on credit bureau information) can be used to rank order customers with respect

**Table 2.1** Explaining Self-activation

| Data | Variables |
|---|---|
| Application data | Age, city (region), occupation, income, number of questions not answered; credit bureau score |
| Credit bureau | Total loan amount, total balance on cards, number of competitor cards (and % of active); number of inquiries in the last 3/6 months |
| Others | Product features—rate, fee, balance transfer taken, credit limit; first/second card; co-brand; channel of sourcing (branch, direct sales, telemarketing; take-one), number of add-on cards; surrogate programme (e.g., club membership); market segment information (e.g., income, lifestyle preferences, socioeconomic classification) |

to activation. Low score customers (low credit worthy) tend to have a higher rate compared to high-score customers (high credit worthy). Further, spend analysis based on data of activated customers can give direction on which categories and merchants to partner with, for sales promotional offers. These offers can be used for both incentivising the first transaction through a parcel of offers in an account opening kit and for increasing spends of actives through promotions. These type of analyses will be discussed in the spend management section.

## 2.3.2 Reactivation: Financial Services

For credit cards, reactivation measures are taken on mature customers, usually after 12 months of account opening and are similar to early activation programmes in philosophy. Since there is enough history of usage

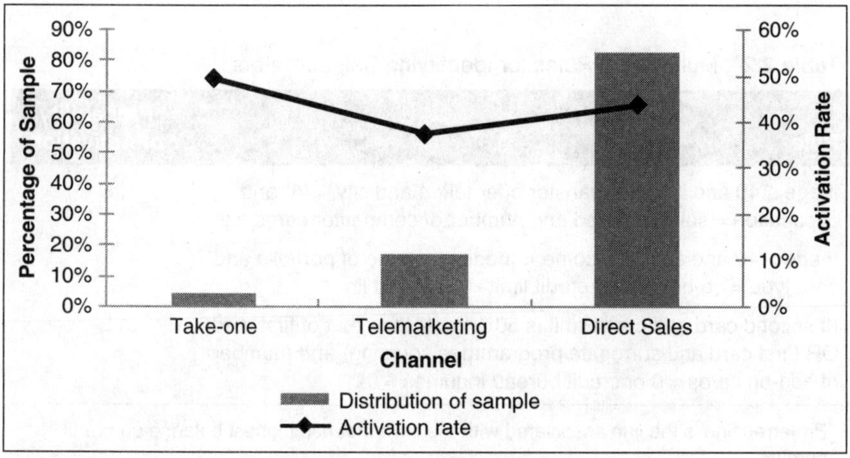


**Figure 2.6** Channel of Acquisition and Self-activation

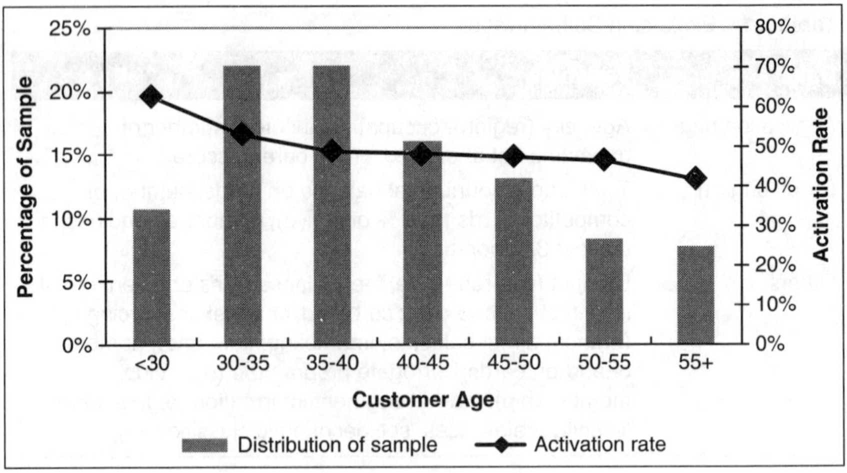


**Figure 2.7** Customer Age and Self-activation

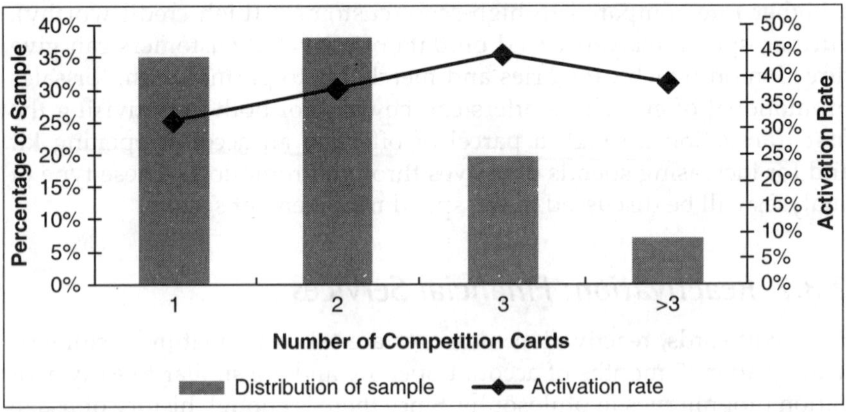


**Figure 2.8** Number of Competition Cards and Self-activation

**Table 2.2** Multivariate Rules for Identifying Self-activators

| Rule | Probability of Activation |
|---|---|
| If age ≤ 40 and balance transfer offer taken and city = "A" and occupation = self employed and number of competitor cards ≥ 2 | H |
| If age > 40 and annual income < median income of portfolio and card type = co-brand and credit limit < preferred line* | M |
| (If second card and credit limit is 50% lower than that of first card) OR (first card and surrogate programmes sourcing) and (number of add-on cards = 0 or credit bureau inquiries = 0) | L |

*Preferred line is the line associated with the card that has highest balance on credit bureau

of 12 months, designing activation programmes are very information and analytically oriented. For example, sales promotional offers can be designed by evaluating spend patterns to determine spend threshold, rebates, and which retail outlets to partner with, by spend category. Also, revenue dynamics of transactor and revolver behaviour and the extent of credit line utilisation provide rich insights into which usage offer should be made (loan on card, balance transfer, line increase, cash rewards). There is no single prescription of the offers palette and continuous testing of offers at a segment level based on history of learning, judgement, and market competitive dynamics is recommended. As mentioned earlier, the sales and statement activation rate are important metrics to monitor for a credit card product. Figure 2.9 elaborates on the flow of inactivity from mild to serious and some of the potential triggers and offers that could be considered. Banks regularly run reactivation programmes. For instance, Bank of America was offering $25 cash back for reactivating the Visa credit card after qualifying purchases of $250[5].

Inactivity is best mitigated when tackled early as the impact of activation programmes decline with duration of dormancy. Figure 2.10 shows that the sales activation rate for the test 7–12 month inactive segment is higher and rises faster than the test 13–24 month inactive segment. Another important point to note is that the differential between the activation rate across test and control narrows down with months post offer. This indicates that the programme effect is the highest during the immediate months following the offer. The impact of a spend hurdle (rebate conditional on frequency or value of transactions/spend) and an upfront credit in the account (reversed if customer does not use the credit card during the promotional period) on sales activation rate is contrasting, as shown in Fig. 2.11.

The returns from reactivation programmes may not be particularly exciting as the profitability of the test group may be only marginally better than the control group at an account level. If rebate costs and incremental marketing expenses are accounted for, the returns may appear even poorer. Activation programmes may not be effective without managing spend, as activation alone may not guarantee significant incremental spend volume. Moreover, sales or spend disengagement is a pre-cursor to inactivity. Therefore, spend management seems to be a much more compelling proposition for promoting usage.

For an investment portfolio, "Promote one more fund" type of campaigns are a good way to reactivate customers who have taken a mutual fund before, and have not done any mutual fund subscription in the last 6 months. A tier-based gift based on the value of investment is an incentive. Other segments such as those who have been active and have taken another mutual fund in

[5]http://www.netbanker.com/2012/04/marketing_bank_of_america_offers_25_to_reactivate_visa_card.html.

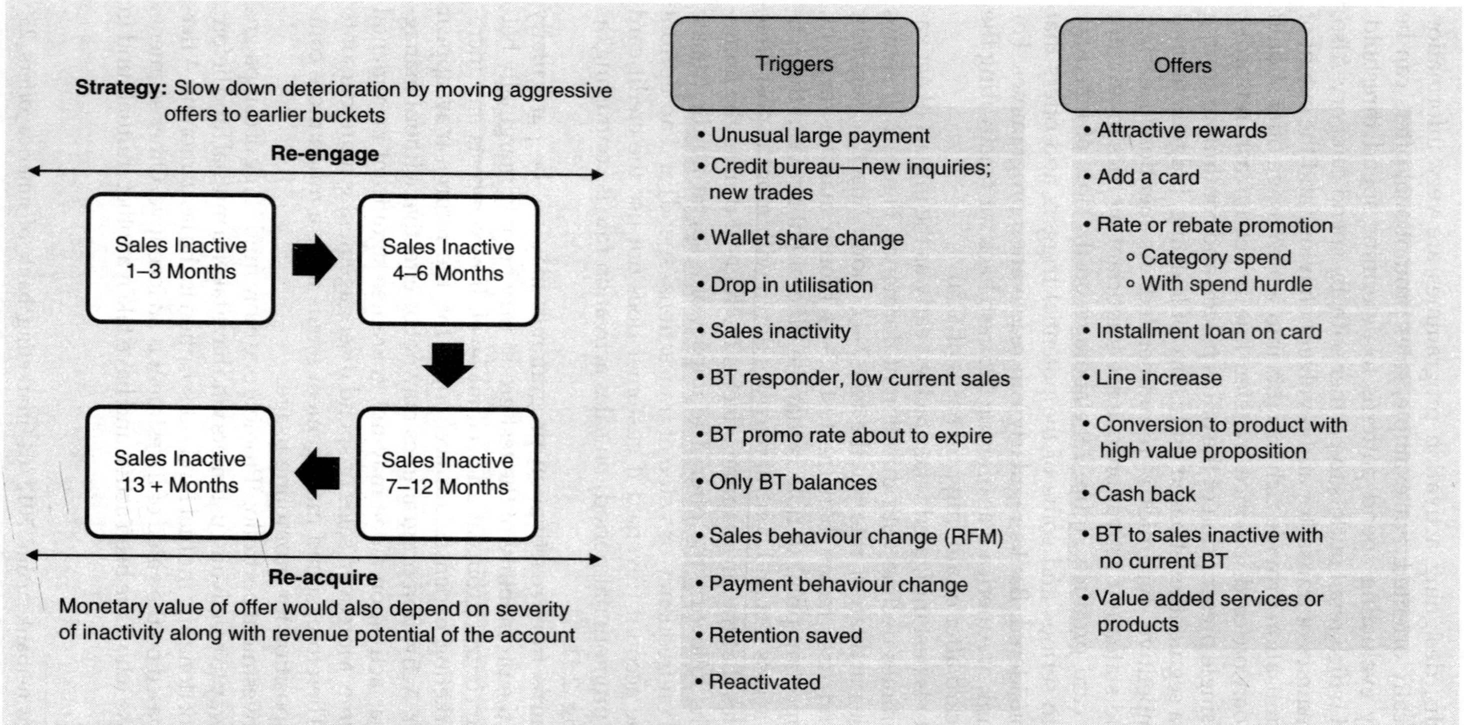


BT= Balance transfer, RFM = Recency, Frequency, Monetary Value

*Note:* There is no one-to-one correspondence across adjacent boxes for triggers and offers.

**Figure 2.9** Reactivation—Sales Inactivity—Segmentation—Credit Card

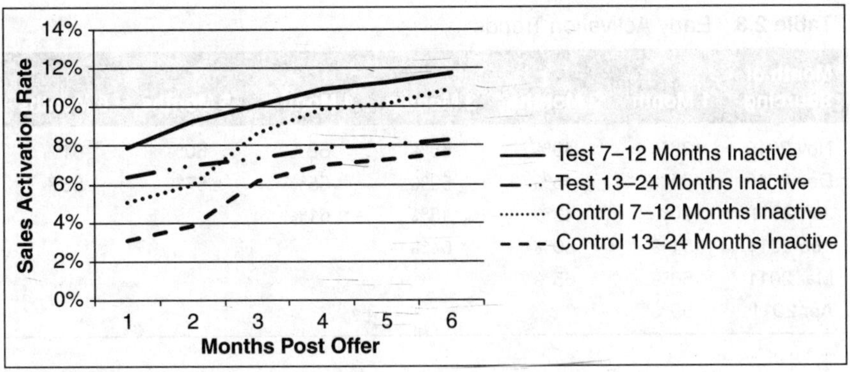


**Figure 2.10** Reactivation Programme Impact by Duration of Sales Inactivity

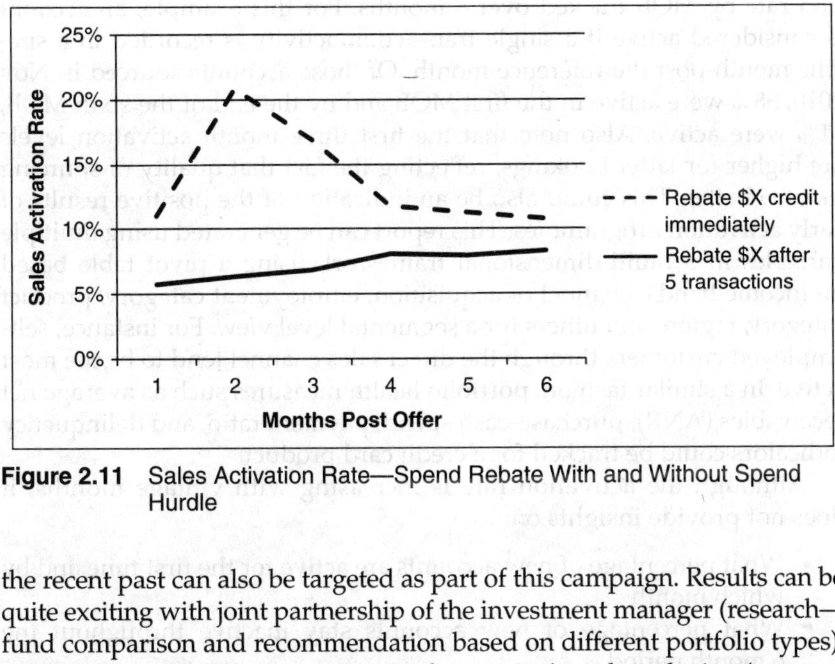


**Figure 2.11** Sales Activation Rate—Spend Rebate With and Without Spend Hurdle

the recent past can also be targeted as part of this campaign. Results can be quite exciting with joint partnership of the investment manager (research—fund comparison and recommendation based on different portfolio types), analytics (segmentation, targeting, and execution), and marketing (communication and gift) teams. A wealth segmentation type of schema, an example of which has been illustrated in the behavioural segmentation section, is a relevant guide for an investment manager to make recommendations based on risk appetite and wealth potential.

## 2.3.3 Activation MIS

Reports on activation by MOB are useful for gauging the momentum of activity as the customer seasons with an understanding of product proposition. The MIS report (Table 2.3) shows the activation rate of those

**Table 2.3** Early Activation Trends

| Month of Sourcing | 1 Month | 2 Months | 3 Months | 4 Months | 5 Months | 6 Months |
|---|---|---|---|---|---|---|
| Nov 2010 | 38% | 49% | 55% | 58% | 60% | 61% |
| Dec 2010 | 34% | 45% | 52% | 55% | 57% | 58% |
| Jan 2011 | 30% | 43% | 48% | 51% | | |
| Feb 2011 | 51% | 60% | 64% | | | |
| Mar 2011 | 56% | 65% | | | | |
| Apr 2011 | 59% | | | | | |

acquired in the reference month (first column) and the cumulative activation rate by MOB tracked over 6 months. For this example, an account is considered active if a single transaction activity is recorded in a specific month post the reference month. Of those accounts sourced in Nov 2010, 38% were active in the first MOB and by the end of the sixth MOB, 61% were active. Also note that the first three month activation levels are higher for latter bookings, reflecting the fact that quality of sourcing may be better. This could also be an indication of the positive results of early activation programmes. This report can be generated using multiple variables in a multi-dimensional framework using a pivot table based on income bands, channel of acquisition, employment category, product category, region, and others for a segmental level view. For instance, self-employed customers through the direct sales channel tend to be the most active. In a similar fashion, portfolio health measures such as average net receivables (ANR), purchase-cash spend, payment ratio, and delinquency indicators could be tracked for a credit card product.

Although the activation rate is increasing with vintage months, it does not provide insights on:

- What percentage of new accounts are active for the first time and by which month
- What percentage of new accounts stay inactive throughout the 6 month period
- Duration of inactivity (till first activation)

These are important points to note and relevant metrics to track before initiating an activation programme. The activation reports can be tailored accordingly, by creating appropriate measures to capture the above mentioned points. Alternatively, survival analysis can be used for this purpose and the results are shown in Figs. 2.12 and 2.13 (using fresh data). Figure 2.12 or the hazard rate function shows the conditional probability of first activation in a particular month, given that the customer has not activated the account till that month. This graph shows that 25% of acquired accounts activate by the end of first MOB. There is a spike in the third month as customers become familiar with the product. Figure 2.13 or the survival function depicts the duration of inactivity till first activation. The figure shows that 50% of new accounts are inactive for at least 3 months. Another observation is that 39% of new accounts never activate during the 6 month period. These statistics should be taken into consideration for the design and timing of activation programmes. For example, duration of inactivity will be used to determine the optimal timing of activation offers and is discussed in Chapter 4. For reactivation programmes, a customer migration analysis across buckets of activity and inactivity is also relevant.

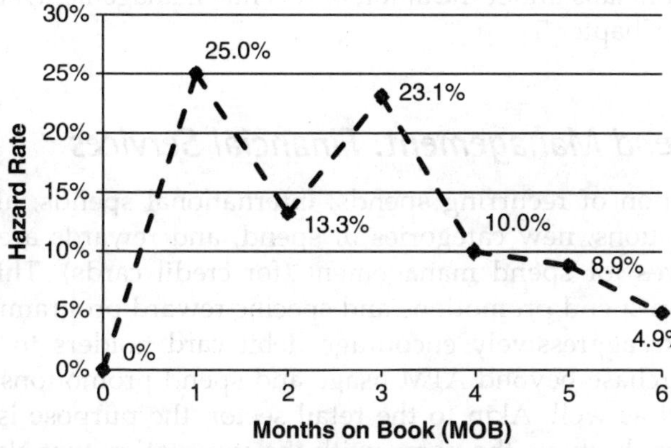


**Figure 2.12** Conditional Probability of First Activation (Hazard Rate)

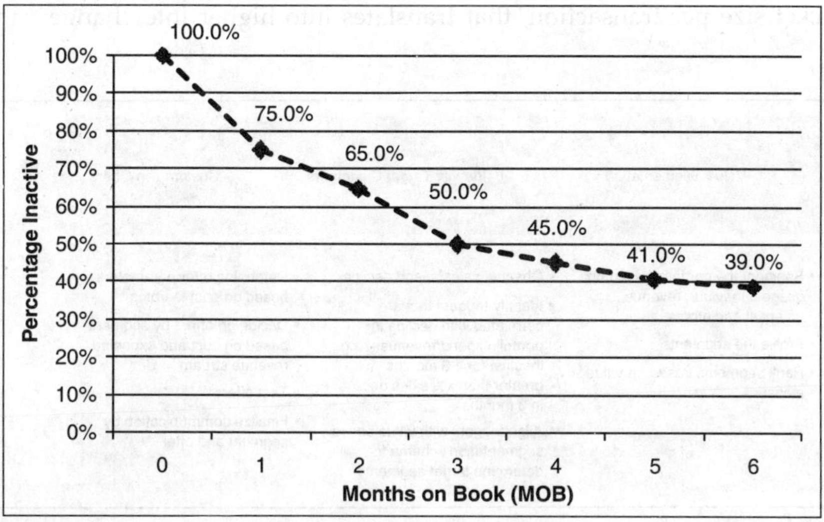


**Figure 2.13** Duration of Inactivity (Survival Function)

## 2.4 Spend Management

The purpose of spend management is to improve spend levels through programmes that affect purchase recency, frequency, and monetary value (RFM). Figure 2.14 provides a succinct description of the spend management process. Spend management also has an important bearing on customer retention. Given the weak impact of reactivation programmes, a more prudent approach is to monitor disengagement which may happen much earlier (6 months to a year), before dormancy sets in. This topic will be covered in the retention management chapter. The subsequent sections will concentrate on spend management by industry, covering financial services, retail, and telecom. Stimulation of demand in the travel and hospitality sectors falls under the ambit of revenue management, and will be reviewed in Chapter 5.

### *2.4.1 Spend Management: Financial Services*

The promotion of recurring spends, international spends, alternative payment options, new categories of spend, and rewards are some of the initiatives for spend management (for credit cards). This section will focus on spend promotions and specific reward programmes (cash back). Banks aggressively encourage debit card holders to use their card for purchase beyond ATM usage and spend promotions apply to this product as well. Akin to the retail sector, the purpose is to drive up spend levels above the norm, with the expectation that elasticity of volume will compensate for the price rebate. Promotions on the card are run during seasonal as well as off-peak periods. The intention is to increase portfolio spend levels through higher activity levels and ticket size per transaction, that translates into higher interchange and

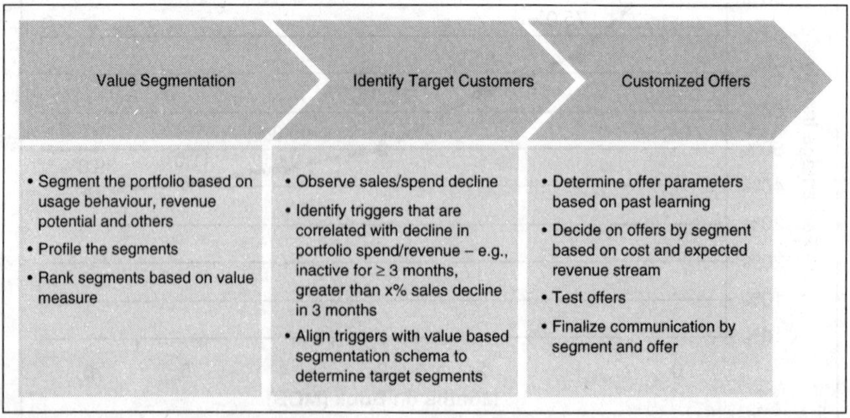


**Figure 2.14** Spend Management Process

interest revenue. In India, festival promotions are popularly offered by credit card issuers. Some additional conditions such as a minimum transaction value, total spend value, or number of transactions is levied to be able to avail the discount. In the case of a store-specific promotion, response is expected to be different for each of these three segments of customers: those who are sales or statement inactive, active customers currently using the card, and active customers not using the card (for purchase at that particular store). Using analytics, one can determine the parameters of spend related offers that include rebate, spend hurdle, period of promotion, minimum transaction, spend categories, and which merchants to tie-up with. Additionally, the evaluation of expected and actual financial gains weighed against costs of the promotion is also carried out. The following example of cash back offer on credit card will provide a flavour of this aspect.

Rich merchant level transaction data can be used to identify the right merchants to partner with and which categories of spends to promote. Although data processing is intensive, dissecting spend level data to the ME (merchant establishment) level is very useful for understanding customer spend patterns and taking appropriate actions for spend building activities across different retail categories. Figures 2.15 to 2.17 of section 2.4.1.2 are examples of MIS that could be useful for this purpose. These reports can be extended to the analysis of international spends for collaboration with international merchant establishments, as many credit card issuers provide special privileges to their domestic card holders travelling abroad.

### 2.4.1.1 Cash Back Offer on Credit Card

The objective of cash back is to enhance spend levels on a credit card and encourage customer loyalty with an offer of cash back as a reward for using the credit card. Many such programmes are tied to grocery or gas purchases as they are frequent transaction categories. These programmes work on the premise of "reinforcing new behaviour" or "modifying spending behaviour".

The workings of a cash back programme and its profitability are shown through an example as per Table 2.4. The offer involves a 10% cash back on retail spend with a cap on the maximum of cash back (e.g., 500 currency units). For a value of 100 currency units of spend, customer receives a cash back of 10 currency units. Communication is through direct mailers and statement messaging. For this example, the assumptions are that the customer is completely inactive (no activity on the card—either spend or payment in the last 6 months) and hence, revenue is nil 6 months prior to the cash back offer. Therefore, any spend is incremental as response to the offer. Interchange and interest income are expected to compensate for rewards cost. This effect can be observed for a spend value of 2000; net revenue is higher at the higher revolve rate. On a familiar trend, cash

**Table 2.4** Cash Back Offer on Credit Card

| Monthly Spend (LCY) | Revolving ANR % | Average ANR Month 1 (LCY) | Cumulative Interest for 3 Months (LCY) | % Cash Back (Capped to 500) | Cash Back (LCY) | One Month Discount Revenue (LCY) | Gross Revenue Over 3 Months (LCY) | Net Revenue Over 3 Months (LCY) |
|---|---|---|---|---|---|---|---|---|
| 9000 | 80% | 7220 | 525 | 10% | 500 | 98 | 623 | 123 |
| 8000 | 50% | 4000 | 207 | 10% | 500 | 88 | 295 | –206 |
| 5000 | 20% | 1000 | 37 | 10% | 500 | 55 | 92 | –408 |
| 2000 | 64% | 1280 | 78 | 10% | 200 | 22 | 100 | –100 |
| 2000 | 50% | 1000 | 52 | 10% | 200 | 22 | 74 | –126 |

*Note:* Only one month spend considered to arrive at revenue stream
LCY = Local currency unit.

rewards are most favourable at highest spend and revolve rate. A threshold spend to break even (rewards cost is compensated by gross revenue) is clearly above a minimum spend level of 8000, and at a revolve rate of around 80%. This seems high for a target base that is inactive. Usually, cash rewards that most issuers offer range from 1% to 5% of spends that seems more financially viable. In this regard, it is important to track the financial impact of a cash back programme beyond 3 months. These effects will include whether the cash back on a specific spend category has encouraged repeat purchase from customers already using the card on this category (higher frequency and spend) and new category spend from non-users. Overall, whether this effect holds up once the promotion is over. In other words, the short-term and long-term impact needs to be assessed, as the immediate term loss may be compensated by future gains. Issuers often pass on cash back costs to the merchant, especially in the case of store brand related offers. An interesting point to note is that in comparison to reward points, the cost of cash back may be roughly 1.5–2 times that of reward points, and becomes more favourable as revolve behaviour increases. Section 2.7.4 also covers rewards in a general industry context.

There are many variants such as cash back rebates given against 3 months of spend, with rebates for the second and third month dependent on qualifying spend criteria in the previous months (step-up structure). Credit card issuers have also packaged this proposition into a regular feature called a "cash-back" card[6]. Banking giant Santander of

[6] For instance, a ranking of cash back credit cards in the US rated Capital One Cash Back Rewards Card with a $100 bonus at first place, earning an average consumer $460 over 2 years. The Blue Cash Everyday Card from *American Express* came in second ($388 over 2 years), and the Blue Cash Preferred from *American Express* ranked third ($354). Available at http://www.forbes.com/sites/mickeymeece/2012/06/19/a-study-ranks-the-top-cash-back-credit-cards/.

Spain introduced a cash back current account ("123 Current Account") in the first quarter of 2012 that pays money back on household bills paid through the current account. Similarly, ICICI Bank of India has an offer of 1% cash back on every EMI for home loan customers that is valid over the full tenor of the loan.

#### 2.4.1.2 Spend MIS: Financial Services

Examples of MIS related to customer spend behaviour on a credit card are shown in Figs. 2.15–2.17. It has also been observed that customers who use the card for purchases in multiple categories tend to be more engaged customers, compared to those who use their card for only specific transactions, like fuel or grocery.

### *2.4.2 Spend Management: Telecom*

In the telecom sector, despite the advent of advanced networks, most operators are struggling to maintain voice ARPU[7] and grow services beyond messaging. ARPU is a key revenue metric used by analysts to track telecommunications firms and markets. Higher ARPU may be the result of higher prices, greater minutes of usage, or a combination of the two. Mobile industry experts believe that the emerging approach of bundled pricing is one of the effective ways to drive usage[8]. The basic premise is to motivate subscribers to adopt and use more services than they would, if the services were purchased individually. Figure 2.18 shows how bundling, cross-selling, and rate plan migration can be tactically used to build up ARPU for new subscribers.

Rate plan migration is used as a usage enhancement strategy for mature telecom customers, by moving customers to more suitable plans based on call patterns, illustrated by Figs. 2.19 and 2.20. How subscriber level rich call records can be used to determine the best plan by customer or customer segments will be discussed shortly. Relating to rate plans, *flat rate* is one such pricing strategy which offers unlimited usage for a fixed price for a certain set of services. Although simplistic, unlimited usage can become ineffective in generating additional revenue from increased usage and may increase susceptibility to price competition.

---

[7]For a leading mobile services company in India, voice ARPU grew just 1 percent to ₹161 in comparison to the previous quarter. However, data ARPU grew from ₹70 to ₹75 for the same period. *Source:* Economic Times, Jan 29, 2014.

[8]Value-added services (VAS) are an important component of bundled pricing. VAS (data and non-data) comprise almost 18% of total revenue for telecom players in India. *Source:* Economic Times, July 26, 2014.

Therefore, a *usage-based tier* pricing strategy may be a better option. There are many more rate plan structures that are beyond the scope of this discussion.

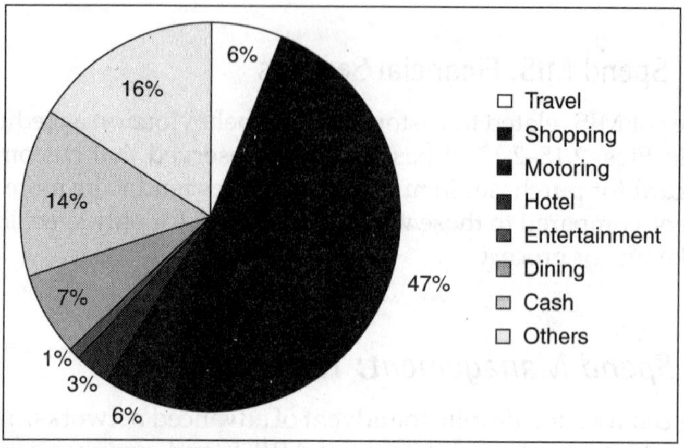


**Figure 2.15** Percentage Share of Local Spend

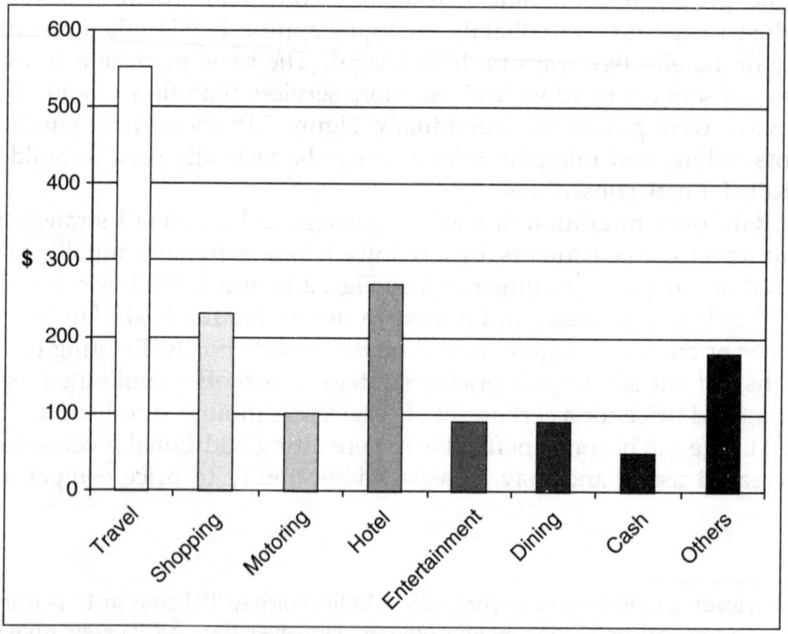


**Figure 2.16** Average Ticket Size by Spend Category

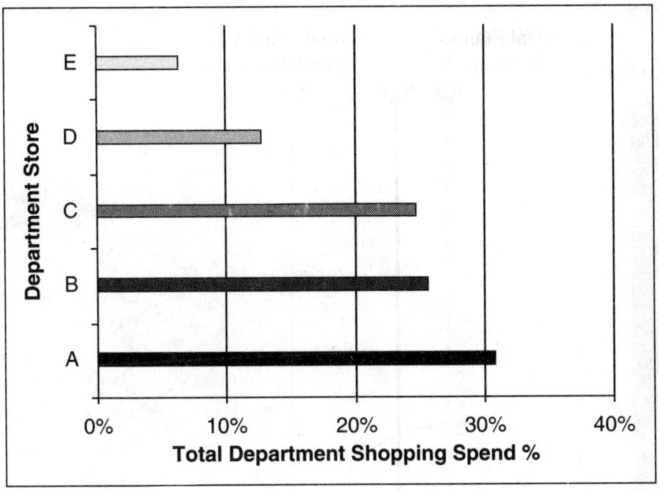


**Figure 2.17** Department Stores: Share of Spend

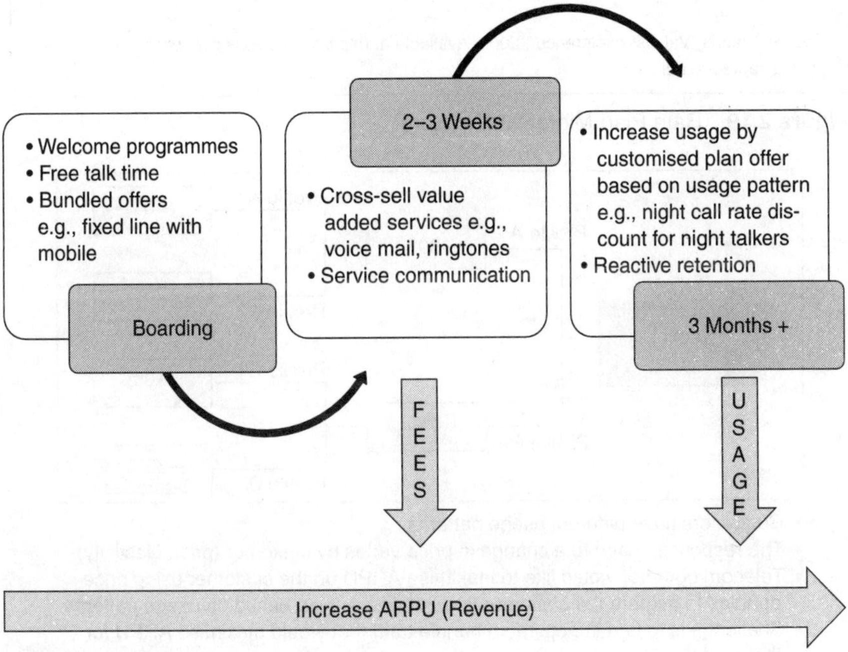


**Figure 2.18** Early Usage Programme: Telecom

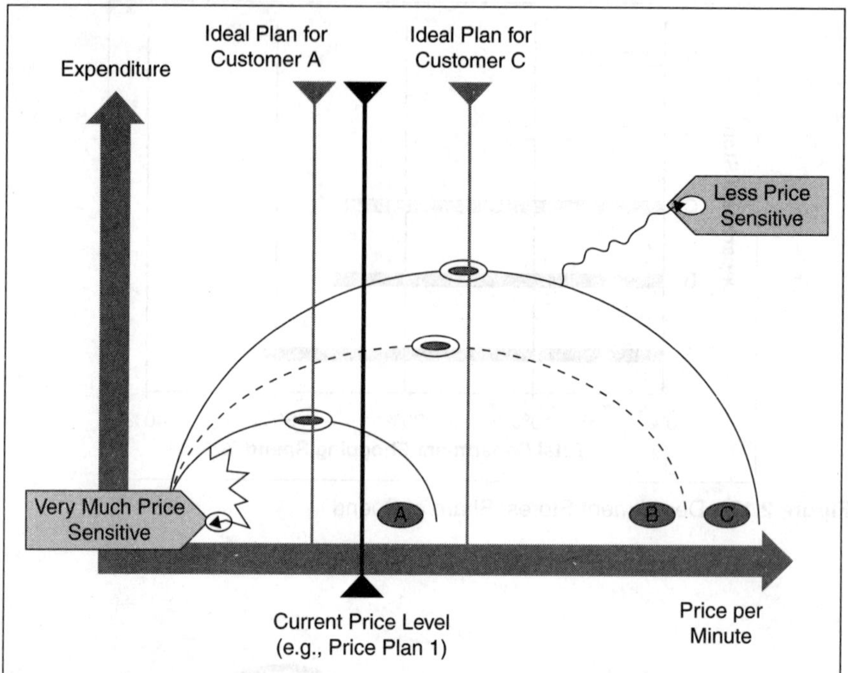


*Source:* Valoris "Val-cial-conference", 2006. Available at http://www.valoris.com/docs/pricingiirapr2006.pdf

**Figure 2.19** Rate Plan Migration: Telecom

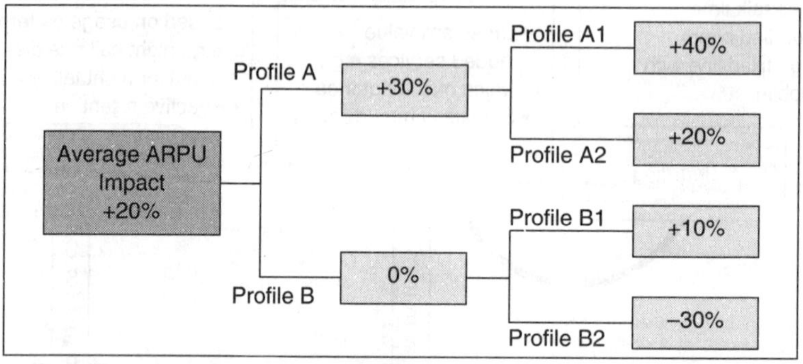


- Customers have different usage patterns
- The response usage to a change in price varies by customer (price elasticity)
- Telecom operator would like to maximise ARPU on the customer using price bundles to migrate the customer to a better rate plan based on usage patterns
- Challenge is to find the optimum bundle tariff that would maximise ARPU for that customer
- Progressively move customers to the optimum price bundle through testing and monitoring impact on usage and ARPU

*Source:* Valoris "Val-cial-conference", 2006. Available at http://www.valoris.com/docs/pricingiirapr2006.pdf

**Figure 2.20** Rate Plan Impact: Telecom

### 2.4.2.1 Telecom Bundling

Bundling is a marketing strategy to promote take-up and usage with added benefits of strengthening the firm's relationship with the customer, encourage retention, and avoid price competition. A bundling strategy involves offering several products/services for sale as one combined product (e.g., package deal), using demand for the dominant product to sell a secondary offer. This combined product is offered at a discount price so that it is cheaper to buy the bundle than products separately. This strategy is often found in multiproduct industries such as telecom, financial services, hardware and software, and fast food. The concept of bundling is discussed in detail in Chapter 3, "Cross-Sell".

A suite of broadband plans from one of the leading telecom companies in India, for both bundled and normal offerings is presented in Table 2.5. The pricing strategy followed is a combination of usage-based tier pricing structure and bundled pricing. Plan B, C, D, and E are bundled offerings of a broadband line with a fixed line and a free phone instrument.

Plan A is a normal offer with value added services and a usage quota. For the same fee, plan B (bundled offer) is a more attractive plan with a fixed line and free local calls to a fixed line on the same network (although the value of value added services is lower). The tier-based structure with a progressive fee based on usage for the bundled offers reflects pricing linked to usage. Higher the data transfer quota, higher the fee for the same download speed. The rate per GB is lower for a higher fee. A customer can take advantage of a price benefit (lower per unit rate), only if the full quota of data transfer for the respective plan is used. Value perception of the higher value of free local calls (with higher fee) on the fixed line will depend on customer calling preferences. This is an example of a usage promoting strategy for both broadband and fixed lines as demand for fixed lines is growing at a much slower pace, when compared to wireless in the Indian market.

### 2.4.2.2 Telecom Rate Plan Migration

Rate plan migration involves moving a customer to an optimal rate plan, with multiple objectives of reducing bill cost for the customer (for same usage), increasing minutes of usage (with new plan), and reducing churn. Optimal rate plan recommendations depend on customer-specific usage patterns. Heavy talkers on low-end plans and low-usage subscribers on high-end plans are examples of non-optimal rate plans. However, the financial viability of this strategy depends on the response of the customer to a new rate plan: conversion, price elasticity, and time taken for minutes of usage (MOU) to increase in reaction to the new rate plan, and may result in a revenue short fall in the short-term. Rate plan optimisation and its impact on churn will be discussed in Chapter 4, "Retention Management".

**Table 2.5** Broadband Plans

| Plan | Offer | Download Speed Till Quota/Bill Cap | Usage–Data Transfer Quota (GB) | Speed after Quota/Bill Cap | Voice Benefits–Free Local Calls to Same Service Provider (₹) | Free VAS–Software Package (₹) | Fee (₹) | Rate Applicable Post Quota per MB Download | Rate per GB for Full Usage of Data Transfer Quota |
|---|---|---|---|---|---|---|---|---|---|
| A | Not bundled | 2 mbps | 10 | 256 kbps post quota | – | 184 | 999 | – | 100 |
| B | Bundled | 2 mbps | 10 | 256 kbps post quota | 500 | 85 | 999 | – | 100 |
| C | | 2 mbps | 30 | 256 kbps post quota | 1299 | 85 | 1299 | – | 43 |
| D | | 2 mbps | 75 | 256 kbps post quota | 1599 | 85 | 1599 | – | 21 |
| E | | 2 mbps | 150 | 256 kbps post quota | 1999 | 85 | 1999 | – | 13 |

Many mobile service providers advertise "The Best Plan for You" on their website, with a wide variety of flexible plan options to accommodate the different types of usage needs and fluctuating usage patterns of a customer. Analysis of call and billing records is an essential requirement to understand call patterns of the customer, recommend suitable tariff plans, and create new plans. The role of data infrastructure (e.g., data warehouse, data marts) is critical for storing voluminous transaction data.

Usage data of Table 2.6 reveals that the customer is a relatively heavy long distance (STD) user with low volume of local calls. The subscriber is currently at 549 plan that has the highest fee and highest long distance rates. The fee structure and free local minutes are tied, and these free minutes are not being fully used up by this particular subscriber. For this usage pattern, the plan that gives the lowest bill amount is the one with the lowest long distance rates and fee (rental), the 199 plan. The bill amount at this recommended plan would be 35% lower than the current bill for the same usage and its pattern. The intention of the service provider is to increase long distance talk time by migrating the subscriber to a more favourable long distance tariff plan, although the minutes of long distance would have to double from the current 748 minutes to 1500 minutes (all else being the same), for the service provider to be billing a similar amount. In this regard, the evaluation of price elasticity is important for assessing the most cost-effective plan by segment and for determining which of these plans would be profitable for the service provider. This would require extensive plan testing.

Some players in the telecom and the credit card industry have attempted to launch programmes whereby the customer has the flexibility of designing their product at the time of acquisition. For example, a telecom customer might choose to have a higher rental and a lower per minute rate, with the option of reducing the rental if the usage crosses a threshold. Similarly, a credit card customer might have the option of paying a lower interest but a higher annual fee. However, such programmes have met with limited success because of the complex process of offer design that the customer has to go through.

### 2.4.2.3 Telecom Segmentation

It would be an impossible task for the service provider to be making recommendations for each subscriber among millions of subscribers. Therefore, customer segmentation is useful for identifying distinct usage patterns, corresponding revenue streams, and for recommending suitable plans by segment. Figure 2.21 is one such usage segmentation schema for post-paid customers based on demographics, call usage patterns, revenue, financial product holding, and cluster system data. The reader may recall that available cluster systems were listed in Chapter 1, "Acquisition". For instance, Armchair Settlers would

**Table 2.6** Mobile Post-paid Plans

| Plan Details (₹) | 549 Plan | 249 Plan | 199 Plan | Usage | Bill 549 Plan | Bill 249 Plan | Bill 199 Plan |
|---|---|---|---|---|---|---|---|
| Activation fee | – | – | – | – | – | – | – |
| Monthly rental | 549 | 249 | 199 | – | 549 | 249 | 199 |
| Local call to same network mobile | 0.30 | 0.50 | 0.30 | 118 | 0 | 59 | 30 |
| Local call to other GSM | 0.30 | 0.60 | 0.50 | 192 | 0 | 26 | 80 |
| Local call to landline/WLL | 0.40 | 0.60 | 0.50 | 154 | 62 | 92 | 64 |
| STD call to same network mobile | 0.75 | 0.50 | 0.50 | 209 | 82 | 105 | 87 |
| STD call to other GSM | 0.75 | 0.60 | 0.50 | 434 | 326 | 260 | 181 |
| STD call to landline/WLL | 0.75 | 0.60 | 0.50 | 105 | 79 | 63 | 44 |
| SMS local | 0.30 | 0.50 | 0.50 | 23 | 0 | 0 | 0 |
| SMS CDMA | 0.30 | 0.50 | 0.50 | 42 | 0 | 21 | 21 |
| SMS national | 0.75 | 0.60 | 0.50 | 79 | 59 | 47 | 40 |
| SMS international | 5 | 5 | 5 | 2 | 10 | 10 | 10 |
| VAS | 3 or 6 | 3 or 6 | 3 or 6 | 0 | 0 | 0 | 0 |
| **Total bill (₹)** | | | | | **1166** | **933** | **756** |
| **Free minutes** | | | | | | | |
| Local call same network mobile to mobile | 800 | – | – | – | – | – | – |
| Local call to any mobile | 200 | 149 | – | – | – | – | – |
| STD call mobile to mobile (same network) | 100 | – | – | – | – | – | – |
| Local call and STD | – | – | 199 | – | – | – | – |
| SMS local | 100 | 200 | 199 | – | – | – | – |

**La Dolce Vita**
- Small and medium enterprise (SME)
- Weekday pattern
- High overage usage
- High international usage
- Medium WAP usage/high VAS utilisation
- Mostly self-employed
- Highly interested in gourmet cooking, fine foods, wine, personal computing
- High proportion own a credit card, personal loan and mortgage
- Prefer Daily Telegraph

**Chatternets**
- Students/new generation
- High in-plan usage
- High weekend usage
- Very long calls
- High WAP/SMS usage

**Family Nesters**
- Weekday (75%), weekend (25%)
- Saturday daylight activity pattern
- High overage usage
- Medium WAP/SMS usage
- High proportion own car
- Interested in gardening, golf, outdoors
- Highest owners of multi-channel TV, broadband internet and TV

**Armchair Settlers**
- Highest international usage
- High weekend usage
- Inbound usage high
- High earning proportion
- Interested in reading books, foreign travel, dining, charity
- Low proportion hold credit cards or loans
- Prefer Financial Times

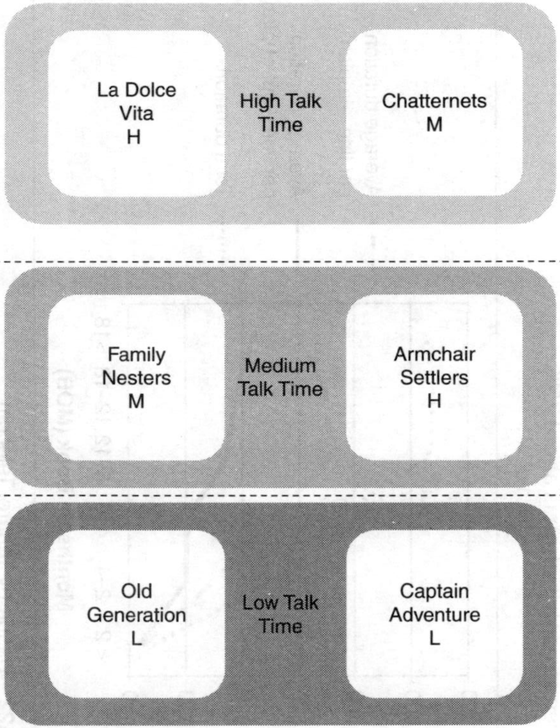


**Old Generation**
- Mostly in-plan usage
- Short calls
- Low SMS/WAP minutes
- Average age late 50's

**Captain Adventure**
- Lowest proportion having an earning occupation
- Lowest PC ownership
- High interest in jogging and physical fitness
- Average age 25–30

H = High ARPU M = Medium ARPU
L = Low ARPU ARPU = Average revenue per user
Overage is out-of-plan which is usually at a higher rate than in-plan

**Figure 2.21** Usage Segmentation: Telecom

respond well to plans with low international calling rates, while La Dolca Vita may prefer plans with competitive tariffs during business hours, and may be willing to pay a high monthly rental for a lower rate. Non-usage related profiles of segments is valuable for communication strategy. A McKinsey Quarterly article, *Getting More from Prepaid Mobile Services*, published in 2008, is a good read for interested readers. The article reviews a targeting schema for inactive customers on the basis of a usage-based segmentation.

### 2.4.2.4 Spend MIS: Telecom

Usage tracking (Fig. 2.22) shows that pick up rates of in-plan usage are much higher as they come under either zero or lower tariff plans. Figure 2.23 shows that vintage of less than 6 MOB cannot be ignored as their revenue contribution is about 25%.

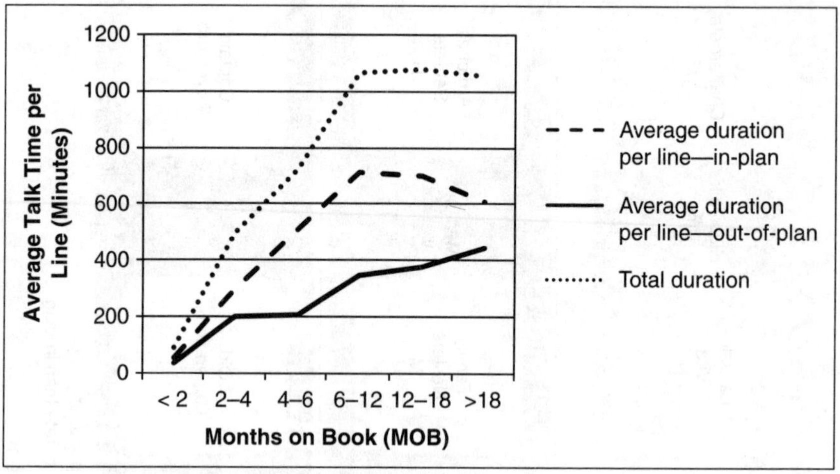


**Figure 2.22** Usage by Tenure: Telecom

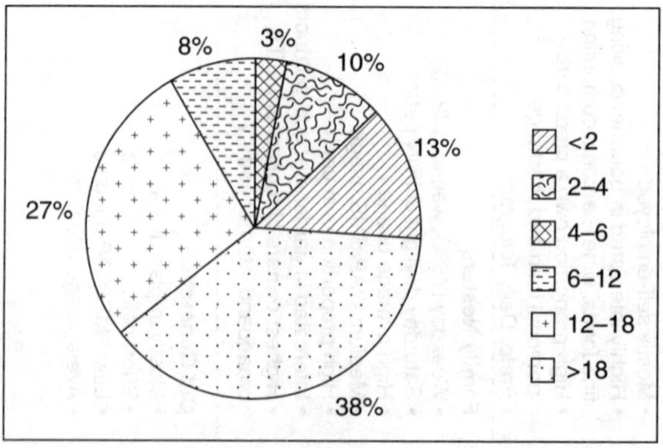


**Figure 2.23** Contribution to Revenue by Tenure: Telecom

## 2.4.3 Spend Management: Retail

Spend management in the retail sector primarily involves brand management, sales promotions, and sales forecasting. In relation to brand analytics, brand managers are usually interested in understanding the estimated brand sales at a constant non-discounted price, and the change in baseline sales over time periods. Regular and promoted price elasticities, the percentage change in revenue due to a percentage change in price are some other areas of interest. The emphasis in this section will be on sales promotions. Further, Chapter 5, "Price Management" will cover this topic as well as sales promotion is an important pricing strategy.

### 2.4.3.1 Sales Promotions

Sales promotions or short-term price reductions are an important element of the marketing mix and the growing managerial emphasis has motivated significant interest and research around its impact. Promotions can be classified into three distinct types based on the initiator of the activity as illustrated[9] in Fig. 2.24.

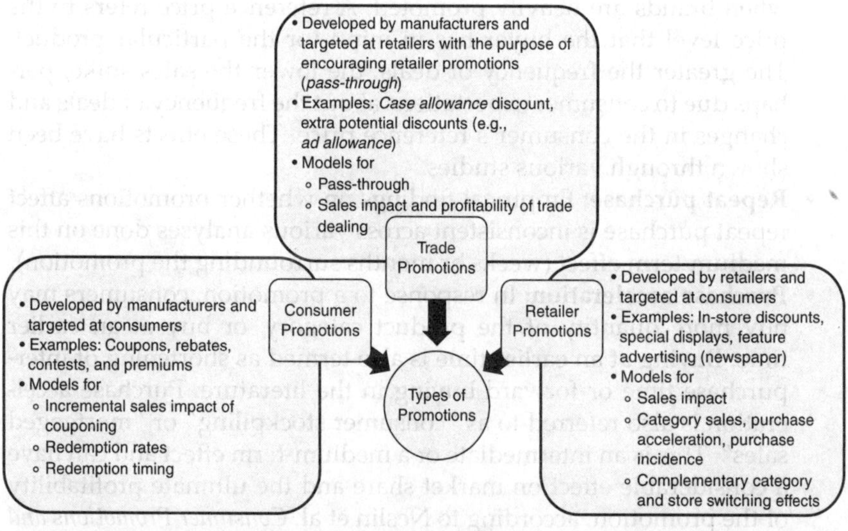


*Source:* Adapted from *Handbooks in Operations Research and Management Science*, Volume-Marketing, Blattberg and Neslin, *Sales Promotion Models*, Pages 553–609, Copyright (1993), with permission from Elsevier.

**Figure 2.24** Types of Sales Promotions

[9] *Case allowance* refers to merchandise purchased by the case, the greater the number of cases, the greater the discount. *Ad allowance* is the discount to cover local advertising or merchandising expenses.

#### 2.4.3.2 Impact of Sales Promotions

There has been significant work done by academicians to understand the impact of promotional activity on sales. Based on literature in this field by Blattberg and Neslin, *Sales Promotion: The Long and the Short of It*, and Blattberg et al. *How Promotions Work*, some interesting hypotheses and observations are noted:

- **Sales impact:** Temporary retail price reductions have a considerable influence on sales of the promoted brand. This sales impact has been substantiated by empirical evidence of a distinct sales spike in the short-term (week or weeks in which the promotion occurs). The increase in sales can be upto 10 fold the normal levels, according to Blattberg and Neslin. Other effects are increased sales of complementary products within the store and increase in store traffic.
- **Switchers:** A significant portion of the immediate increase in sales is contributed by brand-switchers. Although results are mixed, it was found that more than 80% of the volume increase comes from switchers. Also, promoting higher tier brands induces more switching than promoting lower tier brands.
- **Frequency of promotions:** The frequency of discounts alters the consumer's reference price, which explains the loss of brand equity when brands are heavily promoted. A reference price refers to the price level that the buyer has in mind for the particular product. The greater the frequency of deals, the lower the sales spike, perhaps due to consumer expectations about the frequency of deals and changes in the consumer's reference price. These effects have been shown through various studies.
- **Repeat purchase:** Empirical findings on whether promotions affect repeat purchase is inconsistent across various analyses done on this medium-term effect (weeks or months surrounding the promotion).
- **Purchase acceleration:** In response to a promotion, consumers may buy more quantity of the product category, or buy at an earlier time. Buying at an earlier time is also termed as shortening of inter-purchase time or forward buying in the literature. Purchase acceleration is also referred to as "consumer stockpiling" or "mortgaged sales". This is an intermediate or a medium-term effect and can have a considerable effect on market share and the ultimate profitability of the promotion, according to Neslin et al. *Consumer Promotions and the Acceleration of Product Purchases*.
- **Promotional cross-elasticities** have been found to be asymmetric, that is, the impact of Brand A's promotion on Brand B's sales is not the same as Brand B's promotion impact on Brand A's sales.
- **Types of promotion:**
  - Display and feature advertising have strong effects on sales, an expected result. Moreover, the interaction effect between display and feature advertising is a synergetic effect. Advertised promotions are also likely to result in increased store traffic.

  - The individual impact of a promotional tool among several promotional tools bundled together for a promotional offer (e.g., price cut, feature, and display used together) may be difficult to estimate.
- **Impact on product level category sales:** Brand (product) level promotions can increase one brand's sales at the expense of the other brands in the same product category, and may lead to a reduction in sales of the category. A study by Raju, *The Effect of Price Promotions on Variability in Product Category Sales,* published in 1992, analyses the impact of promotions at the product category level. Variability is modeled as a function of promotional activity (magnitude and frequency of discounts) and category characteristics (expensiveness, bulkiness, and competitive intensity). Linear regression is used for this purpose.
- **Whether sales promotions are profitable and its measurement:** Measurement of incremental returns of sales promotions is contingent on the estimate of baseline sales, which are the sales for the brand that would have occurred even if the promotion had not been available. The example of linear regression in Chapter 7, "Quantitative Methods" will elaborate on the intelligent use of test and control for the purpose of estimating the incremental profitability arising from consumer promotions.
- **Brand franchise:** The belief is that long-term effects (years after several promotions are implemented) of promotional activity on brand franchise are negative. One possible reason is that it redirects customer's focus from brand attributes towards finding the best deal. According to Blattberg and Neslin, the factual information is mixed.

#### 2.4.3.3 Sales Promotion Models

For this section, a survey paper by Blattberg and Neslin titled *Sales Promotion Models,* which is a comprehensive and excellent review of these models is used. Data available for analysing sales promotions can be categorised into household panel data and sales-per-period-data. The unit of analysis for household data is the purchase event and for sales-per-period data, it is weekly or monthly sales (market data). Household data consists of historical purchase incidents for a panel of households using supermarket scanner data, e.g., IRI, Nielsen. The benefits of household data are plenty, enabling analyses that encompass purchase incidence, brand choice, brand-loyalty, repeat purchase, and market segmentation. Sales-per-period data takes on the form of a sequence of observations, measured over periodical intervals of time (time series) representing retail sales. This data is more aggregative as compared to household data and is also more readily available. However, sales-per-period data is unable to capture many of the diverse effects of sales promotions as household level panel data.

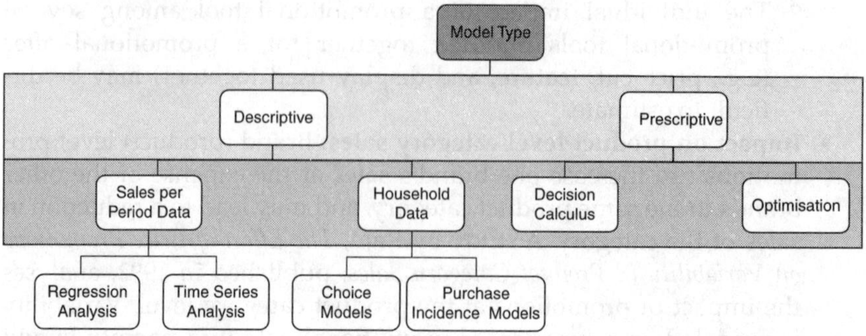


*Source:* Reprinted from *Handbooks in Operations Research and Management Science*, Volume-Marketing, Blattberg and Neslin, *Sales Promotion Models*, Pages 553–609, Copyright (1993), with permission from Elsevier.

**Figure 2.25** Sales Promotion Models

Descriptive models are used to measure the impact of sales promotions, while prescriptive models are used to make managerial recommendations based on descriptive models, such as the extent of price reduction. The approach to model building under descriptive models is dependent on the data available as shown in Fig.2.25. Chapter 7, "Quantitative Methods" will cover linear regression and choice models. The different variants of models, framework, and empirical findings[10] are listed in Table 2.7 for retailer promotions.

## 2.4.3.4 Sales Forecasting

Sales forecasting is pivotal for business planning and operations. At the organisational level, expectation of future demand is an essential input for various functional areas of marketing, sales, finance, purchase, and production. It is also a core requirement for planning and budgeting, revenue management, supply chain and inventory management.

Seasonal variation is a distinct feature of sales data. Some of the quantitative approaches for forecasting are regression analysis, exponential smoothing (ES) and time series (ARIMA) type of models. These forecasting techniques have proven to be effective methods for predicting sales and are in good practice in industry. While regression analysis will be covered in the quantitative methods chapter, readers should refer to the time series text book by Chatfield, *The Analysis of Time Series*, for an easy understanding and detailed exposition of exponential smoothing methods and time series models.

Exponential smoothing (ES) refers to a general class of forecasting procedures that rely on simple updating equations to calculate forecasts for time series data exhibiting both seasonal and time trends. One of the early

[10] A result is called statistically significant if it is unlikely to have occurred by chance and hence, provides enough evidence to reject the hypothesis of "no effect".

**Table 2.7** Sales Promotion Models and Results

| Promotion Impact of Retailer Promotions (*Product–Brand M*) | Models Employed | Dependent Variable | Some Predictor Variables (*Measured at Purchase Occasion or Time t*) | Some Empirical Results |
|---|---|---|---|---|
| **Sales impact** | | | | |
| *Increased sales of promoted brand* | Brand choice model<br>Regression and time series model | Choice of brand M across alternatives; Store or chain level weekly retail sales | • If brand M is on promotion; promotional price of a unit of brand M; regular shelf-price of brand M; deal discount for brand M (discounted/regular); price of competitive item<br>• History of previous promotion purchase of brand M<br>• Brand loyalty and size loyalty (previous purchase history of brand M)<br>• If feature ad run during promotional period<br>• Time since beginning of promotion<br>• If promotional price ends in 9 | • Promotion and regular-price variables are statistically significant<br>• The net immediate effect of a price cut is stronger than that of a change in regular price<br>• Brand and size loyalty variables are positive and highly significant<br>• Display and feature advertising have a positive effect on sales<br>• Response to a retailer promotion is highest in the first week<br>• Promotional prices ending in 9 is an uplifting factor for sales |
| **Purchase acceleration** | | | | |
| *Forward buying by consumers–stocking up due to price discount and use inventory to satisfy needs once retailer price returns to normal* | Recursive regression model<br>Brand choice model, inter purchase timing and quantity model | Purchase quantity by household *i* on purchase occasion *t*; elapsed time for household *i* between purchase occasion *t* and $t-1$ | • Household inventory of the product category immediately after purchase occasion $t-1$.<br>• Whether or not promotion was present for the brand purchased on purchase occasion *t*<br>• Other factors | • Promotions increase purchase quantities and decrease inter-purchase time. However, it was found that promotions have a small but statistically significant positive impact on purchase quantity<br>• Advertised price reductions are most effective |

(*Continued*)

**Table 2.7** Sales Promotion Models and Results (*Continued*)

| Promotion Impact of Retailer Promotions (*Product–Brand M*) | Models Employed | Dependent Variable | Some Predictor Variables (*Measured at Purchase Occasion or Time t*) | Some Empirical Results |
|---|---|---|---|---|
| | Hazard model to predict likelihood of purchase and acceleration<br><br>Time series models | | | • Product-specific results–for coffee, households stockpile by waiting longer until purchasing again<br>• Promotional elasticity–85% from brand switching; 14% from timing acceleration and 2% from purchase of larger quantities<br>• Household level data models find evidence of stock-piling. Weekly sales data models do not find this evidence. |
| **Complementary category and store-switching effects** | | | | |
| | Regression model | Sales for brand M at primary store on purchase occasion *t* (for store-switching) | • Brand M price at primary store<br>• Competitive brand price at primary store<br>• Brand M price at competitive store<br>• Regular and deal prices for brands in both categories (e.g., cake mix and cake frosting)<br>• Brand M feature advertising and display activity at primary store<br>• Brand M feature advertising and display at competitive store | • Promotions in one category can increase sales in a complementary category<br>• Significant and important store switching effect, especially for those stores located within the same geographic area |

*Source:* Adapted from *Handbooks in Operations Research and Management Science*, Volume-Marketing, Blattberg and Neslin, *Sales Promotion Models*, Pages 553–609, Copyright (1993), with permission from Elsevier.

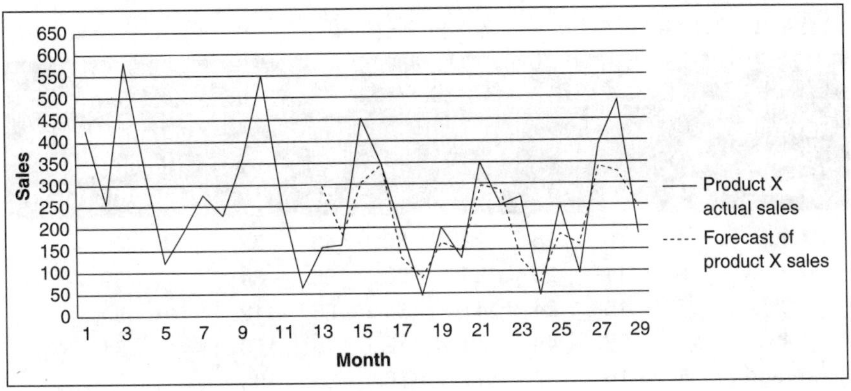


**Figure 2.26** Actual Vs. Forecast of Sales

studies on using ES for sales forecasting was carried out by Winters in 1960 titled *Forecasting Sales by Exponentially Weighted Moving Averages*. In the context of revenue management, Weatherford and Kimes undertake an interesting study titled *A Comparison of Forecasting Methods for Hotel Revenue Management*. Arrivals of hotel guests are forecasted using ES, regression and other methods for US based Choice and Marriott Hotels. Figure 2.26 provides an example of a graphical view of actual vs. forecast sales using time series models.

ARIMA (autoregressive integrated moving average) models were popularised by Box and Jenkins, who developed a three-stage iterative process for time series identification, estimation, and verification. This is popularly referred to as the Box-Jenkins approach.

## 2.5 Balance Build

The discussion will be in the context of financial services as outstanding balances are the primary source of interest revenue for a bank. Interest revenue is the most important and significant contributor to customer revenue[11]. Balance build programmes of interest in this section are early balance build, balance transfer, and top-up programmes.

### *2.5.1 Early Balance Build*

The objective is to accelerate balance build-up in the initial stages of the customer life cycle. The ability to evaluate revenue potential (low–high)

[11] Balance (unsecured and secured) is used as a predictor in delinquency and loss forecast models for lending products. Balance is also an input into EAD (exposure at default) and LGD (loss given default) calculations that are used for Basel norms for capital adequacy. Balance to income and debt-service ratios are used as measures for leverage, and as early warning triggers for loss management.

**Table 2.8** Revenue Score and Months on Book

| | MOB | | | | | | | |
|---|---|---|---|---|---|---|---|---|
| Revenue Score Band | 0 | 1 | 2 | 3 | 4 | 5 | 6 | Average Monthly Revenue for 6 months (LCY) |
| 1 | 4 | 8 | 15 | 22 | 35 | 43 | 53 | 26 |
| 2 | 5 | 11 | 20 | 35 | 50 | 66 | 84 | 39 |
| 3 | 5 | 15 | 24 | 41 | 64 | 86 | 112 | 50 |
| 4 | 10 | 28 | 48 | 72 | 112 | 145 | 170 | 84 |
| Average | 6 | 16 | 27 | 43 | 65 | 85 | 105 | |

early on (at the time of acquisition or soon after) is of use in the determination of the target segment and offers for early balance build activities. However, this is not an easy task with limited customer information from the application form[12] and nascent transactional data of the first month post-acquisition.

Availability of credit bureau is an advantage as it facilitates the development of revenue score (credit card) that can be used as a tool for predicting revenue potential of a customer. A revenue score is a prediction of revenue on an account over a certain time period, usually 12 months from account opening. Although it can prove to be a challenge to forecast revenue, Table 2.8 shows how the revenue score rank orders well with months on book (MOB) based on a quartile distribution across score bands, with 25% equal population. With increasing score band, the actual revenue per account also increases and a similar trend is also observed by MOB. The revenue figures can be annualised using extrapolation methods based on historical revenue curves or a regression analysis (with time as the predictor variable). Figure 2.27 highlights appropriate offers by revenue segment. The revenue score can be used as a proxy for transactor-revolver segmentation as revolvers are significantly higher revenue generators.

For deposit customers, banks take special initiatives by requesting account holders to bring in money from their other banks. These actions are targeted at customers, who are not bringing in new credits post account opening. It has also been observed that online banking facilities promote balance build-up and creating cognisance of Internet facilities may be one such option available to banks.

---

[12] Many fields on the application form are not mandatory and therefore, not filled out by the applicant in emerging countries. The data problem is worse for banking customers in emerging markets, with a high percentage of missing data for key fields such as date of birth of the primary account holder.

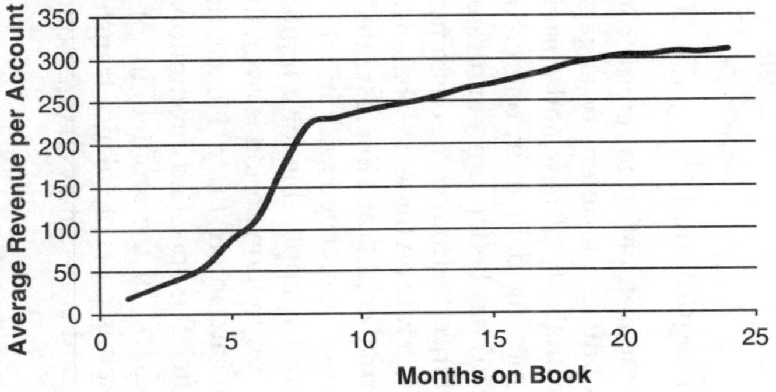


| Product | Potential Revenue Indicator |
|---|---|
| Credit Card | • Revenue score<br>• Credit score |
| Banking—wealth management | • Starting deposit value |
| Insurance | • Annual premium equivalent (APE) |
| Personal loan/mortgage | • Principal loan value |

| Potential | Account Revenue Actions | Customer Revenue Actions |
|---|---|---|
| Potential low revenue<br>*Increase usage* | • Usage/spend related offers at acquisition<br>• Loan on card to credit card account<br>• Balance transfer to credit card account<br>• Balance build-up initiatives for low deposit account | • Personal loan to low balance deposit customer<br>• Bundling of credit card with new deposit account<br>• Value added services |
| Potential high revenue<br>*Ensure high usage* | • Balance transfer to credit card account with utilisation < Y% | • Investment/brokerage to deposit customer<br>• Insurance and mortgage to deposit customer<br>• TD (time deposit) to current/savings deposit customer |

*Note:* A credit score predicts credit behaviour over a certain period of time.

**Figure 2.27** Early Balance Build: Financial Services

### *2.5.2 Balance Consolidation: Balance Transfer*

Balance consolidation involves taking out a single loan to repay debts to several or all creditors at once, often done to take advantage of a lower interest rate, secure a fixed interest rate, or for the convenience of servicing one loan. This option is especially attractive if outstanding debts are at a relatively high rate of interest and is common for unsecured products like credit cards and personal loans. Balance consolidation can take many forms—bundling several unsecured personal loans into one unsecured personal loan (debt consolidation), transferring credit card debt from one issuer to another (credit card balance transfer-BT), moving card balance to personal loans, and unsecured to secured loan (against an asset that serves as collateral such as home). In order to qualify for a debt consolidation loan, a consumer needs to have an acceptable credit rating and threshold income for the lender to determine whether the customer has the capacity to manage the loan payments. Fee on such loans is likely to be high, to take advantage of the attractiveness of these low-interest loans to consumers with high-interest debt balances. Although monthly payments can often be lower, the total amount repaid is often significantly higher due to the long tenor of the loan.

For the purpose of this section, the focus will be on credit card balance transfer programmes that should capture the overall essence, if not all the aspects of a balance consolidation programme.

#### 2.5.2.1 Credit Card Balance Transfer Programme (BT)

Balance transfer is a key portfolio management initiative for credit card issuers, not just to attract new customers but also to intensify engagement, build market share, and improve profitability of new and current customers. Balance transfer is the act of moving debt from one credit card to another, assuming that the newer card has better terms and rates. A balance transfer may increase the interest income from some customers who respond to the offer; however, the interest rate on these new balances (from balance transfer) is lower than the normal credit card interest rate. A balance transfer offer has a promotional period associated with it, which implies that the lower balance transfer interest is applicable for a limited period, e.g., 6 months or one year. Once the promotion period is over, the remaining balance is charged at the normal card interest rate. Hence, the amount of balance that remains unpaid after the specified promotional period (balance retained) is an important driver of the profitability of a balance transfer offer. Due to the high marketing costs of balance transfer driven mostly by low-response rates, credit card issuers may charge a one-time transaction fee.

Usually a customer who accepts a balance transfer or a loan on card offer may decrease purchases on the credit card, because some of the credit limit gets blocked by the transferred balance. Hence, in most cases, these offers may also cause a decrease in interchange income. Net interest margin, the difference between accrued finance charges and cost of funds on the transferred balance can often be negative due to low teaser rates. A trade-off of lower yield relative to the regular card portfolio can be another area of concern. Credit loss is another component of profitability and it is ambiguous whether balance transfer causes incremental loss. The overall programme revenue needs to be measured not just at the programme level (net revenue earned from BT balances), but rather at the card level that also includes revenue from regular (non-BT) balances. Balance transfer is an important revenue component mostly in the US and UK markets. In the Asian markets, loan on card is a much bigger programme.

A balance transfer offer typically consists of three features: offer rate, offer duration and transaction fee. Pricing and its term (duration) are used by credit card issuers to pull balances from competition by offering teaser rates for a duration, either for a fixed period of time or for the life of balance. There is a cap on the amount that can be transferred in from competition and depends on open to buy (of the card account that the offer is made to) and the maximum limit as defined by the offer. Open to buy is the available credit limit; defined as credit limit minus outstanding balance on credit card. With credit card issuers tempted to offer low rates to attract high volume of balances, issuers are faced with balancing the multiple goals of maximising portfolio yield, revenue, and profitability. Hence, applying decision science through experimentation (test and control), segmentation, and optimisation are ongoing activities for credit card issuers in order to manage the bottom-line. As customers get smarter with competition trying to lure them, gamers are a segment that need to be identified and avoided. Gamers surf around for the best bargains, transferring balances back and forth at promotional rates.

Accounts are normally passed through credit criteria and should have a minimum open to buy. One of the surrogates for determining eligibility for a balance transfer offer is eligibility for a card line increase. The prime target groups are traditionally revolvers and low utilisation transactors. Another target segment are those for whom the low-interest rates are attractive for short-term funding of occasional big ticket purchases, like vacations. Communication of offers are generally through direct mail (letters, checks, and statements), telemarketing (inbound and outbound), and online.

At this point, it is important to note that in advanced markets like the US, some of the credit bureaus have come up with enhanced data on the number of times a customer has availed a balance transfer programme in the past. Bureaus have also used predictions to divide a customer's existing balance into revolving and non-revolving balance. This enhanced data provides further insights for a better strategy design. The interested reader could refer to Experian Trend View data for details on the above.

### 2.5.2.2 Balance Transfer Offers

There are different variants of BT offers based on rate and duration of the promotion period. Fee, a component of price is not mentioned here.

- **Purchase rate offer** *(e.g., 2.90% intro rate on purchase and BT for 6 months; 17.24% after that)*
  - Low interest rate on purchases and BT balance for a specified period
  - All balances move to "go-to" rate after promo period
- **Teaser rate offer** *(e.g., 0% rate on BT for 15 months; variable rate 12.99%–20.99% after that based on credit worthiness)*
  - Low-interest rate on BT balance for a specified period
  - All balances at "go-to" rate after promo period
  - Zero percent rate is most common when a new credit card account is initiated
  - Duration of teaser rate varying from 6 to 15 months
- **Fixed life of loan rate offer** *(e.g., 1.99% for 6 months and 3.99% for life of balance; regular rate is 12.99%)*
  - Low rate that is fixed until the transferred balance is paid off
  - Usually higher than the limited duration teaser rate offer, the borrower can save interest on balance transferred without the need to take on another BT when teaser rate expires

### 2.5.2.3 Balance Transfer Optimisation Process

The objectives of a balance transfer programme may include one or a combination of the following:

- Maximise volume of balance transfer value brought in (wallet share)
- Maximise revenue from a balance transfer programme
- Maximise revenue from a balance transfer programme with minimum yield threshold
- Maximise profitability at card account level

Some of these objectives may conflict with each other and therefore, the benefits of taking an optimisation approach as an analytical path for managing the profitability of a balance transfer programme is highlighted in this section. For example, the trade-off between balance growth and yield erosion can be managed effectively. Besides the huge financial benefits associated with optimisation, a structured analytical framework acknowledges and incorporates empirical learnings relating to price sensitivity and other customer behaviours (Fig. 2.28). The optimisation engine can be fully automated and the use of scorecards based on customer behaviour add a dynamic element to this approach. Further, the predictive element permits forecast ability and control over such programmes. For example, historical customer behaviour can be used to simulate expected cash flows and revenue based on the results of rigorous price testing.

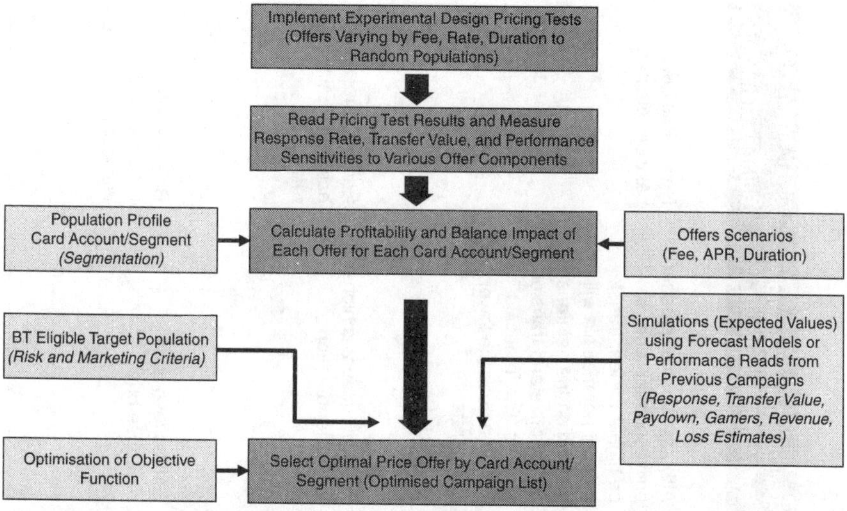


**Figure 2.28** Balance Transfer Optimisation Process

In addition, appropriate score cut-offs can be used to finalize the target population at each price point, depending on the objectives of the programme. The allocation of leads across channels to optimise returns on expenses is also possible.

*Balance Transfer: Price Testing* Since pricing is an important factor that influences the profitability of a balance transfer programme, price testing is quintessential to understand the impact of price on response, balance transferred, balance retained, and other drivers. Balance retained is the percentage of balance of the promotion period that moves to the regular card interest rate, once the promotion period is over. A price testing framework is presented in Table 2.9 and expected sensitivities in Table 2.10. The impact will vary based on the segment being considered and is shown in the following segmentation section.

**Table 2.9** Balance Transfer Price Test: Test Design

| Cell | Test | Purpose |
|---|---|---|
| 1 | 1.99 (6 mon) fee | Fee |
| 2 | 5.99 (6 mon) fee | Fee |
| 3 | 1.99 (9 mon) no fee | Duration |
| 4 | 5.99 (9 mon) no fee | Duration |
| 5 | 1.99 (6mon) no fee | Rate |
| 6 | 3.99 (6 mon) no fee | Rate |
| 7 | 5.99 (6 mon) no fee | Rate |

"Go to" rate the same for all

**Table 2.10** Balance Transfer Price Test: Expected Results

| Test | Test Cells | Fee | Term Duration | Rate | Response Rate | Balance Transfer Amount Per Mail File Account | Balance Retained |
|---|---|---|---|---|---|---|---|
| **Fee test** | | | | | | | |
| | 1 and 5 | Fee to no fee | – | – | Fee depresses response rate | Although transfer amount per responder tends to be higher for fee, transfer amount per mail file will depend on the net impact of response and transfer amount. The impact is similar across the lower and higher rate. | No fee has lower balance retained |
| | 2 and 7 | Fee to no fee | | – | | | |
| **Duration of term rate** | | | | | | | |
| | 3 and 5 | – | Increase from 6 to 9 months | – | Duration increases response rate | Transfer amount is higher for higher duration | Shorter duration has lower balance retained |
| | 4 and 7 | – | Increase from 6 to 9 months | – | Response sensitivity to duration decreases with higher price point | | |
| **Term rate** | | | | | | | |
| | 5, 6, 7 | | – | Rate increase | Response rate decreases with higher rates. The proportionate change is higher for every 200 basis points, which may not hold for the higher rates. | Similar results as response rate | Balance retained increases with increasing rate |

Ideally, design of experiments should be used for price testing as it allows the following advantages. It captures interaction effects and focuses on isolating the impact of each factor, overall, and by segment. It uses data more efficiently, compared to a "one-at-a-time" approach and provides more comprehensive data for determining the optimal strategy in one go. This topic is covered in a comprehensive manner in Chapter 8.

*Balance Transfer: Segmentation* Figure 2.29 highlights the need and relevance of segmentation for balance transfer programmes. A combination of some or all four of the dimensions can be used for a comprehensive behavioural segmentation.

Gamers are a population to identify and avoid as they surf around for the best bargains, transferring balances back and forth at promotional rates. This segment has a tendency to become sales delinquent, leading to a high likelihood of a negative net interest margin on the account. Identifying them is a challenge and some indicators of a gamer profile are:

- BT balance is 90% of total balance
- Accounts with net interest margin less than a threshold, for those who have taken up a balance transfer
- Credit bureau of customer shows an increase in the number of open accounts while total balance outstanding remains constant
- Customer stops spending after balance is transferred in (sales inactivity)

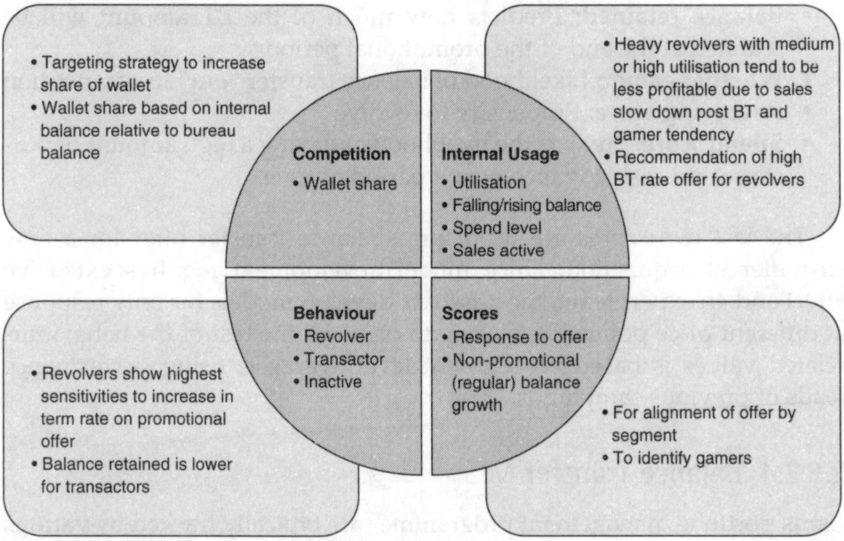


**Figure 2.29** Balance Transfer Segmentation

*Balance Transfer: Balance vs. Revenue Maximisation* The objective of balance maximisation is to maximise balance transferred in, which may not necessarily translate to revenue maximised from a balance transfer programme; nor does it give an assurance of a minimum yield on the programme as the lowest rate usually attracts the highest balance transferred per customer. Noting the example in Table 2.11 based on reads of a price test (rate) for the revolver segment, the optimal interest rate to offer to a revolver to maximise the volume of balance transfer is the lowest rate of 1.99%; while the interest rate that maximises revenue from the programme is 3.99%. The assumption in this example is that the conversion rate from response to acceptance (for a balance transfer offer) is 100%.

*Balance Transfer: Behavioural Models* A model-based framework is a statistically robust decision logic based on the interaction of various behavioural models to determine the optimal offer by customer or segment. Some benefits are the ability to rank order customers by revenue, a fully automated campaign activity, ability to quickly react to competition (e.g., rate drop), manage programme goals appropriately (volume, revenue, yield), revenue forecasting, scenario planning (changes in business assumptions, environment), and channel optimisation. An example of a model-driven balance transfer offer strategy requires the following model inputs:

- **Response propensity by price point for each customer at various price points:** Which profile of customer will respond to which price offer
- **Amount of balance transfer:** Predicts the BT amount transferred "in" from competition
- **Balance retained:** Predicts how much of the BT amount will be retained at the end of the promotional period
- **Whether gamer:** Likelihood of balance transfer "out" to competition
- **Revolving score:** Propensity to revolve
- **Spend score:** Predicts the likelihood of having a high amount of purchase and cash advance over a period of time

The last two scores are used for a balance transfer offer for a new customer at acquisition. Since model development requires extensive effort and an expert team, most issuers develop models for only response at different price points. Sensitivity to price for the rest of the behaviour-related values is based on segment level averages, using performance reads of previous campaigns.

### 2.5.2.4 Balance Transfer MIS

Cards portfolio management programmes are typically tracked by various metrics as in Fig. 2.30.

**Table 2.11** Balance Transfer by Price Point—Revolver Segment

| Rate | Balance Retained | Response Rate | Responses | Average BT Value Per Responder $ | BT Value $ | Revenue/ Responder | Revenue Per $ Transferred | Total Revenue $ | Number of Customers | Revenue Per Customer |
|---|---|---|---|---|---|---|---|---|---|---|
| 10.99% | 93.6% | 1.9% | 1,922 | 5,162 | 99,21,364 | $210 | 0.041 | 4,03,620 | 100000 | 4.03 |
| 7.99% | 90.4% | 2.6% | 2,551 | 5,071 | 1,29,36,121 | $263 | 0.052 | 6,70,913 | 100000 | 6.72 |
| 5.99% | 90.1% | 3.3% | 3,314 | 5,810 | 1,92,54,340 | $255 | 0.044 | 8,45,070 | 100000 | 8.46 |
| 3.99% | 90.0% | 5.4% | 5,404 | 6,860 | 3,70,71,440 | $253 | 0.037 | 13,67,212 | 100000 | 13.66 |
| 1.99% | 89.0% | 6.5% | 6,453 | 6,861 | 4,42,74,033 | $181 | 0.026 | 11,67,993 | 100000 | 11.66 |

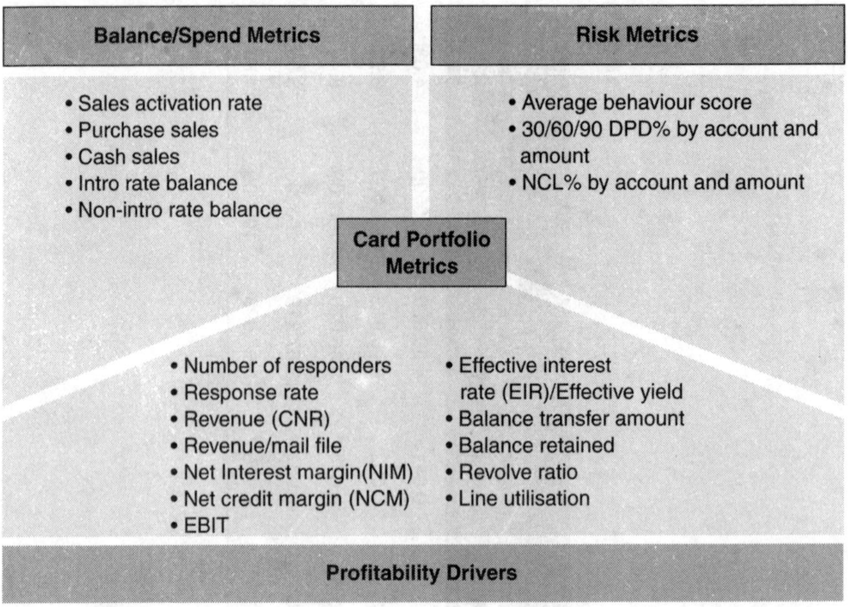


**Figure 2.30** Balance Transfer MIS

## 2.5.3 Top-Up

A top-up loan is a loan taken from a financial institution with whom the customer already has a loan. It is an extra loan that a lender allows for an existing customer that tops up an existing loan to a higher level. The top-up amount is usually determined by the original loan sanctioned, balance outstanding, and repayment track. In the initial first few years of loan tenor, a higher proportion of the EMI amount is paid towards the interest as compared to the principal. Therefore, a top-up offered in the first year would be a lesser amount as compared to later years (top-up with enhancement, total loan amount greater than original loan sanctioned in some cases). For a personal loan, a top-up is offered by lenders as early as in the 9th month after the loan sanction date for a customer with a clear repayment track over these 9 months. The interest rate on a top-up loan is usually lesser than that charged on the original loan and the lender may charge a processing fee for the loan. In many cases, the balance of original loan is re-priced downwards (to the rate of the top-up).

Top-ups are mostly offered as pre-approved offers and aggressively marketed by lenders, primarily to manage run-offs resulting from pre-payment and loan maturity. Top-ups are used as a retention strategy and offered at different points of the tenor of the loan. For example, at MOB signifying high attrition rates and closer to loan maturity. The analytics required for a top-up programme are to address the following:

- Risk eligibility
- Timing of offer (at which MOB)
- Amount of top-up loan
- Interest rate to charge
- Incremental profitability
- Who is likely to respond

The data preparation for analysing performance of top-up customers by MOB can be cumbersome, if the original loan and top-up loan are not linked for a customer. A regular practice in the industry is to close the original loan and open a new loan with a new account number, reflecting the original loan outstanding plus the top-up amount at new terms (rate and tenor). Therefore, there is a requirement to link the original and new loan, using a unique customer key (e.g., customer ID). It needs to be noted that for performance analysis of loans in general, attrition and delinquency vintage curves show a misleading trend, if the link between the original and new loan is not established.

Top-ups are also offered in the insurance industry. A policyholder has an option to contribute additional amounts over and above the regular premium payable under a unit-linked life insurance plan (ULIP). This feature allows a policyholder to take advantage of a well-performing ULIP by increasing the investment share by paying an extra premium at a lower premium charge. Many insurance companies also increase the sum assured by a significant proportion (subject to underwriting guidelines that vary by insurance provider), if the top-up premium exceeds a certain percentage of total premiums paid (e.g., > 25%). In the case of a traditional plan, insurance cover may also get enhanced post top-up. For health insurance, a top-up plan is generally taken to enhance sum assured over and over the health policy already taken. Such policies work on a concept of threshold limits, if sum assured is $X, the top-up would cover hospital bills in excess of $X.

### *2.5.4 Behavioural Segmentation*

The following examples are segmentation schema to help determine the appropriate offer by segment for credit cards, deposits and wealth management. The objective is to build customer value using balance build and other customer management initiatives.

The cards segmentation (Fig. 2.31) is developed using demographics, usage, transactor-revolver behaviour, profit, and credit loss. Recommended portfolio actions are listed subsequently in Fig. 2.32. The analytical technique used for this example is cluster analysis, a discussion topic in Chapter 7, "Quantitative Methods". Another useful segmentation is revolver behaviour plotted against line utilisation. Further, revenue banding (tier-based) decided upon by segmenting the portfolio based

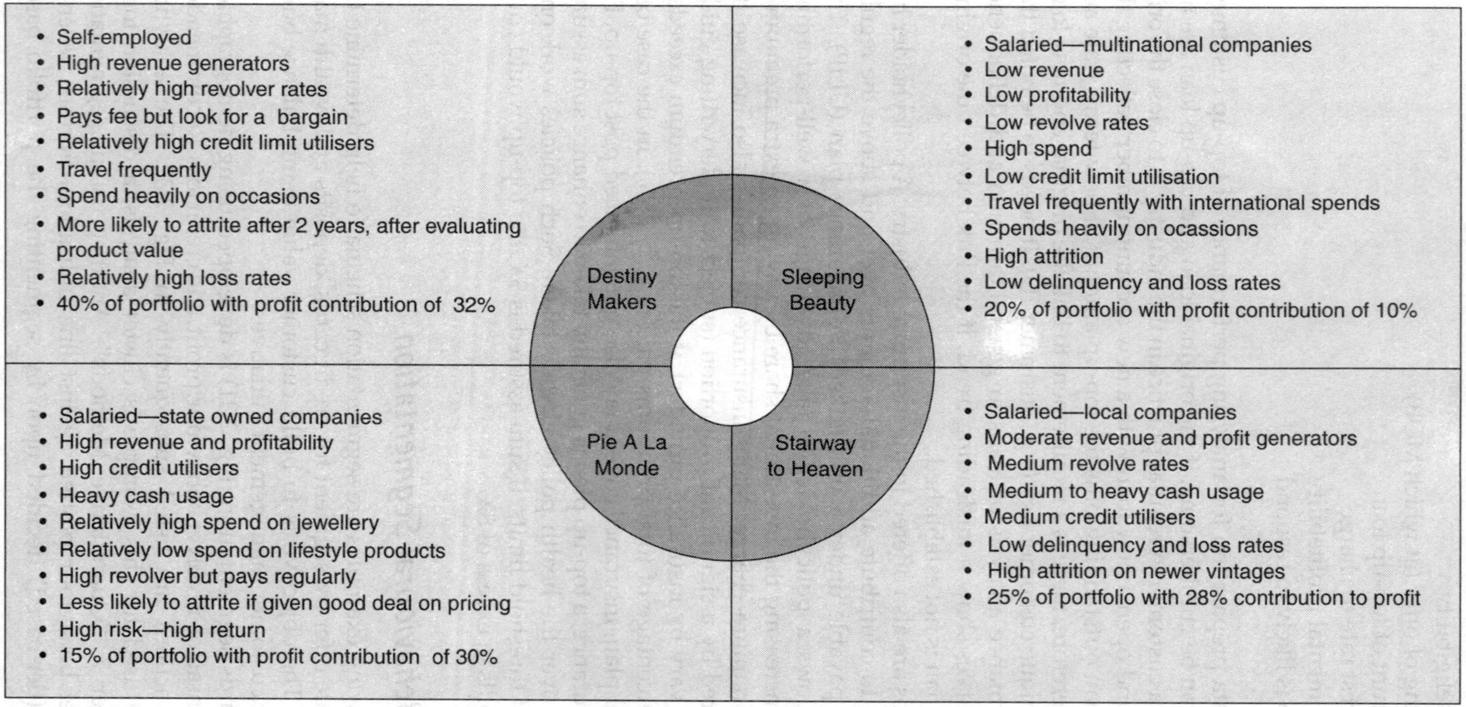


*Note:* Credit bureau data was not available for this segmentation.

**Figure 2.31** Credit Card Segmentation

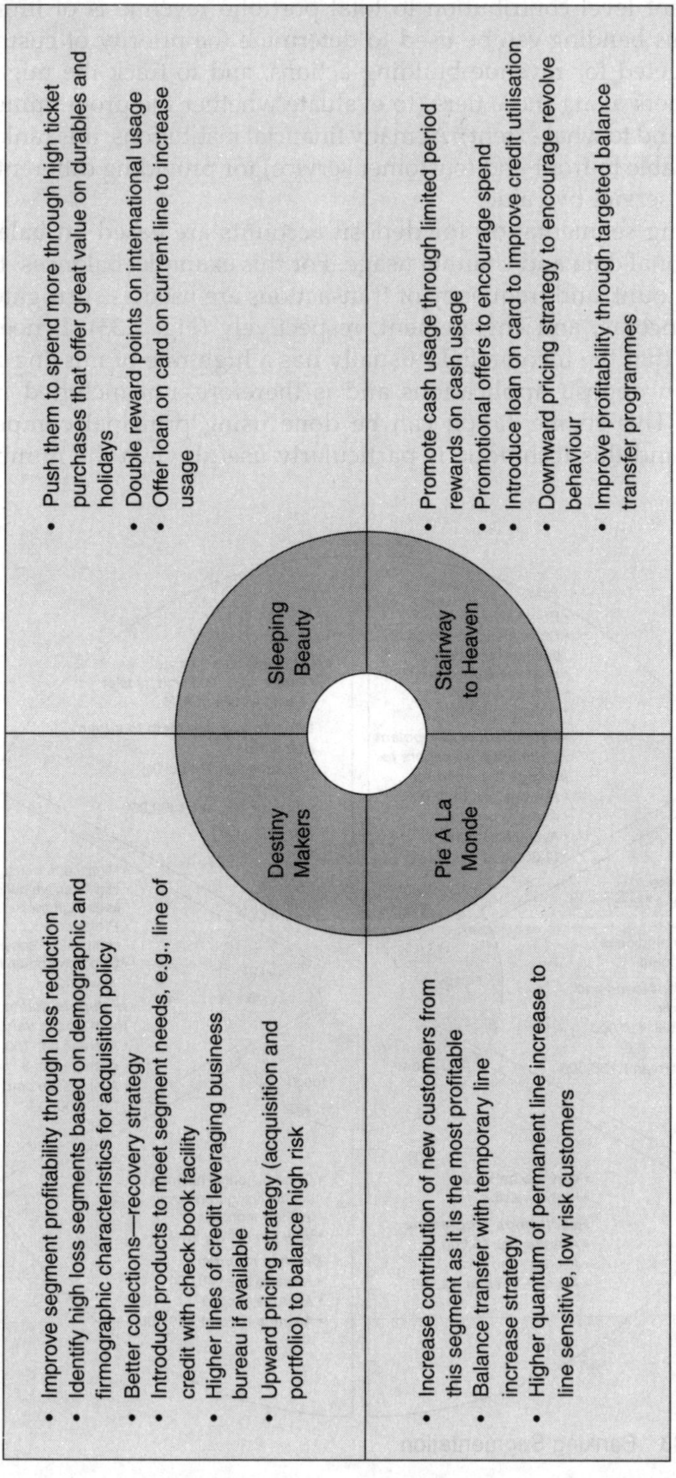


**Figure 2.32** Credit Card Segmentation—Recommended Portfolio Actions

on segment level contribution to total portfolio revenue is of immense value. This banding can be used to determine the priority of customers to be targeted for revenue building actions, and to track the migration of customers along these tiers (to evaluate whether the programmes are working and to what extent). At many financial institutions, this ranking is also available to front-end (customer service) for providing differentiated customer service by value.

Banking segmentation for deposit accounts are based on balances, transactional data and channel usage. For this example, balances, transaction amount, and frequency of transactions are used as surrogates for wealth, income, and engagement, respectively (Fig. 2.33). It needs to be noted that the income field usually has a high rate of missing information on deposit applications and is therefore, not included in the analysis. This segmentation can be done using principal component analysis and this technique is particularly useful when the number of

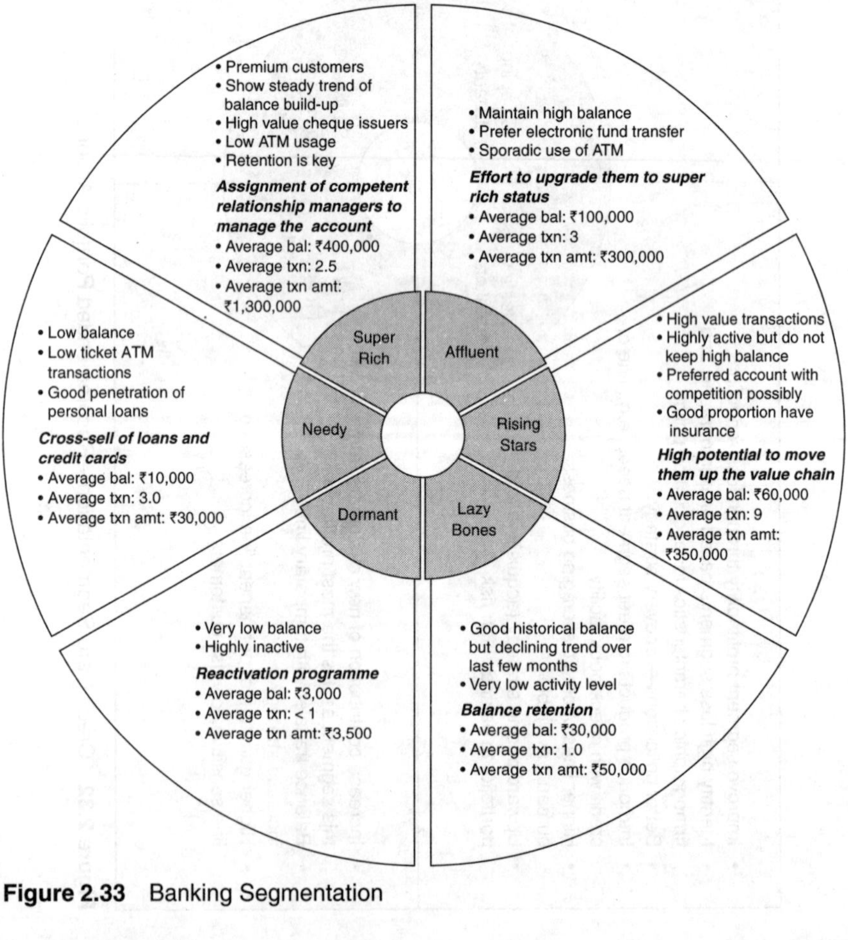


**Figure 2.33** Banking Segmentation

**Table 2.12** Wealth Management Segmentation

| Cluster | Risk Appetite | Average Income | Average Wealth | Average Balance | Share of Wallet (Wealth) | Average Value of Loan Products (% of annual income) | Average Age | Objective | Action Recommended |
|---|---|---|---|---|---|---|---|---|---|
| 1 | L | H | M | M | L | H | Mid 50 | Increase wallet share (wealth) | Low risk investment products such as bonds and monthly income mutual fund plans |
| 2 | H | H | H | H | H | L | Mid 50 | Maintain wallet share (wealth) | High risk investment products and time deposits |
| 3 | M | L | M | L | L | L | Mid 30 | Satisfy financial needs by being the one stop financial services provider | Lending products, products to incentivize inflow of wealth |
| 4 | H | M | L | L | L | M | Mid 40 | Build/grow wealth | Retirement products. Equity and fixed income products. Regular savings and time deposits. |

*Note*: Average wealth is measured across various institutions while rest of the fields pertain to a particular institution.

variables under consideration is very large. This method will be covered in Chapter 7.

Wealth segmentation (Table 2.12) is based on various dimensions of the customer, used for recommending appropriate wealth management products to increase net relationship value (NRV). Risk appetite, income, and wealth can be determined through a questionnaire to the customer. Balance amount, value of savings and investment products, loan products, and age are taken from internal customer data stored with the bank.

## 2.6 Credit Line Management for Financial Services

Credit line and price are important determinants of wallet share and profitability for a lender. Product features of credit line and price are important levers available to a lender to stimulate balances and interest income for credit-related products. According to Gross and Souleles, *Do Interest Rates and Liquidity Constraints Matter for Consumer Behaviour*, published in 2002 and based on US data, a one-percentage point increase in interest rates results in a gross $110 decline in credit card debt on average on the card (within the first 9 months after the rate change).The net impact is $70 as customers move $40 to other cards. Debt sensitivity to line is in the range of 10%-14% resulting in a $350 average increase in debt per dollar line increase. According to another study by Soman and Cheema, *The Effect of Credit on Spending Decisions*, the size of the credit limit is perceived as a signal of future earning potential, and the available credit limit positively influences the propensity to spend.

In its most general definition, credit limit or credit line is the maximum credit that a lender has committed to a borrower and the borrower can use funds upto this credit limit. Credit lines for credit cards and most personal loans require no collateral from the client, also called unsecured loans for the institution. Some credit lines are secured by the equity owned on a home, also referred to as home equity lines of credit (HELOC). Overdraft facility linked to a checking or savings account also involves setting a credit limit. The discussions in this section will apply to unsecured loans. For a credit card, total line assigned is split into a purchase and cash line, with purchase line constituting a higher proportion of total line. The credit limit for unsecured loans such as personal loans is the ticket size, with full 100% utilisation.

For the insurance sector, the credit limit is the maximum amount the credit insurer is willing to insure, and if the outstanding claim exceeds the limit, there is no cover for the exceeding amount. For the telecom consumer, disconnection of service or barring of calls is set into action when usage exceeds the credit limit decided by the operators, similar to the concept of OCL for a credit card[13].

[13] Over credit limit (OCL) customers may be charged a fee for surpassing their assigned credit limit. OCL is considered to be a trigger indicating risky behaviour.

Setting initial credit limits and managing lines gradually (rather than ramping up too quickly) based on customer behaviour and competitive forces are some of the key tasks that lenders face. Line management involves balancing the trade-offs across multiple objectives of fuelling revenue momentum while curtailing credit loss, and keeping customers satisfied (retention). While lower than desired credit line depresses usage, customers with high line utilisation have been found to be more risky, with higher accompanying loss rates[14]. Since credit line is an exposure for the lender, most country-specific regulations require setting aside a loss provision against these lines, which impacts P&L.

Traditional exposure management policies in developing countries such as India are based on demographics (new customer) and in-house payment track record (existing customer). Primarily risk-driven, line management decisions have been largely dependent on demographic fields available on the application form (e.g., income, employment, occupation), and debt servicing ability. Although a good risk policy for line management may work well for the management of credit loss, a limitation is that it tends to ignore both customer need and revenue dynamics. Such an approach is inclined to create average lines which are significantly lower for customers evaluated as potentially risky. However, the returns of a line increase programme for this segment may be promising due to the revenue upside. The consequences are that line management actions may not create the expected lift in balances as credit line may be low relative to need and perceived to be lower as compared to competitors (in the case of low lines). For a good customer, the relatively higher line may not get utilised due to favourable competitors' limits and low demand for credit. Some additional nuances in emerging markets are unreliable income and verification with heavy reliance on surrogates.

The formation of credit bureaus in India has expanded information available for line management, with data on competition that includes external delinquency behaviour, credit bureau score and wallet share (derived) information. Competitor lines are made available by credit bureaus in advanced markets and concepts such as preferred line and highest line are important parameters in the credit line assignment decision. Credit bureaus have been highly leveraged by the US and advanced markets in Europe and Asia Pacific, not just as a source of information but also as a platform to move from a risk to a profitability-based approach for line management. However, India has yet to catch up.

Once lines are assigned, managing line increase programmes in its various forms (e.g., line increase on same product, second product,

[14] A FICO Report, *How are Credit Line Decreases Impacting Consumer Credit Risk,* shows a positive correlation between bad rate (90 days or more delinquent) and credit card utilisation. Bad rate > 20% for utilisation > 80%; Bad rate < 10% for utilisation < 60%. Line utilisation is an important and significant predictor variable in risk and credit bureau scores.

upgrade) is an important portfolio management initiative which impacts customer profitability, customer satisfaction, and retention. A practice among lenders is to be conservative in the initial phase and ratchet up exposure as customer behaviour is observed, by granting line enhancements in periodic intervals (e.g., 6 months). Line decrease programmes are taken on marginal customers who pose a credit threat to the issuer, and are not covered in this section.

In the following sub-sections, priority will given to initial line assignment and line increase programmes at an account level. Both risk and profitability based approaches will be considered. Customer level exposure and its allocation across secured and unsecured products is a topic of serious interest to credit issuers, and outside the purview of this book. Small business and corporate lines with higher limits will also not be covered here as well.

## 2.6.1 Forms of Line Management

Line management can take many forms:

- **New accounts**
  - Line assignment at customer level, the tipping point beyond which chances of default are expected to rise. In India, maximum unsecured exposure (MUE) is usually set as a multiple of verified income
  - Line assignment at account level for customers who have just been approved
  - Line assignment for cross-sold offers, typically for pre-approved offers
  - Line assignment after interactions with applicants perceived to be high risk
- **Existing accounts: Line increase and decrease**
  - Planned periodic increases—target customer, quantum, timing/pacing, and communication
  - Form of line increase (for credit card)—line increase on same card, additional line through second card, upgrade, and personal loan
  - Real-time line increases to credit worthy customers approaching their limit
  - Temporary or contingent line increase (e.g., with balance transfer offer)
  - Line increase requests from customers
  - Line decrease programmes
- **Line structure**
  - *Normal line assignment*—sets initial lines with periodic line increases
  - *Teaser line/contingent line*—sets very high lines to start with for debt consolidation purposes, with the expectation that line will be automatically reduced after 6 months if not used. If used, the lines are automatically ratcheted down with pay down.

- *Flexible line*—sets moderate initial lines and expectations of easy and flexible line increases on customer request
- *Shadow line*—invisible line typically set for charge cards that the customer is not aware of

## 2.6.2 *Initial Line Assignment*

Although research in this area by the academic community is scant, some early studies of the 1960s circuit mostly around the question of "whether to grant credit" based on credit worthiness. Using statistical tools like linear discriminant analysis, focus of early researchers has been on differentiating between good and bad risk customers, by developing a weighted score based on customer characteristics. However, this approach does not take into consideration the future profits of a customer. Bierman and Hausman in their 1970 paper titled *The Credit Granting Decision*, cover some of the shortcomings of the earlier studies by addressing the dual decisions facing an issuer regarding "whether to grant credit" and "how much", in the light of the fact that expected gains from spend and excessive loss from uncollectible accounts have to be balanced. They develop a multi-period Bayesian approach based on debt collection experience and future discounted profits using dynamic programming. As mentioned earlier, industry philosophy around assigning lines and its management have been largely based on risk measures such as credit worthiness and capacity (ability) to pay. Later developments include a profitability-based approach.

### 2.6.2.1 Risk-based Line Assignment Based on Credit Worthiness

A risk-based credit policy for credit line determination can take the form of a rule based system using customer attributes or an expert opinion based score. Figure 2.34 features a rule based policy strategy, in the case of a new to issuer credit card customer. In the exampie, in the absence of a credit bureau, line assignment is based on customer's demographic profile ascertained from the application form, financial statements, and utility bills obtained from the customer. Self-employed are considered more risky and for salaried, income levels are considered for the determination of potential risk.

### 2.6.2.2 Risk-based Line Assignment Based on Capacity to Pay

The concept of capacity to pay is used for the determination of ticket size and is commonly used for term loan products such as a personal loan. Based on the payment capacity of a customer, for a given rate and tenor, the logic

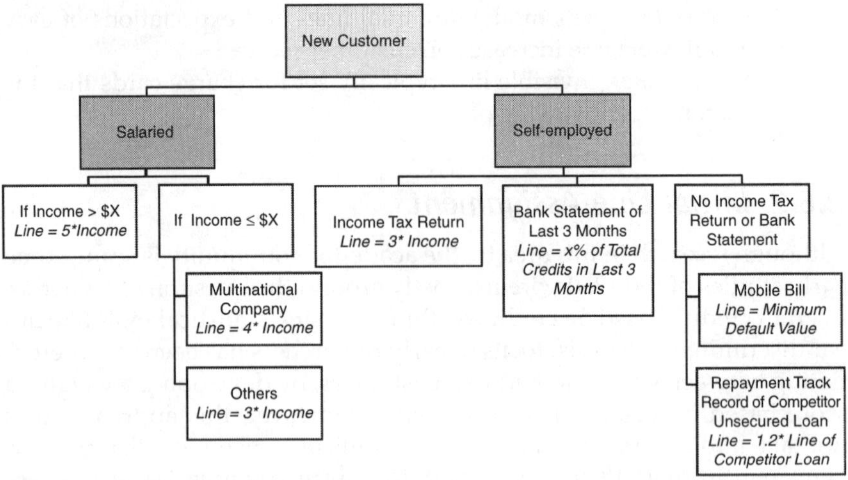


**Figure 2.34** Risk-based Line Assignment Based on Credit Worthiness

outputs the maximum amount of loan that can be approved. Maximum line is determined as a function of capacity. Capacity is taken as the EMI that can be paid with a 100% financial obligations ratio (FOR)[15] in this example. The maximum line can be represented as a geometric series for a given rate and tenor, and calculations are shown in Table 2.13. In reality, lenders lend at a FOR that is below 100% (e.g., 60%–80%) and the same logic can be applied to calculate line size using this upper limit as a constraint.

$$\begin{aligned}
\text{Payments} &= \text{Credit bureau total monthly payments + monthly mortgage/rent + others} \\
\text{Income} &= \text{Verified disposable income from salary and other sources (post tax income)} \\
\text{Capacity} &= \text{Income} - \text{payments} \\
\text{Rate} &= \text{Annual interest rate}/12 \\
\text{Maximum line} &= \text{Capacity} * [((1 + \text{rate})^{\text{term}} - 1)/(\text{rate} * (1 + \text{rate})^{\text{term}})]
\end{aligned}$$

## 2.6.2.3 Risk and Revenue-based Line Assignment

An example of an approach based on risk and revenue is presented in Table 2.14. The original line is set as a multiplier of earning capacity with a higher factor for a potential high revenue-new customer (expected to be

[15] The household debt service ratio (DSR) is an estimate of the ratio of debt payments to disposable personal income. Debt payments consist of the estimated required payments on outstanding mortgage and consumer debt. The financial obligations ratio (FOR) adds automobile lease payments, rental payments on tenant-occupied property, homeowners' insurance, and property tax payments to the debt service ratio. *Source:* Federal Reserve website of the US.

**Table 2.13** Risk-based Line Assignment Based on Capacity to Pay

| Income (Monthly) | Payments (Monthly) | Capacity = Income – Payments | FOR | Rate (Monthly) | Term (Months) | Max Loan Amount (at FOR = 100%) | Income Multiplier |
|---|---|---|---|---|---|---|---|
| $1,000 | $600 | $400 | 60% | 1.3% | 36 | $11,442 | 11 |
| $2,000 | $1,000 | $1,000 | 50% | 1.3% | 36 | $28,604 | 14 |
| $3,000 | $1,200 | $1,800 | 40% | 1.3% | 36 | $51,488 | 17 |
| $4,000 | $1,400 | $2,600 | 35% | 1.3% | 36 | $74,371 | 19 |
| $5,000 | $1,650 | $3,350 | 33% | 1.3% | 36 | $95,824 | 19 |
| $6,000 | $1,800 | $4,200 | 30% | 1.3% | 36 | $120,138 | 20 |

**Table 2.14** Risk and Revenue Based Line Assignment

| | Risk (Based on Risk Score) | | |
|---|---|---|---|
| Revenue (Based on Revenue Score) | Low | Medium | High |
| Low revenue | 2x | 1.5x | Reject |
| High revenue | 2.5x | 2x | |

more sensitive to line). Potential revenue classification into low and high is based on the revenue score as a higher score implies higher potential revenue. In this case, it is difficult to evaluate whether this line is low or high, unless several rounds of testing with the income multiplier are carried out.

### 2.6.2.4 Profitability-based Line Assignment

A conservative credit line strategy may reduce usage and profits while a generous expansive one may be disproportionate (leading to wastage). Further, this strategy may not be able to discriminate between good and bad customers, thereby resulting in higher costs. Therefore, striking the right balance of granting an "optimal" line that balances revenue and credit loss is an ultimate challenge. Approaches that focus on objectives such as improving share of wallet, optimising per account future profitability (e.g., NPV), and maximising incremental profit from an incremental dollar of line granted have been the new paradigm for line management in the US (pre-subprime crisis period). For such an exercise, quantitative techniques such as segmentation, statistical models and optimisation have been best put to use.

One approach for determining the optimal line for each customer is by using the concept of NPV as a measure of future profitability. Analytically rigorous and which leverages on learnings of past customer behaviour, this approach is based on business logic and facts, and less on judgement and negotiation. Credit bureau competitor information of external balance, preferred line and default behaviour are explicitly considered. Similarly, the reality that sensitivity to line can be different across segments is incorporated by identifying distinct clusters and assigning lines accordingly. One such framework is presented in Figs. 2.35 and 2.36 for credit card.

Recommendations result in competitive lines that balance customer need and issuer profitability, and can be revised with changing competition. In cases where the requested line is greater than the optimum, the set line is between the line that meets the profitability threshold and the customer requested line. The challenge is to find a functional form for good and bad balances in relation to line that has a closed form solution. Predictive models need to be developed, which produce accurate estimates, as they are important inputs into the business logic. Pricing has an impact on line usage and can also be incorporated in this approach.

### *2.6.3 Line Increase Programmes*

Line increase programmes are mostly self-initiated portfolio management actions, that issuers normally execute on a periodic basis to increase usage and improve customer profitability, with planned targets to increase outstanding lines. It is also a retention tool and customers also call in proactively for line enhancements. In many countries, card issuers are required to obtain consent from customers such as in South Africa, Netherlands, Australia, and India. The same fundamental approaches to determining the initial credit limit applies to line increase programmes as well. Further, since the relationship has already evolved with the customer, relationship value is another dimension that can be considered, for the determination of the quantum of line increase. To leverage value from line increase programmes, customer communication along with usage-related offers (e.g., balance transfer) is important as most customers do not realise that a line increase has been granted.

Current customers are passed through credit and marketing filters to determine the set of customers eligible for a line increase. A line increase risk policy is usually formulated after reviewing performance of accounts that have been granted a line increase in the past. Typically, the more severe risk exclusions are applied first, followed by less stringent exclusions. The percentage of accounts that are eliminated against each exclusion (single and multiple) are examined. This is also done as an audit check to make sure that the programme is executed properly. The review

**Business Objective**

Find Optimal Line (Line**) that maximises NPV

**Quantitative Techniques**

- Linear regression models
- Discrete choice regression models
- Segmentation
- Optimisation

**Process**

- Fit a functional form and model Good Balance based on historical data
- Estimate probability of write-off and bad utilisation. Model Bad Balance as function of Line.
- Calculate Net Cash Flow from historical data. Fit a functional form and estimate Net Cash Flow as a function of Good Balance and Bad Balance.
- Predict Good Balance and Bad Balance for every customer using different values of Line. Plug in these estimates to predict Net Cash Flows and NPV. Do several iterations and pick the optimal Line (Line**) that maximises NPV.

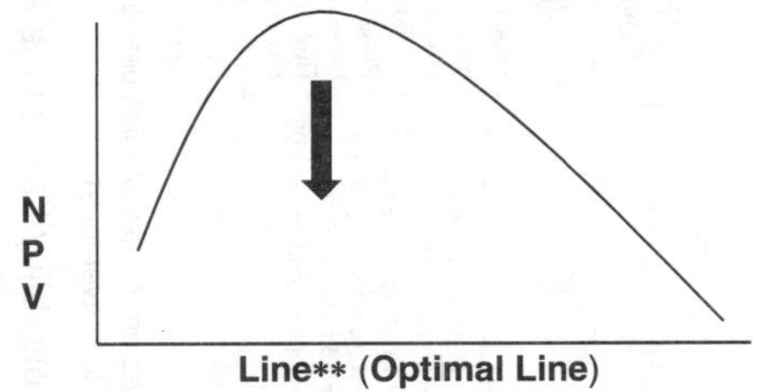


**Business Logic**

- Good Balance = f (Line, External Line, External Balance)
- Bad Balance = h (Line) or equal to Probability of Bad (Write-off)* Expected Bad Utilisation * Line
- Net Cash Flow = j (Good Balance, Bad Balance)
- NPV = Discounted Net Cash Flows over a specified time period

**Customer Data**

- Credit bureau
- Internal historical performance
- Application data

**Estimates—Models**

- Probability of default and write-off
- Credit bureau score
- Bad utilisation
- Good balance
- Bad balance
- Activation and Voluntary Attrition

Good Balance is balance that has not gone bad (write-off or charge-off). Bad Balance is balance that has gone into Write-off.
External Line = Bureau highest line or preferred line on credit card. Preferred line is the line associated with highest balance on bureau.
*Note:* f, h, and j are functional forms which could be linear or non-linear.

**Figure 2.35** Profitability-based Line Assignment Framework for Credit Card

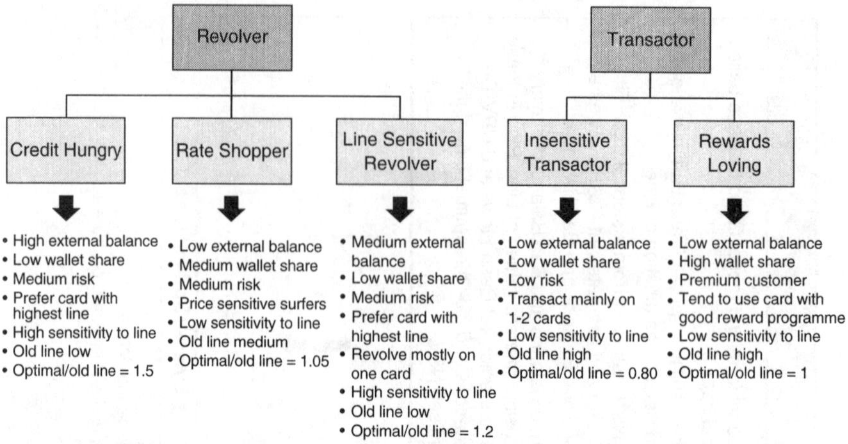


*Note:* Old line is based on traditional rules based system. High and low defined on relative basis (as compared to portfolio averages).

**Figure 2.36** Profitability-based Line Assignment for Credit Card

of exclusion criteria is also important to determine whether the filters are doing their job of weeding out bad risk or low profitable accounts, whether additional criteria need to be added to tighten policy, and to evaluate possibilities of universe expansion through relaxation of policy.

Further, wallet share analysis is insightful for understanding market positioning and associated line management strategy to action, as highlighted in Table 2.15. The report clearly shows that lines are least competitive in the lowest line segment as 60% of this group has an average credit limit that is lower than competition cards held by the customer, thereby resulting in the lowest wallet share. Average external balance is

**Table 2.15** Credit Card–Credit Line: Competitive Landscape

| | Internal Credit Limit | | |
|---|---|---|---|
| | Low | Medium | High |
| % of customers | 30% | 30% | 40% |
| Average internal credit limit $ | 2500 | 5500 | 14000 |
| Average highest external limit $ | 5000 | 8000 | 20000 |
| Average internal balance $ | 2000 | 3500 | 6000 |
| Average external balance $ | 6000 | 8500 | 9200 |
| Open to buy $ | 500 | 2000 | 8000 |
| Average internal utilisation | 80% | 64% | 43% |
| % of customers with internal line < highest external line | 60% | 30% | 20% |
| Wallet share | 25% | 29% | 39% |

thrice the value of internal balance, giving a clear direction that credit line needs to be revised upwards. Another metric that can be added to this report is the percentage of customers who have sufficient internal open to buy, to accommodate external balances. This metric is useful for targeting strategy for balance transfer programmes (with contingent line increase). Readers can also refer to Chapter 6 "Credit Bureau" for another related example on using the concept of wallet share for line enhancement. Risk and profitability based line increase strategies will be discussed subsequently.

### 2.6.3.1 Risk-based Line Increase

Figure 2.37 is an example of a risk based approach to line enhancement that uses both internal and competition information. In this context, classification/decision tree is an effective method for determining good and bad pockets in the portfolio. The segmentation has high inference value as it can be used to finalise the segments that should be offered a line increase, its form (second card, upgrade etc.) and quantum. Chapter 7, "Quantitative Methods" will showcase an example of using classification/decision tree for a credit card portfolio and the following customer management actions at a segment level.

### 2.6.3.2 Example: Profitability-based Line Increase: PORTICO Model

*Summary of PORTICO Model* Markov Chain decision process (MDP) is used to develop the PORTICO model for Bank One[16]. This model recommends price point changes and credit line increases for every card holder, with the objective of maximising net present value (NPV) for the portfolio. The Bank One team comprising of Trench et al. published their research

| Risk (Behaviour score/FICO) | High | Medium | | | | Low | | | |
|---|---|---|---|---|---|---|---|---|---|
| Utilisation | | Low | | High | | Low | | High | |
| Delinquency (Internal performance and credit bureau) | | N | Y | N | Y | N | Y | N | Y |
| Line Increase | $0 | $1000 | $0 | $500 | $0 | $2000 | $0 | $1500 | $0 |

**Figure 2.37** Risk-based Line Increase for Credit Card

[16] Bank One was purchased by JP Morgan Chase in 2004 and thereby operates under this name.

in 2003 titled *Managing Credit Lines and Prices for Bank One Credit Cards*. The PORTICO (portfolio control and optimisation) model decisions price and credit line changes at the account level and is dynamic as it has the functionality to adjust credit lines and prices as customers' behaviour evolves over time.

The BAU (business as usual) strategy for Bank One was a segmentation-based approach using customer's future risk, profitability, and likelihood of discontinuing card usage. Authors claim that this strategy did not give the expected impetus to sales and balances, with a disproportionate incremental credit loss to incremental credit line ratio.

*Choice of MDP Approach* Time series data on customers integrates well with the MDP process as future customer behaviour can be modelled. Using this framework, expected profitability, and other components (e.g., balance and sales) can be estimated. Further, the dynamics of customer performance under different policy scenarios can be incorporated for projections of profitability over time.

*Markov Chain Model*[17] For financial services, some of the applications of Markov Chain are the prediction of default behaviour, pattern of take-up of cross-sold products, and credit line increases. In reference to modelling customer behaviour for marketing applications, Markov Chain is a model that can describe the pattern of changes in behaviour over time. Markov Chain models can range from very simple and easy to understand, to extremely complex models of real-world behaviour and the simplest of Markov Chain models is presented.

In a Markov Chain Model, time is broken into discrete intervals such as hours, days, week, month, quarter or year. Specifically, this is called a discrete-time Markov Chain Model (as opposed to continuous-time models). At any particular point in time $t$, an individual can be in one of a pre-defined set of possible *states*. A *state(s)* can represent the number of products the customer holds, the default status (current, 30, 60, 90+ days past due) or the price and credit line of the credit card held by the customer at time $t$. A Markov Chain attempts to model a customer's behaviour through time by describing the probability that he/she will move from one state to another, or stay in the same state, from one time period to the next (Fig. 2.38). The movement of time from one period to the next is called a *time step*, and a customer's progression from one state to another over that one-time step is called a transition. The probabilities that are assigned to the possible transitions from one state to another over a single time step are called transition probabilities, which are collected into a transition matrix ($P$). The Markovian assumption of memoryless process is that the probability of which state the customer moves to next depends only on the state he/she is in at present. Figures 2.38 and 2.39

[17] *Advanced Marketing Analytics: Markov Chain Models in Marketing*, a White Paper presented by LITYX. Available on their website.

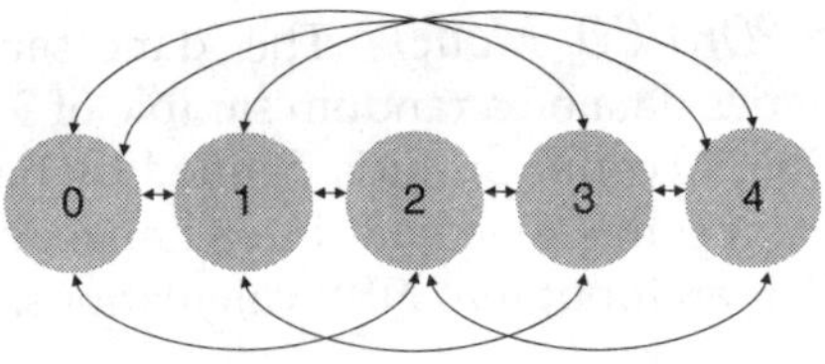


**Figure 2.38** Space Diagram

| | 0 | 1 | 2 | 3 | 4+ |
|---|---|---|---|---|---|
| 0 | 0.95 | 0.04 | 0.01 | 0 | 0 |
| 1 | 0.02 | 0.91 | 0.05 | 0.02 | 0 |
| 2 | 0.01 | 0.06 | 0.90 | 0.02 | 0.01 |
| 3 | 0.01 | 0.03 | 0.06 | 0.85 | 0.05 |
| 4+ | 0 | 0.02 | 0.02 | 0.06 | 0.90 |

**Figure 2.39** One Step Transition Matrix for 5-state Markov Chain Example

are an illustrative example of the possible states and the transition matrix for the products held by the customer, with a time step defined as one month. For example, the probability that a customer with one product will hold two products after one month is 5% and the probability of holding three products is lower at 2% (Fig. 2.39). The probabilities in the matrix are representative of the real behaviour of customers gleaned from historical customer data. Over two time periods (2 months), the transition probability matrix would be $P^2$ and over $n$ periods it would be $P^n$. For example, in Fig. 2.40, the probability that a customer with one product will hold two products in 2 months is 9.2% and three products is 3.6%. Accurate estimation of the transition matrices is one of the biggest tasks of Markov Chain applications.

| | 0 | 1 | 2 | 3 | 4+ |
|---|---|---|---|---|---|
| 0 | 0.9034 | 0.0750 | 0.0205 | 0.0010 | 0.0001 |
| 1 | 0.0379 | 0.8325 | 0.0919 | 0.0362 | 0.0015 |
| 2 | 0.0199 | 0.1098 | 0.8145 | 0.0368 | 0.0190 |
| 3 | 0.0192 | 0.0578 | 0.1076 | 0.7273 | 0.0881 |
| 4+ | 0.0012 | 0.0392 | 0.0406 | 0.1058 | 0.8132 |

**Figure 2.40** Two Step Transition Matrix for 5-state Markov Chain Example

*Data Sample for PORTICO Model* The data sample consisted of 18 months of time-series data on a random sample of 3 million credit card accounts of Bank One. Account profit is defined by net cash flow (NCF) that includes interest income, merchant interchange, operating expenses and credit loss. NCF is an input into NPV calculations.

*Defining the Markov Model for PORTICO Model* As stated earlier, the Markov model requires specifications regarding the following:

- Determination of time set
  - One month was taken as the time period (time set) and 18 months of data was used
  - Projections were made over 36 months
- Defining the states
  - Six behavioural variables and two control variables (price, line) were used to define the states
  - Interval levels for the above variables were also defined to arrive at 14,000 states based on discussions with business stakeholders
- Estimating the transition matrix
  - Some assumptions were made for simplification. For example, an account that is given a credit line increase would behave identically to an account that already has a higher line (at the same levels of behavioural variables).
  - The Markov assumption of memoryless process is satisfied. Readers can refer to the paper for more details.
- A set of actions the decision maker can choose from. Since the bank managed credit line and price changes separately, the algorithms and decisions for price reductions were not combined with line changes. A simplified representation hypothesised by the authors of the book is presented in Table 2.16.
- A set of estimates of the costs and revenues from taking each of the actions. NCF was calculated for each of the 14,000 states.
- Defining the objective function
  - Objective is to select a set of actions for each state that maximises the expected future profits (NPV) over a period of time

**Table 2.16** Portico Model–Example of States

| State | Line | APR | Risk | Payment | Utilisation | Sales Active | Recommended Action |
|---|---|---|---|---|---|---|---|
| 1 | \$10,000–\$12,000 | 10%–15% | Medium | High Revolver | High | Yes | Increase line by \$10,000 |
| 2 | \$18,000–\$20,000 | 10%–15% | Low | Transactor | Low | Yes | Decrease APR by 100 basis points |
| 3 | < 10,000 | 10%–15% | Low | Transactor | Low | No | Increase line by \$5000 |

  - NPV is a function of NCF, transition probability, and other factors. NPV is evaluated at different states and for different actions (line or price change). For a given customer in a given state, the action that maximises NPV is taken as the recommended action. The exact mathematical expression is given in the paper.
  - Optimisation techniques and dynamic programming are used
- Incorporating constraints
  - Tolerance on credit loss
  - Business rules such as not giving line increase to risky customers based on behaviour score value

*Implementation of PORTICO Model* The team at Bank One built up a convincing case for launching the PORTICO model by evaluating the recommendations of the new model against current business as usual (BAU) policy.

- Forecast of a 12.5% improvement in NPV from the PORTICO model
- Monte Carlo simulations to derive the distributions of NPV and balances using PORTICO (to assess volatility)
- Swap set analysis to understand the impact of the different strategies on number of accounts qualified for line increase, quantum of line increase, revenue, and risk. The analysis showed that for accounts fulfilling the criteria of both PORTICO and BAU, the new model recommends an average $ 3500 line increase, a 27% increase over BAU line increase of $2750.
- Test and control
  - Test using PORTICO was launched on 200,000 existing accounts. Several rounds of testing were conducted with learnings from earlier tests fed as inputs into the designs of latter tests. These tests included decisions on credit lines increases, price reductions, both actions and no action.
  - A similar profile of accounts as test sample were put through the BAU price and line strategy that acted as the control

*Strategy Results of PORTICO Model* The implementation of PORTICO model for line increase policies resulted in a 5% increase in 12 month NPV in the test period compared to BAU strategy, with a net impact of a little over $3 per account. Outstanding balances increased over 5% and amount loss ratio increased by 3%. At the time of publication, PORTICO model had already been rolled out to 30% of the cards portfolio at Bank One. The potential was projected to be an incremental $75 million in annual profits over the bank's current methods. Authors conclude that this optimisation-based approach based on Markov Chain model is an important strategic initiative for maximising yield on pricing and credit line programmes.

*Conclusions of PORTICO Model* The example is a real-life industry example of the application of Markov Chain Model for business applications. Markov Chain Model has also been applied in retail for the determination of baseline sales (in the absence of promotions). The assumption of memoryless process is not always the case. In some applications, transition probability matrices are not static (stationary) due to factors such as seasonality and customer behavioural changes over time. With reference to loss forecasting, authors Alexander and Grimshaw develop dynamic delinquency transition matrices for a loan level Markov Chain Model in their published paper titled *Dynamic Delinquency Movement Matrix Loss Forecasting*.

## *2.6.4 Line Increase Programme Priority*

An example of a line increase programme priority is presented in Fig. 2.41. This is based on choices among the different forms of line increase—line increase on the card, and additional lines through upgrade, second card and personal loan. The figure shows recommendations of suitable programmes by customer profiles. As such there is no such guideline and testing should be done to determine the optimal (e.g., profitable) programme by segment.

### 2.6.4.1 Upgrade

One upgrade strategy from "basic" to "premium" status for deposit holders involves identifying potential upgradeable customers. This is done by slicing and dicing the existing premium base. This information is further used to find "look-alike" profiles in the customer pool. Additionally, triggers such as sharp rise in balances for deposit customers or high spend on credit card that indicates premium status are useful. Designing sales and servicing incentives to maintain potential customers at a premium tier is yet another step in this process. Communication strategy as well

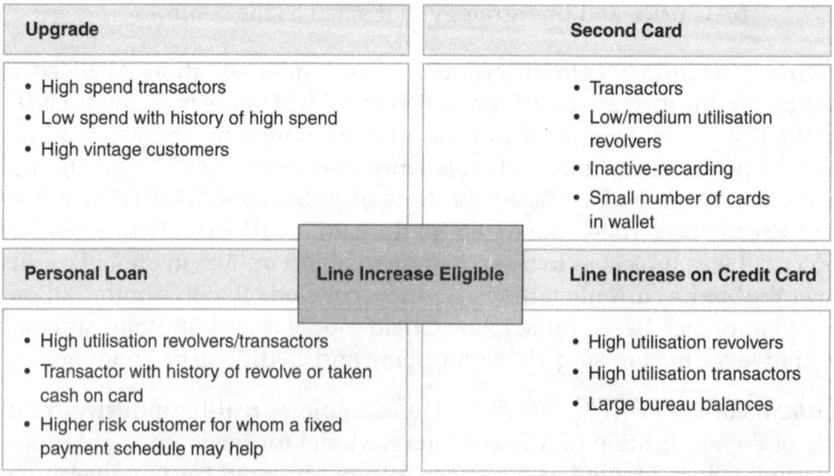


**Figure 2.41** Line Management Priority

as a structured and monitored relationship building process needs to be put in place, with designated relationship managers to support the programme. Retaining customers with an orientation of a superior customer service and its execution is a necessity. An ongoing process for identification of potential premium customers and tracking post-upgrade is also important.

The impact of upgrade (Fig. 2.42) is shown by an example of a regular programme that is normally executed by a credit card issuer. Added benefits of an upgrade may include a higher line of credit, access to airport lounges, better service and improved rewards programme, besides a better plastic in terms of look and feel. The impact can be high and benefits of a line increase of 100% may be far better than the usual lift in balances resulting from an equivalent line increase on the current card. This effect may be attributable to a "feel good" factor of being valued as a customer and the additional privileges that come along with being a premium customer. Upgrade is an effective loyalty and retention strategy for high value customers.

## *2.6.5 Line Management MIS*

As credit line management involves incremental credit exposure for the issuer, it is important to track the returns on these programmes. Variables to track are similar to the ones listed in the balance transfer MIS section (Section 2.5.2.4). An additional metric would be the incremental return to incremental line and credit loss rate. The metrics should be tracked for both test (e.g., line increase) and control (e.g., no line increase) for 3 months prior and 3/6/12 months post-line increase. Line stress testing

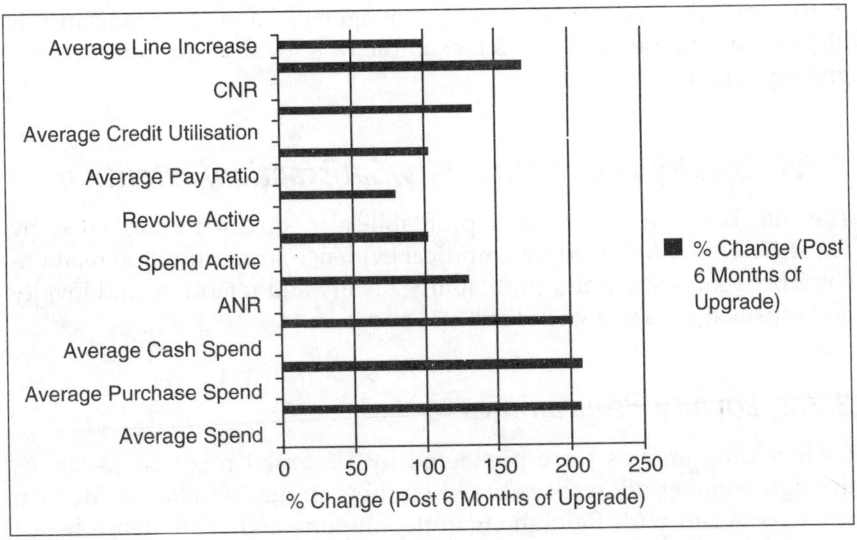


**Figure 2.42** Impact of Upgrade from Basic to Premium Credit Card

at a portfolio level to evaluate the impact on vital portfolio parameters, under different scenarios is also recommended. Tracking should also be carried out by the different forms of line increase (e.g., line increase on card, upgrade, second card) granted, to evaluate the distribution of total/ incremental lines and financial impact.

## 2.7 Loyalty Management

Loyalty management is about building a sustainable and profitable relationship with the customer. This is popularly done using loyalty programmes that encourage repeat purchase and deter switching behaviour. Loyalty programmes have received plenty of attention in the marketing world and billions are spent on such schemes. According to McKinsey, *Loyalty: Is It Really Working for You?*, loyalty programmes can generate as much as 20% of a company's profits. A note worthy example is Tesco, a UK based supermarket and an industry leader in the retail loyalty space. Its market share has risen by 52%, while floor space increased by only 15% since the launch of its loyalty programme ClubCard in 1995 (*Source:* Reinartz, 2010). The section outlines is as follows. The definition of loyalty for the reader's benefit—theoretical as well as its measures are highlighted in Table 2.17. Further, the link between loyalty and profitability, loyalty and retention, and loyalty and satisfaction is elaborated. This is followed by a description of loyalty programmes. Whether loyalty programmes work is a debated issue and exemplars across different industries are presented along with empirical evidence from academic literature. Rewards, the incentive for becoming and remaining loyal, is covered briefly. Customer segmentation is one of the analytical pillars for loyalty management and its importance is highlighted, followed by a P&L example of a loyalty programme for a grocery retailer.

### *2.7.1 Loyalty and Profitability/Satisfaction/Retention*

The link between loyalty and profitability in theory is illustrated by Fig. 2.43. This is followed by empirical evidence supporting the relationships between loyalty and profitability, loyalty and retention, and loyalty and satisfaction as shown in Figs. 2.44 and 2.45.

### *2.7.2 Loyalty Programmes*

Loyalty programmes were pioneered by US-based retail cooperatives through member allowances based on their annual purchases. Modern versions began with Raleigh cigarette coupons and with stamp-based programmes such as the S&H Green Stamp Company that offered

**Table 2.17** Loyalty Definition

| Author | Theoretical Definition | Type | Measure | Comments |
|---|---|---|---|---|
| Reichheld | – | Attitudinal | Net Promoter Score (NPS) based on a single question "How likely is it that you would recommend us to a friend or colleague" | NPS is defined as the percentage of respondents answering 9 to 10 on a 10 point willingness-to-recommend scale, minus the percentage of respondents answering 0 to 6. The best companies get scores between 75% to 80%. Belief is that NPS correlates with revenue growth relative to competitors. GE and Wall Street Journal are some of the big proponents of this score. |
| McGoldrick and Andre (1997) | Various notions of affection, fidelity or commitment. Overall attachment to a product, service or organisation | Attitudinal | Satisfaction | Satisfaction affects buying intentions in a positive way. Strong correlation between satisfaction and loyalty is not found in reality as many customers still defect despite being satisfied. |
| Aasael (1992) | Commitment to a brand rather than just repetitive behaviour | Cognitive/ behavioural | Repeat purchase accompanied by a favourable attitude | Behavioural measures are insufficient as measures of store or brand loyalty. |
| Dick and Basu (1994) | – | Attitudinal/ behavioural | Relative attitude/ patronage/ manifestation | Segments: No loyalty/spurious loyalty/latent loyalty/sustainable. Sustainable loyalty is defined as high relative attitude with high repeat purchase (patronage). |

(*Continued*)

**Table 2.17** Loyalty Definition (*Continued*)

| Author | Theoretical Definition | Type | Measure | Comments |
|---|---|---|---|---|
| O'Brien and Jones (1995) | – | Behavioural | High repeat purchase because of strong preference. Customer modifies behaviour to remain loyal over time. | Sustainable loyalty |
| Zeithaml et al. (1996) | Intention to perform a diverse set of behaviours that signal a motivation to maintain a relationship with the focal firm | Behavioural | Includes allocating a higher share of the category wallet to the specific service provider, engaging in positive word of mouth, and repeat purchase | – |
| Dowling and Uncles (1997) | Polygamous loyalty–customers likely to have preferences for multiple (2–3) brands | Behavioural | Multiple membership in loyalty schemes | Practical definition as 100% loyalty is hard to achieve. Only about 10% of buyers for many frequently purchased consumer goods are 100% loyal over a one year period. |
| Generally Accepted Industry Definition | – | Behavioural | Tenure with product/ service provider | Higher tenure (duration) implies higher loyalty |

consumers points based on purchases (redeemable for a broad section of merchandise). The contemporary version of customer loyalty programmes originated in the 1980s with the introduction of frequent flier programmes by airlines. In 1981, American Airlines introduced the first frequent flier loyalty programme AAdvantage, which was designed to reward customers by utilising the airlines' excess capacity. This was the outcome of the US Airline Deregulation Act of 1978, after which airlines were struggling to keep their competitive advantage. Recognised as a success story, similar loyalty programmes have been adapted by

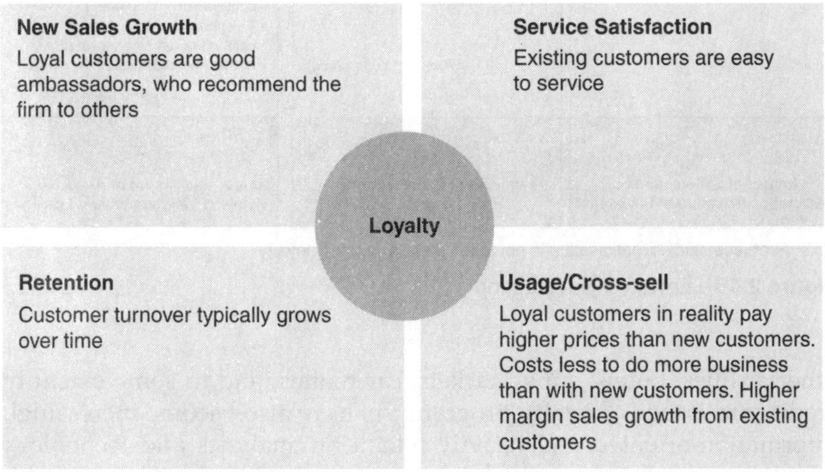


**Figure 2.43** Loyalty and Profitability

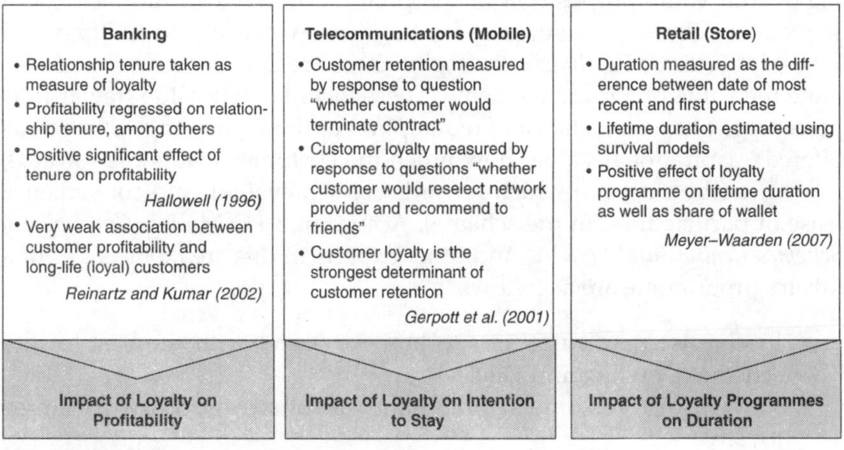


**Figure 2.44** Loyalty—Profitability—Retention

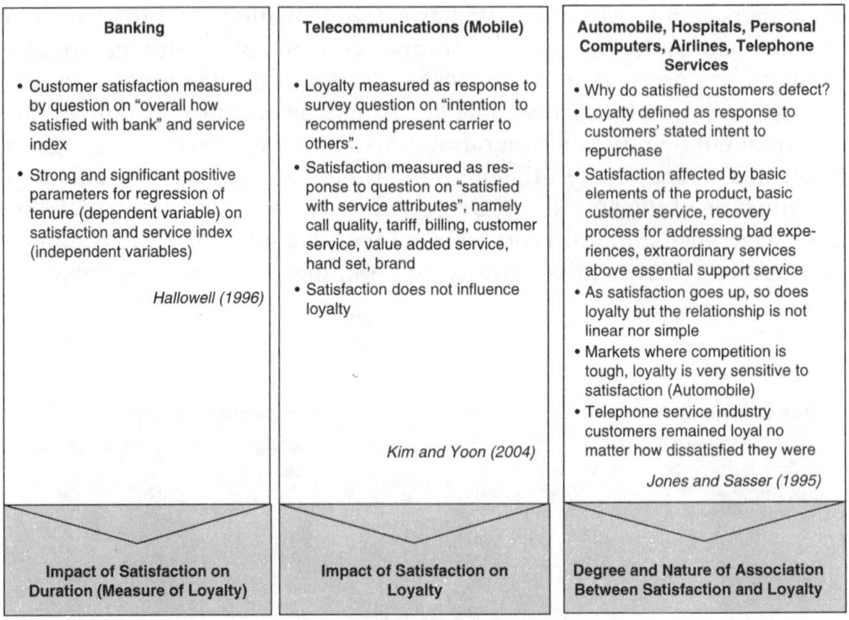


*Note:* For these studies, satisfaction is not taken as a measure of loyalty.

**Figure 2.45** Loyalty—Satisfaction

other airlines, hotels, supermarkets, car rentals, and to some extent by credit card issuers. Loyalty programmes have also become increasingly information-oriented and heavily reliant on analytics and technology. Loyalty programmes can be broadly categorised and are presented in Table 2.18.

According to Dowling and Uncles, *Do Customer Loyalty Programs Really Work*, in competitive times of today, a loyalty programme should enhance the overall value-proposition of the product or service, leading to subsequent purchases and support for the firm. According to O'Brien and Jones, *Do Rewards Really Create Loyalty*, there are five elements that determine the value of a loyalty scheme. These include cash value (rewards as percentage of spend), choice of redemption options (the range of rewards offered), aspirational value (how much the customer wants the reward), relevance (the extent to which rewards are achievable), and convenience (ease of participation in the scheme). According to O'Malley, *Can Loyalty Schemes Really Build Loyalty*, and other experts in this area, objectives of a loyalty programme are as follows:

- Incentivise new customers to buy the brand with the best loyalty scheme (Dowling and Uncles)
- Reward loyal customers by discounts and other rewards, and increase loyalty

**Table 2.18** Types of Loyalty Programmes

| Programme Type | Characteristics of Programme | Examples |
|---|---|---|
| *Type 1:* Members receive extra discount on register | • Membership open to all customers<br>• Clerk will swipe discount card if member forgets or does not have card<br>• Each member receives the same discount regardless of purchase history<br>• Firm has no information base on customer name, demographics, or purchase history<br>• There is no targeted communications directed at members | Supermarket programmes |
| *Type 2:* Members receive "1" free when they purchase "n" units | • Membership open to all customers<br>• Firm does not maintain a customer database | Local car wash, nail salon, SuperCuts, Airport FastPark, PETCO |
| *Type 3:* Members receive rebates or points based on cumulative purchases | • Seeks to get members to spend enough to receive qualifying discount | Airlines, hotels, credit card programmes, Staples, Office Depot |
| *Type 4:* Members receive targeted offers and mailings | • Members are divided into segments based on their purchase history<br>• Requires a comprehensive customer database of customer demographics and purchase history | Tesco, Dorothy Lane Markets, Wakefern's ShopRite, Giant Eagle Supermarkets, Harris Teeter, Winn-Dixie, Harrah's, Hallmark |

*Source:* Berman (2006)

- Influence customers to increase RFM (recency, frequency, monetary value), cross-buy or diversify their basket of goods purchased from the same provider
- Improve per customer value—margin and lifetime duration
- Defensive marketing—combat competition by maintaining wallet share
- Revenue generation from promotional activities, cross-sell, up-sell, and retention using the loyalty database. Shoppers Stop, a retail chain in India, witnessed a 30% jump in sales for a particular category in a three-week period in response to a promotion. The idea behind launching this promotion was based on insights derived from mining their loyalty database[18].

### *2.7.3 Are Loyalty Programmes Effective?*

Despite their rising popularity as a marketing tool, loyalty programmes have been under critical scrutiny. They are often viewed as reactive programmes to competition with a short-term outlook, and with little or no differentiation. Furthermore, the emphasis on short-term results seems to have overshadowed the long-term strategic objectives. O'Malley claims that these programmes are perceived as sophisticated sales promotions and customers have become smart shoppers for rewards, thereby shifting from brand loyalty to scheme loyalty. Dowling and Uncles cast doubt on whether loyalty programmes modify purchase behaviour, and if "heavy spend and users of reward programmes" are simply more loyal. According to O'Malley, a study by Shell in the early 1990s revealed that 85% of petrol buyers were not loyal to any brand or location.

A McKinsey paper authored by Cigliano et al. *The Price of Loyalty* published in 2000, points to some interesting facts relating to the workings of these programmes. *First,* 16 major European retailers had about $1.2 billion tied up in annual discounts to customers and figures were similar for the US. The impact on post-programme enrolment was limited. Survey results showed that only 48% of customers spent more (grocery) and 18% (casual apparel) than what they would ordinarily do. *Second,* a 2% rebate has to translate into a 6% increase in spend for the programme break even on rewards cost alone, while data showed that only 1%–3% was achieved for groceries and 5%–8% increase for department stores in the first year. *Third,* a retailer's rebate of 2% on $500 annual sales translates into a rebate check of $10 a year that does not seem anywhere attractive compared to sales promotions with as much as 50% markdowns. *Fourth,* they claim that as many as 50% of loyalty programme members are "free-riders", enjoying the benefits without spending more at the stores that offers them. Industry exemplars are presented in Table 2.19 and a mixed bag of results in Table 2.20.

[18] *Source:* The Strategist, *Business Standard,* Oct 1, 2012.

**Table 2.19** Loyalty Programmes–Exemplars

| Industry | Company | Programme Name | Feature 1 | Feature 2 | Competing Advantages | Successes | Loyalty Analytics |
|---|---|---|---|---|---|---|---|
| Hotel | Marriott | Marriott Rewards | The programme, which is free lets customers earn points or airline miles for every dollar spent at all of its eleven Marriott brands across 68 countries and other participant hotels. Won multiple awards in 2011 for best loyalty programme. | Members can redeem loyalty points on hotel stays, shopping online, among other items. Can convert points to miles with preferred airline frequent flier programme. Rewards card with Chase with favourable terms (3 points for every dollar spent at Marriott locations). | No blackout dates. Members of its loyalty programme can buy additional points online to earn rewards. Marriott Rewards members can enter their preferences online—foam vs. feather pillows, high floor or low, newspaper choice—and have them communicated to all Marriott brands globally. | Greater than 30 million members belong to Marriott Rewards, with 20% of these members driving 80% of the revenue. Members contribute over 51% of Marriott's total paid lodging room nights. After joining Marriott Rewards, travellers typically double their trip-share to Marriott. | Strong marketing programme backed by data. Using the loyalty database, Marriott can effectively market weekend and leisure stays, recommend new hotels in the portfolio, and suggest business and social events at Marriott properties to their customers. Developed systems to optimise offerings to frequent customers. |
| Airlines | American Airlines | Advantage | Started in 1981, it was the first airline loyalty programme (Frequent Flier) in the world with 230,000 members. Completed 30 years in 2011 with greater than 69MM members as of mid 2012. | Miles are earned on travel on eligible flights of any Oneworld alliance airline. Miles can also be earned through non-travel-related partners including assorted financial and retail partners (more than 1,000 participating companies). | Partnership with Citibank–AAdvatange credit card that allows a card customer to earn 1 Advantage mile for every $1 spent on purchases. Attractive promotional offers such as "Earn 25,000 American Airlines AAdvantage bonus miles after $750 in purchases within the first 4 months". | The first frequent flyer programme revolutionised air travel by creating loyalty towards an airline. Leverages loyalty database to create new revenue streams by monetising programme partnership (third-party offers). | Loyalty analytics supported by internally developed data warehouse. This allows them to store huge amounts of customer and loyalty member data over 13 months and conduct in-depth analysis of their customers and loyalty programme enrolees. |

*(Continued)*

**Table 2.19** Loyalty Programmes–Exemplars (*Continued*)

| Industry | Company | Programme Name | Feature 1 | Feature 2 | Competing Advantages | Successes | Loyalty Analytics |
|---|---|---|---|---|---|---|---|
| Gaming | Harrah's | Total Rewards | Introduced in 2000, it is the casino industry's first national, multi-brand loyalty effort. Customers earn credits each time they visit. Accumulated credits are traded for rewards, cash, coupons or complimentary services, forming the basis of customer loyalty status–gold, platinum or diamond. Associated services and privileges become increasingly valuable with each new level. | Harrah's can track who plays what games, where, when and how often through its total rewards card offers and rewards are most appealing to them. The company can offer special deals aimed at generating repeat business such as free hotel rooms to its biggest spenders and a graduated level of perks such as free movie passes, to its low-rollers. | Tracks non-gaming spending to better attract customers who don't view themselves as big gamblers. More than 18% of Harrah's revenue comes from other sources, including hotel rooms, food, drinks and entertainment. Intent is to further increase its share of non-gambling revenue by learning all it can about how people spend their money, whether they gamble or not. | About 40 million plus members in loyalty programme. Generated 80% of its gambling revenue. Increased share of gambling wallet from 36% to 42%. Generated an additional $165 million per year from top-tier guests. Occupancy rate exceeds 90%, significantly higher than industry average. | Heralded as industry's gold standard in CRM. According to CEO Loveman, "Decision-science based analytic tools allow us to better understand our customers so that we can offer them the best reasons to visit and play at our properties." |
| Financial Services | American Express | Membership Rewards | Every dollar spent earns one membership reward point. No expiry of points while the account | Points can be redeemed for a wide range of gift cards, hotel accommodation, merchandise and | Programme can be customised to individual goals. Straight forward redemption and speedy rewards delivery. Members can redeem | The American Express® Membership Rewards programme was recognised as a | Promoted by industry findings that loyalty programme members spend significantly more compared |

(*Continued*)

**Table 2.19** Loyalty Programmes–Exemplars (*Continued*)

| Industry | Company | Programme Name | Feature 1 | Feature 2 | Competing Advantages | Successes | Loyalty Analytics |
|---|---|---|---|---|---|---|---|
| | | | remains current. Bonus points at select locations. | travel rewards. More than 140 redemption partners and 2 million brand name products. Can also transfer points to other loyalty programmes. | location based deals by swiping their AmEx card. Facebook ads can be purchased with membership reward points. | 5 star product by the 2007 CANNEX Rewards Star Ratings, the first national comparison of rewards programmes. | to non-enrolees post enrolment (comparison of similar profiles). |
| Retail | Nectar | Nectar Scheme | A coalition loyalty scheme in the UK, launched in 2002 with leading UK retail partners such as Sainsbury's and BP. Currently, it has greater than 15 retail partners and 500 online retailers on nectar.com. | Points are accumulated based on purchase value, with point scheme differing across partners. The nectar points are redeemed for free flights, meals, vouchers and others. The high spenders are attracted by rewards like "Flights to Australia" and the low spenders are attracted by rewards like "Free Video Rentals." | The operating costs are low due to shared costs divided between the partners. Allows customer to aggregate points into one single loyalty scheme—quicker route to redeeming a high value award and easier to manage. | Founder of the programme claims that significant growth and market share was observed by partners post launch. Hugely popular, it had 40% of UK households enrolled in the programme in only 2 months after the launch. In 2010, Nectar claimed that it had overtaken Tesco Club card with a total of 16.8 MM members to become UK's most popular loyalty card. | Partners can avail themselves of a much richer data bank of their customers, analysing their purchases across different partners for product offering and targeting. |

*Source:* World Wide Web

**Table 2.20** Impact of Loyalty Programmes

| Author | Industry | Type of Data | Impact of Loyalty Programme |
|---|---|---|---|
| Sharp and Sharp (1997) | Grocery retailing | Survey-panel | Little or no impact on market share, repeat purchase rates, and purchase frequency |
| Benavent and Meyer–Waarden (2000) | Grocery retailing | Scanner | 5% increase in turnover, 3.5% increase in traffic, no impact on purchase volume and value |
| Reinartz (1999) | Charge card mail-order firm | Internal database on customer | No impact on lifetime duration |
| Meyer–Waarden (2006) | Grocery retailing | Panel and POS | Little impact on market share, repeat purchase rates, average and total value of basket, purchase frequency, inter-purchase time. Impact on purchasing behaviour changes is only weak and short-term. |
| Magi (2003) | Grocery retailing | Survey panel | Mixed support for impact of loyalty cards on customer behaviour (share of purchase and share of visits) |
| Lewis (2004) | Online grocery retailing | Online purchase data | Positive impact of rewards on repeat purchase rate, mean annual order per customer and average customer revenue |
| Meyer–Waarden (2007) | Grocery retailing | Panel data | Slight positive effect on lifetime and share of purchase. Multiple card memberships reduces lifetime. |
| Chin (2002) | Airlines | Singapore airlines data (Krisflyer programme) | Membership does have significant positive impact on probability of choosing Singapore airlines and positive impact on market share |
| Whyte (2004) | Airlines | Quantas frequent flier members-survey questionnaire | Only 7% of respondents were highly committed while 45% were quite committed. 23% were not very committed and 6% were not at all committed. Remaining 19% did not share their preference. |

*Source:* Adapted from *Journal of Retailing*, Volume 83, Issue Number 2, Meyer–Waarden, "The effects of loyalty programs on customer lifetime duration and share of wallet", Pages 223–236, Copyright (2007), with permission from Elsevier.

## 2.7.4 Rewards

Rewards are the core of a loyalty programme and there are many types of reward schemes, and some of the familiar ones will be described in this section[19]. *Cash rebate* awards a gift certificate redeemable for the next purchase, when the customer reaches a certain spending level. When there is a wide selection of products, this reward programme can be used to motivate new incremental purchases and increase store traffic. Department stores use cash rebates to build additional sales from existing customers. For financial services, it takes the form of a cash-back offer for credit card that was discussed in section 2.4.1.1. *Reward points* programmes award *points* for purchases that can be exchanged for gifts and perks that may be unrelated to the brand. Points are "earned" according to the amount of business customers do with the firm. A tier structure for points can be used to reward members who increase their purchases over a predetermined level or reward members, who are heavy users of a firm's products or services. Airline and hotel loyalty schemes follow a tier reward system.

A reward points programme, whereby the points have wider usage has more appeal to customers. Recently, aggregators have started creating reward currencies across multiple companies, wherein several companies are enrolled and customer accumulates points based on spends across participating members (e.g., Nectar Scheme, UK). These reward points could be used at a wide variety of online and brick and mortar stores. Many banks with multiple products have introduced a single reward currency across multiple products. For example, a customer could earn points through purchases using a credit or debit card or by maintaining a certain threshold balance in their deposit account. Partnership through alliances allows points accrual with spends with their partners, and rewards a member's accumulated purchases with a partner's products or services. Airlines use this frequently when they give points for renting cars and hotel stays. Redemption options are also plenty, for example, American Express card users can use points for gifts, travel or transfer to an airline frequent flyer programme. *Upgrade* programmes offer special communications, value-added benefits and bonuses, and recognition as a valued customer. Examples are airline frequent flyer premium status and high net worth customers in the financial services sector. An example of an upgrade program for credit card was discussed in section 2.6.4.1.

The basic concepts of rewards are defined as follows:

- **Rewards currency:** The form of rewards issued by the programme operator to the loyalty programme member, who uses them to exchange for awards, e.g., reward points for airlines frequent flier programme members

---

[19] For more information on reward structures, the book *Database Marketing* by Blattberg et al. is recommended.

- **Currency validity:** Evergreen points that never expire or expire after a certain time frame (e.g., 18 months). Usually, validity is conditional on meeting a preset criterion such as redemption activity or purchase
- **Earn rate (velocity):** The rate at which customer earns points, e.g., 5 reward points per dollar spent on a rewards credit card
- **Burn rate:** The price in points for an award, e.g., 50,000 frequent flyer miles for a domestic flight round trip
- **Exchange rate:** The rate at which customers are able to trade the currency with other reward currencies. Hilton Honors programme allows customers to redeem 55,000 points for a 3-day pass at Disneyland worth $100, an implied exchange rate of 550 points per dollar
- **Breakage rate:** The percentage of points issued but not redeemed
- **Liability for unredeemed points:** The allowance for the risk that unredeemed points will be redeemed at some point. This liability that may run into millions and higher, must be shown on the balance sheet as a cost, and is often scrutinised by tax authorities
- **Redemption rate:** The rate at which customers redeem or exchange their points for rewards. The redemption rate should strike a chord between being too low (failing to engage) or too high (too expensive)

From a customer's perspective, the value of rewards to a customer has evolved over time, and so have their expectations. The concept of "implicit value" defined as the returns on every dollar spent is brought out in Fig. 2.46. This is in response to the claim that the loyalty market

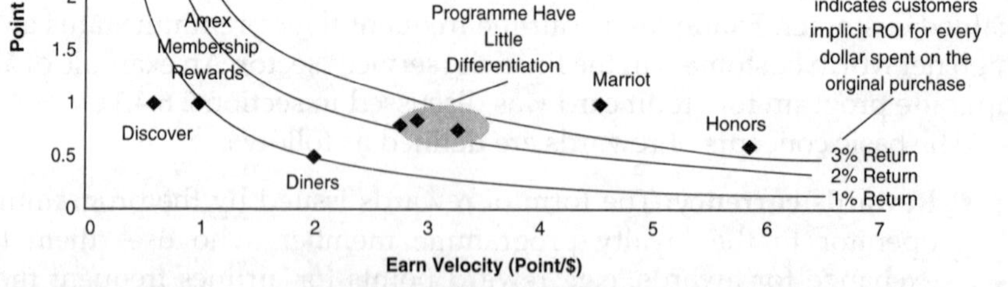


*Note:* Earn velocity assumes $5,000 annual direct spend and $10,000 annual credit card spend; point value shown for burning directly into company product or for highest-returning reward.

*Source:* Oliver Wyman, *The New Economics of Loyalty Programs*, "Copyright Oliver Wyman: used with permission".

**Figure 2.46** Rewards Comparison

in its current state has become a market with many currencies, each with different perceived values and exchange rates.

## *2.7.5 Loyalty Segmentation*

Segmentation is a way forward for understanding the loyal customer and taking the required marketing actions, by flexing the offer and offer value by type of customer. The aim is to take actions that continually build customer loyalty and yield visible benefits for costs incurred. A conviction of loyalty experts is that rewards must be linked to expected consumer behaviour. This is based on the effective use of information generated from the programme. In this regard, the development and maintenance of a loyalty customer database is a key input for loyalty segmentation. This database should integrate profiles of its members, which includes purchase data from each channel and partner, demographics and lifestyle/preferences. With reference to the airline industry, Dolnicar et al. *Key Drivers of Airline Loyalty,* find that the drivers of behavioural loyalty are not the same across different market segments. For example, loyalty programmes are influential for the business traveller, while loyalty for leisure travellers is difficult to attribute to a single factor. This inference was based on data collected from a survey of airline passengers. In a similar context, an airline customer segmentation is presented in Fig. 2.47.

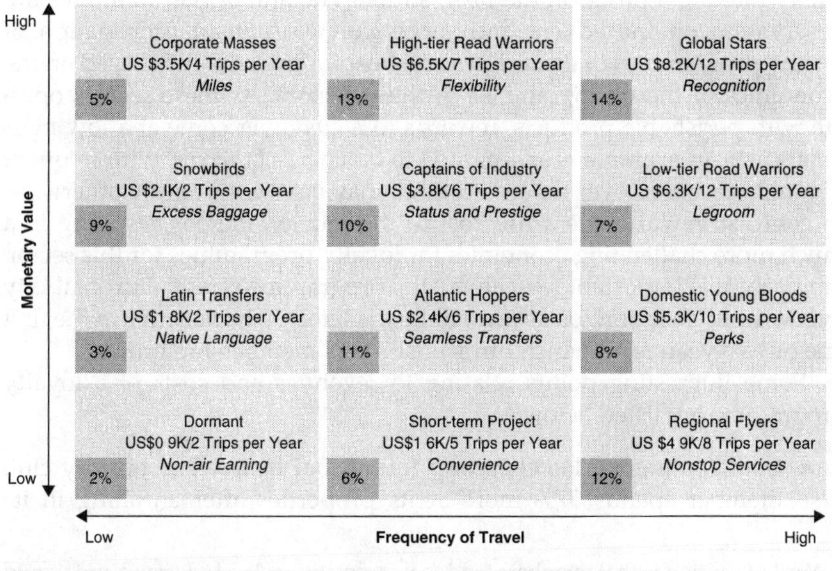


*Note:* Italicized text refers to key driver behind customer satisfaction for each segment.
*Source:* IBM Institute for Business Value, "The Future of CRM in the Airline Industry"
Courtesy of International Business Machines Corporation, © 2002 International Business Machines Corporation.

**Figure 2.47** Airlines Value-based Customer Segmentation

The importance of a rewards design segmentation schema is brought out by Meyer–Waarden and Benavent in their Wall Street Journal (17 Sept 2008) article titled *Rewards that Reward*. They mention five broad categories that are attractive to different preference groups. These are:

1. Economic rewards such as price reductions and purchase vouchers, appealing to customers concerned about their budget
2. Hedonistic and socio-relational rewards such as points that can be exchanged for entertainment—spa services, airport lounges, etc.
3. High on emotional value that customers relating to high society would appreciate
4. Informational rewards expected to attract brand loyal customers such as personalised beauty advice
5. Functional rewards such as access to priority checkout counters or home deliveries of groceries

## 2.7.6 Profitability (P&L) of Loyalty Programmes

Some of the fundamental questions that a loyalty manager needs to address are whether the programme works; is it driving sales; what is the cost of the programme; and its ROI. An example of a P&L[20] of a loyalty programme for a grocery retailer from Reinartz's paper titled, *Understanding Customer Loyalty Programs*, is presented in Table 2.21. For this example, the programme benefits and costs are very close and the supermarket is barely making a profit on the programme. The author has an interesting observation on the advent and successful widespread propagation of loyalty programmes in the airlines and hospitality industries based on the economics of these programmes in these sectors. As these sectors operate with perishable products, rewards to a customer come at a low marginal cost. An example is an upgrade to business class paid with frequent flier miles accrued over time, a seat that may have gone empty otherwise. In contrast, rewards are a full cost to the retailer, thereby resulting in a much more challenging economics for loyalty programmes for this sector. Similarly, it is important to evaluate the programme's annual profitability over a multi-year horizon as profitability is likely to be negative in the first one or two years, and which turns positive as membership grows.

Some interesting points relating to revenues and costs of a loyalty programme are listed below[21]:

- InterContinental Hotels group found that its average priority club member spends 57% more at its properties after enrolling in its

[20] Word of caution is that members tend to be a positive self select group and would expect a higher value (e.g., spend) and lower attrition rate for a member on average compared to a non-member, even in the absence of a loyalty programme.

[21] *Source:* World Wide Web

**Table 2.21** P&L of a Loyalty Programme for a Grocery Retailer

| | | | | |
|---|---|---|---|---|
| **Programme Revenues** | | | | |
| 1 | | Total # of customers | 5,000,000 | |
| 2 | | Yearly spending per non member (€) | 2,000 | |
| 3 | | % Sales increase due to membership | 5 | |
| 4 | | Yearly spending per member (€) | 2,100 | |
| 5 | | % Customers in programme | 50 | |
| 6 | = 5 × 1 | # Customers in programme | 2,500,000 | |
| 7 | = 6 × 4 | Total revenue from members (€) | 5,250,000,000 | |
| 8 | = (4 – 2) × 6 | Additional revenue from members (€) | 250,000,000 | |
| **Programme Cost** | | | | |
| 9 | | Programme reward rate | 2.0% | |
| 10 | = 7 × 9 | Potential outstanding rewards (€) | 105,000,000 | |
| 11 | | % Breakage | 40 | % of assets that never get redeemed |
| 12 | = 10 × (1 – breakage) | Breakage adjusted redemption (€) | 63,000,000 | |
| 13 | | Yearly programme administration cost (€) | 10,000,000 | |
| 14 | = 12 + 13 | Total yearly programme cost (€) | 73,000,000 | |
| 15 | = 14/6 | Yearly programme cost per member (€) | 29 | |
| **Programme Profits** | | | | |
| 16 | | Additional revenue from members (€) | 250,000,000 | |
| 17 | | Variable cost | 70% | Available contribution margin = 30% |
| 18 | = 16 × (1 – variable cost) | Additional contribution margin (€) | 75,000,000 | |
| 19 | = 14 | Total yearly program cost (€) | 73,000,000 | |

[shaded] Fully or partially under management control

*Source:* Reprinted from Reinartz (2006), with permission from Springer.

loyalty programme. Best Buy loyalty members visit its stores twice as often and spend 1.5 times as much as other customers.

- Another interesting number is the breakeven incremental spend (lift), above which the programme must rise in order to pay for itself. Intercontinental Hotel Group break even point is about a 6% increase in spends.
- Airlines receives significant revenue from the sales of miles. It is estimated that all US airlines sell close to $2 billion dollars in miles to over 22,000 businesses.
- It is believed that Shell has spent 20–40 million pounds in developing its Smart Card loyalty programme. Tesco's initial data gathering costs for its loyalty programme ClubCard has been estimated at 10 million pounds.
- The annual costs of maintaining a loyalty programme can range from 1% to 5% of sales.

THREE

# Cross-Sell

## 3.1 Introduction

Cross-sell is a customer management strategy, which involves selling multiple products or services offered by a single provider to a new or existing customer. The objective of cross-selling is to deepen the relationship with the customer in order to maximise customer lifetime value (CLV). For multiproduct industries, cross-selling has become a defining strategy for growth and of major focus in financial services, telecom, retail, hospitality, and T&E sectors. Cross-selling has also become a key initiative in the automobile and computer industry because of the composite nature of the products that characterise these sectors. Moreover, through partner alliances, firms are able to expand their bouquet of offerings and offer a wider choice to their customers; familiar examples being bancassurance for the banking sector and vacation packages in the travel industry.

Up-sell is a strategy which involves selling higher valued products or services to an existing customer. An up-sell offer typically involves selling a higher variant of the current product or service to an existing customer; a platinum membership offer to an existing gold frequent flier airlines customer is a case in point. The very nature of an up-sell strategy suggests that up-sell offers would naturally be made to be the "most valued" customers and hence, the scale of up-sell programmes in most sectors is smaller as compared to cross-sell programmes. It is important to note that in most cases, an up-sell offer to a particular customer is preceded by one or more cross-sell offers and at times the two are used interchangeably. Often used for usage enhancement in the form of product upgrades, up-sell was covered in Chapter 2, "Usage Management".

As a business strategy, cross-selling has transformed rapidly over the last few years, from unstructured selling to a sustainable revenue model with dedicated teams, systematic processes, and investments to support profitable growth. An effective cross-sell strategy requires an integrated view of the customer and a far-sighted customer-centric marketing approach. Hence, the focus has shifted to life cycle and lifestage relationship building with the customer in contrast to simply acquiring one. Cross-selling as a strategy has delivered significant results and the financial successes of role models such as Amazon and Wells Fargo, among many is evidence of this fact. However, often considered the "holy grail" of large banks, there is considerable debate on whether cross-sell strategies have been able to live up to their expectations of delivering quantum jumps to performance and shareholder wealth.

Cross-selling has also evolved with the changing face of industry. Globalisation and competition have resulted in a plethora of choices for the consumer. Therefore, product variety, customization, and differentiated service have become organization level priorities for holding on to a customer in a commoditised market. Traditionally, firms have relied on new customer momentum to grow market share. However, new customer acquisition has become a challenge due to competition and rising per unit acquisition costs. Hence, firms are under pressure to extract the maximum value from their existing customers to retain wallet share and enhance profitability. Industries are also experiencing rapid consolidation[1] globally and are selling each other's products, acknowledging the fact that cross-selling is one of the objectives and outcomes of such merger activity.

With a changing demographic landscape[2] the need for diversification and resulting cross-selling continues to be strong across the globe. In the case of financial services, while the younger generation lead the growth for consumer finance, the ageing look for dependable returns in the form of insurance, retirement, and pension products; private wealth services are the need of the hour for the rich, and small business services for the growing enterprise segment.

The success of a cross-sell programme depends on key enablers such as organisational commitment, well-defined business strategy, effective execution, and regular monitoring. A sound targeting strategy is the core of a cross-sell programme and a pre-requisite for maximising returns

[1] Year-to-date global deal volume as of June 2014 surged to $1.75 trillion, up 75 percent from the year-ago period, according to Thomson Reuters data. That has been the highest level since 2007 when deal volume reached $2.28 trillion.

Source: http://www.reuters.com/article/2014/06/30/us-deals-m-a-idUSKBN0F50A920140630

[2] According to the U.N. World Population Ageing Report (2013), the world is ageing with median age expected to rise from 29 years in 2010 to to 36 years in 2050. The global share of older people at and above age 60 years was 11.7 per cent in 2013 and is expected to reach 21.1 per cent by 2050. Japan, Germany and Italy are the countries with the highest median ages in the world.

on such programmes. The questions to address for a cross-sell targeting strategy are *what* product and to *whom*, *when*, and *how*. Quantitative techniques based cross-sell models to address the four prong targeting strategy of "the right product to the right customer at the right time using the right communication channel" provide indispensable analytic tools for the cross-sell manager. Moreover, infrastructure and technology play a pivotal role in delivering the value of cross-sell analytics to the firm and the customer.

Given that cross-selling is a core business strategy in multiproduct financial services and telecom, the chapter is biased towards these particular sectors. The chapter begins with industry exemplars and a discussion on types of cross-sell offerings–bundling and sequential with several examples. Subsequently, benefits and limitations of cross-selling are highlighted. The next topic is the cross-sell process, with attention given to identifying opportunities and programme implementation. Lastly, cross-sell models for multiproduct marketing, also called next-product-to-buy models (NPTB) are comprehensively reviewed with detailed examples.

## 3.2 Industry Exemplars

To exploit the benefits of diversification, firms across sectors have been expanding into non-conventional areas. For example, retailers like Wal-Mart have expanded into non-traditional areas like financial services, to serve the customer entering their store. To increase customer visits, Wal-Mart has also entered into a relatively low margin food retailing business. This move was a response to the observation that people visit grocery stores more often than a general merchandise store. Professional service firms have become diversified conglomerates, offering "end-to-end" solutions ranging from consulting, technology, outsourcing, alliances, and venture capital. For the big four accountancy firms, consulting revenue continues to grow and generates as much as 33 percent of global revenue[3].

Retailers like Sears and J.C. Penny of the US have been promoting cross-buying through store layout, product packaging, shelving, in-store promotions, and store cards to encourage repeat visits and loyalty. Best Buy's customer centric approach involved moving technology, DVD, software, and wireless communication to the front of the store, after discovering that a significant proportion of their customers were leaving dissatisfied. Table 3.1 focuses on some of the successful industry champions of cross-selling and their business, marketing, and analytical blueprints.

[3] *The Economist*, "Strategic Moves", 9 November 2013

**Table 3.1** Cross-Sell Industry Exemplars

| Industry | Company | Key Success | Business Strategy | Marketing Strategy | Analytical Strategy | Success Metrics |
|---|---|---|---|---|---|---|
| Retail | Amazon | Cross-sell is the core strategy behind the phenomenal success and growth of the world's largest E-retailer. "Earth's biggest selection" is Amazon's click to fame with books, music, video, consumer electronics, jewellery, clothing, and others. | Long-term strength for Amazon lies in its customer centricity and its ability to recognise individuals one-on-one and effectively cross-sell them products across categories, based on targeted recommendations. Diversification leading to a broad range of multiple products, coupled with undercutting and competitive pricing strategy are the major factors behind cross-sell success. Virtual shopping mall for partner sellers (zShops) promotes cross-sell of Amazon products. | Personalisation based on analytics, followed by one-to-one marketing. Strategy of product and price bundling strategy, along with free shipping offers to increase order size and value. | Dynamic pattern recognition based on expanded view of customer purchases and historical behaviour, by pioneering the use of "collaborative" filtering. This system recommends items deemed to be similar to the items that the "user or a similar like minded consumer" liked in the past. Has the advantage of easily including brand new items in the recommendation. | Sales tripled in 6 years from $3 billion in 1989 to $8.5 billion in 2005. Sales of third-party items increased from 6% of all items sold in 2000 to 28% in 2005. Amazon's own retail revenues went up three-fold during the same period. Overall poised for revenues of $100 billion in 2015, according to industry experts. |

(*Continued*)

**Table 3.1** Cross-Sell Industry Exemplars (*Continued*)

| Industry | Company | Key Success | Business Strategy | Marketing Strategy | Analytical Strategy | Success Metrics |
|---|---|---|---|---|---|---|
| | Tesco | Segmentation based cross-sell and diversification has helped Tesco reach top supermarket status in UK, competing against strong competitors like Sainsbury's and Asda. | Diversification across food and non-foods (entertainment, health and beauty, household, clothing, finance, travel and telecom). Strong loyalty programme (Clubcard), one of the most popular in UK. | Branding customised to appeal to different lifestyle segments through private label brands. Lifestyle segments of finer foods, healthy, traditional, mainstream, convenience, and price-sensitive. | Targeting based on differentiated profiles, using segmentation and effective data usage of loyalty programme, demographics, and lifestyle attributes. | Added 10% market share in 5 years (1992–2003) to beat Sainsbury's and Asda, achieving a market share of 27%. |
| | Best Buy | Market leader in consumer electronics in the US, regarded for their customer centric operating model for stores. | Move from a product centric to customer centric approach in 2004. Store layout optimised to encourage cross-sell, after finding that 17% of store space contributed to 67% of revenues. Introduced store "within" a store concept (home entertainment store inside its super-centres). | Shift to a more balanced offering based on product diversification, segment need, and preferences. Cross-sell efforts further enhanced through focus on service. Transaction centres for customers to review service plans, delivery information etc. for complex purchases. | Optimisation of store layout and product bundling based on purchase adjacencies and affinities. Analytical based analysis led to 8 customer segments. | In the year after the makeover, the Best Buy stores that had been converted to the customer-centric model reported same-store sales growth in excess of 9%—more than double that of stores that had not been overhauled based on segmentation and optimisation. |

(*Continued*)

**Table 3.1** Cross-Sell Industry Exemplars (*Continued*)

| Industry | Company | Key Success | Business Strategy | Marketing Strategy | Analytical Strategy | Success Metrics |
|---|---|---|---|---|---|---|
| | Kmart-Sears | Sears merged with Kmart in 2004, threatened by competition from giants such as Wal-Mart and Target. | Expected impact of merger was a stronger brand, greater operational efficiency, and higher returns. Achieved 3rd largest retailer status after Wal-Mart and Home Depot in early 2005. The merger was beneficial for both retailers. The complementary strengths in products created a better retail experience. In addition, Kmart and Sears were both able to save millions of dollars, by streamlining their purchases and offering products to the same customers. | Sears had a reputation for excellent service, while Kmart had a reputation for good prices. Without more products, Kmart faced tough competition from similar stores such as Wal-Mart. Sears also struggled to maintain a steady amount of customers from their mall-based locations. The merger between the two companies was successful because it complemented the strengths and weaknesses of the two companies. | Sears store card is managed by Citigroup, an organisation that has invested heavily in analytics across the globe (Decision Management). | About one-third of financial gains came from cross-sell of each others products. |

(*Continued*)

**Table 3.1** Cross-Sell Industry Exemplars (*Continued*)

| Industry | Company | Key Success | Business Strategy | Marketing Strategy | Analytical Strategy | Success Metrics |
|---|---|---|---|---|---|---|
| Hospitality | Marriott | One of the world's largest hotel chain, Marriott has been very successful at cross-sell, faciliated by investment in Customer Relationship Management (CRM) systems. | Cross-sell backed by a strong loyalty programme. Company measures and monitors income stream on how much a guest spends over multiple stays, time across hotels, resorts and conference centres. | Personalised services by "knowing your customer". Classic example is customer's favourite breakfast. When a customer makes a reservation for one of Marriott's select resorts, the company starts building an itinerary based on customer's requests and preferences. Under the Personal Planning Service programme, personal vacation activities are organised in advance of arrival. | Customer information available for cross-sell at all touch points by sales force automation tools. Advanced systems to help optimise offers to frequent customers. Regular tracking and management of ROI. | Financial benefits achieved soon after implementing CRM systems. Non-room income and cross-chain income generated by cross-selling efforts accounts for a considerable proportion of hotel revenues. Customers participating in Personal Planning Service are found to spend $100 more per day on average beyond the room rate. |
| Financial services | Wells Fargo | One of the largest banks in the US with strong presence in small business lending. Cross-sell is a core strategy for revenue growth. One of the highest cross-sell ratios in industry at 6.16 products per household as of Nov 2013. | Cross-sell is the culture at Wells Fargo. Cross-sell capability built over several years and proven over time. Long-term target of 8 products per household coined as "Gr8". One of every four of its retail banking households has eight or more of its products. | Successful bundling strategy—Wells Fargo Packages comprise of checking account and at least 3 other products-debit card, credit card, savings account or home equity loan. Pioneers in online banking. | Data driven strategies with extensive efforts on increasing the number of products per household. Strong analytics support with excellent tracking and monitoring at business line level. | Almost 80% of new checking account customers purchase Wells Fargo packages. Cross-sell and retention has generated more fee income relative to peers. Significantly higher operating margins. |

*Source:* World Wide Web

## 3.3 Types of Cross-Sell Offering

Sequential cross-sell involves selling different products or services at various points of customer's tenure with the firm. Bundling is the sale of products or services together as a combined offering. It is important to highlight that companies focussed on cross-selling set revenue targets and profitability per dollar disbursed, for both these types of cross-sell offerings. Readers may recall that bundling as a strategy to promote usage was emphasised in Chapter 2, "Usage Management".

### *3.3.1 Sequential Cross-Sell*

In financial services and high-technology industries, customers often purchase multiple products and services from the same provider. Cross-buying takes place consecutively over a period of time in a sequential manner. Life cycle and lifestage marketing are good examples of a multi-stage cross-sell strategy. In the case of life cycle marketing, a checking or savings account is typically the first product with which a customer initiates his or her relationship with a bank. This may be followed by a brokerage account and insurance. Similarly in the technology industry, a customer who buys a personal computer, may also subsequently purchase additional accessories and software from a particular company. So is the case in the telecom industry, as customers of a fixed line or mobile service may subscribe to value-added services and data services from the same service provider in the future. Lifestage marketing is popularly practiced in financial services and insurance sectors. An example of life-stage marketing by age is a personal loan followed by a home loan, and subsequently insurance and retirement products. The behavioural predictability regarding the pattern of cross-buying can be further analysed to determine "the right product to the right customer at the right time". This is done using rich historical data and quantitative models that will be discussed in Section 3.6.

The benefits of sequential offering are multi-fold. Sequential cross-sell creates value both for the firm and customer through relationship building in a systematic, step-wise, and measurable fashion. Timing is of critical importance in the case of implementing a sequential cross-sell strategy. Research has indicated that the foundation of a successful relationship happens within the first 3 months. Hence, the customer experience at the initial stages of the relationship is of paramount importance for implementing a successful cross-sell strategy. According to a McKinsey report titled *Back to the Future: Rediscovering Relationship Banking*, more than 70% of total cross-sales for a bank happens in the first 180 days of account opening and has an important bearing on customer retention as well.

Sequential relationship marketing has some challenges. Aggressive marketing in the form of push mails can lead to customer response fatigue rather quickly. Life cycle and lifestage marketing strategies require synchronisation that may not be practically feasible, given the different product/business stakeholders participating in cross-sell initiatives. The determination of the next best offer to cross-sell, target audience, timing, and contact channel strategy, is a heavy resource-intensive exercise, both from a marketing and analytical perspective, and may not always give the desired outcomes in terms of cross-sell objectives.

### 3.3.2 Bundling

Manufacturers, retailers, and service firms often use bundling strategies to differentiate products and services from competition and enhance market position. For this topic, work done by Stremersch and Tellis from their paper titled *Strategic Bundling of Products and Prices: A New Synthesis for Marketing* is referenced. Bundling terms are outlined in Table 3.2. The authors define products as "separate" if separate markets exist for each of the products, thereby giving consumers the choice to buy products with or without a bundle.

In product bundling, the integration of more than one product (the bundle) provides additional value such as compactness (integrated stereo systems), reduced risk (mutual fund), convenience (telecom packages), and value-added services (extended warranty on consumer durables). Familiar examples of price bundles are large deposits with lower interest home loans,

**Table 3.2** Bundling Terms

| Term | Definition | Examples |
|---|---|---|
| Bundling | Bundling is the sale of two or more separate products in one package | Opera session tickets, Multimedia PC |
| Price bundling | Price bundling is the sale of two or more separate products as a package at a discount, without any integration of the products | Luggage sets, variety pack of cereals |
| Product bundling | Product bundling is the integration and sale of two or more separate products at any price | Multimedia PC, sound system |
| Pure bundling | Pure bundling is a strategy in which a firm sells only the bundle and not (all) the products separately | IBM's bundling of tabulating machines and cards |
| Mixed bundling | Mixed bundling is a strategy in which a firm sells both the bundle and (all) the products separately | Telecom bundles |

*Source:* Reprinted with permission from *Journal of Marketing*, published by American Marketing Association, Stremersch and Tellis, 2002, Volume 66, and Pages 55–72.

six packs of beer, and a combo meal. There is significant research to show that buying behaviour is influenced by features of a bundle such as pure or mixed, functional complementarities, and number of bundle components. Readers can refer to the paper by Herrmann et al. titled *Product and Service Bundling Decisions and Their Effects on Purchase Intention*.

Price bundles provide monetary savings for the consumer. As mentioned earlier, product bundles provide the benefits of value addition of integration, reduction of time and effort to make purchases, etc. Akin to discount sales, price bundling is a short-term strategy used as a pricing and promotional tool. Product bundling on the other hand is more strategic, and is used as a long-term value differentiator.

While the benefits of bundling will be spotlighted in the industry examples of telecom and financial services, the disadvantages of bundling are succinctly discussed. The landmark Microsoft antitrust case of bundling Windows and Explorer exemplifies the possible legal pitfalls of a bundling strategy. While firms may push bundles aggressively as a sales strategy for their low margin products, consumers may get saddled with products or services of low preference. Similarly, the full benefits of a bundle may be passed on to the consumer only if certain usage requirements are met, as in the telecom bundling example of the "Usage Management" chapter.

E-commerce relies heavily on price bundling for its sales strategy. E-retailer Amazon aggressively promotes bundles to boost not only the number of transactions, but also order size. For instance, customers interested in purchasing the movie "Gladiator" may be given the option of purchasing "Spartacus" as well, with a saving of an additional $5 over the single purchase price of both DVDs. Amazon has also pioneered a feature known as "better together", wherein Amazon recommends a book that is similar in subject and price to the one that is browsed. Price bundling is one of the most prevalent marketing practices in hospitality and travel related sectors. Almost all types of firms in these sectors, from suppliers such as hotels and airlines to intermediaries such as travel agents, promote travel "packages" to save money and streamline the purchasing process.

To arrive at an optimal bundle that is expected to satisfy the objectives of a cross-sell strategy, analytics plays a decisive role. Analysis of past buying patterns using analytical techniques such as market basket analysis gives an understanding of customers' preferences regarding which products may be bought together. Further, surveys may prove to be beneficial for understanding segment-level preferences for offer customisation. Online players heavily rely on recommender systems to determine the actual size of the offering and the combination of bundles to offer. An example of using analytics for bundling strategy will be reviewed later in the chapter. Extensive testing of product combinations and pricing is recommended to arrive at optimal bundle offerings by segment.

### 3.3.2.1 Example: Bundling in Telecom

The preceding usage chapter had an example of dual play of fixed line and broadband in the context of usage enhancing programmes. Successful triple-play operators need to look beyond fixed line, broadband, and television to remain competitive. The recent wave of "convergence" in the telecom industry across the globe has led to "quadruple play", the combination of fixed line and mobile, broadband and television. For example, in UK, the merger of NTL and Virgin Mobile has resulted in Virgin Media offering a quadruple play. According to industry experts, the benefits of product bundling in the telecom sector are compelling:

- Offers convenience and price benefits to the customer, like one-stop shopping, flexibility to use any service, and simplicity of one bill
- Lowers advertising, customer acquisition, and other service costs for the company through economies of scale under a single brand. In addition, converged network lowers cost of operations, thereby allowing price benefits to flow through to the customer.
- Protects core business of fixed line that has been on the decline with the mobile boom
- Encourages product stickiness, which in turn has helped companies survive fierce industry competition in the post-consolidation era. Chapter 4, "Retention Management" will have more on this topic in the telecom churn section.

For designing an appropriate bundling strategy, it is necessary to understand consumer preferences. According to a McKinsey survey conducted in Europe, results varied by country, reflecting differences in culture, competition, and market development. The results of the survey, available in the report titled *Bundling Europe's Broadband*, led to five segments—shoppers, basic users, value bundlers, wealthy bundlers, and off-line bundlers. These segments were profiled based on the following dimensions—level of interest in broadband and new services, preference for bundled services, inclination to switch service providers for bundled offerings, and demographics. A similar segmentation schema can apply to retail customers as well—shopaholics, brand conscious, value seekers, and discount seekers.

Bundling strategy is expected to take on a leading role in the growth of the telecom sector. According to an industry market study[4], telecom services revenues on a worldwide basis are expected to grow at a compound rate of 2.1% over the next 5 years, taking global telecom revenues to $2.4 trillion by 2019. Demand for triple play (fixed line, broadband, and television) is expected to play a pivotal role in contributing to telecom growth.

[4] The Insight Research Corporation, "The 2014 Telecommunications Industry Review: An Anthology of Market Facts and Forecasts".

The forecast[5] is that slightly more than 20% of the world's TV households will subscribe to triple-play services by 2018, and China is expected to represent 34% of this total.

### 3.3.2.2 Example: Bundling in Financial Services

For banks, a potential of bundling is the stimulation of demand for additional services by introducing complementary services to the customer. Banks may also use bundling strategies to attract new customers looking for an all-in-one solution for their banking needs. Bundling is also an option for recouping a revenue shortfall, by increasing the number of high margin products in the bundling suite. Among industry exemplars, Wells Fargo has used bundling to build its franchise with cross-selling envisaged as the core of the company's vision and strategy[6]. Sales of Wells Fargo Packages consisting of a checking account and three other products have increased by 16% from 2010, and was purchased by 86% of new checking account customers[7]. Similarly, an ICICI bank bundle consists of a savings, demat and trading account. Moving across geographies, examples of price bundling strategies for the European market based on a survey report by Merja Mankila titled *Application of Price Bundling Strategies in Retail Banking in Europe*[8] are highlighted. The interviews conducted in 2000 were part of the author's doctoral dissertation, which provide insights on the application of price bundling strategies in retail banking. Some of the researcher's interests in carrying out the survey were as follows:

- Does the bank currently practice price bundling? If yes, what do price bundles look like?
- Motivation behind price bundling
- Competitive advantages and challenges
- Factors behind the success of price bundling strategies and the measurement of profitability

Motivation behind a price bundling strategy was found to be different for banks across Southern, Central and Northern Europe, and was mainly driven by image building, customer acquisition, cross-sell, retention;

---

[5] Digital TV Research report titled, "Triple-play revenues to reach $144 billion", 26 Nov 2013

[6] Wells Fargo website.

[7] News Release of 17 January 2012, "Wells Fargo Record Quarterly and Full Year Net Income".

[8] Available at https://gupea.ub.gu.se/handle/2077/2654.

and for migrating customers to use more efficient delivery channels. Measurement of profitability and the success of price bundling strategies varied across banks. Some banks could not measure profitability standalone, and instead inferences were drawn based on aggregate bank level fee, interest revenue, and number of customers; others measured the impact of bundling strategy separately. The results were quite encouraging. One bank reported an increased customer retention rate by 10% and an increased product penetration from 3 to 5 per average customer relationship. Another bank reported an increased market share in a product segment by 3%, and increased customer retention of 30% (over the earlier figures of a pre-bundling strategy). Different approaches to price bundling and various examples are presented in Fig. 3.1 and Table 3.3.

### *3.3.3 Sequential or Bundling*

Taking the example of the financial services sector, sequential cross-sell is practised particularly in cases when

- The products involve risk exposure to the firm and require pacing, for example, a personal loan followed by home loan
- The products are substitutable in nature like credit card and personal loan
- The customer is more risky than the average customer, for example, a sub-prime borrower
- The product offered involves an upgrade
- Lifestage marketing

Similarly bundling is common in cases when

- One of the products is tied to the sale of another product (e.g., credit insurance with a loan)
- One product is a liability and the other an asset to the firm (e.g., checking/savings account with credit card)
- Non-banking and banking product (e.g., life insurance with a savings account)
- A complementary product suite (e.g., equity brokerage account, demat and financial goal planner)
- Cross-sell of services (e.g., SMS banking and inter-bank mobile payment services)

Firms often resort to bundling as a promotional tool for customer acquisition and sequential cross-sell for managing the customer relationship.

**Cost Efficiency Bundling**

- *Day-to-day service bundle:* A current account that includes all basic services (payment services, debit card, cheques, often through several channels) for a certain flat account fee or for reduced individual prices.
- *On-line bundle:* A customer is offered special prices if he or she uses only telephone banking or Internet banking for day-to-day transactions.
- The aim of these bundles is first and foremost to improve efficiency (to reduce servicing and transaction costs). At the same time, the improved customer service may indirectly improve effectiveness (increase revenues) from other banking services.

**Cross-selling Bundling**

- *A bundle of two or more core banking services:* A price bundle based on one primary service (e.g., a current account), in order to increase customer relationships by additional "core" banking services (loans or savings).
- *A bundle of a banking service and a non-banking service:* A price bundle combining a banking product (e.g., a current account), and a non-banking product (e.g., a mobile phone), in order to increase sales of the banking product.
- The aim of these types of prices bundles is to increase sales of certain services.

**Loyalty Bundling**

- *Customer concept:* A price bundle that defines a given type and size of a customer relationship, that in turn affects the total prices paid for the specified services included in the bundle.
- *Loyalty bonus by volume:* A price bundle wherein the customer is given price reductions based on the total customer relationship volume.
- *Loyalty bonus by product:* A price bundle wherein the customer is given price reductions based on the usage of certain products/services (and their respective volumes).
- The aim is to retain the "right" types of customers through price rewards for the "right" behaviour.

*Source:* Mankila (2001).

**Figure 3.1** Price Bundling Strategies—Banking

**Table 3.3** Price Bundling Examples—Banking

| Price Bundle Model | Type | Example-1 | Example-2 |
|---|---|---|---|
| Cost efficiency bundling | Day-to-day service bundle | Savings bundle for customers with low frequency of transactions; five transactions per month with additional transactions charged individually; debit card applicable for all automatic delivery channels | Different account bundles with different service levels; basic bundle includes current account, different transactions; debit card (credit card) and cheques, including all delivery channels; fee charged; upgraded versions include emergency service during travel and premium credit cards at a higher fee |
| | On-line bundle | Internet and telephone bundle applicable for customers who agree to use only Internet or phone platform for transactions; current account, debit card, cheques, medical information and general international travel information are included in this bundle; fee per month | Additionally, personal mortgages and brokerage on-line services at lower rates |
| Cross-selling bundling | Loans/ Savings | Bundle of two debit/credit cards, the second card for 30% less than the normal price; objective is to promote a specific type of debit/ credit card | Mortgage bundle, insurance given free if customer consolidates all competition loans with the bank offering the bundle |
| | Non-banking incentive | Targeted at affluent customers; banking service designed to meet all the personal needs of customers; available only to customers above a certain value in savings and investment with the bank; assigned relationship manager, offered private client services with financial advisory; preferential interest rates on bank account; no annual credit card fee; quarterly magazine; travel services and assistance on tickets for theatres, shows; no account or transaction fee | Bundle combines a current account (plus certain services) with a mobile phone; price of this bundle is about 50% higher than a bundle without a phone; designed for existing as well as new customers, as the idea is that customer will renew the contract due to the phone effect |
| Loyalty bundling | Customer concept | Various price bundles with a set fee for each bundle; current account bundle includes account statement debit card; standing order, automatic and personal phone and Internet banking with a standard fee per month, which can be reduced depending on relationship size | If customer has a current account with regular salary credits, debit card and payment/internet services, a 15% discount on yearly fees for the latter two services; plus an added bonus of additional 175 basis points on interest rate on checking account up to a certain slab |

*Source:* Mankila (2001).

## 3.4 Benefits and Challenges of Cross-Selling

The evolution of an effective business model which brings increasing benefits of cross-selling is brought out best as different stages[9]:

- *Add wallet share*—increase profitability of a customer
- *De-commoditise*—provide value that is highly visible and unique
- *Increase loyalty*—improve customer satisfaction
- *Transform customer perception*—from product vendor to "financial partner"

The industry exemplars emphasised on the business successes of cross-selling in practice. In this section, the benefits and challenges of cross-selling as a strategy will be highlighted by expanding on some of the points of Fig. 3.2. Further examples during the course of the chapter will also explicitly bring out some of these points.

According to Villanueva and Hanssens, *Customer Equity: Measurement, Management and Research Opportunities*, add-on selling (defined as cross-selling, up-selling, and higher quantity of the same product or service) is an important driver for maximising customer equity as it increases CLV of an acquired customer. According to the authors, customer equity (static) is defined as the sum of CLVs of a specific cohort of customers. The impact of cross-buying on CLV in a retail setting is best illustrated by Kumar et al. in their paper titled *Cross-buying in Retailing: Drivers and Consequences.* Figure 3.3 illustrates the factors that affect cross-buy behaviour and the linkages between cross-selling and CLV. Subsequently, the advantages and challenges of cross-selling are presented using a company-wise perspective.

As a market differentiator, the world's largest retailer Wal-Mart diversified into the food business and was followed by financial services. According to American Banker, *Wal-Mart Undeterred*, Wal-Mart Stores Inc. have been offering savings accounts and credit cards in Mexico since 2009. Its Asda subsidiary in UK offers loans and insurance, where rival Tesco already operates a wholly owned banking franchise. Wal-Mart is also experimenting with a "blended retail point-of-sale approach", whereby the entire store is positioned as a branch, and any customer contact is an entry point to meet potential banking needs. Based on a June 2011 *Credit Union Journal* article, the retailer was expected to roll out automated versions of its manned Money Centre offices that provide a gamut of financial services to the shopper—check cashing, bill payment, wire transfer, and other services. These centres are supposed to be one of the most profitable areas in Wal-Mart stores.

According to an Accenture Report, *Banking 2012: Revenue Growth and Innovation*, spreads tend to be lower in developed markets, especially in Europe, and banks rely on an array of strategies and business models.

[9] Ballenger, "Crossing the Balance Sheet", White Paper of 2006. Available at http://www.kendalltodd.com/downloads//crossingbalancesheet.pdf

**Cross-Sell Benefits and Challenges**

**Benefits for Firm**

- Builds customer equity
- Differentiates from competition; enhances market position
- Promotes diversification and innovation
- Stimulates universe expansion and entry into new markets
- Balances growth between new and existing customers, low and high margin products and segments
- Enhances customer profitability
- Discourages customer attrition; improves customer loyalty
- Patronises the brand

**Challenges for Firm**

- May lead to revenue cannibalisation of one product by another
- Over-reliance on cross-sell can be potentially constraining to remain competitive
- May causes high customer level attrition if customer satisfaction levels are low—lose it all
- Increases credit risk from high exposure multiproduct customers in the absence of good credit policies
- Encourages intra-business conflicts regarding product prioritisation and revenue sharing

**Benefits for Customer**

- Broadens choice of products and services from the provider and from competition
- Offers convenience through one-stop shopping, flexibility, consolidated bill, and others
- Increases customer satisfaction
- Lowers price
- Encourages better customer service from relationship marketing

**Challenges for Customer**

- Increases communication fatigue from deluge of offers
- Creates confusion, if offers are not optimised for product suite and price for repeated cross-sell efforts

**Figure 3.2** Benefits and Challenges of Cross-Selling

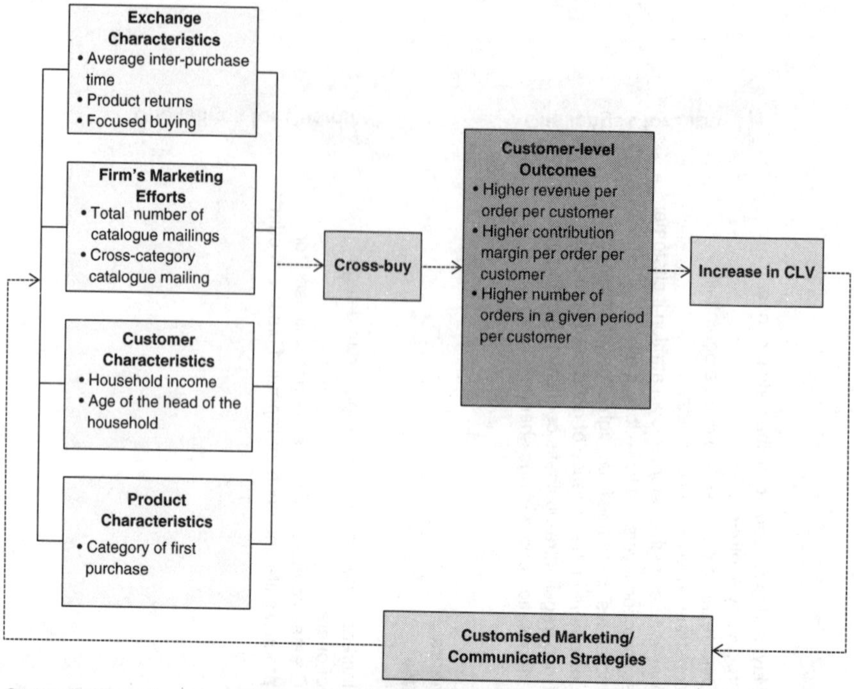


*Source:* Reprinted from *Journal of Retailing*, Volume 84, Issue 1, Kumar et al., "Cross-Buying in Retailing: Drivers and Consequences", Pages 15–27, Copyright (2008), with permission from Elsevier.

**Figure 3.3** A Framework for Analysing the Drivers of Cross-Buy

One of these is a customer-centric model to achieve a higher share of wallet and cross-selling for strong interest and fee income. A quote from the report is "Wells Fargo generated an asset turnover ratio well ahead of its peers through recurring customer revenues". Spanish banking giant Santander, which cross-sells financial products to its huge base of retail customers worldwide, has been aggressive in expanding market share. The bank made its fee-free current account more widely available to its mortgage customers in UK, according to London Evening Standard article of March 2010, *Santander extends Zero Account to Take on Rivals*.

For the aviation industry, the role of ancillary services is expected to play a defining role in abating some of the profitability challenges that the industry has been going through in recent years. Ancillary services include fees added to an "unbundled" air fare (e.g., baggage check-in, seat allocation) and third-party value-added services (e.g., travel insurance, hotel reservations, and car hire). These services can be offered to the airline customer during the booking process. According to a 2011 report by Amadeus and Forrester Research, *Cross-Sell Your Way to Profit*, revenue from third-party ancillary services is forecasted to grow at 30% by 2015.

On successful implementation of a similar cross-sell strategy, the Australian airline Qantas reported a 400% increase in car rental sales revenue, a 100% increase in travel insurance revenue, increased customer satisfaction levels and heighted awareness of the Qantas brand[10].

Customers in effect pay for the cost of several different sales force, when multiproduct firms sell products separately. Bundling is an option to bring all of them together, cut costs, and pass some of the savings onto customers. Examples of product and price bundling were discussed in the earlier section. Small and medium enterprises (SMEs) are increasingly looking at single service providers, who can offer them key services bundled together as per their needs to manage costs. Dell has several bundled technology options for this growing segment. In reference to costs, an empirical study of retail banking customers by Hallowell across 59 divisions shows that account cross-sell and service cross-sell ratios of a bank have a considerable impact on reducing non-interest costs. In the regression model that has non-interest expense as a proportion of revenue as the dependent variable, both cross-sell account and services ratio variables come up as statistically significant factors.

As pointed out in the "Usage Management" chapter, customer satisfaction is an attitudinal measure of customer loyalty while the length of relationship with the firm is a standard behavioural measure. As pointed out by Brian King of Benchmark Consulting, *Consumer Lending Cross-Sell and Product Bundling*, Wells Fargo and Bank of America have seen a significant upside from online banking and online bill payment as a product bundle. It was observed that Wells Fargo and Bank of America customers with online banking are more likely to stay with the bank than other customers. Those who use bill pay services have a significantly lower attrition rate. The telecom bundling results mentioned in the "Retention Management" chapter further impress these findings.

While multiproduct industries such as banking, telecom, retail, and T&E attempt to push their products onto customers, there can be several challenges and limitations to this strategy. In financial services, multi-bank relationships create an upper bound on the extent of cross-selling that can be done in practice. A 2011 PwC customer centricity survey of US consumers revealed that customers have relationships with an average of 3.2 financial institutions. Although customers hold an average of 3.3 products at their primary[11] financial institution, credit cards, insurance, and mortgages are often taken from financial institutions other than the primary one. Moreover, cross-sell programmes are likely to fail if the products and

---

[10] Amadeus Qantas cross-sell case study.

[11] Primary financial institution by the customer is considered as the bank at which the customer has a checking account, according to a PwC report, "Getting to Know You: Building a Customer-Centric Business Model for Retail Banks".

packages being promoted are uncompetitive or do not deliver perceived value to the customer.

Over-reliance on cross-sell can be uncompetitive as observed through an unsuccessful media example. One of the anticipated synergies of the merger of Time Warner and America Online (AOL) was to create a media giant of the future. The expectation was that America Online's Internet subscribers would also enjoy music and publishing information, and use Time Warner's cable operations to deliver data online at superfast speed. The biggest merger in media history came to an end in 2009 as America Online finally separated from Time Warner almost 10 years after they first agreed to merge. The main reason for this debacle is speculated to be the failings by AOL Time Warner management to ever actually integrate the two companies. Another example of a failed attempt at becoming a financial super market, with a clear intention to cross-sell, was the merger of banking giant Citicorp and financial conglomerate Travelers Group. On a similar note, according to Bank of America executives[12], spirit of collaboration and equitable revenue sharing are experiences to learn from, for "cross-selling in practice". This is in reference to the merger of Bank of America with erstwhile Merrill Lynch.

## *3.4.1 Cross-Selling and Profitability: Financial Services*

Cross-selling as a customer management strategy focuses on earning a continuous revenue stream from customers through their life cycle. Reiterating industry exemplars, retailers like Tesco and Best-Buy were able to gear their cross-sell strategy to drive profitability through a segmented approach of their customer base. For financial services, new and current customer is an important segmentation that drives profitability.

### 3.4.1.1 Prospecting vs. Cross-Selling

A specific example of a P&L performa of prospecting compared to cross-selling will be highlighted. Sales for a firm originate from two types of customers: prospects that are converted to new customers and current customers. A new customer acquisition dominated growth strategy has been the most traditional and effective way of growing market share. However, the effectivenss of prospecting has been on a decline, thereby resulting in a rising cost-revenue ratio of acquiring a new customer. Needless to say, new customer acquisition will continue to be critical for baseline growth, while firms balance the gains from new and existing customers.

---

[12] *The Economist*, "Bank of America and Merrill Lynch: Moynihands Full", 15 April 2010.

The factors in favour of cross-selling as a market practice are as follows:

- Higher conversion and approval rates
  - Familiarity and experience with the franchise
  - Availability of behavioural information (internal and external) used for response targeting and credit screening
- Higher profitability
  - *Revenue benefits*. According to a McKinsey cross-sell banking report titled *Back to the Future: Rediscovering Relationship Banking*, customers with two products are disproportionately more valuable in terms of revenue than the combination of two similar customers (each of whom owns one of the products). The relationship multiplier due to higher balances and usage can account up to a 25% increase in revenues (and with retention benefits).
  - *Lower fulfilment costs*. For example, ease of utilising direct marketing channels that are more cost effective than direct sales or relationship managers; the cost of selling to someone already on the books can be as low as one-tenth of attracting a new one.
  - *Risk mitigation*. The McKinsey study reports a 10–25% lower risk from customers that have multiproduct relationships.
- Need for minimal documentation

*Example: Personal Loan to Credit Card Cross-Sell P&L* A simplistic product profitability report or P&L performa for a personal loan portfolio is shown in Tables 3.4 and 3.5. Table 3.4 represents one for a cross-sold personal loan portfolio (of personal loan to a lender's credit card customer) and Table 3.5 is for new customer personal loan portfolio. For definitions of terms used, readers are advised to look up the glossary and the P&L section of Chapter 8, "Analytics Ecosystem". The reported numbers are at "per account" level for a personal loan product.

For a new customer, eligibility for a personal loan offer as per credit policy is based on application and credit bureau information (if available). Documentation required from the prospect is usually proof of income and proof of residence. For this example, new customers are offered a personal loan at an average interest rate of 18%, average loan size of $3000, and average tenor of 18 months.

Cross-sell programmes are usually pre-approved or pre-screened programmes and involve the offer of a personal loan to current credit card customers. Current customers are screened for credit eligibility based on credit card performance (revenue and risk), performance on other products held with the lender, external credit bureau information (if available), and vintage (e.g., 9-12 MOB). Minimal documentation is required from the customer, for example, income proof (if customer requests a higher loan amount than what the lender has to offer). Ticket size and interest rate offered are determined based on current credit exposure—internal

**Table 3.4** Product Profitability: Personal Loan Cross-Sell

| Cross-Sell | | |
|---|---|---|
| | **Year 1** | **Year 2** |
| Number of months | 12 | 6 |
| Average net receivables (ANR) | $2,551 | $677 |
| Interest revenue | $442 | $66 |
| Cost of funds (COF) | $209 | $31 |
| Net interest margin (NIM) | $233 | $35 |
| Fees | $12 | $2 |
| Revenue | $245 | $37 |
| Operating expense | $45 | $7 |
| Operating margin | $200 | $30 |
| Net credit loss (NCL) | $11 | $9 |
| Earnings before interest and tax (EBIT) | $189 | $21 |
| **As % of ANR** | **Year 1** | **Year 2** |
| Interest | 17.34% | 19.45% |
| COF | 8.20% | 9.20% |
| NIM | 9.14% | 10.25% |
| Revenue | 9.61% | 10.77% |
| Operating expense | 1.77% | 1.98% |
| Operating margin | 7.84% | 8.79% |
| Credit loss | 0.42% | 2.57% |
| ROTA | 4.08% | 3.42% |

**Table 3.5** Product Profitability: Personal Loan New Customer

| New Customer | | |
|---|---|---|
| | **Year 1** | **Year 2** |
| Number of months | 12 | 6 |
| Average net receivables (ANR) | $2,073 | $553 |
| Interest revenue | $388 | $58 |
| Cost of funds (COF) | $170 | $25 |
| Net interest margin (NIM ) | $217 | $33 |
| Fees | $10 | $1 |
| Revenue | $227 | $34 |
| Operating expense | $54 | $8 |
| Operating margin | $173 | $26 |
| Net credit loss (NCL) | $12 | $10 |
| Earnings before interest and tax (EBIT) | $161 | $16 |

(*Continued*)

**Table 3.5** Product Profitability: Personal Loan New Customer (*Continued*)

| As % of ANR | Year 1 | Year 2 |
|---|---|---|
| Interest | 18.69% | 20.96% |
| COF | 8.20% | 9.20% |
| NIM | 10.49% | 11.76% |
| Revenue | 10.95% | 12.28% |
| Operating expense | 2.60% | 2.91% |
| Operating margin | 8.36% | 9.37% |
| Credit loss | 0.59% | 3.60% |
| ROTA | 4.27% | 3.17% |

(the lender offering the loan) and external (other lenders), risk factors, price elasticity (reflecting demand), and competition. For this example, the interest rate is 130 basis points lower than that for a new customer, and is an outcome of relationship-based pricing. Average ticket size is $3700 with an average tenor of 18 months.

While approval rate for new customers hovers around 20–30% in India, the same for cross-sell is significantly higher. A low approval rate translates into a higher cost of acquisition of a new customer. Lenders also take special care in minimising reject rates through continuous improvements of selection criteria and processes, in order to keep their customers satisfied.

- Definitions for this example:
  - Average net receivables is calculated as Net Accounts Receivables (current month) + Net Accounts Receivables (prior month) ÷ 2. This is then averaged out for the period of 12 and 6 months, respectively.
  - Net interest margin is interest revenue net of cost of funds
  - Revenue is the sum of net interest margin and fees
  - Gross credit loss is outstanding balance at write-off. Net credit loss is gross credit loss net of recoveries.
  - Operating margin is revenue minus operating expense
  - EBIT simply defined is operating margin minus net credit loss
  - ROTA is EBIT after taxes divided by average net receivables

Profit is defined by earnings before interest and tax (EBIT) and return on investment is measured by return on total assets (ROTA). Both EBIT and ROTA for the cross-sold portfolio are 20% higher than new customer portfolio. This is a compelling reason for firms to move aggressively towards increasing the portfolio contribution from their current customer base. The driving factors leading to higher returns on the cross-sold portfolio are as follows:

- Higher average ticket size for the cross-sold portfolio (23% higher), as credit worthiness can be more accurately determined given the rich customer information that is available—card application, performance on all current and past products held with the bank, and competition products
- Higher net interest margin on the cross-sold portfolio resulting from a higher loan size, which more than compensates the interest differential of 130 basis points
- Lower second year loss rate on the cross-sold portfolio (2.6%) vs. new customer (3.6%), resulting from improved quality of underwriting on an existing customer
- Lower operating expenses (maintenance, technology, and people) for the cross-sold portfolio

### 3.4.1.2 Cross-Sell Profitability Tool Kit

Cross-selling is also used as a strategy to gain entry into new segments. Financial institutions such as Citigroup and HSBC offer products to subprime segments that would not normally qualify for products offered to its prime segments. Pricing strategy such as risk-based pricing is used as a product proposition to offer similar products. Customers are then gradually cross-sold other products based on a periodic review of customer performance. Alternatively acquisition of high volume low margin accounts (e.g., salaried banking accounts) is a strategy to acquire a large customer base, and thereafter migrate the portfolio to higher margin products through cross-selling. For example, Spanish bank BBVA's emphasis for 2009 for their Mexico market was to reach the unbanked segment of the market via payroll banking, and followed by cross-selling to this segment[13].

**Table 3.6** Banking Profitability Tool Kit

| $ Figures are per Customer per Quarter/% are Cross-Sell Penetration | Q1 | Q2 | Q4 | Q8 |
|---|---|---|---|---|
| EBIT with cross-sell $ | (4) | 10 | 87 | 104 |
| EBIT without cross-sell $ | (6) | (6) | 62 | 67 |
| Cards | 12.06% | 10.51% | 4.45% | 2.82% |
| Personal loans | 0.55% | 0.77% | 0.85% | 0.85% |
| Mutual funds | 0.04% | 0.01% | 0.01% | 0.01% |
| Mortgage | 0.06% | 0.06% | 0.08% | 0.08% |
| Auto | 0.08% | 0.03% | 0.05% | 0.05% |

[13] Retailer Banker International, "A Rich and Poor Strategy for Mexico", 20 February 2009.

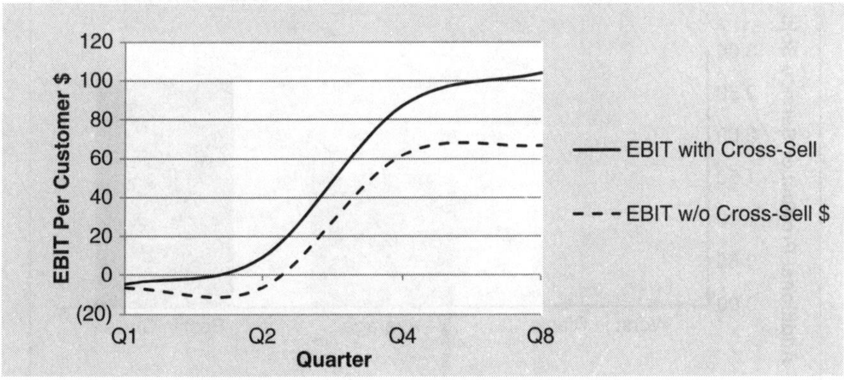


**Figure 3.4** Banking Cross-Sell Profitability Build-Up

A profitability tool kit for evaluating the income stream build-up from cross-selling is a valuable tool for planning and forecasting. Additionally, the product mix to sell and at what point can be assessed (Table 3.6 and Fig. 3.4). Simultaneously, this tool kit could be useful for making decisions on the quality of new customers to acquire, based on the forecast of revenue potential. The tool kit can be supplemented by a segmentation derived from customer net relationship value (NRV) and salary. This segmentation can provide guidelines for cross-sell recommendations.

## 3.5 Cross-Sell Process

In this section, some of the key steps that organisations need to focus on to make their cross-sell vision a successful reality are outlined.

### *3.5.1 Organisational Culture and Focus*

Industry experience suggests that a long-term management commitment combined with a culture that encourages and rewards cross-selling is important for the success of a cross-sell programme. This involves the following:

- Setting goals and benchmarks at all levels—company, business, campaign, employee, and customer. Wells Fargo is a best in class example that strives towards a goal, and this point was earlier emphasized in Section 3.2. Moreover, top management should also regularly and enthusiastically communicate support for the programme.
- Measurement of benchmarks of success (e.g., cross-sell ratio, wallet share, customer satisfaction levels, and loyalty-retention). Some of

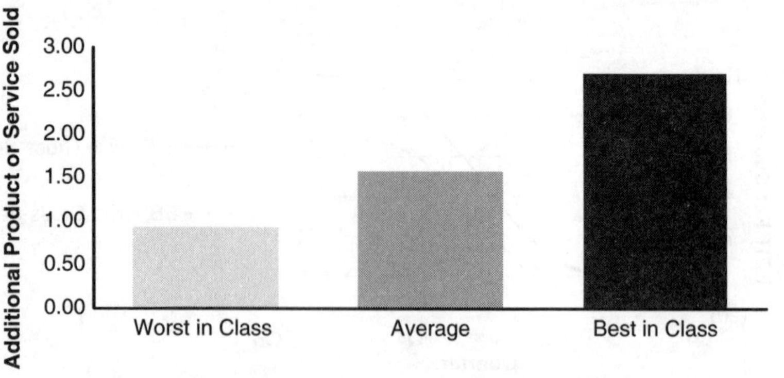


*Source: Consumer Lending Cross-Sell and Product Bundling*, Benchmark Consulting International.

**Figure 3.5** Cross-Sell Success Metrics for Home Equity Lenders

these measures of success are highlighted in Fig. 3.5[14] and later in the discussion on cross-sell grid.

- A "customer first" attitude is very important for designing and driving a cross-sell programme. For example, an aggressive cross-sell target may result in mis-selling, whereby the customer is not adequately informed about the risks and benefits associated with a particular product. It is also important to ensure that the cross-sell programme does not result in customers getting bombarded with communications and offers. Therefore, a proper contact management strategy needs to be adopted, so as to avoid customer fatigue.
- Information and organisational silos need to be minimised. Isolated operational silos and fragmented flow of information between different business units of the organisation involved in the cross-sell programme are detrimental factors.
- Coordination and conflict resolution across business lines. Decisions on next best product recommendations and profit sharing need effective management as team effort.
- A customer-centric approach in contrast to a product-centric approach is necessary to maximise benefits both for the customer and the firm as depicted by Figs. 3.6 and 3.7. It is also important to have the right technology strategy to implement a customer-centric approach, a subject that will be expounded later in Chapter 8, "Analytics Ecosystem". In practice, moving to a customer-centric approach is a long road ahead given the product silos that normally exist in any organisation.

[14] Available at http://benchmarkinternational.com/Articles/Consumer%20Lending%20Cross-sell%20and%20Product%20Bundling.pdf.

| Business Driver | Product Centric | Customer Centric |
|---|---|---|
| Business Objective | Product profitability | Product and customer profitability |
| Business Approach | Build the product irrespective of customer needs | Provide solutions based on present and future customer needs |
| Offerings | Lines of business by products or services | Integrated cross-sell of all existing products and services |
| Service Delivery Approach | Product-based approach | Relationship-based approach |
| Customer Relationship | Customer views the organisation as a provider of a particular product or service | Customer views the organisation as a trusted and committed long-term partner |

**Figure 3.6** Product Vs. Customer View I

| Information Driver | Product Centric | Customer Centric |
|---|---|---|
| Source | Individual lines of business databases | All information sources in the organisation |
| Information | Demographics, behaviour, transactional data | Demographics, behaviour, transactional, relationship, competition data |
| Relationships | Lack of or ad-hoc identification of accounts and products held by a customer with the organisation | Single customer view-cross account and cross-product/ service relationships |
| Value | Individual value of products to line of business | Value of customer to the organisation—historic, present and future potential |
| Needs and Preferences | Partially captured in each line of business | Comprehensive and structured cross-sell |

**Figure 3.7** Product Vs. Customer View II

### 3.5.2 *Identify Opportunities for Cross-Sell*

Before embarking on an organisation-wide cross-sell strategy, it is critical to define the opportunity landscape and decide upon the scale and scope of the programme.

- Understand industry outlook and estimate wallet share for various products. In reference to financial services, interested readers can refer to Chapter 6, "Credit Bureau" on how customer product mapping on the bureau and resulting wallet share can be used for cross-sell decisions.
- Segment the existing customer base for a deeper understanding of the portfolio. This can be based on current product ownership, life-stage (income and age), affluence levels, wallet share, usage, risk, and other relevant variables.
- Identify segments which are under penetrated compared to the average based on cross-sell metrics.
- Prioritise segments based on the organisation's focus. A prioritisation methodology involves identifying the following:
  - *Focus segments:* Segments which the company wants to grow
  - *Quick wins:* Segments where the programme could be implemented to obtain quick success
  - *Long-term focus:* Segments which require long-term attention to obtain success

#### 3.5.2.1 Cross-Sell Grid

As mentioned earlier, it is important to establish metrics and benchmarks for monitoring a cross-sell programme at various levels in the organisation. The concept of a cross-sell grid provides a useful framework for this purpose. The cross-sell grids, Table 3.7 and Table 3.8 are effective multipurpose reports for gauging actual cross-sell penetration; evaluating whether cross-sell programmes are working; and for providing guidance on *whom* to target and for *which* product. A quintessential requirement for creating the cross-sell grid is a "customer one view" or a complete picture of all the products/services held by a customer with the same provider. This depends on a customer identification key (e.g., customer ID) that is unique to a customer and is populated for each of the products (and accounts) held by a customer. Linking of all relationships of a customer to this unique customer ID is the next step. In the absence of such an identifier, the organisation would have to rely on a matching logic based on fields like name, address, and phone number. The quality of the match would depend on the matching algorithm and the quality of information available. There are matching algorithms and related softwares available in the market. The acquisition and credit bureau chapters discuss matching algorithms.

**Table 3.7** Simple Cross-Sell Grid

| | Product A | Product B | Product C | Product D | Product E |
|---|---|---|---|---|---|
| **Product A** | | x.x% | x.x% | x.x% | x.x% |
| **Product B** | x.x% | | x.x% | x.x% | x.x% |
| **Product C** | x.x% | x.x% | | x.x% | x.x% |
| **Product D** | x.x% | x.x% | x.x% | | x.x% |
| **Product E** | x.x% | x.x% | x.x% | x.x% | |

**Table 3.8** Expanded Cross-Sell Grid

| | | | Cross Bought–Sold Products | | | | | PDR |
|---|---|---|---|---|---|---|---|---|
| | | | Family I | | Family II | Family III | | |
| | | | Product A | Product B | Product C | Product D | Product E | |
| Family I | Product A | # Customers | 2,00,000 | 1,00,000 | 10,000 | 20,000 | 50,000 | 1.90 |
| | | # Accounts | 2,50,000 | 1,10,000 | 10,500 | 30,000 | 55,000 | |
| | | Product Penetration | 100.0% | 50.0% | 5.0% | 10.0% | 25.0% | |
| | | % Attrition (Annual) | 12.0% | 10.0% | 9.0% | 7.0% | 4.0% | |
| | | % Eligible | – | 80.0% | 30.0% | 20.0% | 50.0% | |
| | | Avg Customer Revenue (LCY) | $500 | $550 | $1,000 | $900 | $600 | |
| | | Reference Number | 1 | 2 | 3 | 4 | 5 | 6 |
| | Product B | | | | | | | |
| Family II | Product C | | | | | | | |
| Family III | Product D | | | | | | | |
| | Product E | | | | | | | |

*Note:* LCY is local currency

*Simple Cross-Sell Grid* The simple cross-sell grid (Table 3.7) reflects the cross-product holding pattern. More precisely, it shows product penetration, the percentage of customers that hold a product on the vertical axis, and also hold a respective product on the horizontal axis. In the case of sequential cross-sell, the vertical product list could refer to the base or hook product, for example, the first relationship product with the firm, and the horizontal product list could represent the subsequent products sold. Although this simple cross-sell grid is the first step towards quantifying opportunity and measuring the impact of cross-selling, it has limitations as it may not represent a true picture of the outcome of cross-sell efforts. First, the average number of products held by a customer (cross-sell ratio) is a challenge to decipher. Second, it is unclear how multiple accounts (of the same product) for a customer are being categorized. Third, two products may belong to the same business line, for example, a savings account and a checking account, but may not be considered as cross-sell. Therefore, another metric is required to measure cross-sell across business lines. These shortcomings can be overcome by a comprehensive version of the cross-sell grid, that is, the expanded cross-sell grid (Table 3.8).

*Expanded Cross-Sell Grid*

Table 3.8 is the expanded cross-sell grid.

- It is important to note that at the beginning of the exercise, "family groups" should be defined in order to group all existing products into their respective families. One definition of a family is a "business line" consisting of products that are similar in nature and functionality. For example, life and general insurance would be clubbed into the "insurance" family while "deposits" would include current, savings, and fixed or term deposits. In the cross-sell grid, current, savings, and term deposits will be categorised as 3 products under the family "deposits". Similarly, product classification within a family needs to be done.
- Grid entries
  - In the grid, customers refer to the number of customers who hold the respective combination of products
  - Accounts refer to the number of open accounts of the respective product, for example, a customer can have more than one savings account with a bank
  - Cells are not mutually exclusive. For example, a customer holding products B and C will appear in cells 2 and 3.
  - Product penetration for a particular combination of products, say A and B, is defined as the percentage of product A customers that hold product B. It takes a value of 50% in this example.

  - Percent eligible is defined as the percentage of customers that are eligible for an offer of the respective product on the horizontal axis, post credit and marketing screening
  - Average customer revenue is calculated by dividing the total revenue for the respective product combination divided by the number of customers in that cell
- In the grid, 200,000 customers of product A hold 250,000 accounts of this product. This implies that there are multiple account holders of the same product. All the metrics reported would be for this segment of customers holding product A.
- Cross-sell ratio
  - *Product depth ratio (PDR)* is defined as the average number of products per customer. This represents the depth of the customer relationship, which on average is approximately two products per customer and has the potential to go up to a maximum of five in this example.

    PDR = Sum of customers across all products/Number of unique customers

    = 380,000/200,000 = 1.90
  - Normally the definition of cross-sell ratio varies by organisation, and is usually not disclosed when the ratio is published. A guess estimate is that it is the PDR. As of 2008, the industry average for PDR[15] was around 3.69 products per customer for banks. At a specific bank level, Wells Fargo reported a cross-sell ratio of an average of 6.16 different products per household, according to a press release of Nov, 2013. J.P. Morgan Chase reported a cross-sell ratio of 6.68 products per household, according to Wall Street Journal dated 28 February, 2011.
  - Similarly, the cross-sell ratio should be replicated and reported at product, overall business unit, and organisation level.
  - The average number of product families per customer can also be evaluated and the additional information required is the number of unique customers by family group. This metric is termed as the *product breadth ratio (PBR)* and it gauges the extent of the customer relationship at the broader business line level.
- The barometers of *PDR* and *PBR* should be periodically tracked (at least quarterly) to gauge the effectiveness of a cross-sell programme. While it is important that *PDR* increases, *PBR* also needs to be assessed, to evaluate how well the organisation has been able to cross-sell across business lines.
- This grid can be replicated by different segments using key decision criteria like lifestage (age and income) and affluence levels based on relationship value with the firm (Table 3.9)

[15] Banking and Payments Asia, "Bankinter Tops Global Cross-Selling League", May 2009.

**Table 3.9** Segment Level Cross-Sell Ratios

| Segment | PBR | PDR |
|---|---|---|
| Super affluent | 1.8 | 2.6 |
| Affluent | 1.8 | 2.1 |
| Mass market | 1.4 | 1.5 |

- As mentioned earlier, the expanded cross-sell grid can be used to identify potential opportunities:
  - *Improve cross-sell ratio*: Product penetration is high at 50% for cell 2 as products belong to the same family and therefore, easier to cross-sell. A recommendation for next best product offer is an offer of product B to product A customers, who do not currently have this product. Since the incremental revenue benefit of LCY 50 (relative to holding only product A) is not as significant, efforts should also be directed to increase the *PBR* through the range of products sold (outside of the family) and these points are noted subsequently.
  - *Maximise revenue*: Revenue per customer is highest for the product combination A and C (cell 3). Incremental revenue as a result of selling product C is of the order of LCY 500 (relative to holding only product A). Only 5% of Product A customers have product C, and has the potential of going up to 30%. This segment should be further tapped for cross-selling.
  - *Increase eligible universe*: Combination A and D has low eligibility at 20% and requires further evaluation on how it can be enhanced as this combination has the second highest revenue

### *3.5.3 Cross-Sell Programme Implementation*

Till now the organisational strategy and the associated cross-sell metrics for monitoring a cross-sell programme were discussed. Pivotal steps of programme implementation are highlighted in this section (Fig. 3.8).

#### 3.5.3.1 Business Strategy

The first step of a cross-sell business strategy involves finalisation of cross-sell targets, for example, cross-sell ratio, cross-sales volume by product, and revenue goals by business units. This needs to be done after reaching an agreement among different business units. Given the traditional product silos in which most businesses operate, this is probably the most important and difficult step of a cross-sell programme. After finalising targets, some of the next steps are as follows:

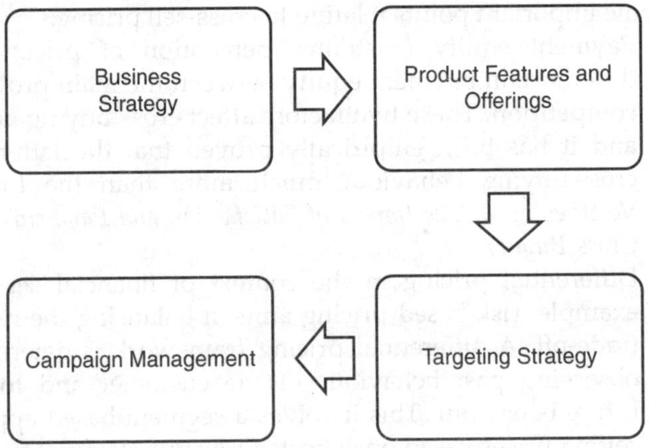


**Figure 3.8** Cross-Sell Programme Implementation

- **Budget planning:** Allocation of budget for cross-sell programmes, and across business lines and products
- **Designing sales force and customer incentives:** A well-defined compensation programme needs to be developed in order to motivate front-line sales and service staff. The same should be communicated properly. Each member of the sales and service team should be made accountable for achieving measurable rates of cross-sell appropriate for their lines of business.

### 3.5.3.2 Product Features and Offerings

A pragmatic approach is to determine product strategy by segment, as it is impractical to be cross-selling everything to everyone. After deciding upon segments to be targeted, it is important to tailor products and pricing by segment based on business objectives that the firm is trying to achieve.

- **Product**
  - Limit strategy to a small number of products for effective cross-selling
  - For bundled offers, construct product bundles in effective combinations. A good example is a student package of checking, debit and intro credit card.
  - Add services to the product bundle so as to enhance value. For example, bill pay and mobile pre-paid recharge facilities.
- **Pricing**
  - In the context of cross-sell, relationship-based pricing is the strategy that most firms adopt to incentivise, reward, and retain existing customers. Pricing is an important lever for boosting profits in a hyper competitive scenario.

- Some important points relating to cross-sell pricing:
  - Payment equity (customer perception of price) and the difference in payment equity between the main provider and competition. These two factors affect cross-buying behaviour, and it has been empirically proven that the latter impacts cross-buying behaviour much more than the former, by Verhoes et al. *The Impact of Satisfaction and Payment Equity on Cross-Buying*.
  - Differential pricing in the context of financial services, for example, risk-based pricing aims at balancing the risk return trade-off. A differential pricing framework is determined by observing past behaviour of the customer and forecasting future behaviour. This involves a segment-based approach of setting prices based on expected revenue streams, costs of service, and expected losses. These drivers are then combined to calculate expected profitability.
  - Alternate approaches to relationship pricing are presented in Table 3.10
  - Readers should refer to Chapter 5, "Price Management" for examples of different pricing structures
- Price testing is recommended to arrive at the optimal relationship price point by segment and experimental design framework is useful in this context. This topic is covered in the last chapter. The impact of pricing needs to be evaluated from many dimensions—propensity to take up the product, usage, profitability, and retention.

### 3.5.3.3 Targeting Strategy

In the last section on cross-sell models for multiproduct marking, different analytical approaches to determine the targeting strategy of what products, to whom, when and how to cross-sell, will be discussed. The execution of this step of the cross-sell process is heavily dependent on a dedicated and specialised analytics team. The targeting strategy can be based on analytical tools of triggers, segmentation, and predictive models. Some of the dimensions of a targeting strategy include demographics and lifestyle, wallet share, response, usage, revenue, risk, and profitability.

### 3.5.3.4 Campaign Management

*Campaign Mail File Creation Process* A cross-sell programme requires a number of campaigns to be executed at regular intervals, usually monthly or at the time of data update. While campaign design will be discussed in the last chapter of the book, the broad steps of campaign mail file creation are outlined in Fig. 3.9.

**Table 3.10** Relationship Pricing

| Behavioural Parameters | Information Used | Cross-Sell Pricing Strategy | Benefits | Challenges |
|---|---|---|---|---|
| Total customer value | Revenue or profitability | Tier structure based on value; lower pricing for higher value | Ability to reward "good" customers | Profitability measures need to be defined and constantly updated. Ambiguity on how to treat customers moving in and out of value buckets |
| Risk | Customer risk profile | Higher pricing covers for higher risk | Expected loss compensated by revenue | Predatory pricing, regulatory issues, transparency and clear communication to the customer |
| Relationship depth | Cross-sell ratio | Lower pricing for customers with higher number of products | Promote cross-buying behaviour | Higher cross-sell ratio does not imply higher customer profitability |
| Contact history | Number of times customer has been contacted, customer feedback | Price reduction in a step-wise manner | Optimising for price and response in a systematic way | Need good information systems with contact and price history |
| Tenure | Length of oldest relationship with the firm | Lower pricing for higher tenure | Reward for loyalty | Not all loyal customers are profitable |

(*Continued*)

**Table 3.10** Relationship Pricing (*Continued*)

| Behavioural Parameters | Information Used | Cross-Sell Pricing Strategy | Benefits | Challenges |
|---|---|---|---|---|
| Cross-buy behaviour/response history | Prior history of whether the customer has taken the product to be "cross-sold" or a like product | Could go either way. High likelihood of future product take-up indicates high demand which supports higher pricing. Alternatively, the firm can afford lower pricing for promoting repeat behaviour (e.g., top-ups on installment loans) | Lower pricing can be a strong market differentiator | Price revisions could be confusing to the customer |
| Attrition based | Event of customer wanting to close the account, predicted risk of attrition | Price discount to save the customer | Ability to leverage cross-selling for retention using pricing as a tool | Tendency to give away any price discount to save the customer irrespective of value. Cost may be higher than value gained. Repeat customers wanting to avail price breaks after knowing tricks of the trade |
| Expected profitability on "cross-sold product" | Futuristic value (e.g., lifetime value) depending on predicted cash flows, response, and expected tenure | Price that maximises lifetime value | Improved portfolio profitability resulting from cross-sell port folio | Highly intensive analytical exercise |

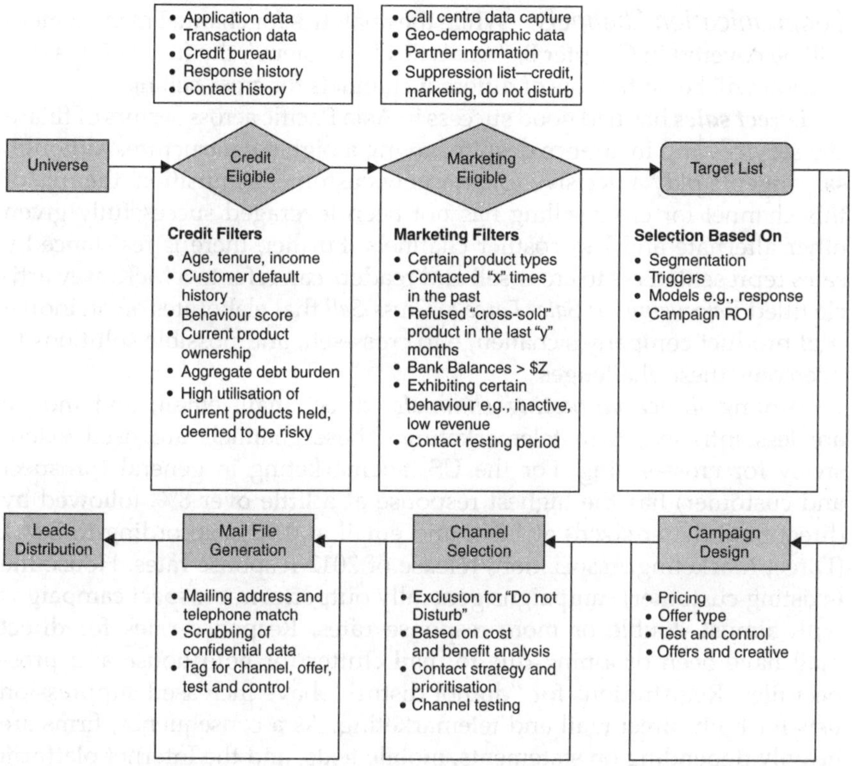


**Figure 3.9** Cross-Sell Campaign Mail File Creation Process

*Contact Management Strategy and Advertising* An important aspect of campaign design and roll-out involves channel selection and the design of customer contact strategy. At times, multiple channels are utilised for a given campaign (e.g., a direct mailer followed by a telephone call and SMS). Historical campaign data is used to analytically evaluate optimal channel selection. Customer contact management will require the following:

- Multi-channel selection based on cost-benefit analysis
- Contact protocol—frequency of contact, channel of contact, interval between two consecutive communications to the same customer, handling "do not disturb" customers
- Improvement of customer contact rate and the use of multiple sources of information for filling in gaps relating to customer contact details
- Creative design and scripting for attracting attention to the offer. Demographic segmentation plays a key role in differentiating the communication message, for example, working, senior citizen, homemaker.
- Channel testing
- Advertising for brand and offer awareness

*Communication Channels* While the analytics for channel management will be covered in Chapter 8, "Analytics Ecosystem", the focus of this discussion will be on the role of different channels for cross-selling.

***Direct sales*** has had good success in Asia Pacific across sectors of financial services and insurance despite having a high cost structure. Although sales agents play a decisive role for new customer acquisition, the role of this channel for cross-selling has not been leveraged successfully given other alternate and less costlier channels. Further, there is resistance by sales representatives to cross-sell and readers can refer to a McKinsey article titled *Refocusing the Sales Force to Cross-Sell* that elaborates on an industrial product company's challenge to cross-sell, and possible solutions to overcome these challenges.

Among ***direct marketing channels***, direct mail, email, and mobile are less intrusive than telemarketing. These channels are used extensively for cross-selling. For the US, telemarketing in general (prospect and customer) has the highest response at a little over 8%, followed by direct mail (letter-sized) at 1.3%, and email at 0.03%, according to DMA (Direct Marketing Association) release of 2012 response rates. House-file (existing customer) campaigns generally outperform prospect campaigns with almost double or more response rates. Response rates for direct mail have been dropping due to mail clutter for both house and prospect files. Registrations for "do not disturb" have increased suppression lists for both direct mail and telemarketing. As a consequence, firms are heavily depending on statements, mobile texts, and the Internet platform to inform their customers about new services, products, cross-sell and up-sell offers.

For managing communication and online sales, the ***Internet*** is playing a pivotal role. BBVA, a leading multinational banking group of Spain, launched a general online banking platform in late 2008, called Tú Cuentas (*Source:* Forrester case study, 2009). This online system is linked to its CRM system, so that it can make personalised product cross-sell recommendations. Banking, investment, and insurance products are tailored to the individual, each constructed from the customers' information DNA (single customer profile), according to an American Banker article titled *Core Matters*, published in July 2010. Similarly, a leader in the online space has been Wells Fargo, who has transformed its online channel into a viable sales channel. This has been done by creating an online product application engine. The website wellsfargo.com is an integrated sales process with one application process for multiple products, and the highest revenue generation from this platform is from cross-selling products during the application process. The applicants choose the product, and cross-sell offers are based on the product applied for, the applicant's state of residence, and whether the applicant is a new or existing member, among others. The bank has witnessed a dramatic increase in cross-sell rates as a result of the fructification of these efforts, according to a Forrester report of 2005 titled *How did Wells Fargo Boost Online Sales*.

***Call centres*** have become one of the most important delivery channels for service-oriented organisations across the globe. Also called phone or customer service centres, customer service representatives (CSR) access the firms' databases and applications and take the role of a delivery channel. Although call centres were set up for servicing, it has become a vital delivery channel for expanding business through cross-selling, and for retaining customers. With the right sales processes and tools, trigger (event) based marketing and next best product to sell recommendations available to the front-end (inbound and outbound), can promote intelligent cross-selling. A McKinsey report, *Using Call Centres to Boost Revenue*, estimates that cross-selling at a bank's call centre can generate significant revenue, equivalent to 10% of the revenue generated through the bank's entire branch network. The inbound service centre of Citibank is a very good example of the metamorphosis of a service channel into a profit centre for the India market.

The primary role of inbound call centres is service, and the volume of service calls varies during a day, creating peak loads in the system load. It may be the case that even for calls presenting high revenue potential, cross-selling during peak times is not advisable due to the detrimental effect it may have on capacity and service. However, customers who have a positive experience with their bank's call centre are about 50% more likely to listen to a sales pitch for additional products or services[16]. Therefore, given the dual objectives of service and sales, a natural question that comes up is whether a bank can have a cost-effective call centre operation, achieve the high standards of customer service, and generate target sales revenue all simultaneously. These trade-offs are addressed by Aksin and Harker in their co-authored paper titled *To Sell or Not to Sell*, for a phone centre of a major US retail bank. They conclude that cross-selling is a costly affair—adding to costs of training and technology and with adverse effects on customer service. This is due to the additional load it creates on service representatives through congestion-related problems (due to additional talk time). Re-staffing is shown as a solution based on a simulation analysis of call centre profits under various scenarios using performance models and optimisation routines.

Additional analytic tools that could be useful for enhancing CSR sales in the context of cross-selling are pre-set business rules, using customer propensity to take up a product. This is based on analysis of historical cross-sell data (mail and response files). Segmenting the customer base into groups based on sales potential and targeting high potential segments (tagged and available to front-end call centre agents) is one possibility. Real-time decisioning is a revenue management approach for dynamic cross-selling in call centres. A cross-sell engine that makes real-time

[16] *American Banker*, "Call Centers Said to Miss Chances for Cross-Sales", 11 February 2009.

decisions based on real-time customer data is a requirement. While all this information is available, the key is to make customer information easily accessible and decipherable for the CSR. A tool based on a thermometer concept that represents a ranking of products for cross-sell can improve sales productivity significantly. Figure 3.10 is an illustration of a sales thermometer. The thermometer ranks products to cross-sell based on propensity to buy that product and recommendations are customized by customer. Other measures such as expected revenue by product can also be used to set the priority.

Despite the Internet revolution, the ***branch network*** has proved to be "the place" where customers open accounts and are persuaded into buying more services through personalised contact. As per BAI (http://www.bai.org), banks are depending on a relationship management tool called "book of business" to achieve deeper household penetration and help manage retention. These customer tags contain information regarding the customer's relationship with the bank, including customer net revenue (CNR). Customers are assigned to the relevant branch based on where the primary checking account resides and customers become part of the branch's "book of business". This approach helps improve a bank's performance by setting objectives for its relationship managers. The objectives could be of retaining the most profitable customers and identifying those that represent cross-sell opportunities. However, the scope for cross-selling through the branch is limited for banks that have a small branch network. According to a Forrester survey-based report, *Driving Sales*

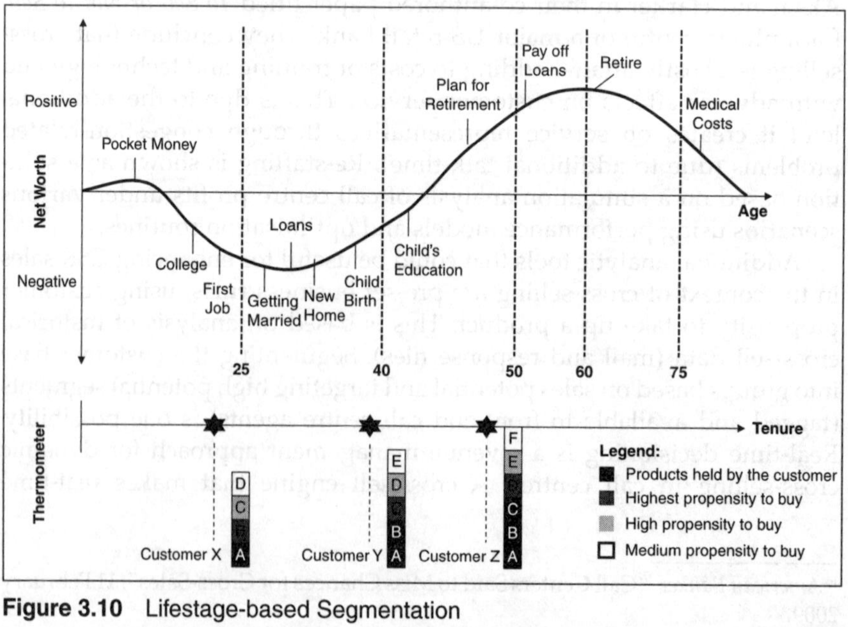


**Figure 3.10** Lifestage-based Segmentation

*through the Branch Network*, low product cross-sell is the biggest challenge faced by a branch.

The ***ATM*** (automated teller machine) remains an important part of the financial services delivery system. Banks have been migrating customers away from tellers at the branch to the ATM, to cut costs and improve efficiency. The ATM can serve as a powerful channel for communicating cross-sell and promotional offers to the customer as it accounts for a high proportion of cash withdrawals for many banks. HDFC Bank, the second largest private bank in India, is the first bank in Asia to offer targeted messaging across all its direct banking channels. More than 45% of HDFC's customers initiate their transactions through an ATM, resulting in more than 300 transactions per ATM on an average day. Three quarters of the bank's customers visit the ATM three times each month to withdraw cash or check statements. More than 4 million customers have been targeted for cross-sell messaging through their ATM network, and has generated more than USD 1.25 million for sales conversions booked to date[17].

***Bancassurance*** is the distribution of insurance by banks, and has been effective in bolstering fee-based income through cross-sell opportunities. It allows banks to leverage their extensive customer base to sell a range of investment and retirement products, and is often bundled with other products. Bancassurance in the Asia Pacific region has been a major success story, according to Bank of International Settlements, May 2014. In China, bancassurance sales increased by 415% during 2004–2009. In Malaysia, bancassurance accounted for 36% of new life insurance business premium.

*Campaign Execution* A cross-sell programme involves multiple cross-sell campaigns. Further, campaign execution needs a proper technology infrastructure. The technology infrastructure should provide an integrated and customer-centric view; execute automated cross-sell campaigns at a customer level; and handle huge volumes of campaign runs. A technology based campaign management framework will be discussed in Chapter 8, "Analytics Ecosystem".

The process also needs to be actively managed, so as to minimise execution risks. Aspects of campaign execution that require attention are the following:

- Sales training
- Right data management tools to enable front-line staff
- Regular communication with all those involved in the programme
- Monitoring of project plan with milestones and the identification of key partners for delivery and execution

[17] ACI Worldwide, "HDFC Transforms Customer Experience at the ATM with ACI Worldwide", Undated.

- Well-defined processes for customer service as improper customer service can become an important roadblock
- Tightly integrated flow of information across all transaction and communication channels, to ensure consistent communication of offers across different channels
- Cross-sell fulfilment process as illustrated in Fig. 3.11
- Regular audit of mail file and quality check on telephone calls made to customers

*Campaign Tracking and Measurement* Tracking and monitoring the programme is as crucial as implementation. Performance metrics should be tracked both at the overall programme level and for individual campaigns. While the cross-sell grid is a high-level tracking mechanism, the following tables are specific reports for campaign and programme-level tracking of cross-sell.

- Track and report success metrics at regular intervals. For example, the cross-sell ratio is a "health-check" barometer closely monitored by the industry.
- Tables 3.11 and 3.12 are simple templates of monthly MIS reports, with the former having general applicability across industries, while

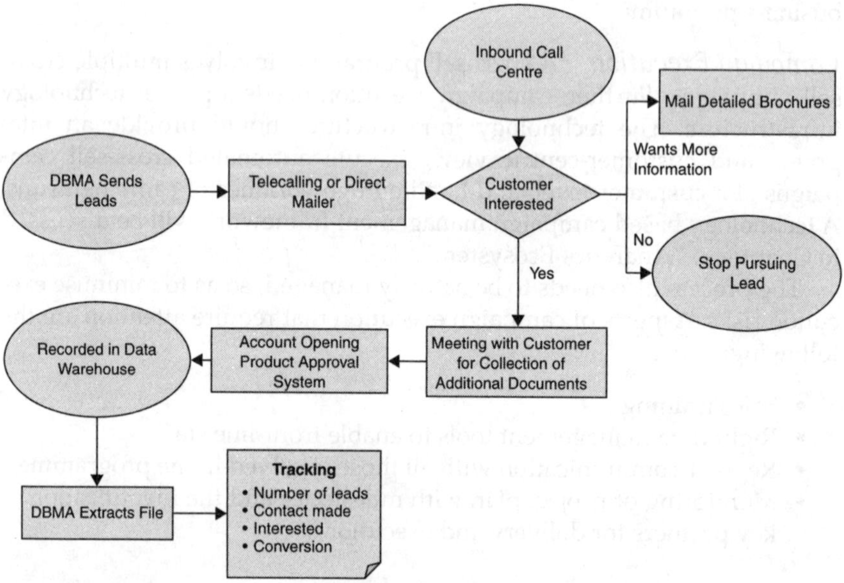


*Note:* DBMA stands for Database Marketing and Analytics.

**Figure 3.11** Cross-Sell Fulfilment Process

**Table 3.11** Cross-Sell Campaign Tracking Report

| | | Direct Mail | | | | Telecalling | | | |
|---|---|---|---|---|---|---|---|---|---|
| City | Price | P1 | P2 | P3 | Total | P1 | P2 | P3 | Total |
| City A | Total mail file number of customers | | | | | | | | |
| | Total contacted | | | | | | | | |
| | Contact rate | | | | | | | | |
| | Response rate | | | | | | | | |
| | Conversion rate | | | | | | | | |
| | Average cross-sale value | | | | | | | | |
| City B | Total mail file number of customers | | | | | | | | |
| | Total contacted | | | | | | | | |
| | Contact rate | | | | | | | | |
| | Response rate | | | | | | | | |
| | Conversion rate | | | | | | | | |
| | Average cross-sale value | | | | | | | | |
| Grand total | Total mail file number of customers | | | | | | | | |
| | Total contacted | | | | | | | | |
| | Contact rate | | | | | | | | |
| | Response rate | | | | | | | | |
| | Conversion rate | | | | | | | | |
| | Average cross-sale value | | | | | | | | |
| Hit ratio (Number of contacts generating unit response) | | | | | | | | | |

the latter is specific to banking (by different channels of acquisition, including cross-sell and up-sell)

- Ensure that information is captured at all contact points and is fed back into the decision-making process—whether contacted, how many times contacted, customer interest, and feedback on offer solicitation

Table 3.12 Channel Report For Banking (Deposits)

| Acquisition Channel/Month of Tracking | | M1 | M2 | M3 | M4 | M5 | M6 | M7 | M8 | M9 | M10 | M11 | M12 | Total |
|---|---|---|---|---|---|---|---|---|---|---|---|---|---|---|
| Cross-Sell | | | | | | | | | | | | | | |
| Existing credit card customers | Number of customers opening basic banking relationship | | | | | | | | | | | | | |
| | Average (mean/median) balances on opening basic banking relationship | | | | | | | | | | | | | |
| | Number of customers opening premium relationship | | | | | | | | | | | | | |
| | Average (mean/median) balances on opening premium relationship | | | | | | | | | | | | | |
| Up-Sell/Upgrade | Number of customers | | | | | | | | | | | | | |
| Existing banking customers | Number of customers upgraded to premium within the month | | | | | | | | | | | | | |
| | Average (mean/median) balances on upgrade | | | | | | | | | | | | | |
| New Customer | Number of customers acquired directly to basic banking relationship | | | | | | | | | | | | | |
| New customer: No prior bank relationship | Average (mean/median) balances on opening basic banking relationship | | | | | | | | | | | | | |
| | Number of customers acquired directly to premium banking relationship | | | | | | | | | | | | | |
| | Average (mean/median) balances on opening premium banking relationship | | | | | | | | | | | | | |

- Measure programme effectiveness periodically and disseminate this information to top management as well as others involved in the process
- Make efforts to incorporate "lessons learned" into programme enhancements

*Example: Cross-Sell Campaign of Personal Loan to Credit Card* This example describes a cross-sell campaign of a lender aimed at selling personal loans to its credit card customers.

*Campaign Details* A campaign mail file is created based on the process highlighted in Fig. 3.9. For proper campaign reads, appropriate test and control cells are recommended (Fig. 3.12).

- **Target** population consists of three distinct segments of occasional revolvers, permanent revolvers, and transactors. Inactive customers are usually not solicited. For this example, the definitions used are as follows:
  - *Revolver:* A credit card customer is termed "revolver" for a particular month if the customer pays the bill partially
  - *Occasional revolver:* A customer who has revolved less than three times in the last 12 months
  - *Permanent revolver:* A customer who has revolved more than six times in the last 12 months
  - *Transactor:* A customer who pays the total bill amount in a given month. For this example, a transactor is defined as one who has paid in full every month over the last 12 months.

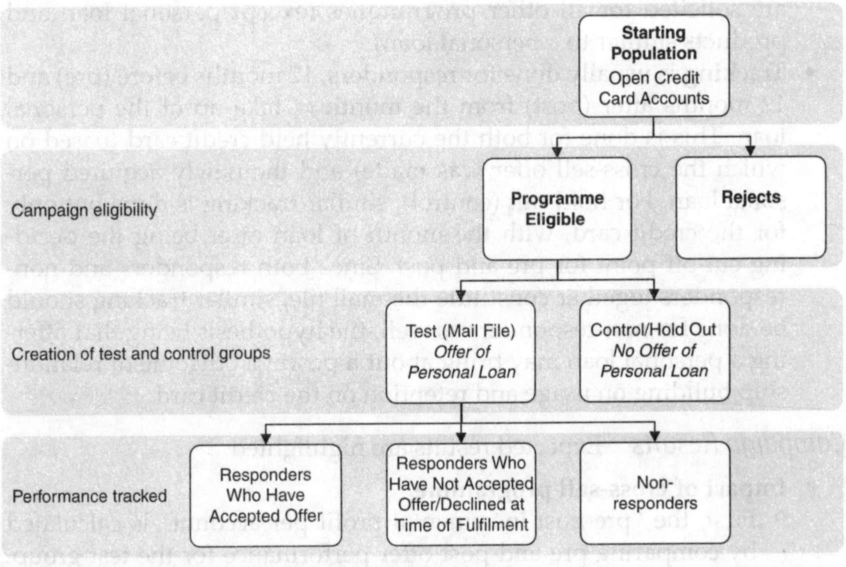


**Figure 3.12** Cross-Sell Campaign File

- **Programme eligible file** is likely to have a higher proportion of transactors, due to the fact that some of the credit related selection criteria (for eligibility) may consider a revolver as a riskier customer. In contrast, the responder file is likely to have a higher proportion of revolvers as this segment is credit needy and has a higher propensity to respond to the offer. An example of factors affecting response are outlined as segmentation output from classification/decision tree in Section 3.6. A corresponding response score is elaborated under logistic regression in Chapter 7, "Quantitative Methods".
- **Pricing**
  - *Relationship pricing* is the interest rate on the personal loan for an existing customer that is considerably lower than that for a new personal loan customer. The interest rate on the personal loan is significantly lower than credit card.
  - *Segment-based pricing* based on revolve behaviour is often used by banks to incentivise response, improve profitability, and discourage cannibalisation for revolvers. There is a risk that revolvers may accept a personal loan offer and pay up balance due on the credit card, thereby reducing the interest income on credit card. This is the cannibalisation effect, the extent of which is highly correlated with the positive price differential between the credit card and personal loan. Therefore, transactors tend to receive the most favourable relationship pricing and heavy revolvers the worst.
- **Control/hold-out group** (selected randomly) are accounts that are passed through the same selection criteria as the mail file, but are not solicited for a personal loan. In terms of revenue and risk profile, this segment is very similar to the mail file, which is a necessary and sufficient condition to qualify as a proper hold-out. These accounts are solicited for all other programmes (except personal loan and products similar to a personal loan).
- **Tracking** is usually done for responders, 12 months before (pre) and 12 months after (post) from the month of take-up of the personal loan. This is done for both the currently held credit card (based on which the cross-sell offer was made) and the newly acquired personal loan. For hold-out (control), similar tracking is done but only for the credit card, with the month of loan offer being the deciding cut-off point for pre and post. Since both responders and non-responders together constitute the mail file, similar tracking should be done for non-responders as well, the hypothesis being that offering a personal loan may bring about a positive outcome of relationship building on usage and retention on the credit card.

*Campaign Results* Expected results are highlighted.

- **Impact of cross-sell programme**
  - First, the "pre-post incremental profit per account" is calculated by comparing pre and post offer performance for the test group.

The same is repeated for the control group as well. For responders, the profit from a personal loan programme includes the combined profit from credit card and personal loan.

- Second, the gain from the cross-sell programme (doing vs. not doing) is calculated and one of metrics is the "test-control incremental profit per account" measured as the *difference* in the "pre-post incremental profit per account" between the test and control groups
- Since in an ideal scenario, the test and control groups are supposed to be identical in terms of characteristics, the "pre-post incremental profit per account" for the test can be taken as the gain from the cross-sell programme
- If the response rate is low, then per responder calculations are done rather than per mail file
- Other metrics that drive the profitability of this programme are also tracked at the mail file and responder level. Readers can refer to Chapter 8, "Analytics Ecosystem" for specifics on campaign tracking.

- **Profitability:** Incremental profit per account is expected to be positive and maximum for transactors followed by occasional revolvers and then permanent revolvers. EBIT is one such measure for profitability
- **Sales/revolve behaviour/balance:** A summary (Table 3.13) is presented to bring attention to the different behaviours by segment, and readers should refer to the glossary for definitions of these terms.
  - Occasional revolvers and permanent revolvers become less active
  - Personal loan may induce a higher degree of revolve behaviour for transactors and occasional revolvers, as inferred from the lower payment ratio. This phenomenon reflects a comfort factor setting in for transactors and occasional revolvers, to revolve to a higher degree on the credit card.
- **Cannibalisation:** Some of the negative consequences are cannibalisation of card balances for revolvers, specifically permanent revolvers. This effect is reflected in a higher payment ratio and lower

**Table 3.13** Personal Loan to Credit Card Campaign—Pre and Post

| | Occasional Revolvers | Permanent Revolvers | Transactors |
|---|---|---|---|
| Per Account $ | Change | Change | Change |
| Sales activation | (–) | (–) | (+) |
| Purchase sales per account | (–) | (–) | (+) |
| Cash sales per account | (–) | (–) | (+) |
| Balance per account | (+)/(–) | (–) | (+) |
| Payment ratio (%) | (–) | (+) | (–) |

balances. However, permanent revolvers utilise this available credit limit (open to buy) to slowly build up spend and balances on their credit card, although it may not quite match up to the prior levels.

- **Credit loss:** Loss rate on the card is expected to increase for responders, due to additional credit exposure and burden on payment schedule
- **Attrition:** Attrition rates for responders should go down in line with the hypothesis that cross-sell and retention are positively related

Although counter-intuitive, industry experience points to the fact that "credit card to personal loan" programme has not been as successful as the "personal loan to credit card" programme. One hypothetical reason is that given the regular payment schedule associated with a personal loan, the customer may experience difficulty in adjusting to a flexible payment structure of a credit card, thereby increasing the tendency to default.

## 3.6 Cross-Sell Models for Multiproduct Marketing

The four pillars of a cross-sell targeting strategy are *what* product to cross-sell, to *whom*, *when*, and *how*. This section on cross-sell models will focus on *what*, to *whom*, and *when* through a survey of "*next-product-to-buy*" models (***NPTB***). These models are in practice in industry and are of research interest to academics. Most ***NPTB*** models have a statistical foundation and some of these techniques will be elaborated in Chapter 7, "Quantitative Methods". One of the challenges of building cross-sell models is that it may reflect historical marketing actions of firms engaged in cross-selling. An ideal approach to overcome this issue is by random testing (of cross-sell offers and target population). The broad philosophies to cross-selling and corresponding models are illustrated in Table 3.14. This will form the backdrop of the discussion on this topic. A summary of cross-sell models is then followed by examples.

### *3.6.1 Summary of Cross-Sell Models*

***NPTB*** recommendations generally rely upon pattern recognition methods that decipher systematic impressions from the data. Simple cross-tabulations like the **cross-sell grid** gives quick insights into patterns of customer product holdings and a snapshot of under-serviced segments for management to act upon. It also provides recommendations on *what* product to sell based on product penetration, and to *whom* based on the observed patterns of product holdings. To a limited extent, the order of products can also be determined, contingent on the value of the cross-sell rate by product combinations.

Based on association rules, **market basket analysis (MBA)** identifies frequently purchased baskets of goods and advocates different combinations

**Table 3.14** Cross-Sell Models

| Approach | Model | What | Whom | When | How |
|---|---|---|---|---|---|
| Need | Lifestage | Y | Y | Y | N |
| | Hierarchy model | Y | Y | Y | N |
| | Triggers/RFM | Y | Y | Y | N |
| Preferences/ response | Cross-sell grid | Y | Y | N | N |
| | Markov Chain | Y | Y | Y | N |
| | Market basket analysis | Y | Y | N | N |
| | Recommender systems—e.g., collaborative filtering | Y | Y | N | N |
| | Segmentation—e.g., classification tree, clustering | Y | Y | N | N |
| | Logistic/multinomial logit model | Y | Y | N | Y |
| | Survival model | Y | Y | Y | N |
| Expected-revenue/ profitabilty/ CLV | Response and revenue optimisation | Y | Y | N | Y |
| | Decision analysis | Y | Y | N | N |
| Return on investment | Share of wallet model | Y | Y | N | N |
| | Optimisation model | Y | Y | N | Y |

of products to bundle, and is generally not personalised. The retail sector is a heavy user of **MBA**. However, the inference value from **MBA** and **cross-sell grid** becomes overwhelming with a large product set under consideration. In contrast, **recommender systems** such as collaborative filtering can be used to discover numerous multiple combinations of product holding preferences based on the concept of similarity of users or items bought. Computationally intensive, **collaborating filtering** uses huge volumes of transactional history data to make personalised recommendations, and has been one of the defining forces behind the success of e-commerce.

Several researchers have found evidence of the existence of a sequential pattern regarding the acquisition of durable goods and financial services. For example, a sequence from checking/savings accounts to credit cards, followed by mutual funds and bonds/stocks. Figure 3.13 is an illustration of this sequential pattern. Based on the premise that discovered acquisition patterns of the past is a good predictor of actual acquisition behaviour, there has been research analysing these acquisition patterns.

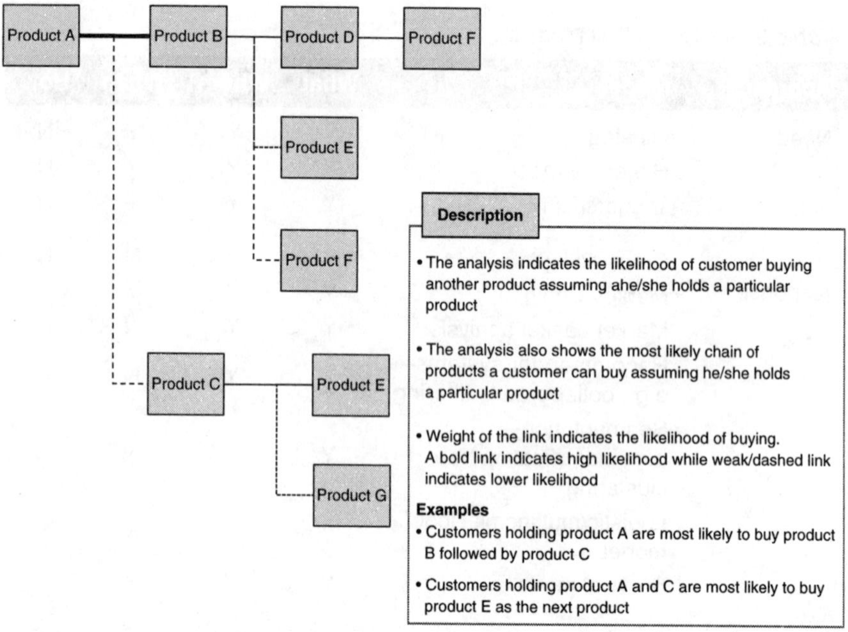


**Figure 3.13** Product-Purchase Sequence Grid

A sequential pattern can be classified into three categories—hierarchical process such as **latent trait analysis**, succession of purchases such as **Markov Chain**, and sequence with focus on time aspect such as **survival analysis**. With respect to the hierarchical process, work done by Kamakura et al. titled *Applying Latent Trait Analysis in the Evaluation of Prospects for Cross-Selling of Financial Services* is a seminal paper in this area. This research takes into account the financial maturity of the customer relative to the acquisition difficulty of the product, for evaluating the observed acquisition sequence of financial products.

In a similar context, stochastic methods like **Markov Chain** analyse customer behaviour over time, to find solutions for *what* product to sell and to *whom*, by tracking customer holding from one period to the next. It does not assume the acquisition pattern to be hierarchical. For example, a banking account followed by an equity stock purchase would be possible in this scheme. However, in the hierarchical sequence, investment in equity stock will come much later in the sequence order as it is a more complex product and depends on customer's financial maturity. **Markov Chain Model**[18] can be restrictive in their applicability given the

[18] Markov models are used for line increase strategy in the usage management chapter and interested readers can refer to this section for basics of Markov theory.

underlying assumptions of Markov theory, and Prinzie et al. attempt this approach in their 2006 paper.

The recommendations based on the preceding cross-models are inadequate, if one wants to drill down further. For example, which specific customer behavioural profile (beyond lifestage or product holding/preference pattern) should be targeted, with a certain order of priority of products, is a challenge to address using these models. Behavioural changes either prompted by personal events or market-driven phenomena are strong indicators signalling need and inclination to respond to an appropriate cross-sell offer. The ability to identify events and behavioural changes in real time is an incentive for firms to practise **trigger-based** cross-selling to a hot lead list, usually defined by a set of one dimensional *"if-then"* rules. However, a conjoint of behavioural and other factors affect a customer's buying propensity, where multivariate segmentation techniques are suitable. One such technique is **classification/decision tree**, which can detect interaction effects and discernibly isolate the dominating factors that influence takers from non-takers of a cross-sell offer. Based on segment averages, the results are robust with a fairly accurate prediction performance over a few implementation cycles, and require no underlying data distribution assumptions. Another segmentation technique of **cluster analysis** involves the natural groupings of observations (clusters) such that observations in a given cluster tend to be similar. For example, a portfolio can be grouped into clusters based on demographic, behavioural, and market data (with cross-product holdings and cross-sell rate mapped to these clusters), to determine the appropriate targeting strategy.

**Scoring models** give more precise and trackable output at an account or customer level. Using these models, linear and non-linear relationships can be mapped between independent and dependent variables, thereby lending high value for prediction and for performing sensitivity analysis. **Scoring models** attempt to explain why customers behave in a certain way and enable one-to-one marketing through the ability to assign a score at the most granular (account or customer) level. With wide applicability to industry applications, the estimation of these multivariate scoring models require a fairly good foundation of statistics. **Discrete choice models** are commonly used scoring methods and among these, **logistic regression** is a popular one. Financial services and other sectors rely heavily on logistic regression for building response and behavioural models for determining the target audience, choice of product, and channel for cross-selling.

The question of timing of cross-sell is also important. Two individual research studies by Knott et al. and Kumar et al. titled *Next Product-to-Buy-Models for Cross-Selling Applications and Knowing What to Sell, When and to Whom* are based on **survival models,** in conjunction with other advanced econometric models. The purpose is to determine the optimal time to offer the right product to the right customer. In this regard, the approach by Kumar et al. is broader and more sophisticated in scope. The model by Knott et al. addresses the timing of cross-buying behaviour using a **survival model**, while the probability of next best product to sell is based on a **discrete choice model**. **Survival models** also have the unique characteristic of incorporating time varying factors such as macroeconomic indicators of unemployment rate and consumer confidence index that can affect propensity to cross-buy.

The approaches discussed so far miss out on the net benefit logic associated with decision-making under uncertainty. **Response–revenue maximisation** and **decision analysis** are appropriate for deriving measures of expected monetary benefit from the cross-sale of products or services under consideration. Additionally, **optimisation** routines are popularly deployed in the face of multiple objectives and constraints. Addressing the four pillars of a cross-sell strategy under multiple constraints is a real-life business challenge that Cohen addresses in his paper titled *Exploiting Response Models—Optimizing Cross-Sell and Up-Sell Opportunities in Banking,* in a multiproduct and multi-channel scenario.

### 3.6.2 Latent Trait Analysis: Hierarchy Model

This discussion is based on research done by Kamakura et al. titled *Applying Latent Trait Analysis in the Evaluation of Prospects for Cross-Selling of Financial Services*. This approach positions both customers and products along a "latent" maturity/difficulty dimension. Customers are ranked on "financial maturity" based on factors such as financial expertise, investment objectives, resources, and family lifestage. Products are ranked on a "difficulty" dimension based on how complex and risky the product is. The more "difficult" products (that require greater resources, are more complex and risky, and have lower liquidity) require highest levels of customer "financial maturity". For example, the more "difficult" products are acquired in the later stages of family lifestage and follow a similar order as suggested by the pyramid of financial advisors (Fig. 3.14). Therefore, foundation products such as a banking account, credit card, and mortgage acquired early on are followed later by more complex investment products. In summary, cross-sell hierarchy is based on realistic assumptions that household needs change over family lifestage, risk aversion decreases with wealth, and knowledge and sophistication increase with time and experience.

Probability of product ownership is calculated as a function of the level of customer "financial maturity" relative to the level of product "difficulty". Figure 3.15 highlights the relationship between "financial maturity" and probability of acquisition based on empirical analysis conducted

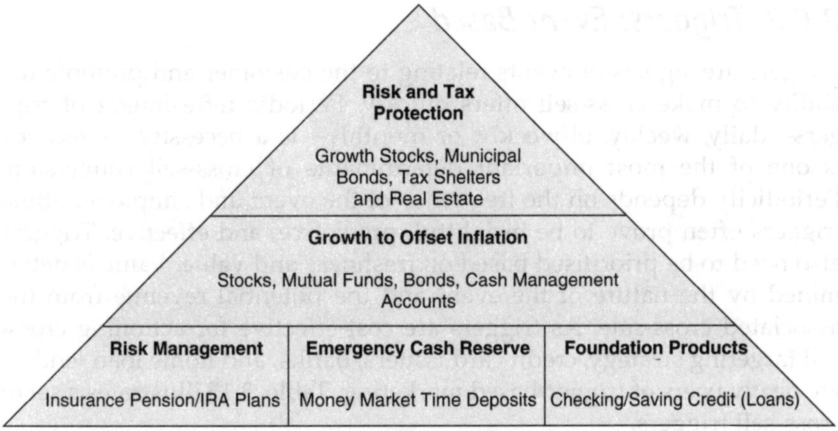


Typical hierarchy of objectives suggested by financial advisors. Transfer of risk/growth and tax investment to safer, income producing products (CD's, annuities) is recommended upon retirement

*Source:* Reprinted from International *Journal of Research in Marketing*, Volume 8, Issue 4, Kamakura et al., "Applying Latent Trait Analysis in the Evaluation of Prospects for Cross-Selling of Financial Services", Pages 329–349, Copyright (1991), with permission from Elsevier.

**Figure 3.14** Product Hierarchy

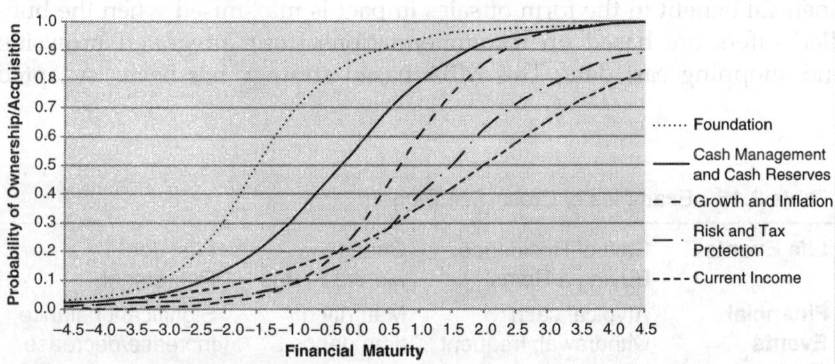


*Source:* Reprinted from *International Journal of Research in Marketing*, Volume 8, Issue 4, Kamakura et al., "Applying Latent Trait Analysis in the Evaluation of Prospects for Cross-selling of Financial Services", Pages 329–349, Copyright (1991), with permission from Elsevier.

**Figure 3.15** Hierarchical Grouping of Financial Products by Objectives

by the authors. The probability of owning a product increases as a function of the customer's financial maturity. However, the ownership probability changes more quickly for the product whose level of product "difficulty" is close to the level of customer "financial maturity".

### 3.6.3 Triggers: Event Based

Triggers are signals of events relating to the customer and promote the ability to make cross-sell offers quickly. Periodic refreshment of triggers—daily, weekly, bi-weekly, or monthly—is a necessity, as recency is one of the most important determinants of cross-sell conversion. Periodicity depends on the frequency of the event and simple real-time triggers often prove to be insightful, predictive, and effective. Triggers also need to be prioritised based on freshness and value. Value is determined by the nature of the event and the potential revenue from the associated cross-sale. As triggers are cost-effective for actioning cross-sell targeting strategy, credit card issuers, banks, and home loan lenders are heavy users of trigger-based marketing. Table. 3.15 illustrates a set of cross-sell triggers.

### 3.6.4 Market Basket Analysis (MBA): Bundling Model

#### 3.6.4.1 Summary

Market basket analysis is used to determine an effective bundling sales strategy for books (online). Three type of information are used: order data, browsing data, and shopping cart data. The results show that the financial benefit in the form of sales impact is maximised when the bundled offers are based on recommendations from integrated browsing and shopping cart data. This MBA based strategy has been "Adapted

**Table 3.15** Examples of Cross-Sell Triggers

| | | | |
|---|---|---|---|
| **Life Events** | Shift of Residence; Buying a Home | Change in Marital Status | First Job/ Retirement |
| **Financial Events** (Transaction Related) | Atypical cash withdrawal, frequent ATM/credit card usage abroad, large transaction value, out of pattern spend | Maturity of time deposit | Significant balance increase/decrease e.g., exceptionally large deposit, standing order of round amount to another bank |
| **Behavioural Changes** | RFM measured over a time period | Significant increase/ decrease in order size, bill amount | Significant change in basket composition, change in calling patterns, shift from revolver to transactor and vice versa on credit card |

from Electronic Commerce Research and Applications, Volume 5, Issue 4, Yang and Lai, *Comparison of Product Bundling Strategies on Different Online Shopping Behaviors*, Pages 295–304, Copyright (2006), with permission from Elsevier".

#### 3.6.4.2 Introduction to MBA

Market basket analysis[19] is an analysis of the composition of a basket of products purchased by a customer during a single shopping experience, with the objective of discovering buying patterns. The technique is frequently used by marketers to reveal affinities between individual products or product groupings and is based on association rules. Rule $A \rightarrow B$ can be interpreted as "If A occurs in the market basket, then B also occurs in the market basket", with *degrees* of association measured in the form of *support* and *confidence. Support* statistic provides a measure of how often the rule occurs in market baskets and enables the marketers to assess whether the rule is worthy of attention. *Confidence* ensures that the rule is true often enough. The support and confidence for $A \rightarrow B$ are defined as follows: *Support*—If *A* and *B* occur together in at least X% of the market baskets, the support for this rule is X. *Confidence*—Of all market baskets containing *A*, if at least Y% also contains *B*, then the confidence of this rule is Y. Interest for retailers comes from the fact that a market basket reflects customers' selection process regarding brand preferences and cross-category purchases. This information is useful for sales promotion activity, advertising, cross-selling, store layout, and product placement. An increase in size and value of the basket is the ultimate objective. Other industry applications include the exploration of menu items assortment, analysis of credit card purchases, and telephone calling patterns.

#### 3.6.4.3 Data Sample

The data on online shopping behaviour is taken from the website of a publisher specialising in information technology and electronic commerce books. Three sources of data were used—order data, browsing data, and shopping cart data. It is important to note that shopping cart data may be different from order data as items can be removed or added at any time, before finalising the purchase.

#### 3.6.4.4 Output

Three strategies based on the three data sources were implemented—order data only, browsing data only, and browsing + shopping cart data.

---

[19] Interested readers can refer to the textbook by Berry and Linoff, *Data Mining Techniques*, 2nd edition.

- Minimum support of 5% was set for all the three strategies. Related confidence measures were not reported in the paper.
- Results vary based on data used. Product associations and summary of association rules are presented in Tables 3.16 and 3.17.
- Browsing and shopping cart data—Chances of both products B18 and B21 being browsed together by the same customers is 8.2%, and the chance of both appearing in the customer's shopping cart is 6.9% (Table 3.16). This combination is given top priority in Table 3.17.

### 3.6.4.5 Implementation

- Nine bundling strategies were selected based on recommendations from using order data only, browsing data only, and browsing + shopping cart data
- Books which were part of the earlier promotion scheme were removed for proper control and test reads
- The promotion ran over a period of 1 month and discounts of about 25% were also implemented as a price bundling strategy
- Bundles based on browsing + shopping cart data had the best results, with 2.1 books per customer as compared to less than 1 for the other

**Table 3.16** Product Associations Based on Browsing and Shopping Cart Data

| Based on Browsing Data | | | Probability of Product Associations Appearing in a Consumer's Shopping Cart | | |
|---|---|---|---|---|---|
| Product Item 1 | Product Item 2 | Support (%) | None (%) | One Product (%) | Both Products (%) |
| B18 | B21 | 8.2 | 78.4 | 14.7 | 6.9 |
| B19 | B21 | 5.6 | 86.2 | 8.7 | 5.0 |
| L001 | L06 | 15.9 | 86.7 | 10.1 | 3.2 |
| B20 | B21 | 11.6 | 83.9 | 13.3 | 2.8 |
| B18 | B20 | 7.8 | 80.7 | 17.0 | 2.3 |
| B21 | B22 | 6.9 | 83.9 | 13.8 | 2.3 |
| L001 | L002 | 6.9 | 89.0 | 10.1 | 0.9 |
| B21 | SB01 | 5.6 | 85.3 | 13.8 | 0.9 |
| B19 | B20 | 5.6 | 89.0 | 10.1 | 0.9 |
| L002 | L303 | 8.2 | 94.0 | 5.5 | 0.5 |

*Source:* Reprinted from *Electronic Commerce Research and Applications*, Volume 5, Issue 4, Yang and Lai, "Comparison of Product Bundling Strategies on Different Online Shopping Behaviors", Pages 295–304, Copyright (2006), with permission from Elsevier.

**Table 3.17** Summary of Association Rules

| Priority | Based on Order Data Only | Based on Browsing Data Only | Based on Both Browsing and Shopping—Cart Data |
|---|---|---|---|
| 1 | (L001, L06) | (L001, S07) | (B18, B21) |
| 2 | (B15, B16) | (L06, S07) | (B19, B21) |
| 3 | (B18, B21) or (L001, T001) | (B21, S07) | (L001, L06) |
| 4 | (B18, B21) or (L001, T001) | (L001, L06) | (B20 , B21) |
| 5 | (L06, T001) or (B15, B18) or (B19, B21) | (S07, T002) | (B18, B20) or (B21, B22) |
| 6 | (L06, T001) or (B15, B18) or (B19, B21) | (S07, T001) or (B20, S07) | (B18, B20) or (B21, B22) |
| 7 | (L06, T001) or (B15, B18) or (B19, B21) | (S07, T001) or (B20, S07) | (L001, L002) or (B21, SB01) or (B19, B20) |
| 8 | (B15, B21) or (B09, B21) | (B20, S07) or (N26, S07) or (L002, S07) | (L001, L002) or (B21, SB01) or (B19, B20) |
| 9 | (B15, B21) or (B09, B21) | (B20, S07) or (N26, S07) or (L002, S07) | (L001, L002) or (B21, SB01) or (B19, B20) |
| 10 | (B14, B15) | (B20, S07) or (N26, S07) or (L002, S07) | (L002, L303) |

*Source:* Reprinted from *Electronic Commerce Research and Applications*, Volume 5, Issue 4, *Yang and Lai*, "Comparison of Product Bundling Strategies on Different Online Shopping Behaviors", Pages 295–304, Copyright (2006), with permission from Elsevier.

two strategies. This is an empirical confirmation of authors' hypotheses that

- Information of shopping cart is more closely related to final shopping decision than browsing data alone, which explains the improved results of browsing + shopping cart data vs. browsing data only
- Order data standalone does not reveal preferences completely, which explains the better results for browsing + shopping cart data vs. order data only

- Implementation was successful with significantly higher customers and orders (post strategy), as shown in Table 3.18

**Table 3.18** Bundling Implementation Results

| Pre and Post Implementation Results (Means Per Month) | | | |
|---|---|---|---|
| | Customers | Orders | Books |
| Pre strategy | 2.7 | 2.8 | 9 |
| Post strategy | 22 | 33 | 78 |

*Source:* Yang and Lai (2006).

#### 3.6.4.6 Advantages and Limitations

The example emphasises on the application of market basket analysis for identifying product associations for bundling offers. This forms the basis for promotional strategies, and the financial results exemplify the benefits of using such an approach. The usage of this technique for marketing bundles hinges on the implicit assumption that it identifies complements. To the contrary, according to a paper titled *Why Promotion Strategies based on Market Basket Analysis do not Work*, Vindevogel and co-authors claim that market basket analysis may not be as effective, as it identifies as many substitutes as complements (and this noise has to be filtered out).

### *3.6.5 Recommender Systems: Collaborative Filtering*

#### 3.6.5.1 Summary

Recommender systems are best known for their use on e-commerce websites, wherein inputs about customers' interests and preferences are used to generate a list of recommendations. The products can be recommended based on the analysis of past buying behaviour of the customer as a prediction for future buying behaviour. Broadly speaking, these techniques are part of personalisation, as the site adapts itself to each customer. Recommender systems enhance e-commerce by helping customers find products they wish to purchase, and by suggesting additional products for the customer to purchase and increase the order. Recommender algorithms often operate in a challenging environment with huge amounts of data, millions of customers, and millions of distinct catalogue items. Most applications require the results set to be returned almost instantaneously in real time, while still producing high-quality recommendations. New users or customers provide limited information based on a few purchases or product ratings, while older customers provide too much information based on thousands of purchases and ratings. Customer data is volatile with customers' preferences changing over time and each interaction provides valuable customer data. The algorithm is expected to respond immediately to new information. The three common approaches of recommender systems are: collaborative filtering, cluster models, and search-based models[20]. Widely used in the last decade for Internet marketing efforts, Amazon is a big proponent and successful user of collaborative filtering for online cross-sell activities.

[20] Search-or-content-based methods treat the recommendations problem as a search for related items. Given the user's purchased and rated items, the algorithm constructs a search query to find other popular items by the same author, artist, or director, or with similar keywords or subjects.

### 3.6.5.2 Introduction

Collaborative filtering (CF) is primarily used to predict customers' preferences and has its roots in information filtering that uses group opinions to recommend items to customers. The term was coined by Dave Goldberg and his colleagues at Xerox PARC. The fundamental premise of CF is that customers with similar tastes tend to like similar types of items. In order to work effectively, it requires a fairly representative sample of customers and a rich record of preferences or purchase histories. The traditional method of collaborative filtering is user-based. The user-based first finds sets of customers with purchase and rated items similar to the user's purchased and rated items, and the algorithm aggregates items from these similar customers, eliminates the one the user has already bought, and recommends the remaining items. CF works by building a database of preferences for items by users, and a new user is matched against the database to find neighbours who have similar preferences as the new user. Items that neighbours prefer are recommended to the new user. However, item-to-item based, invented by Amazon has gained popularity. Item-to-item CF is based on similar items rather than similar customers and matches each of the user's purchased and rated items to similar items, and then combines these similar items into a recommendation. As the relationship between items is relatively static, the item-based recommendation may be able to provide the same quality as the user based recommendation with less online computation. The definition of "similar" varies from system to system and one aspect of making good recommendations is having an appropriate measure of similarity[21]. Collaborative filtering is widely applied by e-commerce sites for cross-selling.

### 3.6.5.3 Advantages and Limitations

CF is a powerful technique that does not require intervention by the user as he/she does not need to state preferences explicitly by filling out on-screen forms before being presented with recommendations. It is computationally demanding, which increases with the number of users. To reach its potential, it has to be integrated with a cross-sell engine or an online store. It suffers from limitations relating to the accuracy of recommendations made as opinions change or when close neighbours do not exist. Requiring large samples, direct insights into factors driving preferences are difficult to comprehend. CF does not necessarily exploit information on customer profiles that have important ramifications on customer purchase behaviour.

---

[21] Some similarity measures are simple key word matching, nearest neighbour algorithms, and cosine similarity.

### 3.6.5.4 Applications

*Amazon*[22] Amazon uses recommendations as a targeted marketing tool on its pages. Clicking on "*Your recommendations*" link directs customers to a site, where they can filter their recommendations by product line and subject area, and rate their previous purchases. Similarly, "*Customers who bought*" is found on the information page for each book in their catalogue and has two separate recommendation lists. The first recommends books frequently purchased by customers, who purchased the selected book. The second recommends authors whose books are frequently purchased by customers, who purchased works by the author of the selected book. Email campaigns and customer level personalisation are also heavily dependent on these recommendations. Since Amazon has a huge database of tens of millions of customers and products, item-to-item CF is able to scale up to massive data sets with high-quality recommendations in real time, irrespective of the number of purchases and ratings.

*Netflix* Netflix, is a provider of on-demand Internet streaming media and flat rate DVD-by-mail in the US. The company was established in 1997 and by October 2012, it had 30 million subscribers (streaming).

The Netflix website automatically makes recommendations based on a system called CineMatch, which includes a database that uses information from different sources to determine which movies customers are likely to enjoy. The CineMatch database updates itself constantly, and makes thousands of recommendations every second or close to a billion total predictions every day. The company's movie recommendation software was already renowned for suggesting rentals based on a customer's previous picks and those of others with similar tastes. Occasionally, the predictive algorithms directed customers to films that were not preferred. After repeated attempts to improve the programme, Netflix announced a million-dollar prize Netflix competition in 2006, with an objective to boost the accuracy of its predictions by 10%. Data of 100 million movie ratings was provided and contestants attempted to predict which movies particular customers would prefer, and these predictions were compared with how customers actually rated these movies later. After a 3 year long contest, two teams of Bellkor and Ensemble (a global alliance with some 30 members) were the winners, after passing the 10% threshold.

[22] Linden et al. *Amazon.com Recommendations*, and Schafer et al. *E-Commerce Recommendation Applications*.

## 3.6.6 Classification/Decision Tree: Response Segmentation

### 3.6.6.1 Summary

The purpose of using classification tree for response segmentation is to identify and differentiate customers with low and high response rates based on customer demographics and behaviour. The implementation benefits of this segmentation can be two-fold—cost reduction from lower mail file volume for the same response volume; higher revenue from response rate lifts for the same volume of mail file. For example, based on practical experience, a doubling of response rate for the same mail file volume, with a similar quantum jump in campaign revenue is feasible. The segmentation can also be leveraged for differential pricing and contact strategy, with higher pricing for higher response segments (based on price elasticity). An example of response based pricing is presented as implementation strategy of a cross-sell response score in the logistic regression section of Chapter 7, "Quantitative Methods".

### 3.6.6.2 Introduction

A classification tree is used to explain and predict outcomes on a categorical variable, using one or more explanatory (predictor) variables. Hierarchical in nature, this method evaluates the effects of predictor variables on the dependent variable by performing multivariate segmentation in a recursive manner. The process can be characterised into three basic steps of selecting splits, determining when to stop splitting, and choosing the "right-sized" tree. Predicting the event of response (to a mail campaign) and payment delinquency are common applications. Marketers use the results for focused targeting, to improve response and ROI on campaigns and for personalised communication. The flexibility, ease of development, and graphical representation makes it a very attractive option.

### 3.6.6.3 Output

Historical campaign data of personal loan to credit card cross-sell has an average response rate of 4.5%. Business as usual (BAU) strategy is a mail file of 34,000 accounts, selected as a random sample from an eligible credit card population of 100,000 accounts. Credit card customer data of demographics, transaction, and product level information is used. The dependent variable is response that takes a value of 1 if response is yes, else 0. The tree with all the relevant information and the Gains Chart is presented in Figs. 3.16 and 3.17, respectively. The reader should focus on the end or

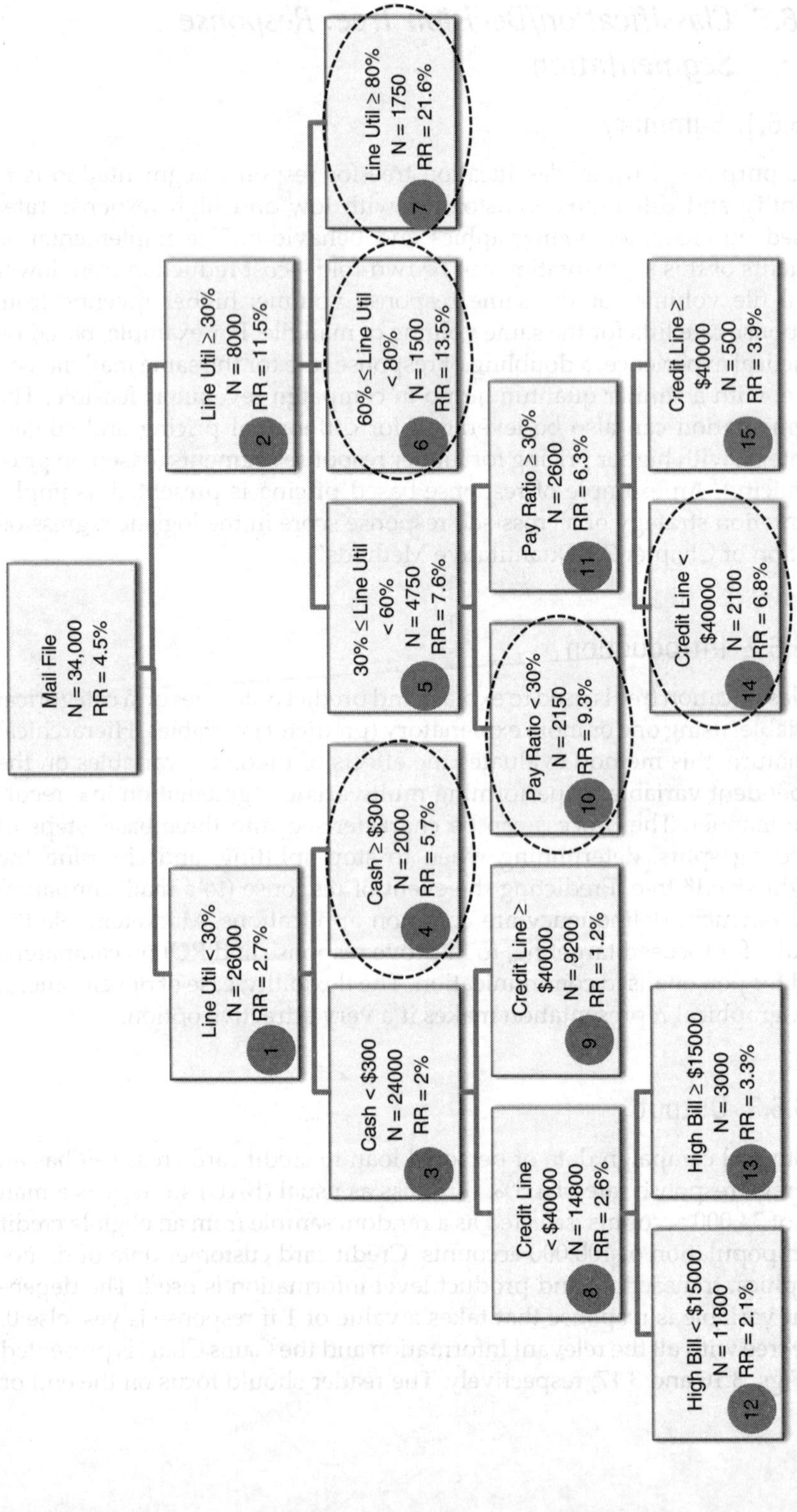


**Figure 3.16** Personal Loan to Credit Card Cross-Sell-Response Segmentation

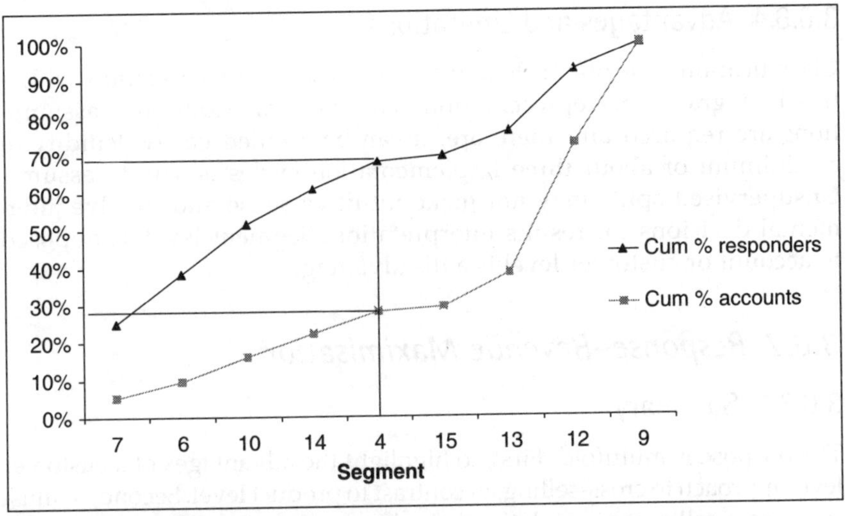


**Figure 3.17** Personal Loan to Credit Card Cross-Sell—Gains Chart

terminal nodes (4, 6, 7, 9, 10, 12, 13, 14, 15). Please do note that relevant statistical measures are not shown in this example.

- The segment with the highest response rate of 21.6% is node 7, a group which has the highest line utilisation of greater than 80%. Propensity to take a personal loan for these credit card customers is more than four times the sample average of 4.5%.
- The segment with the lowest response rate is node 9 characterised by a profile that can also be written as a rule: Line Util < 30% and Cash < \$300 and Credit line ≥ \$40,000
- Nodes 4, 6, 7, 10, 14 have response rates above the average, with a collective response rate of 10.6%, thereby forming the target segments for cross-sell
- Gains Chart shows that close to 70% of responders can be captured by approximately 30% of the sample population. This result translates into a marketing cost reduction as 40% of the sample population does not need to be contacted. This is in comparison to a random selection of 70% of the population for 70% of responders.

RR = Response Rate
N = Sample Size
Credit Line = Credit Line on Card
Cash = Cash on Card
Line Util = Line Utilisation Defined as Card Balance Divided by Credit Line
High Bill = Highest Bill Amount Ever on Credit Card

#### 3.6.6.4 Advantages and Limitations

Classification tree offers flexibility and ease of interpretation with a tree-like graphical representation. No data distributional assumptions are required and therefore, it can be applied easily. Validity of a minimum of about three implementation cycles is safe to assume. Unsupervised splits may not make intuitive sense and involve judgmental decisions for results interpretation. Segment level as opposed to account or customer level is a disadvantage.

### *3.6.7 Response–Revenue Maximisation*

#### 3.6.7.1 Summary

The purpose is multifold. First, to highlight the advantages of a customer level approach to cross-selling, in contrast to product level. Second, to illustrate cross-sell recommendations of what product to offer and to whom based on objectives of maximising response and subsequently revenue.

#### 3.6.7.2 Introduction

A firm has three products to offer and as a simplistic example, the assumption is that the firm is soliciting three customers for these products. Each of these customers has a different demographic/behavioural profile. Product revenue is a yearly unit figure and the implicit assumption is that the customer will stay for at least 1 year after accepting the product offer. It is assumed that the conversion rate is 100%. Each customer is scored for response for every product, and expected revenue by product for every customer is derived.

#### 3.6.7.3 Output

Table 3.19 illustrates the different scenarios being considered.

*Product Level—Scenario 1* The firm has information on average response rates and revenue by product from historical data, and these are assumed to be expected values. Both are at a segment level. The average response rates are the same for all products. If the objective of the firm is to maximise revenue, the best choice would be to offer product C to all three customers since it has the highest revenue per unit. This gives an expected revenue of $117 ($39 * 3). Products A and B are not offered.

*Customer Level—Scenario 2* As the firm's objective is to also offer products A and B as part of its cross-sell focus, the strategy is revisited with the intention of offering the right product to the right customer. The analytics team scores every customer for each of the three products to derive propensity to respond by product. On a re-look, given the huge

**Table 3.19** Optimising Response and Revenue

| Scenario 1: By Product | | | |
|---|---|---|---|
| Product | Expected Response Rate | Revenue per Unit: Cross-Sell Channel | Expected Revenue (Expected Response Rate * Revenue per Unit) |
| A | 3.0% | $1,000 | $30 |
| B | 3.0% | $600 | $18 |
| C | 3.0% | $1,300 | $39 |
| Average | 3.0% | $967 | $29 |
| | Product C for every customer<br>Average response rate = 3%<br>Total expected revenue = $117 | | |

| Scenario 2: By Customer | | | | | | | | | |
|---|---|---|---|---|---|---|---|---|---|
| Products | A | | | B | | | C | | |
| Customers | Expected Response Rate | Revenue Per Responder | Expected Revenue | Expected Response Rate | Revenue Per Responder | Expected Revenue | Expected Response Rate | Revenue Per Responder | Expected Revenue |
| 1 | 2.5% | $1,000 | $25 | 4.0% | $150 | $6 | 0.5% | $2,500 | $13 |
| 2 | 5.0% | $400 | $20 | 2.0% | $1,300 | $26 | 2.5% | $600 | $15 |
| 3 | 1.5% | $1,600 | $24 | 3.0% | $350 | $11 | 6.0% | $800 | $48 |
| Average | 3.0% | $1,000 | $23 | 3.0% | $600 | $14 | 3.0% | $1,300 | $25 |
| | Product C for every customer<br>Average response rate = 3%<br>Total expected revenue = $76 | | | | | | | | |

(*Continued*)

**Table 3.19** Optimising Response and Revenue (*Continued*)

| Scenario 3: Recommendations By Response | | | | | |
|---|---|---|---|---|---|
| **Customer** | **1st** | **2nd** | **3rd** | **Expected Response Rate (For 1st Offer)** | **Expected Revenue (For 1st Offer)** |
| 1 | B | A | C | 4.0% | $6 |
| 2 | A | C | B | 5.0% | $20 |
| 3 | C | B | A | 6.0% | $48 |
| Average | | | | 5.0% | $25 |
| Customer 1 = Product B; Customer 2 = Product A; Customer 3 = Product C<br>Average response rate = 5%<br>Total expected revenue = $74 | | | | | |

| Scenario 4: Recommendations by Revenue | | | | | |
|---|---|---|---|---|---|
| **Customer** | **1st** | **2nd** | **3rd** | **Expected Response Rate (For 1st Offer)** | **Expected Revenue (For 1st Offer)** |
| 1 | A | C | B | 2.5% | $25 |
| 2 | B | A | C | 2.0% | $26 |
| 3 | C | A | B | 6.0% | $48 |
| Average | | | | 3.5% | $33 |
| Customer 1 = Product A; Customer 2 = Product B; Customer 3 = Product C<br>Average response rate = 3.5%<br>Total expected revenue = $99 | | | | | |

variation in response rates and revenue at a customer level, following the preceding strategy (*Scenario 1*) and offering product C to all three customers is expected to give only $76 of revenue, which is 35% lower than the estimate of *Scenario 1*. A customer view is a more representative and accurate measure of expected benefits and highlights the disadvantages of not evaluating the choice of product at a customer or segment level.

*Response Maximisation—Scenario 3* To maximise response, the optimal product to offer to the customer is the one with the maximum expected response rate. Products are prioritised based on ranking of response rates across products for that particular customer. The expected average response rate is 5% with total expected revenue of $74. On a scale beyond three customers, this strategy would yield higher expected revenue for the programme as compared to *Scenario 2*, given the response enhancement in this scenario.

*Revenue Maximisation—Scenario 4* To maximise revenue, recommendations are based on expected revenue. The product with maximum expected revenue is chosen as the first offer to make to the customer. Such an approach gives total expected revenue of $99, which is 33% higher than *Scenario 3*. Given the lower response rate, this scenario reflects a trade-off of response for revenue.

#### 3.6.7.4 Advantages and Limitations

This example clearly highlights the benefits of a customer rather than a product-level evaluation. The approach permits flexibility regarding the priority of product offers by customer/segment, depending on the cross-sell goals of the organisation. An enhancement would be to incorporate expenses and base decisions on profitability measured over a longer period. With millions of customers and multiple products in a multi-objective and multi-constraints scenario, a concrete analytical framework such as optimisation and decision analysis are required, that is discussed subsequently.

### *3.6.8 Optimisation Model*

#### 3.6.8.1 Summary

The aim is to determine *what product* to offer to *which customer* and by *which channel* that would maximise the marketing return on investment (marginal return on additional dollar of investment). This is under a multi-constraint scenario of a budget constraint, multiple sequential campaigns, and other business constraints. Using this framework, some of the objectives that can be achieved are campaign budget allocation, channel capacity planning and sensitivity analysis, and the impact of making different budget allocations on campaign profitability. This has high applicability to financial services with multiple campaigns, multiproduct offers, and channels with different costs and returns. The discussion is "Adapted from Information Systems, Volume 29, Issue 4, Cohen, *Exploiting Response Models-Optimizing Cross-Sell and Up-Sell Opportunities in Banking*, Pages 327–341, Copyright (2004), with permission from Elsevier".

#### 3.6.8.2 Introduction

An optimisation model is used to maximise the return on investment under multiple constraints. The constraints are campaign budget, channel capacity, minimum and maximum number of offers for a product and number of offers per customer. Some of the constraints are as follows:

- Campaign costs cannot exceed $1 million
- Campaign must have an ROI of at least the corporate hurdle rate
- Branch and call centre channels have a certain constraint, for example, 250,000 leads for branch
- Product offer to a minimum number of 20,000 customers
- Standard marketing and risk exclusions

Inputs for this exercise are predictive response models, expected profit at customer level, defined segments, channel costs, optimisation algorithm, and advanced programming skills.

#### 3.6.8.3 Output

Table 3.20 shows optimal product, channel, and resulting return on investment for a sample of customers on the mail file. Reports on frequency of offers, channel recommendation, return on investment, constraint reports, and profit per channel can be systematically and graphically presented, to share with senior management.

#### 3.6.8.4 Implementation

Using the optimisation approach, the campaign expected profit is $3.58 million on an investment of $1 million, resulting in a ROI of 258%. In comparison, the ad hoc method (based on response models and satisfying all business constraints) can generate up to $2.65 million and a ROI of 165%. Cohen claims that the incremental return is attributable to the quality of the solution.

#### 3.6.8.5 Advantages and Limitations

The optimisation routine is a significant improvement over conventional approaches as it incorporates multiple constraints and channels, which impact the value of investment. Optimisation algorithms can handle complex constraints, usually difficult to do with traditional approaches.

**Table 3.20** Optimisation—Sample of the Solution Data Set

| Customer Id | Product | Channel | Return |
|---|---|---|---|
| 00182723 | | | . |
| 00200688 | | | . |
| 00032937 | | | . |
| 00722119 | | | . |
| 02137391 | | | . |
| 00992639 | | | . |
| 00060721 | | | . |
| 00483601 | Offer 2 | Direct mail | 0.0005 |
| 01164964 | | | . |
| 00025469 | | | . |
| 01008244 | | | . |
| 00179891 | | | . |
| 00410488 | Offer 10 | Direct mail | 3.1852 |
| 01484008 | | | . |
| 00184804 | | | . |
| 03350118 | | | . |
| 00983111 | | | . |
| 00387834 | Offer 5 | Call centre | 13.0782 |
| 01100914 | | | . |
| 01507075 | | | . |
| 01559899 | | | . |
| 00309931 | | | . |
| 00657640 | | | . |
| 01095694 | | | . |
| 02075404 | | | . |

*Source:* Reprinted from *Information Systems*, Volume 29, Issue 4, Cohen, "Exploiting Response Models-Optimizing Cross-Sell and Up-Sell Opportunities in Banking", Pages 327–341, Copyright (2004), with permission from Elsevier.

Scalability does not appear to be an issue as the optimisation was worked upon 2.5 million customers, 11 offers, 3 channels, and more than 5 constraints in an acceptable amount of execution time and resources. However, Cohen states the inability of the particular algorithm used, to effectively tackle complex constraints regarding customer contact plan. Inputs require exhaustive data analysis that depend on reads of historical campaigns and the support of a good technology infrastructure (e.g., data warehouse), process, and advanced analytics. Inputs and assumptions need to be periodically revised based on the review of recent campaigns and the accuracy of customer level score estimates need validation.

Alternatively, Sundarajan et al. from GE Global Research take a fuzzy mathematical programming approach to minimise the imprecision relating to these score estimates, and apply it to a retail bank cross-sell example.

### *3.6.9 Decision Analysis*

#### 3.6.9.1 Summary

A decision analysis framework is used for a cross-sell programme of second card. The concept of expected lifetime NPV on the second card is used for making a decision on whether to cross-sell. Specifically, NPV is a measure by which customer behaviour projections (through cash flow) are translated into a value measure for decision making. The framework is based on the synthesis of different behavioural scorecards into a structured analytic architecture for decision making.

Issuers treat second card programmes as a quick route to increase cards in force. A conventional approach relies on the risk profile of the customer based on performance on the first card, other products held with the same institution and competition. A traditional policy for second card eligibility hinges on a set of rules based on observed delinquency-related behaviour on the first card and usually does not evaluate the expected profitability on the second card. Often run as a pre-approved programme, the cross-sell strategy does not necessarily translate into a profitable programme. The reasons are high inactivity and low usage on the cross-sold credit card. Exceptions are perhaps co-brand products perceived to be a high value proposition by the customer and therefore, usage is not a concern. Further, second card involves an increase in credit limit exposure. Therefore, the challenge is to achieve good returns on the incremental line as it comes at an opportunity cost. The opportunity cost is an alternative unsecured product that could have been cross-sold, for example, personal loan with 100% utilisation. Having ramped up this effort early on, many issuers are scaling down this programme and closing down select multiple card accounts in their portfolio as a reaction to low profitability.

#### 3.6.9.2 Introduction

Decision analysis is a logical and systematic method to address a wide variety of problems involving decision making in an uncertain environment. As a method for structuring and analysing managerial decision-making, it refers to the broad quantitative field overlapping operations research and statistics that involves modelling, optimising, and analysing decisions.

Decision making with respect to risk related to uncertainity, requires a specification of a decision rule so that different alternatives or strategies can be evaluated for achieving the stated objective. Some commonly used single-objective decision rules are maximising expected monetary value (EMV) and maximising expected utility. When multiple objectives are at stake, an aggregation into a single measure of performance is of use for decision making. Trade-offs are required for reconciliation by assigning weights of importance to the various objectives. Multi-attribute utility theory provides a framework to assign these weights systematically. For the financial services industry, the multiple objectives of minimising credit loss, maximising profits, and maintaining market share would be one such case.

The process of testing and evaluating how the solution behaves in response to changes in data is called sensitivity analysis or simulation and is as much of an art as it is science. The exercise of performing sensitivity analysis is important to gain confidence in the validity of the model and a necessary step before decisions are taken regarding the final choice across alternatives.

### 3.6.9.3 Framework

The analytical model that is used in decision analysis is called a decision tree. A decision tree is a systematic way of organising and representing the possible decision paths. A decision tree showing the behaviour of a credit card account through the first 12 months on book (MOB) is given in Fig. 3.18 and can be easily extended for a 24 month horizon.

The expected monetary value (EMV) of an account is the weighted average of all possible outcomes, with the probabilities of each of the outcomes used as weights. It is also the expected cash flow.

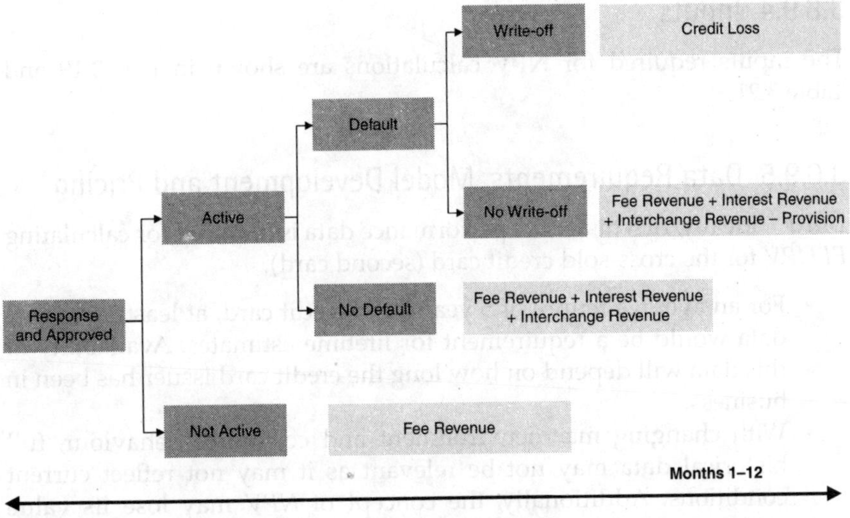


**Figure 3.18** Decision Tree for a Credit Card Portfolio

EMV (Year 1) = *P* (Active & Default & Write-off)* [–Credit Loss] + *P* (Active & Default & No Write-off)* [Fee Revenue + Interest Revenue + Interchange Revenue – Provision] + *P* (Active & No Default)*[Fee Revenue + Interest Revenue + Interchange Revenue] + *P* (Not Active) * [Fee Revenue]

where *P* = Probability of Occurrence of the Event

***Net Present Value (NPV)*** Net present value (*NPV*) is the present value of expected future cash flows. Assuming an average lifetime of 5 years for the cross-sold credit card, *Expected Lifetime NPV (ELNPV)* on the cross-sold credit card account can be estimated as follows:

$$ELNPV = P\,(\text{Response Rate}) * \left[\frac{EMV(Year\ 1)}{1+r} + \frac{EMV(Year\ 2)}{(1+r)^2} + \frac{EMV(Year\ 3)}{(1+r)^3} + \frac{EMV(Year\ 4)}{(1+r)^4} + \frac{EMV(Year\ 5)}{(1+r)^5} + \frac{Terminal\ Value}{(1+r)^5}\right]$$

*r* = Hurdle Rate (e.g., cost of equity, rate of return on equity)

Terminal Value = Residual Value of the Investment, for example, sale value of receivables after 5 years

*P* (Response Rate) = Predicted response rate

*ELNPV* can be estimated at different price points with the necessary inputs. For this example, the assumption is that a co-brand credit card (cross-sold product) is being considered for cross-sell to an account holder of a vanilla classic credit card (base product).

#### 3.6.9.4 Inputs

The inputs required for NPV calculations are shown in Fig. 3.19 and Table 3.21.

#### 3.6.9.5 Data Requirements, Model Development and Pricing

***Data*** Ideally, rich historical performance data is required for calculating *ELNPV* for the cross-sold credit card (second card).

- For an average tenure of 5 years on a credit card, at least 5 years of data would be a requirement for lifetime estimates. Availability of this data will depend on how long the credit card issuer has been in business.
- With changing macroenvironment and consumer behaviour, full historical data may not be relevant as it may not reflect current conditions. Additionally, the concept of *NPV* may lose its value in terms of validity and hence, usability (if calculated over a time

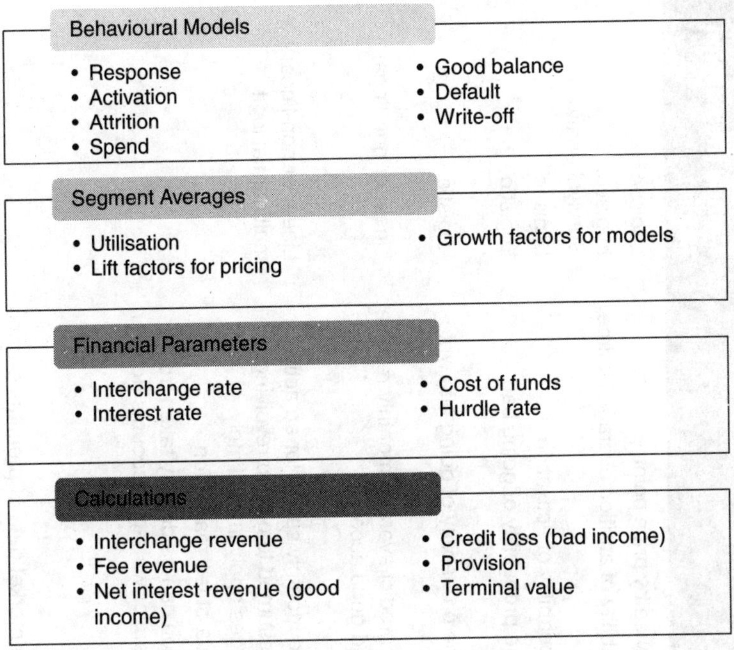


**Figure 3.19** Decision Analysis—Inputs I

frame of greater than 24/36 months). For a prime credit card portfolio, the first 24–36 months on book are important for determining profitability, given the credit cycle.

*Models* Models should be built by MOB (e.g., 1–12 MOB, 13–24 MOB, 25–36 MOB etc.) in order to capture the changing portfolio credit behaviour by MOB, and its differential impact on year-wise P&L. However, developing models for each of the 5 years can prove to be an immensely difficult task. This effort requires a specialised modelling team for the development of scores and their maintenance. In lieu of the above, given constraints of data, time, and skill availability, it is advisable to limit model development to a specific time frame, for example, 24/36 MOB. The choice of time frame would depend on the observed credit cycle of the card portfolio, time taken for the portfolio to break even, and data availability. The next step involves the calculation of *EMV* estimates for the later periods beyond 24/36 MOB. If longer vintage data is available, one approach could be to use estimates of segment-based averages based on historical data for the rest of the periods for all the components of *EMV*. Alternatively, to bring in variability at an account level, an "adjustment growth factor" could be developed based on historical performance data by MOB (later vintage performance pegged to early vintage). This adjustment factor is then applied to the models developed using early period data for later period forecasts, for which models are

**Table 3.21** Decision Analysis—Inputs II

| Input Variable | Definition | Estimate | Method (Regression Model) |
|---|---|---|---|
| Response | | Models to predict response by price point | Logistic |
| Lifetime/attrition | Voluntary attrition | Model to develop probability of attrition/average lifetime (tenure) of the account | Logistic; Survival analysis |
| Activation | Spend or balance active | Model to predict the probability of activation | Logistic |
| Default | Ever 90+ DPD in the next 12 months (bad); else good | Risk Model to predict the probability of going bad | Logistic |
| Write-off | Ever 180+ DPD in the next 12 months | Loss Model to predict the probability of going into write-off, given default | Logistic |
| Interest revenue | (Interest rate – Cost of funds)* good balance | Good balance model to predict average monthly revolve balance for an active and good account. | Linear or non-linear |
| Spend revenue (interchange and cash) | Interchange revenue is interchange* purchase spend | Model to predict average monthly spend for an active account. Cash can be assumed to go into revolving balance as finance charges apply immediately. | Linear or non-linear; multinomial logit |
| Fee revenue | Annual fee and other fees | Actual from historical data of fee realisation | |
| Credit loss | Probability of write-off * bad utilisation* credit line | Estimate for bad utilisation can be directly taken from actual utilisation observed for write-off accounts (total or by segment) | |
| Provision | Percentage of total line exposure | Finance parameter | |
| Terminal value | Value from selling the receivables at end of year 5 | Can be determined from market data of premium earned based on credit card portfolio valuation | |

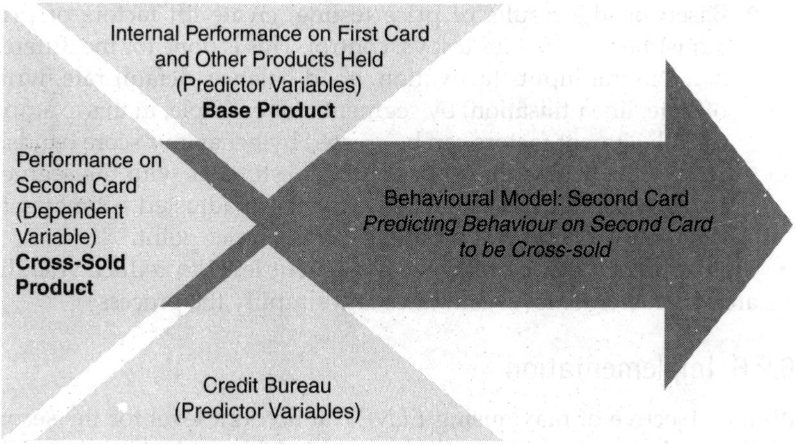


**Figure 3.20** Decision Analysis—Model Related

not available. Alternatively, one can make decisions based on the first 2–3 year period horizon only. Figure 3.20 gives a framework for model development for the cross-sold product.

*Pricing Data* For effective price management, the issuer would need to do one or several rounds of random price testing to understand the sensitivity of rate and fee on response, activation, balances, attrition, delinquency, and credit loss. The tests should be conducted in a controlled manner with a proper champion challenger set-up and if required, design of experiments discussed in Chapter 8, "Analytics Ecosystem" would be useful at this time.

- Some expected results of test price relative to control (base) price on customer behaviour:
  - A lower rate for the same fee has higher response, higher activation, and therefore higher balances
  - Higher fee (for same rate) may depress response but leads to a higher activation rate leading to higher balances. For a lower credit quality customer profile (low behaviour score), a high fee may attract riskier segments (negative selection), which may negate the upside from higher fee earnings.
- Price adjusted framework
  - To build separate models for each price point would be a gigantic task. If additional price points are introduced, this would involve building new models to reflect the new price points.
  - One solution is to develop base models for base price points that are expected to serve as the control, against which all other price points can be compared.

  - Based on the results of price testing, create lift factors or price adjustment factors for test vs. control. This is done for the different behavioural inputs (activation, good balance, default rate, write-off rate, line utilisation) by segment. For example, in this example, the adjustment factors can be created by behaviour score bands.
  - Adjust the account level base model estimates with the segment level price adjustment factors. Use these adjusted estimates for cash flow calculations for the respective price point.
- This approach can be taken at a segment level to reduce volatility around customer level estimates and simplify the process

### 3.6.9.6 Implementation

With the objective of maximising *ELNPV* at account level for the second card, the implementation process is highlighted. First calculate the *ELNPV* at different price points, followed by a swap set analysis, pricing simulations, and then the final pricing strategy before designing and rolling out the campaign. Figure 3.21 gives an insight into the decision rule.

*Swap Set Analysis* For the initial round of implementation and perhaps for some more cycles, it is important to conduct a swap set analysis to determine the eligible population for cross-selling. Further, to understand the profile of accounts brought in and eliminated as a result of the new strategy relative to the existing strategy/policy (Table 3.22).

Contents of each cell should include sample size, means of behaviour score, expected default and loss rates, average balance, revenue, profitability and *ELNPV*, and other metrics. Consequent to the first implementation, the above mentioned variables should be stacked up against this grid.

*Pricing Financials* At most organisations, the final call on pricing strategy is made by the finance department. The cash flow calculations discussed earlier are basic calculations, which do not incorporate important elements that the finance department would typically look at. In other words, a fully loaded profitability measure that accounts for late/delinquency fees, operating expenses, rewards costs, partnership/alliance costs, fraud losses, and others. The recommended price point by segment and related number of expected cross-sold accounts, estimates of predicted behaviour (e.g., balances, default, and loss rate) from the models, are normally provided by the analytics team to the finance department. Table 3.23 is an illustration of one of the outputs to expect from the finance team regarding the recommendations on price points to offer.

### 3.6.9.7 Advantages and Limitations

Decision analysis incorporates the comprehensive use of behavioural models to derive a lifetime value concept for cross-sell offer decision making. This method is highly resource intensive and inputs require

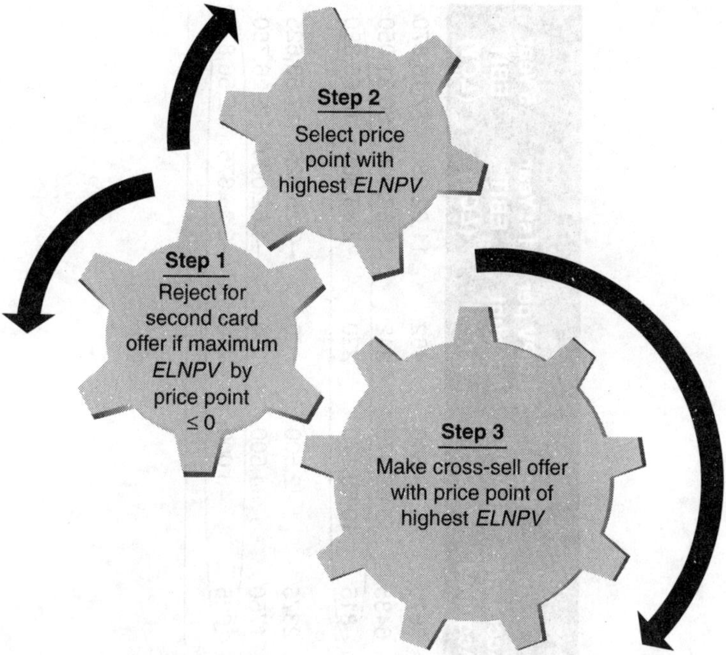


**Figure 3.21** Decision Rule

**Table 3.22** Swap Set Analysis

| | | New Criteria | |
|---|---|---|---|
| | | Pass | Fail |
| Old Criteria | Pass | Offer | No offer/Test |
| | Fail | Offer | No offer |

constant validation and updating (dependent on access to a highly experienced analytics team). Optimisation methods are an additional requirement when a suite of different credit card products are being considered for cross-selling. Moreover, for a holistic and customer-centric approach that is the fundamental philosophy of cross-selling, decision making based on customer profitability at the card level (first and second card together) is recommended (rather than account profitability of the second card only). This should be done, to account for after-effects such as spend and balance migration from the first to second card.

**Table 3.23** Pricing Plan Simulation

| Segment (based on behaviour score) | | Rate | Fee (*LCY*) | Yield | Cost of Acquisition per Account (*LCY*) | Accounts Acquired | Total ELNPV (*LCY*) | ELNPV per Account (*LCY*) | 1st Year EBIT (*LCY*) | 5 Year EBIT (*LCY*) |
|---|---|---|---|---|---|---|---|---|---|---|
| <750 | Proposed | 16% | 150 | 17.9% | 33 | 5670 | 26,19,540 | 462 | 11,62,350 | 77,16,870 |
| | Base | 16% | 100 | 17.3% | 30 | 6485 | 15,69,370 | 242 | 8,68,990 | 60,31,050 |
| | **Incremental** | | | | | –815 | 10,50,170 | 220 | 2,93,360 | 16,85,820 |
| >750 | Proposed | 10% | 180 | 12.0% | 290 | 2375 | 1,42,500 | 60 | –2,25,625 | 17,83,625 |
| | Base | 16% | 100 | 18.7% | 395 | 1750 | 94,500 | 54 | –4,62,000 | 5,26,750 |
| | **Incremental** | | | | | 625 | 48,000 | 6 | –2,36,375 | 12,56,875 |

*Note:* Cost of acquisition is significantly higher for >750 segment as response rate is lower

*LCY is local currency.* USD in this example.

FOUR

# Retention Management

## 4.1 Introduction

Attrition, the converse of retention, is traditionally defined as the end of a relationship between the buyer and seller, either partial or the complete association. Usually defined from the seller's perspective, a more contemporary view also refers to attrition as a decline in engagement between those concerned: firm–consumer, employee–employer, and service provider–client, to quote a few. According to loyalty expert Frederick Reichheld, *The Loyalty Effect*, with customer defection rates in double digits across most industries, firms can lose half their customers in five years, employers can lose half their employees in four, and half their investors in less than one, leading to a depression of corporate performance by as much as 25–50%. It is also a well-known fact that it is multiple times more expensive to acquire a new customer than to retain an existing one, and high attrition rates increase replacement costs of existing customers. Reichheld claims that a good retention strategy creates competitive advantages, provides a boost to employee morale, produces gains in productivity and growth, and reduces cost. The results can be impressive. It has been observed that a 5 percentage point improvement in customer retention can result in a 75% and upwards increase in customer lifetime value (CLV) across a range of industries; account for more than a 20% improvement in productivity; and translate into a growth advantage equal to a doubling of customer inventory every 14 years.

Retention strategies are formulated based on the nature of attrition such as type, severity, consequential financial burden, and overall retention and profitability goals of the firm, among other considerations. Reactive, proactive, and win-back approaches to retention management are options available to the firm. Nevertheless, retention strategies are incomplete without a robust and effective implementation process. This involves putting in place a dedicated retention unit, the required infrastructure, and trained retention personnel.

Attrition is multifarious in character, thereby warranting a discussion on the types of attrition. Account and customer attrition signify partial and complete loss of a relationship, respectively. In the case of multiple associations of a customer with a firm, losing an account is less severe than losing a customer. This is often a good indicator of customer attrition following soon and requiring speed to action. Voluntary closure is initiated by the customer for reasons such as uncompetitive pricing, poor service, and others. Payment delinquency and low profitability can lead to involuntary closure of the account without customer consent. However, the focus of this chapter is on voluntary attrition. Another dimension of attrition is active and passive. Active attrition is measured based on actual formal closure of the relationship, and passive or silent attrition is measured as a decline in engagement. Coyles and Gokey in a McKinsey quarterly paper titled *Customer Retention is Not Enough,* illustrate the pitfalls of relying on active attrition alone. Through a retail bank example, the authors demonstrate that 5% of defecting customers take away only 3% of balances, while 35% who reduced their balances cost 24% of total balances.

Characteristics of attrition also vary by industry based on several factors, which include agreement type, general nature of the product, pricing structure, and switching costs. Attrition also needs to be managed in tune with the life cycle profit pattern of different businesses. For products such as auto/life insurance and credit cards, businesses actually lose money on customers[1] in the first year. Retaining customers until positive returns are made from them becomes important. For contractual relationships with multiproduct providers such as financial services and telecom, retention practices form a part and parcel of the larger customer relationship and portfolio management initiatives of the organisation. In contrast, transaction-oriented hospitality, travel, and retail industries depend largely on loyalty programmes to discourage switching behaviour.

To understand the dynamics of attrition, it is important to analyse the underlying reasons behind churn tendencies. These can be broadly classified as environmental (macroeconomic conditions/competition); product related; acquisition strategy; service related (satisfaction); marketing and distribution strategy; and customer profile/behaviour. The relationship between satisfaction and retention has received plenty of attention and was highlighted in the loyalty section of Chapter 2, "Usage Management". Moreover, there are uncontrollable reasons such as relocation outside of institutional footprint and others, which fall outside the purview of the chapter.

Customer acquisition and retention rates jointly drive customer growth and firm profitability. Customer growth is at its best when acquisition momentum is high and attrition rates are low. This relationship is

[1] Reichheld, *The Loyalty Effect*.

also important from a budget perspective as firms need to make difficult budget allocation decisions across acquisition and retention spends.

Information is vital for detecting attrition and for developing retention strategies to guard market share. While customer demographics and transaction data are readily available, the challenge lies in the systematic capture and availability of data related to reasons for defection as expressed by the customer, discernible service related front-end and customer interaction call records, and customer survey data. Proactive retention programmes require the identification of customers, who are likely to defect in the near future. For this task, ensuring accuracy of analytical tools such as triggers and statistical models is of critical importance, given the high cost implications of running model-based proactive retention programmes. Furthermore, attrition stems from customers who range from low to high profitability and there is a need for offers to be aligned with customer value. Henceforth, the returns and costs of both reactive and proactive retention programmes require due attention as they can be unprofitable, if not monitored.

The chapter outline is as follows. Different types of attrition are introduced followed by the impact of retention on profitability. The relationship between acquisition and retention is highlighted, with a brief review of budget allocation models. The relationship between usage and attrition is established through the inactivity route, and a framework to decide the optimal timing of activation offers is discussed. Next, retention management strategies are elaborated, which includes types of retention programmes and the retention process. Measurement and prediction of voluntary attrition encompass reports and investigative analyses, and an overview of issues relating to predicting attrition. Furthermore, a financial model to evaluate the viability of proactive model-based retention campaigns is examined. Several quantitative approaches to retention management are reviewed, while specific analytic techniques practiced by industry and researched in academia are covered in relation to specific industries. Lastly, sector-specific cases of credit card attrition, mortgage prepayment, telecom churn, and insurance lapse are exemplified. The examples focus on characteristics of attrition, types of retention programmes, analytics, implementation guidelines, and associated financial benefits.

## 4.2 Types of Attrition

Attrition takes on multiple appearances as illustrated in Fig. 4.1. For a single account customer, account attrition is the end of the relationship with the product/service provider. Account attrition can be construed as a trigger for targeted relationship management activities in the case of a multi-account customer. Customer and household level attrition warrants more serious marketing attention to save the relationship. Active attrition

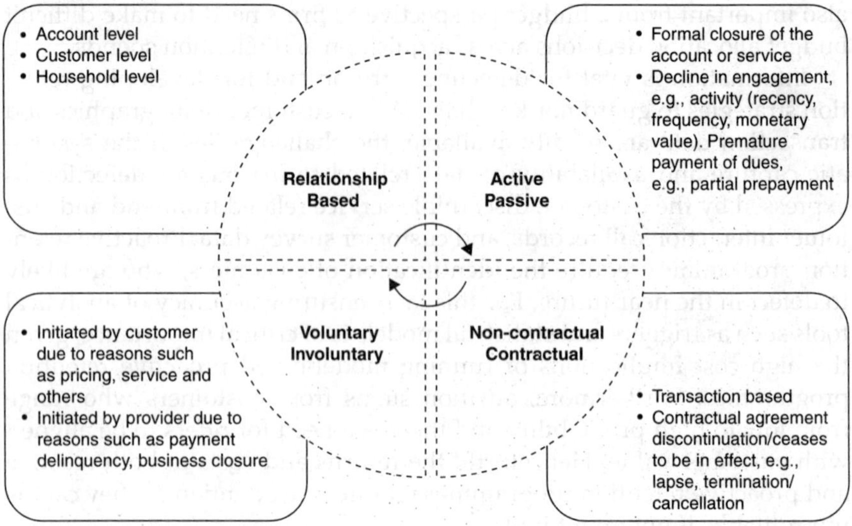


**Figure 4.1** Types of Attrition

involves the formal closure of the account and is subsequently tagged as "closed" on the provider's system. Passive attrition is often invisible unless monitored closely and is therefore, also termed as "silent attrition". In the case of passive attrition, the account is not formally closed but disengagement sets in, and may manifest itself in various forms such as a decline in RFM (either or all) of activity levels, value of the account or customer relationship, etc. Passive attrition may either happen suddenly or gradually over a period of time. Measurement of active attrition needs to be supplemented by passive attrition for a variety of reasons. In the presence of passive attrition, active attrition is a partial or imperfect view of the attrition phenomena as it focuses only on "numbers lost" and ignores value. Passive attrition can also be detected much earlier as it is a trigger for active attrition. Furthermore, there is time to action with a potential for larger value saves if passive attrition can be controlled. Involuntary attrition commands special attention and there are plenty of books on credit risk management for financial services, and is therefore not addressed in this chapter. Taking an example, telecom post-paid churn initiated by the subscriber on a bundled package would be classified as customer, active, voluntary, and contractual attrition.

While attrition is mostly of the active variety in telecom, passive attrition is also a distinct characteristic of financial services. Further, the cannibalisation effect, the trade-off in which sales of a new product or service decrease sales/revenue from existing products or services, is stronger for financial services as compared to telecom. This can be explained by the fact that a financial services provider offers a highly diversified multiproduct suite of products as compared to telecom.

In terms of attrition trends, the first attrition wave could be as early as the first month of billing for telecom. Buyer's remorse during the first three to six months post boarding is quite common for a credit card product. Prepayment on an instalment portfolio can happen at any point as competitors try to lure away customers with lower interest rates. For insurance, the attrition peak happens later as customers are a quick win for competition at renewal, when premium is due. Similarly for some products, attrition rates tend to be high at the end of promotional period and at proximity to renewal. For products such as mortgage and insurance with heavy underwriting costs, criticality of a minimum customer tenure is important for recovering these costs.

Since a contract involves a time bound arrangement between the product/service provider and customer, retention management forms an integral part of customer management activities. In contractual relationships, satisfaction plays a very important role in influencing churn behaviour. For financial services and telecom, usage building and cross-sell strategies are key focus areas for controlling retention on a proactive basis. Further, these programmes can be suitably developed and customised by customer/segment on the basis of rich transaction data. Other sectors such as hospitality, T&E, and retail rely heavily on loyalty programmes to promote retention through repeat purchase. The retail sector also depends on sales promotions to influence transaction RFM (recency, frequency, monetary value) and manage transaction based defection. Sales promotions and loyalty programmes were covered in Chapter 2 "Usage Management".

## 4.3 Retention and Profitability

According to retention experts, the impact of a higher retention rate is reflected in three dimensions: longer tenure, higher revenue, and reduced costs. All these factors have a positive impact on CLV. According to Reichheld, *The Loyalty Effect*, a 90% retention rate implies an average tenure of 10 years, while a 95% retention rate doubles the average to 20 years. With higher customer tenure, purchase volume (repeat sales), and customer referrals are expected to increase. At the same time, relationship maintenance costs are anticipated to come down, as the customer becomes more familiar with products and the firm develops a better understanding of customer needs and preferences. Furthermore, retained customers may pay higher prices than new customers. These hypotheses are validated by Reichheld for a wide range of sectors and interested readers are encouraged to refer to his book mentioned earlier. Further, Van den Poel and Lariviere in a paper titled *Customer Attrition Analysis for Financial Analysis Using Proportional Hazard Models* quantify the relationship between retention and profitability. This is done through a real-life study of a major UK retail bank, illustrated in Fig. 4.2. In a similar context, Gupta et al. in a

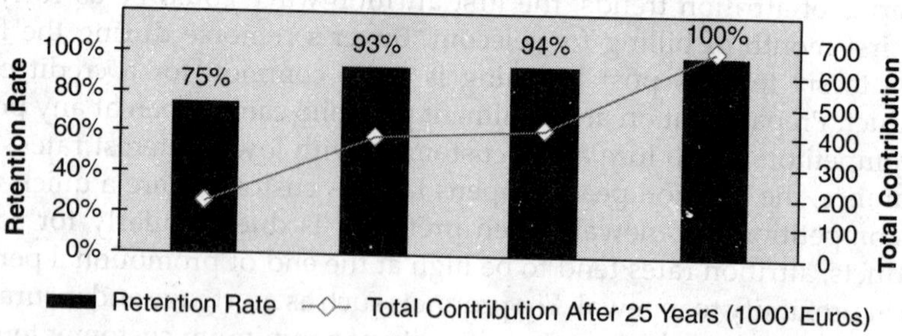


*Source:* Adapted from *European Journal of Operational Research*, Volume 157, Issue 1, Van den Poel and Lariviere, "Customer Attrition Analysis for Financial Services using Proportional Hazard Models", Pages 196–217, Copyright (2004), with permission from Elsevier.

**Figure 4.2** Retention and Profit

2004 study titled *Valuing Customers* demonstrate that a 1% improvement in retention has almost a five times greater impact on firm value than an equivalent 1% change in discount rate or cost of capital.

## 4.4 Acquisition and Retention

### *4.4.1 Acquisition and Retention Link*

The broad linkages between acquisition and retention are highlighted in Fig. 4.3. An important relationship between acquisition and retention is about acquiring the "right customer". The determination of the right customer or ideal profile could be done using analytics based "straw-man analysis". For this exercise, retention rate is an important input parameter. Another link is the transparency of communication regarding product pricing. Often, companies have hidden charges that are not communicated upfront and promotional offers come with conditions in fine print and without adequate disclosure. In relation to the consequences of acquisition strategy on retention, an explicit understanding will be brought out in later sections. Early usage has a bearing on retention in the first few months following product take-up. Buyer's remorse is likely to be high with improper communication and low early engagement. Buyer's remorse is a sense of regret after making a purchase, which prompts early closure of the account by the customer or the lack of visible engagement, often seen within the first three to six months of account opening. The relationship between usage and retention will be further discussed in Section 4.5.

Retention practices are designed with the objective of increasing customer lifetime. A challenge that firms often face is balancing acquisition and retention spends with a limited budget, which is the next topic of discussion.

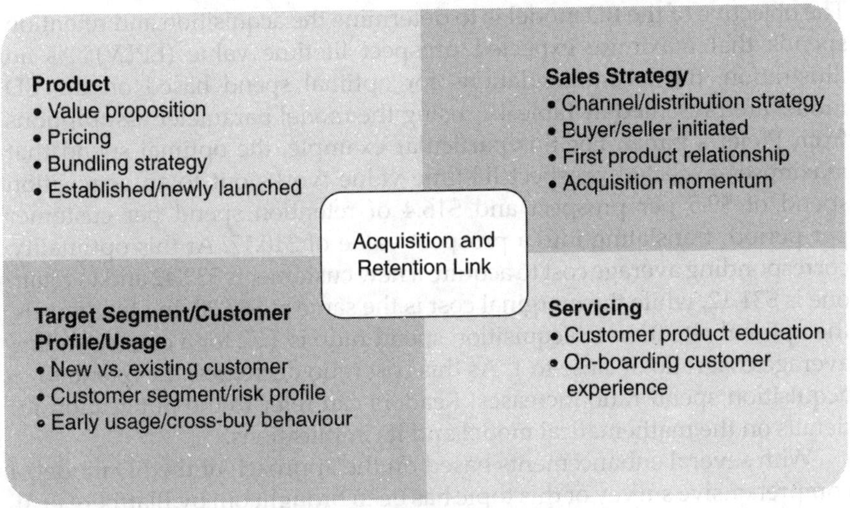


**Figure 4.3** Acquisition and Retention Link

## 4.4.2 Balancing Acquisition and Retention Spends

Traditional marketing wisdom points to the conviction that acquiring a customer is multiple times as expensive as retaining an existing one and therefore, firms should spend more money on retention. According to Pfeifer *The Optimal Ratio of Acquisition and Retention Costs*, there have been considerable deliberations on how this multiplier affects the budget allocation decision across retention and acquisition spends.

Some of factors that influence acquisition and retention spends are the maturity and profitability objectives of the firm. Firms in their infancy are likely to spend more on acquisition to build market share. For established firms, customer profitability may be the primary goal. Budget allocation models are used for optimising acqusition and retention spends. In this regard, the seminal work by Blattberg and Deighton, *Manage Marketing by the Customer Equity Test*, is highlighted. The model is popularly referred to as the "BD model".

The BD model guides managers on how to determine the optimal balance between acquisition and retention spends. This is done by linking customer acquisition and retention rates to marketing spend through independent acquisition and retention response functions. Acquisition rate is defined as the proportion of prospects that are converted to customers, while the retention rate is defined as the proportion of existing customers that are retained. The acquisition rate is assumed to be an increasing function of acquisition spend, with decreasing returns to scale for acquisition outlays. In other words, as acquisition spend increases, the acquisition rate increases but the gains from incremental expenses decreases with every additional dollar spent. The same applies to the retention response function as well.

The objective of the BD model is to determine the acquisition and retention spends that maximise expected prospect lifetime value (EPLV). As an illustration, the recommendations for optimal spend based on the BD model are presented in Table 4.1, using the model parameter assumptions from Pfeier's paper. For this particular example, the optimal spend that maximises expected prospect lifetime value works out to an acquisition spend of $9.5 per prospect and $16.4 of retention spend per customer per period, translating into a prospect value of $10.17. At this optimality, corresponding average cost to acquire a new customer is $32.42 and to retain one is $31.12, while the marginal cost is the same at $67.20. In other words, the optimal retention to acquisition spend ratio is 1.72 for a corresponding average cost ratio of close to 1. As this cost ratio decreases, the retention to acquisition spend ratio increases. Readers can refer to the publication for details on the mathematical model and its implications.

With several enhancements based on the approach of the BD model, a comprehensive survey of this topic has been brought out by Blattberg et al. as a separate chapter in their book titled *Database Marketing*. According to the authors, acquisition spend increases acquisition rate; retention spend increases customer duration; and acquisition and retention spends together increase customer profitability, all at a decreasing rate. In practice, data and resource constraints limit the ability of firms to estimate resource allocation models even when the construct is well established. Blattberg et al. have several practical guidelines for firms to address issues such as the amount of budget to be distributed across acquisition and retention; under what conditions is it better to focus on acquisition vs. retention; and the organisation of resource allocation models in a budget (ready-made toolkit). They also explicitly mention some key aspects that should be considered while building such models:

- Acquisition, retention (customer duration), and profitability should be modelled simultaneously taking into account the inter-relationships.

**Table 4.1** Blattberg–Deighton Model

| Acquisition Spend ($) | Retention Spend ($) | Acquisition Rate | Retention Rate | EPLV ($) |
|---|---|---|---|---|
| 0.96 | 1.82 | 0.05 | 0.10 | 1.70 |
| 2.08 | 3.97 | 0.10 | 0.20 | 3.59 |
| 3.39 | 6.61 | 0.15 | 0.30 | 5.68 |
| 5.00 | 10.00 | 0.20 | 0.40 | 7.86 |
| 7.08 | 14.79 | 0.25 | 0.50 | 9.68 |
| 9.49 | 16.37 | 0.29 | 0.53 | 10.17 |
| 10.00 | 22.97 | 0.30 | 0.60 | 9.21 |
| 15.00 | 31.16 | 0.35 | 0.65 | 3.54 |

For example, the dependency of the retention process on the acquisition process, and the joint impact of acquisition and retention spends on customer profitability.
- Multi-period models that address how much to invest at different points of the customer firm relationship
- Cohort models to incorporate the fact that the pool of available prospects and retention rates change with time
- Segment level models to emphasise the importance of different drivers that impact acquisition and retention
- Wallet share models to reflect competition that influences acquisition and retention strategy that conventionally tends to be ignored

## 4.5 Usage and Retention

### *4.5.1 Relationship Between Inactivity and Voluntary Attrition*

The inter-relationship between inactivity and voluntary attrition is not simple as cause and effect conclusions are hard to draw. However, it is a well-accepted fact that inactivity (passive attrition) is a strong predictor (trigger) of active attrition. Using a numerical example, the association of inactivity (timing and duration) with voluntary attrition is analysed over a 12 month period (by quarter). This type of analysis would be applicable to products or services of a contractual nature that require renewal every 12 months (and may involve a fee). For example, credit card with annual fee and club membership. The following discussion refers to Tables 4.2 and 4.3.

- The first quarter pertains to the three months from renewal for an existing account or three months post-acquisition for a new account
- Sample considered for the analysis are accounts in open status at the start of the first quarter. Accounts which close involuntarily during the 12 month time window are not considered.
- An account is defined as being active for that quarter if a minimum of one activity or transaction is recorded in the respective quarter
- Closure rate is defined as the number of voluntary closures during the four quarters divided by the number of open accounts at the start of the first quarter[2]. In this example:
    - Closure rate is 5% over a period of 12 months
    - There are two states: active and inactive. "A" is defined as active and "I" as inactive. Sixteen possible states are defined in Table 4.2 and with corresponding attrition rates in Table 4.3. Groups 1–8 are first quarter inactives, while Groups 9–16 are first quarter actives.

[2] Assumption is that once an account is in closure status, it does not revert to open status during the 12 months of observation.

**Table 4.2** Inactivity and Attrition I

| Group | Quarter 1 | Quarter 2 | Quarter 3 | Quarter 4 |
|---|---|---|---|---|
| 1 | I | A | A | A |
| 2 | I | A | A | I |
| 3 | I | A | I | A |
| 4 | I | A | I | I |
| 5 | I | I | A | A |
| 6 | I | I | A | I |
| 7 | I | I | I | A |
| 8 | I | I | I | I |
| 9 | A | A | A | A |
| 10 | A | A | A | I |
| 11 | A | A | I | A |
| 12 | A | A | I | I |
| 13 | A | I | A | A |
| 14 | A | I | A | I |
| 15 | A | I | I | A |
| 16 | A | I | I | I |

**Table 4.3** Inactivity and Attrition II

| Group | Closure Rate (% of Voluntary Closed Within the Group) | % of Total Sample | % of Total Voluntary Closures |
|---|---|---|---|
| 1 | 2% | 5% | 2% |
| 2 | 7% | 1% | 2% |
| 3 | 4% | 1% | 1% |
| 4 | 4% | 2% | 3% |
| 5 | 4% | 2% | 2% |
| 6 | 8% | 2% | 2% |
| 7 | 6% | 2% | 2% |
| 8 | 23% | 10% | 40% |
| Average/ Total | 12% | 25% | 53% |
| 9 | 2% | 59% | 24% |
| 10 | 8% | 4% | 6% |
| 11 | 4% | 3% | 2% |
| 12 | 12% | 2% | 6% |
| 13 | 3% | 3% | 1% |
| 14 | 7% | 1% | 1% |
| 15 | 4% | 2% | 1% |
| 16 | 14% | 2% | 6% |
| Average/ Total | 3% | 75% | 47% |

- **Timing**
  - Accounts that are inactive in the first quarter are four times as likely to churn as compared to their active counterparts. First quarter inactives form 25% of the total sample and constitute more than 50% of closures, and with a high churn probability of 12%. Given these statistics, it is important to initiate engagement with the customer as soon as possible, starting with the on-boarding process.
  - The churn probability of an account that is active in the first two quarters, and then becomes inactive in the following two quarters (Group 12), is six fold higher compared to an account that is active over all quarters (Group 9)
  - It would be beneficial if an inactive account (over the first two quarters) can be activated in any of the subsequent two quarters (Groups 5, 6, 7). The likelihood of churn is drastically lower in comparison to an account that is serially inactive over all the four quarters (Group 8).
  - Inactivity preceding renewal is a high attrition risk. Timing of intervention is important, and aggressive retention activities at least three months prior to renewal are recommended.
- **Duration**
  - Serial inactives (Group 8) constitute 10% of the sample, but contribute to 40% of total attrition. Churn probability of a serial inactive account is almost twelve times that of a serial active account (Group 9).
  - An account that is inactive for at least the first two quarters (Groups 5, 6, 7, and 8) has a collective likelihood of attrition of 16%. An account that is inactive over the first quarter has a churn probability of 3% (Groups 1, 2, 3, 4). Sensitivity is very high as churn rates increase by more than five times, if an account is allowed to be inactive for an incremental quarter beyond the first quarter of inactivity. Henceforth, activation programmes are important for minimising roll rate. Roll rate is the percentage of accounts that migrate from one quarter to two quarters of inactivity.

## 4.5.2 Optimal Timing of Activation Offers

Activation programmes can be costly, and intervention using activation offers needs to be aligned with the returns from such programmes. In this regard, one such consideration is the optimal timing of activation offers. Timing is important as targeting early on can lead to wastage of resources due to customer self-activation behaviour. On the other hand, delaying the action may be too late to save the customer. As a reminder to readers, an analytical approach to identify self-activators was discussed in Chapter 2, "Usage Management". In this section, a basic framework to determine the optimal timing of activation offers is presented. The approach is amenable to modifications and improvisation based on the business situation at hand. Readers should refer to Tables 4.4–4.5 and Figs. 4.4–4.5.

- The objective of an activation programme for inactive customers is to create an incremental pool of active customers, defined as the number of responders to the activation programme minus the number who would have got self-activated, in case no offer was sent
- It is possible to estimate the percentage of self-activators based on historical data through control groups. Yet, it is often a challenge to identify which specific customer will self-activate. Therefore, marketing actions are usually targeted at the whole universe of inactives. In this example, percentage of self-activators is an estimate derived from historical data.
- Likelihood of self-activation and potential revenue (if activated) decreases with every month of inactivity. Attrition rates increase with duration of inactivity.
- Customer activated through an offer is assumed to be active for the next month only
- Customer retained through an offer is assumed to have an incremental tenure of 12 months. An assumption for the purpose of this numerical example is that it is possible to save all the potential attritors. A customer has only one account of the product being considered.
- In local currency (LCY), contact cost is LCY 7 per offer sent and fulfilment cost is LCY 100 per response
- Total costs of activation programme is the sum of contact and fulfilment cost

$$\text{Number of inactives at beginning of month } t = \text{Number of inactives at end of month } (t-1) - \text{Number self-activated during month } (t-1)$$

Contact cost = Number of inactives * Cost per contact

Fulfilment cost = Number of responders * Fulfilment cost per response

Total cost = Contact cost + Fulfilment cost

- Total saves is the sum of revenue saves on inactives who responded to the offer and those who have been retained

Number of incremental accounts activated = Number of responders to the activation programme – Number self-activated (if no activation offer is extended) in that month

Number of closures saved = Attrition rate * Number of incremental accounts activated

**Table 4.4** Activation Programme—Costs

| C1 | C2 | C3 | C4 | C5 | C6 | C7 | C8 | C9 |
|---|---|---|---|---|---|---|---|---|
| | $C2_{t-1} - C4_{t-1}$ | | $C2_t * C3_t$ | C2 * 7 | | C2 * C6 | C7 * 100 | C5 + C8 |
| **Number of Months of Inactivity** | **Number of Inactives** | **% Self Activated** | **Number of Self Activated** | **Contact Cost (LCY)** | **Response Rates to Activation Offer %** | **Number of Responses** | **Fulfilment Cost (LCY)** | **Total Cost (LCY)** |
| 1 | 10,000 | 45% | 4,500 | 70,000 | 50% | 5,000 | 5,00,000 | 5,70,000 |
| 2 | 5,500 | 32% | 1,760 | 38,500 | 35% | 1,925 | 1,92,500 | 2,31,000 |
| 3 | 3,740 | 25% | 935 | 26,180 | 28% | 1,047 | 1,04,720 | 1,30,900 |
| 4 | 2,805 | 17% | 477 | 19,635 | 20% | 561 | 56,100 | 75,735 |
| 5 | 2,328 | 15% | 349 | 16,297 | 18% | 419 | 41,907 | 58,204 |
| 6 | 1,979 | 12% | 237 | 13,853 | 14% | 277 | 27,705 | 41,558 |

**Table 4.5** Activation Programme—Saves

| | S1 C7 – C4 | S2 | S3 S1 * S2 | S4 S1 – S3 | S5 | S6 S4 * S5 | S7 | S8 S3 * S7 | S9 S6 + S8 | N S9 – C9 |
|---|---|---|---|---|---|---|---|---|---|---|
| Number of Months of Inactivity | Incremental Accounts Activated | Attrition Rate | Number of Closures | Net Incremental Accounts Activated | Monthly Revenue per Inactive (LCY) | Revenue Saves on Inactivity (LCY) | Yearly Revenue per Closure (LCY) | Revenue Saves on Closures (LCY) | Total Revenue Saves (LCY) | Net Saves (LCY) |
| 1 | 500 | 25% | 125 | 375 | 194 | 72,750 | 3,072 | 3,84,000 | 4,56,750 | –1,13,250 |
| 2 | 165 | 30% | 49 | 116 | 175 | 20,300 | 2,765 | 1,36,858 | 1,57,158 | –73,842 |
| 3 | 112 | 35% | 39 | 73 | 157 | 11,461 | 2,488 | 97,716 | 1,09,177 | –21,723 |
| 4 | 84 | 42% | 35 | 49 | 141 | 6,909 | 2,239 | 79,150 | 86,059 | 10,324 |
| 5 | 70 | 50% | 35 | 35 | 127 | 4,445 | 2,016 | 70,387 | 74,832 | 16,628 |
| 6 | 40 | 60% | 24 | 16 | 115 | 1,840 | 1,814 | 43,077 | 44,917 | 3,359 |

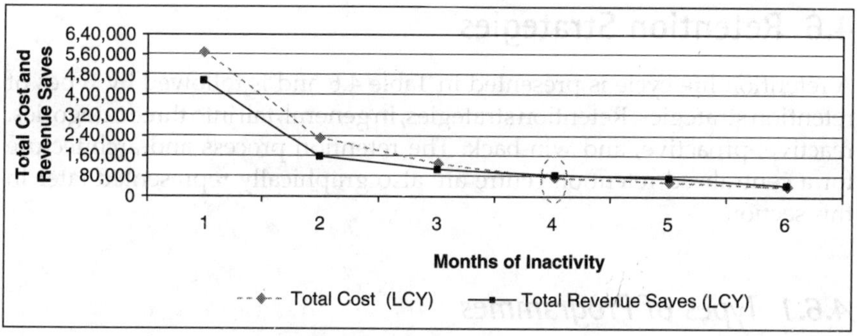


**Figure 4.4** Optimal Timing of Activation Offers

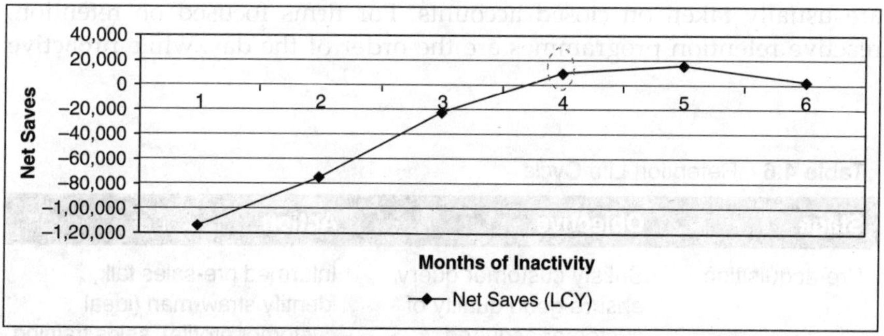


**Figure 4.5** Activation Programme—Net Saves

Number of net incremental accounts activated = Number of incremental accounts activated – Number of closures saved

Revenue saves on inactivity = Monthly revenue * Number of net incremental accounts activated

Revenue saves on closures = Annual revenue * Number of closures saved

Total revenue saves = Revenue saves on inactivity + Revenue saves on closures

- Net saves is total saves due to the activation programme minus total cost of activation programme
- Conclusion is that the optimal time to make an activation offer to inactives is immediately after three months of successive inactivity, as net saves are positive

## 4.6 Retention Strategies

A retention life cycle is presented in Table 4.6 and is followed by types of retention strategies. Retention strategies, in general, fall into three categories: reactive, proactive, and win-back. The retention process and architecture for a centralised retention centre are also graphically represented later in this section.

### 4.6.1 Types of Programmes

The aim of reactive programmes is to prevent attrition after the customer has voluntarily initiated steps towards account closure. On the other hand, the goal of proactive programmes is to take preemptive actions to minimise attrition of identified "at-risk" customers. Win-back actions are usually taken on closed accounts. For firms focused on retention, reactive retention programmes are the order of the day, while proactive

**Table 4.6** Retention Life Cycle

| Stage | Objective | Action |
|---|---|---|
| Pre-acquisition | Satisfy customer query, ensure good quality of customer acquired | Informed pre-sales talk, identify straw-man (ideal customer profile), sales training |
| Acquisition agreement | Healthy negotiation with customer | Trained and responsible sales force |
| Contracting | Customer understanding of terms and conditions | Transparency of agreement signed by customer |
| Welcoming | Early activation | Welcome call/kit, activation-usage offers |
| Early life | Buyer's remorse control | Customer call/visit by sales agent with value re-iteration |
| Early maturity | Control prepayment, resolve early problems | Pricing, good customer service |
| Pre-anniversary or contract end | Customer commitment to renewal | Proactive call reinforcing product proposition to those at high risk of attrition |
| Anniversary or contract end | Renewal | Incentives to non-renewals in tune with expected profitability |
| Post-renewal | Retain profitable customers | Portfolio management actions of building usage, loyalty and cross-selling |
| Voluntary closed | Reinstatement, win-back | Special offer, reduced pricing, swap to value based product |

programmes are generally leveraged by those experiencing high attrition rates. The role of reactive, proactive, and win-back retention practices will be emphasised in the section on industry examples.

### 4.6.1.1 Reactive

The following points highlight the important steps for a reactive retention strategy.

- Establish a centralised and specialised retention centre, to direct all retention activities to this unit for result-oriented actions
- Develop a definition of retention eligibility based on both current and potential profitability
  - In the short-term, eligibility based on current profitability is appropriate
  - In the long-term, an eligibility logic that considers both current and potential profitability is beneficial
- Develop a behavioural retention segmentation scheme that divides the retention eligible population into distinct groups for reactive offers (Table 4.7)
  - Qualified for an offer which involves cost such as fee waivers, value-added offers/services at a discount (aggressive)
  - Qualified only for offers with no direct profitability impact such as benefits re-sell and service resolution (mild)
- Target previously profitable accounts with no current activity on the account
- Develop a retention strategy for attritors with other relationships (existing and closed). Decide if the segment warrants different retention eligibility.
- Direct inbound and outbound reactive retention efforts only to retention eligible. Attempt should be to save retention ineligible accounts only if resources are available.

**Table 4.7** Reactive Retention Offer Grid

| Type of Product | Vintage (Months) | Months Since Recent Closure of Any Account with Same Provider | Number of Current Products Held with Same Provider | Current Customer Profitability | Offer |
|---|---|---|---|---|---|
| Basic | 10 | – | 2 | High | Aggressive |
| Silver | 24 | 12 | 2 | Low | Mild |
| Silver | 36 | 3 | 4 | Medium | Aggressive |

- Test lower pricing targeted to highly profitable accounts
  - As a reactive measure only in the short-term
  - Based on past data, results from past campaigns should be used to establish minimum margin hurdle rates and a long-term reactive pricing strategy
- Analyse retention reasons codes over time, identify, and revise strategies to respond to changes in attrition trends and its reasons
- Enrich database if contact rates are low
- Track retention rate and behaviour of saved accounts for at least six to twelve months to measure stickiness of retention offers

#### 4.6.1.2 Proactive

A proactive retention strategy involves the following steps:

- Inbound toll-free number to address customer grievances
- Expand early engagement programmes such as new account activation and communication programmes involving reiteration of value. For example, welcome kit that includes usage stimulation and cross-sell offers. The purpose is to build brand preference and perception of positive price/value relationship.
- Develop and test a comprehensive activation strategy for customer segments, beginning at three months of consecutive low or no activity
  - Test a variety of offers
  - Different offers to non-responders in fourth, fifth, and six months, with aggressiveness of offers increasing with duration of inactivity
  - Use results to model response propensity and increase effectiveness of future programmes
- Develop a strategy for continuous engagement with the customer by leveraging usage and cross-sell type of programmes
- Promote rewards programmes strategy as rewards can be a successful retention tool
- Use statement and email channels to promote product benefits which may include:
  - A benefit-oriented statement message each month
  - Periodic statement inserts to resell benefits
  - Periodic newsletter to customers
  - Email statement enhancements to accommodate usage and cross-sell activities
- Move towards optimal product mix comprising of products that encourage retention, referred to as "account linkage strategy" by TowerGroup

- Identify the "at-risk" population for proactive targeting based on triggers and attrition prediction models. This is accompanied by a careful assessment of profitability of a model-based proactive retention programme.
- Profitability segmentation with tags by customer value for service and retention:
  - For example, "preferred" and "private bank" customers are offered superior customer service
  - Similarly, credit card customers are flagged on the system based on revenue potential. This information is made available to front-end and many issuers follow this in practice.
  - Telecom companies have also begun differentiating their high value customers and provide a separate service line
- Conduct market research studies to:
  - Confirm understanding of contributing dynamics
  - Test potential appeal of retention offers

#### 4.6.1.3 Win-back

Win-back or re-acquisition programmes are targeted at attrited or lapsed customers with the intention of re-establishing the lost relationship. Insurance companies rely heavily on win-back strategies using reinstatement programmes. Developing a win-back strategy involves the following actions:

- Analysis of historical information on closed/lapsed customers—reasons for defection, previous profitability
- Leverage findings from past campaigns to offer a superior value proposition tailored to the customer. Product offered should be perceived as high benefit. Examples would be a premium product offer to a high value customer who was previously ignored.
- Favourable pricing with acknowledgement of customers' past business
- Communication with the customer to re-establish the relationship by recapitulating product benefits

### *4.6.2 Retention Process*

Figure 4.6 illustrates the step-by-step process of a retention strategy. Figure 4.7 is an architecture for a reactive retention process. The figure shows the process flow from the customer to the retention centre for two modes of communication. The options available to the customer are call-in to front-end/retention centre and a letter for initiating account closure.

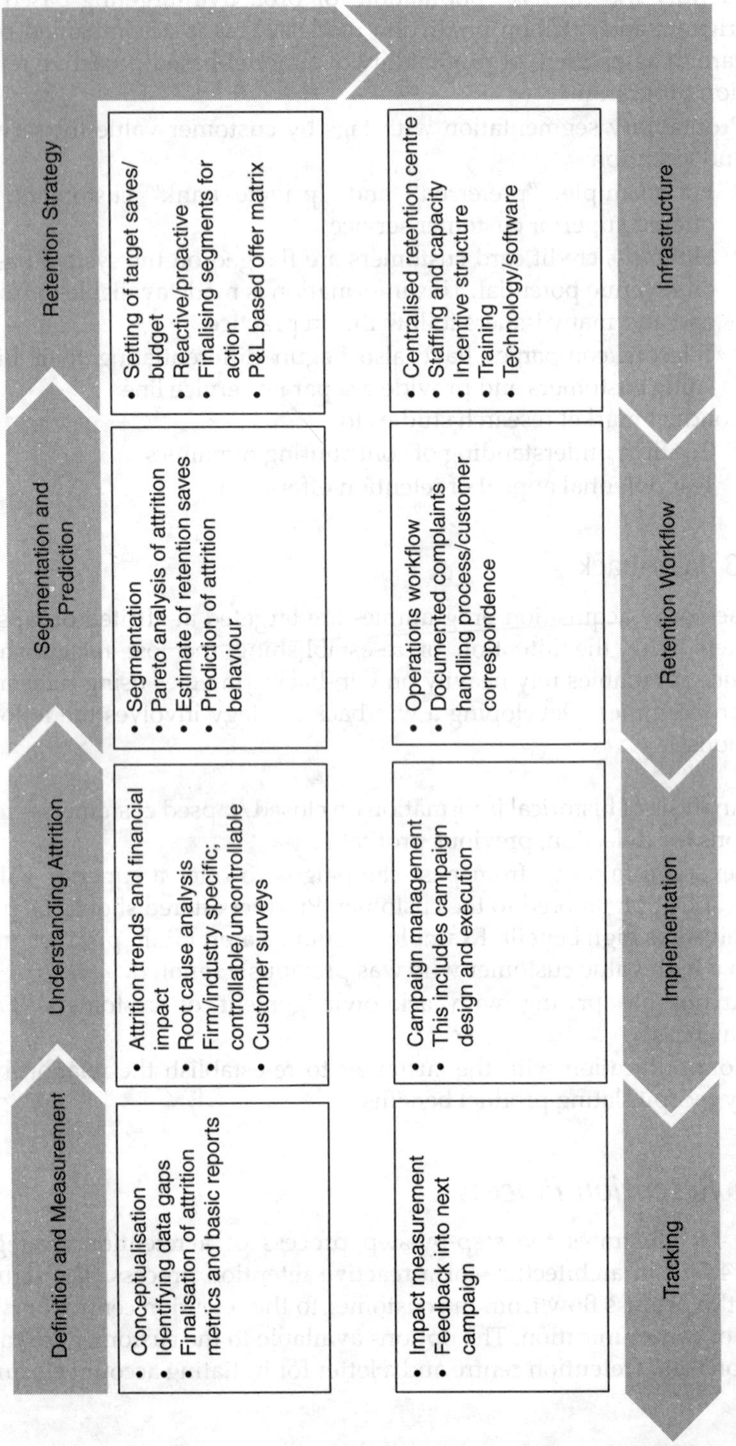


**Figure 4.6** Retention Process

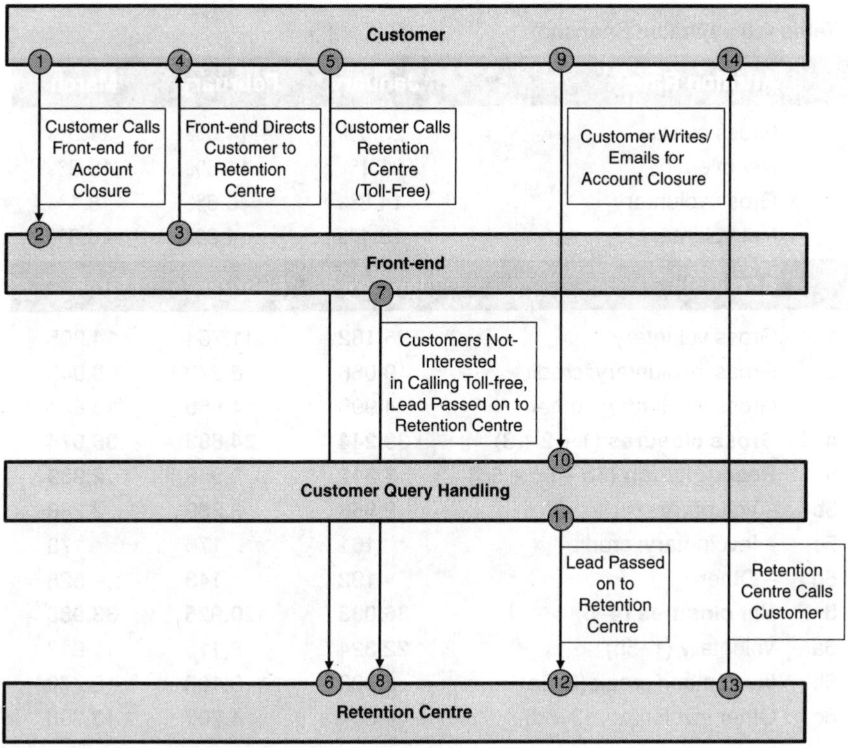


**Figure 4.7** Centralised Retention Centre

# 4.7 Measurement and Prediction

There is no common definition or measurement for attrition as it may vary based on industry; by firms belonging to the same industry; and across different departments within the same firm. The focus of this section is on the measurement and prediction of active and passive attrition.

## 4.7.1 Measuring Attrition

### 4.7.1.1 Active Attrition

*Attrition Snapshot* Attrition snapshot is a month on month portfolio view. Attrition rate as defined in Table 4.8 is calculated as the number of accounts closed (measured at end of period) divided by the total number of open and closed accounts end of period. For this example, period is defined as a month. Attrition is classified as gross (before saves) and net (after saves), voluntary and involuntary. As the report is for all vintages (vintage defined as month and year the account was booked), some of the important attrition trends are masked. For example, the different attrition

**Table 4.8** Attrition Snapshot

| | Attrition Rate | January | February | March |
|---|---|---|---|---|
| | Gross overall | 23.0% | 14.0% | 21.0% |
| | Net overall | 21.1% | 11.8% | 19.3% |
| | Gross voluntary | 14.8% | 6.6% | 8.1% |
| | Net voluntary | 13.1% | 4.6% | 6.8% |
| | **Accounts** | **January** | **February** | **March** |
| 1 | Gross voluntary | 25,182 | 11,754 | 14,205 |
| 2 | Gross involuntary: credit | 9,066 | 8,279 | 8,945 |
| 3 | Gross involuntary: other | 4,996 | 4,850 | 13,824 |
| **4** | **Gross closures (1 + 2 + 3)** | **39,244** | **24,883** | **36,974** |
| **5** | **Reacquisition (5b + 5c + 5d)** | **3,211** | **3,958** | **2,989** |
| 5b | – Voluntary | 2,858 | 3,639 | 2,288 |
| 5c | – Involuntary: credit | 161 | 176 | 173 |
| 5d | – Other | 192 | 143 | 528 |
| **6** | **Net closures (4–5)** | **36,033** | **20,925** | **33,985** |
| 6a | Voluntary (1–5b) | 22,324 | 8,115 | 11,917 |
| 6b | Involuntary: credit (2–5c) | 8,905 | 8,103 | 8,772 |
| 6c | Other involuntary (3–5d) | 4,804 | 4,707 | 13,296 |

behaviour of new and existing accounts, months on book effect, and impact of acquisition sourcing strategy. Therefore, a vintage perspective is presented subsequently.

*Attrition Rates by Vintage I* Table 4.9 is useful for analysing recent attrition trends, identifying vintages that are causing grief, and revalidating sourcing strategy. From the report (based on a different data set than the previous report), it is evident that 85% of attritors are from a certain vintage (2011) that also had the most aggressive sales. Further analysis of this particular vintage, for example, by months on book can be very insightful.

*Attrition Rates by Vintage II* Figure 4.8 is useful for identifying attrition rate trends by months on book (MOB), indicating the effects of buyer's remorse, renewal fee, promotional pricing, and others. The peak around 2 MOB (months on book) may be a reflection of buyer's remorse. Products with promotional pricing induce high rates of attrition as soon as the introductory period is over (e.g., immediately after 6 and 12 months). This impact is reflected as kinks in the attrition curve around this time. Optimal timing of top-up offers for installment loans, which is a usage and retention programme, can be determined from this trend (supplemented by delinquency trends by MOB). For example, 8–10 MOB may

Table 4.9 Attrition Rates by Vintage I

| Vintage | Accounts Booked | Total Voluntary Attrition (Last 3 Months) | Attrition Volume (%) Last 3 Months |
|---|---|---|---|
| 2010Q1 | 5,381 | 42 | 0.43% |
| 2010Q2 | 6,455 | 109 | 1.12% |
| 2010Q3 | 7,258 | 115 | 1.18% |
| 2010Q4 | 9,660 | 580 | 5.96% |
| 2011Q1 | 15,311 | 1,639 | 16.84% |
| 2011Q2 | 22,151 | 2,277 | 23.39% |
| 2011Q3 | 30,871 | 2,929 | 30.10% |
| 2011Q4 | 41,560 | 1,420 | 14.59% |
| 2012Q1 | 51,842 | 622 | 6.39% |
| Total | 1,90,489 | 9,733 | 100% |

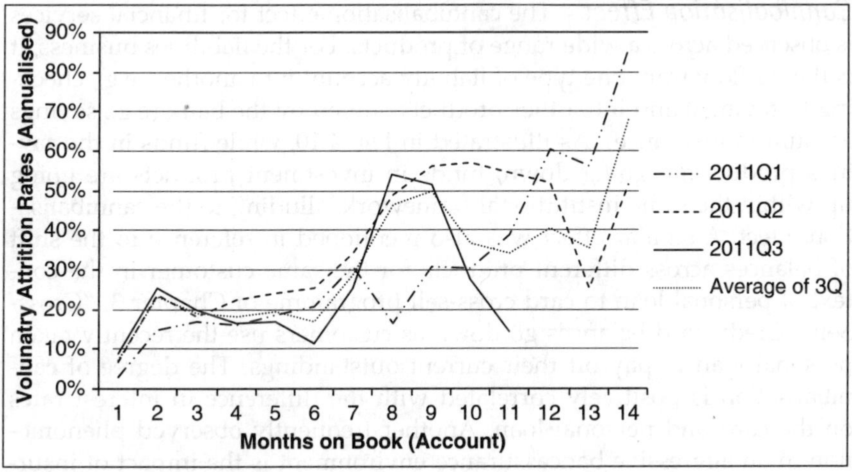


Figure 4.8 Attrition Rates by Vintage II

be an appropriate time to offer top-ups, given the spike in the attrition curve for two vintages. The spike at MOB 14 may be due to low sample size and should be evaluated prior to plotting the graph.

### 4.7.1.2 Passive Attrition

*Flow of Funds* Flow of funds analysis, in the context of financial services is the tracking of flows month-on-month to evaluate inflow/outflow/net flow trends. This analysis can be conducted with respect to destination, whether it is circulating within the system (same provider and its associates) or has moved out-of-system. Referring to Fig. 4.9, 70% of total funds are moving out-of-system and when stock markets are bullish, one does observe significant movement of funds into market-linked investment products within or outside of the bank's franchise. On the other hand, when markets are bearish, outflow of funds into commodities such as gold is generally observed. Funds exiting out-of-system is a retention concern for the firm, while within system fund movement, also called "cannibalisation" is not so much about retention, but about optimisation of balances and profitability across various products offered by the bank. Movement to external sources is managed by retention programmes such as balance consolidation, as discussed in Chapter 2, "Usage Management". For liability accounts, text mining of checks written out is useful for identifying the destination of funds. This information is used for cross-selling of appropriate products. For a better understanding of funds movement and its implications, the flow of funds analysis can be drilled down further based on customer segments, vintage, product type, demographics, channel, and others.

*Cannibalisation Effect* The cannibalisation effect for financial services is observed across a wide range of products. For the liabilities business, it is the outflow from one type of liability account into another (e.g., checking to savings) and into other products offered by the bank (e.g., savings account to insurance). As illustrated in Fig. 4.10, while funds in the savings product are going down, funds in investment products are going up within the same institutional framework, alluding to the cannibalisation effect. A similar effect was also mentioned in reference to the shift of balances across different products for the same customer in the context of personal loan to card cross-sell programme of Chapter 3, "Cross-Sell". Credit card balances go down as customers use the recently taken personal loan to pay off their current outstandings. The degree of cannibalisation is positively correlated with the difference in interest rates on the card and personal loan. Another frequently observed phenomenon in an aggressive bancassurance environment is the impact of insurance on deposit balances. Normally, third party insurance products are

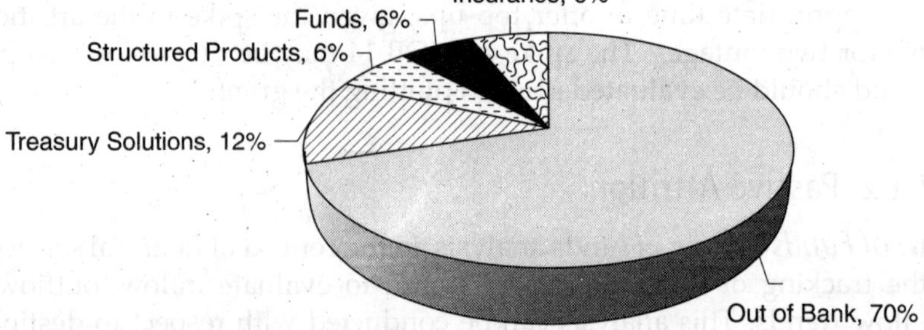


**Figure 4.9** Flow of Funds—Outflow

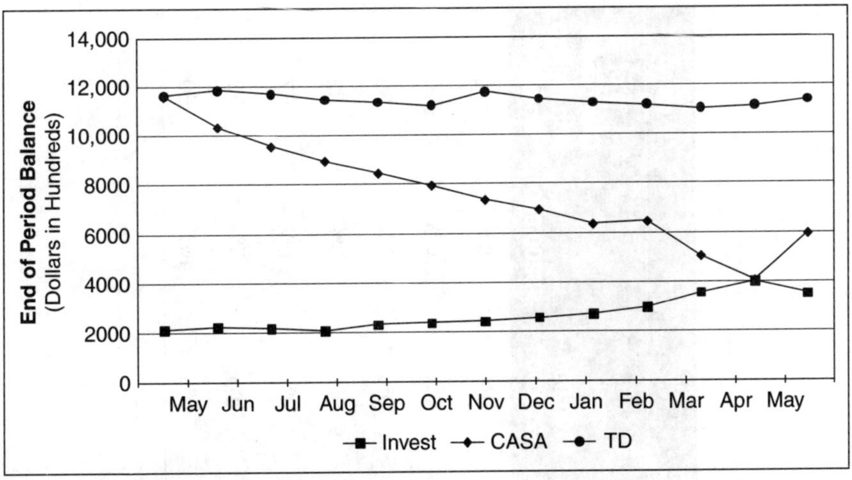


**Figure 4.10** Flow of Funds—Liabilities

cross-sold by banks to their customers as a source of fee revenue and to strengthen the relationship. This may result in an outflow from deposit balances if customers pay from their existing bank account relationship. It is therefore practical that the bank evaluates the revenue lost due to fund outflows against the fee revenue earned from insurance sales, and the benefits from increasing customer stickiness. However, balance build-up has not been too much of a concern, as it has been often observed that balances start to pick up gradually to reach near previous levels. Detecting cannibalisation is a challenge if a customer level view is not available. A customer level view entails that all accounts of a particular customer are mapped to that customer's unique customer ID.

A cannibalisation effect in the retail industry is related to opening new store locations. Cannibalisation often occurs when a retailer opens a new store location in close proximity to an existing store, and the existing store location loses customers to the new store. The older store's sales may decline at the cost of an increase in the new store. Cannibalisation is a risk of opening new stores, but retailers are willing to take this risk with the belief that total sales will increase as a result of the new store (new store will bring in customers who have not been previously shopping at the old store). An example of cannibalisation in the telecom sector is the decline in minutes of usage on fixed lines post the introduction of mobile services, witnessed in countries where demand for mobile services is very strong.

*Value (Balance) Attrition* Balance movement over the course of 12 months is analysed (for a bank deposit portfolio) so that efforts can be directed to control balance attrition. Table 4.10 shows upward and downward movements by balance bands. To control for seasonality, like-to-like quarters are compared. Further, it is important to evaluate the contribution of different segments to total balance depletion as shown in Fig. 4.11.

**Table 4.10** Balance Attrition—Transition Matrix

| Balance Band as of Quarter 1 – Year 1 | | Balance Band as of Quarter 1 – Year 2 | | | | | | | |
|---|---|---|---|---|---|---|---|---|---|
| | Balance Band | ≤$0 | <$10,000 | $10,000 – $20,000 | $20,000 – $50,000 | $50,000 – $100,000 | $100,000 – $200,000 | >$200,000 | % of Customers with Falling Balance |
| | ≤$0 | 66% | 26% | 6% | 1% | 1% | 0% | 0% | 0 |
| | <$10,000 | 0% | 91% | 8% | 1% | 0% | 0% | 0% | 0 |
| | $10,000 – $20,000 | 0% | 39% | 55% | 4% | 2% | 0% | 0% | 39 |
| | $20,000 – $50,000 | 0% | 18% | 44% | 25% | 13% | 0% | 0% | 62 |
| | $50,000 – $100,000 | 0% | 11% | 31% | 15% | 41% | 2% | 0% | 57 |
| | $100,000 – $200,000 | 0% | 13% | 17% | 22% | 30% | 13% | 5% | 82 |
| | >$200,000 | 0% | 0% | 0% | 0% | 60% | 0% | 40% | 60 |

*Note:* Values in the cell are percentage of customers in a specific balance band.

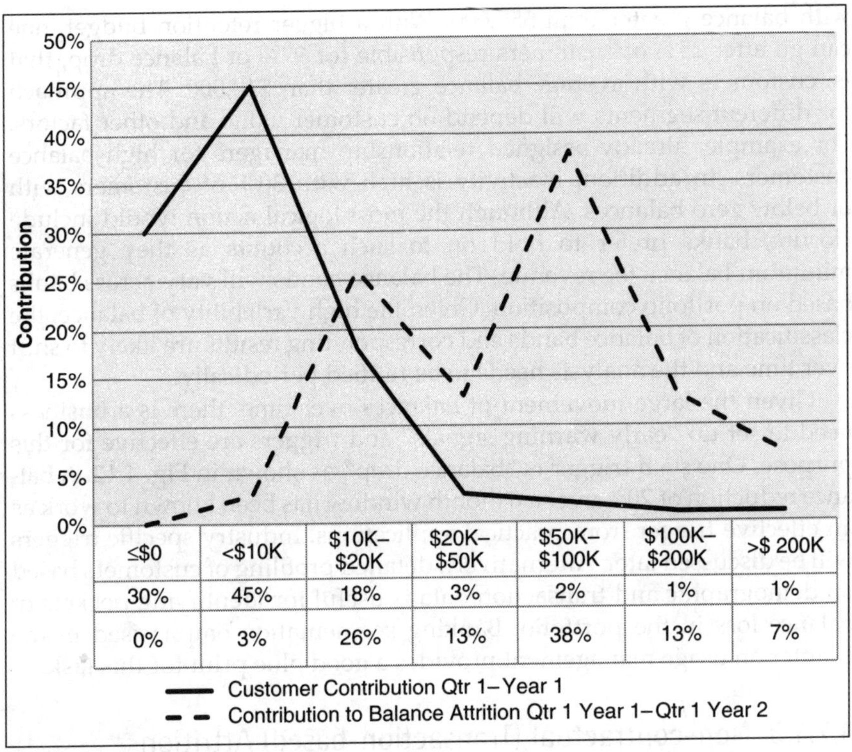


| | ≤$0 | <$10K | $10K–$20K | $20K–$50K | $50K–$100K | $100K–$200K | >$ 200K |
|---|---|---|---|---|---|---|---|
| | 30% | 45% | 18% | 3% | 2% | 1% | 1% |
| | 0% | 3% | 26% | 13% | 38% | 13% | 7% |

**Figure 4.11** Balance Attrition—Contribution

Customer level analysis rather than account level is used for a complete holistic picture as a customer may hold multiple accounts with the same bank, and is likely to move funds between these different accounts. Household level analysis is another option if the bank has linked different member accounts at the household level. This analysis can easily be extended using other profitability-based measures. Subsequent to this exercise, a flow of funds analysis should be conducted to estimate balance outflow (out-of-system).

Customers with an average balance of greater than $50,000 are an area of concern due to multiple reasons—higher starting balance; a good proportion of customers within a balance band are moving to a lower balance band (in the range of 57% to 82%); and significant contribution to total balance decline (close to 60%). On close observation, almost one-third of the $50,000–$100,000 segment reduce balances to one-fifth of starting balances. This segment is also the highest contributor to total balance loss (38%). Another balance depletion segment is the one with an average balance of $10,000–$20,000, which has 18% of customers and contribute 26% to total balance loss.

A recommendation is that retention focus be prioritised for 4% of customers that contribute to 58% of balance deterioration, namely customers with balance greater than $50,000. With a bigger retention budget, one can go after 25% of customers responsible for 97% of balance drop, that is, customers with average balance greater than $10,000. The approach for different segments will depend on customer value and other factors. For example, already assigned relationship managers for high balance customers. In addition, inactivity is high with 30% of customers with or below zero balances. Although the most logical action would include closure, banks prefer to hold on to such accounts as they generate minimum balance fee revenue. The balance bands will vary across banks based on portfolio composition. Given the high variability of balance, the classification of balance bands and corresponding results are likely to shift over time and the analysis needs to be ratified periodically.

Given the large movement of balances over time, there is a business need to set up "early warning signals" and triggers are effective for this purpose. One such trigger is "balance drop" as shown in Fig. 4.12. A balance reduction of 20% over a 6 month window has been known to work as an effective trigger from practical applications. Industry specific triggers will be discussed later. Alternatively, detailed profiling of customers based on demographic and transaction data is useful for identifying pockets of balance loss in the portfolio. Banking segmentation emphasised in the chapter on usage management provides a good blue print for this task.

#### 4.7.1.3 Non-contractual (Transaction-based) Attrition

Given the transaction-based customer–firm relationship in a retail setting, it can be a challenge to determine when customers defect. Defection could be defined by "total defection" and "partial defection". Total defection is defined as the termination of all existing spends with the current retailer. Usually, customers switch a certain proportion of their purchases to a competitor and is termed as partial defection. However, in the long-term, partial defection may lead to total defection. An approach for capturing retail defection is through RFM (recency, frequency, and monetary value) represented by time since last transaction, total number of transactions in the last 3 or 6 months and total value of transactions. This is illustrated in Figs. 4.13–4.14 and Table 4.11. Active and low-value segment constitute a sizeable proportion of the portfolio with 35% of customers. This schema could be used for migration analysis as a follow-up to assess the impact of retention strategies. Furthermore, an RFM score can be developed and readers can refer to the website of database marketing expert Arthur Hughes for details.

According to a 2008 report by Accenture titled *Reducing the Risk of Customer Defection*, customer defection is high in the retail industry despite the entrenchment of loyalty programmes. Estimates are that although 70% of US consumers are loyal to one retailer, 85% of these loyal customers are ready to spend elsewhere, given the right incentives. Loyalty programmes are popular in retail, and readers should refer to

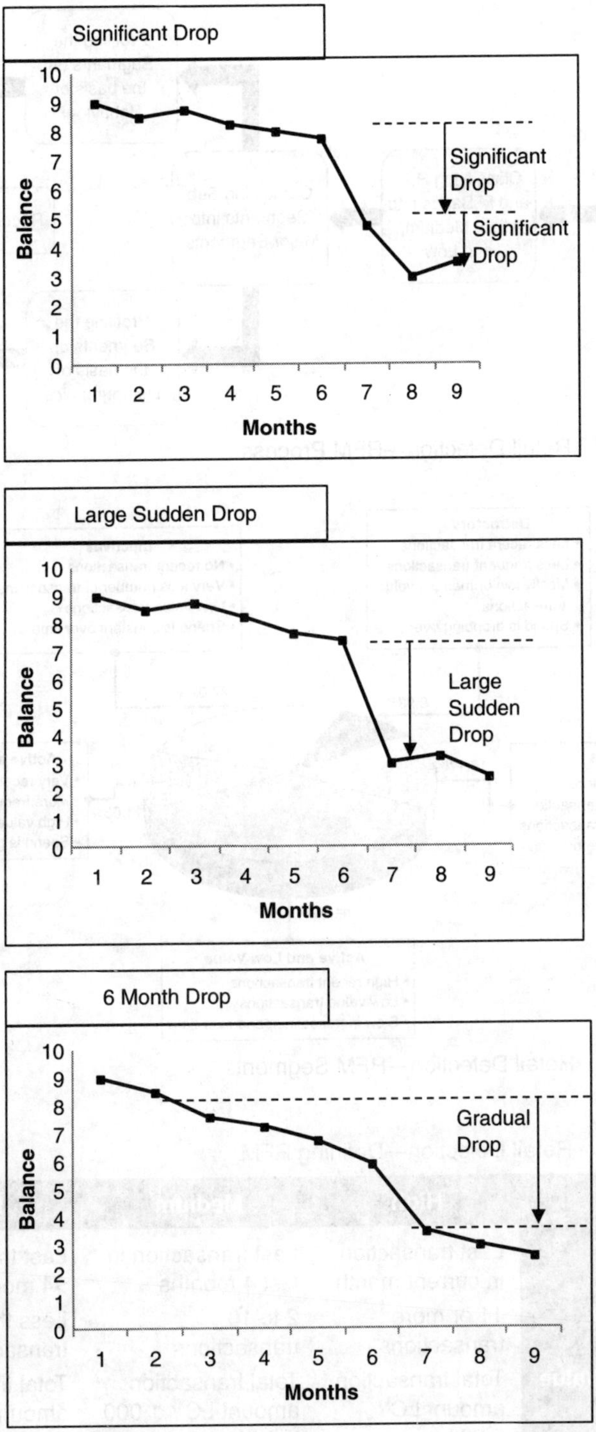


**Figure 4.12** Balance Attrition—Triggers

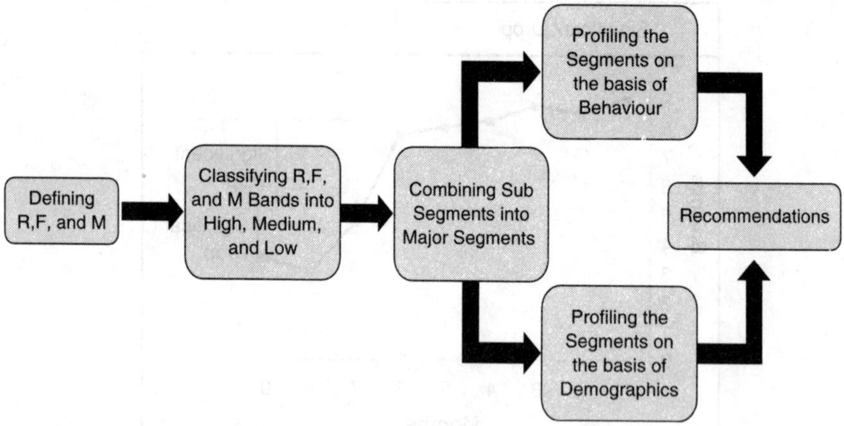


**Figure 4.13** Retail Defection—RFM Process

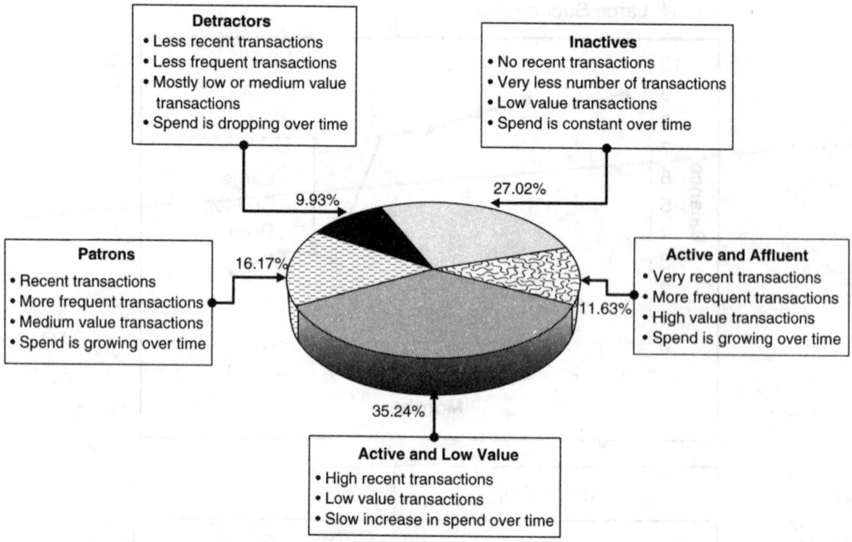


**Figure 4.14** Retail Defection—RFM Segments

**Table 4.11** Retail Defection—Defining RFM

| | High | Medium | Low |
|---|---|---|---|
| **Recency** | Last transaction in current month | Last transaction in last 4 months | Last transaction >4 months |
| **Frequency** | 11 or more transactions | 2 to 10 transactions | Less than 2 transactions |
| **Monetary Value** LCY = Local Currency | Total transaction amount LCY 5,000 or more | Total transaction amount LCY 1,000 to LCY 5,000 | Total transaction amount 0 to LCY 1,000 |

the loyalty section of Chapter 2, "Usage Management" for a P&L performa of a retail loyalty scheme.

In an attempt to understand the reasons for customer attrition in the retail sector, findings from an empirical study by Buckinx and Poel titled *Customer Base Analysis: Partial Defection of Behaviourally Loyal Clients in a Noncontractual FMCG Retail Setting* are presented. This is one of the few studies in this area. Loyalty card customer level data was used to develop a statistical model (probability of partial defection) for a specific segment, namely behaviourally loyal customers.

- **Empirical analysis** was conducted on a large retailer offering fast moving consumer goods (FMCG), having a customer base with average inter-purchase time of 12 days, which indicates an average visit rate of 30 times a year
- **Behaviourally loyal customers** are defined on the basis of frequency of purchase and inter-purchase time, resulting in an activity profile of about 52 visits a year, average inter-purchase time of 7 days, and average spend twice of the average customer. Using this definition, about 20% of customers are termed as loyal customers for modelling partial defection.
- **Partial defection** is defined as
  - Below average frequency of purchase *and*
  - Below average ratio of standard deviation of inter-purchase time to mean purchase time
- Important variables (predictors) considered and the relationship with likelihood of partial defection are summarised as follows:
  - **Inter-purchase time:** Number of days since last purchase; average number of days between customers shop incidences; irregularity of time between purchases. The more recent the purchase, the less the likelihood of defection. Irregular purchase behaviour and defection are positively correlated.
  - **Frequency:** Number of shop visits (with purchase); number of shop visits relative to length of relationship. Frequency of purchase has a negative effect on defection behaviour.
  - **Monetary:** Total value of spend; total value of spend relative to length of relationship and percentage of shop visits with above-average spend. Higher money spent is associated with lower probability of defection.
  - **Brand:** Relative spend of customer across brands (national, own store and private label). Higher the spend on store and private label, higher is the probability of staying.
  - **Length of relationship:** Number of days since first purchase. Time since first purchase positively impacts the stability of the relationship.
  - **Timing:** Average moment of time of shopping; time of last store visit. This relates to diffferences in service quality levels during

the day and week to customer satisfaction and hence, likelihood of defection.
  - **Mode of payment:** Relative amount of money paid in different ways, for example, cash, check, debit card, credit card, reward vouchers, etc. High usage of vouchers indicates stickiness to retailer.
  - **Promotions:** Number of shop incidences when coupon was used, number of loyalty points earned because of special product purchase. Customers who are more sensitive to promotions are likely to have a higher probability of switching.
  - **Demographics:** Household size, language, region classification (postal code based). Smaller households are more deal-sensitive and expected to have a higher likelihood of switching.
- **Conclusions**
  - RFM (recency, frequency, and monetary value) are the best predictors of partial defection
  - Variables such as length of relationship, mode of payment, and promotions are some of the other influencing factors
  - No major differences were reported in the performance of techniques such as logistic regression, neural networks, and classification/decision tree (random forest)

## *4.7.2 Predicting Attrition*

### 4.7.2.1 Issues

The ability to predict voluntary attrition behaviour is important for managing retention activities in the context of the earlier discussion on proactive retention programmes. The questions that researchers and practitioners attempt to answer using analytics are identifying which customers are at risk of attrition and the timing of this event. According to a PwC report of 2002, "the poor management of customer churn is a poor value destroyer and that the key to prevention is to predict and avert attrition of the *right customer*". The quantitative methods used for this purpose include segmentation, triggers and statistical models. While the industry examples will elaborate on the research and industry applications of these methods, the several issues specific to attrition models are outlined in this section.

Whether churn is latent or observable influences the *overall approach* to modelling. Passive attrition is not directly observed while active attrition is clearly visible. Segmentation methods seem to work well for both. Triggers are most effective for identifying passive attrition early on. Regression methods can be used for predicting passive as well as active attrition. In the earlier analysis of balance attrition and retail defection, RFM formed the basis of these triggers. Among regression models, discrete dependent or choice models like logistic regression have been favoured due to their easy interpretation. There is significant evidence pointing to the fact that these models perform well. This point is also ratified by Neslin et al., *Defection Detection: Measuring and Understanding the Predictive Accuracy of Customer Churn Models*, a study that was an outcome of a tournament conducted by them. Survival models can address timing of attrition and can accommodate time varying macroeconomic factors. A joint paper by Van den Poel and Lariviere evaluates the use of this technique for customer attrition for financial services.

Alternative methods of classification/decision tree, neural networks[3] and a Bayesian framework have also been applied. Hu in his 2005 paper titled *A Data Mining Approach for Retail Bank Customer Attrition Analysis* concentrates on predicting active attrition for a loan type service for a retail bank. The findings show that among the models used, neural networks has the best performance while a hybrid model developed from the different models outperforms all other methods. Non-parametric methods such as neural networks, although difficult to interpret, are relevant when the attrition rate is very low. The telecom industry example will showcase the financial benefits of using this procedure. The appropriate methodology for predicting attrition is dependent on various factors such as the extent of data availability, its richness, nature of the event, value of event rate being modelled, criteria for model performance assessment, and other factors.

It is important to build *effective models* due to the high risk of wasted efforts that come with the application of attrition models. In this regard, some evaluation criteria need to be assessed. According to Kamakura et al., *Choice Models and Customer Relationship Management*, one such criterion is the relative importance given to interpretation vs. prediction as models that are better at interpretation may not necessarily be good at prediction. For example, parametric methods such as logistic regression are easy to interpret, but since churn is a behaviour that can be a challenge to predict, it may require new approaches from data mining, machine learning, and non-parametric methods (e.g., neural networks) that stress on *predictive ability*[4]. Selection of the most appropriate model for implementation across several model alternatives, whether by statistical measures or campaign profitability is yet another consideration. It is also important to note that churn models are vulnerable with stability at risk of compromise, given the changing market environment and customer response to competition.

---

[3] Neural networks is a data mining technique that attempts to mimic human cognitive processes. Bayesian is a method of inference in which Bayes' rule is used to update the probability estimate for a hypothesis as additional evidence is learned.

[4] One of the dimensions of predictive ability is an accurate probability estimate. Readers can refer to the model evaluation section of Chapter 7, "Quantitative Methods" for more information on this topic.

One of the inferences drawn from the competition conducted by Neslin and team is that model *staying power* (measured by predictive ability over time) does not diminish appreciably, even after a period of roughly three months. Nevertheless, an out-of-time validation before finalising the model is highly recommended.

There are also heavy dependencies on the *quality and quantity of data* available. One constraint is the low attrition rate on samples available for model development after all exclusions are applied. This can become a challenge for isolating the distinguishing characteristics of defectors and stayers. An option is to bias the sample in order to boost up the attrition rate. Attrition trends are also a reflection of retention efforts by the organisation, thereby leading to an inherent bias in the data being modelled. This aspect makes it difficult to discern attrition stemming from customer behaviour vs. reinstatement efforts by the firm. Good quality of historical information of previous churn, reason codes for closure, service call data, and detailed transaction data are very useful. Customer defection is caused by multiple reasons. This requires appropriate reason codes to be captured on data information systems and categorised for analytical usage. Complaint logs from service call data (using text mining), often not available for analysis purposes, have been found to be a good predictor of attrition behaviour. Transaction data makes the model dynamic as the attrition score responds to changes in customer behaviour at the time of data update. Satisfaction strongly influences attrition and this information is generally available only through customer surveys or feedback at the retention centre. This data is normally stored on disparate data sources and not readily accessible.

Switching to a competitor vs. cancelling the service are different behaviours and combining them together in a model may increase the heterogeneity of the predicted variable. The difficulty of predicting attrition is further amplified with much of the personal reasons explaining a good percentage of churn tendencies, and this data is almost impossible to capture. For example, one of the co-author's experience in developing a prepayment model for Korea proved to be futile as loan customers are seriously inclined to borrow from family and make a lump sum payment in this market. Moreover, caution should be exercised regarding the *inclusion of variables* in the model. Some of these variables may not just be factors influencing attrition behaviour, but may also be characteristics of the attrition phenomena itself, for example, inactivity, and months on book[5].

---

[5] If included in the model, variables such as inactivity and months on book may overshadow many of the customer and transaction related behavioural factors. One of the solutions to inactivity is to model on the active segment only as inactivity or passive attrition is a highly predictive trigger for active attrition.

#### 4.7.2.2 Triggers

Triggers are useful in instances where speed of execution is of utmost criticality. In this case, business experience is useful (to determine the possible triggers) as predictive models take time to build. Moreover, in situations of limited data availability, triggers have been found to serve the purpose successfully. During model development, it is also advisable to keep strong triggers out of the model. For example, separate models for customers with history of churn; and first incidence of churn. Many of the explanatory variables that are included in a predictive model can also be used as triggers, and examples of triggers are shown in Table 4.12. The potential of triggers lies in real-time decision making along with an integrated application of triggers and models. This can be illustrated through a relationship marketing initiative of gaming company Harrah's. Harrah's manages its usage and retention through its coveted and successful loyalty programme which issues a total rewards card (a medium to derive insights of real-time extensive behavioural information of each customer). Rewards card usage captures information on different triggers such as what games the customer is playing, how much is the wager, how long is the duration of the play, what is the outcome, is the spouse accompanying the player, what has been ordered at the restaurant, and is player responding to an offer. These triggers are then processed by a model that determines the predicted behaviour and opportunity for each customer[6]. An example of a dynamic real-time experience would be an instant offer of a free meal triggered by a rule, in response to a first-time customer losing at the slot machine. A corresponding and a less intense strategy of using a combination of triggers and models for financial services (new bank deposits) is highlighted in Fig. 4.15.

#### 4.7.2.3 Profitability of Model-based Proactive Retention Programmes

The reader will recall that proactive retention actions are pre-emptive steps or early measures that are taken by the firm, to minimise the risk of losing the customer. The framework for this strategy is based on predicting whether a customer will attrite in the future (defined over a time period). This prediction is derived from triggers that signal attrition or statistical models. There are certain points that need to be kept in mind while implementing a model-based retention programme.

---

[6] Gary Loveman, "Creating Actionable Business Intelligence to Drive Customer Loyalty and Profitability", Balanced Scorecard Collaborative, A Palladium Company, May 1–19, 2006, The Drake Hotel, Chicago.

**Table 4.12** Attrition Triggers

| Industry | Sub-industry | Triggers |
|---|---|---|
| Financial services | Credit card | No purchase or cash transaction in last 3 months; fall in number of monthly transactions; change in spend (lower); decrease in revolve behaviour; drop in balances; decrease in utilisation; fall in revenue; increase of call-in complaints; fall in number of product holdings with same provider; balance transfer out; recent reward redemption; increase in rate/fee |
| | Personal loan/mortgage | Price drop by competition; closer to maturity date; customer query on lower rates; movement from promo to higher rate |
| | Deposits | Sudden drop in balance (e.g., >20% in 3 months); change in transaction activity; increase in withdrawals (number of transactions and amount); fall in deposit transactions; ATM service issues |
| Wealth management | Mutual funds/insurance | Fall in stock market index; customer query on fund value; discontinuation of SIP (systematic investment plan); completion of stipulated (minimum) number of premium payments for Insurance |
| Telecom | Mobile | Sudden drop in number of calls or total minutes or bill value; increase in customer complaints; higher incidence of call drop-offs; revisions in plan subscribed to; increase in plan fees/callrates; billing errors |
| Travel and entertainment | Hotel/airlines | Recent service complaints; change in tariff; scheduling changes; package deal revisions |
| Retail | | Last visit > "x" months ago; drop in frequency or purchase value; change in store location; promotional offers by competition |

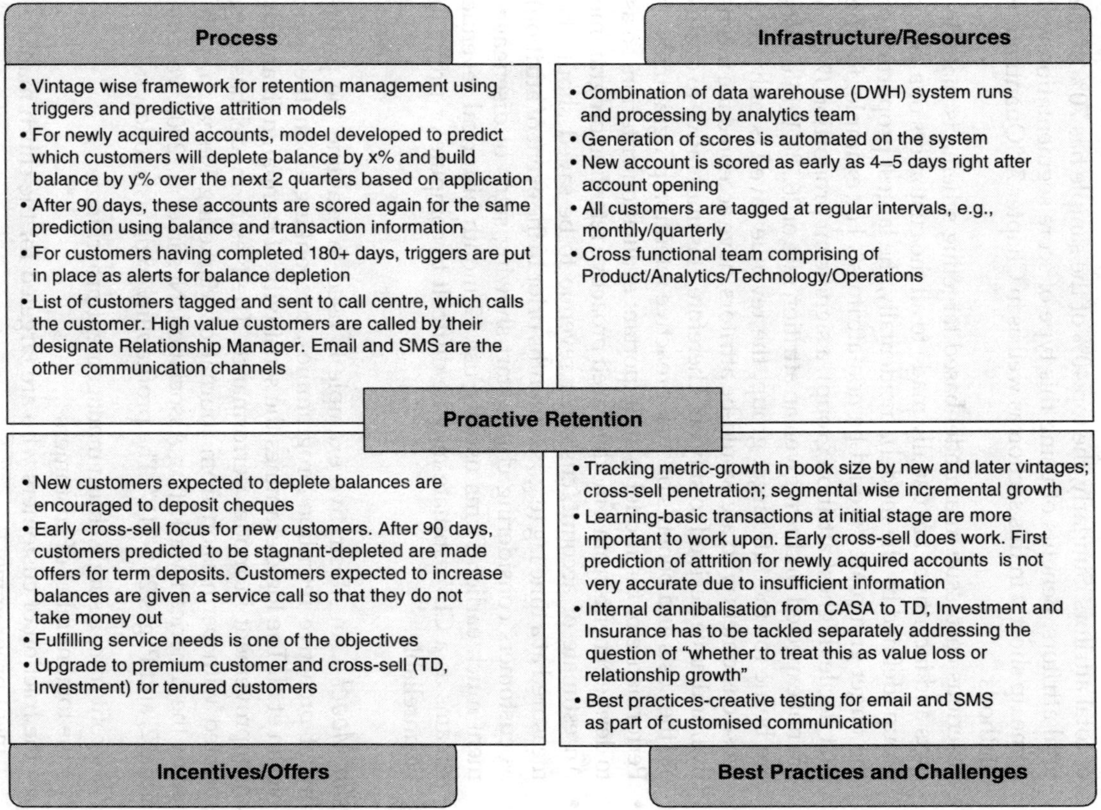


**Figure 4.15** Example of Trigger and Model-based Retention Strategy—Banking

- If based on a prediction model, it is advisable to divide the scored sample into groups based on the probability score and its ranking (Table 4.13). One such grouping is decile based (10 equal groups). Decile-1 has the highest and Decile-10 has the lowest attrition rate. Decile-1 has 10% of the sample with an attrition rate of 26.7% (2.6 times the average sample attrition rate) and constitutes 26.4% of total attritors. Similarly, the top 40% of the sample has 70% of the total attritors. Benefits of using this type of score segmentation will come up shortly in this section as well as in Chapter 7, "Quantitative Methods".
- A serious cost issue in a model-based targeting schema is that contacts and incentives are usually made to all the customers of a target group (defined by the model). Incidentally, the largest proportion of the target group are "would-be non-attritors". For example, for the first decile (highest attrition group), a significant proportion (73.3%) are not expected to churn given an attrition rate of 26.7%. While costs are borne for the full target group, the revenue saved is only from those customers who are would-be attritors, have accepted the incentive, and have decided to stay on. Therefore, it is imperative to evaluate the costs and benefits of such proactive retention programmes.
- Performance of the model is an important evaluation criterion, so as to derive benefits from a model-based proactive retention programme
- An estimate of account/customer revenue to be saved should be measured at a time lag (e.g., six months prior to the event of attrition) as customers considering churn start showing signs of disengagement much earlier. Firms usually use 12 month historical revenue streams as a CLV estimate may be difficult to compute or prove to be unreliable.

*Neslin Model* An illustrative example is used to examine the profitability of proactive retention programmes, by banking upon the logic by Neslin et al. The logic examines the sensitivity of campaign financials to an improvement in model performance. The Neslin model has been "Reprinted with permission from Journal of Marketing Research, published by the American Marketing Association, Neslin et al., 2006, Volume 43, Issue 2, and Pages 204–211". The profitability logic is as follows:

$\Pi$ = profit from a single churn management programme
N = the total number of customers
$\alpha$ = the fraction of customers who are targeted for the churn management programme
$\beta$ = the fraction of customers of targeted customers who are would-be churners
$\delta$ = the cost of customer incentive to the firm
$\gamma$ = success rate of the incentive; the fraction of targeted would-be churners who decide to remain because of the incentive

**Table 4.13** Attrition Score Deciles

| Deciles (Based on Predictive Model) | Customers | Attritor | Attrition Rate ($\chi$) | % Attritor | % Cumulative Attritor | Non-attritor | % Non-attritor | % Cum Non-attritor | KS | Lift ($\mu$) |
|---|---|---|---|---|---|---|---|---|---|---|
| 1 | 3,000 | 800 | 26.7% | 26.4% | 26.4% | 2,200 | 8.2% | 8.2% | 18.3% | 2.64 |
| 2 | 3,000 | 488 | 16.3% | 16.1% | 42.5% | 2,512 | 9.3% | 17.5% | 25.1% | 1.61 |
| 3 | 3,000 | 445 | 14.8% | 14.7% | 57.2% | 2,555 | 9.5% | 26.9% | 30.3% | 1.47 |
| 4 | 3,000 | 399 | 13.3% | 13.2% | 70.4% | 2,601 | 9.6% | 36.6% | 33.8% | 1.32 |
| 5 | 3,000 | 262 | 8.7% | 8.6% | 79.0% | 2,738 | 10.2% | 46.7% | 32.3% | 0.86 |
| 6 | 3,000 | 220 | 7.3% | 7.3% | 86.3% | 2,780 | 10.3% | 57.0% | 29.3% | 0.73 |
| 7 | 3,000 | 152 | 5.1% | 5.0% | 91.3% | 2,848 | 10.6% | 67.6% | 23.7% | 0.50 |
| 8 | 3,000 | 113 | 3.8% | 3.7% | 95.0% | 2,887 | 10.7% | 78.3% | 16.7% | 0.37 |
| 9 | 3,000 | 92 | 3.1% | 3.0% | 98.1% | 2,908 | 10.8% | 89.1% | 9.0% | 0.30 |
| 10 | 3,000 | 58 | 1.9% | 1.9% | 100.0% | 2,942 | 10.9% | 100.0% | 0.0% | 0.19 |
| **Total/ Average** | **30,000** | **3,029** | **10.10%** | **100.0%** | | **26,971** | **100.0%** | | | |

c = the cost of contacting a customer to offer him or her the incentive
CLV = customer lifetime value (i.e., the value to the firm if the customer is retained)
A = the fixed administrative costs of running the churn management programme

$$\Pi = N\alpha[\beta\gamma(CLV - c - \delta)] - N\alpha[\beta(1 - \gamma)(c)] - N\alpha[(1 - \beta)(c + \delta)] - A$$

= Profit from contacted would-churners who decide to stay on the basis of the incentive—Cost of contacting would-be churners who do not accept the offer and leave—Cost of contacting customers who are not would-be churners but accept the offer—Fixed administrative costs of churn management programme

The term $\beta$ can be expressed as

$$\beta = \lambda\beta_0$$

$\beta_0$ = fraction of all the firm's customers who will churn (e.g., model sample attrition rate)
$\lambda$ = lift (i.e. how much more are contacted group of customers likely to churn than all the firm's customers?)

If $\lambda = 1$, the model provides no predictive power as the targeted group is as likely to attrite as the sample as a whole. For gains from the model, this value should be greater than 1.

Gain in profit from a unit increase in the lift factor ($\lambda$) is expressed as

$$GAIN = N\alpha\{[\gamma CLV + \delta(1 - \gamma)]\beta_0\}$$

*Neslin Model—Example* Based on a prediction model, the scored population is divided into 10 groups (deciles) based on the probability of churn as shown in Table 4.13. A simulation based on the Neslin model was done by the authors of this book to evaluate the sensitivity of campaign profitability to changes in customer value, success rate and model performance (lift factor). Assumptions are stated in Table 4.14 and simulations are given in Table 4.15 for a cost of customer incentive of \$50. For the highest lift of 2.64 and for the highest value group of \$2500, positive returns from the programme are achieved starting from a success rate of 10%. For the next lower lift group, a higher success rate of 30% for the same high value group is required. For the lowest lift group, success rate would have to be higher than 50%, which would be a challenge to achieve. One can also use the same framework to examine the sensitivity of campaign profitability to incentive cost (offer value). From this case in point, it is clear that aligning offers with parameters of risk of attrition, customer value, and success rate is a basic requirement for a profitable proactive retention programme.

**Table 4.14** Neslin Model—Assumptions

| Parameters | Values | Parameters | Values |
|---|---|---|---|
| N | 30,000 | $\gamma$ | 10%, 30%, 50% |
| $\alpha$ | 10% | c | $10 |
| $\beta$ | Based on model decile | CLV | $500/$1500/$2500 |
| $\delta$ | $50 | A | $30,000 |

**Table 4.15** Neslin Model—Campaign Profit Simulations

| | | Success Rate | | |
|---|---|---|---|---|
| **Profit Per Contact** | **CLV** | **10%** | **30%** | **50%** |
| Top deciles | 500 | −45 | −21 | 3 |
| Attrition rate = 26.7% | 1500 | −18 | 59 | 137 |
| Lift = 2.64 | 2500 | 9 | 139 | 270 |
| | | **Success Rate** | | |
| | **CLV** | **10%** | **30%** | **50%** |
| Top 4 deciles | 500 | −53 | −37 | −22 |
| Attrition rate = 17.6% | 1500 | −36 | 15 | 66 |
| Lift = 1.76 | 2500 | −18 | 68 | 154 |
| | | **Success Rate** | | |
| | **CLV** | **10%** | **30%** | **50%** |
| Bottom 6 deciles | 500 | −65 | −61 | −56 |
| Attrition rate = 5% | 1500 | −60 | −46 | −31 |
| Lift = 0.49 | 2500 | −55 | −31 | −6 |

Authors demonstrate an impact of $400,000+ from contacting 10% of a 5 million customer company for CLV of $500; success rate of 10%; base 1.8% churn rate. They also show that logistic regression performs the best as compared to classification/decision tree, discriminant analysis, and others using the metric of profit impact per contact. Similarly, for an application to telecom churn, Verbeke et al. improvise on the profitability framework of Neslin in a data-intensive empirical study of 11 telecom operators in their 2012 published paper, *New Insights into Churn Prediction in the Telecommunication Sector: A Profit Driven Data Mining Approach.*

# 4.8 Industry Examples

## 4.8.1 Credit Card Attrition

### 4.8.1.1 Business Scenario

Credit card annual attrition rate (including both voluntary and involuntary) in most markets is a double digit figure, with the voluntary attrition rate hovering around 10%. Further, given the tightened credit market of recent years, retention strategies will need the required focus; it is expected that the cost of replacing a credit card customer will increase as the number of credit worthy prospects decline. However, many issuers lack consistent retention strategies based on a study[7], which covered large financial services providers in Europe and US. The study revealed that only 50% of the survey participants had systems to predict which cardholders were at risk of leaving and to prevent them from defecting. Moreover, methods for dissuading cardholders from switching were different. Methods of measuring results were also erratic. Success rates were found to be in the range of 10–15% and for one issuer, the success rate was as high as 30%. Success rate is measured as the percentage of cardholders prevented from cancelling accounts among those who wanted to cancel[8].

Credit card attrition is a multifaceted phenomenon with both active and passive attrition. Active attrition (voluntary) involves formal closure of the account that is initiated by the customer. Passive attrition manifests itself as low usage in several forms—spend inactivity, spend deterioration, balance depletion, and statement inactivity. Each of these needs to be closely managed in order to tackle passive attrition. Both reactive and proactive retention strategies are practiced by issuers to manage credit card attrition. Reactive retention strategies, focused at customers who call or write in to cancel their accounts, encompass many best-in-class practices with a specialised retention unit in place. In general, issuers look at customer's spending history or total relationship with an institution to determine whether efforts to retain the customer are warranted. As proactive measures, issuers have a formal pre-attrition strategy and implement portfolio management initiatives across the customer life cycle. Additionally, triggers and attrition models are used for determining the set of accounts/customers who are at high risk of attrition. Both these strategies will be discussed later in this section.

[7] Fitzgerald, "As Card Use Slows Retention Strategies Gain Importance", American Banker, 21 June 2011.

[8] Erstwhile credit card issuer MBNA realised that a 5-point increase in retention lifted per-customer profit by more than 125%. Readers can refer to Reichheld, "The Loyalty Effect", for more information regarding retention strategies of MBNA.

### 4.8.1.2 Factors Affecting Attrition

Some of the primary reasons behind voluntary credit card attrition are highlighted.

- **Environmental factors**
  - Saturated marketplace with increased competition, multiple cards in wallet[9], and educated and increasingly sophisticated consumers[10].
  - Macroeconomic conditions affect consumer confidence, which has an impact on usage and hence attrition.
- **Acquisition strategy**
  - Channel of acquisition. For example, direct sales through agents, common in emerging countries is the primary channel of sourcing of new credit cards. Forced selling by agents leads to buyer's remorse and subsequent inertia to use to the card and early closure.
  - Poor quality of acquired customers, an outcome of the trade-off of low retention rates for acquisition momentum, linked to reasons such aggressive sales and inappropriate product vs. target market mapping.
  - Multiple cards from same issuer. Closure of inactive cards for multiple card holders is a regular practice among issuers.
  - Target segment: sub-prime/prime/super-prime. Super-prime segment tends to have the highest voluntary attrition rates.
- **Product specific**
  - Basic vs. premium product. Attrition rates on premium cards are usually lower.
  - Lack of unique utility for consumers with no perceived differentiation of solutions.
  - Insufficient credit line or dissatisfaction with line enhancements is likely to depress utilisation and retention.
  - Pricing at acquisitions and customer management.
    - Promotional interest rate effects show up as spikes in attrition rates as soon as the promotion period is over. In this context, Hu in a paper titled *A Data Mining Approach for Retail Bank Customer Attrition Analysis*, shows that teaser rate along with others (current balance and payment pattern) have a strong influence on attrition for a retail loan product.
    - Role of first year and renewal fee. Voluntary attrition rates tend to be positively correlated not just with the level of fee, but also with the gap between first year and renewal fee.
    - Variable pricing, e.g., penalty pricing (rate goes up suddenly) encourages voluntary attrition.

---

[9] A credit card customer in the United States is believed to carry an average of more than 3 cards in his/her wallet.

[10] TowerGroup, "Credit Card Attrition: Causes and Countermeasures".

- **Service issues** and billing complaints
- **Customer related**
  - Demographic profile: age, gender, occupation, income, others
  - Credit worthiness

### 4.8.1.3 Retention Strategy

*Reactive*

- **Inbound retention unit** to handle customers who call or write-in to cancel their accounts. This would be one of the first critical steps towards managing retention.
- **Channel rationalisation** based on activation and retention trends. Monitoring of productivity at direct sales agent level.
- **Behavioural segmentation** scheme that divides the retention eligible population into distinct segments for reactive offers based on vintage and behavioural variables such as revenue (CNR), line utilisation, additional product ownership, and behaviour score. A revenue ranking is of high practical use for value-based retention offers. These segments include:
  - Qualified for an offer which involves a cost such as fee waivers or discounted cross-sell offers
  - Qualified only for offers with no direct profitability impact such as benefits re-sell
  - Attritors with a retail relationship
- **Pricing**
  - Test discounted prices targeted to highly profitable or low-risk accounts for cross-sold products and services at the point of retention
  - Fee break based on profitability. Note of caution is that repeat behaviour from serial attritors is common. For example, call-in for closure to avail of a fee break that was offered at last renewal.
- **Customer feedback** to identify priorities for improving customer retention using exit survey

*Proactive*

- **Welcome call** after customers receive their first bill (to minimise buyer's remorse)
- **Inbound call to activate**
  - Continue to position as a fraud prevention tool
  - Leverage the customer conversation to cross-sell insurance and fee services, add-on products
- **Lower price** offers to credit worthy customers. For example, first year and renewal fees should be appropriately set based on retention impact and other profitability-related metrics using fee testing.
- **Usage promoting programmes** to encourage statement and sales activity levels

- **Cross-sell/Up-sell** of products and services to improve stickiness. According to a paper by Agarwal et al. titled *Benefits of Relationship Banking: Evidence from Consumer Credit Markets*, for credit card accounts with at least one other relationship with the bank, the marginal probabilities of attrition and default are 12% and 10% respectively. This is lower than accounts with no relationship, ceteris paribus. Additionally, the benefits to the bank generally increase with the strength of the relationship.
    - Free or reduced fee additional card
    - Second card offer with a specific value proposition card based on spend patterns, e.g., petro/telecom card
    - Bill pay, insurance and recurring payment offers
    - Value added services of online and mobile facilities. Consumer research conducted by Forrester reinforces the idea that mobile banking increases customer retention; 30% of US mobile banking users claim that mobile banking has made them more likely to stay with the bank from which they receive the service[11].
    - Product mix with products that have anti-attrition characteristics, for example, a savings account
    - Product upgrade with and without line increase. An example would be a premium product upgrade for a high value customer.
- **Segmented** first year pre-renewal strategy targeted to customers at 9–10 months on books (in case of renewal fees). Test strategies such as:
    - Customer appreciation letters or calls to high value/profitable customers
    - Proactive credit line increases for profitable low-risk customers with high line utilisation, for example, 70%+
    - Balance transfer offers priced at profitable yet competitive rates targeted to transactors and revolvers with low line utilisation
- **Rewards**
    - The Capital One Cash card requires card holders to stay with the company for at least a year to earn all the promised rewards, according to an article by Fitzgerald (American Banker, 26 Aug 2011). The belief is that the one year commitment will counteract attrition for the affluent card segment.
    - For Citibank, the introduction of Thank You Rewards programme reduced customer attrition by 50% since its introduction in 2004, according to an article titled *Citi: ThankYou Lowers Attrition*, in American Banker, 10 Oct 2008
- **Credit line management** involving a robust automated credit line management strategy. Review all accounts for credit line increases every six months. Promote increased spending power and usage incentives as part of notification. Test to selected segments such as:

[11] Bank Technology News, May 2011.

  - Inactives who were previously active and profitable
  - Low-risk customers with high attrition risk
- **Review selected segments** at least quarterly
  - Accounts with high card profitability, high line utilisation and low risk
  - Accounts with high attrition risk

### 4.8.1.4 Analytics

The focus in this section will be on models for proactive retention management.

*Predictive Models* Attrition scores that predict the probability of the event of attrition (active or passive) are important inputs for analytical-based proactive retention strategies. While banks have their own proprietary models, significant research has been conducted by academicians having access to bank data. Considerations while modelling attrition behaviour include the type of statistical model (dependent on whether event attrition or time to attrition is of interest), account vs. customer, and active vs. passive attrition. Nie et al. in their 2011 paper, *Credit Card Churn Forecasting by Logistic Regression and Decision Tree*, develop a model for passive attrition using transaction activity at the card account level as the dependent variable. This is done for the Chinese market using a very comprehensive set of bank data variables and logistic regression performance is better than decision tree. A survival model-based study by Poel and Lariviere for the European financial services industry titled *Customer Attrition Analysis for Financial Services using Proportional Hazard Models*, is a highly referenced paper for active attrition models at a customer level. This model incorporates macroeconomic variables. Findings reveal the significant impact of demographics (e.g., age, education, social status) and macroenvironment factors (e.g., prosperity index measured by GNP per capita). Customer behavioural attributes (e.g., inter-purchase time, total product ownership) take a secondary role. Some more considerations while developing such scores are further highlighted.

*Dependent Variable*

- Event of attrition (yes/no) over a selected time frame—passive (balance drop of greater than x%; spend inactivity, statement inactivity), and active attrition (actual event of voluntary closure)
- Models—binary choice models, survival/hazard rate models, neural networks
- Card account level or card customer level (for multiple card holders)
- Defining the event of active attrition based on the selection of appropriate closure reason codes (stored on the system)

### *Explanatory Variables*

- Factors used for modelling attrition are defined in Table 4.16 for event attrition and Table 4.17 for passive (balance) attrition
- Balance attrition results also include the order of importance of the variables (both internal and credit bureau variables). The percentage contribution is the percent of variation in the dependent variable that is captured by the independent variables. Number of revolving cards with balance and number of inquiries in 0–3 months are the most and least important, respectively. The relationship of these variables with balance attrition, whether positive or negative, is left to the readers to determine.

### *Sample for Model Development*

- Inactivity and attrition are highly correlated as discussed earlier. Therefore, it is ideal to model the active segment only.
- If voluntary attrition rates are low, for example, below 10%, a common practice is to bias the sample for model development. This is done so that a higher attrition rate is modelled for better differentiation between attritors and non-attritors. Nie et al. conclude that 1:1 ratio of attritor to non-attritor (50% attrition rate) yielded the best model results.
- Timing is another important factor as vintage has a significant impact on attrition rates. For instance, in the case of fee-based products, customers approaching first renewal and those who have completed at least one cycle of fee renewal behave differently, with significantly higher attrition for the former group. Also attrition rates drop significantly for high-tenured customers. Separate models can be built by customer vintage depending on exploratory analysis of whether drivers of attrition differ by vintage.
- Predictor variables measured as of less than 3 and 6 months prior to the event of attrition should be used. With the exception of change-related variables (e.g., average monthly decline in spend over the last 6/12 months), historical information beyond 6 months is not very effective in explaining attrition based on authors' experience.
- Recent changes in rate, fees or rewards should be explicitly considered while finalising the sample data for model development.

### *Model Performance*

- The Gains Chart is a measure of model discriminatory power (separation of attritors and non-attritors). Figure 4.16 shows that if this model is not used, one would expect to capture 10% of the total attritors by targeting 10% of the sample population. Similarly, to capture 70% of total attritors, one would have to reach out to 70% of the

**Table 4.16** Variables for Active Attrition Prediction Model—Credit Card

| Category | Variable | Relationship with Voluntary Attrition Rate (Empirical Evidence) |
|---|---|---|
| Customer demographics | Age* | Negative |
| | Single* | Positive |
| | Income | Positive |
| Customer relationship | Number of non-card relationships or products with the same issuer | Negative |
| | Number of credit cards with same issuer | Positive/Negative |
| | Number of add-on cards | Negative |
| | Number of active cards | Negative |
| Card features | Value proposition card | Negative |
| | Credit line | Negative |
| | Whether/amount of renewal fee | Positive |
| | Proximity to fee renewal | Positive |
| Card performance | Months on book | Positive/Negative |
| | Sales or statement inactive | Positive |
| | Time since last activity (e.g., spend/cash transaction) | Positive |
| | Spend, balance, highest balance | Negative |
| | Cash user | Negative |
| | Line utilisation | Negative |
| | Revenue | Negative |
| Rewards | Number of times redeemed in the last "x" months | Positive |
| Credit bureau | Number of credit card inquiries | Positive |
| | Max or 2nd max balance/credit line on card relative to other competitor cards | Negative |
| | Bureau score (higher is better credit worthiness) | Positive |
| Customer care/service | Number of calls made to customer service; unresolved queries | Positive |
| Other | Number of times card lost by customer | Positive |
| | Bill pay, insurance | Negative |
| | Recent switching behaviour on other products held with issuer | Positive |

*Regulatory environment in some countries do not permit use of the variable.

**Table 4.17** Variables for Passive (Balance) Attrition Prediction Model—Credit Card

| Description | Percentage Contribution |
|---|---|
| Number of revolving cards with a balance | 25% |
| Aggregate credit utilisation | 20% |
| Ending of promotion period | 14% |
| Days since card open | 10% |
| Last cash advance 3 months ago | 9% |
| Spend active on debit card | 9% |
| Number of months with finance charge in past 6 months | 9% |
| Number of inquiries in last 0–3 months | 4% |

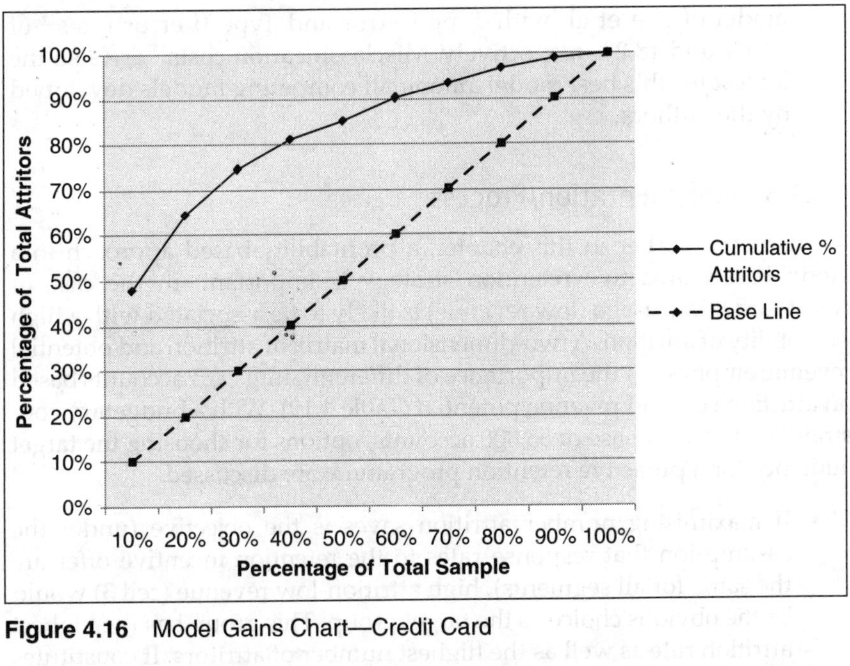


**Figure 4.16** Model Gains Chart—Credit Card

sample population. Using this model, one can capture 74.5% of total attritors by targeting only the top 30% of the sample population. This leads to direct saves on marketing costs on 40% of the sample population, thereby enhancing marketing efficiency.

- The confusion matrix is a measure of model predictive power (classification accuracy). Table 4.18 is confusion matrix of the best

**Table 4.18 Confusion Matrix—Credit Card**

| Observed | | Predicted: No Churn/Churn: No Churn | Churn | Sum | Percentage Correct (%) | Error (%) |
|---|---|---|---|---|---|---|
| Good/Bad | Good (*No Churn*) | 4179 | 593 | 4772 | 87.6 (*4179/4772*) | 12.4 (*593/4772*) |
| | Bad (*Churn*) | 41 | 184 | 225 | 81.8 (*184/225*) | 18.2 (*41/225*) |

*Source:* Adapted from *Expert Systems with Applications*, Volume 38, Issue 12, Nie et al., "Credit Card Churn Forecasting by Logistic Regression and Decision Tree", Pages 15273–15285, Copyright (2011), with permission from Elsevier.

model of Nie et al. with Type I error and Type II error rates[12] of 12.4% and 18.2% respectively. Misclassification costs[13] are also the lowest for this best model among all competing models developed by the authors.

### 4.8.1.5 Implementation/Process

As discussed earlier in this chapter, a profitability-based approach to a model-based proactive retention strategy is important. In the case of credit cards, low usage (low revenue) is likely to be associated with a high probability of attrition. A two-dimensional matrix of attrition and potential revenue emphasises the importance of differentiating card accounts based on attrition risk and revenue potential (Table 4.19). With a budgetary constraint of a contact base of 55,000 accounts, options for choosing the target audience for a proactive retention programme are discussed.

- If maximising number attrition saves is the objective (under the assumption that response rates to the retention incentive offer are the same for all segments), high attrition-low revenue (cell 3) would be the obvious choice as the target group. This group has the highest attrition rate as well as the highest number of attritors. It constitutes 17% of credit card accounts; contributes to 44% of total card attrition; and forms 13% of total value loss.

---

[12] Type I error—customer who did not churn is misclassified as a churner. Type II error—customer who churned is misclassified as non-churner.

[13] Type II error is generally considered to be much more costly (5–20 times higher) than Type 1 error. Therefore, the measure of misclassification costs based on Type I and II error rates and an economic cost is used as an additional model evaluation criterion by Nie et al.

**Table 4.19** Revenue at Risk Grid—Credit Card

| Expected Attrition | | High Revenue > *LCY* 3000 | Medium Revenue *LCY* 1000 – *LCY* 3000 | Low Revenue < *LCY* 1000 | Total |
|---|---|---|---|---|---|
| High attrition | Total accounts | 15000 | 40000 | 55000 | |
| | % of total accounts | 4.5% | 12.1% | 16.6% | 33.2% |
| | Total attritors | 525 | 2000 | 3410 | 5935 |
| | % of total attritors | 6.8% | 26.0% | 44.3% | 77.1% |
| | Attrition rate | 3.5% | 5.0% | 6.2% | 5.4% |
| | Average revenue | 5,000 | 1,500 | 500 | 1,235 |
| | Potential revenue loss | 26,25,000 | 30,00,000 | 17,05,000 | 73,30,000 |
| | **Cell** | **1** | **2** | **3** | |
| Medium attrition | Total accounts | 35000 | 39000 | 36000 | 110000 |
| | % of total accounts | 10.6% | 11.8% | 10.9% | 33.2% |
| | Total attritors | 350 | 468 | 432 | 1250 |
| | % of total attritors | 4.5% | 6.1% | 5.6% | 16.2% |
| | Attrition rate | 1.0% | 1.2% | 1.2% | 1.1% |
| | Average revenue | 5,500 | 2,000 | 600 | 2,496 |
| | Potential revenue loss | 19,25,000 | 9,36,000 | 2,59,200 | 31,20,200 |
| | **Cell** | **4** | **5** | **6** | |

(*Continued*)

**Table 4.19** Revenue at Risk Grid—Credit Card (*Continued*)

| Expected Attrition | | High Revenue > *LCY* 3000 | Medium Revenue *LCY* 1000 – *LCY* 3000 | Low Revenue < *LCY* 1000 | Total |
|---|---|---|---|---|---|
| Low attrition | Total accounts | 60000 | 31000 | 20000 | 111000 |
| | % of total accounts | 18.1% | 9.4% | 6.0% | 33.5% |
| | Total attritors | 300 | 155 | 60 | 515 |
| | % of total attritors | 3.9% | 2.0% | 0.8% | 6.7% |
| | Attrition rate | 0.5% | 0.5% | 0.3% | 0.5% |
| | Average revenue | 6,000 | 2,500 | 800 | 4,341 |
| | Potential revenue loss | 18,00,000 | 3,87,500 | 48,000 | 22,35,500 |
| | **Cell** | **7** | **8** | **9** | |
| Total | Total accounts | 110000 | 110000 | 111000 | 331000 |
| | % of total accounts | 33.2% | 33.2% | 33.5% | 100.0% |
| | Total attritors | 1175 | 2623 | 3902 | 7700 |
| | % of total attritors | 15.3% | 34.1% | 50.7% | 100.0% |
| | Total attrition rate | 1.1% | 2.4% | 3.5% | 2.3% |
| | Average revenue | 5,404 | 1,648 | 516 | 1,647 |
| | Potential revenue loss | 63,50,000 | 43,23,500 | 20,12,200 | 1,26,85,700 |

- If the goal is revenue loss minimisation (defined as *revenue per attrited account* attrition rate* number of accounts* for a particular cell), high attrition and low-and medium-revenue segments (cells 1 and 2) would be the candidate target groups. These two groups contribute to 44% of total revenue loss with 17% of card accounts and 33% of total account attrition.
- For a random selection of 55,000 customers with an average sample attrition rate of 2.3%, the potential is saves of only 1265 attritors, constituting only 17% of total account and revenue attrition

### 4.8.1.6 Financial Benefits

The financial results of model implementation for a retail loan product based on a paper by Hu titled *A Data Mining Approach for Retailing Bank Customer Attrition Analysis*, are quoted. The model predicts the probability that the customer voluntarily closes the account within the next "x" months.

- Customers were sorted on the basis of the attrition sore
- Top 4% of the existing customers were contacted and this target group was divided randomly into test and control
- Test group was offered an incentive package as part of a proactive retention strategy. Control group was not contacted.
- Tracking revealed that the test group cumulative attrition rate for 2 months was as low as 1.1%. For the control group, the attrition rate was close to 5.6%. This result is a reflection of the effectiveness of the retention marketing program.
- The high actual attrition rate on the control group is also a validation of the model's ability to identify attritors

## *4.8.2 Mortgage Prepayment*

### 4.8.2.1 Business Scenario

One of the challenges faced by the mortgage industry is prepayment risk, the risk associated with the early unscheduled return of principal on the loan. Prepayment is payment made by the borrower over and above the scheduled mortgage payment. If the additional payment pays off the entire balance, it is termed as "prepayment in full"; otherwise, it is a "partial prepayment." Prepayment is beneficial for the borrower as it draws down debt, although it reduces interest earned by the lender that would have been received otherwise. As a result, some lenders attach prepayment penalties to loans in order to disincentivise prepayments. Prepaying in the early years of the tenor of the loan is more financially beneficial for the borrower as interest burden is relatively higher when compared to later years. In general, a negative relationship between the overall level of interest rate and level of refinancing activity has been observed. (*Source:* FRBSF Economic Letter, *Mortgage Prepayments and Changing Underwriting Standards*, 19 July 2010)

In a scenario of increasing prepayments, the objective of lenders is to manage runoffs by controlling prepayment rates to maintain portfolio book size, manage the economic and accounting impact of unexpected loan turnover, maximise return on investment in the customer, and achieve favourable pricing of securitisation deals. According to a PwC study titled *Customer Retention in the Consumer Finance Industry*, almost all lenders have been focused on tracking retention rates rather than profitability of retained loans. Although reactionary programmes based on rate reductions have been able to deliver a retention rate of 20–25% of paid-off loans, their financial simulation analysis showed that improving the annualised retention rate from 15% to 40% (through a 20 basis point price discount) may result only in a fractional increase in portfolio profitability. Henceforth, it is important to track the incremental benefits of retention programmes for a mortgage portfolio.

### 4.8.2.2 Factors Affecting Prepayment

Besides interest rate and macroeconomic related factors, prepayment behaviour is also influenced by other factors. An empirical paper written by Hakim titled *Autonomous and Financial Mortgage Prepayment*, is a good study on the factors influencing prepayment behaviour for the US market, with some observations noted below:

- **Property/loan related**
  - Level and trends in mortgage interest rates. An increasing trend is associated with a lower likelihood of prepayment and vice-versa for a decreasing trend.
  - Difference in the present value of mortgage at market rate and at contract rate minus the refinancing cost. Higher this differential, higher the inclination to prepay.
  - Property age and prepayment behaviour have a positive relationship
  - A higher loan to value ratio (at the time of purchase) is associated with a higher prepayment probability
  - Mortgage age is an important indicator and takes the form of an inverted U or V shape curve, increasing with mortgage age and then decreasing. This is expected as interest burden is much higher in the early years of life of the loan, making it more beneficial for the customer to prepay earlier than later.
  - Movement from a lower fixed to higher floating rate has a positive effect on prepayment behaviour

- **Customer related**
  - *Income:* High income is a surrogate for social and income stability that indicates a lower probability of moving to another lender. On the other hand, increase in earnings may make a move more likely as part of the process of upgrading the home.
  - *Family size:* Number of dependents increases the risk of prepayment, given the need to move to a larger property
  - *Age:* Customers with high prepayment risk tend to be older and own an older property
  - *Family related:* For example, divorce often leads to sale of the shared dwelling
  - *Credit Worthiness:* A sub-prime customer is less likely to prepay than a prime customer
  - *Geographic state of home:* regional variations are significant with state mobility rates highly correlated to mortgage closures

### 4.8.2.3 Retention Strategy

A highly segmented retention plan is recommended and a need for both proactive and reactive strategies in action. A dedicated retention team for inbound and outbound calling is a quintessential requirement.

*Reactive Strategy*

- A retention process to handle customers calling or writing in to close their accounts. Price breaks to hold on to the customer, besides addressing service issues.
- Price calculator to determine the optimal rate to offer will be discussed in the implementation/process section
- Customer surveys to those who have already closed

*Proactive Strategy*

- Identification of customers at high risk of churn using triggers and predictive models
  - Calls to customers termed as "health check", to understand and resolve service problems; interest rate breaks are usually not considered due to its low profitability
  - Loan anniversary message along with a summary of features of mortgage and current conditions of the mortgage market
  - Calls to customers prior to expiry of the fixed rate in an attempt to re-fix the rate; it has been observed that customers who re-fix are less likely to defect as compared to customers who are not contacted or choose not to re-fix

- Cross-sell of debt consolidation; cross-sell at point of sourcing that include general insurance and wealth management products
- Customer service centres for financial education
- Feedback calls to customers walking into the branch

### 4.8.2.4 Analytics

- MIS shared periodically with senior management
  - Monthly/weekly/daily attrition MIS at portfolio and segment level
  - Broker-wise MIS on sales, profitability and attrition
  - Tracking reports relating to the impact of retention activities
- Deep analysis of customer survey results and feedback from the retention unit to understand reasons for attrition
- Retention offers based on profitability will be discussed subsequently as mortgage rate break calculator
- Triggers which signal risk of attrition, for example, significant decrease in outstanding balances
- Proactive retention model to identify customers most likely to attrite.
  - Some significant variables that positively impact churn: number of calls by customer in the last 3 months, tenor, latest outstanding balance, interest rate above "x", unsettled request by customer for change in terms of the product, and enquires regarding terms and conditions (Ts and Cs)
  - Due to possible differences between borrowers who take out variable and fixed rate mortgages, separate models may need to be developed for these segments
  - Besides logistic regression, a popular modelling technique is competing risks survival model as survival risks are "competing"; mortgages can terminate in two different ways—prepay or default/foreclosure

### 4.8.2.5 Retention Unit Incentive Structure

- Sales or broker commissions are usually a function of volume with no penalty for active churn. Compensation scheme should also be based on retention rather than just sales. One such approach is to stagger commissions over time based on observed customer retention rates by broker.
- Setting performance metrics and incentives for retention officers
  - An example of a performance metric is balance amount saved at individual and team levels. Incentives are based on benchmark levels that are four to five times the targets at individual and team level.

- Incremental bonus linked to the difference between negotiated interest rate and the floor price (break-even below which it is not profitable for the mortgage provider).

#### 4.8.2.6 Implementation/Process

*Reactive*

- Service calls for closure are routed to the retention team
- Reasons for attrition are captured by the retention unit and then analysed and quantified
- A mortgage rate break calculator[14] to determine rate cuts based on profitability is illustrated in Table 4.20. It is important to note that it is not always necessary to drop rate as a retention strategy, as customers are sometimes in the "wrong product".

*Proactive*

- Service calls by the retention team to hot leads identified by triggers and scoring models
- Identified customers are called for assessment regarding satisfaction with the product, features and service issues, with follow-up action by retention staff
- Communication in the form of a letter is sent to customers who cannot be reached
- Campaign design to address which segments to target for retention activities. Creation of control and test cells is illustrated in Fig. 4.17, to measure the difference in observed attrition rates post-implementation resulting from model impact, model and retention strategy, and retention strategy alone. Control Group (1) and Test Group (1) are selected based on the model, for example, top 2 deciles of a model that predicts attrition. These specific high attrition control and test groups should have the same attrition rate as well as other characteristics. Control (1a) is a random sample which reflects the average attrition rate for the sample under consideration, before any model is applied. On control groups, no retention action is taken. Customers are further segmented into low interest (less than "x") and high interest (greater than or equal to "x") and the determination of "x" can be based on the lowest competition market rate, for example.
  - Control (1) and Control (1a)—Incremental impact of retention model
  - Test (1) and Control (1)—Incremental impact of retention strategy
  - Test (1) and Control (1a)—Incremental impact of model and retention strategy.
  - Further additional test groups can be created for offer testing

[14] Authors would like to thank Nitin Agarwal for the mortgage rate break calculator.

**Table 4.20** Mortgage Rate Break Calculator

| | | |
|---|---|---|
| **MORTGAGE RETENTION Offer: Rate Break** | | |
| **Inputs** | | |
| Original principal amount | $1,00,000 | |
| Original tenor | 240 | (months) |
| Month of attrition | 60 | (months) |
| Interest rate | 10.00% | (annually) |
| Cost of funds | 7.00% | (annually) |
| Prepayment penalty | 3.00% | of the outstanding balance at the time of attrition |
| Refinance charges | 1.00% | of the refinance amount |
| Average risk free rate for the tenor of the loan (same as cost of funds %) | 7.00% | |
| Cost per year of maintaining a loan (statementing, servicing) | $30 | |
| Customer reinvestment rate | 7.50% | Return on alternative investment opportunity |
| Best available interest rate for refinanced loan in the market | 8.00% | |
| **Customer Profitability—What is the rate below which customer is better off switching?** | | |
| Current EMI at current interest rate 10% | $965 | |
| Principal outstanding at possible attrition month | $89,802 | |
| Prepayment + refinancing charges | $3,592 | |
| New installment to be cash neutral | $945 | (Sum of installment amounts for the remaining tenor—cost of refinancing/ remaining tenor) |
| New rate required to be cash neutral | 9.63% | Customer—loses cash if he refinances above this rate |
| New installment needed to be value neutral for the customer | $932 | (Old installment—monthly receipts from annuity payment by investing the refinancing amount at the alternative investment rate for the remaining term of the loan) |
| New rate required to be value neutral | 9.39% | Customer—loses value below this rate |
| **Competition—What is the best rate available in the market currently?** | | |
| Best rate in the market | 8.00% | Competition—market spoiler rate |

(*Continued*)

**Table 4.20** Mortgage Rate Break Calculator (*Continued*)

| | | |
|---|---|---|
| **Bank Profitability—What is the minimum offer rate below which bank starts losing money?** | | |
| Net present value of the loan in case of no attrition at point of evaluation | $11,174 | (NPV of all the future cash flows—opportunity lost in prepayment penalty—cost of maintaining the loan over the tenor of the loan) |
| Min rate bank can afford | 7.69% | Banks affordability—profitability breaker rate |
| **Negotiation Strategy** | | |
| 1. Manage attrition only reactively as a high number/percentage of customers who don't attrite, but are identified by the predictive model as 'Highly Likely to Attrite' will never let a price break strategy justify itself financially<br>2. Offer customer rates in the below explained range<br>3. Retention incentive should be a function of the rate of interest at which the customer is retained. Incentive should have a skew towards higher rate | | |
| **Negotiation Range** | | |
| Current rate | 10.00% | |
| Negotiation start rate | 9.63% | Customer loses in cash terms if competition offers a higher rate than this. A "demi-intelligent" customer will not want to attrite unless offered below this rate by the competitor |
| Negotiation start rate—stage 2 | 9.39% | Customer loses in value terms if competition offers a higher rate than this. An "Intelligent customer" will not want to attrite unless offered below this rate by the competitor |
| Last rate for negotiation | 8.00% | Below this rate, either giving the loan would be unprofitable for the bank or bank will be spoiling the market (and thus lowering the pie for everyone) |

## *4.8.3 Telecom Churn*

### 4.8.3.1 Business Scenario

With the boom of the telecom mobile industry, wireless churn has become a serious concern with rising subscriber churn rates in the backdrop of a global trend of declining ARPU. For the Indian wireless market, analysts estimate the rate of monthly subscriber churn rate to be in the range of 6–8% among pre-paid and 1–3% among post-paid subscribers. The post-paid customer segment constitutes 5% of total subscriber base and

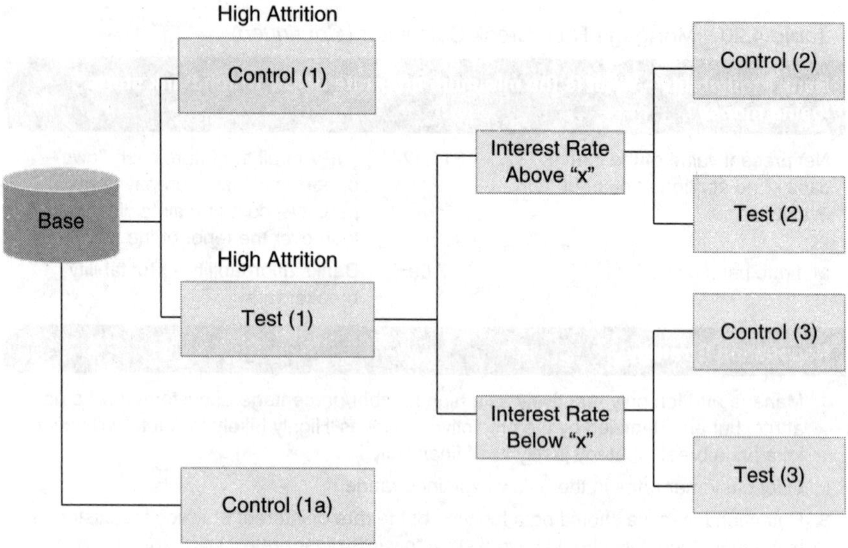


**Figure 4.17** Campaign Design—Mortgage

contributes to about 20% of revenues for the larger telecom players[15]. In relation to costs of churn, it is estimated that subscriber churn costs the telecom industry billions of dollars. According to a report by WDS titled *Industry Briefing Mobile Churn*, for a mobile operator with 1.5 million net additions in the year, ARPU of $39 and a 3.5% quarterly churn rate, decreasing the churn rate by 50 basis points to 3% would yield an additional $40 million of revenue and $22 million of profit in 36 months (from the original collective of net additions). Net additions are the increase in total subscriber base from the start to the end of the period. Some salient features of telecom churn are highlighted:

- One definition of churn rate is the number of subscribers who leave an operator's network in a month as a percentage of its total subscriber base (as of that month).
- Mobile churn rates vary across different markets and depend on various factors such as maturity of the market, price sensitivity of customers, the percentage of pre-paid subscribers in the market, competitive landscape, and pricing and competitive strategies of different operators within that market. Mature European markets are at a monthly churn rate of around 2%. For emerging countries with high pre-paid subscribers and price sensitivity such as Indonesia, it exceeds 10%[16].

[15] DNA, *Portability Launch Spurs War for Post-paid Users*, 20 Jan 2011.

[16] CommsMEA, *Customer Acquisition*. Report available at http://www.commsmea.com/11306-customer-acquisition/

- On average it costs a service provider $60 to retain a customer and around $200 to acquire a new one in the US market, and as much as $350–$400 for a smart phone (iPhone)[17]. Cost of acquisition in the European market is almost three times higher than in the Middle East, according to the CommsMEA article.
- New accounts tend to be less profitable due to the huge discounts and promotions offered to a new customer. In Europe, a subscriber plan offer commonly includes a subsidised handset including a bundle of minutes and data, and a minimum commitment of six months to a year.
- In markets where there are low-end subscribers and high penetration levels, the focus is more on aggressive promotions. In these markets, operators launch two to three promotions every day targeting different customer segments.
- Churn can occur early as a new customer may review plans of other carriers as early as 60–90 days after sign up. For a contractual relationship, high churn rates are observed during weeks prior to the expiration of the contract.
- "Artificial" churn may be encouraged by so called "spinners", who disconnect and reconnect to the same network by taking advantage of offers available.
- Segmental-based approach to churn management
  - Pre-paid subscribers have a higher propensity to churn than post-paid and constitute a high proportion of the total subscriber base. The ARPU of a pre-paid subscriber is about one-third or less than that of a post-paid subscriber in some countries. The task of retaining customers can be demanding as this segment is likely to be price-sensitive.
  - Since the revenue and cost dynamics vary across the two segments, telecom operators are inclined to tailor retention strategies by segment. According to a McKinsey report, *Profiting from Pre-paid Phone Customers*, the attractiveness of the pre-paid segment is that the economics are lucrative with faster payback on investment due to lower acquisition and activation costs. A European operator recovered its investment on the pre-paid segment in only 9 months as compared to 13 months for the full subscriber base.
  - Pre-paid churn in India is also induced by retailers, who shift pre-paid customers from one operator to another, depending on who offers a better commission. (*Source:* Business Standard, *Telecom Industry makes Hay while the Industry Whines*, 23 Sep 2012).
  - Consumer, small business (SME) and corporate segments behave differently and the focus of this section is on the consumer segment.

---

[17] WDS report, "Industry Briefing Mobile Churn". Available at http://www.wds.co/enlightened/churn/WDS_Churn_2011.pdf.

**Table 4.21** Sensitivity of Profitability to Churn Rate—Telecom

| Quarterly Churn Rate | Average Customer Lifetime (Months) | Blended APPU |
|---|---|---|
| 2.5% | 150 | $30.46 |
| 3% | 100 | $29.92 |
| 3.5% | 86 | $29.66 |
| 4% | 75 | $29.39 |
| 4.5% | 67 | $29.12 |
| 5% | 60 | $28.85 |

- Churn is primarily of the active variety as customers fade away at a snap. Promoted by advertising, customers are updated about competition and are likely to make decisions regarding account closure, soon after a decision is made on a probable alternate service provider. Therefore, a proactive orientation to retention management is expected to be more effective than a reactive one. An early warning system is a necessary requirement for managing churn in this sector.
- Increasing demand from customers is compelling telecom operators to invest in new technology and increase their network capacity. These initiatives are expected to provide better customer experience to help reduce churn. While incumbents tend to focus on retention of existing customers, new operators are focused on acquiring new customers.
- The impact of a reduction in churn rate on average lifetime and per user profitability is shown in Table 4.21. Based on the WDS report, profitability measure used is APPU[18] (average profit per user). A few interesting observations from this report are mentioned:
  - Relating to the cost relationship between acquisition and retention, for a 3.5% quarterly churn rate, it takes 2.73 gross additions to achieve 1 net addition, according to the WDS report. Gross additions is the total number of new subscribers connected to the network. Net additions is the increase in total subscriber count from the start to the end of the period.
  - In financial terms, the cost burden on remaining subscribers to replace a churned subscriber with a new subscriber for the different service providers in the US is of the order of $4.50 for AT&T

[18] APPU is the gross revenue contribution per user, per month. APPU is the monthly profit per user after all costs have been factored. CPGA (cost per gross addition) is the cost of acquiring a new subscriber to the business and this acquisition cost includes retail, administration, marketing and handset subsidy costs. Calculations assume 1.5 million net additions on a 20 million subscriber base, ARPU $50, CPGA $160 and CPU $18.50.

and \$11 for T-mobile[19], as of the fourth quarter of 2010. Readers can refer to the report for the derivation of these calculations while the P&L section of the last chapter will cover the revenue and cost dynamics for the telecom sector.

### 4.8.3.2 Factors Affecting Churn

Factors driving telecom churn behaviour are noted.

- **Competition**
  - Pricing plans have been very aggressive as providers have been focused uni-dimensionally on growing new subscribers. Promotions and discounts for new customers are likely to promote churn behaviour.
- **Rate plans**
  - Customers don't fully understand rate plans of a provider—various combinations of call charges, free minutes, service features, and others.
  - Inappropriate plans in relation to customer-specific needs (either low usage for the plan or exceeding allotted rate plan minutes). Light users will be overpaying if they subscribe to high-end plans and the same for heavy talkers if they subscribe to low-end plans.
- **Pricing structure:** Two-part tariff (TPT) and pay-per-use (PPU) have been found to have an impact on consumer preferences and retention. Raghuram Iyengar et al. in their 2011 paper titled *The Impact of Tariff Structure on Customer Retention, Usage, and Profitability of Access Services*, show that TPT structure has lower marginal utility as compared to PPU plans and leads to an average decline of 9.6% in the annual retention rate, and an average decrease of 38.1% in yearly usage relative to PPU pricing. PPU plans feature only marginal price per use and with no access fee, whereby a customer is charged only for the minutes used. TPT pricing structure has an initial access fee plus a marginal price per use. Pricing field experiment data for a new telecommunication service was used for this study.
- **Service issues**
  - Handset issues for plans where handset is part of the offer plan—equipment problem, lost or stolen handset.
  - Problems relating to network coverage, blackouts, dropped calls, etc.
  - Customer care and billing concerns.

---

[19] Monthly churn rate for the same period for T-Mobile in the United States was 2.5% for post-paid compared to 1.4% for AT&T (*Source*: Rosenfeld, M+R Strategic Services).

- **Customer profile**
  - Younger customers have a higher percentage enrolled in pre-paid services, and since switching costs are lower, they are likely to unsubscribe faster. For the US market, "youth churn" as is so described, is a double digit multiple of the national average.

#### 4.8.3.3 Retention Strategy

According to an interesting study by Booz-Allen Hamilton[20], a fundamental concern related to retention management is the low strategic importance given by telecom operators. More importantly, expected results from anti-churn activities are not met, as symptoms rather than root causes of churn are addressed. Some of the proactive retention efforts taken by telecom operators are the following:

- **Rate plans:** Periodic reviews of rate plans based on call pattern data. In this context, Wong conducted several studies in an attempt to understand the drivers of mobile churn and in particular, the impact of rate plans. The 2011 multivariate and longitudinal study (same set of subscribers were observed over a period of 44 months) for the Canadian wireless telecommunications industry, was published as a paper titled *Using Cox Regression to Model Customer Time to Churn in the Wireless Telecommunications Industry*.
  - The definition of an optimal rate plan for a given customer is based on usage of the particular customer, and which results in the lowest monthly expense. A subscriber is flagged to be using an optimal rate plan if he or she has been on an optimal plan for more than 50% of the time during the period of the study.
  - It was observed that post-paid customers with non-optimal rate plans are 1.85 times more likely to churn than customers with optimal rate plans. This effect was isolated after adjusting for the effects of all other variables.
  - Another finding was that about half of the subscribers of the telecom company of interest were not at their optimal rate plan. Customers are less likely to churn if they had moved to a different rate plan, as compared to those who have not, during the study period.
  - Rate plan optimisation can contribute to customer churn reduction, although short-term profitability has to be given up.
- **Promotions that stimulate usage**
  - Address dormancy or inactivity; a good percentage of pre-paid subscribers may become inactive if they do not talk for a given period, for example, 14 days. An offer like, for a recharge value greater than $X, a 10% immediate bonus.

[20] Insights, "Winning the Customer Churn Battles in the Wireless Industry", 2001 available at http://www.boozallen.com/media/file/Winning.pdf

- Increase likelihood of buying more minutes; 11th hour promotions of discounted calling time for renewal can be offered to those whose minutes are about to run out
- Discounted fees for lock-in (6/12 months) in a rate plan

- **Cross-selling**
  - Bundling through converged offers—multiple home entertainment and connectivity services to increase lock-in. Figure 4.18 for a mobile service provider in Europe shows that subscribers opting for 4-play bundle (4 services) show a quarter of the churn rate as compared to 1-play subscribers (*Source:* Solon White Paper). The "Cross-Sell" chapter has a section on bundling for interested readers.
  - Exclusive availability of key handset models in a defined market, for example, AT&T's four year exclusivity on the Apple iPhone has helped the company to bring down churn rates since the second quarter of 2010 (for the US market).
- **Billing:** Improve billing accuracy and increase payment options
- **Service:** A centralised service culture and infrastructure for customer experience management
  - Verizon in the United States has remained the leader for achieving low-churn rates through good customer service and a reliable network
  - At some of Vodafone's call centres in the United States, different language options are available making it easier to interact with customers. In India, this is the norm across most telecom players.

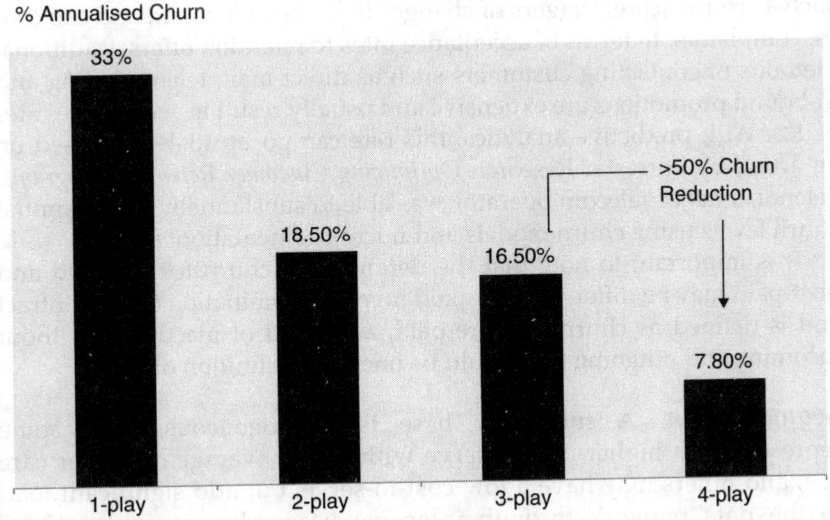


*Source:* Solon Telecoms White Paper (2011).

**Figure 4.18** Churn Levels Among Subscribers to Different Product Bundles

- **Network operations:** To improve call quality and reduce dropped calls
    - Loop Mobile (Mumbai-India circle) was offering compensation to subscribers for every dropped call, according to the DNA article, quoted earlier
    - T-Mobile of US uses their data from cell towers and switches for drop call analysis and has overcome challenges from its disparate IT infrastructure, to move towards a more advanced churn management solution. They have invested in a sophisticated information management architecture to consolidate subscriber and network data from multiple databases and source systems[21].
- **Loyalty programmes:** Although the wireless telecom sector is not known for its loyalty programmes, there are several operators in Asia with loyalty initiatives. Celecom Malaysia's website of March 2012 quotes an Anniversary Reward "We make your anniversary with us every year memorable with up to 30 minutes of free calls to any Celecom numbers. Your supplementary account holders get up to 20 minutes on their anniversary with us too!" Singtel of Singapore has "Earn 1 point for every 1 dollar eligible spend on your SingTel bill" for their post-paid customers and has several redemption options as well.

#### 4.8.3.4 Analytics

Typically in mature markets, most operators have sophisticated churn models that analyse different behavioural patterns of customers, and allows operators to predict which customers are likely to churn. The operator identifies "at-risk" customers based on multiple evaluation criteria such as churn score, triggers of changes in usage behaviour, and call centre complaints. In terms of acceptance rates to retention offers, traditional methods of contacting customers such as direct mail, telemarketing and in-bound promotions are expensive and usually result in acceptance rates of 1%. With predictive analytics, this rate can go up to 4–5%. Based on an article by Forrester Research *Optimizing Customer Retention Programs*, Telenor, a major telecom operator was able to substantially lower annual churn levels using churn models and micro-segmentation.

It is important to note that the definition of churn for pre-paid and post-paid may be different. Post-paid involves termination of the contract and is defined as churn. For pre-paid, a "period of inactivity" without incoming and outgoing calls could be one such definition of churn.

*Segmentation* A subscriber base is heterogeneous, with some representing a higher cost-to-serve with above average customer care use; and others may have a low cost-to-serve, but add significant load to the data network through intensive usage. For example, AT&T

---

[21] O'Reilly radar, "T-Mobile Challenges Churn with Data".

moved to a tier-based pricing structure in 2010. This was in reaction to a finding that fewer than 2% of their Smartphone customers made heavy use of the network and slowed it down (*Source:* New York Times, *Heavy Users of Phone Data will Pay More*, 2 June 2010). Segmentation of the subscriber pool is insightful for understanding usage, profitability, cost drivers and churn dynamics, as presented in Table 4.22. The segmentation uses variables such as contract type (pre-paid vs. post-paid), age, usage, churn, cost, and CLV as differentiating factors. These characteristics are further used to devise differential retention strategies by segment. CLV depends on customer profitability and average lifetime, and the latter can be simplistically approximated as the reciprocal of churn rate. The focus on CLV is important, as a high-paying subscriber may not be a good revenue benefit if such a subscriber churns in a few months post sign-up.

Some observations relating to Table 4.22 are as follows. The pre-paid segment has the highest churn rate and lowest CLV. This segment usually constitutes a sizeable proportion of a wireless subscriber account base, and the retention budget should be optimally allocated based on retention objectives of the firm. Among post-paid subscribers, retention strategies can differ based on usage. For example, a lower flat fee for the segment with low data usage (to increase stickiness) as opposed to a higher flat fee with unlimited usage. For the post-paid segment with highest usage and low CLV, bundling plans which lock in the customer for more than 12 months can be effective; the long-term revenue potential from this segment looks promising.

**Table 4.22** Telecom Churn Segmentation

| Contract Type | Post-paid | Pre-paid | Post-paid | Post-paid |
|---|---|---|---|---|
| Age range | 25–35 | 45–55 | 45–55 | 25–35 |
| Usage summary | Smart phone, heavy data user | Light pre-paid minute usage (off-peak). No data usage | Smart phone, limited data use. Uses all monthly voice minutes | Smart phone, heavy data user. Cancels after 12 months |
| Usage value | $350 | $10 | $350 | $400 |
| ARPU | $50 | $15 | $50 | $50 |
| Cost p/user | $20 | $10 | $15 | $20 |
| Churn | 3% | 4% | 2.5% | 3% |
| CLV @ 1 year | $110 | $50 | $170 | $60 |
| CLV @ 2 years | $479 | $119 | $608 | – |
| CLV @ 3 years | $880 | $202 | $1095 | – |
| CLV @ 4 years | $1316 | $300 | $1636 | – |

*Source:* WDS Report.

*Predictive Models* Considerable amount of research has been conducted in the area of telecom churn prediction models. Kim and Yoon's study titled *Determinants of Subscriber Churn and Customer Loyalty in the Korean Mobile Telephony Market*, emphasises on the importance of satisfaction, service issues and brand image for the prediction of loyalty and churn behaviour. This is done using econometric models to determine "intention to switch" using rich survey data. The limitation of the fact that intention to switch does not always mirror actual switching behaviour is overcome by Hung et al., *Applying Data Mining to Telecom Churn Management*. The study uses actual churn behaviour to predict the probability of churn based on customer demographics, billing, call records, customer care, and service data. Gerpott et al. in their 2001 study review the causal inter-linkages between retention, loyalty and satisfaction for the German mobile industry, and show that the lack of number portability is one of strongest drivers of customer retention. Ferreira et al[22]. in their paper, *Data Mining Techniques on the Evaluation of Wireless Churn*, find that calling patterns have a significant impact on churn (roaming time, night usage, and long distance air time).

Model performance by technique depends on factors such as metric used to gauge effectiveness of the model, nature of data sample, and sample size. The AT&T team of Au et al. *Applying and Evaluating Models to Predict Customer Attrition using Data Mining Techniques*, show that classification/decision tree performs better than logistic regression and neural networks. The authors attribute this observation to the fact that decision tree is a non-parametric method and uses the lowest number of predictor variables, thereby making it more stable. In addition, it is also less affected by missing data issues. However, based on Owczarczuk, *Churn models for Prepaid Customers in the Cellular Telecommunication Industry using Large Data Marts*, although both logistic regression and classification/decision tree have similar performance results, the former is more stable and holds up better over time as compared to the latter. Both Ferriera et al. and Hung prove that neural networks outperforms other statistical methods. Wong in his 2011 study uses a hazard rate model to predict churn for a Canadian operator, and some key results relating to rate plans were mentioned earlier. There are many more academic studies concerning advanced quantitative methods for churn prediction, and interested readers can refer to two papers in this regard: Lemmens and Croux, *Bagging and Boosting Classification Trees to Predict Churn*, and a more recent publication by Verbeke et al. *New Insights into Churn Prediction in the Telecommunication Sector*. Application of these models is very similar to strategies in other sectors. Variables used for churn prediction models are highlighted in Table 4.23.

---

[22] Available at https://www.elen.ucl.ac.be/Proceedings/esann/esannpdf/es2004-23.pdf.

**Table 4.23** Variables for Churn Prediction Model—Telecom

| Category | Variable | Relationship with Churn Rate (Empirical Evidence) |
|---|---|---|
| Customer demographics | Age; marital status; income | Younger customers tend to have a higher churn rate |
| Customer relationship | Duration of subscription; switching experience; number of lines by customer | Longer tenure with the mobile service provider is associated with a lower probability of churn Customers with previous history of switching carriers have a higher likelihood of churn |
| Rate plan | Post-paid/pre-paid; base cost of calling plan (recurring cost); current rate plan; plan vs. usage | Pre-paid has higher churn rates. High overage (out of plan) minutes would indicate churn tendency |
| Bill and payment | Monthly payment; overdue payment; cost of roaming | Average monthly payment and churn are negatively correlated. Customers who have at least 1 overdue payment in the past are more likely to attrite than none |
| Usage | Calling pattern by hour of day (number of calls and minutes)—in-plan and overage; weekday-weekend; local-long distance; peak-off-peak; domestic-international; outgoing-incoming to same/different operator. Change in quarterly usage. Last month's usage. Average time between calls | Users of international plans on a competitive rate plan are less likely to churn; declining usage and churn are positively correlated |
| Marketing variables | In promotion target list; responders to mail offers/telemarketing | Responders to previous retention offers are more likely to respond to another retention offer and are less likely to churn |
| Quality and customer service | Number of calls made to customer service; call quality and network coverage, e.g., number of dropped calls | Higher number of dropped calls is associated with higher probability of churn |
| Others | Age of hand set (provided by telecom operator); current handset price | Customers with longer ownership of handset have a higher probability of switching |

**Table 4.24** Savings from Telecom Churn Model

| Model | Monthly Churn Rate of 1.25% | | Monthly Churn Rate of 3% | |
|---|---|---|---|---|
| | Monthly Savings per Subscriber | Total Annual Savings | Monthly Savings per Subscriber | Total Annual Savings |
| Neural networks | $44.20 | $13,260,000 | $97.87 | $70,464,000 |
| Decision tree | $5.45 | $1,635,000 | $75.45 | $54,324,000 |

*Source:* Ferreira et al. (2004).

#### 4.8.3.5 Financial Benefits

The study by Ferreira et al. titled *Data Mining Techniques on the Evaluation of Wireless Churn*, with a monthly churn rate of 1.2%, demonstrates that neural networks gives the maximum expected savings based on a profitability[23] metric (cost of an incentive and cost of loss of a profitable customer). The results are shown in Table 4.24. Furthermore, a leading telecom operator in India reported a 10 times increase in response rate and a 80–90% lift in ARPU per responder. This was in response to its retention campaigns based on an analytics driven segmented approach and a structured usage and retention framework (*Source:* Business Standard, The Strategist, 13 Aug 2012).

### *4.8.4 Life Insurance Persistency*

#### 4.8.4.1 Business Scenario

Life insurance plans are promoted as long-term financial products for security and for savings and investment. Policyholders rely on insurance among other financial instruments to fulfil their lifestage financial goals. As life insurance contracts depend on the continuation of the contract, retention management for insurance is about managing lapse or persistency rates. A lapsed[24] policy refers to a policy which has been terminated (no longer in-force) due to non-payment of renewal premium

[23] Assumes that 50% of possible churners offered an incentive will be retained; average monthly bill of subscribers is $80; cost of an incentive is $25 per subcriber; only 20% of those predicted as churners can be contacted in a given month; total subscriber base is 2 million.

[24] Lapse rate is the ratio number of life contracts that have lapsed within a specified time period to the number in force during the period. It can be defined using premium as well.

by grace period[25]. Persistency rate[26] is a metric that measures the percentage of "issued" policies that remain in-force (and premium paying), after a certain period of time.

In the Indian context, although the life insurance business has been rapidly growing since the liberalisation of this sector, retention rates have been lagging[27]. One of the key drivers of profitability for the life insurance business is persistency of the existing base of policyholders. According to figures from the Insurance Regulatory and Development Authority of India (IRDA), the proportion of lapsed policies in the private sector doubled in 2011–12 (range of 36–51%), in comparison to 2008–2009[28]. The 13-month persistency ratios in India[29], were in the range of 36–72% in FY 2013, far below that for Asia.

Lapse has repercussions on the overall health of the insurance business. Pricing for insurance products assume a certain level of lapses and surrenders for the determination of premium rates and marketing terms. Given the high costs of acquiring new business and peak distributors commissions during the early years of a policy, life insurance issuers are at risk of losses if the policy lapses early on as initial expenses may not be recouped. As the life insurer earns a sizeable chunk of its profits in later years, P&L forecasts are a challenge without an accurate estimate of lapse. For the customer, lapse is a policy interruption that may result in the loss of risk coverage and investments, particularly in the early years, when the policy may have not acquired any paid-up value. Some additional features of lapse are stated below:

- For traditional life insurance policies, a distinction is made between lapse where premium is discontinued before the policy acquires

[25] Grace period is the period after the premium due date during which the policyholder can make premium payments so that the benefits of the policy continue.

[26] Insurance Regulatory Development Authority (IRDA) of India, has standardised the definition of persistency rate. Persistency calculations are on a "cohort basis" involving both "premium" and "number". For example, if 2,250 policies are issued in a financial year and 1,762 and 1,200 of these are in force at the end of the first and second years, respectively, then the first year persistency is 1,762/2,250 or 78% and the second year persistency is 1,200/2,250 or 53%. (*Source*: LiveMint, 3 June 2012. Available at http://www.livemint.com/2012/06/03215556/J-Hari-Narayan–Regulatory-re.html.)

[27] IRDA Report, 2008. Available at http://www.irdaindia.org/Final%20Report%20on%20Lapse%20Study.pdf

[28] *Hindu Business Line*, 18 May 2013, "Investors fail to renew ₹1.9 lakh cr of insurance policies" Annualised lapse ratio during the year = Lapses during the year/Arithmetic mean of the business in force at the beginning and at the end of the year.

[29] *Times of India*, 2 Jan 2014, "LIC Most Consumer Friendly: IRDA".

any value (paid-up or surrender value[30]); and lapse thereafter. The former is termed as a pure lapsed policy and does not acquire any policy benefit payable to the policyholder. In the case of paid-up policy, while premium has not been paid, it continues to be in-force. A broader definition of lapse covers surrendered policies as well. *Source*: IRDA Journal, 2008.

- Reinstatement is the process of bringing a lapsed policy into force (revival) by payment of all un-paid premiums, subject to certain other requirements relating to health (beyond a certain time window post-lapse)
- In India, the insurance business relies heavily on agents and financial advisors as insurance is a complex financial long-term product, which requires customer education. As a large percentage of insurance purchases are through agents, agent behaviour in this market has significant consequences on lapse through rampant agent mis-selling, absence of a need-based selling approach (appropriate product based on customer profile), disinterest in renewal depending on the specific commission structure of the product sold, and orphaned policies. An orphaned policy is one where the original agent who sold the policy is no longer responsible for servicing it and no other agent has been assigned.
- Lapse trends differ by premium frequency and annual frequency policies have the lowest lapse rates (Fig. 4.21 in Section 4.8.4.4)
- Months on book (duration since inception) has an important effect, with a peak in lapse rates around 12 months on book for annual frequency policies. There is a pick-up at 3–5 years and later, as policies acquire surrender/paid-up value. By months on book, a considerable proportion of lapse occurs by the first renewal for annual premium policies, with marginal incremental lapse thereafter. This is a relevant point for consideration while modelling for lapse event.
- Traditional and Unit-Linked Insurance Plans (ULIP) policies[31] differ dramatically in terms of lapse rates, with traditional being lower

[30] Paid-up value is the reduced amount of sum assured paid by the insurer, in case the policyholder discontinues payment of premiums. This is applicable only when the policyholder has paid the premiums in full for the stipulated period (e.g., 3 years). Surrender value is the value payable to a policyholder in the event of his/her deciding to terminate the policy, before the maturity of the policy.

[31] **Traditional** life insurance plans offer multiple benefits in terms of risk cover, return, safety, and tax benefit. Considered risk-free as they provide fixed income returns in case of death or maturity of the policy.

**Unit-linked** is an insurance plan linked to stock market. Offers a combination of investment and protection with flexibility and choice to the policyholder on how premiums are invested.(Contd.)

than ULIP, as market-linked policies are viewed more as investment opportunities that move in tandem with the stock market. Pension products tend to have lower lapse rates compared to non-pension products. These points are to be duly noted while developing segmentation and prediction models for lapse.

- Attrition is a mix of passive (lapse) and active (surrender) varieties. Retention strategies are a combination of proactive and win-back. Proactive programs involve premium reminder contacts for due and over-due policies. Win-back actions involve revival of lapsed policies.
- Revival of lapsed policies is done through reinstatement efforts, with a potential of collecting 50% (recovery rate) and upwards of premium due/over-due. This is from the current lapsed premium pool over a 12 month window, starting from the month of lapse.
  - Seasonality is observed as recovery rates of a lapsed pool are higher in months preceding the end of the financial year, and in markets where tax benefits are associated with premium payments
  - Recovery potential declines dramatically with ageing of lapse premium pool; significantly lower recovery rates for policies that have lapsed more than 6 months ago; high premium collections within the first 6 months post lapse
  - The above points need to be considered while building probability of reinstatement models for win-back retention programmes

## 4.8.4.2 Factors Affecting Lapse

The mismatch between actual and expected returns of an insurance plan for a policyholder is one of the major reasons causing lapse. Price is also frequently rated as one of the top most reasons for switching to a new

---

**Pension/annuity** is an investment that is made either in a single lump sum payment or through instalments paid over a certain number of years, in return for a specific sum received every year, half year or every month for either life or for a fixed number of years, after reaching a certain age as stipulated in the contract.

**Whole life** covers policyholder for entire life and not just for a specific period such as term insurance. As there is no fixed end date for the policy, only the death benefit exists and is paid to the named beneficiary.

**Endowment** is designed primarily to provide a living benefit. Thus it is more of an investment than a whole life policy.

**Term** covers risk only during the selected time period. If the policyholder survives the term, the risk cover comes to an end. Primarily designed to meet the needs of those policyholders who are initially unable to pay the larger premium required for their whole life or endowment policy.

*Source:* SBI Life Insurance and Life Insurance Company of India websites.

insurance company[32]. The broad factors affecting lapse can be classified as follows:

- **Environmental**
  - Macroeconomic factors such as unemployment, income and inflation, stock market performance, and their changes over time are expected to have an impact on investment behaviour in life insurance policies. For example, for unit-linked plans, a correlation between equity market and lapse behaviour has been observed. This fact has been corroborated by various studies and will be highlighted later in this section.
  - Government policies with respect to taxation and fiscal incentives for life insurance premiums and benefits influences demand for such products.
- **Alternative investment options**
  - Mutual funds, direct equity, property, savings deposits, and retirement schemes compete against life insurance plans.
- **Policy related**
  - Lower value policies in the form of low surrender value or premium tend to have higher lapse rates. Other factors that affect lapse are frequency of payment (annual, quarterly), traditional vs. unit-linked, presence of riders, etc.
- **Marketing and distribution strategies**
  - Distribution channels have a significant bearing on lapse rates as life insurance companies transact a considerable volume of business through multiple channels such as sales agents, direct marketing, and banks (bancassurance).
  - Policies sourced through bancassurance have a lower lapse tendency. Agent profile and orphaned status are strong influencing factors on persistency.
  - A key observation worth noting is that the private Indian insurance industry is plagued with the highest agent attrition among the large insurance markets in the world. The average life span is 9 months against the worldwide standard of 10 years[33].
- **Incentive framework, service and processes**
  - Commission structure, quality of training of sales agents and other personnel, service issues, and processes affect lapse rates. According to a study in the United States, 26% of insurance customers will switch insurance providers based solely on a bad experience with the contact service centre[34].

[32] For Germany, France and Japan according to a report by BCG, "Leveraging Customer Insight in Insurance".

[33] *Business Standard*, 20 Sep 2010, "Private Insurers Need Upside Down Biz Model to Survive", E&Y.

[34] Jacada White Paper, "Insurance Providers: Improving Customer Retention through the Contact Center".

- **Customer specific**
  - Empirical evidence shows the impact of age, income, marital status, rural/urban on lapse behaviour. Age and income are clear differentiators of lapse rates.

#### 4.8.4.3 Retention Strategy

As mentioned earlier, retention strategies are a combination of proactive and win-back measures. For regular premium policies, insurance companies send premium due and lapse notices to policyholders from time to time. An example of a contact strategy for reminder calling for premium due policies is highlighted in Table 4.25. A revival or reinstatement initiative for lapsed policies is a routine practice. Other than competitive pricing, a few other retention enhancing initiatives are highlighted:

- **Product related**
  - Innovations in the form of various product add-ons, better use of product features, and flexibility to alter policy elements easily. To the contrary, features such as supplementary cover(s) have been found to have a negative impact on lapse rates, according to a 2011 working paper by Eling and Kiesenbauer, *What Policy Features Determine Life Insurance Lapse? An Analysis of the German Market*. Policies with supplementary covers (e.g., disability insurance) come with a higher premium compared to a stand-alone product and are often offered as a bundle. The inability to pay a higher premium in the event of financial distress or a later realisation that the product bundle does not fit into the policyholder's needs, affects lapse rates. The influence of the regulator is greater felt in product design; France, Germany, and Spain have put restrictions on the features available to combat lapse risk[35].
- **Persistency incentives and rewards to policyholders and staff**
  - Rewards to policyholders for keeping policies in-force for a long duration such as a one-time increase in death benefit for traditional fixed premium traditional products (IRDA, 2008)

**Table 4.25** Contact Protocol—Insurance

| Stage | Mode | Timeline (T = Premium Due Date) |
|---|---|---|
| Due | SMS | Within T–25, T–3, T+7 |
| | Reminder call | Within T–15, T+15 |
| | Emails | Once a month |
| | Letter | T–30 |

[35] "Estimating and Reducing Lapse Risk" http://www.risk.net/life-and-pension-risk/feature/2024005/estimating-reducing-lapse-risk.

- Ensuring minimum return on market linked type of products
- Benefits such as free portfolio rebalancing and automatic fund switches to encourage continuation of ULIP policies
- Incentive contests and rewards for top performers linked to premium collection amount have proved to be successful initiatives in the insurance industry

- **Distribution channels**
  - Training of agents/financial advisors through professional education programmes. Improving hiring standards using agent profiling tools (e.g., tool for agent evaluation based on agent characteristics).
  - Commission structure that involves staggered payouts on renewal premiums over a period of policy duration and balancing the commission structure mix across products. According to IRDA guidelines, the commission paid to distributors and expenses charged by insurers will no longer be front-loaded, but will be distributed over the lock-in period of the product. Further, maximum commission has also been reduced. Similarly, life insurance agents in India will have to ensure that at least 50% of their clients do not default on premium payment from 2011–12 and 75% from 2014–15, as license renewal will depend on meeting this persistency requirement[36]. According to Reichheld, *Loyalty and the Renaissance of Marketing*, Great-West Life Insurance of the US paid 50% of group-health insurance premium to its brokers for meeting customer retention targets.
  - Channel optimisation for reducing distribution costs, benefits of which can be passed on to policyholders. Analytics is useful for assessing the costs vs. returns of these different channels.
  - More premium payment channels with wider geographic coverage
- **Process**
  - Improve contactibility rate by improving capture of contact details on form, address/phone number verification through field visits and skip tracing efforts. Skip tracing is done to locate a policyholder's whereabouts. This segment forms a sizeable volume of the collectible premium base for many insurers.
  - Investment in infrastructure and information technology to reduce unit costs and improve service turn around efficiencies
  - Robust sales process through financial need analysis. Underwriting of the appropriate product and premium value should be based on customers' current as well potential financial capabilities. Segmentation can play a very important role.
  - Leveraging service calls for proactive retention steps. For example, policyholder queries on fund value, surrender value and

[36] LiveMint.com, "Customers may Gain from New IRDA Guidelines", 16 Feb 2011.

lock-in-period would be a good opportunity for a CSR to reiterate policy benefits and anticipated gains from holding the policy.

- **Customer**
  - Customer education in the form of service camps to explain privileges, product features, claims processing, grievance addressing process and other policy servicing aspects
  - Servicing initiatives to reduce customer service complaints is important for the insurance sector given the high value of such products
  - Cross-selling and top-ups to increase relationship value and reduce lapse behaviour, although cross-sell opportunities may be limited in the life insurance sector and more relevant for general insurance. Top-ups for insurance products were discussed in the balance build section of the "Usage Management" chapter.

### 4.8.4.4 Analytics

An analytics based strategy can significantly improve customer retention. Further, the resulting retention initiatives are most effective when they are integrated into daily operations. Some of these analytics-related efforts are simply mapping product features with policyholder needs through segmentation based on lifestage. Targeting the right set of customers for collections through lapse and reinstatement type of predictive models is another analytics dependent retention effort. According to the McKinsey study on insurance churn titled *Limiting Churn in Insurance*, an Italian insurer nearly doubled its retained capital within a year, while a German firm reduced churn in its property and casualty business by 25% through analytics-based retention actions.

*Segmentation* Lifestage based approach is a norm for prospect segmentation in the insurance sector and is geo-demographic based. An example is PersonicX Insurance Groups, a cluster system that uses over 120 insurance-related questions, demographics and socio-economic characteristics to derive 13 clusters of households grouped by similar inclinations for insurance products. This allows for quick and easy identification of target markets for insurance marketers for acquisitions. Similarly, BCG, *Leveraging Consumer Insight in Insurance*, had conducted a cross country study of consumer perceptions relating to the insurance industry and its major brands (France, Germany, Japan, and the United States). Their findings are very interesting. It was observed that Japanese consumers have the most positive inclination towards specific products of insurance, perceived as bringing peace of mind. US consumers associate life insurance and retirement products with safety, security, and protection. At the opposite end, German consumers have a negative view of insurance, its complexity and lack of transparency. The survey was followed by a segmentation schema. This schema would enable insurers to take actions that stimulate growth and encourage retention through refined understanding of consumer segments. In each country, behavioural segmentation gave distinct groups based on the perceived value of insurance, preference for channel and price sensitivity, among others. The impact of retention efforts on profitability are promising based on a McKinsey paper on insurance churn that segments auto policyholders based on profitability—most valuable, valuable, value destroying. Their simulation results of a 10% churn rate impact demonstrated that total profit of the "most valuable" decreased by almost 40%, while that of the "valuable" segment reduced by 17%. Chapter 7, "Quantitative Methods" has a section dedicated to segmentation methods and their workings.

*Predictive Models* There have been several approaches to model development for the prediction of lapse behaviour, starting with academic literature (since 1970s). The focus of these studies has been to use macroeconomic data to test two main hypothesis—interest rate and emergency fund hypothesis. The interest rate hypothesis assumes that savings through life insurance is sensitive to rates of return. Policyholders lapse in order to exploit higher interest rates and/or lower premiums in the market when interest rates rise. In other words, increasing interest rates are an opportunity cost for owning life insurance. The emergency fund hypothesis conjectures that personal financial distress forces policyholders to lapse their contracts, in order to access the cash surrender value. To test some of these hypotheses, Kim's paper considers a large set of explanatory variables (economic variables and policyholder attributes), reported in a paper titled *Modelling Surrender and Lapse Rates with Economic Variables*, for the Korean market. Following research by Kiesenbauer, *Main Determinants of Lapse in the German Life Insurance Industry*, extends Kim's work by evaluating company level data along with macroeconomic data. Multiple explanatory variables are considered indicating the economic environment, for example, the impact of stock market movements on lapse behaviour. From a practitioner's perspective, most insurance companies have their own proprietary in-house built models developed using customer, policy, agent, transaction, and service information. The results of these models will be discussed subsequently.

### *Dependent Variable to Model and Statistical Techniques*

- Probability of lapse/reinstatement event (binary choice and hazard rate models)
- Time to lapse (survival models)
- Number of times lapsed (Poisson model)
- Percentage of times premium has been paid (linear regression model)

The hazard rate and survival functions are shown graphically in Fig. 4.19. Simply defined, hazard rate is the conditional probability of lapse during a time interval (e.g., month, year) given that the policyholder has not lapsed till then. It can also be interpreted as the probability of first lapse for a policyholder. Since annual frequency policies constitute a high proportion of policies in this data file, the hazard rate function is at its peak at year 1 (the first renewal premium for such policies). Half of the policyholders will lapse for the first time at first renewal. The survival curve shows the probability that a policyholder "survives" (policy is in-force) for at least a specified period of time. In this case, the probability that a policy will be in force for at least 2 years is 46% and this probability decreases with years on book. Readers should look up the quantitative chapter for details on survival models and the inter-relationship between hazard and survival functions.

*Explanatory Variables* As mentioned earlier, macroeconomic factors of interest rate, economy growth rates, stock market movement, and unemployment rates have been used in some of the empirical studies.

- Interest rate related variables, for example, market rate minus crediting rate and current yield are used to test the interest rate hypothesis. Crediting rate is the interest rate offered on an investment type insurance policy.
- Unemployment rate, buyers confidence (private spending), economy growth rate are variables used to test emergency fund hypothesis
- Micro level attributes are presented in Table 4.26

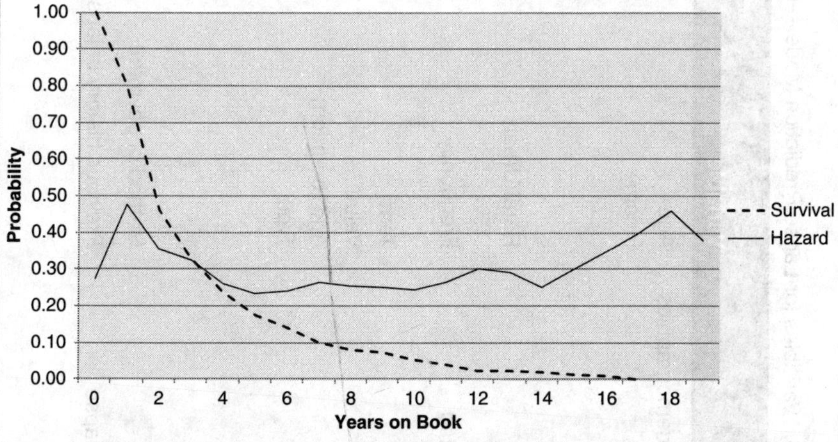


*Source:* Loi et al. (1993) available at http://www3.ntu.edu.sg/nbs/sabre/working_papers/11-96.pdf

**Figure 4.19** Survival and Hazard Functions—Insurance

**Table 4.26** Variables for Lapse Prediction Model—Insurance

| Category | Variable | Relationship with Lapse Rate (Empirical Evidence) |
|---|---|---|
| Customer demographics | Age | Lower for older age groups given lifestage need |
| | Income | Higher income policyholders have lower rates. Products sold to high net worth customers as single premium investment products have lower rates as compared to regular premium products sold to mass market as savings products |
| | Rural/Urban | Different persistency behaviour attributable to lack of communication, access to service and others; regional variations of urban/rural |
| Policy related | Frequency | Quarterly/monthly modes tend to have lower persistency as compared to annual/bi-annual |
| | Term | Higher the term, higher the lapse rate |
| | Value | Low sum assured/low premium have higher lapse rates |
| | Age (duration) | Lapse rate decreases with policy duration |
| | Type | ULIP have higher rates compared to traditional plans due to sensitivity to stock market; pension plans have better persistency as they are viewed as long-term policies for building up a corpus to meet retirement needs; Whole life products show higher lapse rate than endowment products; Medical lower than non-medical |
| | Method of payment | ECS (Electronic Clearing System) has better rates than non-ECS |
| History of lapse | Previous history of lapse | Strong indicator of future lapse behaviour |

(*Continued*)

**Table 4.26** Variables for Lapse Prediction Model—Insurance (*Continued*)

| Category | Variable | Relationship with Lapse Rate (Empirical Evidence) |
|---|---|---|
| | Number of renewals before first lapse | Higher the number of renewals, lower the probability of lapse |
| | Channel | Bancassurance has lower rates than others |
| Marketing and distribution | Agent profile | The more the time an agent has spent with the company, lower is the lapse rate for contracts sourced by him/her; contracts sourced by agents with less than "x" years left for expiry have a higher lapse rate. Most insurance companies capture this information |
| | Orphaned/Not orphaned | Higher lapse rates for orphaned policies where the original agent is no longer responsible for servicing it |
| | Customer contactibility | Inadequate details provided by customer/data capture issues/no address update. Relocation influences lapse as customer does not receive communication regarding renewal notices (if address not updated) |
| | Commission structure | High commission rates of new business for agents and variation by product types has huge bearing on overall persistency levels |
| Service | Service complaints | Poor servicing is correlated with higher rates; complaint log data is a good source for modelling purposes |

*Source:* Adapted from IRDA Report and Journal, 2008. Both available at http://www.irda.gov.in

*Research Studies*

- Kim's study takes a sample period (1997–2000) using data of a Korean life insurer:
  - Surrender rates (dependent variable) have a sudden peak during the financial crisis, the period from December 1997 to December 1998. A flag is created for this period and included in the model.
  - Market rate minus crediting rate, unemployment rate, and economy growth rates are some of the primary variables in the model.
  - Separate models are developed by product type.
  - For protection plans, the variables influencing surrender rates are interest rate, policy age since issue, unemployment rates, economy growth rates, and seasonal effects.
- Kiesenbauer's research covers the period from 1997 to 2009 for Germany:
  - Transformed change variables of current yield, GDP growth rate, unemployment rate, private spending, and stock market index are some of the predictors in the model. Lagged variables for all economic indicators are also added in the model along with current values, to account for the fact that policyholders might react with a certain time gap to changes in economic conditions.
  - Separate lapse models for unit-linked and traditional life insurance products (e.g., endowment, annuity, term life) are considered.
  - Interest rate and emergency fund hypothesis holds only for unit-linked business.
  - An increasing stock market index (lagged) has a positive effect on lapse rates for unit-linked products in the long-term. For all other product categories, a positive relationship between stock market index (current) and lapse rates is observed only for annuities in the short-term.

*Relationship with Lapse (Univariates)* The univariates are based on a study[37] by the Insurance Regulatory and Development Authority of India titled *Lapsation and its Impact on Indian Life Insurance Industry for the Period 2002–07*, which uses data of all life insurance companies in India. Premium lapse rate is based on premium value and is an annualised figure, defined as the amount lapsing during the year divided by the amount exposed to lapse during the year. These graphs (Figs. 4.20–4.23) are self-explanatory.

---

[37] Available at www.irdaindia.org/Final%20Report%20on%20Lapse%20Study.pdf.

### 4.8.4.5 Implementation/Process

A lapse model that predicts the probability of lapse is scored on due (premium to be paid by due date) and over-due (premium to be paid after due date and within the grace period) policies. The due and over-due policies

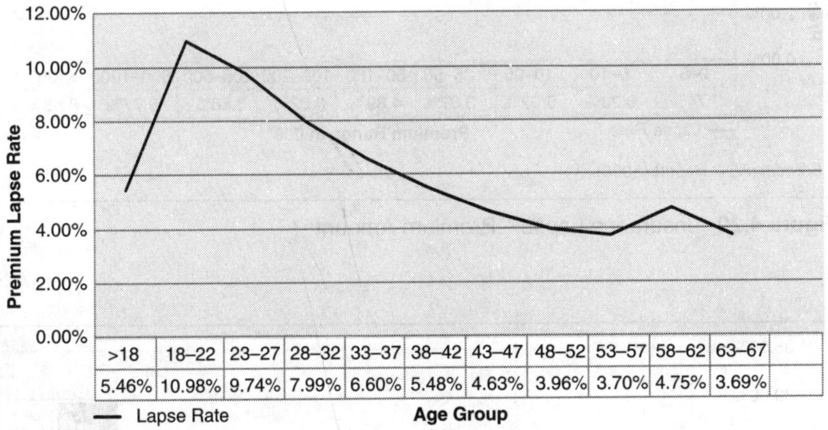


*Source:* IRDA Report (2008).

**Figure 4.20** Insurance Lapse—Customer Age

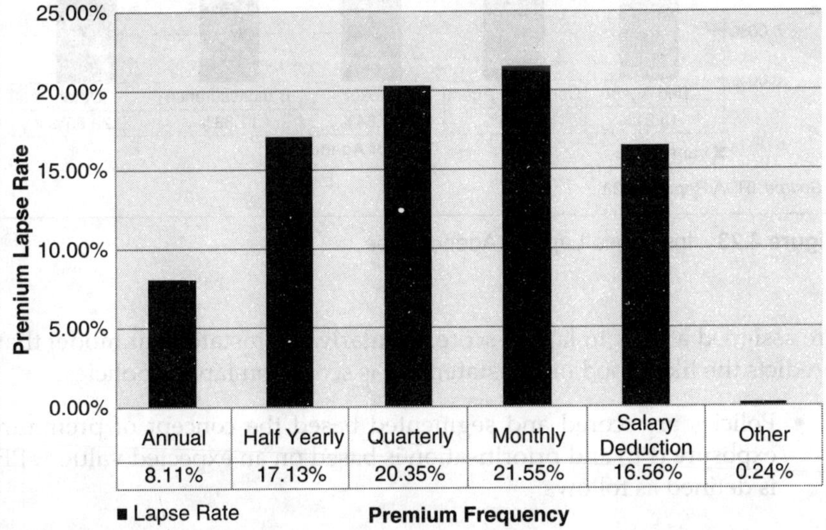


*Source:* IRDA Report (2008).

**Figure 4.21** Insurance Lapse—Premium Frequency

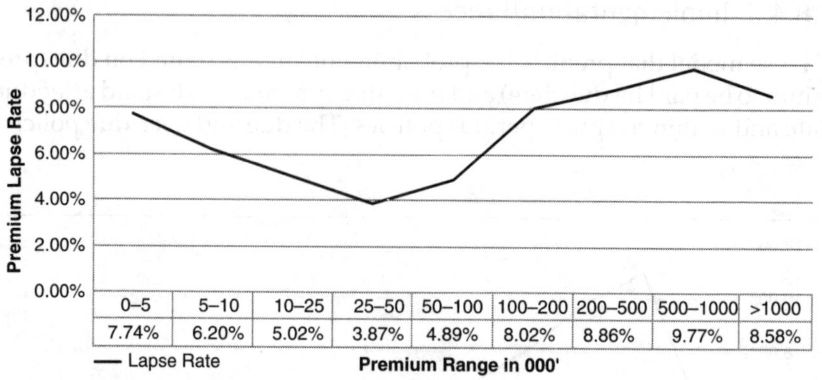


*Source:* IRDA Report (2008).

**Figure 4.22** Insurance Lapse—Premium Amount

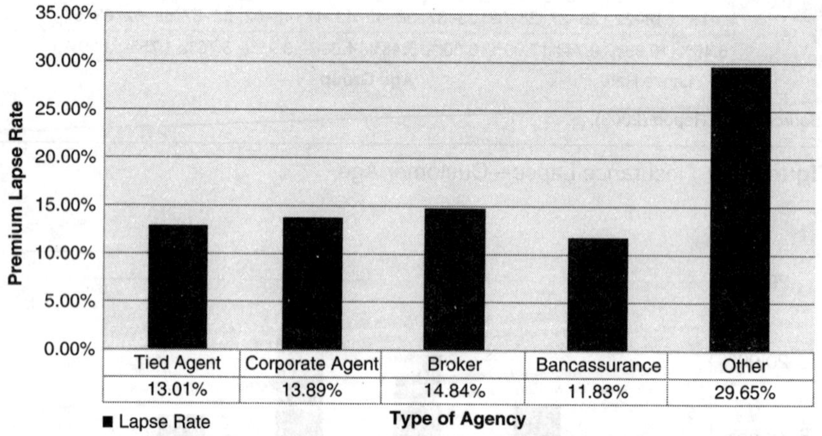


*Source:* IRDA Report (2008).

**Figure 4.23** Insurance Lapse—Agency Type

are assigned a "risk to lapse" score. Similarly, a reinstatement model that predicts the likelihood of reinstatement is scored on lapsed policies.

- Policies are scored and segmented based the concept of premium exposure (PE) and prioritisation is based on an expected value[38]. PE is defined as follows

[38]Traditionally, prioritising customers for a retention strategy based on risk of lapse alone does not ensure a high collection of premium as low premium is associated

**Table 4.27** Insurance Lapse Risk Category

| Risk Category based on PE Bands | % Policies | % Premium |
|---|---|---|
| High | 15% | 46% |
| Medium | 36% | 34% |
| Low | 33% | 15% |
| Very Low | 16% | 5% |

PE = "probability of event (lapse)" * APE[39]

- The computed PE is used to categorise the customer into 3 or more classes such as "High", "Medium" and "Low". Based on Table 4.27, the high and medium risk segments constitute 50% of the policies and 80% of total premium value
- A model based proactive strategy facilitates focused attempts and helps address over/under contacting to ensure effective utilisation of resources of the retention unit and their potential to collect. An example would be to make a reminder call only to high risk policyholders at T–7 and another reminder call at T+7 (T = premium due date). Perhaps even a special payment collection facility for this segment (insurance companies do this typically for high premium policyholders). For low risk, promoting use of SMS and limiting the extent of telecalling is one possible collection action.
- Appropriate test and control samples should be created and process followed to measure the impact of the model, impact of the strategy and impact of the model and strategy together. Insurers are continually improving retention processes and increasing staff as part of their retention initiatives to reduce lapse and improve reinstatement rates. Therefore, test and control for estimating financial benefits of a score-based strategy become even more important.

### 4.8.4.6 Financial Benefits

- A miniscule 100 basis points improvement in recovery rates (reinstatement) collected can translate into a significant increase in incremental premium collected, given the high value of the lapsed premium pool (base).

---

with a high lapse rate. The concept is very similar to Balance at Risk (BAR) measure of collections analytics.

[39] APE (annual premium equivalent) is used for comparison by determining what the price would be, if paid once a year. This is specifically used when sales contain both single premium and regular premium (varying frequency) policies. Alternatively, premium due till date can also be used.

- US based Nationwide Insurance found that a 1 percentage point increase in customer retention rates increased annual premiums by $1 million[40]. Similarly in the Indian context, each percentage point increase in persistency across all insurers can result in $270 million of additional revenue based on the financial year 2009, according to Live Mint, 5 May 2010 edition.
- US-based MetLife launched a multi-part retention campaign in the US, reminding customers of the value of insurance products for auto and home[41]. A pivotal part of this campaign was segmentation based on length of customer relationship, the channel of sale, products held and profitability. They also used control cells (no offer) to measure success. After a year-long campaign, MetLife saw a lift in retention of 0.87 percentage points for those customers who received the letter. This campaign was profitable as a quarter percentage point lift was enough to cover the cost of the campaign.

[40] *Insurance Technology—CRM in Global Insurance*, Datamonitor, 2008.

[41] DM News: http:\www.dmnews/metlife-retention-campaign-boss-loyalty/print article/1373....

FIVE

# Price Management

## 5.1 Introduction

Companies use a variety of marketing tools to drive their marketing objectives. A combination of all these tools is defined as the marketing mix. Broadly speaking, marketing mix consists of four components, namely; product, price, place (distribution), and promotion, or the 4Ps as they are called in marketing parlance. Each of these component represents a number of marketing tools that can be leveraged by the marketer. For example, product represents a set of product-related marketing attributes such as variety, quality, design, features, and packaging. Price represents dimensions such as list price, discounts, payment term, and credit term. Place represents distribution-related dimensions such as channels, coverage, location, inventory levels, and transportation. Promotion represents attributes like sales, advertising, public relations, and direct marketing. The 4Ps together comprise of all the factors that marketers can control to satisfy their target customers while generating profitable growth. Of these 4Ps, price is the most flexible marketing mix element. Price is also one of the most visible element of the marketing mix and a key determinant of buyer's choice.

Price has a direct impact on demand, revenue, profitability, and market share, and an indirect impact on a host of other marketing objectives such as brand image, brand positioning, etc. An increase in price reduces the demand for the product but the revenue realised per unit sale goes up and hence, the total revenue can increase, decrease or remain the same. The indirect effects of price are more difficult to observe. For instance, a credit card company offering a very attractive promotional interest rate on balance transfer at the time of acquiring new customers, will be able to build large balances from new customers. However, in the long-run, when the promotional interest rate expires, a significant proportion of these new customers, may not use their card extensively. While the short-term effect of attracting higher balances is easier to observe, the long-term impact of this pricing strategy may be difficult to ascertain.

Historically, prices have always been set by negotiations between a buyer and a seller. This resulted in a price that was specific for each transaction and hence, sellers were able to use price discrimination to match the reservation price of the buyer for every single transaction. The advent of the industrial revolution and large-scale retailing brought in the concept of *One Price Fits All* and a one price policy. Though this was critical for harnessing the economics of scale, yet it left companies with little room for deriving the maximum value from each transaction. According to Ross and Dixit as discussed in their paper titled *Customer-centric pricing: The surprising secret for profitability* this approach also gave birth to the product-centric "cost plus" approach to pricing. A "cost plus" pricing approach, entails determination of price based on a fixed mark-up over the cost involved in producing a good or rendering a service.

Today's technology capability allows firms to vary prices almost in real time. This coupled with the increasing usage of analytical techniques are providing firms across industries the tools to adopt a dynamic view of pricing. As a result there is an apparent reversal of trend wherein companies are trying to fix a different price for each customer and each transaction. Dynamic pricing strategies have resulted in significant revenue increase for companies across industries. American Airlines, for example, was able to increase their revenue by $1.4 billion in the first three years after implementing a dynamic pricing strategy (Berry C Smith, John F Leimkuhler and Ross M Darrow; paper titled *Yield Management at American Airlines*). Marriott has reported a 20% lift in revenue from transient business, which is attributed to its revenue management system*.

As per Phillip Kotler, the pricing decision of a firm involves three key decisions. The first decision on pricing involves setting a pricing philosophy for the firm's products and services. This needs to be devised in line with brand positioning and broad competitive dynamics. For example, a firm needs to decide whether it aims to adopt a premium pricing strategy or an aggressive low-price strategy. The second decision involves the pricing structure, wherein the firm decides how it will charge its customers. In some industries like consumer packaged goods, there are limited or no options of using a flexible pricing structure. However, in many industries like consumer durables, automobiles, financial services, telecom, and industrial products, firms enjoy the flexibility of designing various pricing structures to suit customer needs. The third pricing decision involves determining the exact price that the firm will charge its customers. With companies across industries adopting a dynamic pricing strategy, the price charged, and the pricing structure adopted, are being determined differently for each customer segment. This chapter focuses on usage of analytical strategies for determining the price charged and the pricing structure adopted.

---

* (http://www.marriott.com/Multimedia/PDF/Hotel_Development/PowerofMarriott_brochureEMEA.pdf)

The first part of the chapter is focused on the economic theories that serve as the conceptual building blocks of price management strategies. The section discusses economic theories pertaining to types of competition and price discrimination. Next, a section has been dedicated to discussion of dynamic pricing strategies and how the same can be adopted across industry verticals. This is followed by, a description of the common pricing structures that are adopted across industries. Special discussion is focused on financial services and enterprise software markets where a wide variety of pricing structures exist. Having illustrated the foundations and the approaches to dynamic pricing, the next section discusses the implementation details around dynamic pricing. This is followed by a discussion on pricing in the e-commerce world; this section also discusses the relevance of auctions as a pricing mechanism. The chapter concludes with the discussion of three industry examples across airlines, utilities, and credit card industries.

## 5.2 Economic Theories of Pricing

Pricing is governed by two key economic principles: one involves the firm's pricing power and the other involves the consumer's willingness to pay. This section focuses on some of these principles. The first set of theories illustrate the competitive environment and thereby the firm's pricing power; the second set of theories analyse how firms can price their products differently based on the consumer's willingness to pay.

### *5.2.1 Types of Competition*

The competitive structure within a particular market determines the pricing power of a firm. Economists have proposed three common types of competitive structures. These structures are generalisations, yet they serve as reasonable models for analysing firm behaviour with regards to pricing.

- **Perfect competition:** Under perfect competition, the firm has absolutely no pricing power in the market and so it acts as a price taker. Typically, commodity markets (wheat, metals, etc.) belong to this category. In a perfect market, the firm has no control over the price it charges and has to sell at the prevailing market price. The other characteristic of perfectly competitive market is that there are a large number of buyers and sellers and hence, each firm supplies only a negligible amount of the total supply.
- **Monopoly:** A monopoly arises when the firm has complete pricing power and is the sole supplier in a particular market. Like perfect competition, monopoly rarely exists in reality. A monopolist tries to charge the maximum amount that each customer is willing to pay

and thereby tries to maximise profit. In many countries, utilities like electricity are operated as monopolies. But in most of these countries, such monopolies are owned by the government and hence, the price charged by them is regulated by government policy.

- **Oligopoly:** An oligopoly is a situation wherein a limited number of firms compete to supply same or similar goods. Each firm has significant pricing power and their actions affect market demand. These firms also observe each other's pricing actions and design their pricing strategy accordingly. To model this kind of firm behaviour, economists have extensively used game theory to analyse the move of each firm, given the strategy of other firms in the market. The discussion of game theory for modelling firm behaviour is beyond the scope of this book. The interested reader can refer to standard texts on strategic behaviour and industrial organisation for details. Among models which do not use game theory, the two most common models for oligopoly are the Cournot model, and the Bertrand model. Both of these are static single stage models where it is assumed that firms make their decisions simultaneously. Simultaneous decision making implies that a particular firm cannot observe the decision of other firms and hence, is not able to change its strategy accordingly.

The Cournot model analyses two firms competing on quantity and the Bertrand model looks at two firms competing on price. Details of these models are beyond the scope of this book, and the interested reader can refer to any standard micro-economics textbook for further detail. In many markets, there are two or three dominant consumer packaged goods companies and there exists fierce price competition among them. Similarly, in a country like India, mobile telecom is another area where there are only two to three dominant operators in a particular region.

### 5.2.2 Price Discrimination

The second set of economic theories that play an important part in pricing involves understanding the customer's willingness to pay. The customer's willingness to pay is governed by the demand curve. It is well known that the demand curve is a downward sloping curve, with price on the X-axis and the quantity demanded on the Y-axis. This implies that as price increases there will be lower demand for the product or service. However, it is important to note that even at the higher price point there exists some demand for the product, which means that some customers are willing to pay the higher price. Hence, if the firm knows the willingness to pay for each and every customer, then the firm can price the product or service differently for each customer. This strategy enables the firm to maximise the money that it can make. The idea of charging a different price to each customer is referred to as price discrimination in economic literature.

Charging each customer the exact amount, that he or she is willing to pay is the best possible situation for a firm because it will generate the maximum revenue. This concept is described as perfect price discrimination or first degree price discrimination. However, first degree price discrimination is not possible in most real-life situations. Some examples which are very close to *first degree price discrimination* are pricing for industrial contracts, where the firm negotiates with the customer to understand the exact amount that the customer is willing to pay. In industrial purchases, the price is decided after a detailed negotiation process between the buyer and the seller. As part of the negotiation process, the seller tries to find out the price that the buyer is willing to pay and creates a customised price for each buyer. An effective pricing strategy will allow customers to select the pricing contract that matches their willingness to pay.

At this point it is important to note that the firm determines the right price not only based on the customer's willingness to pay but also taking into consideration the firm's long- and short-term business objectives. Some of the common business objectives that determine the pricing strategy include need for increasing market share, penetrating a new market, increasing profitability, introducing new products and the like. A firm which aims to penetrate a new market may price its products lower than competition; on the other hand, luxury brands which adopt a premium pricing strategy may set a relatively higher price so as to maintain the premium image of the product.

Though *first degree price discrimination* is the most effective pricing strategy it is very difficult to implement it in real life. Owing to this difficulty in implementation, firms devise alternate strategies for differential pricing. One of the strategies involves pricing based on volume of sale, whereby customers who buy higher volume are charged a lower price. This type of pricing is referred to as *second degree price discrimination. Second degree price discrimination* is practiced in cases where fixed costs are high or where the product is perishable. In both these cases the firm tends to lose heavily if some of its stocks remain unsold and hence, a strategy of offering volume-based discount is quite effective. Another example of *second degree price discrimination* involves usage-based pricing, where heavy users are offered special discounts.

In some cases, the firm separates the customers into distinct groups and offers a different price to each group. All the customers in a group pay the same price but are not allowed to purchase at the price prescribed for the other groups. This idea is referred to as *third degree price discrimination.* Airlines and hotels practice third degree price discrimination quite extensively. Airlines, for example, offer different prices for the same seat for early booking vis-à-vis late booking, similarly the price can differ for a refundable and non-refundable air ticket. In many industries special prices are offered to long-term loyal customers, which involves segmenting customers based on current or expected future loyalty. Readers can refer to

Chapter 2, "Usage Management" for further details on loyalty and usage-based price setting.

The pricing strategies adopted by firms across industries attempt to implement an effective second or third degree price discrimination. Major enhancements in technology and implementation capabilities have equipped companies to harness the power of price discrimination. The "one size fit all" pricing (also referred to as uniform pricing or cost plus pricing) strategy is being replaced by differential pricing strategies which aim to deliver higher revenue and profit.

While implementing price discrimination strategy it is important to note that sometimes customers may adopt stockpiling behaviour. Stockpiling behavior entails that customers tend to buy more if the price is lowered but they do not consume the increased amount that they purchase, instead they tend to store the item for the future, anticipating a price increase. This phenomenon has mostly been observed for non-perishable consumer packaged goods. Consumers also have a reservation price in mind for a particular product and will not purchase if the price is higher than the reservation price. Any price discrimination strategy that prices the product above the reservation price of a particular segment of customer can pose challenges for the firm.

## 5.3 Uniform Pricing

As already discussed, many firms have limited pricing power, which results in a uniform pricing strategy. Multiple factors may limit the pricing power of a firm. The type of competition, the market structure and legal restrictions are often the most important reasons which force firms to adopt a one-price policy. In many cases firms in the commodity market like minerals, bulk metals, etc., adopt a uniform pricing strategy.

Firms tend to adopt innovative strategies to implement dynamic pricing even in cases where a uniform price seems to be the most likely scenario. For example, in the consumer packaged goods industry a particular unit (called a stock keeping unit or SKU) of a product has to be sold at the same price to every buyer. However, firms in these industries always adopt innovative strategies to price their products differently for different customers. Consumer packaged goods companies try to create different pack sizes of the same product, each pack size is targeted to a different customer segment and hence, bears a different price tag. For example, a 200ml bottle of shampoo, which is targeted at more affluent customers, may cost 12 times (and not 10 times) more than a 20ml sachet of the same shampoo, which is targeted at relatively low income and rural consumers. This innovative packaging allows the firm to create different SKUs out of the same product and hence, makes it possible to price them differently. It is important to note that companies also adopt different distribution strategies for different SKUs so that the intended customer segment can only buy a particular

SKU. For example, the 200 ml bottle of shampoo is sold mostly in relatively higher end stores while the sachet is sold in small grocery stores (mom and pop shops). Similarly, companies in the commodity market like metals try to offer discounts to long-term buyers. They also offer special services like just-in-time delivery for buyers who have integrated their supply chain with the seller.

In addition to market structure, there are regulatory constraints which limits the extent of price discrimination that a seller can implement. For example, financial services companies are not allowed to charge different interest rates based on sociodemographic factors such as race, ethnicity, and other factors. These companies are allowed to charge different interest rates based on the risk profile of the customers. However, there are strict guidelines on types of customer behaviour that can be considered for differential pricing. For example, a credit card company might find that some of its existing customers are not paying their utility bills on time. It is also observed that most of these customers end up defaulting on their credit payment. Hence, defaulting on utility bill payment is definitely an indicator of risky behaviour. To account for the same, the credit card company may want to increase price for customers who have defaulted on their utility bill payment. But regulators in most markets do not allow them to do so. Credit card companies are only allowed to increase price if the customer defaults on payments to the particular credit card company.

In cases where a uniform pricing strategy is the only option that a company has, it fixes the uniform price based on either the prevailing market price (e.g., standard commodity prices) or uses a cost plus approach to arrive at the price that will ensure the expected level of profit margin.

## 5.4 Dynamic Pricing: Background

### *5.4.1 Introduction of Dynamic Pricing in the Airlines Industry*

Dynamic pricing refers to the strategy of charging different prices to different customers based on their characteristics. The first impetus to dynamic pricing was provided by the Airlines Deregulation Act of 1978 in the United States of America. The airlines industry witnessed a dramatic transition from a completely regulated environment to an environment where pricing and schedule were determined by competitive dynamics. This led to a major wave of mergers and acquisitions in the industry; at the same time, the industry witnessed the emergence of a number of low-cost airlines. Dynamic pricing was one of the key approaches that carriers had to adopt in order to survive in the new environment. There were few other characteristics of the airlines industry which made it amenable to a dynamic pricing strategy. These characteristics were:

- **Instant perishability of inventory:** A flight seat is an instantly perishable inventory and will have zero value if the plane takes off with an unfilled seat.
- **Availability of information systems which enabled instant distribution of information:** Electronic price distribution systems like SABRE and APOLLO provided airlines the ability to communicate price instantly and also to monitor bookings in real time. This helped them to match bookings with expected demand and change price instantly.
- **Possibility of creating differentiation of the product offering:** Though an airline seat is an undifferentiated product (apart from the basic differences in first class, business class and economy class), yet airlines are able to create differentiation in their offerings by having a flexible structure like refundable vs. non-refundable tickets, early booking vs. late booking, flexibility of changing journey date, and the like. These differentiations allow the airline to justify a different price for the otherwise same product.
- **A segmentable customer base with varied willingness to pay:** The airline customer base can be segmented based on customer needs. For example, a significant number of customers (mostly leisure travellers) are more concerned with price and are willing to have a flexible journey date; another segment may not be flexible about the date but are willing to be flexible about the time of the flight. There may also exist segments which are not price conscious but have a need for a particular schedule or a flexibility of changing the journey date. The existence of these segments allow the airlines to design offerings to address the needs of each segment.

Initially, the price management process in the airline industry was a manual one. In 1985, American Airlines introduced the first automated yield management system. The system was used for forecasting demand for future flights and utilised optimisation techniques for determining the right price for each fare class so as to maximise profitability. Furthermore, the system was used to track actual bookings and change prices accordingly.

### *5.4.2 Adoption of Dynamic Pricing in Other Industries*

Other industries within the travel and entertainment sector were the next in line in the adoption of a dynamic pricing approach. Hertz was the first car rental company and Marriott was the first hotel to install a full-fledged dynamic pricing and revenue management system. Quantity and price based revenue management are the two common revenue management approaches. Both hotels and airlines commonly use price-based revenue management principles to maximise revenue. The airlines pricing example in Section 5.8 explains this principle in detail. The 1990s saw the adoption of the dynamic pricing philosophy in other industries as well. The retail industry which was initially focused mostly on efficient and dynamic supply management started recognising the importance of dynamic pricing as a driver for maximising revenue. The concept was initially thought about as demand management (contrary to the earlier paradigm of supply management) wherein price was used as the primary tool for managing demand.

In the retail space, two basic approaches emerged for managing dynamic pricing. The first approach involved managing price for lifestyle goods, gifts, and related products. These products witness a seasonal peak in demand and have low-salvage value after the peak-demand period. This is particularly true for the Christmas shopping period. Garments and other non-perishable products which remain unsold after the Christmas season have very little salvage value. In addition, it is also difficult to predict the style that will become popular with customers. Hence, retailers need to manage "markdown" of the published prices in such a way so as to maximise revenue.

Another approach to dynamic pricing involved managing the price promotions for consumer packaged goods. Lot of pioneering work was undertaken at Procter & Gamble and Wal-Mart to estimate short- and long-term impact of price promotions and how the same could be combined with other marketing mix elements to design the optimal marketing mix strategy. Significant academic research has also been conducted to evaluate the effects of price promotions on consumer behaviour. For details on the effect of promotions and the results in the context of Consumer Packaged Goods (CPG) industry, the reader may refer to Chapter 2, "Usage Management" which provides the mathematical models used for measuring the effect of promotion.

In the consumer financial services industry, dynamic pricing has taken the form of risk-based pricing and relationship-based pricing. Risk-based pricing is used in two stages. First, at the new customer acquisition stage wherein application data and credit bureau data (where available) are used to ascertain the risk profile of the customer, and depending on the risk profile, the customer is charged a particular interest rate. During the ongoing relationship, the risk profile of the customer is monitored based on transaction data and credit bureau data. In cases where a significant worsening of the risk profile is observed, the bank or financial institution attempts to increase price (interest rate) so as to offset the increase in risk. However, in many markets strict regulatory guidelines limit the flexibility that banks and other financial institutions have in this regard. On the other hand, for low-risk customers, the institution offers various promotional offers.

Common promotional pricing include:

- Balance transfer offer wherein the customer can bring in balances from other lenders and enjoy a lower rate for a specified period
- Top up on loans at a lower interest rate where the customer is extended more credit at a favorable rate

Some of the common non-pricing promotional offers include the following (the interested reader may refer to Chapter 2, "Usage Management" for an understanding of these types of offers)

- An increase in the credit line on a revolving product like credit card
- Waiver on certain types of fees like over limit fees, foreign transaction fees, etc.
- Additional features like no pre-set spend limit on credit cards

In cases where the customer is less risky, the financial institution also aims at rewarding customer loyalty through relationship-based pricing. Figure 5.1 illustrates the concept of risk- and relationship-based pricing. Risk-based pricing is used mostly to manage the cost of credit loss. Relationship-based pricing, on the other hand, is aimed at enhancing the total revenue from the customer. The reader can refer to Chapter 3, "Cross-Sell" for detailed information on relationship-based pricing.

Segment-based pricing is also used for pricing books, computer games, toys, and the like where a special collector's edition of the product is launched at a higher price so as to satisfy the needs of consumers who have a special attraction for the product. In the technology industry, many firms tend to adopt the skimming strategy. As part of a skimming strategy, a new product or technology is very highly priced at the time of its launch and subsequently, the price is brought down to increase product penetration. In the utility industry, price is used as a tool for manipulating demand during peak periods. An interesting pricing experiment performed in California post the utility crisis has been described in Section 5.9.

### 5.4.3 Conditions Necessary for Adopting a Dynamic Pricing Strategy

Certain enabling pre-conditions are critical for the successful implementation of a dynamic pricing strategy. In the absence of these pre-conditions, implementing a dynamic pricing strategy becomes almost impossible. Dynamic pricing becomes most relevant under the following conditions:

- **Segmentable customer base:** As already discussed in the airline example, dynamic pricing tends to produce the maximum benefits when the customer base can be segmented depending on willingness to pay. The firm may have a different offering for each segment or have the same offering with a different price point. It is important to note that the prevalent regulatory and competitive environment may dictate the

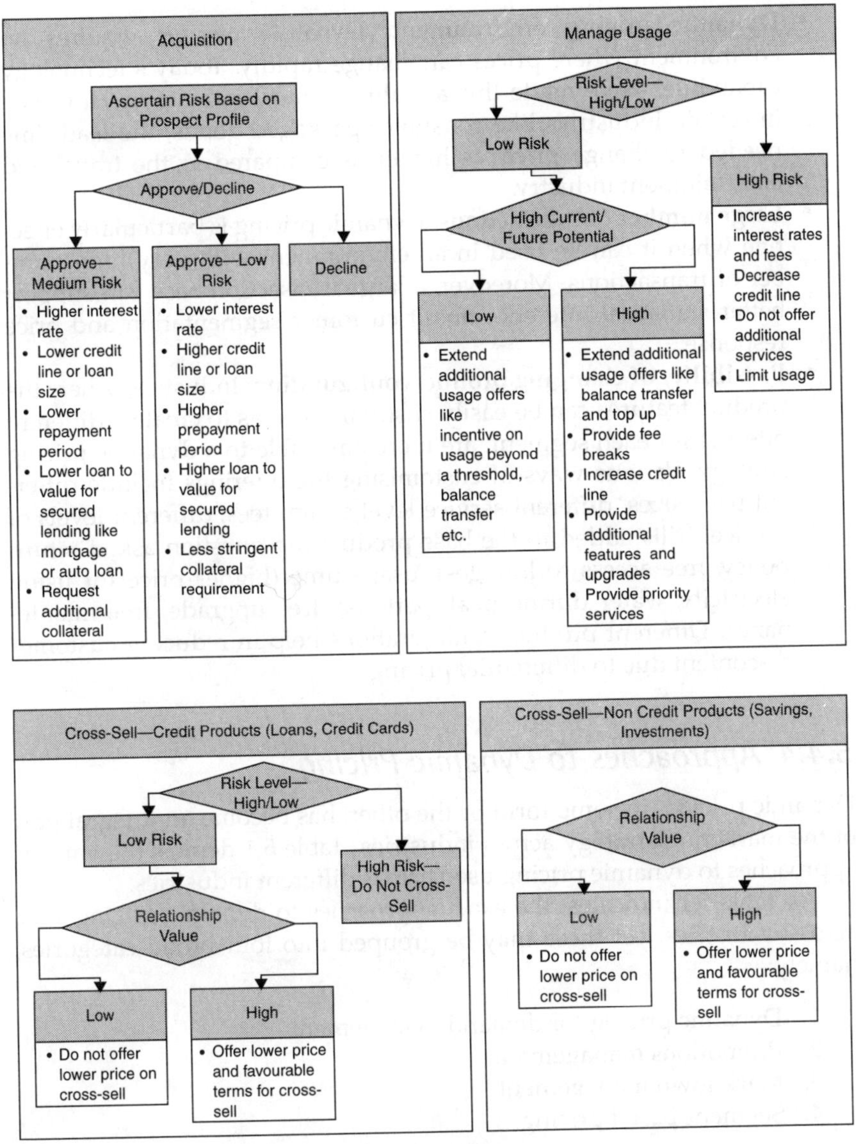


**Figure 5.1** Risk and Relationship Based Pricing

amount of flexibility the firm may have for charging different prices to different segments. For example, strict regulatory norm in the United States dictates a financial services company to explicitly inform the reasons for charging a higher interest rate. The competitive dynamics and customer perception are also important. While customers do not complain about paying a different fare for the same seat in an airline, yet there has been huge customer discontent regarding Amazon's use of transaction data for differential pricing.

- **Dynamic pricing environment:** Dynamic pricing requires an environment where prices can change rapidly. Today's technology capabilities have made this a reality in most industries. However, in certain industries like consumer packaged goods, the lead time needed to change prices is higher as compared to the travel and entertainment industry.
- **Large number of transactions:** Dynamic pricing is particularly effective when it can be used in an environment with very high number of transactions. Moreover, a large transaction base can support better statistical inference about customer segmentation and price response.
- **Possibility of changing product configuration:** Industries where the product features can be easily customised so as to create a different offering for each segment, are more amenable to a dynamic pricing strategy. Various ways of customising the offerings include different pack sizes, different service level guarantees, different levels of service, frills added to the base product (no question asked return policy, free access to lounges), usage time (higher price for using electricity, water during peak periods), free upgrade, free maintenance. Different product configurations help in reducing customer discontent due to differential pricing.

## 5.4.4 Approaches to Dynamic Pricing

Dynamic pricing, in some form or the other, has become an integral part of the marketing strategy across industries. Table 5.1 depicts the various approaches to dynamic pricing used across different industries.

As Table 5.1 indicates, the exact approaches to dynamic pricing vary across industries; yet these may be grouped into four broad categories, namely:

1. Dynamic pricing for demand management
2. Promotions management
3. Markdown management
4. Segment-based pricing.

The next section will highlight the major features of each of the approaches.

### 5.4.4.1 Dynamic Pricing for Demand Management

As pointed out by Talluri and Van Ryzin in their book titled *Revenue Management*, demand management aims at generating the maximum revenue from a limited capacity over a finite time by selling each unit to the right customer at the right time for the right price. Littlewood has been the pioneer in creating frameworks for demand management.

**Table 5.1** Examples of Dynamic Pricing Across Industries

| Basis of Segmentation | Industries | Examples of Dynamic Pricing |
|---|---|---|
| Time of purchase | • Travel and hospitality<br>• Utility | • Lower price for early booking<br>• Higher price during peak demand periods |
| Demographics/ Characteristics of the commercial entity | • Financial services<br>• Enterprise software | • Higher price for younger population who are deemed to be more risky<br>• Lower price for Small and Medium Enterprises |
| Options and product configuration | • Enterprise software<br>• Travel and hospitality | • Additional price for annual maintenance contracts<br>• Lower price for bookings with restrictions like no cancellation, no rescheduling, etc. |
| Channel | • Financial services<br>• Travel and hospitality | • Higher fees for providing personal financial advisors<br>• Lower price for Internet purchase |
| Frequency of purchase | • Travel and hospitality<br>• Entertainment | • Redemption of loyalty points |
| Psychographics | • Computer games, music and, entertainment | • Special collector's edition at higher price for ardent fans |
| Risk profile | • Financial services<br>• Insurance | • Lower price for less risky customers based on internal and credit bureau data<br>• Risk of occurrence of the event being insured for and risk of policy lapses |
| Usage behaviour | • Financial services<br>• Utility<br>• Telecom | • Relationship-based pricing for cross-sell to existing customers<br>• Higher prices for heavy users<br>• Price discounts for higher usage |

Since then a variety of solution methods have been investigated. These methods can be broadly categorised into quantity-based revenue management and price-based revenue management. The current section provides an overview of Littlewood's approach, assuming only two fare classes for a single leg flight. The approach involved closing the lower fare class, when the expected revenue from selling the seat at a higher price exceeds the revenue of selling the seat at the lower price. It needs to be noted that this is a simplistic example and real-life revenue management problems are more complex. However, the approach adopted here forms the building block for solving complex revenue management problems.

To illustrate Littlewood's principle one can assume:

- There are only two fare classes one at $100 and the other at $150 and the flight has a finite capacity "C" which is essentially the number of available seats
- "X" seats are reserved for the higher fare class

If the actual demand for the higher fare class is greater than or equal to X, then the revenue will be 150*X + 100*(C-X). Now if its assumed with only p% surety that the demand for the higher fare class will be greater than X.

- Then the expected revenue will be "Revenue = 150*p*X + 100*C – 100*X"
- Which can be re-written as "Revenue = 100*C + (150*p*X – 100*X)"

The above expression shows that in order to maximise revenue, the expression within the bracket, that is, "(150*p*X – 100*X)" should be greater than or equal to zero (its of course better if the term is positive). This implies that

- 150*p*X should be greater than or equal to 100*X. Hence, one can see that "p" needs to be greater than or equal to 100/150

More formally stated this means that

- If Probability (Demand for higher fare class > X) = Ratio of the fares then the optimal strategy will be to reserve X seats for the higher fare class.

Belobaba extended this concept for multiple fare classes; he coined the term "expected marginal seat revenue (EMSR)". There are two related methods called EMSRa and EMSRb which are most commonly used. Both methods generate the number of seats protected for a particular class and all higher classes. EMSRb uses a weighted average price instead of the actual price for each fare class, while EMSRa uses the actual fares. EMSRb is more widely used in the industry. In the last section of this chapter, these methods will be illustrated with a numerical example.

### 5.4.4.2 Promotions Management

In the context of dynamic pricing, promotions can be defined as short-term price reductions which are mostly used for consumer packaged goods. Promotions are mostly of three types:

1. **Trade promotions:** Promotions which are run by the manufacturers and may or may not be passed by the retailer to the final consumer
2. **Retail promotions:** Promotions run by the retailer
3. **Direct discounts to consumers (Consumer Promotions):** In these cases, the manufacturer gives a discount directly to the consumer in the form of rebates, percentage offs, mail in coupons, etc.

From the manufacturer's perspective, a promotion is used to address the following:

- Lowering of price to clear excess inventory
- Gaining market share by encouraging prospects to try out its products
- Gaining market share by increasing usage (more purchase from existing customers)
- Tackling the higher advertising budgets of big players (for small manufacturers)

From the retailer's perspective, a promotion is used to address the following:

- Finding the optimal price points of various stock keeping units and brands
- Targeting price-sensitive customers who look for attractive deals
- Increasing visibility and store traffic

For a more detailed analysis of the impact of promotions, the reader can refer to Chapter 2, "Usage Management". Promotions can be either advertised or un-advertised. Most manufacturers advertise their direct promotions or rebates. This is particularly true for emerging economies where there are limited numbers of large retailers and the Consumer Packaged Goods (CPG) landscape is dominated by small mom and pop stores.

Enormous volumes of empirical research has been conducted (particularly in the developed markets) using point of sales data to estimate the effects of promotion on consumer behaviour and purchase pattern. Blattberg et al. have summarised the common trends among these findings in their paper *How Promotions Work*. Some of the important findings highlighted in the above paper include:

- Temporary decrease in retail price does increase sales but the increase is lower for higher market share brands
- More frequent promotions tend to lower the consumer's reference price. A reference price refers to the price level that the buyer has in mind for a particular product. If there are very frequent price promotions then buyers start using the lower price as the reference point when they start thinking about the particular product.
- More frequent promotions tend to reduce the quantum of the temporary jump in sales

- Promotions in one category tend to decrease sales of complimentary categories or competitive products
- Promotions which are advertised tend to increase store traffic

In spite of the extensive research there are still unanswered questions regarding the long-term effects of promotions. By long-term impact marketers generally refer to the effects after the promotion period has expired. For example, there is still no definite answer whether the decrease in sales after the promotion is due to customer's advancing their purchase and stockpiling or an inherent decrease in demand because the price has gone up. However, promotions tend to affect the manufacturers and retailers not only from a customer behaviour perspective, but also has tremendous implications on supply chain management. Extensive research suggests that supply chain planning becomes extremely difficult when there are frequent price promotions because it changes the stocking behaviours of the channel partners and hence, magnifies the bullwhip effect. Though a discussion of this effect is beyond the scope of this chapter, it is important to note that in most supply chains it has been found that a small change in demand by the end customer triggers much larger changes up the supply chain (this effect is called the *bullwhip* effect in supply chain parlance). Thus in the presence of frequent promotions supply chain management becomes difficult. Owing to these difficulties Wal-Mart has introduced the famous "Every Day Low Price" strategy.

In spite of the supply chain problems involved and the temporary nature of their impact, promotions are widely used across industries to drive short-term sales increase. The consumer packaged goods industry uses promotions most frequently. In order to design an effective promotions strategy, marketers need to predict the effect of promotions. Blattberg and Neslin in their work titled *Sales Promotion Models* have provided a broad overview of the commonly used models for predicting the effects of promotion for consumer packaged goods industry. A list of common variables that have been found important for predicting an increase in sales (driven by a promotion) are listed below.

- Weekly retail price
- Regular shelf price
- Observed price (the actual price paid by the customer)
- The deal discount
- Competitor price for similar products
- Presence of display in the store
- Presence of feature advertisement
- Time since the beginning of the deal
- Pricing of multiple items together, for example, "buy ten boxes for $10"
- An indicator if the promotional price ends with 9

In conclusion, it needs to be noted that while designing a promotions strategy, a marketer needs to balance the short-term benefits with the long-term impact and the hidden implementation costs. Once all these factors are taken into consideration, an effective promotions strategy is definitely an important pricing tool that can be leveraged by the marketer.

#### 5.4.4.3 Markdown Management

Markdown is an important component of the pricing strategy for apparels and other lifestyle goods. These products commonly demonstrate a seasonal demand and therefore need to be ordered well in advance of the sales season. Forecasting is a key element of managing the sales of these seasonal products. The forecasting becomes extremely difficult because the same needs to be performed for each size, colour style, etc. It is also important to note that due to change in consumer preferences, forecasts based on historical data are also less reliable. A set of mathematical tools called Bayesian techniques are used to combine historical data, observed sales, and the manager's prior belief to forecast expected demand. In this scenario, the initial price setting is mostly performed based on judgement. Once prices are fixed, observed sales patterns is then used to model the trend in demand and accordingly the markdown price is calculated. Past trends and seasonality are two key inputs in calculating the markdown price.

#### 5.4.4.4 Customised Pricing

Customised pricing refers to the practice of segmenting the customer base and charging a different price (or sometimes a different pricing structure) for each segment. Though customer segmentation is a key element of any dynamic pricing approach, in this case the segmentation forms the only basis of charging different prices to different customers. The key segmentation criteria that are used across industries include risk profile of the customer, affluence, and other demographic characteristics, psychographic characteristics, past purchase pattern, etc. Each segment is offered a different pricing and it is ensured that customers in a particular segment can only buy at the price set for the particular segment. Table 5.1 in the beginning of this section provides a list of segmentation criteria used across industries.

## 5.5 Dynamic Pricing Structure

Pricing structure involves answers to the questions on how the firm will charge its customers. In some cases, the firm can only charge a single one-time payment (consumer packaged goods), while in other cases, like enterprise software and hardware, firms can create a set of complex licensing and maintenance contracts—sometimes customised separately for each customer.

Industries like consumer durables, automobiles, financial services, telecom, and industrial products enjoy the flexibility of designing various pricing structures to suit customer needs. Some common examples of flexible pricing structure are:

- A fixed up-front price and subsequent yearly or monthly maintenance fee
- A fixed regular fee and a variable price based on usage
- A service charge or fee if the usage is below a certain level
- A pricing based on usage or number of transactions
- Unlimited usage with a fixed fee

### *5.5.1 Common Pricing Structures*

This section focusses on some of the common pricing structures that are used in various industries. It is possible to have different pricing structures for different types of customers (similar to dynamic pricing).

Optional feature pricing refers to customizing product features for each individual customer. The firm decides on a base price for the basic product (which is most often relatively low) and an additional price for each of the additional features that the customer wants to incorporate. This is most commonly observed in industries like automotive and industrial goods and is increasingly being used for pricing in the software industry. Most software products are being designed in a way that they can be componentised, providing customers the flexibility to buy a basic version and add extra modules if necessary.

Captive product or captive service pricing refers to the case where the product requires the use of ancillary products or services. This is most often referred to as the razor blade strategy where the base product is priced lower and the ancillary product or service is sold at a higher margin. Gillette was an early adopter of this strategy whereby the various brands of Gillette razors were priced relatively lower. However, the blades which had to be replaced frequently were priced much higher. Gillette did not generate a large revenue by selling the razor but made up for it by selling the blades at a higher margin. Similar examples are found in other industries like gaming devices wherein the basic gaming device like a Microsoft XBOX is sold at a relatively lower price. However, each game that needs to be loaded in the XBOX is sold at a relatively higher margin.

Two-part pricing is used mostly in the services industry as it involves a fixed up-front fee and a regular charge based on usage. A typical example is telecom pricing where various tariff plans have various combination of up-front fees and usage charges. Telecom companies use tariff plan analysis to find the optimal plan for a customer. Another commonly adopted strategy involves bundling of one or more products so that the price of the bundle is more attractive for the customer compared to the price of the individual products. For details on the analysis of telecom tariff plans, the readers may refer to Chapter 2, "Usage Management". A detailed analysis of bundling strategies can be found in Chapter 3, "Cross-Sell".

## 5.5.2 Pricing Structure: Financial Services

The financial services industry uses different pricing structures to suit the needs and the risk profile of various types of customers. Because of the diversity of pricing structures in the financial services industry, the current section provides a detailed outline of the various pricing structures used in the financial services industry. In the financial services industry, a combination of various fees and interest is most commonly used. Some of the typical ways of charging fees in the financial services industry include:

- Up-front fee or processing fee
- Late payment fee
- Prepayment fee
- Fees for any special services (e.g., cash withdrawal on credit cards, check book issue)
- Fees for foreign currency transactions
- Penalty fees (e.g., balance in savings account going below the minimum cut-off, customer going over-limit on credit cards)

These fees are either charged as a fixed dollar amount or are charged as a percentage of the outstanding amount involved. In the latter case, the bank also puts a minimum dollar value for the fee. For example, a typical late payment fee on credit cards is charged as "$10 or 1% of the outstanding amount whichever is higher". In many cases, the bank or financial institution uses a tiered-fee structure. Banks attempt to structure the tiers for all the fees in such a manner so as to maximise the total fee revenue. The following is a typical example of a tiered-late payment fee structure:

- For outstanding balance less than $100
  - 1% of the outstanding or $10, whichever is higher is charged as late payment fee
- For outstanding balance between $100 and $500
  - 2% of the outstanding or $20, whichever is higher is charged as late payment fee
- For outstanding more than $500
  - 5% of the outstanding or $25, whichever is higher is charged as late payment fee

The fee income represents a relatively stable income stream because the net contribution from fees is not subjected to interest rate variation. Given that the cost of funds fluctuates with interest rates, banks are able to generate a more stable net income if more of their income comes from fees as against interest. In order to tide over the problem of fluctuating net income, banks and financial institutions have started offering floating interest rate products (as against fixed interest rate products). This is particularly true for mortgage where the loan period is significantly long. In the US markets, most credit card issuers offer a flexible interest rate where the credit card annual percentage rate (APR) is a function of the prime lending rate (most banks disclose rates in the form of "Prime plus 5.99", "Prime plus 9.99"). However in the Asian and Indian markets the credit card APR is still not linked to the prime rate. An annual percentage rate which is independent of the prime rate makes it difficult for the credit card issuers to maintain a stable net interest margin. This is because the cost of funds incurred by the issuers for funding the receivables fluctuates based on changes in the overall interest rates. To tide over this problem, most banks use various methodologies for hedging the interest rate risks on their receivables.

As opposed to a short-term debt (e.g., credit cards and personal loans), mortgages in most markets are sold at a variable interest rate. In the case of variable rate pricing, the interest rate charged to the customer changes in tandem with the interest rate in the economy. Most banks provide customers a reference rate like the interbank offer rate, which is used as a benchmark for calculating the variable interest rate on the mortgage during its lifetime. Though a variable interest rate for a product like mortgage helps the lenders in maintaining a stable interest rate margin, yet it is not an unmixed blessing. During the mortgage crisis in the US market, adjustable rate mortgages have proved to be a major cause of concern. An upward adjustment of the mortgage rates meant a significant increase in the obligation for the borrower, and in many cases the borrower was unable to pay the increased obligation. This made the borrower default not only on his or her mortgage, but also on other credit obligations. At this point it is important to note that in many markets mortgage pricing has attracted a lot of scrutiny from regulators because of the pricing structure adopted by mortgage lenders. Most mortgage lenders tend to adopt a strategy of a lower fixed interest rate during the first few years of the mortgage loan. After the lapse of the promotional period, the lower fixed interest rate is replaced by a higher flexible rate (linked to a benchmark rate). The peril of this pricing strategy is that the customer's obligation increases significantly after the promotional period and there is a risk that this will push many customers into delinquency. To tide over this, mortgage lenders generally do not increase the equated monthly instalment (EMI) when the interest rate goes up but increases the tenor of the loan keeping the monthly EMI the same. But many regulators like the Reserve Bank of India have adopted a very stern view of mortgage pricing and have instructed lenders to avoid a promotional pricing for mortgage loans.

Another interesting example of a differential pricing structure involves the balance transfer offers on credit cards. Balance transfers are offered to customers who are willing to transfer balances from competition credit card to the credit card of the particular issuer. The balance transfer provides a lower rate (also called promotional rate) on the transferred balance for a specific period of time. After the specified time, the remaining balance is charged at the normal interest rate, which is higher than the promotional rate. The pricing structure of a balance transfer consists of the following three components:

1. The promotional rate that is offered
2. The period for which such lower rates are offered
3. The up-front fee that the customer has to pay to avail the offer

The three components can be altered to create the most suitable pricing structure for a particular segment of customer. Sometimes customers are allowed the flexibility to choose from multiple offers. The following is an example of three offers which a particular customer could choose from:

1. **Offer-A:** Promotional interest rate of 9.99% for a period of 12 months and 1% of the transferred balance charged as up-front fee
2. **Offer-B:** Promotional interest rate of 12.99% for a period of 24 months with no up-front fee
3. **Offer-C:** Promotional interest rate of 0% for a period of 6 months and 5% of the transferred balance charged as up-front fee

The interested reader may refer to Chapter 2, "Usage Management", for a detailed understanding of the impact of balance transfer pricing structures on customer behaviour.

### *5.5.3 Pricing Structure: Enterprise Software*

Significant innovation has taken place in designing pricing structures for enterprise software and hardware. In order to cater to a wide variety of customers ranging from small and medium enterprises to large corporations, software vendors have designed a large variety of customised pricing structures. Owing to the widely different pricing structures in this industry, a separate section has been dedicated to the pricing structures typical of this industry. A recent PricewaterhouseCoopers study on software pricing has indicated that customers today are less willing to pay a high up-front license fee. As a result software revenues are shifting from license fees to maintenance fees and the companies are exploring new pricing models like term licensing, commercial open source, software-as-a-service, customisation and integration services, user based and/or usage based pricing in order to maximize their revenues. These changes have significant effects on revenue realization for software vendors. The first is an immediate negative impact on revenue recognition; the high up-front revenue will now be spread over a much longer time period. However, the second impact of this strategy is that it will provide a more predictable long-term revenue stream because once the software sale is made it will ensure that the regular fees will keep on accruing for a much longer time frame. These new pricing structures also help software vendors to enhance their market penetration particularly in the small and medium enterprises segment. Many SMEs who were earlier unable to afford high up-front license fees, will be able to afford the changed pricing terms.

In a flat pricing structure, customers pay a fixed price for unlimited use of the software for a given period, as per Robert Harmon et al. The license fee can be structured differently to provide discounts to key segments. An example of the above is Oracle's pricing model of 11i for small and medium businesses. It involves a monthly fee (without any up-front payment) covering all the basic modules and outsourced software management by Oracle.

Earliest innovations in software pricing was brought about by IBM which used a tiered pricing for its mainframes. As part of the tiered pricing, the price of the software was increased when it was run on a powerful system, the rationale being, that a more powerful system increased the user's benefits from the software. The next phase of innovation involved user or usage-based pricing. User-based pricing took the form of "per user license fee" or "limit to the maximum number of concurrent users". The usage-based model involved MIPS (million instructions per second) based pricing, per click based pricing, number of transaction based pricing, pricing based on type of processor used and the like. The underlying assumption involved in this pricing strategy is that, higher usage by a customer implies that the customer is deriving more benefit from the product. That is why, a higher price is charged.

## 5.6 Implementation of a Dynamic Pricing Strategy

As already discussed, the last and possibly the most important part of the pricing decision process involves setting the actual price for the firm's products and services for each type of pricing structure that the firm uses. This section will focus on the basic steps which are involved in the price setting process. Figure 5.2 depicts the components of the price setting decision.

### *5.6.1 Segmentation of the Customer and Prospect Base*

As discussed by Cross and Dixit in their paper titled *Customer-centric pricing: The surprising secret for profitability*, the first step towards a price setting exercise involves a segmentation of the firm's current customer base and the prospect universe. This needs to be performed to know whether different group of customers or prospects have different needs and different willingness to pay. As part of the segmentation exercise, firms also try to estimate the wallet size of the key segments.

Most firms start this process as an "Inside out" process, wherein they start the exercise with their existing customer base and map them into segments based on the revenue generated, demographic/firmographic

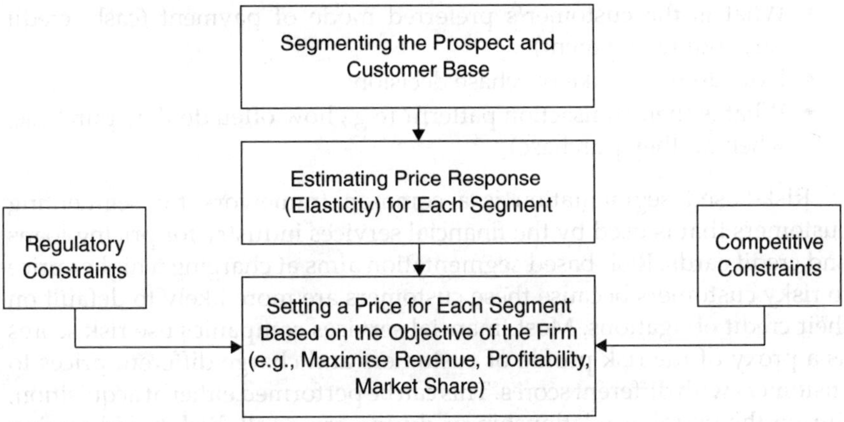


**Figure 5.2** Components of the Price Setting Decision

characteristics and transaction behaviour. In case certain key variables (which the firm thinks are important) are missing in the customer data, a primary survey is performed on a sample of the customers to gather the missing link. Post segmentation of the customer base, many firms also use market research to obtain deeper qualitative and quantitative information about the key segments. Focus group discussion is a tool that is used very often to gather qualitative information about the purchase decision process and psychographic factors. Details of analytical techniques used for segmentation will be discussed in Chapter 7, "Quantitative Methods". The next phase of the "Inside out" process of segmentation involves looking at the prospect universe and segmenting the prospect universe, sometimes on similar lines as the existing customers. Many firms also measure penetration and wallet share of the target universe based on the segmentation of the existing customer base. The interested reader may refer to Chapter 1, "Acquisition" for detailed understanding of methodologies for segmenting the prospect universe.

In the case of consumer packaged goods, transaction data available in some markets in the form of scanner data is also used for performing the segmentation exercise. Marketers in this industry tend to use extensive primary market research for the purpose of segmentation. After the segmentation exercise the firm attempts to derive answers to the following questions for each segment.

- What types of customer does each segment comprise of?
- How much are customers willing to pay?
- What is the wallet size?
- What are their needs? (e.g., some segments will look for price alone some other segment will look for enhanced features, better service, convenience of shopping, return or cancellation policy)
- What is the customer's preferred channel?

- What is the customer's preferred mode of payment (cash, credit card, online payment)
- How do they make purchase decisions?
- What is their transaction pattern? (e.g., how often do they purchase, when do they purchase)

Risk-based segmentation is a common framework for segmenting customers that is used by the financial services industry for pricing loans and credit cards. Risk-based segmentation aims at charging a higher price to risky customers because these customers are more likely to default on their credit obligations. Most financial services companies use risk scores as a proxy of the risk profile of customers and charge different prices to customers with different scores. This can be performed either at acquisition, during the ongoing relationship or during cross-sell. Risk-based pricing at acquisition is possible only in markets where a positive credit bureau exists because a strong risk score for discriminating between risk profiles of new customers is only feasible in the presence of a credit bureau. The reader may refer to Chapter 6, "Credit Bureau" for further details on credit bureau scores. Other than credit bureau scores, lenders also use the loan ticket size, tenor, and sometimes the occupation type of the customer to price new unsecured loans. For pricing secured loans, the loan to value ratio, that is the ratio of the cost of asset (e.g., house) to be financed by the loan and the ticket size of the loan is also a very important determinant of price. Table 5.2 depicts a sample pricing grid for pricing unsecured personal loans. It is to be noted that a higher loan size amounts to higher

**Table 5.2** Pricing Grid for Personal Loan

<table>
<tr><th colspan="2">Personal Loan Pricing Grid: New Loans</th><th colspan="7">Risk Score</th></tr>
<tr><th>Loan Size as Multiple of Monthly Income</th><th>Tenure</th><th>850+</th><th>760–850</th><th>720–760</th><th>680–720</th><th>650–680</th><th>600–650</th><th><600</th></tr>
<tr><th></th><th></th><th colspan="7">Annual Percentage Rate</th></tr>
<tr><td>3X</td><td>Upto 3 years</td><td>16%</td><td>17%</td><td>19%</td><td>20%</td><td rowspan="2">Reject</td><td rowspan="4">Reject</td><td rowspan="8">Reject</td></tr>
<tr><td></td><td>3–5 years</td><td>16%</td><td>17.5%</td><td>20%</td><td>21%</td></tr>
<tr><td>2X</td><td>Upto 3 years</td><td>15%</td><td>16%</td><td>18%</td><td>19%</td><td>20%</td></tr>
<tr><td></td><td>3–5 years</td><td>16%</td><td>17%</td><td>19%</td><td>20%</td><td>21%</td></tr>
<tr><td>1.5X</td><td>Upto 3 years</td><td>14%</td><td>15%</td><td>17%</td><td>18%</td><td>20%</td><td>22%</td></tr>
<tr><td></td><td>3–5 years</td><td>15%</td><td>16%</td><td>18%</td><td>19%</td><td>21%</td><td>22%</td></tr>
<tr><td><1.5X</td><td>Upto 3 years</td><td>12%</td><td>13%</td><td>15%</td><td>18%</td><td>20%</td><td>22%</td></tr>
<tr><td></td><td>3–5 years</td><td>13%</td><td>14%</td><td>16%</td><td>19%</td><td>20%</td><td>22%</td></tr>
</table>

leverage by the customer and hence, is more risky. In this particular example, three dimensions, namely, ticket size of the loan, tenor of the loan and risk score are used for determining pricing. For a given income, higher ticket size indicates more risk, hence a higher price is charged. A lower risk score indicates higher risk, which translates into higher price. Similarly, higher tenor indicates higher risk and hence a higher price is charged for loans with a higher tenor.

In many cases usage-based segmentation is a common segmentation methodology for price discrimination. In cases where a usage-based product like a credit card is involved, customers are offered price breaks if their usage is above a threshold. Sometime special discounts are offered if the customer is ready to shift from competition. For example, a special price is offered to credit card customers who are willing to transfer significant amount of balances from a competitor card.

A key aspect of segmentation for pricing involves segmenting based on willingness to pay. As pointed out by Smith and Nagel in their work titled *How much are your customers willing to pay?*, traditional segmentation based on demographic and psychographic variables are less important in this case. It is more important to judge the customer's willingness to pay on the basis of the circumstances of the purchase. As pointed out by Cross and Dixit in their paper titled *Customer-centric pricing: The surprising secret for profitability*, it is important to ascertain the customer's willingness to pay at a particular point in time. Segmentation by buying behaviour is required to determine the same. Unlike demographics and psychographics that attempt to define who the customers are, segmentation by buying behaviour focuses on predicting how they will respond at the time of a purchase. A typical example of the above is travel purchase behaviour. The same customer demonstrates different willingness to pay based on whether the travel is an official travel or a personal vacation. For vacation travel, a particular customer may be very price conscious but is willing to compromise on schedule, whereas the same customer may be willing to pay much more for his/her business travel if he/she is offered the desired schedule. Hence segmentation based on demographic factors alone is of little use from a pricing perspective.

Transaction data is very important to predict the purchase behaviour and is of critical importance for segmentation for pricing. For example, a mobile telecom company uses the transaction behaviour of a customer to offer various pricing offers like lower roaming charges, lower charges on data usage, lower download charges for downloading games, etc. In some cases, the mobile telecom company may find that the transaction pattern of the customer does not match the plan that a customer has purchased. In such cases the company offers the right pricing plan to the customer. The interested reader may refer to Chapter 2, "Usage Management" to obtain a better idea of rate plan migration.

In case of limited or no availability of transaction data (e.g., in the consumer packaged goods industry in the emerging markets, where scanner data is not available) the firm needs to use primary research findings to judge purchase behaviour and incorporate the same along with demographic and psychographic variables for segmentation. Some industries may face the opposite problem. For example, airlines and e-commerce companies may have a rich set of transaction data for their customers but may have very few fields related to demographic data (other than age and gender). In such a case the firm needs to create an initial segmentation based on transaction data and perform primary survey for each of these segments in order to obtain the missing demographic and psychographic data.

### *5.6.2 Demand Estimation and Price Elasticity*

The next step after segmentation, involves estimating the price response function (sometimes for each segment separately). Price response functions are essentially the short-term demand curve which tells the firm's decision makers the quantity that can be sold at each price point. The price response functions or demand estimation is the most important and the central piece of quantitative insight that drives the price setting process. Building a demand estimation model involves looking at past data and building econometric models to forecast demand at various price points. In case past data is not representative, or the firm is looking to change price way beyond what has been the norm in the past, or market conditions and competition has changed drastically, then the firm needs to perform pricing tests and use the results of the same to estimate demand. In many cases, firms use design of experiments concepts to determine the optimal number of experiments that need to be performed, to ascertain the response of sales to change in the price and/or other market mix variables. A detailed discussion on design of experiment is beyond the scope of this chapter; the interested reader can refer to Chapter 8, "Analytics Ecosystem" for an understanding of design of experiment and its use for pricing.

In countries like the United States, Consumer Packaged Goods (CPG) companies extensively utilise scanner data collected by companies like IRI or ACNielsen to determine how sales of various units are affected by price and other marketing variables like advertising, in store promotions, etc. Companies also utilise price and promotions offered by competing brands in order to forecast expected sales. The mathematical models used for the purpose of this forecast are popularly known as market mix models. Market mix models describe logarithm of sales as a function of various marketing variables such as price, promotions, discounts, advertising. Many of the marketing variables like advertising may have a lagged impact on sales and hence, lags of those are considered for forecasting sales. Similarly, price of a particular SKU may impact its own sales and sales of other SKUs as well. Such cross price elasticity is also taken into account while building such a model. In markets where such scanner data does not exist, CPG companies utilise panel data to estimate price elasticity.

### 5.6.2.1 Limitation of Demand Estimation Models

At this point it is important to note that there are significant limitations of demand estimation models. All demand estimation models are based on the assumption that past demand patterns will be reflected in the future, which need not always be the case. As pointed out by Talluri and Van Ryzin in their book titled *Revenue Management* most of these models also assume that customers are myopic, that is, they purchase as soon as the offered price is less than or equal to their willingness to pay and they do not adopt complex strategies like postponing the purchase in the hope that prices will go down further in the future. The long-term base-line price refers to the price that is charged in the absence of promotions. Usually demand estimation models are used to predict the demand corresponding to the long-term base-line price. The effects of promotions are accounted for by models that predict the effects of short-term promotions. Some of the key limitations of demand estimation models are listed below:

- **Postponing purchase:** In certain cases where consumers expect future prices to drop further, they may postpone their purchase decision. A typical example is end of season sales wherein consumers expect prices to go down and sometimes postpone their purchase decisions.
- **Stockpiling:** In certain cases researchers have shown that customers adopt a stockpiling behaviour. Customers sometimes tend to buy more if the price is lowered but they do not consume the increased amount that they purchase; instead they tend to store the item for future, anticipating that prices will rise. This has mostly been observed for non-perishable consumer packaged goods. On the other hand, many customers seem to have a reservation price in mind for a particular product and will not purchase if the price is higher than the reservation price. Stockpiling and postponement of purchase tend to alter the natural relationship between price and demand, hence estimation of price response functions become difficult.
- **Stable customer behaviour:** Another assumption of the myopic models is that customer's buying behaviour does not change over time. In case customer behaviour changes a new estimation model needs to be built.
- **Stable market conditions:** A key limitation arises out of the assumption that market conditions will remain stable over time. This implies that competition and size of the prospect population will remain unchanged in future. If a competitor drastically reduces price or a new competitor enters the market then the demand estimation model will not be able to predict demand accurately.

However, most of the above limitations can be overcome to some extent by tracking the estimation model very closely over time and rebuilding the models once degradation in performance is observed. The "myopic customer" model seems to a fair approximation in most cases, though it is possible to arrive at a game theoretic specification for demand estimation whereby there is a strategic game between the firm and its customers. However, this makes the model too complex and hence, very difficult to implement. A game theoretic model involving a strategic game between the buyer and the seller uses principles of game theory to predict the behaviour of the buyer or the seller in anticipation of the behaviour of one another.

### 5.6.3 Price Setting

The final price for each segment is determined based on the estimated demand and elasticity of demand for each segment. However, these are not the only factors that determine the final price for a particular segment. The short- and long-term business goals of the company and competitive activity are also an important determinant of the final price for each segment. As discussed earlier (in the section on economic theories of pricing), if a company wants to penetrate a particular segment where it has a lower market share, then it may price its offerings much lower. Similarly, companies sometimes adopt an aggressive pricing strategy to limit entry of competitors in the market. In some cases, companies adopt a low-price strategy for their primary product and expect to make money by cross-selling more products to the same customer at a later stage. A typical example is current and savings accounts, where the bank adopts an aggressive pricing strategy and expects to sell fixed deposits, investments and insurance at a later stage. Detailed examples on cross-sell pricing have been discussed in Chapter 3, "Cross-Sell".

Most companies monitor the profit and loss at a segment level and adopt a pricing strategy to maximise profitability over a period of time.

### 5.6.4 Key Issues in Implementing Dynamic Pricing

In spite of the revenue impact of dynamic pricing there exists multiple constraints which limit the extent to which a dynamic pricing strategy can be implemented. The key issues that limit a dynamic pricing strategy are regulatory constraints and negative customer feedback. Certain industries like consumer lending and insurance are heavily regulated. The regulator limits the flexibility that a company has with regards to pricing. One of the best examples of recent regulatory constraints on dynamic pricing involves the implementation of the CARD Act (Credit Card Accountability Responsibility and Disclosure Act) in the

United States. Prior to the implementation of the CARD Act, credit card companies were allowed to increase the interest rate for customers who demonstrate risky behaviour such as being delinquent by 30 days or more, having a cheque bounce, and the like. The CARD Act limits the set of risky behaviours that can be considered for increasing interest rates. The law specified that customers who have paid late by 60 days or more can only be re-priced. The law also mandates credit card companies to provide 45 days of advance notice to customers before increasing their interest rates. The CARD Act also includes a number of other key regulatory changes for the credit card industry but that is beyond the scope of this section.

In some cases companies have faced the wrath of the consumer, for adopting a differential pricing strategy. In recent times, Amazon had faced a lot of protest from consumers regarding the way it uses the clicking pattern of customers to price its products. The most famous backlash against dynamic pricing took place when Amazon used the customer's clicking pattern to price DVDs differently for different customers.

### *5.6.5 Pricing and Customer Loyalty*

With increased competition more and more companies are realising the importance of retaining existing customers. Pricing in many cases, is an important tool for driving customer loyalty. Some of the major pricing structures for fostering loyalty include:

- Quantity-based discounts, wherein discounts are offered if higher quantities are purchased. For example, an annual subscription of a magazine would fetch a discount compared to a six month subscription.
- Earn back offers, wherein the customer can earn discounts or fee waiver based on a specified usage level. For example, many credit card companies waive off the annual membership fee if the customer spends more than a threshold. In some cases, the credit card company charges a fee at the beginning of the year but gives it back to the customer if the customer spends more than a threshold.
- Award of loyalty points which can be exchanged for future discounts
- Price bundling, wherein a lower price is offered if the customer buys multiple products
- Price guarantees, wherein loyal customers are guaranteed the lowest price

However, it needs to be noted that pricing is just one of the levers for fostering loyalty. The reader should refer to Section 2.7 on "loyalty management" in Chapter 2, "Usage Management" for a complete view of customer loyalty programmes.

# 5.7 Price Setting in E-commerce and Auctions as a Price Setting Mechanism

## 5.7.1 Price Setting in E-commerce

E-commerce has changed the pricing paradigm in three major ways: it has made price comparison much easier, it has provided e-retailer the power of changing price at almost zero cost and it has increased the use of auctions as a price setting mechanism. This section will explore these three key aspects of e-commerce which are relevant from a pricing perspective.

The first major change that has been facilitated by the Internet involves almost instant and real-time price comparisons at zero cost. Price comparison sites collect pricing information from thousands of sellers and make price comparisons fast and effective. However, contrary to intuitive conclusion, a McKinsey survey of Internet shoppers indicate that only 8% of them are bargain hunters. This finding has important implications for both e-retailers and brick and mortar players. While price comparison has become readily available, significant differentiation in terms of product features, terms of purchase, and other factors should be used to sustain a price differential. Today there are a number of online applications which scans through the web for the lowest price and sends automated emails to customers. One such example is a set of applications which leverages Amazon's policy of refunding the difference if the products purchased by a customer goes down in price in the next 30 days. Once the user has keyed in the items that he has purchased from Amazon, these sites track the price of these products in Amazon for the next 30 days, and in case of a price decrease, it sends an automated email to the user. The user can then log on to Amazon to claim the refund.

The second way in which the Internet promises to change pricing strategy is through real-time dynamic pricing. Such real-time dynamic pricing is based on a particular customer's past purchase behaviour, the pattern of "clicks" observed in the current shopping session, the inventory position and the expected demand for the product. Tools like collaborative filtering creates bundles that appeal to a particular customer (based on his/her past purchase and current pattern of clicks) and attractive discounts are offered for the bundle. For more details on use of collaborative filtering, the reader can refer to Chapter 3, "Cross-Sell". Though the above approach has become an accepted standard in the e-retailing environment, dynamic pricing for individual products based on the customer's clicking pattern has not been well received by consumers.

The other major shift that has been brought about by e-commerce is the increased use of auctions for price determination. eBay has been at the forefront of this change. As eBay does not take possession of the articles it does not incur the high distribution costs like e-retailers. The success of the Internet as an auction platform stems from its ability to create real-time collaboration. For example, eBay not only provides users the platform for auctions, it also allows users to share their views and comments about the reliability of each buyer and seller and about the details of products that are on sale. These reviews and comments have helped in reducing information asymmetry, thereby providing a boost to auctions.

## *5.7.2 Auctions*

The theory of auctions is quite complex and a huge amount of theoretical and empirical research has been carried out for modelling and understanding auctions. Researchers have used game theoretic models to predict the behaviour of participants in an auction. However, the current section will outline the types of auctions and the industries where auctions are most frequently used as a price setting mechanism.

Apart from the online space, auctions are predominantly used by the government for sale of public assets like spectrum, public land, etc. Industrial purchasers also use auctions wherein a bidding process is used for selecting the supplier after initial qualification. In the financial markets, auctions take the form of a bid and ask price for selling treasury bonds and currency. Investors bid for a particular rate and the sellers of the instrument quote a minimum asking rate at which he/she is willing to sell the instrument. The institution which organises the auction gets to keep the difference between the bid and ask rates which is called "bid ask spread". Traditional auction houses like Sotheby's and Christie's have been organising auctions for selling art objects and collector's items for the past 300 years.

The common types of auctions that are primarily used for price setting are:

- **Open ascending price auctions (also called English Auctions):** In this type of auction, the seller announces a progressively increasing price and the participants indicate their willingness to pay the price. Finally, if there is only one participant left at a particular price, then the good is sold to that participant at the particular price. The most important factors that underline this type of auction is the fact that each participant can observe the bidding pattern of every other participant and can alter his strategy accordingly. Secondly, as the price goes up with each bid, participants can match the maximum amount that they are willing to pay. In practice, most auctions of art work is conducted using English auction.
- **Open descending price auction (also called Dutch Auctions):** In this type of auction, the price progressively decreases and the first customer willing to buy at the announced price gets to buy the product. Dutch auction is commonly used for sale of commodities in commodity exchanges.

- **First price sealed bid auctions:** Participants submit sealed bids of the amount that they are willing to pay and the participant with the maximum bid gets to purchase the product. An important feature of this type of auction is that participants are unable to observe each other's strategy. Sealed bid auctions are mostly used by governments for the sale of public assets.
- **Second price sealed bid auctions (also called Vickrey Auctions):** This is very similar to the first price sealed bid auction; the only difference is that the highest bidder gets to purchase the product but pays the price indicated by the second highest bidder. This type of auction is not commonly used in practice.

### 5.7.3 Group Buying and Discount Vouchers

Group buying as a pricing mechanism is of relatively recent origin. Group buying and discount sites have changed the price discovery mechanism in the e-commerce world. E-commerce sites such as http://www.letsbuyit.com/, http://chennaionline.com, etc., offer various group buying mechanisms where the seller is able to discover the price that the buyer is willing to pay for a particular volume of goods. Buyers, on the other hand, collaborate with other buyers to achieve scale and therefore can ask for a better price. These sites aid sellers in achieving second and third degree price discrimination. The group buying sites allow sellers to price their products differently based on the volume of purchase and also based on the buyer's willingness to pay.

Each group buying site differs a little in the way they structure their offer. However, a few common offer structures exist. As per Anand and Aron in their paper titled *Group Buying on the Web: A Comparison of Price-Discovery Mechanisms* some of the group buying sites offer an initial ceiling price (maximum price) to interested buyers. As more buyers start putting in their orders the price decreases from the initial ceiling price and is broadcasted on the web site. Finally every buyer is offered the last price achieved during the group buying process. In some cases, buyers can provide options as to whether they want to buy only at the best price or they would like to buy at the ceiling price if the price does not decrease as part of the group buying process. Anand and Aron also point out the example of aggregators like Independent Restaurant Purchasing Group (IRPG) which brings together more than 3,000 restaurants across the United States and negotiates volume-based discounts with suppliers on their behalf.

The other recent developments in e-commerce are sites like Groupon (http://www.groupon.com), offering deep discount vouchers across various product categories. Sites like Groupon attempt to bring diverse set of merchants under a single platform and offer deep discount vouchers to consumers through the web sites. A print of the voucher or a downloaded copy in a smartphone can be used at the merchant outlet for availing discounts. These deep discounts will be profitable for the seller if they attract first time customers who later pay the full price for additional purchase. However, if these discounts attract more of existing customers, then it may not be profitable for the seller. The interested reader can refer to the working paper titled *To Groupon or Not to Groupon: The Profitability of Deep Discounts* by Benjamin Edelman, Sonia Jaffe, and Scott Duke Kominers for a more detailed explanation of the economic theory behind deep discount vouchers.

## 5.8 Industry Example: Price-based Revenue Management (Airlines and Hotel Pricing)

Airline revenue management systems utilise a host of complex forecasting and optimisation techniques, most of which are very computation intensive and require a very high amount of mathematical sophistication for understanding. The current example outlines a sample case study which provides a rather simplistic visualisation of the process of revenue management without venturing into many of the complexities involved. This example has been adopted from the note on *Yield Management* by Serguei Netessine (University of Pennsylvania) and Robert Shumsky (University of Rochester). The book titled *Revenue Management* by Talluri and Van Ryzin has also been used as a reference for creating the example.

As a simple example, one can consider a single itinerary flight having a total capacity of 200 seats across four booking classes. The fares for these classes are \$500, \$800, \$900, and \$1000, respectively. Before the start of the booking process, the pricing problem essentially boils down to finding the optimal number of seats to be reserved for each of these fare classes. Analysis of past booking data is used to estimate an expected demand for each of these fare classes. The estimation is corrected for factors like seasonality, changes in pricing pattern, macroeconomic scenarios, etc. As the demand varies with the time of the year (holiday season) and with macroeconomic conditions, such adjustments are necessary to correct the estimate arrived using historical data.

It is assumed that demand for each fare class is normally distributed. The mean and standard deviations have been calculated using 100 days of data. Table 5.3 summarizes the above information.

**Table 5.3** Sample Demand Pattern by Fare Class

| | Class 1 | Class 2 | Class 3 | Class 4 |
|---|---|---|---|---|
| Fare | 500 | 800 | 900 | 1000 |
| Expected demand | 75 | 39.6 | 45.1 | 17.3 |
| Standard deviation | 11.3 | 13.2 | 15 | 5.8 |
| Ratio of fare between the immediately lower fare class and the particular class | | 0.63 | 0.89 | 0.90 |

Littlewood's principle described earlier in the chapter, is utilized for solving the problem. As already discussed, Littlewood's principle involves comparing a pair of fare classes at a time. If one compares fare class-4 and fare class-3 then the ratio of fares between the two classes is found to be 0.9. The next problem is to determine with 90% certainty the demand for fare class-4? The normality assumption is used to find the answer.

From past data it is known, that the demand for class-4 is distributed normally with a mean of 17.3 and a standard deviation of 5.8. If one looks up the normal distribution table or uses the function NORMINV (1-confidence, mean, standard deviation) in Microsoft XL, then one can find the answer. In this case, if one plugs in the number as follows: Confidence – 90%, Mean – 17.3, Standard deviation – 5.8. Then the result will be 9.9. This means that one can say with 90% certainty that demand for fare class-4 will be more than 9.9. Hence, one should reserve 10 seats for class-4.

Fare class-4 is the highest price class. If one wants to find the number of seats to be reserved for lower-priced classes, then one needs to adopt a slightly different approach. This is because past research suggests that the use of pooled mean and standard deviation provides more accurate results. Which means that for fare class-3 one should use the mean and standard deviation of fare class-3 and fare class-4 put together. Similarly for fare class-2, one should use the mean and standard deviation of fare class-2, fare class-3 and fare class-4 together. Hence, the number of seats to be reserved for fare class-3 is arrived as follows:

- One can combine the standard deviation of 15 for fare class-3 with the standard deviation of 5.8 of fare class-4 to come up with the pooled standard deviation of 11.37, which is arrived as 100 days of data has been used for calculating mean and standard deviation

$$\sqrt{\frac{(100-1)*15^2+(100-1)*5.8^2}{(100-1)+(100-1)}}$$

- One can combine the mean of fare class-3 with the mean of fare class-4 to obtain the combined mean. Combined mean = mean of fare class-3 + mean of fare class-4 (45.1 + 17.3 = 62.4)
- Ratio of fares between the immediately lower-fare class (i.e. fare class-2) and the particular class (i.e. fare class-3) is 0.89
- Hence, if one has to find with 89% confidence, what the demand will be. One can use the following function in

  MS-EXCEL (NORMINV(1-0.89, 62.4, 11.37) = 48.45)

  to find the demand. As the number of reserved seats can only be an integer, hence the number of seats is rounded off to 49.

Similarly, the number of seats to be reserved for other fare classes can be calculated accordingly. Table 5.4 depicts the results for all fare classes. The above example illustrates the use of EMSRa (expected marginal seat revenue) methodology for arriving at the booking limits.

**Table 5.4** Seat Reservation for Each Fare Class Using EMSRa

| | Class 1 | Class 2 | Class 3 | Class 4 |
|---|---|---|---|---|
| Fare | 500 | 800 | 900 | 1000 |
| Expected demand | 75 | 39.6 | 45.1 | 17.3 |
| Standard deviation | 11.3 | 13.2 | 15 | 5.8 |
| Ratio of fare between the immediately lower fare class and the particular class | | 0.63 | 0.89 | 0.90 |
| Expected demand (mean) of all class equal to or higher than the particular class | 177.00 | 102.00 | 62.40 | 17.30 |
| Standard deviation of all class equal to or higher than the particular class | 11.84 | 12.01 | 11.37 | 5.80 |
| Number of seats reserved for the class | 43 | 98 | 49 | 10 |

As discussed earlier, another similar methodology called EMSRb is also used for determining the booking limits. As per the EMSRb methodology, the ratio of fares is calculated in a slightly different manner. As per the EMSRa methodology, the ratio between fare class-2 and fare class-3 is simply the ratio between the two fares ($800/$900). As per the EMSRb methodology, the ratio is calculated as the fare of the lower-fare class divided by the expected fare of all higher classes. If one considers fare class-2 and fare class-3, then the expected fare of all higher classes is calculated as follows:

- Expected fare of all higher classes (class-3 and class-4)
    - Which is calculated as follows
        - Consider Fare of class-4 → F4, Fare of class-3 → F3
        - Consider Expected demand of class-4 → D4, Expected demand of class-3 → D3
    - Expected fare of all higher classes = (F4*D4 + F3*D3)/(D3 + D4)
- Hence, based on the numbers in Table 5.4, the expected fare of class-3 and class-4 together will be (1000*17.3 + 900*45.1)/(17.3 + 45.1) = 927.7
- Hence, the ratio to be used for fare class-2 and fare class-3 will be 800/927.7 = 0.86. As per EMSRa methodology, the ratio would have been 0.89 ($800/$900).
- Hence, one needs to find at 86% confidence, what the demand will be. The following function in MS-EXCEL (NORMINV(1-0.86, 62.4, 11.36) = 50.12) can be used.
- It can be seen that the EMSRb suggests a relatively higher booking level for the higher fare class

Both these approaches of price optimisation take into account two factors. The first is the uncertainty in forecasting the demand for a particular fare class. This uncertainty is represented by the standard deviation. Higher the standard deviation, more is the uncertainty. The next factor is, given an amount of standard deviation how many extra seats should we reserve for a particular class.

As pointed out by Berry C Smith, John F Leimkuhler, and Ross M Darrow in their paper titled *Yield Management at American Airlines* (published in 1992), American Airlines quantified the benefit of revenue management systems at $1.4 billion for the first three years and expected an annual revenue contribution of over $500 million in the future.

The hotel industry shares a lot of characteristics with the airline industry. Similar to an airline seat, a hotel room is also a perishable commodity which is impossible to store (one cannot store a room night). Similar to airlines it is possible to have various fare classes. A hotel room can be sold at various prices based on when the sale is made and the terms and conditions of the sale. For example, a booking made one month in advance with a non-refundable clause attached to it will sell at a very low rate. The same room booked one week in advance with a refundable clause will be sold at a relatively higher price.

Similar to airlines, the commitment to book a room at a particular price has to be made in advance before the hotel is aware of the full demand. For example, on the 20th of January if a leisure traveller inquires about availability of a room for 3rd March and wants to make a booking, then the hotel has to accept or decline the request. It may be the case that the last available room is booked for the leisure traveller at a discounted rate on 20th January. On 25th February, a request might come from a business traveller and the hotel has no option but to forgo the higher revenue it could have made on the same room.

Hence, the same principle of expected marginal revenue maximisation can also be used to allocate hotel room inventory to various fare classes. Typically the fare classes in hotels involve the following:

- Leisure travellers with no refund
- Leisure travellers with refund
- Business travellers
- Corporate bulk bookings

## 5.9 Industry Example: Pricing for Demand Management (Utilities Pricing)

The following case study on utility pricing is based on a University of Michigan report titled *Dynamic Pricing Tariffs for DTE's Residential Electricity Customers* by Arie Jongejan et al. and a paper by Ahmad Faruqui and Stephen George titled *Quantifying Customer Response to Dynamic Pricing*.

Managing demand and supply of electricity is very critical because electricity has to be generated and delivered at the same moment that it is consumed. In other words, it cannot be stored. Hence, supply always has to be equated with demand. Daily electricity consumption experiences a peak during the working hours and a trough during the late hours (11 pm to 6 am). Electricity companies need to manage this fluctuating demand by altering the amount of power generated during different times of the day. Over and above the daily peaks electricity demand also exhibits a critical peak period during the year when consumption is at the highest. The critical peak periods are the months of extreme summer or winter, when most consumers run air conditioners or heaters. Satisfying the yearly critical peak period becomes even more challenging for utility companies.

In order to serve such a fluctuating demand, electricity companies need to maintain reserve capacity. However, high reserve capacity in turn implies higher cost of operation and lower profits. In the report titled *Power of Five Percent* by Ahmad Faruqui of the Brattle Group, it is estimated that a 5% reduction in US peak demand for electricity would result in $35 billion of savings over 20 years. Dynamic pricing is used for shifting demand from the peak period to the non-peak periods. However, implementing dynamic pricing, based on time of usage needs additional investments in technology on the part of the utility companies.

Figure 5.3 depicts a sample pricing scheme based on the time of the day. The pricing scheme charges a higher price for the peak periods and a lower price for non-peak periods. In addition, the pricing scheme is different for the summer months of April to June when power consumption is at its peak.

| | | | | |
|---|---|---|---|---|
| Monday to Friday | 7 am–10 am Low Price | 10 am–8 pm High Price | 8 pm–11pm Medium Price | 11 pm–7 am Low Price |
| Saturday and Sunday | Low Price | | | |

**Pricing Between July and March**

| | | | | |
|---|---|---|---|---|
| Monday to Friday | 7 am–10 am Medium Price | 10 am–8 pm Very High Price | 8 pm–11 pm High Price | 11 pm–7 am Medium Price |
| Saturday and Sunday | 7 am–10 am Medium Price | 10 am–11 pm High Price | | 11 pm–7 am Medium Price |

**Pricing Between April and June**

**Figure 5.3** Dynamic Pricing Scheme for Electricity Pricing

Having decided the pricing structure, the next step involves determining the right price for each of these periods so that the electricity company is able to match demand and supply. For this purpose, one needs to estimate the demand curve for various periods. The paper titled *Quantifying Customer Response to Dynamic Pricing* by Ahmad Faruqui and Stephen George provides a framework for estimating the demand curve for electricity consumption. In order to derive the demand curve the authors used a price testing framework, wherein three different pricing frameworks were tested:

- **Time of usage:** As per this pricing structure, the price during peak period was 70% higher than the standard rate and about twice of the off-peak period
- **Fixed critical peak period price:** This structure had a fixed critical peak period and a day-ahead notification before the critical peak period pricing kicks in. For example, the critical peak period would always be from 10am to 8 pm.
- **Variable critical peak period price:** This structure had a variable critical peak period and a day-ahead notification before the critical peak period pricing kicks in. It also involved an option of having energy saving and monitoring technologies like smart thermostat installed free of cost.
- A control group that stayed at the standard rate

The price levels for each of the schemes were varied to obtain the demand at various price points. The results were used to create the demand curve. The demand curve was used to estimate the demand for electricity for a particular period, given a particular pricing. Along with price, other factors like income, size of household, housing type, presence of central air-conditioning, use of electric cooking, etc. were used to estimate demand for electricity.

The University of Michigan report quantified the savings in peak-period demand using dynamic pricing and enabling technologies like smart thermostats and notification technologies. The report found that time of usage and critical peak period (e.g., summer months) based dynamic pricing could reduce peak period demand by 17%. If enabling technologies like smart thermostats are provided to the customers, the reduction could be as much as 36%. However, the report also pointed out that the cost of enabling technologies may outweigh the higher reduction in peak period demand.

## 5.10 Industry Example: Risk-based Pricing (Credit Card Pricing)

In the consumer financial services industry, dynamic pricing takes the form of either risk-based or relationship-based pricing. Risk-based pricing is driven by the fact that the financial institution is expected to incur higher credit loss on the risky segment and hence, needs to earn higher interest or fees to offset that loss. As described earlier, risk-based pricing is adopted both at the acquisition phase and during the ongoing relationship phase. The example described here outlines risk-based pricing for a credit card portfolio. In this case, the risk-based pricing is implemented during the ongoing relationship phase so as to increase price for the riskier segments. In some cases, low-risk customers are offered lower promotional rates on new purchase or on balance transferred from other cards. Some card issuers also lower the overall interest rates for low-risk customers but that is not a very commonly adopted strategy.

The first task for implementing a risk-based pricing involves identifying the risk drivers that can be used to identify a risky segment. A host of customer behaviour needs to be analysed to find out if the same qualifies as a risky behaviour. To illustrate the point, a segment of the customer base is considered, which had more than one bounced cheque in the last six months. If this cohort of customers are identified and tracked for a particular period (say six months or one year) and the loss data on this segment is measured, then it can be ascertained whether this segment produces loss rate higher than the portfolio average. If this segment demonstrates a loss rate higher than the portfolio, then it will qualify for higher pricing (sometimes also called punitive pricing). Similar analysis needs to be performed on historical data to identify all customer behaviours (also called triggers) which indicate a higher than portfolio average loss rates. Table 5.5 illustrates the above idea. In this case, three triggers have been selected because a portfolio analysis on historical data points that these customer behaviours result in more than average loss rates.

The APR or annual percentage rate indicates the interest rate that is charged for customers who revolve on their credit cards (that is, who pay their bills partially). The cost of funds (which is an annual percentage) indicates the interest rate that the credit cards business has to pay in order to fund the receivables. In this case, the revolving receivable is calculated as the total receivable multiplied by the revolve ratio. Revolve ratio has been defined as the receivable of all the revolvers (in the particular segment) divided by the entire receivable of the segment. It is important to note that there are a few similar but not exactly identical definitions of revolve ratio. As only revolvers pay interest to the credit card company, the interest earned is calculated as revolving receivables multiplied by the APR and divided by 12 (to account for the monthly interest calculation). The net credit loss indicates the percentage of the receivable that finally gets written off, and this is also given as an annual percentage.

Table 5.5 indicates that the bank is able to generate higher interest margins from the riskier segments but it gets offset because of the higher credit loss that it has to bear for this segment. Hence, it makes sense to charge a higher interest from these customers so as to offset the higher loss rates. Therefore, the APR for these group should be higher than the average portfolio APR of 22%. The additional interest income is expected to

**Table 5.5** Risk Based Pricing for Credit Cards

| Profit and Loss Items | Overall Portfolio | Behavioural Characteristics: Twice or More Number of Times Overlimit in Last Six Months | One or More Cheque Bounce in the Last One Year | Once 60 Day Past Due in the Last Six Months |
|---|---|---|---|---|
| Number of accounts | 327,123 | 31,534 | 27,789 | 24,283 |
| Average net receivable (monthly) | $123,500,000 | $14,820,000 | $11,115,000 | $17,290,000 |
| Receivable per account (Average net receivable/Number of accounts) | $378 | $470 | $400 | $712 |
| Revolving receivable as % of total receivable (Revolving balance/ Average net receivables) also called revolve rate | 34% | 42% | 45% | 50% |
| Revolving receivable | $41,990,000 | $6,224,400 | $5,001,750 | $8,645,000 |
| Annual percentage rate (APR) | 22% | 22% | 22% | 22% |
| Interest earned (Annual percentage rate* Revolving receivables)/12 | $769,817 | $114,114 | $91,699 | $158,492 |
| Annual yield (Interest earned/Average net receivables)* 12 Can also be calculated as APR* Revolving balance as percent of total receivables | 7.5% | 9.2% | 9.9% | 11.0% |
| Fees earned | $152,169 | $25,868 | $19,782 | $23,852 |
| Cost of funds (Annualized rate) | 3% | 3% | 3% | 3% |
| Cost of funds (Average net receivables* Cost of funds rate)/12 | $308,750 | $37,050 | $27,788 | $43,225 |
| Interest margin = Interest earned – Cost of funds | $461,067 | $77,064 | $63,911 | $115,267 |
| Net credit loss as % of Receivable (Annualized NCL Percent) | 3.00% | 6.00% | 8.00% | 12.00% |
| Net credit loss (NCL Percent* Average net receivables)/12 | $308,750 | $74,100 | $74,100 | $172,900 |
| Net credit margin = Interest earned – Cost of funds – Credit loss | $152,317 | $2,964 | $(10,189) | $(57,633) |
| Net revenue = Interest earned + Fees earned – Cost of funds – Credit loss | $304,486 | $28,832 | $9,593 | $(33,781) |
| Interest margin as % of receivable (Interest margin/Average net receivables) | 0.37% | 0.52% | 0.58% | 0.67% |
| Net credit margin as % of receivable (Net credit margin/Average net receivables) | 0.123% | 0.020% | –0.092% | –0.333% |
| Net revenue as % of receivable (Net revenue/Average net receivables) | 0.247% | 0.195% | 0.086% | –0.195% |

offset the incremental loss and the bank is expected to generate the same net credit margin (on these risky segments) as the rest of the portfolio. To determine the price (annual percentage rate) for a particular segment, one needs the following inputs:

- Expected revolve rate
- Cost of fund
- Expected loss rate

The expected margin is calculated as follows:

- Yield = Annual Percentage Rate * Expected Revolve Rate
- Net Interest Margin = Yield – Cost of Fund
- Net Credit Margin = Net Interest Margin – Loss Rate

The detailed methodology for calculating net revenue has been outlined in Table 5.5. The price which produces the threshold expected margin is set as the price for the particular segment. If the APR of the segment, with one bounced cheque is increased from 22% to 27%, then the net revenue as percentage of receivable, is expected to increase from 0.086% to 0.274%. Similarly for the segment, which has been once 60 days past due, if the APR is increased from 22% to 33%, then the net revenue as percentage of receivable, is expected to increase from –0.195% to 0.263%.

An interesting point to consider is the resultant change in customer behaviour due to the above pricing action. It is intuitive to expect that such a punitive pricing action may result in the following:

- **Account attrition:** Some customers may not consider the pricing action as favourable and hence decide to leave the bank and seek credit elsewhere
- **Reduction in balance:** Some dissatisfied customers may spend less on the particular credit card and may either limit spending or spend more on competition cards
- **Increase in credit loss:** Punitive pricing may increase the debt burden for some customers and accelerate default. It will also increase the outstanding balance (which might include earlier interest) for defaulting customers, thereby increasing the loss as a percentage of receivables.

Thus it can be seen that the change in customer behaviour may erode some of the expected upside of the differential pricing. However, in spite of such erosion in margin, the new margin on the risky segment is expected to be higher than what the bank used to make on these segments earlier.

It is certain that all of the above downsides will exist for any punitive pricing but it is not possible to estimate each of them beforehand. Hence, the bank needs to set up a control group to estimate the impact of these changes. To set up a control group, a certain random sample of the segment (say 10% of the cheque bounced segment) is kept at the original APR and the rest (90%) is charged the higher APR. Then a comparison of the control group with the treatment group will provide an estimate of the possible changes in customer behaviour. For detailed methodologies on setting up control groups, the interested reader may refer to the section, on "Campaign Management" of Chapter 8, "Analytics Ecosystem".

At this point, it is important to consider some of the regulatory aspects relating to dynamic pricing in the credit card industry. The dynamic pricing methodology discussed above was widely used by most card issuers in the United States; however, recently (early 2011) the US government implemented the CARD Act which eliminated most of the drivers that were used for dynamic pricing. Earlier multiple risk drivers or triggers were used for dynamic pricing. Some of the common triggers were "cheque bounce", "late payment", "30 days past due", "60 days past due" and "delinquency with other lenders as reported in credit bureau". The credit card issuers did not provide any advance notice to customers before increasing interest rates. The CARD act mandated that credit card issuers can only reprice customers if they do not pay for 60 days or more. All other risk drivers or triggers were deemed too harsh and were excluded from the permissible set of risk triggers. In addition, credit card issuers were mandated to provide 45 days of advance notice before increasing interest rates. The requirements of the CARD act limited the scope of credit card dynamic pricing in the United States. Other regulators across the globe may also adopt a similar view with regards to dynamic pricing.

SIX

# Credit Bureau

## 6.1 Introduction

The sale of most products and services involve credit extension to the customer. This is particularly true for the financial services industry but assumes importance in many other industries including telecom, utility, retail, consumer durables, and health care. Many of these industries are also vulnerable to identity and transaction fraud. Effective information sharing between companies within and across industries have evolved as an effective mechanism for ascertaining credit eligibility and minimising the incidence of fraud in these industries. Credit bureaus and credit registries have emerged as the chief information aggregators for achieving seamless information exchange for these purposes. Though these information aggregators have historically focused on the financial services industry, the scope and purview of their operations have been extended over time to cater to other industries as well.

A credit bureau or a credit registry is the repository of credit information for the entire economy; all credit grantors by regulation must submit information about their borrowers to the credit bureau or credit registry. A credit registry is a credit information collection and dissemination agency owned and operated by the government and hence, is a non-profit entity, whereas credit bureaus are mostly privately owned companies. To explore the critical value of credit information, the first step involves distinguishing between negative and positive credit information.

Negative information includes only history of past default or derogatory information like bankruptcy, litigation, etc. In case of credit bureaus which collect only negative information, lenders submit information of defaulted loans or credit lines only and not of loans or credit lines where default has not occurred. Even if a consumer has multiple loans or credit lines with a lender and defaults on only one of them, the lender will still submit the information of the defaulted loan only.

The value of negative information alone is quite limited because borrowers are "punished" for their negative actions but are not "rewarded" for their positive actions. Positive information credit bureaus capture information on all credit that has been granted by a lender, irrespective of the mode of payment by the consumer. A positive credit bureau provides a richer set of information for credit decision making, both for granting new credit and managing existing credit.

Credit bureaus have become the most important data source for many of the industries described above. The current chapter provides an overview of credit bureau data and illustrates how the same can be utilised for building strategies for optimising profitability. Most of the discussions in this chapter are in context of the financial services industry, which is the biggest user of credit bureau information; however, the concepts can be utilised in other industries as well.

The chapter starts with an illustration of the role of a credit bureau in enhancing access to credit in the economy. This is followed by a section on the historical evolution of bureaus and the current state of credit bureaus around the globe. Next, the credit bureau data sources and the data structure of the bureau are discussed. A section is dedicated to the explanation of the common credit bureau products such as credit score, credit characteristics, etc. The chapter concludes with an explanation of how credit bureau information can be used as an enabler in formulating key business strategies across the customer life cycle.

## 6.2 Role of a Credit Bureau in the Economy

A credit bureau helps the economy in increasing access to credit, particularly for individuals and small businesses. It also helps in enhancing the quality of credit granted by lenders, thereby reducing the level of credit loss in the economy. These two drivers help in creating a strong and broad-based financial system.

### 6.2.1 Addressing Moral Hazard

In the credit market, the lender extends credit immediately to the borrower but has to wait for a period of time to get back the principal and the interest. This exposes the lenders to the problem of moral hazard, whereby the borrower has an incentive not to pay back. To address this problem, the lender takes recourse to penalties to enforce borrower discipline. The legal system in the country acts as another vehicle for enforcing discipline among borrowers. The credit bureau acts as an additional mechanism for addressing the problem of moral hazard, whereby the borrower knows that any negative behaviour will be reported to the credit bureau and can be used in future against the borrower if he or she applies for new credit. Hence, the presence of a credit bureau acts as an incentive for the borrower to pay on time. A negative credit bureau is sufficient in addressing the problem of moral hazard and in forcing borrower discipline. Sharing of positive information, in fact, lessens the efficacy of the credit bureau as a means of enforcing borrower discipline. This is because borrowers with good payment behaviour on multiple (and mostly large loans) may have the tendency to default on smaller loans, assuming that prospective lenders will consider their regular payment of large loans and thus will not put a very high penalty on their default on the smaller loan.

### 6.2.2 Addressing Information Asymmetry

While extending credit, the lender has lesser information about the borrower's paying potential and intention compared to the borrower and hence, tends to adopt a conservative outlook. This leads to more frequent denial of credit to borrowers and high interest rates. This is a big hurdle in increasing access to credit, which in turn impedes economic development. A potential solution to this problem for a lender is to enquire with other lenders about a particular borrower. However such information sharing may be difficult to implement because a lender may not want to share information because of competitive pressure. In addition, information sharing may not be possible in case of an economy which has a huge geographical expanse. A credit bureau serves as the perfect solution for addressing this problem. It provides a lender with objective and reliable information about the risk profile of a potential borrower and allows the lender to arrive at an objective decision for accepting a new borrower and pricing the risk involved in extending credit. Because of this effect, a credit bureau serves as a key lever for increasing access to credit and accelerating economic development.

Information asymmetry also becomes a key hindrance for a central bank to monitor the risk levels and lending disciplines of lenders. Some of the lenders can become very aggressive risk takers and thereby may have very high chances of failure. A credit bureau helps the regulator to objectively monitor the quality of retail assets in the bank's books. In the absence of a credit bureau, the regulator has to take recourse to a costlier audit mechanism to investigate the amount of risk in the bank's book. In some of the emerging markets, credit bureaus and credit registries have been established as a central bank initiative mostly to address such regulatory challenges.

### 6.2.3 Addressing Adverse Selection

Adverse selection is another hurdle which impedes the growth of credit market in any economy. Consumers who are credit hungry have relatively higher risk and hence lenders always tend to charge higher cost of credit (interest and fees) to mitigate the risk. But a higher cost of credit deters the less risky consumer from seeking credit. This forms a vicious cycle, whereby the cost of credit increases to a very high level in the economy. It is also important to note that once a lender has extended credit to a particular consumer then it has no control over the behaviour of the consumer in future. The consumer may take more credit from other lenders and thereby increase his or her risk level from the time when he or she was extended credit by the first lender. As it can be easily seen, the presence of a credit bureau helps in addressing both these problems associated with adverse selection. Credit bureau information provides the lender an objective assessment of the risk profile of a consumer and hence, the lender does not need to charge high costs to every potential borrower. A lender can also monitor the risk level of each existing customer and can change the terms of credit if any consumer shows a significant worsening of his/her risk profile. As it will be discussed later, credit bureau information is important for lenders to judge risk levels while acquiring new customers and for managing the risk level of its existing customers.

## 6.3 Evolution of Credit Bureaus

### 6.3.1 Historical Evolution of Credit Bureaus

Historically, one can trace the first formal institutions of credit information sharing to 17th century Paris where notaries used to share data on debtor's credit worthiness; the source of their information used to be their private archive of contracts. However, as noted by Federico Ferretti in his paper titled *A Historical Primer on Consumer Credit Reporting Systems* these notaries used to function mostly as brokers rather than credit reporting agencies, in the sense that they did not provide their services to lenders. These notaries rather used their information for deal making between parties.

More formal credit reporting agencies evolved in the United States in the second half of the 19th century. These early credit reporting agencies focused on business credit reporting rather than consumer credit reporting. The major driver for credit reporting in those early days was the attempt of managing the risk of selling goods on credit. Till the early 19th century, merchants used to rely on personal ties and on the experience and information of others, for credit assessment. However, with the rapid geographical expansion of trade in the United States, following the establishment of railroads, such first-hand information and experience was no more useful and hence, a more formal mechanism of information collection and sharing became important.

In order to gather credit information, groups of whole sellers used to hire private investigators or travelling salesman for providing data about unknown customers, but the quality and reliability of such data used to be a challenge. On the other hand, bigger international banks had their own agents for collecting credit information. These agents used to provide very high quality information but at very high costs. As noted by Feretti, the inadequacy of both of these methods prompted private entrepreneurs to start a new type of organisation to cater to this need for information. The first credit reporting agency named "The Mercantile Agency" was established in New York in 1841; the company was founded by Lewis Tapan. R. G. Dun, an employee of the Mercantile Agency, became the sole proprietor of the company in 1859 and changed the name to R. G. Dun & Co. Later in 1933, the company merged with another credit reporting company founded by John M. Bradstreet, to form Dun & Bradstreet, Inc. Dun & Bradstreet is still the premier source of credit information in the business to business space, particularly for small, medium, and micro enterprises.

Soon a number of such agencies started coming up. These agencies were able to collect and dispense information over a wide territory at an affordable cost. To do so they turned information into a commodity which they could sell to anyone willing to pay a price. In order to have wide territorial coverage, these agencies started having networks of branches across the country. As pointed out by Norris in the paper *Development of Credit Reporting in the 19th Century (1978)*, it is interesting to note that the information provided by these agencies were rarely financial information; creditors were more interested in the borrower's character which included character traits like honour, honesty, punctuality, experiences, vices (like drinking and gambling), etc. Due to content of the information shared and the manner of their collection and dissemination, credit reporting agencies started attracting a number of law suits for defamation. In those early days, the credit reporting agencies argued that the information shared between the credit reporting agency and the buyer of that information is confidential and hence, the person being reported on should not have any access to it. The counter argument to this was the fact that the information supplied by the credit reporting agency was available to a large number of subscribers and hence, is not really confidential. Following these lawsuits, credit reporting agencies started focusing on quality and accuracy of their information to avoid legal charges. As discussed later in this chapter, some of these early challenges for the industry also became key building blocks of the regulations that govern the industry in various markets, at present.

Consumer credit reporting which also started in the United States is a much more recent phenomena compared to business credit reporting. In the United States, retailers were the pioneers in expanding consumer credit; they used to charge a credit price which was higher than the cash price and the differential was the interest cost. As per Hunt (2005), as indentified in his paper *A Century of Consumer Reporting in America,* most of these retailers were limited to a particular city and hence, the initial consumer credit agencies developed as local non-profit associations or cooperatives, established by these community retailers. Hundreds of such small cooperatives emerged across the country. These cooperatives restricted their data only to negative or derogatory information. With the expansion of some of the larger retailers across the country and with increase in the volume of consumer credit it became imperative to share consumer credit information across the country. The National Federation of Retail Credit Agencies was formed in 1906 as a not-for-profit organisation to share information between the cooperative agencies. Towards the end of the 1920s, the consumer credit market expanded further with banks and finance companies participating more aggressively in the consumer credit market. At the same time, technologies were beginning to emerge which made it feasible to operate a consumer credit agency at a national scale. Another driver which propelled the creation of national credit reporting agencies was the emergence of the credit card industry. Credit cards made lenders realise the critical value of credit information, particularly for pre-screening, whereby lenders were interested in knowing certain characteristics of potential customers. Alongside these market developments, two key regulations, namely, the Fair Credit Reporting Act of 1971 and the Equal Credit Opportunity Act of 1974 paved the way for the consolidation of the consumer reporting agencies in the United States. Finally, three principal credit reporting agencies, namely, Experian, Equifax and TransUnion emerged in the United States. The development of credit reporting agencies in markets outside the United States followed at a slower pace. Most of the Western European countries developed along similar lines as the United States, though the credit reporting business in these countries are regulated to a larger extent by the government as compared to the United States. The development of credit bureaus in the Asian and African markets is a very recent phenomenon. In most of these markets, the credit bureau is established by the central bank of the country either directly or through private operators. The Central Banks in these countries have two primary motives for creating credit bureaus; the first is to increase access to credit, because most of these markets have a significant population, which is not adequately served by the commercial banks. The second is to help banks in reducing the level of non-performing assets and to monitor their performance and measure their risk levels.

## 6.3.2 Credit Bureaus in Asia Pacific

Most Asia Pacific markets have a single credit bureau, usually controlled by the government. However as markets mature, the credit bureaus become "for profit" organisations. In addition, markets usually experience the introduction of more than one credit bureaus, thereby fostering competition. Increased competition in turn propels the bureaus in providing better service, advanced products, and accurate data. In highly matured markets, credit bureau information is used for the purposes of marketing as well as risk management. The use of credit bureau information for marketing not only hinges upon a rich credit bureau from an information perspective but also a set of legislation and monitoring which can handle the complexities involved in allowing lenders to use the credit bureau information for marketing purposes. In most Asia Pacific markets, the regulation allows the use of credit bureau data only for credit granting. In some of the Asia Pacific markets, specialised microfinance bureaus have come up to cater to the need of the microfinance sector. Himark, for example, is setting up a microfinance bureau in India.

Table 6.1 collated from the work of Dr Rita Chakravarti and Beng-HaiChea titled *The Evolution of Credit Bureaus in Asia-Pacific*, published in 2005 outlines, the maturity of credit bureaus across the Asia Pacific region.

### 6.3.3 Credit Bureaus in North America

The credit bureau market in North America is the most evolved in terms of richness of data and span of credit bureau solutions that are available. The United States has three bureaus: Experian, Equifax, and TransUnion, while in Canada, currently, TransUnion and Equifax are the major players. Bureaus in North America aggregate information across a wide variety of sources including lenders, telecom companies, utilities, retail, government sources, etc. The bureaus also serve a wide variety of industries beyond financial services.

### 6.3.4 Credit Bureaus in Europe

The current section on the state of credit bureaus in Europe has been adopted from the work of Nicola Jentzsch and Amparo San José Rientra titled *Information Sharing and its Implications for Consumer Credit Markets: United States vs. Europe*, published in 2003, and from the report titled *The European Information Landscape—An Analysis of a Survey of Credit Bureaus in Europe* by Marc Rothemund and Maria Gerhardt, published in 2011.

The European countries have a more conservative culture to credit and stricter regulations around data sharing as compared to the United States. In western Europe, the United Kingdom closely resembles the United States in terms of regulation and the purview of operations of credit bureaus. France, on the other hand, has been most reluctant in opening its markets to private credit reporting companies. In fact, France only allows the collection of negative credit information, which is controlled by the central bank. The key markets in Europe that have a positive credit bureau include the United Kingdom, Germany, Netherlands, Italy, and Spain. Belgium, which used to have only a negative bureau is moving towards a full positive credit bureau. As pointed out by Nicola Jentzsch and Amparo San José Rientra, credit bureaus in Europe are mostly of the following types:

- State-owned agency for information aggregation and sharing
- An agency formed as a consortium of credit providers
- Private company owned by financial institutions
- Private company not owned by financial institutions

**Table 6.1** Overview of Credit Bureaus in Asia Pacific

| Country | Name of Credit Bureau(s) | Maturity of Credit Bureau |
|---|---|---|
| Australia | Baycorp advantage D & B Australia | The bureaus have limited positive information, particularly because of regulatory hurdles. Absence of a common ID is also a key limitation |
| India | Credit Information Bureau of India Limited (CIBIL). D & B and TransUnion are the major provider of technology and analytics to CIBIL. In addition new players like Experian and Equifax are planning to enter the Indian market | The reserve bank of India has granted licenses for new bureaus to start operation however at the current point in time CBIL is the only bureau. The bureau has both positive and negative information and two generic bureau scores. However the quality and frequency of credit reporting from the nationalised banks remain a challenge particularly because of the large and diverse geographical expanse |
| China | State Credit Bureau under the aegis of the people's Bank of China | Contains both negative and positive information including utility bills. However the geographical coverage of the bureau is limited mostly to big cities |
| Hong Kong | TransUnion information services | Currently has both positive and negative information (started as a negative information only bureau). The first bureau score was launched with negative data only. Currently there is a bureau score with both positive and negative information |
| Philippines | No credit bureau exists | Negative lists exists in the country. The central bank is in the process of creating a framework for a positive and negative bureau |
| Thailand | National Credit Bureau (NCB) | Both positive and negative information exists along with a generic bureau score |

(*Continued*)

**Table 6.1** Overview of Credit Bureaus in Asia Pacific (*Continued*)

| Country | Name of Credit Bureau(s) | Maturity of Credit Bureau |
|---|---|---|
| Indonesia | No credit bureau exists. The country has two key negative information sources, the debtor information system and the credit card association negative information list | |
| Singapore | Credit Bureau Singapore (CBS), Credit scan (only negative list) | Bureau contains both positive and negative information and a generic credit score exists |
| Malaysia | Consumer credit bureau under the aegis of the central bank. Commercial bureau operated by D & B | Contains both negative and positive information. However no credit score exists in the country due to regulatory limitations |
| South Korea | Korea Information Service (KIS), Korea Credit Bureau (KCB) | Both positive and negative information exists. The risk management standards in the country became much stricter after the financial crisis of 2003 and the government subsequently has put more restrictions on credit growth. Generic bureau score also exists in the market |
| Japan | Japan Information Centre Corporation (JIC or Zenjoren)<br>Japan Banking Personal Credit Information Centre (or Zenginkyo)<br>Credit Information Centre Corporation (CIC)<br>Central Communication Bureau Corporation (CCB)<br>Tera Net Corporation | The Japan Information Centre Corporation was the first credit bureau in the country. The Credit Information Centre and the Tera Neta Corporation focuses more on credit cards. FICO has a generic score for the Japanese market. FICO and Experian's web based decision systems are also widely used in the Japanese market |
| Taiwan | Joint Credit Information Centre | Both positive and negative information exists, however no generic bureau score exists |

Table 6.2 provides a broad overview of the state of bureaus in key European markets.

**Table 6.2** Overview of Credit Bureaus in Europe

| Country | State of Credit Bureau |
|---|---|
| Austria | Austria has a positive bureau (KSV) which is operated by a consortium of credit providers |
| Belgium | Belgium has two negative bureaus (UPC and NBB) one operated as a state owned agency and the other as a consortium of financial institutions. Lending and leasing institutions contribute to the bureau |
| Denmark | Denmark has a negative bureau (RKI ) which is operated by a consortium of lenders. Lenders and official registries contribute to the bureau. It also has a privately owned positive bureau (Experian) |
| Finland | Finland has a negative bureau (Suomen Asiakastieto Oy) which is owned and operated by the state |
| France | France has a negative bureau which is operated by the central bank. Lenders only contribute to the bureau |
| Germany | Germany has two positive bureaus (Schufa and CEG Credit reform Consumer GmbH) which are owned and operated as a private company owned by the financial institutions |
| Ireland | The Irish credit bureau is a positive credit bureau owned and operated by the financial institutions |
| Italy | Italy has three positive credit bureaus (CRIF, Consorzio per la Tuteladel Credito and Experian Information Services). Only lenders contribute to the bureau |
| Netherlands | Netherlands has a positive bureau (Stichting Bureau Krediet Registratie) which is privately owned. Only lenders contribute to the bureau |
| Portugal | Portugal has a state owned and a privately owned positive bureau |
| Spain | Spain has a state owned and privately owned positive bureau. Experian Bureau de crédito S.A. is the private bureau in Spain |
| Sweden | Sweden has a positive bureau (UCAB) owned by the financial institutions. Along with information from lenders, the bureau contains information from utilities and telecom companies. It also contains information on property owned |
| UK | UK has three privately owned positive bureaus namely Experian, Equifax and Callcredit. In addition to information from lenders, the bureau also contains information from utilities, telecom companies and retailers |

## 6.4 Legal Framework for Credit Bureau Operations

It is important to note that in order to ensure effective functioning of a credit bureau, a legal, and regulatory framework is very essential to balance various competing interest of lenders and borrowers. As per a World Bank and International Finance Corporation (IFC) study, key regulations that govern the functioning of a credit bureau are as follows:

- **Scope of the credit bureau and permissible purpose:** This involves the types of institutions who can participate in a credit bureau. Regulations mostly allow all types of lending institutions, namely, banks, non-banking finance companies, and companies who sell goods on credit (including telecom companies and utilities) to participate in submitting information to a credit bureau. The Fair Credit Reporting Act in the United States is an example of a legislation which outlines the type of institutions who can participate in a credit bureau and the type of information that they can submit. In most countries, there are regulations which enforce mandatory submission of information from all credit grantors. Usually, there are no restrictions on collection of information from public sources like police records, court judgments, bankruptcy filings, etc. The other key regulation that governs the scope of a credit bureau's function involves regulations around permissible purpose, which restricts access to credit bureau information. Permissible purpose has two components: one restricts institutions that can have access to information in the credit bureau and the other restricts the purpose for which an institution (which has permission of accessing the credit bureau information) can access the credit bureau information. Most countries use the principle of reciprocity for defining access to the credit bureau information. The principle of reciprocity entails that an institution which submits data to the bureau can only access data from the bureau. However, in some countries like the United States, a broader set of permissible purpose is allowed. Recruiters, for example, can access the credit report of a potential employee before extending an offer of employment. The other corner stone of permissible purpose involves the purpose for which an institution can access the credit report of an individual. In most cases, the individual needs to provide written consent for an institution to fetch information from the credit bureau. In some countries, a signed application for credit is considered written consent by an individual. Most countries also allow lenders to access credit information of their existing customers who have an open credit relationship with the lender.
- **Limit of the time period for which information is stored and distributed:** Most countries have a time limit for which information can be stored and distributed by a credit bureau. This is particularly true for negative information like default or bankruptcy. In most

countries, any default information which is older than five to seven years is not distributed and the credit bureau has to clean up the record for any past default or bankruptcy which had happened before five to seven years. In some countries, information on only open credit relationships are stored and distributed by the credit bureau; any information on closed accounts is not distributed by the bureau.

- **Data protection and data safety:** Data protection and data safety laws govern information security standards for credit bureaus. In some countries the credit bureau data is not allowed to be shared across the geographical boundary of the country. However, most countries rely more on industry self-regulation for ensuring data safety.
- **Data collection notification:** In most countries, lenders need to obtain written permission from the borrower for sharing the borrower's information with the bureau. Consent is usually obtained while granting credit, and it is valid till the life of the credit facility.
- **Consumer protection:** Consumer protection is another key component of legislation that governs the functioning of a credit bureau. Consumers are allowed to access their own credit reports and can point out inaccuracies and errors in the credit report. Most countries allow consumers to access their credit report free of cost at least once a year. Credit bureaus are required to constitute a non-judicial panel for resolving disputes and discrepancies regarding the credit reports as pointed out by consumers. The other aspect of consumer protection involves adverse action notification in case of refusal of credit. If a lender refuses credit to a potential borrower, or changes credit terms for an existing borrower based on credit bureau information, then the lender is required to provide a justification for the adverse action. Also the lender cannot use information like age, race, gender, etc., for refusing credit or for changing credit terms for an existing customer. The Equal Credit Opportunity Act of the United States is a typical example of this regulation, driving fair credit. Most credit bureaus have multiple credit scores for predicting future events such as default or bankruptcy. Today lenders depend heavily on these scores for credit decision making. All credit scores are required to provide top three to four adverse action reasons which point out the reason why a particular consumer has been awarded a lower score. In most advanced countries, financial institutions must disclose the adverse action reason to customers, in case they decline credit.

## 6.5 Credit Bureau Data Sources

As discussed earlier, both positive and negative credit bureaus capture data from a wide range of sources which must include lenders like banks and finance companies and some public data sources like police records, court judgments, customs records, etc. However, with the evolution of credit bureaus in various markets, the bureaus have tried to tap into a wider array of data sources to increase the richness of their information content. In most countries, banks and finance companies, which come under the regulation of the Central Bank, are legally bound to submit information about the credit performance of their consumers to at least one credit bureau in the country. The central bank also lays down the minimum frequency at which these lenders must submit information to the bureau. In most countries lenders are required o submit information at least once every month. Beyond banks and finance companies, credit bureaus have tried to expand the purview of credit information to other entities which also extend credit. The most common of these entities are retailers who sell their goods at credit and telecom and utility companies which extend their services to consumers on credit. Other than credit and public records data, credit bureaus also need to capture data on different types of frauds. In addition to data from various types of lenders and public records; insurance data provides a rich source of information with respect to frauds. Data on mortgage deeds is also another key data source that many credit bureaus use to identify cases of fraud and for helping users in verifying the correctness of information for either buying or financing mortgages. In some countries, mortgage data is collected by other agencies and users (e.g., lenders or property buyers) overlay that data along with the credit bureau data for decision making. A typical case in point is First American Corporation of the United States which is the largest repository of mortgage data. Public records which form the biggest source of derogatory information include the following key data sources:

- **Courts data:** Data from court records is mostly used to identify cases of suits filed against an individual or a corporate entity, cases of liens on property belonging to an individual or a corporate entity, cases of bankruptcy filing, cases of favourable or unfavourable court judgments
- **Police records data:** Police records data is used for identification of criminal activities reported against an individual

It is very important to note that sometimes public records data is difficult to match with the credit data because of the inadequacy of identifiable personal information provided by the public records. In addition, at an overall level in the entire credit bureau files, public records data tend to be sparsely populated. Hence, in most cases, all derogatory public records information is combined to create a single indicator of derogatory public information.

## 6.6 Data Matching and Merging of Credit Files

A key success criterion of a credit bureau lies in its ability to match information from various data sources and grouping together all information pertaining to a particular consumer. In countries with a unique identification number (like the US social security number) the matching process is relatively easier. However, in these countries also sometimes the unique identification number may be missing from some data source or may be truncated.

In countries like India which lack a common unique identification number, the process of matching data from various sources is a formidable task. Credit bureaus use various matching algorithms for this purpose. Details of the matching algorithm are beyond the scope of this book. However, a broad overview of their use is described in this section.

For data matching a set of search paths are identified and a score is awarded for each search path based on the strength of the match that has been observed. The total score for each path is added to evaluate the strength of the match; if the match is strong enough then the two records are said to have matched.

## *6.6.1 Example of Matching and Merging*

The following example helps in illustrating the above methodology. A particular bureau, for example, can have the following search paths:

- **Path1—name match:** If the name field of an incoming record (from any data source) has a perfect match with the name field of an existing record then a score of 5 is awarded, if there is an imperfect but strong match then a score of 3 is awarded, if there is a loose match then a score of 1 is awarded to the name search path. The definition of strong and loose match is derived by using various text matching algorithms (like fuzzy matching) which are tuned or trained using data specific to a particular country.
- **Path2—address match:** Similar to name, match points are awarded for perfect match, strong match, and loose match. Similar scores are provided for perfect, strong, and loose matches. For example, 7 for perfect, 3 for strong, and 2 for loose.
- **Path3—ID match:** In most Asian countries where a unique and common ID is not available, there are multiple IDs which are used for various purposes like passport number, tax ID, social security ID, etc. A search path is provided for each ID type; in most cases only a perfect match or sometimes strong matches of IDs are considered. The highest points are awarded for ID matches. For example, if there are three IDs in a country, then say a 7 point is awarded for each perfect match of IDs.
- **Path4—telephone number match:** Telephone numbers is another key criteria for matching records; for each perfect match of telephone numbers, points are awarded for the match. For example, if an incoming record has two telephone numbers and the existing record has three telephone numbers, then each telephone number match is awarded 4 points. Table 6.3 illustrates the example:

**Table 6.3** Sample Search Paths for Data Matching

| Path | Field for Matching | Perfect Match | Strong Match | Weak Match |
|---|---|---|---|---|
| 1 | Name | 5 | 3 | 1 |
| 2 | Address | 7 | 3 | 2 |
| 3a | ID1 | 7 | | |
| 3b | ID2 | 7 | | |
| 3c | ID3 | 7 | None | |
| 4 | Telephone | 4 (for each telephone number match) | | |

Hence, in the above example, if an incoming record has the following matches with two existing records:

1. **Record 1**
   - strong name and address match
   - perfect match on at least one of three IDs
   - match for one telephone number
   - incoming record will receive a score of 19 (5 for name match, 3 for address match, 7 for ID match, 4 for telephone number match) to match with record 1
2. **Record 2**
   - strong name match
   - loose match with address
   - perfect matches on two IDs
   - no match for telephone number
   - incoming record will receive a score of 21 (5 for name match, 2 for address match, 14 for ID match, 0 for telephone match) for match with record 2

If this record receives a score of less than 21 for all other existing records in the bureau file, then this record will be matched with record 2, provided the cut-off score for defining a match for that particular credit bureau is lesser than 21. As can be seen from the above illustrative example, the criterion for defining matches in a particular credit bureau has to be customised and derived by studying the sample data pattern in a particular country. The available search paths, the definition of strong vs. loose match, the points awarded for various types of matches are all derived by studying empirical data and the search algorithm for each credit bureau is a proprietary algorithm perfected over time. Similar to matching of incoming records, merging is used for identifying records in the credit bureau file that belong to the same individual consumer and these records are merged while creating a holistic view of the credit profile of an individual consumer.

## 6.7 Credit Bureau Data Structure

Credit bureau data is mostly structured as a relational database wherein specific tables store specific types of information and are linked by a set of unique keys generated by the matching process described earlier.

### 6.7.1 Header Information

The first sets of tables are the ones which house information pertaining to the identification of the individual or the bureau record. These set of information is often termed *"header information"* as they mostly appear in the first section of the credit report. These tables are most critical in the matching and merging process. The information contained in these tables are typically information like name, address, ID information, telephone numbers, etc. When an incoming record hits the credit bureau's information system, the information in the incoming record pertaining to the identification of the individual is matched against the header information to check if that individual already exists in the bureau. If the individual does exist in the credit bureau, then the bureau ID (which is an unique ID generated in the credit bureau data system) is used to match the rest of the information contained in the incoming record with the relevant bureau table. If the individual does not exist then a new record (with a new unique bureau ID) is created in the bureau data system. Similarly, if a lender seeks information about any particular individual then the individual's identity information is matched with the header file to identify the bureau ID pertaining to the individual. Once the bureau ID pertaining to the individual is known, then information from all other bureau tables pertaining to that particular ID is collected together to create a complete information set for the individual.

Though the header files in the bureau are mostly associated with identification of an individual, for some purposes the information contained in the header file is used for decision making. The most common use of header file information involves fraud detection and fraud score calculation. For cases of identity frauds, fraudsters most commonly steal the identity of an unsuspecting victim and use the stolen identity for obtaining loans, credit cards, etc., which they never intend to pay back. To detect such cases of identity frauds the incoming header information (which has been wrongly obtained by the fraudster) is matched with the existing header information. Content of the header information and changes in the header information are used along with other credit bureau information for identifying cases of suspected frauds. Typically fraudsters try to steal identities of individuals with good credit history and hence, header information along with other information in the bureau file is important to point out cases of suspected fraud. Moreover, unexpected pattern and mismatches with the existing credit pattern of the individual can be observed in many cases of suspected frauds. In case where the identity of the individual is stolen, it is referred to as third party fraud. On the other hand, in some cases an individual may never pay after being granted credit, these cases are mostly referred to as first payment default or first party fraud. Here the fraud is committed by the individual in question and there is no case of identity theft. Credit bureau data proves very useful in predicting each of these types of frauds. Most credit bureaus have fraud scores and fraud alerts which can be used by lenders for managing cases of suspected fraud. Though the header information stores the current information, it is possible to re-create the bureau data at any older date and thereby obtain information on changes in the header information.

### 6.7.2 Trades Information

The next set of tables in the bureau data system involve the trades table. The trades table contain each individual credit (e.g., each loan, each credit card, each utility line, etc.) that is present in the bureau. Each of these records in the trade file is termed a trade or a credit facility. Each trade is attached to two unique IDs: one associates the trade with an individual, most cases this is the bureau ID from the header table as discussed earlier; and the second one is an ID that is unique to that trade itself and associates that trade with the history of information for that trade. The set of information pertaining to a particular trade that is stored in the trade table include the following:

- **Open date:** The date on which the trade or the credit facility was opened
- **Close date:** The date on which the trade was closed. For open trades a default value is stored in the close date field to indicate that the trade is in an open status
- **Type of trade:** An indicator which identifies the type of trade (e.g., mortgage loan, home equity line of credit, auto loan, hire purchase, over draft, credit card, personal loan, business loan, etc.)
- Name and type of lender pertaining to the trade
- **Credit limit:** The limit provided for a credit line (e.g., credit card, home equity line of credit, overdraft, etc.) or the sanctioned amount of a loan
- **High credit:** The highest amount of credit ever taken in the life of the particular trade. For credit lines like credit card, this is the maximum balance ever reached in the life of the line. For loans, this is disbursed amount of the loan (which sometimes may be lower than the sanctioned amount of the loan).
- **Current balance:** The current outstanding amount on the trade
- **Last payment amount:** The latest amount that has been paid by the borrower
- **Last payment date:** The date on which the last payment was made

- **Current mode of payment:** Mode of the latest payment; whether the payment was made on time or if it was late, in case it was late the number of days past due. In case no payment was made then the number of days past due reflects the number of days for which the payment is due. This field is also referred to as the current days past due (dpd) status. It is usually zero for loans that are being paid on time.
- **Historical mode of payment:** The mode of payment for past payments. In case no payment was made, then it represents the days past due for the trade. In most cases information up to 24 or 36 months is stored.
- **Derogatory information associated with the trade (if any):** If the trade has any derogatory information like suit filed, write-off, foreclosure, tax lien, collection activity, etc., associated with it
- **Additional trade specific information:** Some bureaus contain additional information for some types of trades like purchase and cash balance for credit cards, collateral value for loans with collateral, etc. However, these additional information are mostly not captured and not used extensively in any bureau product.

## *6.7.3 History Information*

The next set of information relates to history of each trade in the bureau file. While the trade table contains current information about all trades, the trade history table provides historical information for the trade for each month starting from the date when the trade was opened till the current date. Information contained in the trade table is replicated for each month in the history table. While some of the information pertaining to the trade are relatively static in nature, some information like balance and high credit change over time. However, it needs to be noted that information like credit line which is relatively static in nature may also change. Lenders can provide credit line increase on a revolving credit line or a top up on an existing line which will change the credit line. The trade ID in the trade table is used to link the trade table with the trade history table. Commonly the history table contains historical information like:

- Balances
- Past due amount
- Payment
- Mode of payment (also part of trade table)

## *6.7.4 Inquiry Information*

The other set of key information pertains to the inquiries made by various lenders on an individual. At this point it is important to categorise the types of inquires made by lenders. The first are inquiries which are usually called "hard inquiries". Hard inquiries are ones where a prospective lender obtains consent from the prospective borrower for making inquiries at the bureau with respect to application for a new credit facility. The second type is portfolio review inquiries where a lender inquires about the credit health of its existing customers. The third category of inquiries are promotional inquires and pertains to cases where a lender wants to access the bureau to send out offers for new credit to prospective borrowers. These are promotional or marketing offers, and in this case the inquiry is not made with reference to an application of credit by the prospective borrower. The section on use of credit bureau for marketing details this aspect of using the credit bureau for marketing purposes. It is to be noted that only hard inquiries are the ones which can be used in evaluating the credit worthiness of an individual and hence, bureaus need to separate out each of these types of inquiries. Higher number of hard inquiries signifies high credit seeking behaviour which is considered a risky behaviour. For some purposes, discrimination is made among various types of hard inquires. This is performed in order to take into account credit shopping behaviour wherein a consumer normally applies to multiple lenders for high ticket loans like mortgage and auto loans in order to obtain better credit terms but intends to accept the loan from one lender only. Hence, though the data suggests high number of hard inquiries and consequently a high credit seeking behaviour yet in reality the consumer is seeking only one loan and is merely trying to get the best terms by applying for credit with multiple lenders. For each hard inquiry, the bureau usually stores the following information:

- The date of the inquiry
- The type of credit facility for which the inquiry was made
- The lender who has made the inquiry
- The ticket size of the prospective credit facility for which the inquiry was made

The bureau ID is used to match the inquiry information with other bureau information. In most cases, the D-U-N-S number is used as the identification in commercial bureaus. In some cases, particularly for very small businesses, the data from the commercial bureau is matched with the consumer credit data of the owner to obtain a holistic view of the business.

## 6.8 Credit Bureau Products

### *6.8.1 Overview of Credit Report*

The credit report is the most basic and most common credit bureau product; a credit report provides a summary of the credit profile of the individual for whom information has been sought for. As pointed out earlier, any lender who has the consent of a prospective customer can pull the credit report for the prospective customer from the credit bureau; lenders can also pull credit reports of their existing customers. Most countries have a provision for individual customers to pull their own credit reports. A credit report has the following key sections:

- Header section that contains name, address, phone numbers, national identification number, etc.
- Section on credit scores and the reason codes which provides the credit score/s for the individual and the reasons for the credit score being low
- Section on inquiries which has the number and purpose of inquiries made by credit grantors for the particular consumer
- Section on public records, that is, suit filed, tax liens
- Section on the performance of each credit facility that the consumer has in the credit bureau record. The information for each credit facility are as follows:
  - Type of credit facility, and in some cases the type of financial institution that has extended the credit facility
  - The date of opening of the credit facility (and the date of closure for closed ones)
  - The amount of loan or the credit limit of a revolving credit facility like credit card
  - The latest payment date
  - The status of each payment made (if the payment was made on time or whether it was late and if so then by how many days). This is also referred to as the days past due (DPD) status.
  - The amount currently outstanding
  - The amount currently past due in case the customer has not paid in time
  - The payment term (monthly, quarterly)
  - For a closed credit facility, the status at the time of closure (satisfactory, write-off)

In general, the most negative information is provided first in the credit report followed by less negative information. For example, public records section is displayed first before the section that describes mode of payment for each credit facility. Similarly, a credit facility with a write-off or delinquent is displayed before a credit facility that is satisfactory. Figure 6.1 is a sample credit report from Experian (http://www.experian.com/credit_report_basics/pdf/samplecreditreport.pdf).

### 6.8.2 Market Intelligence and Market Overview

Market intelligence and market overview solutions are unique in nature compared to all other bureau solutions, in the sense that these products and solutions provide an aggregate or macro view of credit in the market, whereas most other bureau solutions provide a consumer or individual

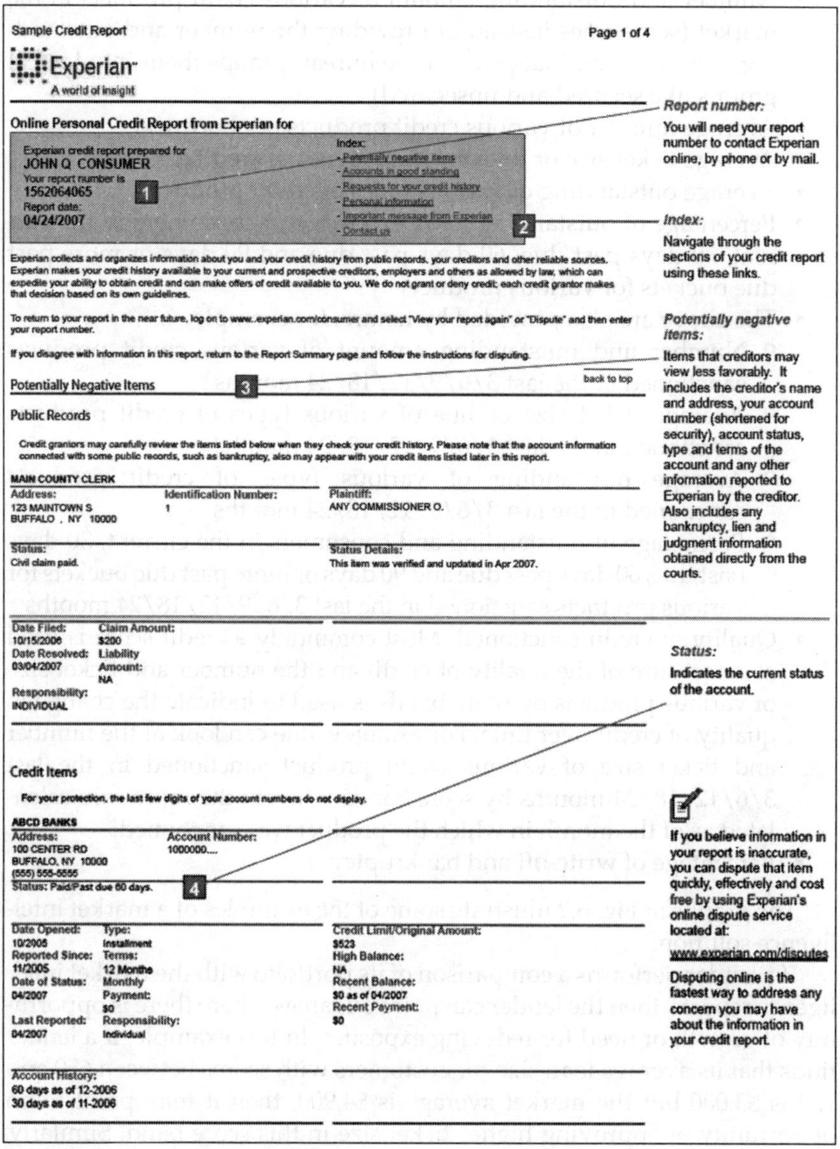

Sample Credit Report

Page 1 of 4

Experian

A world of insight

Online Personal Credit Report from Experian for

Experian credit report prepared for
JOHN Q CONSUMER
Your report number is
1562064065
Report date:
04/24/2007

Index:
- Potentially negative items
- Accounts in good standing
- Requests for your credit history
- Personal information
- Important message from Experian
- Contact us

Experian collects and organizes information about you and your credit history from public records, your creditors and other reliable sources. Experian makes your credit history available to your current and prospective creditors, employers and others as allowed by law, which can expedite your ability to obtain credit and can make offers of credit available to you. We do not grant or deny credit; each credit grantor makes that decision based on its own guidelines.

To return to your report in the near future, log on to www..experian.com/consumer and select "View your report again" or "Dispute" and then enter your report number.

If you disagree with information in this report, return to the Report Summary page and follow the instructions for disputing.

back to top

Potentially Negative Items

Public Records

Credit grantors may carefully review the items listed below when they check your credit history. Please note that the account information connected with some public records, such as bankruptcy, also may appear with your credit items listed later in this report.

MAIN COUNTY CLERK

Address: 123 MAINTOWN S BUFFALO , NY 10000
Identification Number: 1
Plaintiff: ANY COMMISSIONER O.

Status: Civil claim paid.
Status Details: This item was verified and updated in Apr 2007.

Date Filed: 10/15/2006
Claim Amount: $200
Date Resolved: 03/04/2007
Liability Amount: NA
Responsibility: INDIVIDUAL

Credit Items

For your protection, the last few digits of your account numbers do not display.

ABCD BANKS

Address: 100 CENTER RD BUFFALO, NY 10000 (555) 555-5555
Account Number: 1000000....
Status: Paid/Past due 60 days.

Date Opened: 10/2006
Type: Installment
Credit Limit/Original Amount: $523
Reported Since: 11/2005
Terms: 12 Months
High Balance: NA
Date of Status: 04/2007
Monthly Payment: $0
Recent Balance: $0 as of 04/2007
Last Reported: 04/2007
Responsibility: Individual
Recent Payment: $0

Account History:
60 days as of 12-2006
30 days as of 11-2006



**Figure 6.1** Sample Credit Report

level micro view of credit. Market intelligence solutions provide an aggregate view of credit for the entire economy and for various smaller geographical units such as province, regions or metropolitan service areas. These solutions provide either a snapshot view of the market or a view over time or sometimes both. The exact content and structure of such solutions vary across markets and across bureaus. The current section provides a set of examples for illustrative purpose only. Some of the common elements of a market intelligence report include the following:

- Number and outstanding amount of various credit products in the market (sometimes instead of providing the number and outstanding of each individual product the bureau groups them into logical groups like secured and unsecured)
- Average number of various credit products per borrower
- Average ticket size or line of various types of credit products
- Average outstanding of various types of credit products
- Percentage of outstanding and percentage of consumers in the current, 30 days past due, 60 days past due and 90 days or more past due buckets for various products
- The above are also provided by tenure, for example:
  - Number and outstanding amount of various credit products sanctioned in the last 3/6/9/12/18/24 months
  - Average ticket size or line of various types of credit products sanctioned in the last 3/6/9/12/18/24 months
  - Average outstanding of various types of credit products sanctioned in the last 3/6/9/12/18/24 months
  - Percentage of outstanding and consumers in the current, 30 days past due, 60 days past due and 90 days or more past due buckets for various products sanctioned in the last 3/6/9/12/18/24 months
- Quality of credit sanctioned. Most commonly a credit score is used as a measure of the quality of credit and the number and ticket size of various products by score bands is used to indicate the change in quality of credit over time. For example, one can look at the number and ticket size of various credit product sanctioned in the last 3/6/12/18/24 months by score bands wherein the scores are calculated as of the month in which the product was sanctioned.
- Percentage of write-off and bankruptcy

The graphs in Fig. 6.2 illustrate some of the examples of a market intelligence solution.

If a lender performs a comparison of its portfolio with the market intelligence reports, then the lender can point out areas where there is opportunity of growth or need for reducing exposure. In this example, if a lender finds that its average loan size for customers with scores between 650 and 720 is $3,000 but the market average is $4,900, then it may point to an opportunity of approving higher ticket size in this score band. Similarly, if a lender finds that 30% of its portfolio is in the less than 650 score range compared to the market average of 20%, then it makes sense to reduce exposure to this high-risk segment.

### *6.8.3 Credit Bureau Scores*

Credit scores are possibly the most extensively used credit bureau solution after credit reports. A credit score includes all dimensions of credit that are relevant in predicting credit behaviour in future and hence, is the most comprehensive future looking summary of the credit profile of the

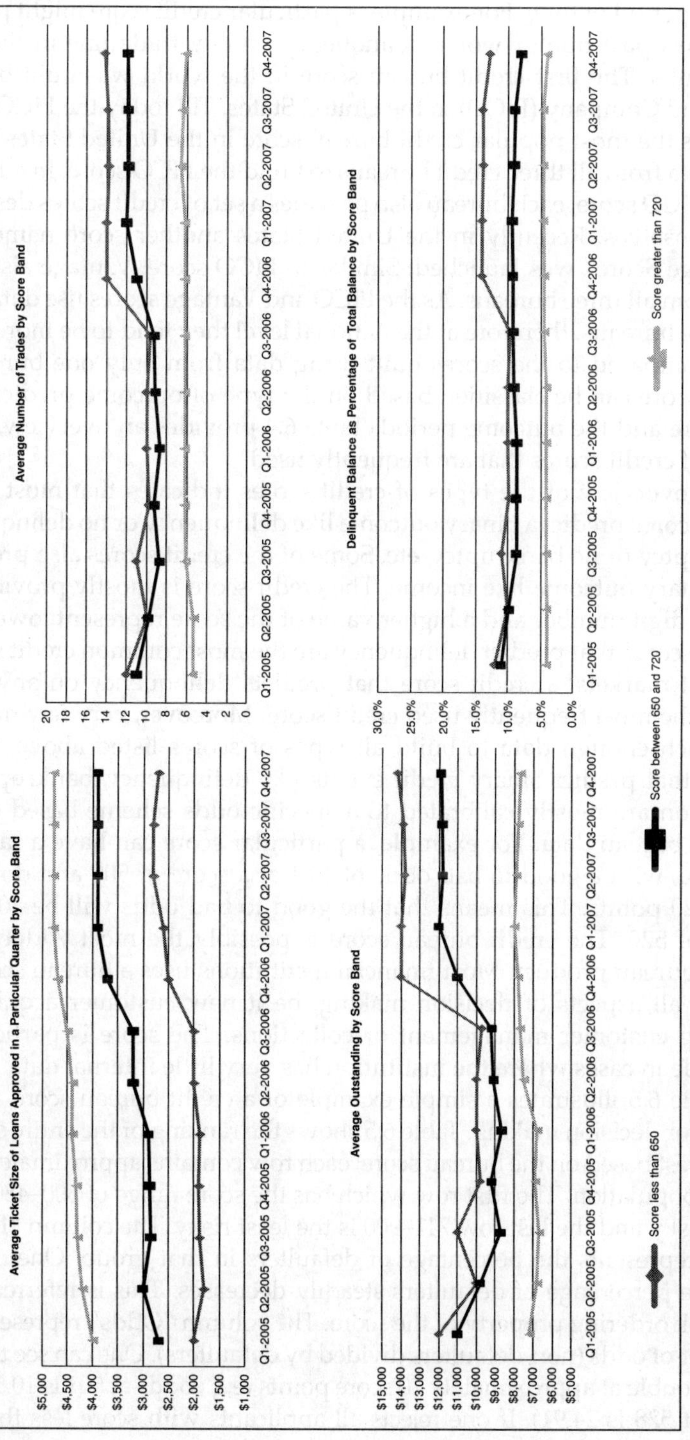


**Figure 6.2** Sample Benchmark Analysis

consumer. A credit score predicts specific future credit behaviour over a certain period of time. For example, a particular credit score might predict a 90 days past due or worse delinquency on any trade line in the next 12 months. The first credit bureau score in the world was built by Fair Isaac and Company (FICO) in the United States. Till today the FICO score remains the most popular credit bureau score in the United States. FICO uses data from all three credit bureaus to build the FICO score. In addition to the FICO score, each bureau also provides a set of credit scores designed by themselves. Recently in the United States another score named the "Vantage Score" was launched. Similar to FICO score, Vantage also uses data from all three bureaus. As the FICO and Vantage scores use data from all three bureaus, therefore at the national level they tend to be more powerful compared to the scores built using data from only one bureau. A credit score can be classified based on the type of outcome predicted by the score and the outcome period. Table 6.4 provides an overview of the types of credit scores that are frequently used.

An overview of the types of credit scores indicates that most of the credit scores predict a binary outcome like delinquency or no delinquency, bankruptcy or no bankruptcy, etc. Some of the credit scores also predict a non-binary outcome like income. The credit score is mostly provided as a three digit number and a higher value of the score represent lower risk. Credit scores that predict delinquency are the most common credit scores. In most markets, a credit score that predicts delinquency on any trade line is the most frequently used credit score. Moreover, very few markets have rich enough data to build all types of scores listed above. Credit scores that predict binary credit events like delinquency, bankruptcy or collection are mostly calibrated to a specific odds scheme based on the overall bureau data. For example, a particular score can have a range of 300–900, with a good to bad odds of 10:1 at a score of 500 and doubling every 20 points. This means that the good to bad odds will be 20:1 at a score of 520. The credit bureau score is possibly the most widely used credit bureau product. Most financial institutions uses a bureau score for almost all aspects of decision making, be it new customer acquisition, existing customer management or collections. The score is particularly valuable in cases where the institution has very little internal data.

Table 6.5 illustrates a simple example of a credit bureau score and its usage for decision making. Table 6.5 shows the ranking of the entire sample of interest based on the bureau score; each row contains approximately 10% of the population. The first row which has the score range of 300–480 is the most risky and the last row 711–900 is the least risky. The column "Default Rate" represents the percentage of defaulters in that group. One can see that the percentage of defaulters steadily decreases. This is referred to as the rank ordering property of the score. The column "Odds" represents the number of odds (non-defaulters divided by defaulters). One can see that the odds double at approximately 20 score points (e.g., odds at 501 is 10.5 while odds at 528 is 24.91). If one rejects all applicants with score less than 533

**Table 6.4** Common Types of Credit Bureau Scores

| Outcome Type | Outcome Description | Outcome Period |
|---|---|---|
| Delinquency | Delinquency (60 days past due or worse or 90 days past due or worse) on any trade line | 12 or 24 months |
| | Delinquency (60 days past due or worse or 90 days past due or worse) on a specific type of trade (like credit card, consumer loan, mortgage etc.) | |
| | Delinquency (60 days past due or worse or 90 days past due or worse) on a trades which have been opened in the last 3/6/12 months | |
| | Delinquency (60 days past due or worse or 90 days past due or worse) on a mature trade lines | |
| Bankruptcy | The consumer going bankrupt | 12 or 24 months |
| Insurance loss | Event of insurance loss | 12 to 36 months |
| Collection and recovery | Delinquent consumers paying back more than a specified amount of money | 3 or 6 months |
| | Delinquent consumers becoming current (non-delinquent) | |
| | Dollar amount that the delinquent consumer is expected to pay back | |
| | Consumers delinquent on a specific type of trade paying back more than a specified amount of money | |
| | Consumers delinquent on a specific type of trade becoming current (non-delinquent) | |
| | Dollar amount that the delinquent consumer (with delinquency in a specific type of trade) is expected to pay back | |
| Identity fraud | New customer application that has been received is a case of identity theft | Immediate |
| Estimated income | Estimated income of the consumer (the score mostly predicts income in bands rather than the exact income) | Immediate |
| Ability of taking on additional debt | Uses income prediction and current debt to predict consumer's ability of taking on more debt | Immediate |
| Response to a particular type of marketing offer | Identify credit worthy consumers most likely to respond to a particular type of offer | Immediate |
| Prospect identification models | Identify credit worthy consumers who are looking for products like home loan or auto loan | Immediate |

**Table 6.5** Sample Risk Rank Ordering for a Credit Bureau Score

| Bureau Score Range | Average Score | Number of Accounts | Non Defaults | Defulats | Defualt Rate | Percentage of Non-defaults | Percentage of Defaults | Cumulative Percentage of Defaults | Cumulative Percentage of Non-defaults | Odds (Number of Non-default Divided by Number of Defaults | Ln (Odds) |
|---|---|---|---|---|---|---|---|---|---|---|---|
| 300-480 | 423 | 12227 | 9660 | 2567 | 21.0% | 8.1% | 39.9% | 39.9% | 8.1% | 3.76 | 1.33 |
| 481-521 | 507 | 12386 | 11346 | 1040 | 8.4% | 9.5% | 16.2% | 56.1% | 17.6% | 10.91 | 2.39 |
| 522-533 | 528 | 12481 | 11582 | 899 | 7.2% | 9.7% | 14.0% | 70.0% | 27.3% | 12.88 | 2.56 |
| 534-545 | 540 | 12522 | 11984 | 538 | 4.3% | 10.0% | 8.4% | 78.4% | 37.4% | 22.28 | 3.10 |
| 545-561 | 553 | 12586 | 12183 | 403 | 3.2% | 10.2% | 6.3% | 84.7% | 47.6% | 30.23 | 3.41 |
| 562-575 | 568 | 12594 | 12254 | 340 | 2.7% | 10.3% | 5.3% | 89.9% | 57.9% | 36.04 | 3.58 |
| 576-593 | 582 | 12632 | 12354 | 278 | 2.2% | 10.4% | 4.3% | 94.3% | 68.2% | 44.44 | 3.79 |
| 594-640 | 610 | 12633 | 12469 | 164 | 1.3% | 10.5% | 2.5% | 96.8% | 78.7% | 76.03 | 4.33 |
| 641-710 | 682 | 12798 | 12644 | 154 | 1.2% | 10.6% | 2.4% | 99.2% | 89.3% | 82.10 | 4.41 |
| 711-900 | 724 | 12819 | 12768 | 51 | 0.4% | 10.7% | 0.8% | 100.0% | 100.0% | 250.35 | 5.52 |

(the first three shaded rows) then one would be able to avoid 70% potential defaults but will have to sacrifice 27.7% of non-defaulters (good applicants). The first three rows (30% of population) accounts for 70% of the defaults, this is referred to as the capture rate. The interested reader could refer to the section on binary choice model evaluation in Chapter 7, "Quantitative Methods" for details on evaluation of a score. Section 6.9 provides additional details on usage of credit bureau score for decision making.

### *6.8.4 Credit Characteristics*

Credit characteristics are a set of variables which summarise the credit information that is available for a consumer at the credit bureau. Typically a set of 500–2000 credit characteristics are derived from credit bureau information and these form inputs to credit scores and many other credit bureau products. In most markets, credit bureaus also provide these credit characteristics to lenders for using them into customised models, segmentation criteria, risk management strategies and in some cases, marketing strategies.

For creating credit characteristics the credit data is summarised and measured in various ways to create information that look at various aspects of the credit profile of an individual. Some of the common ways of measuring and aggregating credit data involve:

- Counts of various types of trades; for example, number of trades of various types, number of trades that are delinquent, not delinquent, ever delinquent, number of various types of inquiries
- Time since the occurrence of certain key credit event for the individual, for example, time since last delinquency, time since the opening of the most recent trade
- Aggregation of various amounts, for example, total balance, total balance of specific types of trades, total high credit or credit limit
- Ratios of various types, for example, percentage of satisfactory trade, percentage of trade ever delinquent, utilisation of various types of trades
- Change of certain key credit variables over time, for example, number of trades with a certain percentage change in balance or utilisation over a certain period
- Indicator for certain credit events or characteristics which are not directly identifiable from the credit information. For example:
    - Transferring of credit balance from one credit line to another (most commonly for credit cards). Though the credit bureau will have information on balances on all the trade lines for the individual, it is not possible to point out cases where an individual transfers his or her balance from one credit line to another (existing or newly opened) because it is very difficult to separate a balance transfer from the phenomena where a consumer pays down one credit line and starts using another.

- The presence of adjustable rate mortgage (for example, the credit bureau certainly contains information about the loan value of the mortgage but may not have information about the type of interest rates and the detailed terms and conditions about the same. Hence, the bureau needs to use proxies to identify whether a mortgage is an adjustable rate mortgage or a fixed rate mortgage). During the fallout of the crisis in the mortgage market in 2007 and 2008, it was found that the presence of adjustable rate mortgages do present an elevated level of risk of default for most types of trades.

Most of the type of credit characteristics described above are created at an overall level and for various types of trades. For example, if there is a characteristic which calculates "Number of trades opened in the last 24 months", then the same is calculated for various types of trades, for example, "Number of bank card trades opened in the last 24 months", "Number of instalment trades opened in the last 24 months", "Number of retail trades opened in the last 24 months", etc. The following provides a list of common credit characteristics that are frequently used in credit bureaus across markets. For the purpose of calculating credit characteristics the trades or credit facilities are categorized based on their type (e.g. revolving, credit card, installment loan, mortgage, auto loan) and based on the type of lender (e.g. bank card, bank installment, retail, finance). It should be noted that this is only an indicative example and is definitely not exhaustive.

- **Count of various types of trades**
  - Number of credit cards/instalment loan/mortgage/retail trade/finance trade
  - Number of open credit cards/instalment loan/mortgage/retail trade/finance trade
- **Delinquency** (the delinquency characteristics are calculated for all trades and for various types of trades e.g. revolving trades, installment trades, mortgage, auto, secured, unsecured, retail trade, finance trade)
  - Number of trades 30/60/90/120/write-off in the last 3/6/12/24 months
  - Number of trades 30/60/90/120/write-off ever
  - Number of trades 30+/60+/90+/120+/write-off in the last 3/6/12/24 months
  - Number of trades 30+/60+/90+/120+/write-off ever
  - Number of times 30/60/90/120/write-off in the last 3/6/12/24 months
  - Number of times 30/60/90/120/write-off ever
  - Number of times 30+/60+/90+/120+/write-off in the last 3/6/12/24 months
  - Number of times 30+/60+/90+/120+/write-off ever
  - Months since most recent 30/60/90/120 or 30+/60+/90+

- Months since most recent delinquency
- Months since worst delinquency
- Number of satisfactory trades
- Amount past due
- Number of trades currently past due
- Balance on trades which are currently delinquent
- Credit limit of trades which are currently delinquent
- Balance of trades which have been delinquent in the last 3/6/12/24 months
- Balance of trades which are 30/60/90 (or 30+/60+/90+)
- Credit limit of trades which are 30/60/90 (or 30+/60+/90+)
- Number of times the customer has an improvement in delinquency status in the last 3/6/12/24 months
- Number of collections
- Number of write-off
- Number of public records or derogatory items
- Number of times the customer has a deterioration in delinquency status in the last 3/6/12/24 months
- Ratio of number of times the customer has an improvement and number of times the customer has a deterioration in delinquency status in the last 3/6/12/24 months

- **Balance and utilisation**
  - Balance/utilisation on various types of trades
  - Balance/utilisation on trades of various types opened in the last 3/6/12/24 months
  - Balance/utilisation of youngest trade (usually calculated for revolving trades, all trades, installment trades, secured trades, unsecured trades)
  - Utilisation of the trade with the highest balance (usually calculated for revolving trades, all trades, installment trades, secured trades and unsecured trades)
  - Utilisation of the trade with the second highest balance (usually calculated for revolving trades, all trades ,installment trades, secured trades and unsecured trades)
  - Number of trades with balance greater than zero (usually calculated for revolving trades, all trades, installment trades, secured trades and unsecured trades)
  - Number of trades with no balance (usually calculated for revolving trades)
  - Number of trades with utilisation greater than 50%/75%/90% (usually calculated for revolving trades)
- **Credit activity**
  - Number of trades opened in the last 3/6/12/24 months
  - Number of trades of various types opened in the last 3/6/12/24 months

- **Age of trades**
  - Average age of trade
  - Age of oldest trade
  - Age of youngest trade
  - Age of oldest trade of a particular type
  - Age of youngest trade of a particular type
- **Inquiries**
  - Number of inquiries of various types (credit cards, loan, etc.) in the last 3/6/12/24 months
  - Number of inquiries and purpose of inquiry
  - Number of collection inquiries

It is possible to create more credit characteristics from the raw bureau data or combine the above for creating more variables. A few examples show how these characteristics can be used for creating new characteristics.

- Percentage satisfactory trades = number of satisfactory trades/total number of trades
- Percentage satisfactory trades = 1 – (number of trades currently past due/total number of trades)
- Percentage of balance owed on recently opened trades = balance of trades opened in the past 3 months/balance of all trades
- Incidence of serious delinquency or derogatory information = If (number of trades 120+ in the last 24 months >0 OR number of public record in the last 24 months >0 OR number of collection in the last 24 months >0 OR number of write-offs in the last 24 months >0)
- Ratio of trades opened to inquiries made = number of trades opened in the last 12 months/number of inquiries made in the last 12 months
- Percentage of credit cards = number of open credit card/number of open trades

It is a difficult task to determine which credit characteristics are important and needs to be calculated, and how many credit characteristics are enough to provide a sufficient and comprehensive view of the credit profile. Past experiences in various markets are often a starting point in designing the initial set of credit characteristics. However, one has to be cognizant of the fact that many of the credit characteristics that are important for a particular market may not be important or may not even be calculable in another market. As an instance of the above, characteristics which look at number of retail revolving trades, for example, "Number of retail revolving trades", "Number of retail revolving trades opened in the last 6/12/24 months", "Number of retail revolving trade inquiries in the last 6/12/24 months", etc., have been found to be very important predictors of risk in the United States market. This is because in the United States, the presence of multiple retail revolving trades indicate that these consumers are unable to secure revolving credit from a bank and hence, have to rely mostly on retail credit cards, which mostly carry higher interest rates and fees. But most of the emerging markets have a very small proportion of retail revolving trades and in many cases the presence of retail revolving trades does not necessarily indicate a higher level of risk.

It is also important to note that the richness of the information in the bureau is a function of the maturity of credit reporting in a particular market and the regulations; hence some of the characteristics which are very important in a matured bureau with a longer history may not be as important in a bureau with a shorter history and less accurate reporting. A typical case in point is the characteristic like "months since most recent delinquency", in some bureaus with a long and accurate reporting history this characteristics is very important; however, for a bureau where the history is limited to three to four years or where regulation restricts the use of historical information longer than a particular span (two to three years), this characteristic is of significantly lesser importance.

It is a common practice to start the process of creating characteristics for a new bureau with characteristics that capture information on all types of trades. In order to ascertain if enough characteristics have been created, one uses some statistical method of studying the dimensionality of the data to see if the characteristics cover sufficient number of dimensions to describe the data. One common technique of measuring the dimensions involves the use of principle component analysis which groups the characteristics into components wherein characteristics which belong to the same component represent a similar aspect of the overall data. Credit bureaus provide a set of characteristics to the lenders for customers who have a credit relationship with the lender. Lenders commonly use the credit characteristics for building their own internal risk or marketing models or for building segmentation or policy rules.

## *6.8.5 Credit Triggers*

To tide over the limitation of a monthly quarterly or biannual update of the credit information and credit characteristics for the portfolio of a lender, credit bureaus have come up with online triggers, which provide real-time notification to lenders if there is any significant change (mostly deterioration) in the credit profile of their customers. A lender can specify the segment of its portfolio on which it wants the bureau to provide real-time alerts, it can also select a set of credit event on which it wants real-time notification. The efficacy of the trigger process depends to a large extent on the speed at which lenders provide information about their portfolio to the bureau. In markets where the update takes longer, the effectiveness of the trigger process gets reduced to a large extent. Some of the common examples of credit bureau triggers include incidence of delinquency, incidence of payment of delinquent trades, opening of credit lines and special types of inquiries.

### 6.8.6 Fraud and Identity Management Solutions

Along with credit information credit bureaus also provide information on potential fraud. For this purpose, the credit data is combined with the header information (address, telephone number, national ID), information from public records like police and court, and information from various types of insurance claims to create indicators which point to potential identity theft. A detailed discussion of fraud identification is beyond the scope of this book. In most cases lenders use the bureau for checking identity theft at the time of new applications. Sophisticated lenders use tools which run fraud check while applicants fill up applications for credit over the Internet. In case the information already filled, in triggers a fraud alert, the applicant is not allowed to complete the rest of the application.

### 6.8.7 Macroeconomic Trend and Forecasting

In markets where considerable historical data is available in the bureau, it is possible to correlate credit performance of various types of credit products with major macroeconomic variables. It is also possible to understand and estimate how macroeconomic variables like GDP growth, unemployment, interest rate, house price index, etc., can act as leading indicators for forecasting the trend of different types of defaults in the consumer credit market. It is important to note that most applications of the credit bureau data tends to take a snapshot view of the overall consumer credit data and attempts to rank order credit behaviour based on the same. For example, consumers with higher balances and with past delinquencies tend to be riskier compared to consumers with lower balances and clean credit histories. However, these methodologies do not take into account a time series view of how credit behaviour has changed over time. An incorporation of the time series trend of credit data can possibly help risk managers in accurately forecasting losses in addition to rank ordering of customers and accounts based on their credit risk.

In order to add a time series trend of credit behaviours with the snapshot view of the credit data, one needs a historical aggregate view of the credit data for a period of nearly seven to ten years or more. The key aspect of this data is the aggregation of the credit data as individual credit performance will not be available for such a long history. It is imperative to aggregate the credit data at various levels to get a holistic picture of the credit behaviour at an aggregate level. For example, one can look at a time series trend of delinquencies like 60 or 90 days or more past due, charge off amount rate, delinquent balance rate, etc. by specific products like revolving debt, mortgage, etc. These aggregations can be performed at different levels, starting from the national level to specific province or even at a metropolitan service area or a zip level. However, one needs to keep in mind that the reliability of the data reduces if the aggregation is performed at a very small geographical level. Usually the aggregate credit data is viewed at a province level. Most often the aggregation of the credit data is performed at a quarterly level because most macroeconomic indicators are available at a quarterly frequency (and not more frequently). In order to build a time series forecast, one needs to find out how these aggregate measures of credit, change with various macroeconomic indicators. But in order to be utilized for forecasting, it is necessary find out the correlation of the credit measures with various lags of the macroeconomic indicators. For example, if the house price index in a particular geographic region tends to change then the effect of that change is felt on delinquencies after two quarters; however, if the unemployment rate goes up then the effect of that on rising delinquencies is felt in the next quarter itself. On the other hand if the unemployment rate goes down, then the positive change on delinquency takes three quarters to materialise. Various time series regression techniques like ARIMA (Auto Regressive Integrated Moving Average) type of models may be used for this purpose. All these time series data tends to have seasonality built into them. For example, delinquencies in many markets tend to be higher after the festive season, hence all these data including the aggregate credit data and the macroeconomic indicators have to be deseasonalised to reflect actual changes in their values.

As mentioned earlier, these macroeconomic models can help risk managers in forecasting the trend of their portfolios based on current macroeconomic indicators. This in turn helps in stress testing, whereby risk managers are able to predict how bad their portfolios will look if certain macroeconomic scenarios happen in future. For example, it assists risk managers in answering questions like "if the unemployment rate rises to 12% how severely will the portfolio get affected?" However, one limitation of these methods is the fact that these effects will vary by the type of the portfolio; for example, if unemployment rises by a certain level then the way a subprime portfolio will be affected is very different from the way a super prime or a prime portfolio will be affected. The macroeconomic indicators that are significant for predicting risk may vary by geography, type of portfolio and risk levels. To tide over this problem one has to aggregate the credit behaviour by geographical regions, by product types and by credit score and can model the effect of macroeconomic indicators based on these combinations. Though the aggregation of credit behaviour by scores solves the problem to some extent, it is obviously not the best solution. Consider, for example, two customers with the same credit score but only one having a mortgage. The direct effects of house price index will be different for these two consumers. But house price index will also affect the economy in general, which in turn will have similar effects on the two consumers. Hence, it is important to combine customer characteristics with the macroeconomic trend variables for building models that accurately predict delinquencies at a customer level by taking into consideration the macroeconomic environment. For this purpose, seven to ten years of customer data needs to be aggregated along with macroeconomic indicators for building a customer level model of credit that incorporates customer level characteristics and macroeconomic variables for predicting credit behaviour like delinquency. Research has shown that an analysis of seven to ten years of data is necessary for deriving the long-term effects of macroeconomic factors. Current binary choice model-based approaches can be modified for accommodating these macroeconomic variables, or alternate techniques like survival analysis can also be used for the same. Details of survival analysis has been outlined in Chapter 7, "Quantitative Methods". In binary choice model-based approaches, the macroeconomic data can be used as an adjustment to the model so that the relative rank ordering of accounts does not change with changes in macroeconomic conditions. However, the expected chance of default of a given customer changes with the macroeconomic environment.

One key usage of macroeconomic trend data is for stress testing portfolios to understand how the portfolios will behave in times of economic stress situations, like higher unemployment, lower house price, high inflation, etc.

## *6.8.8 Marketing Solutions*

The use of the credit bureau data for marketing purposes is mostly a topic of intense legal debate around privacy concerns and permissibility issues. It is a moot question whether the data available in the credit bureau in the form of data submission by member institutions can be used by the bureau for aiding the latter in marketing their products directly to consumers. No doubt, the credit data provides predictive insights into the financial needs of the consumers and can therefore add tremendous value in identifying the right customer for the right product. The use of the bureau for marketing purposes may be closely traced with the evolution of credit bureaus. In most developed markets, regulations do allow the banks and member financial institutions to access the bureau data, to some extent, for marketing purposes, while in most of the emerging markets regulations do not allow members to harness the credit bureau for marketing purposes. When the potential of using the bureau data for marketing purposes is considered, there are essentially two aspects to it: the first is the possibility of using the bureau data for acquiring new customers and the second is to use the bureau data to cross-sell to existing customers. In the following section, the two aspects have been discussed separately.

### 6.8.8.1 Marketing Solutions for Customer Acquisition

Prior to embarking on a discussion on usage of credit bureau information for marketing, it needs to be noted that in most cases marketing is not one of the "permissible purposes" for which the credit bureau information can be used. However, in some markets it is possible to use the bureau data, to a limited extent for marketing purposes. It is critical to consider local regulations before using any credit bureau data for marketing purposes. For new customer acquisition there are two primary regulatory aspects that financial institutions need to take care of. The first is the use of an independent third party for accessing and processing the credit bureau information and the second is the requirement of approving the customer if he or she applies in response to the marketing solicitation sent by the institution. Only in very rare cases, when the prospect's credit quality has worsened very significantly between the time when the marketing solicitation was sent and the prospect has responded, can the institution decline the prospect. In order to access the credit bureau information for new customer solicitation, institutions need to create a set of criteria which they can send to the independent third party. The third party will run those criteria on the entire credit bureau file and then send solicitation on behalf of the institution to those prospects that satisfy the criteria. This is referred to as pre-approved offers.

The selection criteria used by institutions to generate the list of prospects from the bureau generally consists of four components:

1. A set of risk criteria which ensures that the prospect's credit quality is within the acceptable limit
2. A set of criteria which predicts the chance of the prospect responding to the marketing solicitation
3. A set of criteria which predicts future revenue in case the prospect responds to the offer
4. A set of disaster checks. Common examples being, the customer has not been a recent victim of fraud, or is not in the list of individuals who have registered themselves in the do-not-disturb category, etc.

For designing the first three set of criteria, the financial institution normally uses random tests on the credit bureau file to generate enough sample on which it can build the criteria. For the purpose of the risk criteria, a combination of a generic bureau score like the FICO score is used in conjunction with an internal (custom) acquisition risk score built by the institution. For building criteria around response and profitability, the institution needs to develop models on the random population that satisfies the credit eligibility criteria. In order to predict likelihood of response, institutions mostly use classification models based on logistic regression to rank order prospects. In the fiercely competitive direct marketing environment, in most developed markets, the overall response rates of all marketing solicitation is quite low (in the range of less than 2%) and hence, a strong predictive model around response can prove to be a major competitive advantage. Most of these response models are based on the prospect's credit bureau characteristics like the number of trades of various types, credit activity (e.g., number of trades of various types opened recently, number of inquiries), etc. In most cases, variables pertaining to the economic environment, competitive activity, and the relative attractiveness of the institution's offers in comparison with offers extended by competitors are not included in these models but are used as overlays or judgement on top of the result of the response model. In addition to response models, it is possible to build revenue models based on the credit bureau data. These models are mostly used for credit cards acquisition, the model predicts revenue for the first 12 to 18 months post-acquisition. For credit cards, revenue consists of a number of components like interest income, interchange income, interest income from balance transfer, and the like. In some cases separate models are used for predicting each of these components. For example, one may have a model for predicting propensity for revolve (generating interest income) and another for predicting propensity of accepting a balance transfer offer.

For designing a profitability criteria, most institutions use the result of the random test to predict the most significant dimension of profitability. As profitability is a more complex measure compared to response, building a predictor of future profitability mostly turns out to be a more difficult exercise compared to predicting response. Profitability consists of a number of revenue and cost items and predicting each one of them is quite complex. At the same time, if one attempts to predict an overall profitability, it may also turn out to be quite difficult because the drivers of each of the components of profitability are mostly different; and hence, the error in prediction of overall profitability is normally quite high. Hence, most institutions predict major revenue drivers. For example, for credit cards, most of the profit is generated by customers who revolve (that is, who do not pay in full). Therefore most credit card issuers attempt to predict the probability that the particular prospect will revolve in the future. Similarly for telecom companies, profitability is mostly driven by the continuation of the customer beyond the initial offer period and hence, they try to predict the probability of the prospect being with the company after expiration of the introductory offer.

Bureaus in some of the advanced markets provide lists and scores for targeting prospects who are most likely to respond. For example, Experian in the United States provides a score that predicts propensity of responding to a credit card offer, it also provides various prospect lists like consumers who might be looking for auto loans or mortgage.

### 6.8.8.2 Marketing Solutions for Cross-Sell and Existing Customer Management

The legal hurdles for using credit bureau data for cross-sell are considerably limited compared to the use of bureau data for new customer acquisition. This is because the institution has a permissible purpose to fetch bureau information about existing customers.

The bureau data serves as a very valuable source of information for understanding the wallet share that the institution enjoys for a particular customer. The example in Table 6.6 illustrates the same. Consider four consumers (A to D).

**Table 6.6** Usage of Credit Bureau Data for Cross-Sell: An Illustrative Example

| | Consumer-A | Consumer-B | Consumer-C | Consumer-D |
|---|---|---|---|---|
| Age of oldest trade in the bureau | 122 months | 176 months | 80 months | 65 months |
| Number of credit cards with the particular institution | 2 | 1 | 1 | 1 |
| Total number of credit cards | 4 | 6 | 4 | 4 |
| Credit card wallet share—Credit card balance with the particular institution/total credit card balance | 20% | 34% | 43% | 27% |
| Presence of auto loan with the institution | 1 | None | None | None |
| Presence of open auto loan in the bureau | 1 | None | None | 1 |
| Presence of a closed auto loan | 1 | 1 | 0 | 0 |
| Percentage of the auto loan paid off | 80% | | 0 | 25% |
| Credit score | 830 | 780 | 820 | 780 |

As seen in Table 6.6, a Particular institution can enhance its share of wallet for credit card for Consumer-D, but cannot cross-sell an auto loan as the consumer already has an auto loan with competition. Consumer-C, on the other hand, seems like a good target for an auto loan because he or she has a lower (80 months) age of oldest credit line, which suggests that he or she is not very old. In addition, the bank enjoys a high (43%) credit card wallet share for Consumer-C, which indicates that he or she is a loyal customer. Because of all the above reasons, the institution may target the consumer for an auto loan. Consumer-A and B are relatively older consumers and the institution can target Consumer-B for an auto loan as well, because it can possibly be the right time for her/him to buy another car. This can be inferred from the closed auto loan for Consumer-B. The table illustrates that multiple information can be used for making decisions pertaining to cross-sell. The institution can use a set of criteria or build a score to combine all these information to predict likelihood of response to a cross-sell offer.

As in the case of acquisition, a set of criteria for risk and response are used for selecting existing customers for cross-sell programmes. In case of cross-sell, internal data is also used in conjunction with bureau data for predicting response and in most cases internal data seems to add significant value. So the criticality of bureau data for cross-sell is lesser compared to acquisition.

Credit bureaus offer various additional data fields and scores that can help an institution in generating more revenue from existing customers. The bureaus in the United States use their data to identify additional characteristics about customers. For example, Experian's trend view data examines 24 months of credit card balance history for each credit card trade and thereby tries to identify consumer behaviour patterns like:

- **Rate surfing activity**—transferring balance from one card to another
- **Revolving activity**—partial payment of credit card balance
- **Transacting activity**—paying off most of the credit card balance every month
- **Consolidation activity**—transferring multiple credit card balances to one credit card or consolidation loan
- **Inactive**—never uses credit card or only uses it once
- **Seasonal user**—uses credit cards at specific times of the year

In addition, bureaus also use their data to predict the total spend on credit card. This in turn may help institutions to calculate the spend wallet share along with the balance wallet share, which can be calculated from the data available in the credit file. As already pointed out, most of the advanced market bureaus also provide an estimation of the income of the customer that can be used as an important input in several marketing strategies.

Data elements like the trend view data or the estimated income, are not directly available in the customer's credit file but the bureaus utilise long-term data to infer these characteristics. The addition of these characteristics in models and strategies can help institutions to significantly enhance their cross-sell and usage enhancement strategies.

## 6.8.9 Credit Bureau Solution for Insurance

In most developed markets, insurance companies use credit data for predicting insurance loss. Though it is difficult to point out any direct intuitive reason as to why credit data can predict insurance losses, multiple studies conducted by various academic and regulatory institutions have shown a strong correlation between credit data and insurance loss. As per Peter Wu and James C Guszcza in the paper titled *Does Credit Score Really Explain Insurance Losses? Multivariate Analysis from a Data Mining Point of View* it is pointed out that credit data possibly reflects the level of stress that the individual is subjected to; it also takes into account, the degree of planning, organising, and risk taking on the part of the individual. These characteristics cannot be measured directly by any other insurance attributes like age, driving style, past accident record, etc. and hence, credit data emerges as a major predictor of insurance losses in combination with other insurance attributes. As pointed out in the same paper, credit data is not only highly correlated to the absolute insurance loss but also to the loss ratio. Insurance loss measures the absolute loss from a policy, whereas loss ratios measure the loss in comparison to the premium payment. For example, if a credit variable like age of the oldest trade is used to predict the incidence of loss then it can be argued that the variable is actually a proxy of the driver's age and credit data is not the real predictor but age of the driver is the real predictor of loss. However, auto insurance premium naturally takes care of age; that is, the premium for a matured driver is usually lower than the premium for a young driver. Given the fact that the premium amount already takes care of the age of the driver, if age of oldest trade is still predictive for forecasting profitability or loss ratio relatives, then it cannot be said that the predictive power of the characteristic stems from the fact that it is a proxy of consumer age.

Most credit bureaus and credit score providers like FICO have come up with customised scores based on credit data which predicts insurance losses for various lines of personal insurance like auto insurance, home insurance, etc. FICO credit insurance models first introduced in 1993 uses consumer credit data to predict loss ratio relatives for auto and home insurance for both new applicants and existing policyholders. Such scores use all types of credit information described above including derogatory information and inquiries, but does not use information like gender, age, geography, etc.

Though there has been significant legal debate in the United States around the practice of using credit data (and scores based on credit data) for deciding insurance premiums, till now most insurers do use credit data and scores in addition to traditional insurance attributes in their underwriting strategy.

## 6.9 Application of Credit Bureau Information

### *6.9.1 Application of Credit Bureau for Risk Management at Acquisition*

Credit bureau data and score are key measures of risk assessment at the customer acquisition stage for all industries where credit is granted to customers. The industries where this is most important are financial services, telecom (for post-paid customers), retail (where goods are sold on credit) and insurance (where there is a chance of the customer committing fraud or defaulting on premium payment). During acquisition, two key risk decisions need to be made: the first is whether to approve credit to a particular customer and the second is how much credit to approve? Both of these decisions tend to involve a trade-off between risk and return. In most markets where a credit bureau score exists, it forms one of the key ingredients in the acquisition risk management strategy. However, most lenders also use a customised application score to judge the credit quality of prospects at the time of application. Customised application scores use the bureau data and some other data that is part of the application process. However, the bureau data is mostly the major driver of all customised application risk scores. The application score provides an added advantage over the bureau score because it is built for the specific population which is targeted by a particular bank or financial institution, whereas the bureau score is built on the entire population. Consumers who do not have any credit (at the current point in time or in history), will have no trade related information in the credit bureau, though they may have some inquiry information. For these consumers, the credit bureau score, or the application score based on credit bureau data have very low predictive power. Consumers who have very limited credit history (very few tradelines or very limited historical credit information) are said to have a thin file in the bureau. For such thin file consumers the credit bureau information (and score) have limited predictive power.

Most financial services and telecom companies use more than one score and multiple policy rules for evaluating risk at the acquisition stage. In most advanced markets these companies create their own customised acquisition scores and provide the algorithm to the bureaus. The bureaus score all acquisition credit inquiries by that company using the specific algorithm and provide the score along with the credit report and other credit characteristics. However, many emerging market credit bureaus do not offer the flexibility of hosting customised scoring algorithms within the bureau environment and hence, companies seek the credit report and credit characteristics from the bureau and calculate the scores themselves.

Very often companies use a dual score matrix based on bureau score and custom score for building credit policy rules. Table 6.7 provides a sample dual score matrix, while Fig. 6.3 depict a simple policy rule framework, usually a dual score matrix is used within a policy rule framework. The lender uses a bureau score which ranges between 300 and 800 and a custom score than ranges between 0 and 1000.

## 6.9.2 Application of Credit Bureau Information for Managing Existing Customers

Credit bureau information provides companies an outsider's view of their existing customers which proves to be very critical both for risk management and for cross-sell or up sell. Most companies perform a credit bureau update of their existing customer base at a monthly or quarterly frequency so that they are instantly aware of any change in the customer's credit profile and their credit scores. As discussed earlier, companies also utilise credit bureau triggers for some of their more risky customers so as to immediately know any changes in the customer's credit quality. Similar to acquisition, most companies also use customised credit scores

**Table 6.7** Sample Dual Score Matrix

<table>
<tr><th colspan="2"></th><th colspan="9">Custom Score</th></tr>
<tr><th colspan="2"></th><th><600</th><th>600–720</th><th>721–756</th><th>755–775</th><th>776–810</th><th>811–840</th><th>841–880</th><th>881–900</th><th>>900</th></tr>
<tr><th rowspan="10">Bureau Score</th><td>300–510</td><td rowspan="8" colspan="3">Application Code – A0</td><td rowspan="4" colspan="2">Application Code – A2</td><td rowspan="4" colspan="4">Application Code – A5</td></tr>
<tr><td>511–521</td></tr>
<tr><td>522–533</td></tr>
<tr><td>534–545</td></tr>
<tr><td>545–561</td><td rowspan="4" colspan="4">Application Code – A3</td><td rowspan="3" colspan="2">Application Code – A6</td></tr>
<tr><td>562–575</td></tr>
<tr><td>576–593</td></tr>
<tr><td>594–640</td><td rowspan="3" colspan="2">Application Code – A8</td></tr>
<tr><td>641–672</td><td rowspan="2" colspan="2">Application Code – A1</td><td rowspan="2" colspan="3">Application Code – A4</td><td rowspan="2" colspan="2">Application Code – A7</td></tr>
<tr><td>673–800</td></tr>
</table>

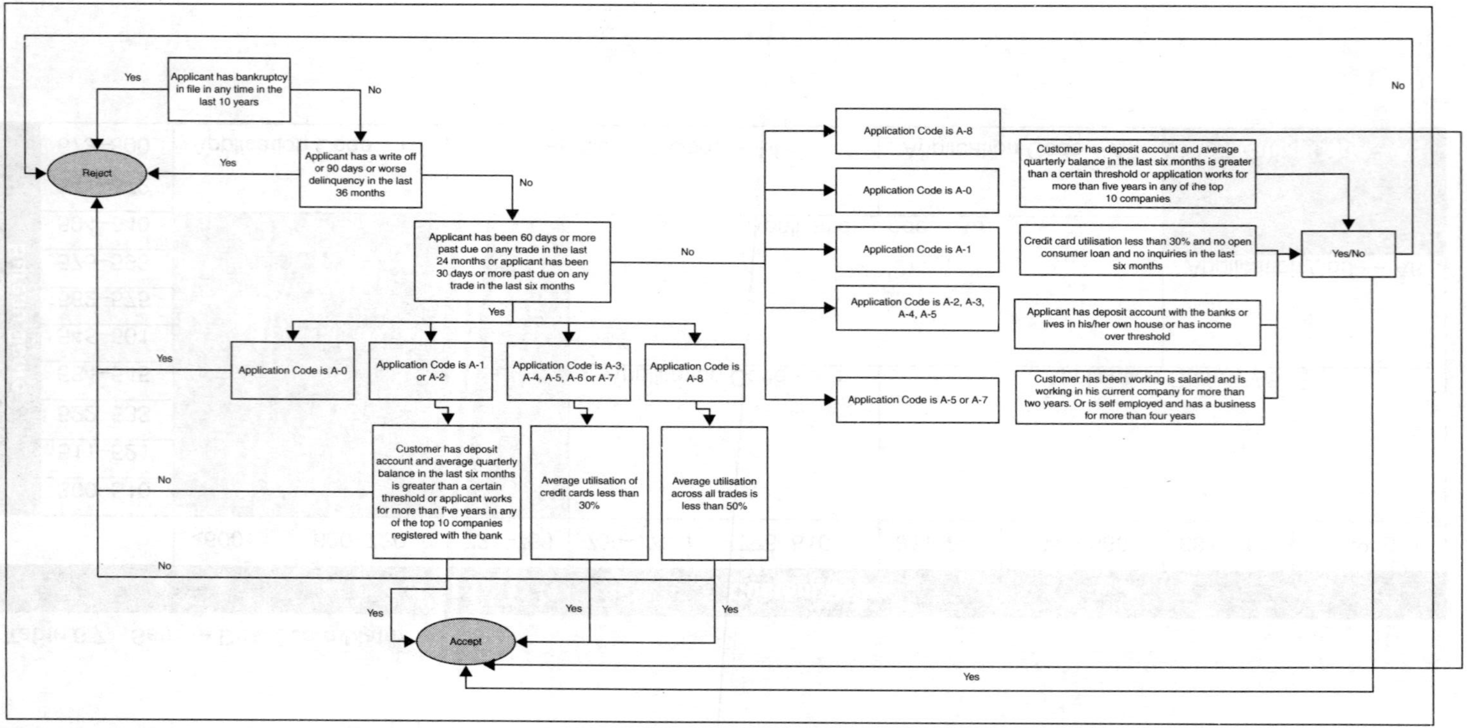


**Figure 6.3** Sample Acquisition Policy Framework

(also called behaviour score or account management scores) for managing risk from existing customers. Such scores include information both from the credit bureau and information internal to the company. Such internal information include information on payment pattern, activity, usage type, etc. In many cases, for an existing customer, information internal to the company tends to be more useful in predicting delinquency compared to credit bureau information. Some of the key uses of risk assessment of existing customers include:

- Considering risky customers for credit limit decrease
- Including risky customers in various programmes like debt restructuring for helping them tide over financial difficulties
- Providing automated reminders to risky customers for making their payments on time
- Enrolling risky customers in programmes where the monthly payment will be deducted from their savings or current account
- Providing risky customers incentives to pay on time and for not accumulating further debt
- Considering whether a particular customer is eligible for credit limit increase or cross-sell
- Considering risk associated with, reactivating customers who have silently attrited without closing their account

Similar to acquisition, multiple scores and rules are used for determining strategies for managing existing customers as well. At this point, it is important to note that most lenders do not refresh the credit bureau data for existing customers on a monthly basis. Usually lenders refresh credit bureau data on a quarterly basis. However, for high risk accounts, the bureau data is refreshed more frequently.

### *6.9.3 Application of Credit Bureau Information for Managing Collection and Recovery*

For all companies that extend credit to consumers, managing the collection and recovery process is a key business challenge. Companies need to prioritise accounts for collections and recovery effort and focus their effort on accounts which are more likely to pay. A focussed collection strategy helps companies in enhancing the efficiency of their collection process. Across industries, collection and recovery can be divided into three key phases based on ease of collection. The first is early bucket collection, which focuses on customers who have not paid their dues for up to 30 or 60 days, that is, they are at most two cycles delinquent. The next phase consists of late bucket collection which focuses on customers who have not paid for a period of more than 60 days upto the point of charge off. The third phase consists of customers who have not paid for 150/180 days or more and have moved into charge off. Typically, the first two phases are part of the collection process and the third is part of the recovery process. However, the exact definition of early, late stage and recovery may vary by industry.

In case of early bucket collection, it is important to predict the chances of the following events:

- The account will roll over to a worse delinquency status
- The customer will pay and self cure without any collection action
- The customer will pay in response to a collection action

However, unlike acquisition or portfolio management, collection-related outcomes need to be predicted over a very small outcome period in future (typically one to four months). For early bucket collection, it is also important to optimise the collection action. There can be various collection actions that are available like soft calling, hard calling, letter, legal notice, etc. As some of the customers in the early collection bucket may be good customers who have faced a temporary payment problem and may roll back to a good status, it is very critical to protect them against very harsh collection actions. Typically, bureau data proves to be a very rich source of information for predicting collection outcomes and chances of the customer self-curing.

The bureau data also provides information about the customer's delinquency status and the outstanding loans with other lenders; this information provides valuable information on how to target the customer for collection. Every lender tries to be the first in line in obtaining the amount to be paid by the customer. At this point, it is important to note that consumers having multiple credit obligations usually demonstrate a payment hierarchy. If a consumer has a home loan, an auto loan, a personal loan, and a credit card then he or she will first pay the home loan, followed by the auto loan. The personal loan and credit card shall be the last in line. However, during unusual times, the payment hierarchy may get reversed. A case in point was the mortgage crisis, wherein consumers who knew that they would almost inevitably lose their homes paid off their credit card dues instead of their home loan dues. This helped consumers to have some credit line available during times of extreme crisis. In case, a customer makes payment to any other creditor, then that information can be an important input in designing the collection strategy.

A collection score is a good starting point of aggregating the bureau information for the purpose of collection. However, a collection score is seldom the only criteria used for prioritising accounts for collection actions; mostly a dual score matrix is used with the collection score and a generic bureau score in order to filter out the good from the bad. A first level filtering is performed based on the generic bureau score followed by the collection score. For each combination of the two scores the optimal collection treatment is designed so as to maximise the total dollar collected.

Similar to the example discussed in the acquisition section, lenders usually build a set of policy rules including multiple scores, internal and credit bureau information. Based on these set of rules, the lender designs the optimal collection action for each delinquent customer. Figure 6.4 depicts a sample collection strategy for early delinquent accounts. In the boxes marked 1 through 6, 1 represents the most aggressive collections strategy and 6 represents the most lenient. It needs to be noted that this is a simple example and real strategies are far more complex in nature.

For late bucket collection and recovery, it is less important to consider the chances of falsely targeting a possible good account. At this stage, the lender uses three key actions, namely, attempting an in-house recovery, selling off the distressed assets to a third party agency, or offering a debt restructuring programme to the customer. Bureau information and internal information are used to determine the optimal action for each account.

Generic bureau scores are also used to price some of the written off accounts that are sold off to a collection or recovery agency. The scores provide a common metric that can be used to evaluate the credit quality of the bundle of distressed loans that are sold off. Hence, the agency buying such a bundle of receivables from a bank or a telecom company can judge the credit quality and recoverability from the average credit score and recovery score of the bundle. In this regard, the scores provide a mechanism of pricing a bundle of stressed assets.

### 6.9.4 Application of Credit Bureau Data and Score for Securitisation, Asset Sell, Pricing and Capital Markets

Credit bureau data and credit scores are the best indicators of the quality of a retail asset. Higher the credit score of a borrower, the lesser the risk of the loan and hence, higher is the quality of the retail asset. Most of the applications of credit data and credit score discussed till now in this chapter hinges upon the use of the same for evaluating the credit quality of a particular borrower. However, in certain cases, it is important to access the credit quality of a pool of retail loans rather than the credit quality of a particular borrower. Typical cases arise when a lender wants to securitise a pool of retail assets or when an investment bank wants to create derivatives like mortgage backed securities where the underlying asset is a pool of retail asset and not a single loan. In these cases it is important to access the credit quality of the entire pool of loans under consideration and not the risk of a single borrower. The practice of pricing such pools of retail loans has gained maximum maturity for the mortgage market where mortgage-backed securities has been quite popular with banks and investors for quite some time. However, it must be noted that the financial crisis of 2008–2009 which involved a meltdown of house prices resulting in skyrocketing of mortgage delinquencies had cast a strong negative perception around mortgage-backed securities in general and the pricing and risk evaluation methodologies in particular.

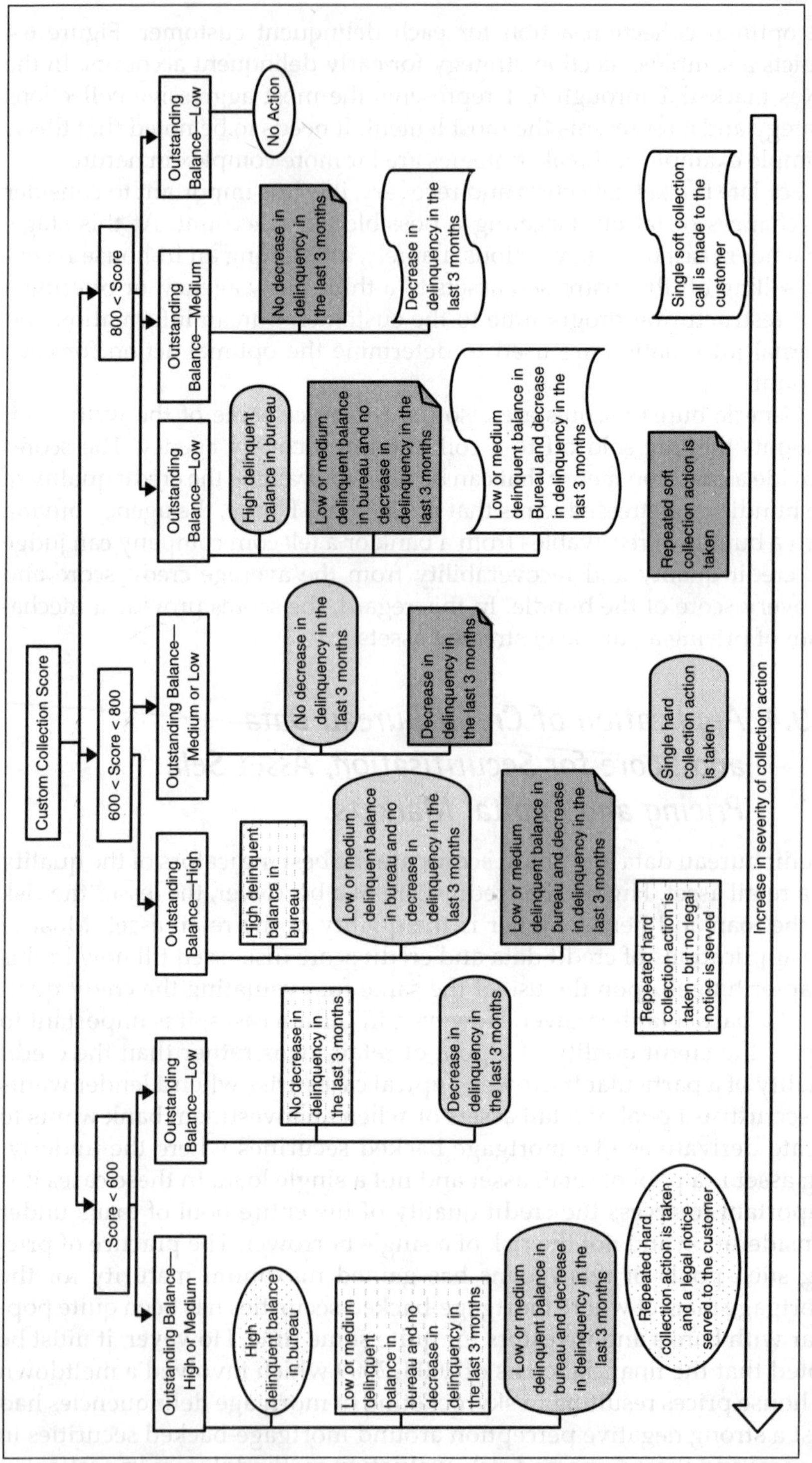


**Figure 6.4** Collection Strategy Grid

This has brought into question much of the analytical techniques used for evaluation of risk of such pools of retail assets.

For assessment of risk of any pool of retail assets the four key components that are used are credit bureau scores, loan characteristics (like to loan to value ratio of a home loan), trend of delinquency and house price in various regions or province, and macroeconomic factors (both at a local and national level). These sets of information are used in a multivariate regression framework for predicting the severity of losses that the pool might experience. A scenario analysis is performed based on the assessment of macroeconomic factors. One important aspect in the evaluation of risk of the overall pool of assets involves an assessment of correlation of defaults of individual loans. In most simplistic analysis of consumer credit risk, each individual loan is assumed to behave independently of any other loan and the correlation of defaults between individual loans are not explicitly considered. However, correlation of defaults between individual loans can greatly enhance the overall risk of the pool of retail asset particularly because research has pointed that such correlation tends to go up significantly during times of economic stress. To illustrate this point further, if one assumes that job loss is a major factor that drives default then the event of each individual borrower losing his or her job is an independent event in a normal economic environment. However, in times of economic stress when there are mass layoffs, the event of individual borrowers losing their jobs become highly correlated, which in turn makes the event of default highly correlated as well. Hence, a stressed economic environment affects the pool in two ways; first it increases the probability of default of each individual loan and second it increases the correlation of defaults between individual loans. As part of conventional risk assessment methodologies it is relatively easier to estimate the increase in probability of default with changes in economic conditions; however, estimating the change in default correlation is quite difficult. Default correlation also depends on the overall risk level of the pool or subpools within the pool. For example, a risky pool may have higher correlation compared to a less risky pool; this means that credit data can be used as a component for determining the correlation as well. However, most current methodologies only use macroeconomic factors for estimating the correlation.

Most risk assessment methodologies use the bureau score at the time of sourcing the loan as the indicator of the risk of the individual loan. But this may lead to problems where there are significant changes in the risk of the borrower between the time when the loan was originated and the time when the risk assessment was carried out. In addition, a customised risk score that predicts default on the particular type of trade can have an added advantage over a generic bureau score like FICO.

A detailed discussion of the methodologies used for pricing pools of retail assets is beyond the scope of this book. But the concept essentially involves an estimation of individual loss probabilities which is used for measuring expected loss and an estimation of the default correlation which is used for measuring the unexpected loss. If one uses the concept of value at risk, then the individual loss probabilities (along with an estimation of the dollar value of the loss) helps in determining the expected or mean loss and the correlation helps in estimating the standard deviation of the loss distribution from which one can estimate value at risk.

## 6.9.5 Application of Credit Bureau Data and Score for Optimising Risk and Marketing Strategy

The objective of any financial institution is to optimise risk and return in such a way so as to maximise overall profitability. Credit bureau information is vital in designing strategies for driving revenue while limiting the level of risk exposure. This section illustrates an optimisation strategy which uses bureau score, custom risk score, custom response score, and other credit bureau data to optimise overall profitability. Figure 6.5 depicts the strategy for credit cards. The strategy uses the following:

- Custom behaviour score which is used to estimate the risk level of existing customers based on internal data only
- Bureau risk score which is used to estimate the risk level of existing customers based only on credit bureau information
- Comparison between the credit limit on the particular card and the credit limit of other cards in the bureau. At this point, it is important to note that in some cases, the bureaus do not report credit limit on cards. In those cases one needs to use high credit (which is the highest billed amount ever on that card) as a proxy.
- Wallet share which is calculated as the ratio of balance on the particular credit to all other cards in the bureau
- Utilisation of all credit cards in the bureau, which is calculated as total balance of all credit cards in the bureau divided by sum of credit limit of all cards in the bureau
- A response score for balance transfer which is derived using bureau information and internal information

For details on line management strategies the reader may refer to Chapter 2, "Usage Management". Similar strategies are used for line assignment at the time of sourcing new accounts, cross-sell and other programs. This example illustrates how bureau information can be useful both for risk mitigation and revenue enhancement.

## 6.9.6 Harnessing Multiple Credit Bureaus

Multiple credit bureaus exist in most advanced markets. In such cases it is important to determine which credit bureau to use. Usually each credit bureau has relatively better data coverage in either a particular geography

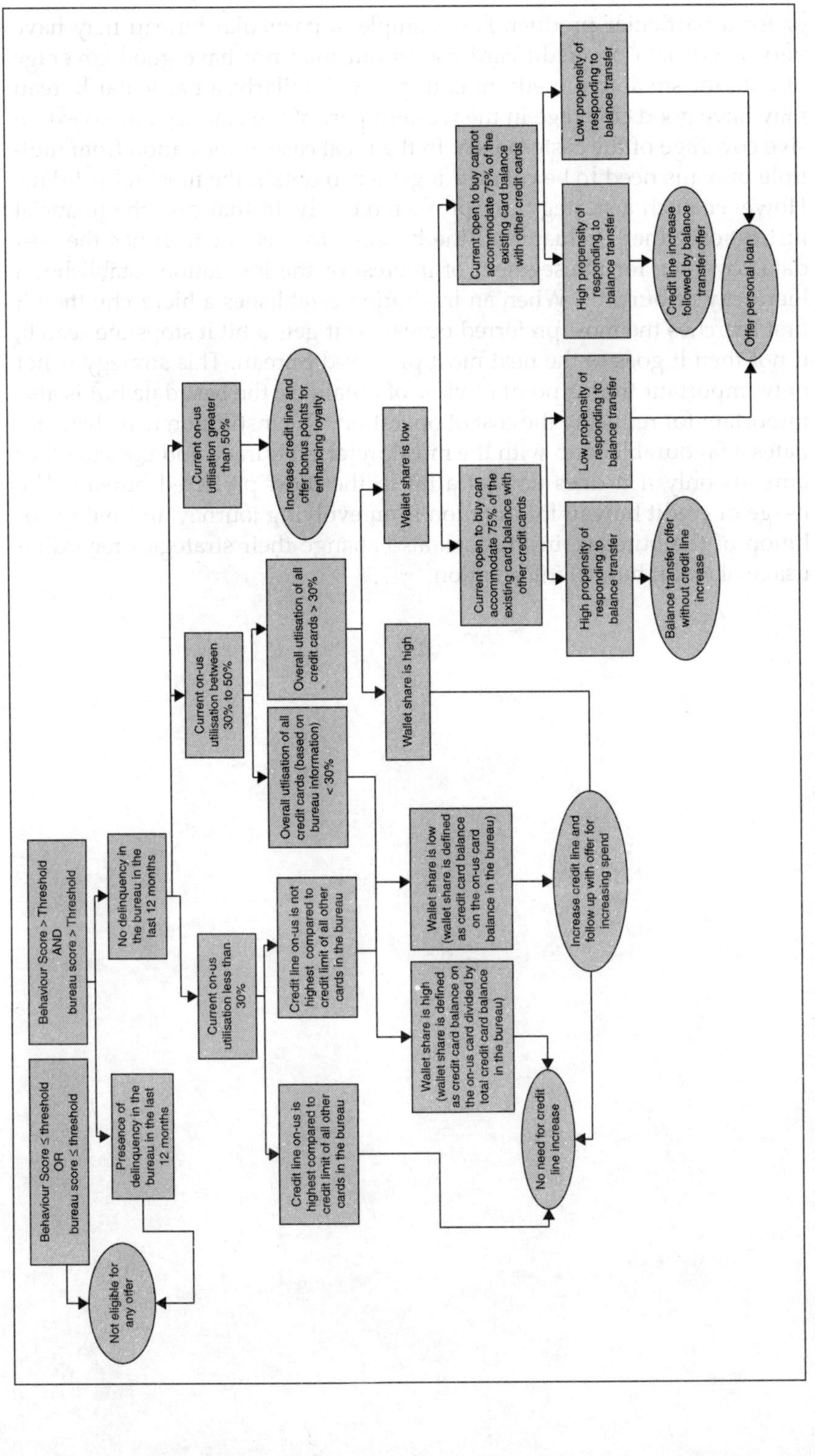


**Figure 6.5** Optimizing Risk and Revenue using Credit Bureau Data

or for a particular product. For example, a particular bureau may have very good data on credit card trades but may not have good coverage of data for small and medium enterprises. Similarly, a particular bureau may have good coverage in the western part of the country but no extensive coverage of the eastern part. In the ideal case, information from multiple bureaus need to be collated together to obtain the most robust data. However, such a strategy can prove too costly. In that case the financial institution either evaluates all the bureaus to access which has the best data coverage for the segment of interest or the institution establishes a hierarchy of bureaus. When an institution establishes a hierarchy then it first searches the most preferred bureau. If it gets a hit it stops the search, if not then it goes to the next most preferred bureau. This strategy is not only important from a point of view of obtaining the best data but is also important for reducing the cost of operation. The institution usually negotiates a favourable term with the most preferred bureau and goes to other bureaus only if it does not get a hit in the most preferred bureau. The usage of credit bureau information is an evolving journey and with evolution of the bureaus, institutions also change their strategies regarding usage of credit bureau information.

SEVEN

# Quantitative Methods

## 7.1 Introduction

Quantitative methods provide decision analytic tools for data driven business strategies that were emphasised in the preceding chapters. A sound acquisition strategy requires the identification and segmentation of the addressable universe, creation of a targeting strategy for each of the segments, and finally a prioritisation among the segments. Once the segments of interest are prioritised, the marketer needs to determine the right price, the right offer, and the right channel for each segment. Usage, cross-sell, and retention are important drivers of customer lifetime value (CLV) and related programmes are key initiatives for delivering profitable growth. The profitability of these programmes is contingent on the intelligent use of customer segmentation, behavioural models, and optimisation for offer testing strategies. Next best product to buy models covering the four prong approach of what product and to whom, when, and how are indispensable tools for the cross-sell manager. Proactive retention programmes require forecasting of which customer is likely to defect in the near future. Credit bureau information is vital for revenue growth, while limiting the level of risk exposure. For this purpose, credit bureau data and custom risk scores can be gainfully leveraged to optimise overall profitability for a financial institution. Dynamic pricing that takes the form of revenue management, risk-based pricing, and relationship pricing is a P&L focused approach, contingent on the premise that customers behave differently. All these analytical strategies involve the identification key segments of interest within customer or prospect pools; prediction of certain outcomes (like response to a campaign, event of attrition); and campaign optimisation. A number of quantitative techniques need to be harnessed for each of these purposes. The analytical marketer uses these (and many more) techniques, along with deep data and business understanding, for formulating data-driven business strategies.

Micro marketing requires segmentation of the prospect and customer database for differentiated management actions. Quantitative methods of cluster analysis and classification/decision tree are widely used techniques for creating these heterogeneous segments. While supervised[1] classification methods of CHAID (Chi-square Automatic Interaction Detector), CART (Classification and Regression Trees), and Random Forests require the objective to be stated as the basis for segmentation, cluster analysis is an unsupervised method based on the measure of similarity. Classification/decision tree has become a very popular segmentation method as the results can also be used for prediction.

A good insightful analytical output requires vast amounts of data, both in terms of the number of observations and the number of attributes. For the determination of the potential set of important attributes, principal components and factor analysis are used for data reduction of the attribute space. Inferences from principal components that are linear composites of the original variables (that capture the maximum variance of the data being analysed) form the basis for further investigation, whether it is exploratory data analysis, segmentation, or regression models.

Moreover, in the presence of multiple attributes, decision-making relating to the choice of alternatives based on these attributes requires trade-offs, with a need for multi-criteria decision analysis (MCDA). Methods such as analytic hierarchy process (AHP), principal components analysis, and regression models can provide tools for the decision maker to arrive at the final choice. For multi-objective decision-making, the need for optimisation techniques is referenced in the business chapters, although not elaborated, given the availability of application-oriented operations research publications.

The ability to predict customer behaviour at the most granular level is an underpinning for productive and cost-effective marketing programmes. This prediction takes the form of a regression-based score, representing the probability of an event of interest or a value prediction. This score is unique for every customer and is futuristic. Industry popular methods for score development (event-based) are discrete choice regression models (such as logistic regression and multinomial logit) and survival analysis. Logistic regression has become the most popular method for event-based modelling due to its multiple advantages.

There are many other alternate techniques available, such as advanced variants of cluster analysis (hard vs. fuzzy and deterministic vs. stochastic) and decision tree (hill climbing method for multivariate splits) for

[1] Supervised methods are methods that attempt to discover the relationship between the input variables (independent variables) and the target variable (dependent variable). There are two main supervised methods: classification models and regression models. *Source*: Maimon and Rokach, *Introduction to Supervised Methods, Data Mining and Knowledge Discovery Handbook*.

segmentation; outranking method for multi-criteria decision analysis; and artificial neural networks (ANN), Bayesian approaches, and support vector machines (SVM) for score development. Panel data and time series methods are customised models for evaluating panel and time series data, respectively. However, this chapter focuses on some of the common quantitative techniques used for analytic decision-making and comprehendible from business users' perspective.

Quantitative techniques such as Markov Chain Model, Market Basket Analysis, and Collaborative Filtering were discussed in the context of business applications in the preceding chapters. The chapter outline is as follows. Segmentation methods are discussed in Section 7.2 followed by multi-criteria decision analysis and regression models in Sections 7.3 and 7.4. The model framework is supplemented by a practical business-oriented application for each of these methods. A detailed review of model validation for logistic regression is conducted in Section 7.5.

## 7.2 Customer Segmentation

### *7.2.1 Introduction*

Customer segmentation is the subdivision of a customer pool into discrete segments, with the feature that customers within a segment share similar characteristics while customers across segments are differentiated. The same applies to prospects as well. By tailoring offerings with distinct competitive advantages (by segment), a business can use customer segmentation as the principal basis for allocating resources to product development, marketing, risk management, pricing, and service. Revenue growth and cost reduction are the major benefits of segmentation, and some of these points were highlighted in the chapters on acquisition, usage, cross-sell, retention, pricing, and credit bureau. The numerous examples of segmentation of the preceding chapters are listed in Table 7.1, which are business as well as statistical technique-based segmentation results.

Customer segmentation involves the following process:

- Division of the customer pool into meaningful and measurable segments based on customer needs, demographic/geo-demographic/socioeconomic profiles, past behaviour, share of wallet, and others
- Determination of the profit potential of each segment by analysing the revenue and cost impact of each segment
- Targeting segments with differentiated customer management programs based on profit potential and the ability to service them in a unique way
- Tracking performance of each segment
- Validation and revision of segmentation approach over time with changing market conditions

**Table 7.1** Types of Segmentation

| Type | Segmentation | Table/Figure | Chapter |
|---|---|---|---|
| Need/Response | Lifestage Based Segmentation<br>Personal Loan to Credit Card Cross-Sell Response Segmentation | Fig. 3.10<br>Fig. 3.16 | Cross-Sell |
| Costs/Benefits | Sample Incentive Structure | Table 1.11 | Acquisition |
| | Reactive Retention Offer Grid<br>Credit Card—Revenue at Risk Grid | Table 4.7<br>Table 4.19 | Retention Management |
| Behaviour | Telecom Usage Segmentation<br>Balance Transfer Segmentation<br>Credit Card Segmentation<br>Banking Segmentation<br>Wealth Management Segmentation<br>Line Management Section | Fig. 2.21<br>Fig. 2.29<br>Fig. 2.31<br>Fig. 2.33<br>Table 2.12 | Usage Management |
| | Segment Level Cross-Sell Ratios | Table 3.9 | Cross-Sell |
| | Balance Attrition—Transition Matrix<br>Retail Defection—RFM Segments<br>Telecom Churn Segmentation<br>Insurance Lapse Risk Category | Table 4.10<br>Fig. 4.14<br>Table 4.22<br>Table 4.27 | Retention Management |
| | Risk And Relationship Based Pricing<br>Examples Of Dynamic Pricing Across Industries<br>Pricing Grid for Personal Loan<br>Risk Based Pricing For Credit Cards | Fig. 5.1<br>Table 5.1<br>Table 5.2<br>Table 5.5 | Price Management |
| | Sample Risk Rand Ordering for a Credit Bureau Score<br>Sample Dual Score Matrix<br>Collection Strategy Grid | Table 6.5<br>Table 6.7<br>Fig. 6.4 | Credit Bureau |
| | Decision Tree Risk Segmentation | Fig. 7.5 | Quantitative Methods |
| Attitudes/Loyalty | Rewards Comparison | Fig. 2.46 | Usage Management |
| Demographics/ Geo-demographics | Segmentation of Individual Prospects<br>Major Geo-Demographic Classification Systems/ Others<br>Socioeconomic Classification<br>Age-Income Grid<br>Classification of Cities<br>Customized Clusters | Fig. 1.3<br>Table 1.4/ Table 1.5<br>Table 1.6<br>Table 1.7<br>Table 1.8<br>Fig. 1.7 | Acquisition |

For segmentation to be beneficial for the objective at hand, the segmentation scheme should meet some key requirements:

- Segmentation should be aligned with specific business goals. Henceforth, input data should be considered accordingly.
- Customer segments should be differentiated by characteristics/ profile
- Size of customer segments should be large enough to take actions
- Actionable segments need to be identified, to ensure that practical and effective programmes can be formulated

Business segmentation is based on business experience and intuition and does not necessarily depend on statistical techniques for its derivation.

Segmentation by one variable (univariate), two variables (bivariate), and more than two variables (multivariate) is possible without relying on statistical methods. For multivariate segmentation, one can use pivot tables in excel. An example of a univariate business segmentation is presented in Table 7.2 from the consumer packed goods industry based on a IRI White Paper[2] titled *Store Segmentation*. IRI conducted an analysis of over 8 million shopping trips and identified 31 distinct trip types, which were aggregated into four primary trip missions. Manufacturers and retailers can leverage trip mission insights to build marketing and merchandising plans that impact sales and satisfaction. Identifying store layout, products to display, and quantities to promote are some other applications. Age and income is a classic example of a bivariate segmentation that has proven to be a powerful and intuitive standard for demographic segmentation, an example of which, was illustrated in Chapter 1 "Acquisition".

The dependence on statistical methods is heavy under either of these situations—large number of variables in the consideration set; no-apriori hypotheses; and purpose of segmentation is prediction. It is important to note that for statistical method based segmentation, business experience is also an important element of creating and finalising the segments. Statistical technique-based segmentation methods that are popular in industry are cluster analysis and classification/decision tree. These are

**Table 7.2** Trip Missions Typology

| Type | # Items | All Outlet Average $ Spent | Mindset | % of All Outlet Trips | % of All Outlet CPQ $ |
|---|---|---|---|---|---|
| Quick trip | 1–5 | < $40 | Need it now, have to make a trip | 54% | 21% |
| Special purpose | 2–10 | $20–$50 | Buying for a specific event (not routine) | 17% | 18% |
| Fill in | 5–15 | $30–$80 | Routine fill-in on heavy use categories | 16% | 21% |
| Pantry stocking | 15+ | $50+ | Prepare for the coming week | 14% | 40% |

*Source:* IRI Shopper Insights™.
*Note:* The IRI Trip Typology™ is based upon an assessment of consumer purchase behaviour across 8 million trips captured over a 52 week period; 31 distinct trip types were identified that roll up into the 4 trip mission trypes represented here.

[2] Available at http://www.symphonyiri.gr/portals/0/articlePdfs/Store_Segmentation_White_Paper.pdf

multivariate techniques and will be discussed in detail in the following sections. Principal components analysis (PCA), a data dimension reduction technique can also be used for segmentation. The banking segmentation of Chapter 2 "Usage Management" is an application of this method.

## 7.2.2 Cluster Analysis

### 7.2.2.1 Introduction

Cluster analysis is a segmentation technique which organises observations into groups or clusters based on similarity. Intuitively, observations within a cluster are more similar to each other than they are to observations belonging to a different cluster. Purely data exploratory in nature, this technique belongs to the class of unsupervised learning (undirected knowledge discovery) methods. This is unlike supervised or confirmatory analysis such as discriminant analysis and classification/decision tree, which aim to label observations with a segment membership[3] based on a goal or dependent variable. There is no underlying statistical rationale behind clustering algorithms as it draws upon measures such as geometric distance to evaluate the extent of similarity. The biggest upside of using this approach is that the analyst can harness huge volume of multi-dimensional data for deriving insights, without having prior information or hypotheses about data inter-relationships. Cluster analysis does not require any assumptions regarding the underlying statistical distribution of sample data. The output can provide rich descriptions of natural groupings for further interpretation, depending on the objective of the exercise. A figurative illustration of the concept of clustering is shown in Fig. 7.1. This figure highlights the impact of retail promotions of a premium product on revenue for a particular manufacturer across its franchise stores. A larger size of the cluster indicates a higher number of stores belonging to that cluster. The results indicate that Clusters 2 and 5 have the highest contribution to revenue from this product. The success of the promotion is highest for Cluster 2, with incremental revenue in the range of $110,000–$140,000. For Cluster 6, the incremental gains are the least.

Although there has been a proliferation of applications of cluster analysis for pattern recognition, image processing, and information retrieval, it also has a rich history in other disciplines such as biology, psychiatry, geology, geography, and marketing. Extensive geo-demographic clustering systems discussed in the acquisition chapter, and telecom usage and credit card portfolio segmentation of the "Usage Management" chapter are relevant examples of clustering applications in the marketing area.

---

[3] Membership indicates the segment to which the observation belongs to.

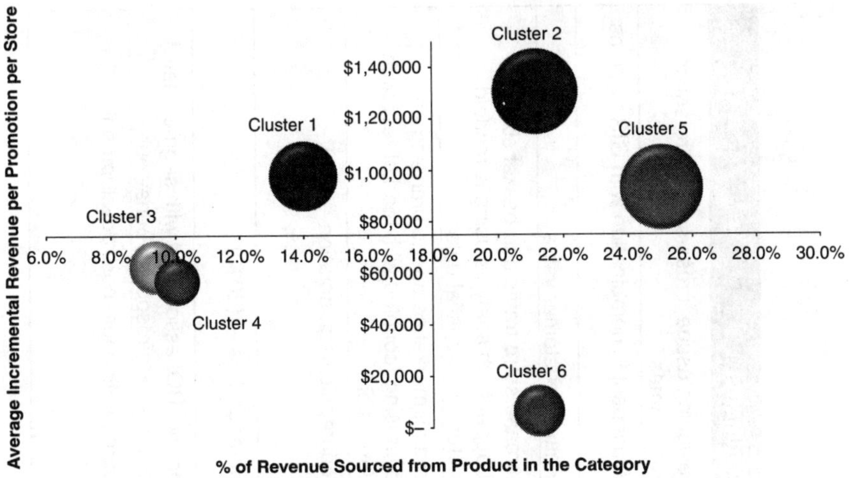


**Figure 7.1** Cluster Analysis—Retail Promotion

For detailed readings on this topic, readers are advised the following books: *Marketing Research* by Malhotra, *Data Mining Techniques* by Berry and Linoff and *Database Marketing* by Blattberg et al.

### 7.2.2.2 Applications

Table 7.3 spotlights applications of cluster analysis across various sectors.

### 7.2.2.3 Process

The process for cluster analysis is summarised in Fig. 7.2.

*Selection of Variables* The choice of variables for the development of customer related clusters depends on the objective of the clustering exercise and its application. The customer variables in the consideration set could range across geo-demographics, demographics, behavioural, revenue and cost, and others. Market research and competitive metrics are generally overlaid as profile characteristics on the developed clusters as these variables are usually not available at a customer level. One approach is to use as many variables as possible if the researcher is not well informed on which variables could be potential discriminators. On the other hand, variables that are most suitable for the objective at hand is strongly linked to theory or expert judgement in the subject. For example, a credit card portfolio segmentation for targeted customer marketing programmes will require customer demographics (e.g., age, income, occupation), behavioural (e.g., history and pattern of spend, revolve propensity, credit line utilisation), wallet share, and customer revenue. Cluster analysis

**Table 7.3** Applications of Cluster Analysis

| Industry | Area | Objective | Comments |
|---|---|---|---|
| Financial services/ Insurance | Portfolio analysis | Understanding your customer | Designing usage, cross-sell and retention programmes |
| | Branch location planning | Identify location based on potential sales, customer density/quality/dispersion | Works best in combination with GIS systems |
| Telecom | Usage | Increase MOU (minutes of usage) | Enhance customer value |
| Retail | Store planning | Store clustering | Increase store traffic and basket size. Shopper path analysis using K-medoid clustering for spatial data. |
| | Assortment planning | Display of items and its positioning | |
| General | Market strategy | Market entry/product innovation | Product/market segment, branding and advertising (coupled with market research information) |
| | Selection of test markets | Grouping cities into homogeneous clusters and selecting comparable cities to test various marketing strategies | Geographic segmentation |
| | Sales forecasting | Weighted clustering to improve sales forecasting | Kumar and Patel (2010) |
| | Marketing programmes/ Promotional offers | Targeted campaign management | Improve ROI associated with segment level customisation/response behaviour |
| | Model development | Indicators of cluster membership as predictor variables; separate scoring models by cluster | Segmentation for score development |

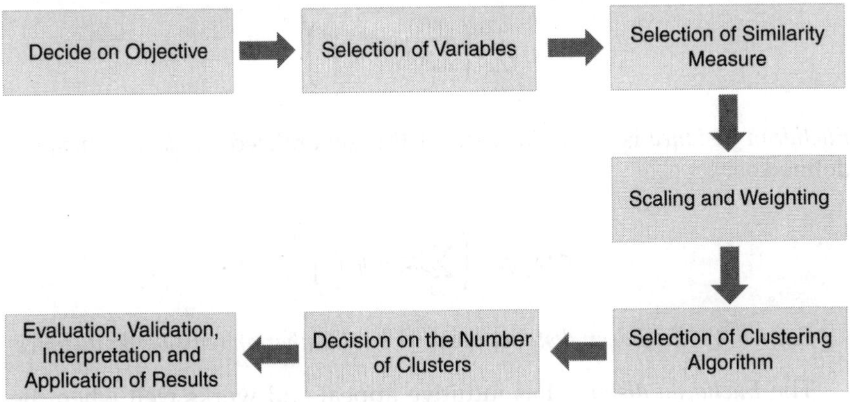


**Figure 7.2** Process for Cluster Analysis

for store location planning would depend on demographics, regional macroeconomic indicators, store location characteristics (e.g., malls, site details), and competition.

Although there is no hard and fast rule, it is advisable to:

- Limit the number of variables for easy interpretation and minimise issues of scaling
- Distinguish between variables for clustering and those for profiling
- Use principal components/factor analysis to determine the variable set for consideration (for high multi-dimensional data) and to address multicollinearity
- Remove outliers (observations with atypical values)

For very large sample sizes, it is practical and efficient to create a random sample and run the cluster analysis on this sample to come up with candidate cluster solutions. The candidate clusters are ultimately run on the full data file for finalisation. It is important to note that variable selection is a highly iterative process. The deletion and addition of variables depends on the evaluation of cluster output with every trial run.

*Selection of Similarity Measure* The concept of similarity is fundamental to the definition of a cluster as different similarity measures give diverse cluster results. Therefore, it is advisable to compare the respective results using different similarity measures. Although there are many such measures available, the focus will be on those that are frequently used.

**Distance Measure** Geometric distance between observations is their distance in a metric space. It is most common to calculate their dissimilarity using this measure. *Euclidean distance* (*d*) between two observations *x* and *y*, with *d – dimensional attribute set* is defined as:

$$d(x,y) = \left( \sum_{k=1}^{d} (x_k - y_k)^2 \right)^{1/2}$$

*Euclidean distance* is a special case of the generalised *Minkowski distance* defined as:

$$d(x,y) = \left( \sum_{k=1}^{d} |x_k - y_k|^p \right)^{1/p}$$

For $p = 2$ = *Euclidean distance* and $p = 1$ = *Manhattan (city-block) distance*

The *Euclidean distance* has intuitive appeal and works well when the data sample is "compact" or is characterised by "isolated" clusters, according to Jain et al., *Data clustering: A Review.* If variables have large ranges, *Manhattan distance* is preferred as distances are not squared. Therefore, it is less sensitive to large variance of one or more variables.

**Other Similarity Measures** Statistical or *Mahalanobis distance* takes into account the correlations between variables. For categorical variables, *matching type* similarity measures are appropriate, which evaluates the ratio of the number of matching attributes to the total number of attributes considered. *Angle* evaluates data points as vectors (which have both magnitude and direction) and measures the angle between them as a measure of similarity.

*Scaling and Weighting* Scaling is an important step in the clustering process. Variables are most often measured in different units and those that have a large range are given more importance in defining a cluster than those with a smaller range. This can lead to misrepresentation of the true underlying clusters. The purpose of scaling is to convert the variables into a common scale, in order to bring them into a comparable range. Weighting is done to incorporate information that some variables are more important than others, and involves a-priori knowledge or managerial importance of different clustering variables. Therefore, it is a subjective decision.

Scaling methods that are widely practised are listed:

- **Limiting range between 0 and 1 by using the transformation:** [X – L(X)]/[(H(X) – L(X)] where H(X) and L(X) are the highest and lowest value of the variable based on sample data
- **Indexing** by dividing each variable by sample variable mean
- **Standardising using the z-score transformation:** [X – M(X)]/STD(X) where M(X) and STD (X) are the mean and standard deviation of the variable based on sample data
- **Vector normalisation** which scales all the variables at once (Berry and Linoff)
- **Mahalanobis distance** measure standardises the variables

The trade-off of scaling is the loss of information as all variables are on equal standing with identical variances, although the original variances were originally unequal. Possible solutions to this issue are to compute the clusters with and without scaling and review its impact on the outcome.

*Selection of Clustering Algorithm* Selection of an appropriate clustering algorithm is critical to the effective use of cluster analysis. There are fundamentally two approaches to clustering—hierarchical and non-hierarchical.

**Hierarchical** Hierarchical methods proceed on the lines of a tree-like structure, by either a series of successive mergers (*agglomerative*), or a series of successive divisions (*divisive*).

The *agglomerative* algorithm starts with each observation representing a single cluster, with N clusters for N observations. The number of clusters is reduced to N – 1 based on a measure of *similarity* between them, by combining the two most similar observations. This process goes on until the desired numbers of clusters are formed. An initial step is to create a similarity matrix, a table of all pair-wise distances between clusters. An initial input is the pair-wise distance between individual pair of observations. There are variants for the agglomerative approach based on the distance used to measure similarity (Table 7.4).

*Divisive* method operates in the reverse direction, by starting with one group of N observations and divides the group into smaller groups based on a measure of *dissimilarity (distance)* between them. This process continues until the desired number of clusters are created, and stops when each observation becomes one cluster. According to Ketchen and Shook, *The Application of Cluster Analysis in Strategic Management Research,* there should be a match between the algorithm selected and the underlying structure of the data. Factors to be considered are—sample size, sample distribution, and types of variables, i.e., nominal, ordinal, ratio or interval.

**Non-hierarchical** Non-hierarchical method (also known as partitional method) partitions the data into a pre-specified number of clusters. The process involves selecting a cluster centre and then grouping/re-grouping all the observations using a criterion function. Cluster centres are the initial starting points for non-hierarchical cluster methods and clusters are built around these centres or seeds.

*K-means* is a very popular partitional clustering method as it is computationally faster than agglomerative techniques, especially for large datasets. It first starts with randomly assigning the N observations into K disjoint clusters, and iteratively improvises on the partitions by changing the cluster membership of each observation. The distance between the observation coordinates and centroid are calculated and the observation is either allocated to a different cluster or remains in the same cluster, depending on distance (assigned to the group with the nearest centroid). Cluster centroids are recomputed and multiple

**Table 7.4** Agglomerative Method—Variants

| Variant | Definition of Distance Between Clusters | Comments 1 | Comments 2 |
|---|---|---|---|
| **Linkage method** *Single linkage* | Distance between the closest members | Clusters have the feature that every member of a cluster is more closely related to at least one member of its cluster than to any member outside it | Based on nearest-neighbour rule. Does not perform well when clusters are poorly defined. |
| **Linkage method** *Complete linkage* | Distance between their most distant members | Clusters have the feature that all members in a cluster are within some known maximum distance of one another | Based on farthest-neigbourhood rule. Clusters are more compact than single linkage and is therefore preferred to the former. |
| **Linkage method** *Average linkage* | Average of the distance between all pairs of observations, where one member of the pair is from each of the clusters | Uses all information on all pairs of distances | Usually preferred to the single and complete linkage methods as it uses more information. |
| **Centroid method** | Distance between centroids | Centroid of a cluster is its average observation (mean values of the variables for all the observations in a particular cluster) | Less sensitive to outliers as cluster means are compared. Bias towards creating irregularly shaped clusters. Recommended to be used with interval or ratio data. |
| **Variance method** *Ward's minimum variance method* | Squared Euclidean distance to the cluster means | Distance measure is minimised | Suitable when number of observations in each cluster are expected to be approximately equal and there are no outliers. |

passes through the data set continue until a convergence criterion is met to arrive at an optimal solution (for example, no observations change cluster membership).

Another non-hierarchical method is probabilistic technique that incorporates uncertainity about cluster membership. This method overcomes some of the limitations of hierarchical (agglomerative) and K-means. These limitations are the assumption that each observation belongs to only one cluster with no reference to the degree or strength of cluster membership, and the issue of overlapping clusters. Readers can refer to Blattberg et al. and Malhotra, for more information on these techniques. The survey paper by Jain et al. is an advanced reading for analytics experts.

**Comparison of Hierarchical and Non-hierarchical Methods** Although easy to apply and understand, a critical limitation of the tree based hierarchical algorithm is that poor cluster assignment cannot be improvised, given only one pass of the data in a given iteration. Selecting the appropriate algorithm within the hierarchical approach can be demanding, and solutions are often unstable when observations are dropped, especially for low sample data size. Non-hierarchical have potential advantages over hierarchical methods. Non-hierarchical methods are less impacted by outliers as observations are allowed to switch cluster membership. Given the multiple passes through data, the final solution optimises within-cluster homogeneity and between cluster heterogeneity. K-means is computationally faster, translating into faster processing speed for large data files. It is also less stringent regarding requirements of store space as it does not save distance matrices. Although K-means is easy to implement, a limitation of this technique is that it is sensitive to the selection of the initial partition (Jain et al.), and requires pre-specification of the number of clusters and selection of cluster centres. It has been suggested that both algorithms be executed sequentially as a two stage process. Run the hierarchical algorithm to tentatively define the number of clusters and cluster centroids, which are then further used as inputs for the non-hierarchical method.

*Decision on the Number of Clusters* Determining the number of clusters is a challenge as it tends to be subjective, often depending on the method used and the application. For example, for an action and result oriented clustering objective of portfolio management, it is advisable to limit the number of clusters to ensure easy implementation. A few guidelines suggested by subject matter experts in this area are mentioned:

- For hierarchical (agglomerative) clustering technique, inspection of the dendogram. Dendogram or tree graph is a graphical devise for displaying cluster results and vertical lines represent clusters that are joined together. The distances at which clusters are combined are calculated from the dendogram, and the number of clusters is chosen at the point where the distance increase is suddenly high.

- For K-means clustering technique:
  - Fix the lower bound of K for the number of clusters and develop K clusters. Using a diagnostic measure, evaluate the cluster results and attempt another value of K. At every iteration, the overall strength of the collection of clusters is evaluated using a measure such as the ratio of the mean distance of cluster members from the cluster centre to the mean distance between clusters (Berry and Linoff).
  - The ratio of total within-group variance to between-group variance in relation to the number of clusters is plotted. The point at which an elbow or sharp bend occurs indicates an appropriate number of clusters (Malhotra).
- Maximise the function $G$ to find the optimal number of clusters (Blattberg et al.)

$$G(k) = \frac{(n-k)(T-W)}{(k-1)W}$$

where $k$ = Number of clusters
$n$ = Number of observations
$W$ = Square sum of the distances of observations to the centre of its cluster
$T$ = Square sum of the differences of each observation to the average observation (centre of the full data)

- Relative size of the clusters should be meaningful (Malhotra)
- Non-statistical basis such as a-priori theory or managerial judgement

### *Evaluation, Validation, Interpretation and Application of Results*

Evaluation of cluster analysis results is a highly subjective exercise. In general, clusters should have members that have a high degree of similarity, while the individual clusters should be different from each other. The strength of the resulting clusters can be assessed by comparing the average distance of the observations from the centroid to the average distance between cluster centroids. This can be carried out for each cluster separately and for the entire collection of clusters (Berry and Linoff). Other pointers that involve eye-balling the results are highlighted:

- Whether cluster output is making business sense. A critique of cluster analysis in management research is that it has the potential to offer inaccurate descriptions of groupings and impose groupings when none exist (Ketchen and Shook).
- One should be able to put a descriptor on the various clusters using clustering and profiling variables. This description should highlight segment differences. If it is not possible to do so, the process should be re-run with a modified set of clustering variables.

- The variable that is important for the objective of the exercise should be scrutinised. For example, for insurance lapse, the clusters should be evaluated by lapse rate and should rank order using a lift factor (cluster lapse rate by the average sample lapse rate). Table 7.5 shows that Cluster 6 has the highest lapse rate, while Cluster 2 has the lowest lapse rate based on the field "Lift".
- Compare the individual clusters by the clustering and profiling variables. This can be done by creating an index as shown in Table 7.6 and Table 7.7. Table 7.6 is the distribution of customers by age and APE (annual premium equivalent), and by cluster and sample population. Table 7.7 is an index table created by dividing the cluster distribution by the population distribution (for the respective variable and its category bands). Clearly, Cluster 6 is characterised by younger customers (age group 25–35) and lower

**Table 7.5** Cluster Output

| Cluster | Frequency | Pop | Centroid | Lapse Rate | # Lapse | Percentage of Lapsed Cases | Lift |
|---|---|---|---|---|---|---|---|
| 1 | 279618 | 24.4% | 1.9702 | 22.7% | 63473 | 15.6% | 0.64 |
| 2 | 137096 | 12.0% | 1.4855 | 18.4% | 25174 | 6.2% | 0.52 |
| 3 | 174231 | 15.2% | 2.0868 | 21.5% | 37529 | 9.2% | 0.61 |
| 4 | 104703 | 9.1% | 1.4855 | 33.6% | 35194 | 8.7% | 0.95 |
| 5 | 323432 | 28.2% | 1.7783 | 47.1% | 152366 | 37.5% | 1.33 |
| 6 | 128150 | 11.2% | 1.7783 | 72.3% | 92606 | 22.8% | 2.04 |
| | 1147230 | | | 35.4% | 406342 | 100% | |

**Table 7.6** Cluster Profile

| Cluster | Description | 1 | 2 | 3 | 4 | 5 | 6 | Pop |
|---|---|---|---|---|---|---|---|---|
| Age | 25–35 | 39.2% | 22.4% | 23.0% | 24.5% | 30.8% | 64.8% | 33.9% |
| | 35–40 | 17.0% | 19.6% | 11.3% | 20.6% | 19.6% | 10.6% | 16.8% |
| | 45–55 | 15.2% | 28.8% | 22.9% | 29.7% | 21.2% | 4.2% | 19.8% |
| APE | 0–5000 | 0.8% | 2.4% | 0.0% | 1.5% | 0.4% | 19.0% | 2.9% |
| | 5000–7500 | 17.7% | 1.2% | 17.4% | 16.6% | 12.7% | 20.5% | 14.5% |
| | 7500–10000 | 14.9% | 4.3% | 18.2% | 21.0% | 13.4% | 24.1% | 15.3% |
| | 10000–12500 | 10.7% | 1.4% | 9.6% | 59.3% | 14.6% | 9.5% | 14.8% |
| | 12500–25000 | 33.8% | 43.1% | 21.0% | 1.5% | 33.8% | 17.3% | 28.2% |
| | >25000 | 22.1% | 47.6% | 33.8% | 0.1% | 25.2% | 9.6% | 24.4% |

**Table 7.7** Cluster Profile Index

| Cluster | Description | 1 | 2 | 3 | 4 | 5 | 6 |
|---|---|---|---|---|---|---|---|
| Age | 25–35 | 1.16 | 0.66 | 0.68 | 0.72 | 0.91 | 1.91 |
| | 35–40 | 1.01 | 1.17 | 0.67 | 1.22 | 1.17 | 0.63 |
| | 45–55 | 0.77 | 1.45 | 1.16 | 1.50 | 1.07 | *0.21* |
| APE | 0–5000 | *0.28* | 0.86 | *0.00* | 0.53 | *0.12* | 6.67 |
| | 5000–7500 | 1.22 | *0.08* | 1.20 | 1.15 | 0.87 | 1.42 |
| | 7500–10000 | 0.97 | *0.28* | 1.19 | 1.37 | 0.88 | 1.58 |
| | 10000–12500 | 0.72 | *0.09* | 0.65 | 4.00 | 0.99 | 0.64 |
| | 12500–25000 | 1.20 | 1.53 | 0.74 | *0.05* | 1.20 | 0.61 |
| | >25000 | 0.91 | 1.95 | 1.39 | *0.00* | 1.03 | *0.39* |

premium (APE < 5000) than other clusters. Cluster 2 is a relatively higher premium (APE > 12,500) segment.

- Similar profile clusters should be combined together, making the results amenable to interpretation and application
- Low sample size of a cluster is a concern, leading to low confidence in the results. Therefore, cluster size should be kept above a threshold level based on total sample size.

The goal of validation is to ensure that a cluster solution is stable and representative of the general population of interest. This can be achieved by running multiple trials of cluster analysis by changing algorithms; changing distance measures; splitting sample into two random samples and analysing the cluster centroids separately; validating the results on hold out (in-sample and out-of-sample). For non-hierarchical methods, the order of observations may impact results and multiple runs using different order of observations should be conducted until the solution stabilises (Malhotra). Interpretation and application of results will be brought out using the telecom usage segmentation example.

### 7.2.2.4 Strengths and Challenges

- Does not require assumptions regarding the underlying statistical distribution of the data sample
- Exploratory in nature and data speaks for itself
- Results are easy to understand and can be presented easily to a non-technical audience
- Sensitive to outliers and results vary based on the starting cluster centres
- Subjective interpretation of results
- Resource intensive that requires several iterations to come up with valid clusters that are heterogeneous, of acceptable cluster size, and with purposeful interpretation

- Lacks (low) predictive capability, limiting its usage beyond current requirements of segmentation. Limits the ability to precisely assign cluster membership to a new observation. Cluster membership prediction requires regression modelling.
- Difficult to assess the relative importance of variables that represent cluster characteristics due to the lack of statistical measures to evaluate
- Interval data cannot be inputted directly as a variable into the algorithm, e.g., age groups 25–30, 30–35. These need to be transformed into indicator variables.

#### 7.2.2.5 Example—Telecom Usage Segmentation

*Objective* Segment based approach for usage enhancement programmes and improve ARPU for a telecom operator (fixed line).

*Data*

- Last 3 months of call transaction data, for example, call duration, number of calls, time of calls, domestic vs. international, in-plan vs. overage (out of plan) available at the line level, revenue per user (ARPU), plan type
- All consumer lines, mostly single account

*Methodology*

- K-means clustering algorithm was used
- Analysis was based on usage related variables, a consequence of the business objective of the exercise
- Factor analysis was first conducted on the variables and several sets of variables for cluster analysis were selected. After multiple cluster runs with these various sets, 7 variables were finally selected as clustering variables as they gave reasonable clustering solutions from a result and business reasoning perspective.
    - **Variables for factor analysis:** Total call amount, total call duration, total number of calls. Classification by inbound and outbound, in-plan and overage, peak and non-peak, weekday and weekend, domestic and international.
    - **Variables selected for clustering:** Total call amount, domestic outbound duration, international outbound duration, weekend outbound duration, in-plan duration, and plan type
- Eight clusters were finalised
- Revenue and usage tags are based on ARPU and average total outbound duration per month, respectively. Revenue includes revenue from outbound calls plus plan fees. Duration is in minutes and is an average value per line per month.

- Alpha-numeric tags for revenue and usage. The number denotes ranking, with 1 as the highest among all segments and L/M/H is the classification into low-medium-high.
- High outbound call minutes do not necessarily imply high ARPU as the pattern of calls is the primary driver of revenue

*Results* Output of cluster analysis is presented in Tables 7.8–7.13. A brief description and recommended actions are outlined.

- **Cluster 1:** Low usage segment. However, revenue ranking is not as low due to peak usage. Increase usage by migrating them to an attractive bundled offer. For example, data plan plus lower peak rates.
- **Cluster 2:** Second highest revenue segment mostly driven by domestic overage calls. Can further increase revenue by increasing average talk time per call through customised plans (average talk time on overage is similar to the average).
- **Cluster 3:** Highest usage with outbound call duration, 90% from in-plan. Increase revenue by making overage calling attractive.
- **Cluster 4:** Overall fourth highest usage segment and most calling is during in-plan hours. Usage on this segment can be improved by migrating them to plans with good balance of in-plan and overage tariffs.

**Table 7.8** Cluster Profile—Revenue and Usage

| Cluster | Distribution of Lines Across Clusters | Contribution to Revenue | Revenue Tag | Usage Tag |
|---|---|---|---|---|
| 1 | 17% | 16% | M/4 | L/6 |
| 2 | 7% | 14% | H/2 | H/3 |
| 3 | 7% | 9% | M/3 | H/1 |
| 4 | 18% | 15% | L/5 | H/4 |
| 5 | 7% | 17% | H/1 | H/2 |
| 6 | 21% | 14% | L/6 | L/5 |
| 7 | 19% | 10% | L/7 | L/7 |
| 8 | 4% | 5% | M/3 | L/6 |

| Revenue | % of Lines | % of Revenue |
|---|---|---|
| H | 14% | 31% |
| M | 28% | 30% |
| L | 58% | 39% |

| Usage | % of Lines | % of Revenue |
|---|---|---|
| L | 61% | 45% |
| H | 39% | 55% |

**Table 7.9** Cluster Profile—Inbound and Outbound

| Average of Variables Across the Clusters | | | | | | | |
|---|---|---|---|---|---|---|---|
| Cluster | Total Duration | Total Transactions | Outbound Duration | Outbound Transactions | Inbound Duration | Inbound Transactions | Average Talk Time (outbound) |
| 1 | 256 | 82 | 179 | 56 | 76 | 26 | 2.2 |
| 2 | 790 | 211 | 618 | 162 | 172 | 49 | 2.9 |
| 3 | 1609 | 294 | 1294 | 218 | 315 | 76 | 4.4 |
| 4 | 795 | 176 | 511 | 112 | 285 | 64 | 2.9 |
| 5 | 1134 | 188 | 848 | 133 | 287 | 55 | 4.5 |
| 6 | 254 | 72 | 188 | 51 | 66 | 21 | 2.6 |
| 7 | 27 | 12 | 19 | 7 | 9 | 6 | 1.5 |
| 8 | 228 | 70 | 178 | 51 | 50 | 18 | 2.5 |
| Average | 506 | 115 | 370 | 80 | 136 | 35 | 3.2 |

*Note:* Figures denote average per line per month. Duration is in minutes.

**Table 7.10** Cluster Profile—Domestic and International

| Average of Variables Across the Clusters | | | | |
|---|---|---|---|---|
| Cluster | International Outbound Duration | Domestic Outbound Duration | Average Talk Time per Call (International) | Average Talk Time per Call (Domestic) |
| 1 | 26 | 153 | 6.6 | 2.9 |
| 2 | 58 | 560 | 6.3 | 3.7 |
| 3 | 27 | 1267 | 4.9 | 5.9 |
| 4 | 26 | 485 | 5.8 | 4.5 |
| 5 | 336 | 512 | 9.9 | 5.2 |
| 6 | 8 | 180 | 5.0 | 3.7 |
| 7 | 3 | 15 | 5.4 | 2.6 |
| 8 | 19 | 159 | 5.0 | 3.4 |
| Average | 43 | 327 | 7.6 | 4.4 |

- **Cluster 5:** Second highest usage and highest revenue per line. Highest international calls (duration and transactions). Highest overage call duration but still less than in-plan. Competitive international rate plans.
- **Cluster 6:** Low usage segment, mostly in-plan. Potential to increase usage and revenue through plans with high fees/lower rate and bundled offers of value-added services.

**Table 7.11** Cluster Profile—Weekday and Weekend

| Average of Variables Across the Clusters | | | | |
|---|---|---|---|---|
| Cluster | Weekend Outbound Duration | Weekday Outbound Duration | Average Talk Time per Call (Weekend) | Average Talk Time per Call (Weekday) |
| 1 | 16 | 163 | 4.7 | 3.2 |
| 2 | 95 | 523 | 4.3 | 3.9 |
| 3 | 296 | 998 | 6.9 | 5.8 |
| 4 | 106 | 405 | 5.0 | 4.5 |
| 5 | 188 | 660 | 7.3 | 6.2 |
| 6 | 36 | 153 | 4.1 | 3.6 |
| 7 | 3 | 15 | 2.6 | 2.9 |
| 8 | 22 | 156 | 3.3 | 3.5 |
| Average | 72 | 298 | 5.5 | 4.5 |

**Table 7.12** Cluster Profile—Peak and Non-peak

| Average of Variables Across the Clusters | | | | |
|---|---|---|---|---|
| Cluster | Peak Time Outbound Duration | Non Peak Outbound Duration | Average Talk Time per Call (Peak) | Average Talk Time per Call (Non-peak) |
| 1 | 141 | 38 | 3.1 | 3.5 |
| 2 | 398 | 220 | 3.7 | 4.0 |
| 3 | 610 | 684 | 4.9 | 7.4 |
| 4 | 278 | 233 | 4.1 | 5.4 |
| 5 | 392 | 456 | 5.2 | 7.9 |
| 6 | 112 | 76 | 3.3 | 4.6 |
| 7 | 12 | 7 | 2.8 | 2.9 |
| 8 | 129 | 49 | 3.4 | 3.7 |
| Average | 205 | 165 | 4.0 | 5.7 |

- **Cluster 7:** Lowest usage and average talk time per call is less than 3 minutes. At the lowest end of revenue spectrum, customer feedback on understanding reasons for low usage is recommended.
- **Cluster 8:** Low usage segment, revenue upside from peak time and overage (50% of total outbound duration). Increase call volume through plans such as "friends and family" on the same network.

**Table 7.13** Cluster Profile—In-plan and Overage

| Average of Variables Across the Clusters | | | | |
|---|---|---|---|---|
| Cluster | Overage Call Duration | In-plan Call Duration | Average Talk Time per Call (Overage) | Average Talk Time per Call (In-plan) |
| 1 | 52 | 127 | 3.7 | 3.0 |
| 2 | 247 | 371 | 4.0 | 3.7 |
| 3 | 131 | 1163 | 3.4 | 6.5 |
| 4 | 72 | 439 | 3.3 | 4.9 |
| 5 | 286 | 562 | 5.7 | 6.9 |
| 6 | 33 | 155 | 3.1 | 3.9 |
| 7 | 6 | 12 | 3.4 | 2.4 |
| 8 | 87 | 91 | 3.9 | 3.1 |
| Average | 81 | 289 | 3.9 | 4.9 |

*Conclusions* Overlaying attrition on the existing framework can address both usage and retention together in one stroke as they are intertwined behaviours. An enhancement would be to integrate geo-demographic segmentation with the above usage clusters for media advertising and other subscriber-related actions. To this effect, Nielsen Company launched Mobile-PRIZM in 2008. This is a customised analysis of mobile usage patterns for PRIZM's 66 consumer segments that allows advertisers to make more informed decisions about where to place mobile advertising and target mobile customers more effectively.

## 7.2.3 Classification/Decision Tree

### 7.2.3.1 Introduction

Decision tree is a powerful and intuitive rule-based data exploratory method for discrimination, classification, generalisation, and prediction. Discrimination is the process of deriving classification rules from samples of classified observations. Classification is applying the rules to new observations of unknown class. Generalisation is uncovering a mapping from independent to dependent variables, that is useful for prediction of the dependent variable. Graphically depicted as a hierarchical and sequential tree-like structure, it works on the principle of recursively splitting a prospect or customer population into smaller and more distinct groups (with distinct classification rates based on the target variable). The splits are defined on the basis of predictor (independent) variables. Examples of a target variable are response to an offer, event of default, churn, and spend value. Belonging to the class of supervised learning, an advantage of this non-parametric multivariate technique is that it also identifies interactions among independent variables during the tree-building process. Using simple statistical tests, the results are easy to comprehend, communicate and quick to estimate. The output in the form of if-then rules are easy to interpret and can be used for classification and prediction. Widely applicable and popular, decision tree often constitutes an important preliminary step towards statistical scoring. In terms of nomenclature, it is termed as classification or decision tree if the dependent variable is categorical, and regression tree if it is continuous. However, decision tree is more frequently used.

The origin of decision tree was motivated by the requirement to analyse survey data. Statistical programmes such as AID (automation interaction detector) were developed by Sonquist et al. in the 1960s. A decade later, Hartigan modified AID to develop CHAID (Chi-square Automatic Interaction Detector). Subsequently, Breiman et al. (1984) developed an alternative algorithm called CART (Classification and Regression Trees). One of the latest developments in this area is RANDOM FORESTS by Breiman. Random forests is a collection of CART-like trees following specific rules for tree growing, tree combination and self-testing; data visualisation for high dimensional data; anomaly, outlier and error detection; analysis of small sample data; explicit missing value imputation; and generation of strong (accurate) predictive models[4].

Applications of decision tree extend from statistics to pattern recognition, decision theory, signal processing, machine learning, and artificial neural networks. While responder and non-responder profiles of personal loan to card cross-sell using decision tree were described in the "Cross-Sell" chapter, risk segmentation is discussed as the example in this section. A pictorial example of a travel-related decision tree is presented in Fig. 7.3. The objective of this segmentation is to assess the factors influencing the likelihood of a repeat visit to an international country. Description of this tree is done subsequently.

Berry and Linoff, *Data Mining Techniques* and Blattberg et al., *Database Marketing* are recommended books for this topic. A good survey journal article is by Murthy titled *Automatic Construction of Decision Trees from Data: A Multi-Disciplinary Survey*.

### 7.2.3.2 Applications

Table 7.14 brings to attention examples across various sectors.

---

[4] Salford Systems, "Data Mining with Random Forests: A Brief Overview to Random Forests", 2004.

**Table 7.14** Applications of Decision Tree

| Industry | Area | Objective | Data Used | Comments |
|---|---|---|---|---|
| Financial services/ Insurance | Portfolio risk segmentation | Understanding your customer—risk and reward | Demographics, product related behaviour, attrition, revenue-risk, credit bureau | Design programmes to manage portfolio profitability |
| | Acquisition | Determine "Straw-man" profile of a desirable customer | Application data, market research, market/census data, and competitor information (credit bureau) | |
| | Lapsation/ Reinstatement for insurance | Understanding profile of lapsed customers and reasons for lapse, for proactive retention and win-back strategies | Customer demographics, policy information, service/contact data, agent profile | Low–medium–high risk of lapse segments for differentiated contact strategy |
| Telecom | Churn | Attrition prediction | Call transactions— time, type, call drop information, service, and complaint log | Segment based retention strategies. Refer to Xevelonakis (2004). |
| Retail | Wallet share | Identify store specific shopper profile and purchase—cross buying behaviour to improve share of customer spend | Demographics, shopping behaviour, composition and value of basket of goods, and cross-buying data | Private label credit card study (US). Refer to Moore and Carpenter (2010). |
| | Sales promotional analysis | Which in-store activities most influence purchase decision? | Survey data, data related to promotions e.g., coupons, inserts, in-store vs. external | CHAID done for 4 customer categories. Refer to Shultz et al. (2011). |
| Hospitality | Hotel segmentation | Market segmentation for hotel guest rooms by benefits sought, to improvise benefits offered and increase sales | Hotel room attributes, service related factors, average room rate, and customer information | Factor Analysis, Cluster Analysis and CHAID are used for Korea market. Refer to Chung (2004). |
| General | Marketing programmes/ Promotional offers | Targeted campaign management to improve ROI through response, purchase history, and contact profiling | Psychographics, demographics, transaction data, loyalty data, marketing history | RFM, CHAID, and LOGISTIC are compared. Refer to McCarty and Hastak (2007). |

### 7.2.3.3 Basics

The starting point of a decision tree is the full sample (root node) under consideration. This root node is successively split into mutually exclusive groups and each observation is assigned to one group or the other. The entire sample is one root node that is split into two or more child nodes and subsequently split until the tree is complete based on the algorithm. The final child nodes are called terminal (or leaf) nodes, as they are the ends of the tree. Non-root and non-terminal nodes are called internal nodes. Classification rate indicates the probability of classification. For example, in Fig. 7.3, the target variable is whether a repeat visit to an international country will be made (1 = Yes, 0 = No). Predictor variables for this example are travel purpose, age, income and repeat visit status. The terminal nodes are Segments 1–6. Segment 1 has a classification rate of 70%, which is the probability of revisiting an international country for customers with travel purpose of vacation or leisure and less than or equal to 45 years in age. A split of the variable income (< $100,000 and ≥ $100,000) grows the tree to create Segments 4 and 5. Rule for Segment 5 can be expressed as: Travel purpose = Business and Income ≥ $100,000.

### 7.2.3.4 Process

The decision tree process is summarised in Fig. 7.4.

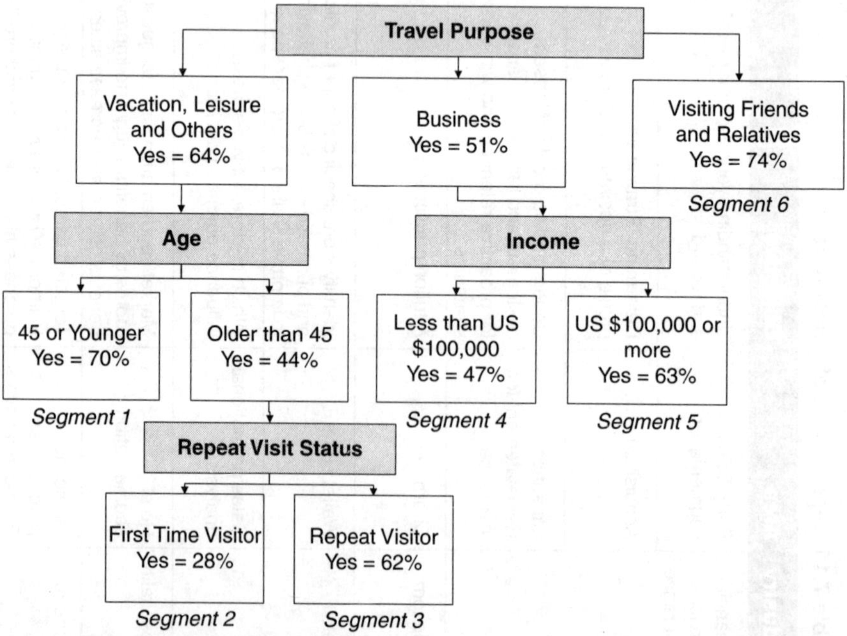


**Figure 7.3** Travel Segmentation

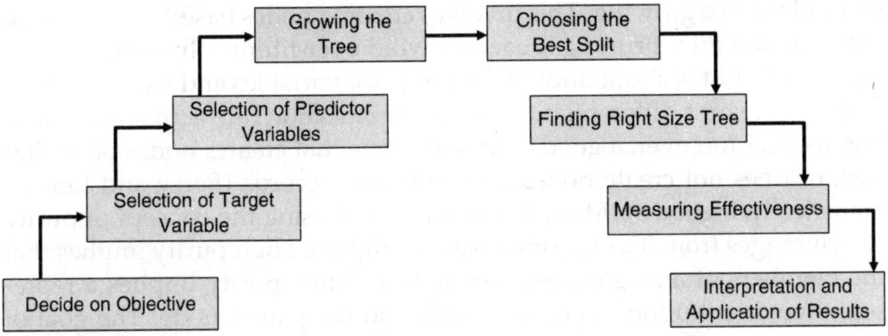


**Figure 7.4** Decision Tree Process

*Selection of Target (Dependent) and Predictor (Independent) Variables* The process of selection of the target and predictor variables for construction of a decision tree is guided by the objective of segmentation. Examples of categorical dependent variables with two classes are response to a marketing offer (yes–no); revolver–transactor; attrited (yes–no). For greater than two classes—number of days of stay (0–3 days, 3–5 days, 5–7 days, >7 days); low-medium-high revenue. For response—marketing history, demographics, and behavioural related variables are likely to be relevant. For an event such as attrition—behavioural, and service-related issues would tend to dominate. If the goal is prediction, it is important to confirm that the predictor variables used for the development of the tree will be available for classifying a new observation.

The choice of predictors for tree construction is a highly iterative procedure. Relevant predictors available in the data file are entered into the algorithm that outputs specific predictors and the associated splits as selected by the algorithm. Subsequently, the tree is re-constructed with a choice of predictors from the predictor set that was selected by the algorithm from the preceding step. The user may also force the entry of some predictors and its splits based on a-priori hypotheses. A few important predictors are also entered one at a time (univariate) to determine the individual influence of the predictor on the target. This step also aids in the evaluation of splits in a multivariate scenario. With every run, the resulting predictors and splits are evaluated from a statistical and business point of view and this process continues, until the tree is finalised. A high degree of judgement is involved by the analyst for determining the predictors that should be considered for tree construction. Factors such as multicollinearity is accomodated by the algorithm as it picks the predictor which has the best split (among competing variables). It is advisable to isolate multiple trees with different predictors and splits as "candidate" trees for finalisation.

*Growing the Tree and Choosing the Best Splits* Construction of a tree is generally top–down with greedy trees being the most commonly used method for tree growing. This involves creating nodes based on a criterion function and then pruning it back to avoid over-fitting[5]. Intuitively, finding a good split is about finding the predictor variables and its values, that result in the best differentiation of the classification rate across the resulting nodes. Moreover, a good split is also one that creates nodes of similar size, or does not create nodes with very few records (Berry and Linoff). Statistically, a good splitting rule is measured using the concept of purity which ranges from 0 to 1, from lowest to highest. High purity implies that the members of a single class dominate and low purity implies a representative distribution of classes, relative to the parent node. The goal of growing a tree is to maximise purity and it continues until it is no longer possible to increase purity. Purity measures are listed in Table 7.15. According to Murthy (1998), different purity measures are similar from a functional perspective. This observation explains the findings that performance is similar, although the resulting trees look different. In addition to purity measures, it is also important to ensure that each node in the tree contains sufficient number of total observations and sufficient number of target observations.

While decision tree commonly uses one predictor variable at a time for splitting rules, readers can refer to Murthy for applying multiple variables (multivariate splits), that is, a linear combination of predictors using advanced techniques. The CART algorithm has this functionality.

*Finding Right Size Tree* Finding the right size tree is guided by the objective that the classification should capture only the true characteristics of the data, and not the noise and randomness. Stopping rules aid in deciding when to stop adding branches (or child nodes) and are listed in Table 7.16. It has been observed that the quality of the tree depends more on a good stopping rule than on splitting rule (Breiman). Results vary based on the method deployed. Readers should refer to the example of CHAID and CART algorithms applied to direct mailing by Blattberg et al. (for comparison of results using these methods on the same data set).

*Measuring the Effectiveness of a Tree* Tree quality measures to evaluate "goodness" of a tree in order to decide which tree is better than the other will be discussed. The example of credit card risk segmentation will address the interpretation and application of results. Essentially, a choice among multiple "candidate" trees needs to be made, on the basis of the fact that several trees can correctly represent the same data. Table 7.17 is a list of evaluation criteria and corresponding measures to determine the "goodness" of a tree.

[5] To detect an over-fit model, readers should refer to the model evaluation section for logistic regression in Section 7.5.

Table 7.15 Purity Measures

| Purity Measure | Dependent Variable Type | Definition | Goal | Comments |
|---|---|---|---|---|
| **Gini score/ Population diversity** | Categorical | Weighted sum of squares of the proportion of classes | Choose split if Gini score increases | Employed by CART. Challenge when number of classes is large. |
| **Entropy reduction/ Information gain** | Categorical | Entropy is a measure of disorganisation in information theory. Shannon's entropy formula can be referenced from Berry and Linoff and Blattberg et al. | Choose split that reduces entropy or uncertainty by the greatest amount | Uncertainty reduces from root to internal to terminal node. |
| **Chi-square test** | Categorical | Tests the null hypothesis that there is no significant difference between expected and observed data. The statistic is defined as the sum of squares of the standardised difference between expected and observed frequency of an occurrence, between multiple disjoint samples | Chose split if chi-square value is higher, implying higher purity | Oldest splitting rule. Employed by CHAID. |
| **Reduction in variance** | Continuous | Variance of target variable | Choose split which reduces target variable variance | |
| **F-test** | Continuous | Test the null hypothesis that variances of two populations are equal | Larger value indicates that proposed split has successfully split the population into sub-populations with significantly different distributions | |

**Table 7.16** Stopping Rules

| Stopping Rule | Method | Definition | Comments 1 | Comments 2 |
|---|---|---|---|---|
| **Pruning** (merging smaller leaves to address spurious/unstable results). Generates a number of candidate sub-trees | CART pruning algorithm | Employs greedy algorithm to grow a complete tree, until no new splits can be found to increase purity. Calculates/uses an adjusted error rate, based on an in-built cross-validation procedure to identify weak nodes for pruning, to create a more stable model. | Adjusted error rate is misclassification rate, adjusted for the number of leaves, with a penalty factor. Misclassification rate is the percentage of observations classified incorrectly. Tree with lowest validation error rate is selected as the final model. | Developed by Breiman et al. (1984). Validation data required may be a constraint; large variance for small samples. |
| | C5 pruning algorithm/Quinlan pessimistic pruning | Similar to trees grown by CART. It calculates an estimate of the worst error rate based on sampling and a given confidence interval. Examines error rate at every node and assumes true error rate to be significantly worse. | Decision is based on development/training data only. | |
| | Stability based pruning | Chi-square test for pruning. | Split is pruned when the confidence interval is less than the user defined threshold. | Useful as CART and C5 may fall short of pruning nodes that are unstable. |

*(Continued)*

**Table 7.16** Stopping Rules *(Continued)*

| Stopping Rule | Method | Definition | Comments 1 | Comments 2 |
|---|---|---|---|---|
| **Threshold stopping** | Impurity e.g., Chi-square (CHAID) | Threshold imposed on the value of splitting criterion. If it falls below threshold, tree growth is terminated e.g., stopping based on p-value of chi-square test. | Can be at a local (individual node) or entire tree level (global). | Does not guarantee problem of over fitting. p-values can be varied and the resulting trees can be analysed. |
| | Number of observations in node | Node is not split if number of observations is less than a threshold number/ % of starting number of observations. | Typically 1–5% of starting sample (root node) or minimum of 100 observations is a guideline. | Judgemental factor of analyst. This rule should be used with all other rules. |
| **Business/Logic** | Tree to Rule conversion | Simplicity of rules. Whether rules are making intuitive sense/in line with business logic. | Complex rules based on over-grown trees/ill-defined predictors may miss the bigger picture with low inference value. Implementation challenges with too many segments. | Should use this rule in combination with pruning and threshold stopping. |
| **Costs** | Misclassification costs | Based on a cost function with cost structure based on Type-1 and Type-2 error. | Cost function assigns weight to the probability of misclassification. | Also a good measure for evaluating effectiveness of a tree. |

*Note*: Leaves are the terminal nodes

**Table 7.17** Evaluation Criteria

| Evaluation Criteria | Measures | Comments |
|---|---|---|
| Quality of the branches | • Number of records entering the nodes<br>• Proportion of observations in each class across nodes<br>• Whether predictor variables and splits make business sense | This should hold for development and validation samples |
| Classification accuracy | Misclassification error and costs (in-time and out-of-time sample) | Error rate on out-of-time validation is expected to be higher than in-time validation. But a large difference reflects an unstable model. |
| Generalisation accuracy | Cross-validation or boot-strapping on a sample independent of development | 10 fold cross-validation is a good rule for assessing tree quality (Murthy) |
| Discrimination power | Gains table/lift factor | Gains table and lift factor will be discussed in the risk segmentation example |

In case of significant differences of results across development and validation, it is generally advisable to:

- Compare the development and validation sample as a preliminary step of the process (variable statistics and sample data distribution)
- Identify predictors and splitting rules that do not hold for the validation file and re-run the decision tree on the development file, by removing the predictors that are not holding up and/or revising the splitting rule
- Pass validation data through the decision tree algorithm to evaluate potential predictors. Some of this information can be incorporated back for re-developing the tree on the development sample.
- The trade-off is that the purity measures may not be as high as the original versions. However, for prediction purposes, it is important to optimise results to make sure that validation results are satisfactory.

### 7.2.3.5 Strengths and Challenges

- Easy to interpret with visual and intuitive appeal and wide applicability
- Non-parametric method that can handle broad spectrum range of data distributions, including uni-modal and multi-modal

- No/Low sensitivity to outliers or monotonic transformations of predictor variables
- Missing data is classified as a separate category
- Good at capturing interaction effects among multiple predictors beyond two variables (joint effect on the target variable)
- Concluding rules have crisp, insightful, and predictive inference value and therefore, useful for actionable strategies
- Practical experience is that the method is robust as the results are usable for a few implementation cycles
- Valuable for pre-modelling analysis to determine segmentation schema for developing separate models (if required); the set of initial predictor variables; interaction effects; imputation of missing values
- Fast algorithm and data preparation is less intensive than others as it can handle both discrete and continuous variables
- Hierarchical partitioning implies computational efficiency in classification (Murthy)
- Requires cautious interpretation of inter-relationships between variables in line with hypothesis and expected outcomes
- Complex rules may have low inference value
- Spurious results due to small sample size, mostly observed at terminal nodes, and which may warrant further investigation
- No clear weighting scheme for the splits. Based on the chi-square value of the splits, it is not possible to assign number weights as in regression analysis.
- Classification tree splits are conditional (and therefore the hierarchy). Hence, if a satisfactory predictor variable is taken out from the decision tree, there is a risk of losing significant value from subsequent predictor variables in the hierarchy.

### 7.2.3.6 Example—Credit Card Risk Segmentation

*Objective* To understand the risk-reward dynamics based on a behavioural segmentation of a credit card portfolio. To facilitate distinct segmental level portfolio management actions to improve profitability.

*Data* Data consists of a credit card open accounts as of Month X, which has not been delinquent during the past 6 months prior to/at Month X. Performance of these accounts over the next 12 months from Month X is used to determine the delinquency related target variable. The predictor variables include application data, account-related performance information (the past 12 months from month X), and recent credit bureau snapshot. The starting sample (after exclusions) is 200,000 accounts with

12 month account delinquency rates: Ever 30+ = 3.63%, Ever 90+ = 2.41% and NCL account rate (Loss Rate) = 2.53%.

### *Methodology*

- CHAID is used to construct the decision tree, with manual pruning to delete smaller unstable nodes
- All three definitions of the target variable—Ever 30+/Ever 90+ (Delinquency) and Ever NCL Status (Write-off or Loss) were attempted and separate decision trees were run using all these definitions. Ever is defined as the occurrence of the event at least once during the next 12 months, starting from month X. 30+ and 90+ delinquency implies non-payment of full credit card dues beyond 1 and 3 billing cycles, respectively. Do note that definitions vary by organisation.
- The target variable Ever 90+ (If Ever 90+ = 1, then BAD; else GOOD) was selected based on the following evaluation criteria:
    - Whether BAD RATE and number of BADS are sufficient for classification
    - How good is the separation of the GOODS and BADS across nodes (Value of BAD RATE, Chi-square and significance values of splits, and lift factor)
    - Whether splitting rules are making business sense
    - Commonly followed definition of BAD that is used by the lending institution, so that results can be synchronised with other findings/analysis
    - Roll back from 90+ is much lower; a very small percentage of accounts migrate to a lower delinquency state

### *Results*

- The top most node of Fig. 7.5 (which has not been numbered) is the root node which has the starting population as well as the basic sample statistics. The nodes, which have been numbered from 1 to 12 are the terminal nodes that will form the basis for actions.
- Numbers reported in the boxes are the sample size of the node and delinquency statistics. Ever 90+ is highlighted in bold to reflect the sample BAD RATE of 2.41%. The delinquency rates and the corresponding number of accounts in delinquent and NCL status are stated for each node.
- Chi-square values and associated p-values are reported. As one goes down the hierarchy, the declining order of importance is clear as Chi-square values drop from top to bottom. The p-value cut-off can be specified while developing the tree at 1%, 5% and 10%, respectively. In this case, 1% is taken as the cut-off.

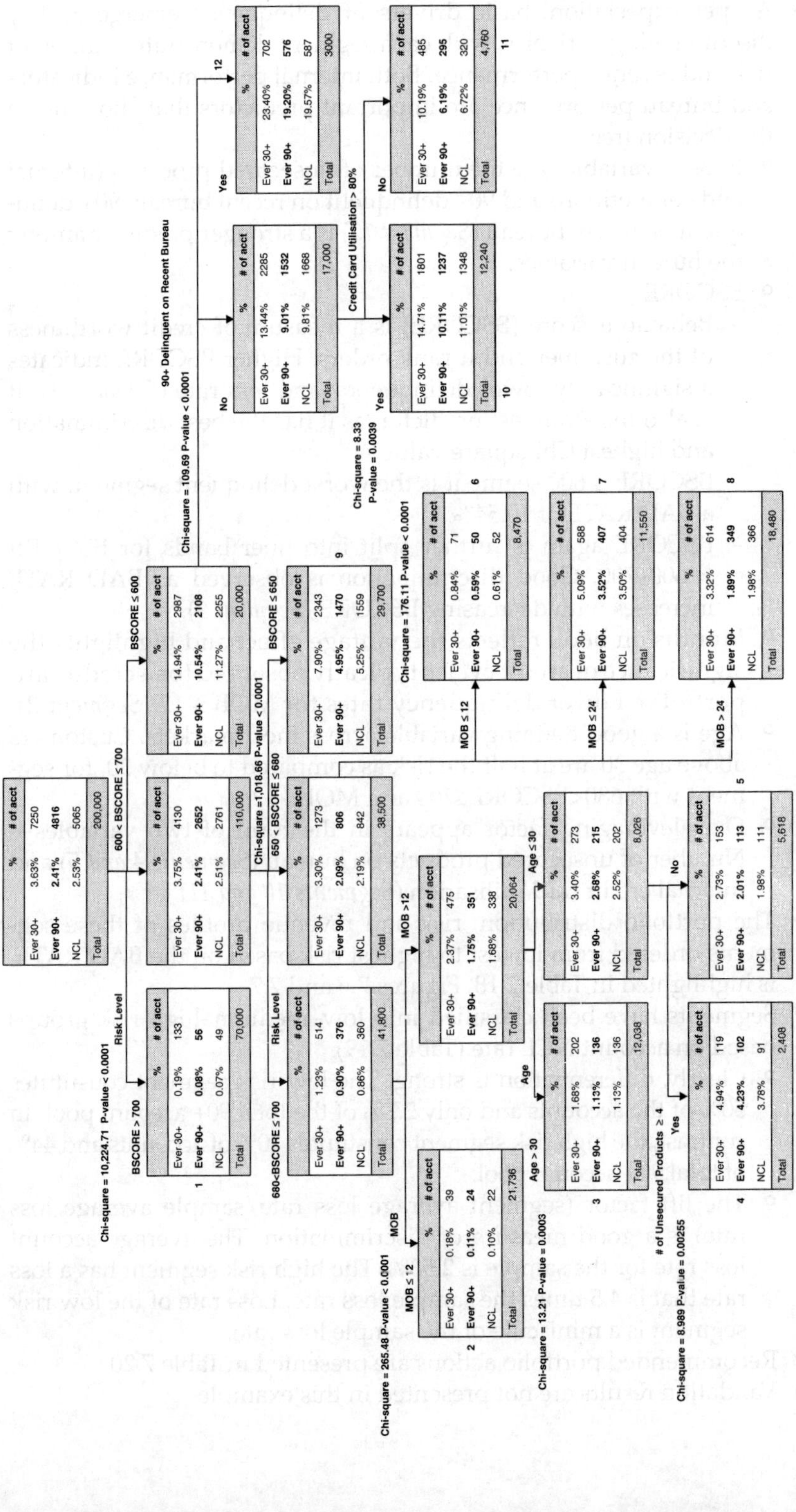


**Figure 7.5** Decision Tree Risk Segmentation

- As per expectation, basic drivers of delinquency emerge as key discriminating variables, with each segment demonstrating different risk and revenue performance. Both internal performance indicators and bureau performance are important predictors that show up in the decision tree.
  - Bureau variables are the number of unsecured products (internal and competition) and 90+ delinquent on recent bureau. 90+ delinquent on recent bureau (*Segment 12*) is a stronger predictor among the bureau variables.
  - BSCORE
    - Behaviour score (BSCORE) is a measure of credit worthiness of the customer and it rank orders. Higher BSCORE indicates a significantly lower delinquency and loss rate (*Segment 1*). It is also the strongest predictor, as it has the best discrimination and highest Chi-square value.
    - BSCORE ≤ 600 segment is the worst delinquent segment, with a BAD RATE of 10.54%.
    - BSCORE again is further split into finer bands for BSCORE = 600–700. Good discrimination is observed as BAD RATE increases with decreasing BSCORE (*Segment 9*).
  - Months on book reflects the vintage effect and highlights the significance of credit cycles typically observed for a credit card portfolio. Lower delinquency rates for MOB ≤ 12 (*Segment 2*).
  - Age is a good defining variable across most markets. Customers above age 30 are at half the risk as compared to below 30, for segment with 680<BSCORE≤700 and MOB> 12.
  - Over-leveraging factor appears in the form of two variables—Number of unsecured products on bureau (*Segments 4 and 5*) and internal credit card utilisation (*Segments 10 and 11*)
- The portfolio distribution, risk and revenue profiles of these segments ordered from lowest to highest risk based on the BAD RATE, is highlighted in Table 7.18, Figures 7.6 and 7.7
- Segments have been classified into low–medium–high risk groups based on account NCL rate (Table 7.19)
  - Clearly, differentiation is strong. The low risk segment constitutes 50% of the accounts and only 2.7% of the total 90+ account pool. In contrast, the high risk segment constitutes 10% of accounts and 44% of total 90+ account pool.
  - The lift factor (segment average loss rate/sample average loss rate) is a good measure of discrimination. The average account loss rate for the sample is 2.53%. The high risk segment has a loss rate that is 4.5 times the sample loss rate. Loss rate of the low risk segment is a miniscule of the sample loss rate.
- Recommended portfolio actions are presented in Table 7.20
- Validation results are not presented in this example

**Table 7.18** Portfolio Distribution by Risk Segment

| Risk Segment | Account Distribution % | Contribution to Balance % | Share of Wallet (SOW) |
|---|---|---|---|
| 1 | 35.0% | 7.50% | 4.11% |
| 2 | 10.9% | 3.40% | 19.10% |
| 6 | 4.2% | 2.70% | 22.30% |
| 3 | 6.0% | 1.40% | 19.13% |
| 8 | 9.2% | 14.30% | 19.30% |
| 5 | 2.8% | 9.50% | 22.10% |
| 7 | 5.8% | 6.10% | 21.10% |
| 4 | 1.2% | 3.40% | 13.14% |
| 9 | 14.9% | 26.50% | 19.50% |
| 11 | 2.4% | 5.40% | 21.41% |
| 10 | 6.1% | 18.40% | 15.58% |
| 12 | 1.5% | 1.40% | 8.00% |
| Average | | | 17.72% |

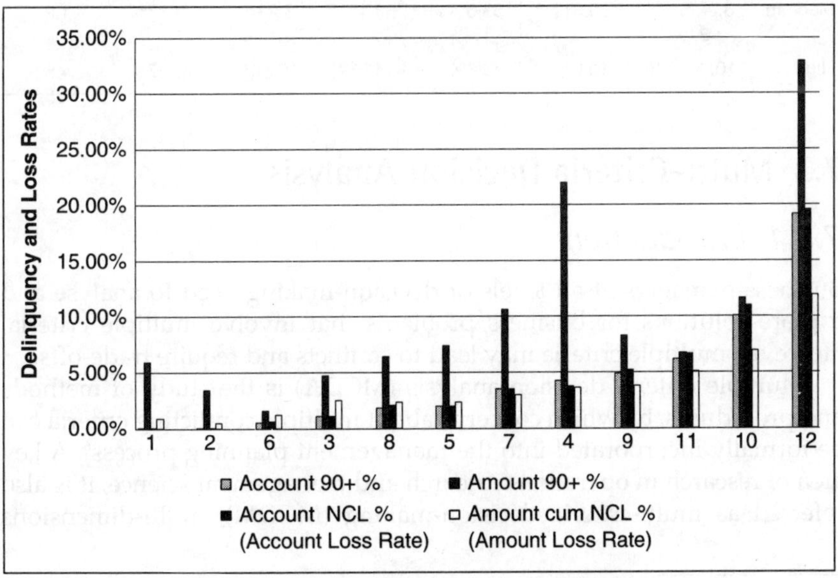


**Figure 7.6** Delinquency and Loss Metrics By Risk Segment

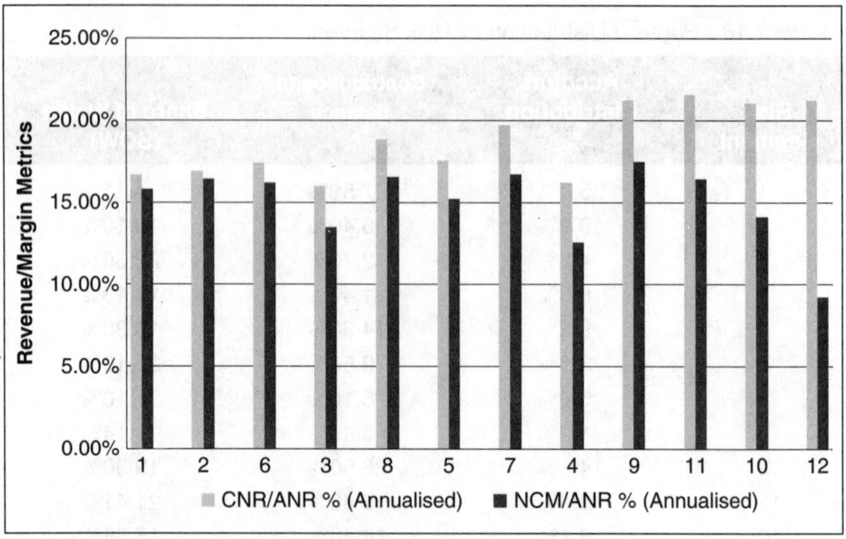


**Figure 7.7** Revenue and Margin Metrics By Risk Segment

**Table 7.19** Risk Distribution

| Risk | Segments | % of Accounts | % of 90+ Accounts | % of NCL Accounts | Account 90+ Rate | Account NCL Rate (Account Loss Rate) | Lift (Based on Loss Rate) |
|---|---|---|---|---|---|---|---|
| Low | 1, 2, 6 | 50.1% | 2.7% | 2.4% | 0.13% | 0.12% | 0.05 |
| Medium | 3, 4, 5, 7, 8, 9 | 39.9% | 53.5% | 53.1% | 3.23% | 3.37% | 1.3 |
| High | 10, 11, 12 | 10.0% | 43.8% | 44.5% | 10.54% | 11.27% | 4.5 |

# 7.3 Multi-Criteria Decision Analysis

## *7.3.1 Introduction*

Business managers at all levels of decision-making need to analyse and explore solutions for business problems that involve multiple criteria. However, multiple criteria may lead to conflicts and require trade-offs.

Multiple criteria decision analysis (MCDA) is the study of methods and procedures, by which concerns about multiple conflicting criteria can be formally incorporated into the management planning process[6]. A key area of research in operations research and management science, it is also referred as multi-criteria decision-making (MCDM), multi-dimensions

[6] As defined by the International Society on Multiple Criteria Decision Making.

**Table 7.20** Action Plan for Risk-based Segmentation

| Risk Segment | Node | Profile | Strategy | Programme |
|---|---|---|---|---|
| Low risk | 1 | Low revenue/low risk mass segment. More than one-third the population with less than 10% contribution to balance, lowest SOW. | Increase usage to increase SOW | Spend incentives, balance transfer, loan on card, profitability based line increase if required (to accommodate potential incremental balance) |
| | 2, 6 | 15% of accounts with 6% contribution to balance. Good share of wallet. | Potential to increase balance contribution | |
| Medium risk | 3, 5 | 9% of accounts and 11% of balance. Lower than average NCM/ANR% | Improve revenue | Cross-sell of value added services for fee revenue |
| | 7, 8, 4 | 16% of accounts and 24% of balances. Mature vintage with 2 segments having above average 90+ delinquency rate. | Improve collection strategies at early and later buckets for segments 4 and 7 | Early warning systems. Collection scores to improve collections efficiency. Segment 4 seems to be over-leveraged. Curtail lending to this segment. |
| | 9 | Best performing segment with highest NCM/ANR % with more than a quarter of balances. | Grow this segment, increase portfolio contribution | Acquisition strategy to increase through the door population. Identify ideal customer through "straw man" analysis, using classification tree based on acquisition customer information. |
| High risk | 10 | NCM/ANR% below average due to high loss rate. Highly leveraged group with high credit card utilisation. | | Risk-based pricing |
| | 11 | Good risk return trade-off with highest CNR/ANR %. Good share of wallet. | Grow this segment | Given good share of wallet, offer balance transfer to a selected cherry picked lot. Since sample is small, evaluate viability. |
| | 12 | Lowest return segment with highest loss rate. | Do not acquire | Sample size small. Monitor closely as this segment is delinquent on competitor products. |

decision-making (MDDM) and multi-attributes decision-making (MADM). MCDA is designed to help the decision-maker finalise a choice among a set of pre-specified alternatives. Each MCDA problem is associated with multiple attributes and these attributes are also referred to as "decision criteria". As different attributes represent the different dimensions from which the alternatives can be viewed, they may conflict with each other. These conflicts can be resolved through trade-offs that require a relative ranking of the attributes. Most MCDA methods require that attributes be assigned weights of relative importance, and these weights are usually normalised. Further, these multiple attributes must be aggregated into a single measure of performance (score) using the calculated weights, to which a decision rule can be applied. One short coming of trade-offs is the failure to capture interactions among criteria.

Among MCDA methods, the analytic hierarchy process (AHP) has become increasingly popular in recent years and is discussed in Section 7.3.2. An application of AHP to the determination of a credibility score for credit evaluation of manufacturing firms is elaborated. AHP involves a good degree of judgement on the part of the decision-maker through pair-wise ranking of the criteria that are used to derive the weights. Principal components analysis (PCA), traditionally used for reduction of data dimensionality, can also be deployed for multi-criteria decision-making. In this case, weights can be calculated objectively from the resulting principal components. Section 7.3.3 presents an example of the application of PCA for the development of a performance score relating to the choice of vendor supplier.

## *7.3.2 Analytic Hierarchy Process (AHP)*

### 7.3.2.1 Introduction

Analytic hierarchy process (AHP) is a subjective multi-criteria evaluation approach for decision-making that handles complexity with intuitive appeal. Originated by Saaty in the 1980s, AHP is a theory of measurement through pair-wise comparisons and relies on the judgements of experts to derive priority scales based on relative importance. AHP works on the basis of three basic principles—decomposition, comparative judgements, and synthesis of priorities. Decomposition of the problem into a hierarchy implies that each level of the hierarchy consists of a set of criteria, which is further broken into sub-criteria for the next level of hierarchy. Pair-wise comparisons are done using Saaty's scale of absolute judgments that represents how much more, one criteria dominates another (at the same hierarchy level), with respect to its immediate higher level (parent) criteria in the hierarchy. Using these pair-wise comparisons, relative priorities (local weights) are established for each of these sub-criteria and criteria, at every level of hierarchy. These local

**Table 7.21** Applications of AHP

| Broad Application | Examples* |
|---|---|
| Selection | Software selection; project management—vendor/contractor selection and project delivery method; warehouse site selection |
| Evaluation | Credit worthiness; quality of journals; environmentally conscious manufacturing programmes; highway transportation |
| Cost-benefit analysis | Evaluate success factors and develop strategies for environmental management system; linking investment decisions to activity based costing; whether concurrent engineering for an electronics company should be implemented? |
| Allocations | Geographic location allocation decisions; resource allocation; sales plan with limited production capacity |
| Planning and development | Scenario planning for conflicts in a country; planning a health care system; integrated approach for reactive power price |
| Priority and ranking | Model quality control systems; decision regarding quality control measures in the service industry |
| Decision-making | Education decision problem; decision support model to identify successful new ventures |
| Forecasting | Inventory demand forecasting; technological forecasting; forecasting exchange rate |

*AHP is used stand alone or in conjunction with other analytical methods

*Source:* Derived using information from Vaidya and Kumar (2006).

weights are further transformed into global weights for the final level of the hierarchy (representing the decision-maker's weights for the set of alternatives). Calculation of the evaluation score is the final step in the AHP process. This method encourages a consensus or a group approach as the determination of hierarchy and relative evaluations can be made through collective participation and discussion by experts. Among the numerous publications by Saaty on this topic, a good example-oriented overview journal paper is *Decision Making With the Analytic Hierarchy Process*, published in 2008.

Some of the successful applications of AHP in academia, industry, and government, are shown in Table 7.21. Readers can also refer to an extensive survey article by Vaidya and Kumar's paper titled *Analytic Hierarchy Process: An Overview of Applications* for examples across the globe. The subsequent example that discusses the development of credit worthiness score using AHP will elaborate on the detailed methodology.

### 7.3.2.2 Process

The process is explained in Fig. 7.8.

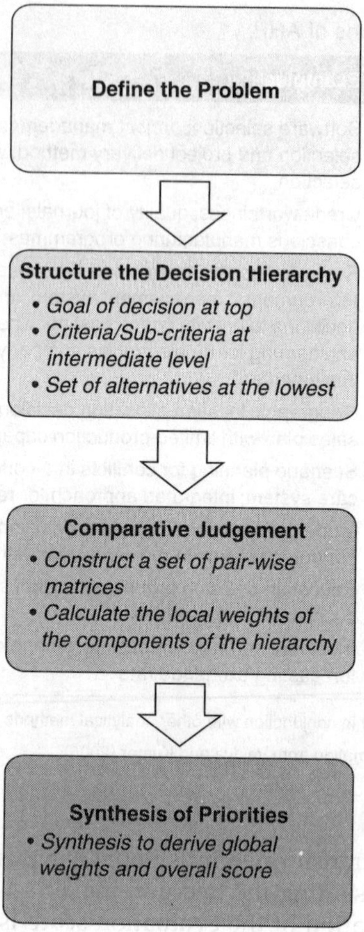


**Figure 7.8** AHP Process

### 7.3.2.3 Example—Credibility Score

A decision analytic tool (credibility score) is developed for evaluating the credit worthiness of manufacturing firms and is used for credit granting decisions by banks. AHP is employed to construct a credibility score based on both financial and non-financial information. The authors Yurdakul and Tansel in their 2004 published paper, identify the need for using a multi-criteria approach on the basis of technical, financial, and economic performance. All these factors are considered in order to compensate for the existing challenges relating to the credit evaluation process in Turkey. As stated by the authors, some of these gaps are the lack of structured and uniform decision-making framework; high reliance on financial factors (e.g., financial ratios, company financial statements) in an environment of unreliable information and unstable economic and political conditions. This example is "Adapted from *International Journal of Production Economics*, Volume 88, Issue 3, Yurdakul and Tansel, *AHP Approach in the Credit Evaluation of the Manufacturing Firms in Turkey*, Pages 269–289, Copyright (2004), with permission from Elsevier".

*Define the Problem* The goal is to develop a credibility score, combining both financial and non-financial factors.

*Data* Textile firm data (one of the largest cotton yarn and fabric producers in Turkey); credit evaluation reports prepared by credit experts (as opposed to technical and financial experts); financial statements of the firm; interviews of credit experts of the bank and management of the firm involved; data from the textile industry; and data published by a Turkish government organisation.

*Structure the Decision Hierarchy* The top level of the hierarchy is the goal and for this example, it is the firm's credibility score as illustrated in Table 7.22. Credibility score is a combination of both financial and

**Table 7.22** AHP Hierarchy

| | | |
|---|---|---|
| Goal–Hierarchy–Level 1 | Credibility score | |
| Criteria–Hierarchy–Level 2 | Financial score | Non-financial score |
| Criteria–Hierarchy–Level 3 | Capital structure and long-term solvency | Revenue generation capacity |
| Criteria–Hierarchy–Level 4 | • Debt to equity<br>• Bank debt to equity<br>• Short-term bank debt to short-term liabilities<br>• Fixed assets to total capitalisation<br>• Net sales to equity | |
| Criteria–Hierarchy–Level 3 | Short-term liquidity | Cost control capacity |
| Criteria–Hierarchy–Level 4 | • Cash-flow liquidity ratio<br>• Current ratio<br>• Account receivables turnover<br>• Inventory turnover<br>• Debt turnover | |
| Criteria–Hierarchy–Level 3 | Operating efficiency and profitability | Other factors |
| Criteria–Hierarchy–Level 4 | • Percentage of increase in net sales<br>• Net profit margin<br>• Return on assets<br>• Return on equity<br>• Operating profit margin | |

*Source:* Derived using infomation from Yurdakul and Tansel (2004).

non-financial factors that take the form of two separate scores (criteria–hierarchy–level 2). The focus of this section is the calculation of financial score.

- Four levels of hierarchy are defined. Goal is defined as the top of the hierarchy (level 1), followed by criteria as subsequent levels in the hierarchy (levels 2–4). Criteria–level 4 is the lowest level in the hierarchy and forms the set of alternatives. For criteria–hierarchy–level 3, parent criteria is criteria–hierarchy–level 2 and sub-criteria is criteria–hierarchy–level 4.
- Three distinct categories of "capital structure and long-term solvency", "short-term liquidity", and "operating efficiency and profitability" (criteria-hierarchy-level 3) are defined.
- Further, financial measures in the form of financial ratios under each of these separate categories are identified. Each category has five different financial ratios as measures (criteria–hierarchy–level 4). These financial ratios were derived from financial statements of the firm.
- Performance ratings for all the 15 financial ratios of the particular firm were assigned. This was done by benchmarking with the average values for the industry, as reported by the Central Bank of Turkey (assigned a rating of 0.5). For example, if cash-flow liquidity ratio takes a value of less than 0.45, a performance rating of zero is assigned, and if it takes a value greater or equal to 1.40, a performance rating of 0.3 was given.

*Comparative Judgement* To obtain local weights, each set of criteria is evaluated using a pair-wise comparison matrix with respect to their parent category in the hierarchy. This is based on a measurement methodology. The measurement relies on a 9-point scale of Saaty[7] as per Table 7.23. Pair-wise comparisons indicate the degree to which one criteria dominates another criteria at the same level, with respect to its parent criteria. Pair-wise comparison matrix is shown as a matrix for all the 5 financial ratios—for the category "capital structure and long-term solvency" in Table 7.24.

- Debt to equity is considered slightly more important than all the other financial ratios, with respect to the category (parent criteria) "capital structure and long-term solvency". Based on Saaty's scale, the ranking takes the value of 2 (comparing rows to columns). Similarly, the reciprocal of 2 is entered into the corresponding cells (comparing columns to rows).
- Normalised pair-wise comparison matrix is calculated by dividing each value in the cell by its respective column total that is not

[7] Saaty, "How to Make a Decision: The Analytic Hierarchy Process", 1990. Available online at http://www.elsevier.com/authored_subject_sections/S03/Anniversary/EJOR_free16.pdf.

**Table 7.23** Saaty's Fundamental Scale

| The Fundamental Scale | | |
|---|---|---|
| **Intensity of Importance on an Absolute Scale** | **Definition** | **Explanation** |
| 1 | Equal Importance | Two activities contribute equally to the objective |
| 3 | Moderate importance of one over another | Experience and judgment strongly favor one activity over another |
| 5 | Essential or strong importance | Experience and judgment strongly favor one activity over another |
| 7 | Very strong importance | An activity is strongly favored and its dominance demonstrated in practice |
| 9 | Extreme importance | The evidence favoring one activity over another is of the highest possible order of affirmation |
| 2, 4, 6, 8 | Intermediate values between two adjacent judgments | When compromise is needed |
| Reciprocals | If activity *i* has one of the above numbers assigned to it when compared with activity *j*, then *j* has the reciprocal value when compared with *i* | |

*Source:* Saaty (1990).

represented here. The sum of the rows for the normalised pair-wise matrix is called the eigenvector and is "column f" of Table 7.24.

- Local weights are calculated by dividing each normalised row sum by the number of financial ratios in the matrix (5). This is "column g" of Table 7.24.
- Similar pair-wise comparisons were done for the other 10 financial ratios (for each of the other two financial categories of "short-term liquidity" and "operating efficiency and profitability").
- CR (Consistency Ratio) is a measure of inconsistency of judgements and should be less than 0.1. Readers can refer to Saaty (1990) for the formula.
- Local weights for all the 15 financial ratios are presented in Table 7.25. Debt to equity, cash-flow liquidity ratio, and percentage of increase in net sales are considered the most important in their respective financial categories. This importance is reflected by the magnitude of the respective local weights.

**Table 7.24** Pair-wise Comparison Matrix for Capital Structure and Long-term Solvency

| Capital Structure and Long-term Solvency | D/E | BD/E | STBD/STL | FA/TC | NS/E | Eigen Vector = Sum (Cell Value/Column Sum) | Local Weight = Row Sum/Number of Criteria |
|---|---|---|---|---|---|---|---|
| Column label | *a* | *b* | *c* | *d* | *e* | $f = (a/3 + b/4.5 + c/6 + d/7.5 + e/9)$ | $g = f/5$ |
| Debt to equity (D/E) | 1 | 2 | 2 | 2 | 2 | 1.60 | 0.32 |
| Bank debt to equity (BD/E) | 1/2 | 1 | 2 | 2 | 2 | 1.21 | 0.24 |
| Short-term bank debt to short-term liabilities (STBD/STL) | 1/2 | 1/2 | 1 | 2 | 2 | 0.93 | 0.19 |
| Fixed assets to total capitalisation (FA/TC) | 1/2 | 1/2 | 1/2 | 1 | 2 | 0.72 | 0.14 |
| Net sales to equity (NS/E) | 1/2 | 1/2 | 1/2 | 1/2 | 1 | 0.54 | 0.11 |
| Column sum | 3 | 4.5 | 6 | 7.5 | 9 | | |

*Source:* Adapted from *International Journal of Production Economics*, Volume 88, Issue 3, Yurdakul and Tansel, *AHP Approach in the Credit Evaluation of the Manufacturing Firms in Turkey*, Pages 269–289, Copyright (2004), with permission from Elsevier.

**Table 7.25** Calculation of the Financial Score

| Financial Ratios | Performance Value | Performance Rating | Local Weight | | Global Weight | Performance Score |
|---|---|---|---|---|---|---|
| | | | Financial Ratio | Category | | |
| Column label | a | b | c | d | e = c*d | f = b*e |
| **Capital structure and long-term solvency** | | | | | | |
| Debt to equity | 0.87 | 1.0 | 0.32 | 0.50 | 0.16 | 0.160 |
| Bank debt to equity | 0.32 | 1.0 | 0.24 | 0.50 | 0.12 | 0.121 |
| Short-term bank debt to short-term liabilities | 0.39 | 0.8 | 0.19 | 0.50 | 0.10 | 0.075 |
| Fixed assets to total capitalisation | 1.00 | 1.0 | 0.14 | 0.50 | 0.07 | 0.072 |
| Net sales to equity | 2.49 | 0.7 | 0.11 | 0.50 | 0.06 | 0.038 |
| **Short-term liquidity** | | | | | | |
| Cash-flow liquidity ratio | 0.91 | 0.9 | 0.35 | 0.25 | 0.09 | 0.078 |
| Current ratio | 1.41 | 0.9 | 0.27 | 0.25 | 0.07 | 0.061 |
| Account receivables turnover | 4.00 | 0.6 | 0.18 | 0.25 | 0.05 | 0.027 |
| Inventory turnover | 6.35 | 1.0 | 0.11 | 0.25 | 0.03 | 0.027 |
| Debt turnover | 6.40 | 0.5 | 0.09 | 0.25 | 0.02 | 0.012 |
| **Operating efficiency and profitability** | | | | | | |
| Percentage of increase in net sales | 66.50 | 1.0 | 0.34 | 0.25 | 0.09 | 0.084 |
| Net profit margin | 0.03 | 0.1 | 0.26 | 0.25 | 0.07 | 0.006 |
| Return on assets | 0.05 | 0.1 | 0.18 | 0.25 | 0.05 | 0.004 |
| Return on equity | 0.01 | 0.2 | 0.13 | 0.25 | 0.03 | 0.007 |
| Operating profit margin | 0.07 | 0.4 | 0.09 | 0.25 | 0.02 | 0.009 |
| **Sum of "column f"—Financial score** | | | | | | 0.781 |

*Source:* Reprinted from *International Journal of Production Economics*, Volume 88, Issue 3, Yurdakul and Tansel, *AHP Approach in the Credit Evaluation of the Manufacturing Firms in Turkey*, Pages 269–289, Copyright (2004), with permission from Elsevier.

*Note:* Numbers have been rounded off to 2 decimal places.

- By category, weights can be calculated for all the three categories, using pair-wise comparison matrices with respect to the financial score (parent criteria). This is reflected in "column d" of Table 7.25. Highest importance is given to "capital structure and long-term solvency" with the highest local category weight of 0.5, followed by a weight of 0.25 for the other two categories. The rationale for these weights is that the amount and proportion of debt in a firm's capital structure is an important factor for predicting the long-term financial health of a firm in Turkey.

*Synthesis of Priorities* The calculation of the financial score is presented in Table 7.25. Global weights for the set of alternatives are derived by multiplying the weights for financial ratios with category level weights for the respective category ("column e"). Cross-product of global weights and performance rating gives the performance score for the respective financial ratio ("column f"). The sum of all performance scores over all the 15 financial ratios gives the financial score. The non-financial score is calculated using the same approach as the financial score, and is further integrated with the financial score to derive the creditability score. The weighting scheme is 0.50 each (average of the two scores).

*Conclusions* A distinct advantage of this study is the use of both financial and non-financial factors for credit evaluation. The final credibility score reflects both quantitative and qualitative criteria as the non-financial score incorporates measures such as brand image (firm characteristics), attractiveness of the industry to global competitors (competition intensity), and others. Similar research has been done in the area of credit extension and credit limit assignment for corporate lending by Srinivasan and Kim titled *Credit Granting: A Comparative Analysis of Classification Procedures.* AHP can be extended to develop a judgemental credit score for a retail bank. This is of particular relevance to situations characterised by the absence of/or limited credit history. This score can be used for applicant screening for new business launches, a stop-gap arrangement before a full-fledged traditional credit score is developed. Nonetheless, despite these attractions, AHP has come under criticism and this discussion is not within the scope of this chapter.

## *7.3.3 Principal Components and Factor Analysis*

### 7.3.3.1 Introduction

Principal components analysis (PCA) is a multivariate statistical technique used for data dimensionality reduction and summarisation. The primary objective is to extract a few uncorrelated linear composites of the original variables (called principal components), that account for the maximum variance in the data. As a data exploration and compression technique for high dimensional data, principal components analysis can enhance understanding and further usefulness of a data structure composed of a large number

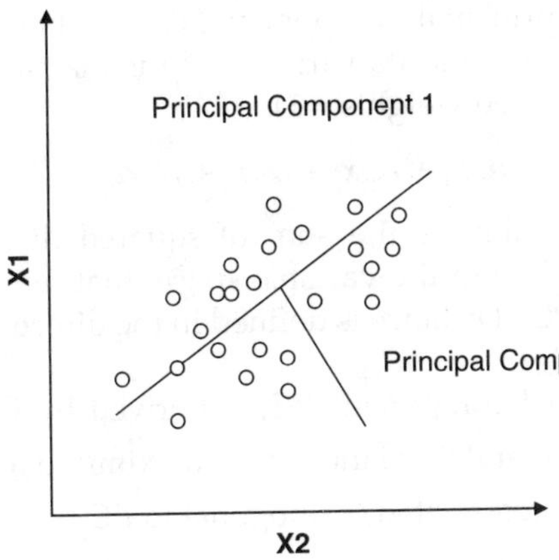


**Figure 7.9** Graphical Representation of Principal Components

of correlated variables. Moreover, principal components analysis can aid in the selection of candidate variables for inclusion and deletion in a model as a practical remedy for addressing multicollinearity for regression methods. For cluster creation and detection, the use of principal components for detecting outliers and the graphical visualisation of principal components can be very useful. Regarding segmentation, principal components analysis was the basis of banking segmentation in the "Usage Management" chapter. Figure 7.9 is a graphical description of principal components.

While both principal component and factor analysis work towards the goal of reducing dimensionality of the original data set, principal components analysis maximises the total variance accounted for in the original variables. On the other hand, factor analysis (FA) focuses on explaining the common variance among the original variables on the basis of few underlying factors. Principal components analysis is also used prior to factor analysis for determining the dimensionality of a common factor space. The prime focus will be on principal components analysis, with a brief write-up on factor analysis later in the section.

The earliest description of principal component analysis is by Pearson (1901) and Hotelling (1933). Applications of principal components and factor analysis are very diverse and range across disciplines such as biology, meteorology and social sciences, besides industry. For this topic, a simple and intuitive read is a book by Dunteman titled *Principal Components Analysis*. For factor analysis and its applications to marketing research, *Marketing Research* by Malhotra is recommended.

### 7.3.3.2 Basics

Assume a $p$ random vector of standardised variables $(x_1, x_2, x_3, \ldots\ldots x_p)$ with a covariance matrix defined over $n$ observations. The objective is to find $k$ principal components that maximise the variation of $p$ original variables, with $k \leq p$. The first principal component $PC_1$ is a linear combination of $(x_1, x_2, x_3, \ldots\ldots x_p)$ such that its variance $(\lambda_1)$ is maximised, subject to $\Sigma_{i=1}^{p} \alpha_{1i}^2 = 1$ (sum of squared weights = 1).

$$PC_1 = \alpha_{11}x_1 + \alpha_{12}x_2 + \alpha_{13}x_3 + \cdots \alpha_{1p}x_p$$

Geometrically, it minimises the sum of squared distances of the $n$ observations from the line in the variable space, that represents the first principal component $PC_1$. Distance is defined in the direction perpendicular to the line.

The second principal component $PC_2$ is derived by finding weights $(\alpha_{21}, \alpha_{22}, \ldots\ldots \alpha_{2p})$ such that its variance $(\lambda_2)$ is maximised and $\sum_{i=1}^{p} \alpha_{2i}^2 = 1$ and $\sum_{i=1}^{p} \alpha_{1i}\ \alpha_{2i} = 0$ (uncorrelated/orthogonal to $PC_1$).

This process continues for the third principal component $PC_3$ and so on.

*Features*

- **Uniqueness:** The principal component solution is unique
- **Eigenvector:** The initial output of principal components analysis are variable weights $\alpha_{j1}, \alpha_{j2}, \ldots \alpha_{jp}$ for $PC_j$ for $j = 1, 2, \ldots. k$. The pattern of variable weights for a particular principal component are used to interpret the principal component. The relative size of the weights associated with a particular principal component indicates the relative contribution of the variable to the variance of the principal component. It is also termed as ***latent vector***.
- **Eigenvalue:** Variance of a principal component. The maximisation of variance $(\lambda)$ of a principal component is equivalent to maximising the sum of squared correlations of the principal component with the original variables. It is also termed as ***latent root***.
- **Variance:** The first principal component accounts for the largest amount of variation in the sample, followed by the second principal component, and so forth.
- **Loading matrix:** Loadings are the correlation of the variables (appearing in the principal component) with the principal component, and is relatively easier to interpret than the eigenvector. Loading $(l_{ji})$ for variable $x_i$ is equal to $\sqrt{\lambda_j}\alpha_{ji}$, for principal component $PC_j$. Sum of squares of all loadings for a principal component is equal to the eigenvalue or variance of that principal component.
- The sum of variances of all principal components is equal to the sum of variances of the original variables. Therefore, it is important to find the first few principal components $(k < p)$ that account for most of the variation of the original variables.

### 7.3.3.3 Process

The process is outlined in Fig. 7.10.

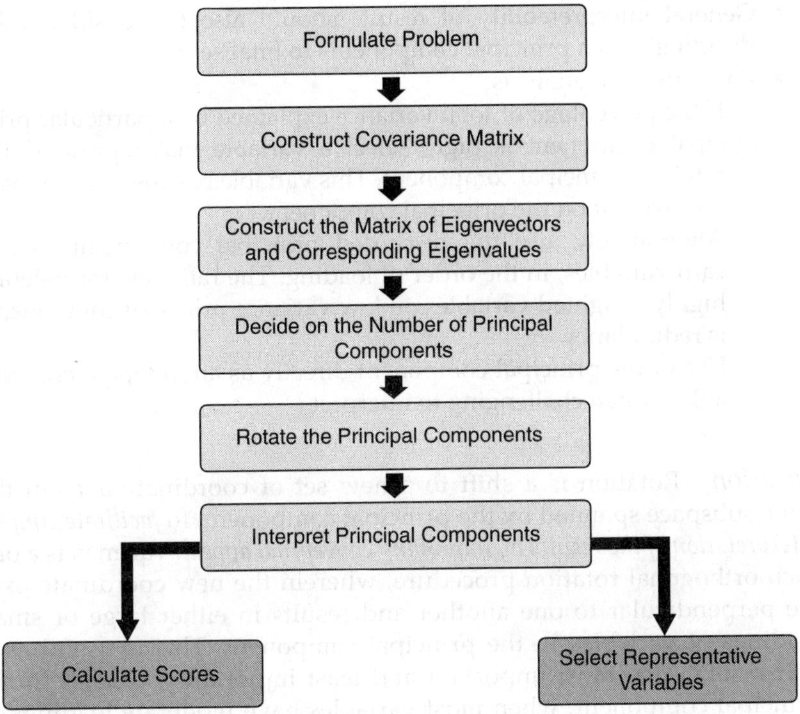


**Figure 7.10** Process for Principal Components Analysis

*Decision on Principal Components* How many and which principal components to retain is discussed. An important point to note is that the more principal components retained relative to the number of variables, the less parsimonious is the outcome (Dunteman). A few guidelines are highlighted:

- Drop principal components which have an eigenvalue $\leq 1$ as standardised variables have a variance of 1 (Kaiser's rule). According to Dunteman, this may result in discarding principal components, although small, but important. Jolliffe recommends a more reasonable cut-off of eigenvalue $\geq 0.70$, to take into account sampling variation and avoid the problem of retaining too few principal components.
- Scree graph by plotting the latent roots. Reject those principal components after which a steep fall in variance is detected.
- Retain the principal components that comprise up to 80% or 90% of total variation, depending on the particular data set
- Bartlett's test for unequal eigenvalues. Using this test for various values of *k*, it can be determined as to how many principal components have a substantial contribution to variation and how many are noise (Joliffe).

- General interpretability of results should also be considered for deciding which principal components to finalise
- For regression analysis:
  - If the percentage of total variance explained by a particular principal component is high, select a variable that represents the retained principal component. This variable has the highest loading/weight on the principal component.
  - Alternatively, use the discarded principal component to discard variables, in the order of loading. The rationale for deleting highly weighted variables on low variance principal components is redundancy.
  - Use of the principal component directly as an independent variable is often challenging to interpret

*Rotation* Rotation is a shift to a new set of coordinate axes in the same subspace spanned by the principal component, to *facilitate simpler interpretation of the results by improving conceptual appeal*. Varimax is a one such orthogonal rotation procedure, wherein the new coordinate axes are perpendicular to one another and results in either large or small loadings of variables in the principal component. This is useful as it helps isolate the most important and least important variables in the principal component, when most variables have moderate loadings in the principal component. Choice between rotated and un-rotated results depends on interpretability from the analysts' perspective. It needs to be noted that the total variance of the original principal components and rotated versions are equal.

### 7.3.3.4 Comparison to Other Multivariate Methods

Discriminant analysis focuses on difference among groups, and calculates weights for a linear composite that maximises the between group variance relative to within group variance on that linear composite. Linear regression also give results of a line of closest fit, by minimising the sum of squared distances of the points from the line (in the direction of the dependent variable). These distances are not perpendicular to the line as in principal components analysis.

### 7.3.3.5 Factor Analysis

Based on an underlying model, factor analysis focuses on explaining the common variance, unlike the total variance in principal components analysis. The common variance among the observed variables is assumed to reflect the correlation of the observable variables to some underlying, but not directly observable (latent) variables. A variable in the data set can be expressed as a linear combination of hypothetical unobserved common factors plus a factor unique to that variable. Unlike principal components analysis, it does not provide a unique transformation from variable to factors. Principal components analysis is one of the methods to estimate the factor loading matrix. Another factor analysis procedure is maximum likelihood factor analysis that assumes multivariate normality of the variables. Some examples of latent variables are quality of life, consumer confidence, and willingness to pay.

The similarity of results for principal and factor analysis depends on the values of communalities; communality for each variable is defined as the portion of total variance shared with the remaining variables. When communalities are small or vary considerably, the results will differ. When it is closer to the value of 1, the results will be close. Results will also be similar if the number of variables under consideration is large.

The choice of principal components versus factor analysis depends on the particular situation and the objective of data analysis, according to C. R. Rao, *Principal Component and Factor Analysis.* The recommendation is to use principal components analysis when the purpose is reduction of data dimensionality and factor analysis when the objective is to explain the correlations or association between the original variables. According to Dunteman, factor analysis is recommended when the variables in the data set contain a substantial amount of measurement error. Measurement error is a part of unique variance, which is uncorrelated with common variance.

### 7.3.3.6 Strengths and Challenges

- Useful data summarisation technique in the case of highly correlated variables, while maintaining the inherent properties of the data analysed
- Helpful secondary tool for customer segmentation, especially when the combinations of variables for the creation of customer segments is not well known or understood
- Outlier detection is possible, by plotting the principal component scores
- Quick to estimate with most software packages having canned programmes
- The resulting principal components may be hard to interpret, while the variables themselves are easy to comprehend. As C. R. Rao mentions in his paper, "While the roles of PCA and FA in exploratory data analysis are clear, the exact use of the estimated principal components and factors in inferential data analysis, or in planning further investigations do not seem to be satisfactorily laid out".
- If relationships between variables are non-linear, principal components analysis or factor analysis may not be a suitable method for dimension reduction (Fair Isaac White Paper, 2003)
- A high degree of subjectivity is involved in the interpretation of results

### 7.3.3.7 Example—Vendor Selection

*Objective* To develop a decision support tool for vendor selection based on multi-attribute evaluation criteria of price, delivery, quality and others. A single evaluation measure (score) is proposed for appraising supplier performance. This example is from *Journal of Supply Chain Management*, Volume 36, Issue 2, Petroni and Braglia, *Vendor Selection Using Principal Component Analysis*, Pages 63–69, Copyright (2006), John Wiley & Sons, Inc., Adapted with permission of John Wiley & Sons, Inc.

*Data* A medium-sized bottling machinery/complete packing line firm is faced with a supplier choice decision among 23 suppliers. Actual data considered includes supplier-related attributes for a sample of 23 suppliers. The original attributes include product price; technology capabilities; management capabilities; production facilities and capacity; shipment quality; and delivery compliance. These variables are further transformed into output/input ratios (d1–d6) as measures of performance. The data related to performance measures are reflected in Table 7.28.

d1 = Product price/technological capability
d2 = Product price/management capabilities
d3 = Shipment quality/management capabilities
d4 = Shipment quality/technological capability
d5 = Delivery compliance/production capability
d6 = Delivery compliance/management capabilities

*Methodology*

- Input data was first standardised. Results are sensitive to scaling and it is important to get it right before commencing on component extraction. One recommendation is to scale the original variables by the inverse of the standard deviations.
- Correlation analysis was done by creating the correlation matrix to test whether there is significant correlation among the variables. Bartlett's test of sphericity, to test the null hypothesis that correlation matrix is an identity matrix (off-diagonal elements are zero), could not be rejected at .001 level of significance. This result implies that variables are correlated, thereby warranting a multivariate analysis of this kind.
- Principal components analysis was conducted using six performance variables (d1–d6), with the objective that the decision maker would prefer to select the supplier that provides the best combination of these six performance variables
- For better interpretability, varimax rotation of the principal components was used for the three principal components selected

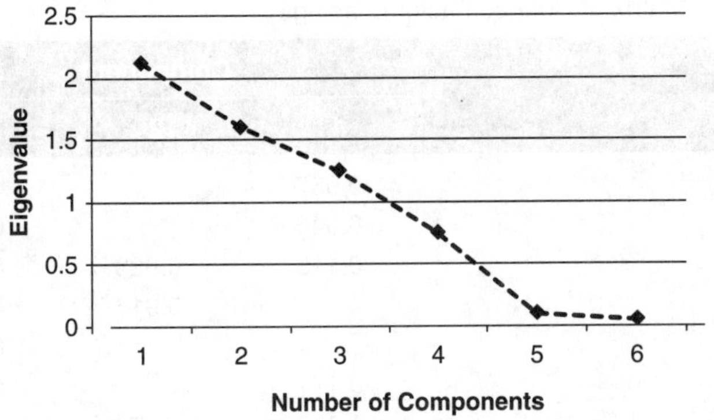


*Source: Journal of Supply Chain Management*, Volume 36, Issue 2, Petroni and Braglia, "Vendor Selection Using Principal Component Analysis", Pages 63–69, Copyright (2006), John Wiley & Sons, Inc., Reproduced with permission of John Wiley & Sons, Inc.

**Figure 7.11** Scree Plot

### *Results*

- The eigenvalues of the six principal components are presented in Fig. 7.11 in the form of a Scree plot. The variance drops significantly after three principal components. This result explains the selection of the first three principal components.
- Rotated factor loading matrix (Table 7.26)
  - The first three principal components represent 83.3% of the variance of the total sample (based on eigenvalues)
  - The first principal component represents delivery compliance as the loadings are the highest on variables $d_5$, $d_6$
  - Similarly, the second principal component represents shipment quality with very high loadings on variables ($d_3$, $d_4$)
  - The third principal component represents price with strong price-related variables ($d_1$, $d_2$)
  - Authors did not report loadings for values $< 0.1$
  - The squared sum of the factor loadings for a principal component is approximately equal to the eigenvalue of that component. Readers can verify this.
- Further scoring weights were calculated for all the six variables. Scoring weights are derived based on the factor loadings weighted by the percentage of variance captured by each of the three principal components. Weights are given in Table 7.27.

$$w_1 = 0.171 \times 0.31885 + 0 \times 0.28508 + 0.749 \times 0.229249$$

**Table 7.26** Matrix of Rotated Factor Loadings

| Variable | Component 1 | Component 2 | Component 3 |
|---|---|---|---|
| d6 | 0.987 | | |
| d5 | 0.946 | | 0.247 |
| d3 | 0.115 | 0.923 | 0.256 |
| d4 | | 0.918 | 0.282 |
| d2 | | | 0.778 |
| d1 | 0.171 | | 0.749 |
| Eigenvalue | 1.913 | 1.71 | 1.377 |
| % of variance | 31.885 | 28.508 | 22.949 |
| % of cumulative variance | 31.885 | 60.393 | 83.342 |

*Source: Journal of Supply Chain Management*, Volume 36, Issue 2, Petroni and Braglia,"Vendor Selection Using Principal Component Analysis", Pages 63–69 Copyright (2006), John Wiley & Sons, Inc., Adapted with permission of John Wiley & Sons, Inc.

**Table 7.27** Scoring Weights

| Weights | Value |
|---|---|
| w1 | 0.2264 |
| w2 | 0.1785 |
| w3 | 0.3585 |
| w4 | 0.3264 |
| w5 | 0.3583 |
| w6 | 0.3147 |

*Source:* Derived using data from Petroni and Braglia (2006).

A final performance score was calculated for each of the 23 firms based on the following logic. Firm 4 had the highest score as shown in Table 7.28.

$$\text{Score} = w_1 \times d_1 + w_2 \times d_2 + w_3 \times d_3 + w_4 \times d_4 + w_5 \times d_5 + w_6 \times d_6$$

*Conclusions* Principal component analysis is less subjective than AHP as the weights are derived from the principal components. There has been extensive work done in the area of vendor choice models, and readers can refer to a survey paper by Boer et al. titled *A Review of Methods Supporting Supplier Selection* for rich information on this topic.

**Table 7.28** Derived Variables and Score

| | Product Price/ Tech Capability (d1) | Product Price/ Management Capabilities (d2) | Shipment Quality/ Management Capabilities (d3) | Shipmen Quality/ Tech Capabilities (d4) | Delivery Compliance/ Production Capacity (d5) | Delivery Compliance/ Management Capabilities (d6) | Score |
|---|---|---|---|---|---|---|---|
| 1 | 1.436 | 1.540 | 0.161 | 0.150 | 0.467 | 0.196 | 0.936 |
| 2 | 1.751 | 2.000 | 0.400 | 0.350 | 0.601 | 0.400 | 1.352 |
| 3 | 2.338 | 1.269 | 0.180 | 0.333 | 0.389 | 0.227 | 1.140 |
| 4 | 2.214 | 1.439 | 0.266 | 0.410 | 3.497 | 1.464 | 2.701 |
| 5 | 2.395 | 2.119 | 0.885 | 1.000 | 0.113 | 0.088 | 1.633 |
| 6 | 1.219 | 1.916 | 0.328 | 0.209 | 0.032 | 0.063 | 0.835 |
| 7 | 1.651 | 0.943 | 0.333 | 0.583 | 0.358 | 0.179 | 1.037 |
| 8 | 1.722 | 1.263 | 1.285 | 1.751 | 0.139 | 0.120 | 1.735 |
| 9 | 2.072 | 1.544 | 0.280 | 0.376 | 0.341 | 0.101 | 1.122 |
| 10 | 1.000 | 1.894 | 0.420 | 0.222 | 0.090 | 0.093 | 0.849 |

*Source:* Derived using raw data of 10 firms from Petroni and Braglia (2006).

## 7.4 Regression Models

### *7.4.1 Introduction*

A regression model is a formal expression of a statistical relation between a single dependent (*outcome or target*) variable and one or more independent (*explanatory or predictor*) variables. A statistical relation can be characterised by two basic features:

- A tendency of the dependent variable to vary with the independent variables in a systematic fashion
- A scattering of points around the line representing the statistical relationship

However, it is important to note that the existence of a statistical relation between the dependent and independent variables does not imply a cause-and-effect relationship. To ascribe causality one must invoke a-priori or theoretical considerations.

Regression analysis serves the major purposes of *description (explanation)* and *prediction*. *Description* is the understanding of the nature of the relationship in order to explain the differences in the dependent variable, that may depend on the independent variables. *Prediction* is a forecast of the value of the dependent variable based on specific values of the independent variables. A classic example of a regression model for marketing is the estimation of a sales response function to explain the relationship between sales (dependent variable) and advertising-promotional activities (independent variables), and to forecast sales for impact measurement.

The term "regression" was introduced by Sir Francis Galton in the latter part of the 19th century. During his study of the relationship between heights of parents and children, he observed that the heights of children of both tall and short parents appeared to "revert" or "regress" to the mean of the group. According to Galton, this tendency was considered as a regression to "mediocrity". Galton developed a mathematical characterisation of this regression tendency, the antecedent of modern regression analysis[8].

Specific issues of interest relating to a regression model are summarised as follows:

- The model specification that represents the association between the dependent variable and independent variables.
- The econometric specification (model for estimation) and associated estimation procedure
- The direction of the associations, whether there is a positive or negative association between the dependent variable and the independent variables. This is inferred from the sign (value) of the estimates of the regression coefficients.
- Determination of which independent variables are important. Statistical hypothesis testing relating to regression coefficients, in conjunction with the standardised values of the coefficient estimates.
- Whether the association between the dependent and an independent variable is confounded by other independent variables. This involves including other independent variables that may be associated with both the independent variable of interest and the dependent variable.
- Predicting values of the dependent variable based on values of the independent variables. How well this can be done depends on "goodness-of-fit" of the model, that is, whether the model is "good" enough?

The focus of this section is on regression models that have been referenced in the preceding business chapters, and are also popular from a practitioner's perspective. Based on the nature of the dependent variable, the regression models of interest in this chapter are:

- Continuous (*linear regression model*)
- Discrete (*logistic regression and multinomial logit model*)
- Time to event (*survival model*)

For each of the regression models, the model specification is followed by a business application. Section 7.4.2 is the description of the linear regression model followed by discrete choice models in Section 7.4.3. Survival models are discussed in Section 7.4.4.

[8] Neter et al., *Applied Linear Statistical Models*.

## 7.4.2 *Linear Regression Model*

### 7.4.2.1 Introduction

Linear regression is one of the most commonly used regression techniques and has wide-ranging applicability across all disciplines. In linear regression, the dependent variable is continuous, that is, values can be any real number, positive or negative, e.g., sales, credit card spend, account balance, credit utilisation and minutes of usage. Forecasting has been dominated by linear regression as it is easy to develop and implement, and is simple to understand and interpret. However, a linear regression model does not capture non-linear relationships in the data sample. In this discussion, the specification of the model is followed by an application of linear regression to the estimation of a sales response function. The sales response function is used to measure the impact of sales promotions and to forecast the profitability of such promotional efforts.

### 7.4.2.2 Model Specification

The multiple linear regression model is specified for 2 independent variables and can be easily generalised to a regression framework with more than two independent variables.

$$Y_i = \beta_0 + \beta_1 x_{1i} + \beta_2 x_{2i} + \varepsilon_i$$

$Y_i$ = Dependent variable for observations $i = 1, 2, \ldots n$

$x_{1i}, x_{2i}$ = Independent variables (regressors or explanatory or predictor variables) for observation $i$, where $x_i$ is a given value of $x$

$\varepsilon_i$ = Random error term (disturbance) for observation $i$ with mean zero and variance equal to $\sigma^2$

$\beta_0, \beta_1, \beta_2$ = Partial regression coefficients (parameters) to be estimated

The mean and variance of $Y_i$ given $x_{1i}$ and $x_{2i}$ (also called the conditional mean and variance) can be expressed as

$$Mean\ (Y_i|x_{1i}, x_{2i}) = \beta_0 + \beta_1 x_{1i} + \beta_2 x_{2i}$$

$$Variance\ (Y_i|x_{1i}, x_{2i}) = \sigma^2$$

*Fitted Regression Line* The *fitted regression line* is the line of the average relationship between $Y$ and $x$ and takes the form of the following equation.

$$\tilde{Y}_i = b_0 + b_1 x_{1i} + b_2 x_{2i}$$

$$Y_i = \tilde{Y}_i + e_i$$

$\tilde{Y}_i$ = Fitted value of $Y_i$ for observation $i$

$b_0, b_1, b_2$ = Estimators of the parameters $\beta_0, \beta_1$, and $\beta_2$ respectively, also known as sample statistics

$e_i$ = Residual error term

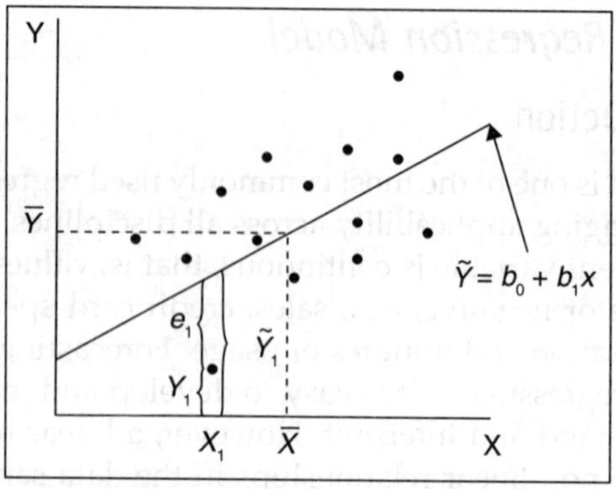


**Figure 7.12** Graphical Representation of Linear Regression

An *estimator* is a rule or formula or method for estimating the population parameter from a given sample. An *estimate* is the particular numerical value obtained by the estimator. A graphical representation of the two variable regression line (one independent variable) is depicted in Fig. 7.12.

*Important Features*

- The dependent variable $Y$ is the sum of two components—the systematic term $\beta_0 + \beta_1 x_1 + \beta_2 x_2$ (explained/deterministic) and the random term (unexplained/stochastic). The error term frequently represents factors omitted from the model that may affect $Y$ and which vary at random without reference to the independent variables.
- The parameters $\beta_1$, $\beta_2$ are called partial regression or partial slope coefficients
    - $\beta_0$ is the intercept and for $x_1 = 0$ and $x_2 = 0$, the mean of $Y$ is equal to $\beta_0$
    - $\beta_1$, $\beta_2$ is the slope of the regression line with respect to $x_1$ and $x_2$ respectively. $\beta_1$ is the change in the mean value of $Y$ for a unit change in $x_1$, holding the value of $x_2$ constant. $\beta_2$ is the change in the mean value of $Y$ for a unit change in $x_2$, holding the value of $x_1$ constant.
- Standardised coefficients calculated from the regression of standardised variables are necessary to interpret the relative importance or strength of the independent variables (for explaining the dependent variable). This is because regressors measured in different units affect the values and interpretation of the estimated regression coefficients in relation to one another. For example, in a regression model to evaluate the impact of advertising on sales (with advertising expenditure and price as independent variables), the coefficient of expenditure will be a minuscule when compared to the coefficient of price.

### 7.4.2.3 Estimation Methods

*Ordinary Least Squares (OLS)* The method of least squares involves finding estimators $b_0$, $b_1$, and $b_2$ that minimise the sum of squares of residuals $\left(\sum_{i=1}^{n} e_i^2\right)$ for the given sample of $i = 1, 2, 3, \ldots n$ observations.

$$\sum_{i=1}^{n} e_i^2 = \sum_{i=1}^{n} (Y_i - \tilde{Y}_i)^2 = \sum_{i=1}^{n} (Y_i - b_0 - b_1 x_{1i} - b_2 x_{2i})^2$$

Given the assumptions of classical linear regression model, OLS provides point estimators $b_0$, $b_1$, and $b_2$ that are BLUE[9] and have minimum variance among all unbiased linear estimators. OLS estimator is considered the "optimal estimator" and is the standard against which all other estimators are compared. This method is very popular because of its desirable properties.

**Assumptions of OLS**

- The regression model is linear in parameters and these parameters are assumed to be constant. Linear in parameter as the parameter appears with a power of 1 and is not multiplied (divided) by another parameter. Models that are non-linear in variables can be estimated by linear regression after suitable transformations (Table 7.30).
- Observations of the independent variables ($x$) are considered fixed in repeated samples. In other words, the independent variables are assumed to be non-stochastic (exogenous). This assumption is for mathematical convenience.
- Number of observations is greater than the number of independent variables
- Mean of error term is zero. Error terms, all have the same variance ($\sigma^2$). Violation of this assumption is termed heteroscedasticity.
- The error terms are assumed to be uncorrelated, which implies zero correlation for $Y_i$ and $Y_j$ for $i \neq j$. Violation of this assumption is called autocorrelation.
- Zero correlation between error term and the independent variables
- No perfect or exact linear relationships between the independent variables. Violation of this assumption is termed perfect multicollinearity.

Under the above assumptions, linear regression is referred to as classical linear regression model. Under the additional assumption of normally distributed error terms, linear regression is referred to as classical normal

[9] BLUE—Best Linear Unbiased Estimator. Linear—linear function of a random variable; Unbiased—its average or expected value is equal to the true value; Minimum Variance in the class of all such linear unbiased estimators. Unbiased estimator with the least variance is known as an efficient estimator.

linear regression model. There are serious consequences to the quality of the estimators under violation of these assumptions and readers are advised to refer to the popular text book *Basic Econometrics* by Gujarati and *A Guide to Econometrics* by Peter Kennedy for details on related issues and solutions.

**Properties of the Fitted Line**

- The sum of residuals is equal to zero
- The sum of squared residuals is a minimum
- The sum of the observed values of $Y_i$ is equal to the sum of the fitted values $\tilde{Y}_i$
- The regression line always goes through the mean values of the dependent and independent variables
- The sum of the weighted residuals – residuals weighted by the independent variables; and residuals weighted by the fitted values is zero

*Maximum Likelihood Estimation (MLE)* For a specified probability distribution of the error terms, the estimators can be derived from the method of maximum likelihood. This has stronger theoretical properties than the method of OLS. Fundamentally, the method of maximum likelihood is concerned with estimating the unknown parameters such that the probability of obtaining the observed set of data is maximum. Under the standard assumption of normality, the maximum likelihood estimators are the same as the least squares estimators and have all the properties of least squares estimators.

### 7.4.2.4 Model Evaluation

Model evaluation is based on multiple criteria and this section provides a brief description of some of the commonly used measures. Evaluation measures that are specific to prediction (e.g., forecast error) are not discussed.

*Model Fit (Goodness-of-Fit)* Goodness-of-fit of the fitted regression line represents how "well" the regression fits the data. One measure of goodness-of-fit is the coefficient of determination ($R^2$) that measures the proportion of total variation in the dependent variable that is explained by the independent variables.

$$R^2 = 1 - \frac{RSS}{TSS}$$

$$R^2 = 1 - \frac{\Sigma_{i=1}^{n} e_i^2}{\Sigma_{i=1}^{n} \left(Y_i - \overline{Y}\right)^2}$$

$$0 \le R^2 \le 1$$

$RSS$ = Residual sum of squares

$TSS$ = Total sum of squares

$\overline{Y}$ = Average value or mean of $Y$

If $R^2$ takes the value of 1, then the regression is a perfect fit and if zero, there is no relationship between the dependent variable and independent variables. A high $R^2$ is often called a good fit, although there is no generally accepted answer to the question of what is a high $R^2$. For time-series data, value of the coefficient of determination is inflated (due to common trends) as compared to cross-section data. Adjusted $R^2$ is $R^2$ adjusted for the number of explanatory variables as the unadjusted measure has a tendency to increase with number of regressors[10]. It is appropriate to use the adjusted measure when the number of regressors is high relative to the number of observations, particularly in the case of small samples.

*Statistical Significance (Hypothesis Testing)* Assuming that the fitted model is a reasonably good approximation of reality, suitable criteria are required to evaluate whether the estimates obtained are in line with the expectations of theory (or a-priori expectations) that are being tested. This involves evaluating the values and signs of the estimates and its statistical significance. Such confirmation or refutation of theory on the basis of sample evidence is based on a branch of statistical theory known as statistical inference (hypothesis testing). The purpose of hypothesis testing is to make inferences about a population parameter, by analysing differences between observed sample statistics and the results one expects to obtain if some underlying assumption is true. A method for testing statistical hypotheses is the test of significance, a procedure by which sample results are used to verify the truth or falsity of a null hypothesis. The process of hypothesis testing consists of four steps.

1. Formulate the null hypothesis $H_o$ (commonly, that the observations are the result of pure chance) and the alternative hypothesis $H_a$
2. Identify a test statistic that can be used to assess the null hypothesis (Table 7.29). For this purpose, normal distribution of error terms is assumed.
3. Compute the p-value; p-value is the probability of obtaining a test statistic at least as extreme as the one that was actually observed, assuming that the null hypothesis is true. The smaller the p-value, the stronger is the evidence against the null hypothesis.
4. Compare the p-value to an acceptable significance value (sometimes called $\alpha$ value). $\alpha$ is a probability threshold for a decision and takes the value of .01, 0.05 and 0.10. If $p \leq \alpha$, then the observed effect is statistically significant, the null hypothesis is rejected, and the alternative hypothesis is accepted. When the null hypothesis is rejected, the result is said to be statistically significant.

---

[10] Adjusted $R^2 = R^2 - [(k - 1)/(n - k)](1 - R^2)$; $N$ = Number of observations; $k$ = Number of independent variables.

**Table 7.29** Hypothesis Testing

| Purpose of Test | Testing Hypothesis | Example | Test |
|---|---|---|---|
| Whether dependent variable *Y* is related to independent variable $x_1$ | Individual regression coefficient | $H_o: \beta_1 = 0; H_a: \beta_1 \neq 0$ | t-test |
| Overall significance of the estimated multiple regression model | Linear equality restrictions | $H_o: \beta_1 = \beta_2 = 0; H_a$: Not all slope coefficients are simultaneously zero | F-test |
| Partial regression coefficients satisfy certain restrictions | | $H_o: \beta_1 = \beta_2; H_a: \beta_1 \neq \beta_2$<br>$H_o: \beta_1 + \beta_2 = 1; H_a: \beta_1 + \beta_2 \neq 1$ | |

### 7.4.2.5 Functional Forms

Through appropriate transformations, a regression model that is non-linear in variables (and linear in parameters) can be estimated using the linear regression model. Table 7.30 shows two examples of such forms.

**Table 7.30** Examples of Functional Forms

| Model | Form | Transformed Form (Linear Regression) | Type of Model | Interpretation of $\beta_1$ |
|---|---|---|---|---|
| Exponential Regression Model | $Y = \beta_0 x^{\beta_1} e^{\varepsilon}$ | $\ln Y_i = \ln \beta_0 + \beta_1 \ln x_i + \varepsilon_i$ | Log-log/ double-log or log-log | Percentage change in *Y* for percentage change in *x*; Elasticity of *Y* respect to *x* |
| Growth Rate Model | $Y_t = Y_0(1+g)^t$ *g is compound rate of growth of Y* | $\ln Y_t = \beta_0 + \beta_1 t + \varepsilon_i$<br>$\beta_0 = \ln Y_0$<br>$\beta_1 = \ln(1+g)$ | Log-lin | Relative (constant) change in *Y* for a given absolute change in the value of the regressor (instantaneous rate of growth) $g = antilog(\beta_1 - 1)$ |

#### 7.4.2.6 Example—Impact of Promotions on Sales

*Introduction* Sales promotions represent a considerable proportion of the marketing spend of an organisation. Among the available promotion tools, couponing is a popular one for incentivising sales. According to a NCH report of 2014 for the US, marketers distributed 315 billion coupons for consumer packaged goods (CPG) in 2013, and coupon volume of \$2.8 billion was redeemed by consumers. Unlike promotions involving regular shelf price cuts which are available for every shopper, coupon promotions benefit those consumers who spend the time and effort to redeem coupons. Profitability of couponing depends on the incremental sales generated, relative to costs. According to Leone and Srinivasan, *Coupon Face Value: Its Impact on Coupon Redemptions, Brand Sales, and Brand Profitability,* coupon profitability can go either way. Data on coupon profitability is hard to obtain, and this is further compounded by the lack of good methods to calculate this metric. Analysing the impact of coupon characteristics (e.g., face value and method of distribution) on coupon profitability is a challenge in the absence of data. Henceforth, an example that focusses on a data based experimental approach is discussed. The example is "Adapted from *Journal of Retailing,* Volume 62, Issue 1, Chapman, *Assessing the Profitability of Retailer Couponing with a Low-Cost Field Experiment,* Pages 19–40, Copyright (1986), with permission from Elsevier".

*Objective* Chapman in his study uses the linear regression model framework to estimate a sales response function based on data compiled from a couponing experiment conducted for a pizza restaurant. The purpose of the sales response function is to:

- Understand the short-term and long-term impact of coupon promotions on sales; and the influence of other factors on sales
- Assess the impact of different promotional offers on sales
- Estimate base sales (sales in the absence of couponing) and sales from couponing
- Quantify the impact of couponing on incremental sales (sales from promotion minus base sales)
- Predict profitability and return on investment of the couponing promotion

Noteworthy features of the model are the use of test and control to derive incremental sales and profitability; the inclusion of variables representing the lagged effects of coupon distribution on sales (to capture the long-term impact of the promotion). The impact of promotions on sales is affected by many factors and were emphasised in the spend management section of Chapter 2 "Usage Management". Chapman's model is being used as an example to illustrate the use of linear regression for modelling and predicting the impact of promotions on sales.

*Data/Design of Experiment* The experiment included one control and two test (treatment) groups as stated in Table 7.31.

- For distribution of coupons, boundaries of market area of the restaurant were finalised by the restaurant manager based on experience of take out patterns. 12 census tracts or market subareas defining the market area were identified with a total of 27,365 households, and each census tract ranging from 500 to 3730 households.
- Research design, the split of total market into control and experimental groups is not random, but rather largely based on restaurant management's judgement on expected success of the couponing experiment. However, a true test and control should be random samples with similar average household characteristics, GDP per household, household size, type of dwelling, distance from the restaurant, and other factors that could influence response to the promotion. Chapman also acknowledges this point. Alternatively, factors that are not considered (controlled for) while creating the sample for experimental and control groups could be included as predictor variables in the regression.
- Coupons were delivered at the beginning of the starting week. Experimental period is defined as three weeks (from the starting week that is inclusive). The coupon is invalid after the end of three weeks.
- Measurement window: A nine-week window was designed with three weeks each for pre-experimental, experimental and post-experimental. Sales were tracked for all the nine weeks, for both control and experimental groups.
- The sales revenue per household for the control group is relatively flat and for the experimental group, the results are promising with a rising curve till week 6 (Figures 7.13 and 7.14). For the experimental group, a rise in sales is clearly visible during the 3 weeks experimental period (weeks 3–6).
- A more formal analysis is required to isolate the effects of the coupon promotion on sales by controlling for other factors that affect sales such as census tract characteristics and time trend. This is done by estimation of the regression model.

**Table 7.31** Experiment Design

| Group | Experiment/Offer |
|---|---|
| Control group | No promotion |
| Experimental group 1(EG1) | $1 coupon, menu, information brochure |
| Experimental group 2(EG2) | $1 coupon, menu |

*Source:* Derived using information from Chapman (1986).

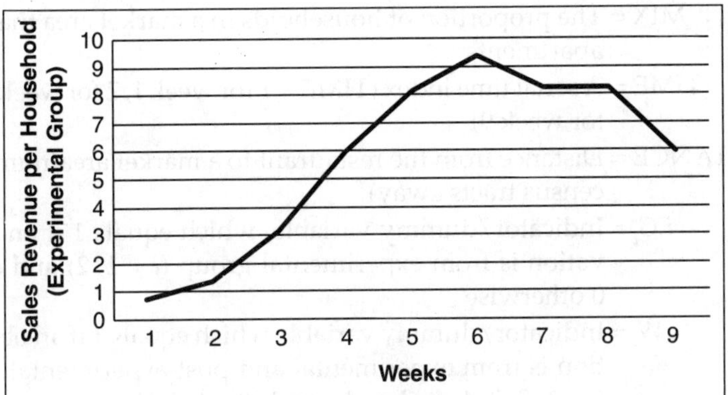


*Source:* Derived using data from Chapman (1986).

**Figure 7.13** Sales Revenue—Experimental Group (Both)

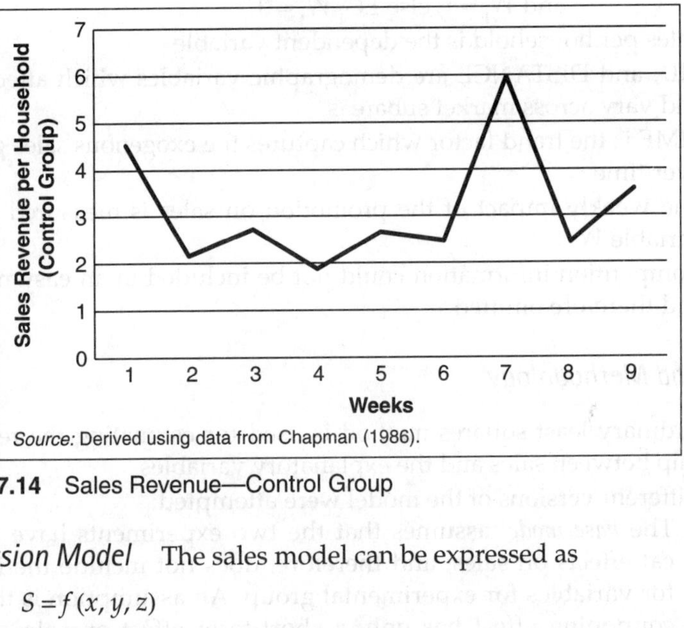


*Source:* Derived using data from Chapman (1986).

**Figure 7.14** Sales Revenue—Control Group

*Regression Model* The sales model can be expressed as

$S = f(x, y, z)$
$S$ = Sales
$x$ = Marketing decision variables (pizza restaurant)
$y$ = Marketing decision variables of competitors
$z$ = Market-specific demographic variables that influence demand

The specification of the sales model for the purpose of estimation is stated as:

$$\frac{S}{H} = f\,(\text{MIX, TIME, DISTANCE}, EG1, EG2, W1, W2, W3)$$

$S$ = Sales from a market area in a week
$H$ = Number of households in an area

MIX = The proportion of households in a market area that were apartments

TIME = A serial time index (TIME = 1 for week 1, 2 for week 2 ....,9 for week 9)

DISTANCE = Distance from the restaurant to a market area(number of census tracts away)

$EG_i$ = Indicator/dummy variable, which equals 1 if an observation is from experimental group ($i$ = 1, 2) and equals 0 otherwise

$W_j$ = Indicator/dummy variable which equals 1 if an observation is from experimental and post-experimental weeks ($j$ = 1, 2, 3, 4, 5, 6) and equals 0 otherwise

$EG_i\ W_j$ = Interactive dummy between experimental group and experimental week. For example, $EG_1\ W_1 = 1$ if $EG_1 = 1$ and $W_1 = 1$; else $EG_1\ W_1 = 0$

- Sales per household is the dependent variable
- MIX and DISTANCE are demographic variables which affect sales and vary across market subareas
- TIME is the trend factor which captures the exogenous sales growth over time
- The weekly impact of the promotion on sales is measured by the variable $W_j$
- Competition information could not be included in an easy manner and therefore omitted

## *Data and Methodology*

- Ordinary least squares method is used for estimating the relationship between sales and the explanatory variables
- Different versions of the model were attempted:
    - The *base model* assumes that the two experiments have identical effects on sales, and therefore, does not include the indicator variables for experimental group. An assumption is that the couponing effect has only a short-term effect on sales within the three-week experimental period and hence, references this period alone.
    - The *extended model* assumes that the two experiments have a different impact on sales, with the inclusion of the interactive dummy variables (between $EG_i$ and $W_j$). This version is not presented.
    - *The final model* measures the long-term effect of couponing, with the addition of variables representing the three weeks of post-experimental period ($W_4$, $W_5$, $W_6$) to the *base model*
- The 108 observations were derived from nine weeks of sales data for all the control and experimental groups, with one data point for sales for every week for each of the 12 market sub-areas (12 × 9)

*Model Results* Two versions of Chapman's model are presented. The final model is used as the sales response function for evaluating the sales impact and profitability of coupon promotional activity (Tables 7.32 and 7.33).

**Table 7.32** Base Model

| Variable | Coefficient Estimate | t–value | Impact | p–value |
|---|---|---|---|---|
| Constant | 0.054 | 4.32 | | <.001 |
| Mix | – 0.009 | 0.700 | – | >.10 |
| Time | 0.002 | 2.34 | + | <.05 |
| Distance | – 0.011 | 3.27 | – | <.01 |
| W1 | 0.073 | 6.83 | + | <.001 |
| W2 | 0.053 | 4.92 | + | <.001 |
| W3 | 0.040 | 3.68 | + | <.001 |
| R-square | 0.465 | | | |
| N (sample size) | 108 | | | |

*Source:* Adapted from *Journal of Retailing*, Volume 62, Issue 1, Chapman, "Assessing the Profitability of Retailer Couponing with a Low-cost Field Experiment", Pages 19–40, Copyright (1986), with permission from Elsevier.

**Table 7.33** Final Model

| Variable | Coefficient Estimate | t–value | Impact | p–value |
|---|---|---|---|---|
| Constant | 0.067 | 5.109 | | <.001 |
| Mix | – 0.010 | 0.837 | – | >.10 |
| Time | – 0.001 | .764 | – | >.10 |
| Distance | – 0.011 | 3.34 | – | <.01 |
| W1 | 0.083 | 7.55 | + | <.001 |
| W2 | 0.066 | 5.81 | + | <.001 |
| W3 | 0.057 | 4.71 | + | <.001 |
| W4 | 0.023 | 1.83 | + | <.10 |
| W5 | 0.034 | 2.46 | + | <.05 |
| W6 | 0.039 | 2.64 | + | <.05 |
| R-square | 0.509 | | | |
| N (sample size) | 108 | | | |

*Source:* Adapted from *Journal of Retailing*, Volume 62, Issue 1, Chapman, "Assessing the Profitability of Retailer Couponing with a Low-cost Field Experiment", Pages 19–40, Copyright (1986), with permission from Elsevier.

- Objectives of the study and associated results:
  - *Whether offer had an impact on sales (Base Model)*
    - The short-term effect is clearly visible as the coefficient estimates of variables $W_1$, $W_2$, $W_3$ are positive and highly significant. This result implies that couponing had an additive effect on sales during all the three weeks of the experimental period.
  - *Differential impact of offer on sales (Extended Model)*
    - Both offers have a comparable influence on sales. This is based on the F-test with null hypothesis that the effects of $EG_1\ W_1$, $EG_1\ W_2$, and $EG_1\ W_3$ simultanously equal the effects of $EG_2\ W_1$, $EG_2\ W_2$, and $EG_2\ W_3$. The authors conclude that F-test is statistically insignificant, thereby accepting the null hypothesis that both experiments/offers have a similar impact on sales. Henceforth, this model is not used.
  - *Long-term effect on sales (Final Model)*
    - Evidence of a long-term effect beyond the three-week experimental period is reflected by the positive and statistical significant estimates of the variable $W_j$ for weeks 4, 5 and 6, and which is further substantiated by the statistical F-test. The null hypothesis for the F-test is that the addition of the three additional indicator variables adds no extra value to the explanation of sales, and this is rejected. According to Chapman, this result in general represents forward buying, repeat purchase and buyers' awareness.
    - The impact on sales reduces with increasing duration from coupon drop as observed from the decreasing estimate values of the indicator variable $W_j$ as $j$ increases (till Week 4). The impact is highest in week 1.
- Model evaluation
  - Most coefficient estimates are all highly significant (rejecting the null hypothesis that coefficient estimate is equal to zero) based on the p-values. The exception is variable MIX for both specifications.
  - The variable TIME is becoming insignificant in the final model, perhaps due to multicollinearity with variables representing the lagged effects for weeks 4, 5, and 6
  - The result of the DISTANCE variable is intuitive. A sales (per household) reduction of .0117 units on average, for every additional census tract of distance of the restaurant away from the market subarea, ceteris paribus.
  - Values of the standardised coefficient estimates are not reported in the paper
  - The value of $R^2$ which is explained variation as a percentage of total variation (measure of model fit) is satisfactory, with 50% of sales variability being explained by the regressors. As $R^2$ depends on the data and the objective of the modelling effort, an acceptable standard for the value is difficult to ascertain.

*Interpretation* The results of the final model can be expressed as an equation that represents the sales response function. The final model or sales response function could be used for impact assessment from the couponing experiment. This could also be used for forecasting sales and profitability of the couponing experiment. The incremental sales per household from couponing measured over 6 weeks is \$0.3039 (\$0.7065 – \$0.4026), which is a 75% increase over base sales as shown in Table 7.34. The intercept of the final model is taken as base sales per week (sales without couponing).

$$\frac{S}{H} = 0.0671 - 0.0108 \times \text{Mix} - 0.0013 \times \text{Time} - 0.0117 \times \text{Distance} + 0.0831 \times W_1 + 0.0663 \times W_2 + 0.057 \times W_3 + 0.0237 \times W_4 + 0.0342 \times W_5 + 0.0396 \times W_6$$

*Profitability Model* In the short-run, an ideal promotion is expected to stimulate sales such that the incremental sales at the lower margins can offset the costs of the promotion. Incremental sales can be from higher purchase frequency/quantity from current customers; switchers from competition; and non-customers of the product category trying out the brand during the promotional period. The profitability of coupon distribution (drop) depends on the volume of incremental sales generated in the short- and long-run relative to the costs of distributing the coupon, retailer reimbursement and costs of other third parties for face value, and processing costs.

The expression for incremental profit from couponing is "Reprinted from *Handbooks in Operations Research and Management Science*, Volume-Marketing, Blattberg and Neslin, *Sales Promotion Models*, Pages 553–609, Copyright (1993), with permission from Elsevier".

**Table 7.34** Sales Impact from Couponing

| Week | Sales per Household Impact from Couponing | Base Sales per Household |
|---|---|---|
| | Intercept + Coefficient of $W_i$ | Intercept |
| 1 | \$0.1502 | \$0.0671 |
| 2 | \$0.1334 | \$0.0671 |
| 3 | \$0.1241 | \$0.0671 |
| 4 | \$0.0908 | \$0.0671 |
| 5 | \$0.1013 | \$0.0671 |
| 6 | \$0.1067 | \$0.0671 |
| **Total** | **\$0.7065** | **\$0.4026** |

*Source:* Derived using information from Chapman (1986).

$D$ = Number of coupons distributed
$f$ = Face value per coupon
$c$ = Processing cost per coupon
$d$ = Distribution cost per 1000 coupons distributed
$r$ = Redemption rate; percentage of distributed coupons redeemed
$i$ = Incremental sales per redemption generated by the coupon drop
$p$ = Profit margin per unit
$\Pi$ = Incremental profit generated by the coupon drop

Incremental profit from couponing can be expressed as:

$\Pi$ = Incremental benefits – incremental costs
$= d \times r \times i \times p - D \times d - D \times r\,(f + c)$
= Profit contribution from incremental sales – Distribution costs – Redemption costs

Incremental sales from couponing and redemption rate need to be modelled (estimated). Distribution costs are fixed and redemption costs are variable with respect to the redemption rate.

Chapman uses a slightly different version of the preceding profitability equation. The sales response function representing the final model is used to predict incremental sales from couponing (sales from coupon promotion minus base sales). Costs incorporate delivery costs, coupon printing costs and menu printing costs. The outcome of the calculations are predicted couponing profits of \$191.67 for Offer 2, which represents a return on investment of 10.9%.

*Conclusions* Chapman's results indicate that couponing has a consequential effect on short-term sales and some long-term residual impact beyond the experimental period. Couponing can also be a profitable proposition. While the focus of this section was on the application of linear regression in the retail sector, this is just the tip of the iceberg as advanced research in this area has resulted in innovative econometric model specifications and techniques. Another interesting application of the linear regression model is related to the impact of price promotions on the variability of category sales by Raju titled *The Effect of Price Promotions on Variability in Product Category Sales*. Readers should refer to the survey paper by Blattberg and Neslin mentioned earlier, for advancements in this area. The impact of advertising on sales is another interesting and deeply researched topic.

## *7.4.3 Discrete Choice Regression Models*

### 7.4.3.1 Introduction

Discrete choice regression models are used for modelling discrete dependent variables as a function of independent variables (which can be continuous or categorical or both). There are different variants of these models based on whether the dependent variable is categorical or a count, and within categorical, whether binary or multiple outcomes are observed. Explanation of discrete choice dependent variables is given in Table 7.35. Also known as event-based models, the term discrete choice models has roots in economic theory based random utility models. Discrete choice models provide a framework to analyse and predict consumers' choices among alternatives, and how their choices are influenced by their personal characteristics and the different attributes of the finite set of alternatives available to them. For example, the choice of which consumer durable to buy is influenced by personal factors such as income and family size; and attributes of the product such as price and brand. The general framework is specified later. The focus is on logistic regression model for binary choice and multinomial logit model for multiple choice, motivated by their universal and multifarious applications in business.

From a historical perspective, the logistic distribution was studied in the 19th century for the description of the growth of populations and has been prominently used in the field of biostatistics. It was introduction by Berkson in the 1940s, who coined the term "logit". In the 1970s, McFadden introduced a set of methodological based concepts that developed into the modern econometric analysis of discrete choice models (with the influential empirical study of household travel). Industry applications have popularised these models in financial services, insurance and telecom. Event-based

**Table 7.35** Explanation of Discrete Choice Dependent Variables

| | Example | Values | Comments |
|---|---|---|---|
| Binary/Dichotomous | Response to an offer, whether defaulted | Yes/No coded as 1/0 | |
| Multiple/Polytomous—Unordered | What products will customer purchase? | 0 = Credit card<br>1 = Personal loan<br>2 = Housing loan | Not ranked |
| Multiple/Polytomous—Ordered | Opinions about a particular product/service. Level of insurance coverage | 0 = Strongly like<br>1 = Like<br>2 = Neutral<br>3 = Dislike<br>4 = Strongly dislike<br>Level of insurance coverage-none, full, or part | Ranked—Difference between outcome represented by 0 and 1 is not necessarily the same as between 2 and 1 |
| Count | Number of accidents in a week; number of 30 days past due in six months | 0, 1, 2, 3 4, ... | Count data can also refer to rare or infrequent occurrences e.g., winning more than one lottery within two weeks |

models are used to predict customer behaviours such as response, churn, default-loss, fraud, and recovery. The retail sector relies on discrete choice models to predict demand for a product, and to understand which customer and brand attributes influence brand preference or choice. In the transport sector, development of discrete choice travel demand models reflecting choice behaviour of travellers is a common application. In the health industry, understanding and quantifying patient's preferences for treatment alternatives using these choice models is one such practice. Economic applications include labour market models of understanding entry and exit variables influencing recruitment and retention. Applications of discrete choice models are listed in Table 7.36. Later, a response model for a cross-sell programme and an insurance fraud model will be discussed in detail. Model evaluation is discussed elaborately in Section 7.5. Interested readers can refer to books by Greene, *Econometric Analysis* and Gujarati, *Basic Econometrics* for detailed information on this topic.

### 7.4.3.2 General Structure

Figure 7.15 provides the general framework for discrete choice regression models.

### 7.4.3.3 Applications

Applications for logistic and multinomial models, by purpose and industry are noted in Table 7.36.

**Table 7.36** Applications of Discrete Choice Regression Models

| Applications | Industry | Model |
|---|---|---|
| Cross-sell/Up-sell | Financial services/ Insurance | NPTB (next best product to buy) models to predict which products customers will buy next |
| Risk scores | Financial services (retail, SME and corporate) | Default, loss, collection, recovery, fraud models |
| | Insurance | Fraud models |
| Attrition/Lapsation | Financial services | Attrition models |
| | Insurance | Lapsation/Reinstatement models |
| | Telecom | Subscriber churn and customer loyalty models |
| Brand choice | Retail | Choice models |
| Portfolio valuation | Financial services | Prediction of default, loss, and prepayment |
| Response | General | Direct marketing—response models by channel |

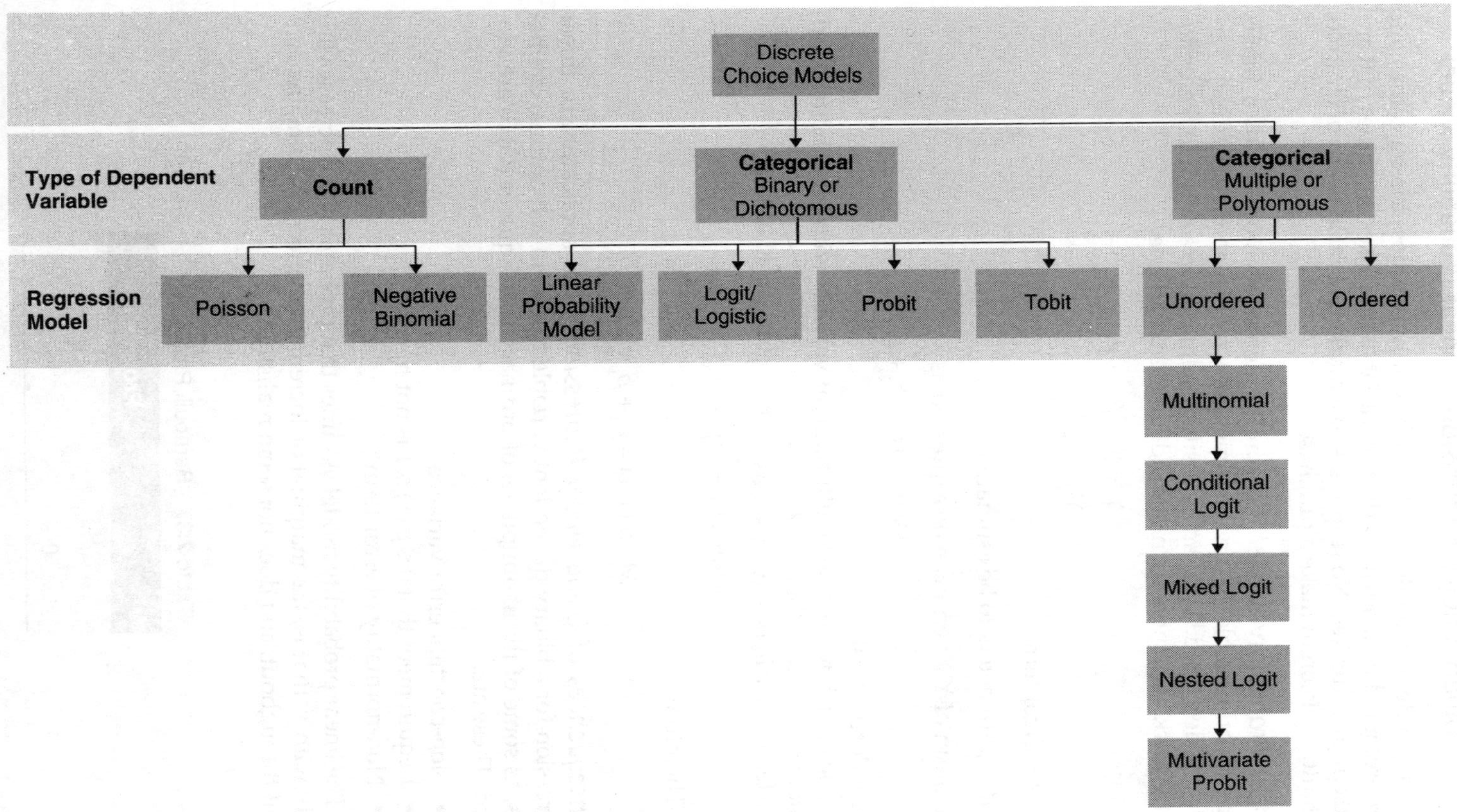


**Figure 7.15** Framework for Discrete Choice Regression Models

### 7.4.3.4 Binary Choice Regression—Linear Probability Model

The dependent variable of interest has only two possible outcomes and is represented by a binary indicator variable that takes on values of 0 and 1. Examples are: Yes–No responses to a marketing offer, event of churn or default, decision to make a purchase.

*Linear Probability Model* A simple regression model with a binary dependent variable $Y$, and independent (explanatory/predictor) variable $x$ is described. This can be easily generalised to a multiple regression framework with more than one independent variable.

$$Y = \beta_0 + \beta_1 x + \varepsilon$$
$$Y = 0,1$$

$\varepsilon$ = Error term

$\beta_0, \beta_1$ = parameters to be estimated

The mean of $Y$ given $x$ can be expressed as

$$Mean\ (Y|x) = \beta_0 + \beta_1\ x$$

Since Mean $(\varepsilon) = 0$

Consider $Y$ to be a Bernoulli random variable with probability distribution as shown in Table 7.37.

Mean of $Y$ can be expressed as

$$Mean\ (Y) = 1\ (p) + 0\ (1 - p) = p$$

Therefore,

$$Mean\ (Y|x) = \beta_0 + \beta_1\ x = p\ (x)$$

*Consequences of Using Linear Regression* The application of linear regression for a binary dependent variable results in sub-optimal estimators, as some of the assumptions of ordinary least squares (OLS) are violated. These are:

- Non-constant error variance
- Requirement that $0 \leq p\ (x) \leq 1$ is not met
- Non-normality of error term

The linear probability model assumes that probability ($p$) increases linearly with $x$, that is, the marginal or incremental effect of $x$ remains constant throughout, and does not seem realistic.

**Table 7.37** Bernoulli Probablility

| *Y* | Probability |
|---|---|
| 1 | $p$ |
| 0 | $1 - p$ |

### 7.4.3.5 Binary Choice Regression—Logistic Model

The logistic regression model is discussed.

*Logistic Probability Model* The mean of $Y$ can be represented by a logistic response function as follows:

$$\text{Mean}\,(Y|x) = p\,(x) = \frac{e^{\beta_0+\beta_1 x}}{1+e^{\beta_0+\beta_1 x}}$$

- $0 \le p(x) \le 1$
- $P(Y=1|x) = p(x)$ and $P(Y=0|x) = 1 - p\,(x)$
- Non-linear regression (in parameters and independent variables)

*The Logit Transformation* The logit transformation $g\,(x)$ is the equation that is estimated and is expressed as follows:

$$g(x) = \ln\frac{p(x)}{1-p(x)} = \ln\frac{P(Y=1|x)}{P(Y=0|x)}$$
$$= \beta_0 + \beta_1 x$$

- Logit transformation is linear in parameters and independent variables, may be continuous and can range from $-\infty$ to $+\infty$
- Logit transformation is also referred to as the log of odds, where

$$\text{Odds} = \frac{p\,(x)}{1-p\,(x)}$$

*Properties of the Logistic Response Function*

- Response function is shaped either as a titled S or as a reverse tilted S
  - Relationship between probability and independent variables is monotonic, probability increases as $x$ increases (for $\beta > 0$); and probability increases as $x$ decreases (for $\beta < 0$). Figure 7.16 is a relationship between mean response to an offer (probability of response) and income.
  - Relationship between probability and independent variables is non-linear
- Meets the constraints of probability, that it is bounded between 0 and 1
- The logistic distribution function is similar to the normal distribution function except at the tails
- Although the log of odds is linear in parameters and independent variables, the probabilities themselves are not
- Marginal effect is the change in mean response due to a unit change in the value of $x$ and is defined as

$$\text{Marginal effect} = p\,(x)\,[1 - p\,(x)]\beta_1$$

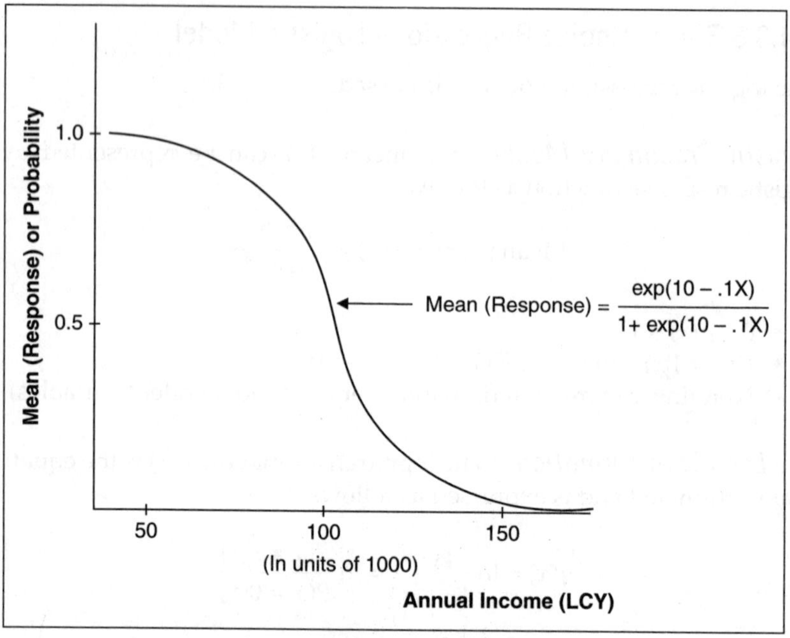


**Figure 7.16** Logistic Response Function

 - Effect of a unit increase depends on the level of probability from which this change is measured. Probability depends on the independent variable ($x$).
 - One such standard practice is to evaluate the marginal effect at the means of the independent variables
- The slope coefficient ($\beta_1$) denotes the change in the log of odds due to a unit change of the independent variable
- The *odds* ratio (OR) is a measure of the odds of the outcome for one group relative to another group or the change of odds for a unit change in the $x$ variable. Assume that the independent variable $x$ takes on the value of either 0 or 1. For evaluating the odds ratio at $x = 1$ versus $x = 0$, OR is defined as:

$$\text{OR} = \frac{p(1)/[1-p(1)]}{p(0)/[1-p(0)]}$$

Alternatively,

$$\text{OR} = e^{\beta_1}$$

If estimated OR = 4 for a credit card attrition study (event defined as churn) and if $x = 1$ (cash or spend inactive) and $x = 0$ (cash or spend active), this implies that the odds of churn of an inactive customer is 4 times the odds of churn of an active customer.

*Random Utility Model (RUM) Specification* Random utility models are the theoretical construct behind discrete choice models (e.g., to make a purchase or not to make a purchase). Consumer utility of an alternative is a function of product characteristics, personal characteristics of the individual making the choice, and a stochastic individual level taste shock. The decision is based on customer's marginal benefit and marginal cost, a calculation based on the utility achieved by making the purchase and not making the purchase. The net benefit ($y^*$), defined as marginal benefit minus marginal cost, is latent and is not observed, while the observed outcome of the choice ($Y$) for a customer is observed. The net benefit can be expressed as a function of product and individual attributes ($x$) and taste shock. The outcome of the choice decision depends on whether $y^*$ is higher than the threshold value, which is zero in this case.

$$y^* = \beta_0 + \beta_1 x + \varepsilon$$

$Y = 1$ if $y^* > 0$ — Makes the purchase

$Y = 0$ if $y^* \leq 0$ — Does not make the purchase

$$p\,(x) = p\,(Y = 1|x) = P\,(y^* > 0) = P\,(\varepsilon < \beta_0 + \beta_1 x)^{11} = F\,(x\beta)$$

$F\,(x\beta)$ = cumulative distribution function

If $F\,(x\beta)$ is a **logistic** distribution, then it is a ***logistic*** regression model.
If $F\,(x\beta)$ is a **normal** distribution, then it is a ***probit*** regression model.

*Estimation Method* The method of maximum likelihood (ML) outputs values for the unknown parameters that maximise the probability of obtaining the observed set of data. This is achieved by first specifying the *likelihood function,* which expresses the probability of obtaining the observed set of data. The maximum likelihood estimators of the parameters are chosen such that those values maximise the likelihood function. For a sample of $n$ independent observations for $i = 1, 2, \ldots n$, the likelihood function $l\,(\beta)$ is a product of expressions for observations with $Y = 1$ and $Y = 0$. To obtain full maximum likelihood estimator of $\beta$, the log-likelihood function $L\,(\beta)$ is maximised with respect to $\beta$, by taking the derivatives of $L\,(\beta)$ with respect to $\beta$, setting the equations to zero, and solving for $\beta$.

$$l(\beta) = \prod_{i=1}^{n} p(x_i)^{Y_i} \times [1 - p(x_i)]^{1-Y_i}$$

$$p\,(x) = p\,(Y = 1|x)$$

$$1 - p\,(x) = P\,(Y = 0|x)$$

The solution algorithm is iterative and programmes are available in most statistical softwares.

---

[11] Since logistic distribution is symmetric, $P(\varepsilon < \beta_0 + \beta_1 x) = P[\varepsilon > -(\beta_0 + \beta_1 x)]$

*Strengths and Challenges*

- A useful and popular description of the relationship between mean response and independent variables
- Very flexible and easily used function
- Lends a meaningful interpretation
- For rare events (event rate < 1%), logistic regression (and probit) tend to underestimate the probability of the occurrence of the event (Blattberg et al.)
- Difficult to capture complex interactions between more than two independent variables
- Non-suitable when the relationship between log odds and independent variables is non-linear

## 7.4.3.6 Binary Choice Regression—Probit and Tobit Model

As mentioned earlier, a probit regression model assumes a normal response function. In comparison to the normal distribution, the logistic response function is slightly fatter at the tails, implying that probability approaches 0 or 1 at a slower rate than in probit. Although there is no compelling reason to choose one over the other, logistic is preferred due to its mathematical simplicity and ease of interpretation.

Tobit model is an extension of the probit model with censored data, that is, information on the dependent variable is available only for some observations (while independent variables are available for the full sample). Therefore, the model has to be corrected for a bias termed as "sample selectivity" using a two-step process. An example of censoring is the following—amount spent on a consumer durable is only observed for customers who have bought the consumer durable. This model is often referred to as censored regression model.

## 7.4.3.7 Multiple Choice Regression Models

Multiple choice models are an extension of the binary model, with more than two categories of the outcome variable. Logit models for multiple choice, termed as multinomial logit, are formulated to incorporate multiple outcomes/responses or choices among alternatives as a function of set of independent variables. In the literature, the terminology for multinomial logit is referenced in more than one way. Traditionally, the term "multinomial logit" is used to represent the model described in this section, while in contemporary research multinomial logit encompasses a variety of multiple choice logit models in a broad sense (Table 7.38).

*Multinomial Logit* Assume multiple choices with the dependent variable taking on three outcomes or alternatives, with $Y = 0, 1, 2$. One of the outcomes is used as the baseline and therefore two logits are estimated.

**Table 7.38** Multiple Choice Logit Models—Unordered

| Multiple Choice Logit Models | | | | |
|---|---|---|---|---|
| **Type of Model** | **Individual Specific Predictors (attributes of customers making the choice)** | **Choice Specific Predictors (attributes of alternatives)** | **Feature of the Model** | **Example** |
| Multinomial Logit | ✓ | | Parameter values are different by alternatives | Corporate bankruptcy (bankrupt, not bankrupt, financially weak) |
| Conditional Logit | | ✓ | Parameter values are same by alternatives* | Choice of travel mode |
| Mixed Logit | ✓ | ✓ | Parameter values are same by alternatives for choice specific predictors* and different by alternatives for individual specific predictors | Brand choice model with heterogeneity |
| Nested Multinomial Logit | ✓ | ✓ | The choice process is viewed as a 2 step procedure in a hierarchical manner. At first level, choose among choice sets. At the second level, make a specific choice within the chosen set. Parameter values are same by alternatives*. | First level—whether fraud is committed<br>Second level—If yes, type of fraud committed |

*Intercept value can differ by alternatives

The procedure involves the estimation of several binary logits with customer characteristics or attributes used as independent variables. Taking $Y = 0$ as the baseline, the two logits can be expressed as:

$$g_1(x) = \ln\frac{P(Y = 1|x)}{P(Y = 0|x)} = \beta_{10} + \beta_{11}x$$

$$g_2(x) = \ln\frac{P(Y = 2|x)}{P(Y = 0|x)} = \beta_{20} + \beta_{21}x$$

Probability is expressed as:

$$P(Y = 0|x) = \frac{1}{1 + e^{g_1(x)} + e^{g_2(x)}}$$

$$P(Y = 1|x) = \frac{e^{g_1(x)}}{1 + e^{g_1(x)} + e^{g_2(x)}}$$

$$P(Y = 2|x) = \frac{e^{g_2(x)}}{1 + e^{g_1(x)} + e^{g_2(x)}}$$

The mentioned formulae can be generalised to incorporate up to $j$ choices. Maximum likelihood procedure is used to estimate the unknown parameters. Odds ratio can be computed in the same manner as logistic regression. This is possible if the assumption of multinomial logit called "independence of irrelevant alternatives (IIA)" is true. That is, the ratio of probabilities between two alternatives is independent of the other alternatives. This may be a restrictive assumption and there are several statistical tests (Hausman test) to validate this assumption.

#### 7.4.3.8 Example I—Logistic Model—Personal Loan to Credit Card Cross-Sell Response Model

*Objective* The business objective is to increase cross-sell penetration of personal loans in the credit card portfolio, given the profitability potential of this programme. This aspect was highlighted in the "Cross-Sell" chapter. The analytical objective is to increase marketing efficiency. A segmentation based approach was discussed in the section on multiproduct models in Chapter 3 "Cross-Sell".

The analytical output is a score that serves as a guide for selecting the target population, and for providing the prioritisation logic for corresponding direct marketing activities. As a part of the objective, the aim is to identify customer profiles that are most likely to respond to the offer (by differentiating between potential cross-sell responders and non-responders) and suggest appropriate strategies to increase response rates/response volume.

*Data* Campaign files for the past six months consisting of both responders and non-responders and file details are shown in Table 7.39.

**Table 7.39** Model Development Sample Statistics

| Dependent Variable: Response = 1 If Customer Responds to the Offer; = 0 If No | |
|---|---|
| Number of eligible card accounts (a) | 100,000 |
| Number of cards accounts in mail file (b) | 30,000 |
| Average response rate per campaign (c) | 4.0% |
| Average number of responders per campaign (d) = (b)*(c) | 1200 |

**Campaign Contact History Over Six Months** Whether contacted; channel of contact—telecalling or direct mail during offer period. All accounts in the mail file were contacted.

**Product Details** Personal loan product offered (rate, loan amount, tenor); card product related features.

**Card Customer Demographics** Age, occupation, gender, income, city/state; private or public sector, industry type, internal company rating, salaried or self employed, number of years on current job.

**Card Level Behavioural Information** Spend (cash and purchase), bill value; cash and credit line; payment ratio, revolve ratio; behaviour score, application score; and others. These variables are measured prior to the month of campaign file creation e.g., previous month, last 3/6 months.

**Credit Bureau** Data is not available

**Relationship** Number of total bank products held, number of credit cards held; whether prior history of having a personal loan, whether deposit holder.

## *Methodology*

- Logistic regression is used to predict the binary outcome of response as a function of customer demographics, credit card level and other behavioural variables (independent variables or predictors)
  - The response score is developed such that a higher score implies higher response probability.
  - The sample is segmented into 10 equal groups (deciles) based on score bands. Each decile has 10% of total sample accounts.
- Analysis is done at the credit card account level as the offer is made at an account level, ≥ 2 card customers are made only one offer.
- Pre-modelling analysis was conducted and some of these steps are:
  - Creation of derived variables (from raw variables) e.g., payment ratio, utilisation
  - Segmentation using cluster analysis or classification/decision tree method

  - Outlier detection and treatment
  - Missing value imputation
  - Check for multicollinearity
- Three samples were taken out from the final sample—development; hold out (within sample); out-of-time. Hold-out and out-of-time were used for validating the model.
- Several candidate models were evaluated for model finalisation on the basis of coefficient estimate values/signs and statistical significance; discrimination power; and validation results

*Model Results* Results of the final model selected by using logistic regression are presented. Variables are listed in the order of importance by statistical significance based on the Wald Chi-square statistic (Table 7.40).

- Credit need
  - Revolvers, those with low payment ratio are more responsive to a loan offer than transactors
  - Prior history of loans or balance transfer has an odds ratio of 2 implying that the odds of response for a customer who has taken a loan product earlier is twice that of a customer who has not, everything else being constant
  - Cash usage is a good trigger. The positive coefficient value signifies a positive relationship. For a cash utilisation increase of 1 percentage point, odds of response is 2.7 fold, ceteris paribus.

**Table 7.40** Response Model

| Variable | Impact | Coefficient Estimate | Wald Chi-square | p-value | Odds Ratio |
|---|---|---|---|---|---|
| Average payment ratio | Negative | –1.452 | 358.9 | < 0.001 | .234 |
| If balance transfer or installment loan on card or personal loan in last 12 months | Positive | 0.683 | 301.5 | < 0.001 | 1.98 |
| Credit line | Negative | –0.062 | 156.5 | < 0.01 | .939 |
| Cash utilisation in last 3 months | Positive | 1.01 | 146.9 | < 0.01 | 2.74 |
| Age | Positive | 0.025 | 95.9 | < 0.01 | 1.02 |
| If self employed | Positive | 0.520 | 40.5 | < 0.05 | 1.68 |
| If average credit utilisation (over 6 months) > 60% | Positive | 0.286 | 24.8 | < 0.05 | 1.33 |
| Has ≥ 1 non-card product with the bank | Positive | 0.182 | 11.0 | < 0.10 | 1.20 |

*Intercept not reported. Gini = 0.570; Concordance = 79.5

- Credit utilisation (balance/credit line) is a good predictor of response. A card customer having an average utilisation >60% is more likely to respond, ceteris paribus.
- Demographic variables affect response. Age is a surrogate for life-stage needs and the estimate is positive. Self-employed individuals tend to have a 70% higher odds of response relative to salaried, perhaps due to reasons of cash flow management.
- Cross-selling is a self-fulfilling proposition. The odds of response for a customer having one or more non-card products is 20% higher than a customer with card product only, ceteris paribus.
- It may be worthwhile to segment the population based on variables that have high odds ratio such as prior history of loan type product and cash usage. Separate models for each segment if warranted (based on pre-modelling segmental analysis of factors driving response). Or alternatively, a trigger-based approach for prior history or cash usage segment and a model-based approach for the rest.

*Model Evaluation* Readers are advised to look up model evaluation, Section 7.5 for an elaborate discussion of the measures.

- Coefficient estimates are all statistically significant at different levels of significance and with expected signs
- Gains Table and the Gains Chart—Table 7.41 and Fig. 7.17 show that the model rank orders and provides good discrimination of responders and non-responders. Corresponding deciles of the Gains Table is derived by segmenting the sample into 10 equally sized groups based on response score. Decile-1 corresponds to the highest response score band.

**Table 7.41** Gains Table—Response Score

| Decile | Response Rate | Lift | Cumulative % of Responders | Cumulative % of Non-responders | KS |
|---|---|---|---|---|---|
| 1 | 16.5% | 4.13 | 41.3% | 8.7% | 32.6% |
| 2 | 8.6% | 2.15 | 62.8% | 18.2% | 44.6% |
| 3 | 4.9% | 1.23 | 75.2% | 28.1% | 47.0% |
| 4 | 3.2% | 0.79 | 83.1% | 38.2% | 44.9% |
| 5 | 2.0% | 0.50 | 88.1% | 48.4% | 39.7% |
| 6 | 1.7% | 0.44 | 92.5% | 58.6% | 33.8% |
| 7 | 1.2% | 0.29 | 95.4% | 68.9% | 26.5% |
| 8 | 0.8% | 0.19 | 97.3% | 79.3% | 18.0% |
| 9 | 0.7% | 0.18 | 99.1% | 89.6% | 9.5% |
| 10 | 0.3% | 0.09 | 100.0% | 100.0% | 0.0% |
| Average | 4.0% | | | | |

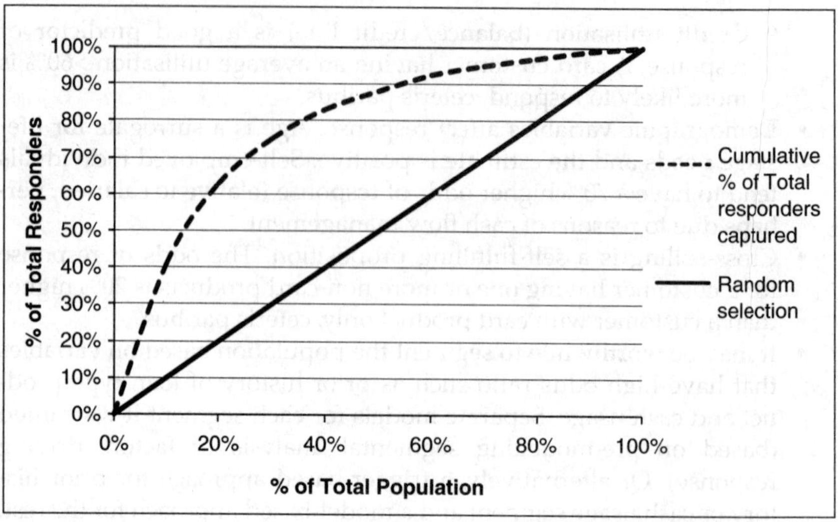


**Figure 7.17** Gains Chart—Response Score

- Model rank orders—lower actual response rate for a lower score band/lower decile.
- Good distinction of segments. *High:* Deciles 1/2/3 with average response rate of 10% ; *Medium:* Deciles 4/5/6/7 with average response rate of 2% ; *Low:* Deciles 8/9/10 with average response rate of 0.6%. Response rate of the top 30% is almost 17 times the response rate of the bottom 30%.
- Response rate of the top decile is 4 times the average response rate based on lift. The lift is calculated by dividing the response rate of the respective decile by sample average response rate.
- The top 30% of the target population captures 75% of the responders, and the KS statistic is also at its maximum at the third decile.
- Based on model statistics, good discrimination is further corroborated by a satisfactory Gini coefficient[12] and a high concordance.
- Comparison to the segmentation example of the "Cross-Sell" chapter reveals some commonality of predictor variables; percentage of responders captured by top 30% of the population is similar. Using logistic regression, the number of predictor variables is higher. The distinct advantage of scoring is the ability to make more granular decisions (one-to-one marketing strategies).

*Implementation Strategy* Three different strategies are proposed for the determination of the target population (mail file) to be contacted for the offer.

[12] Gini greater than 0.5 based on a good data set is acceptable, although there are many factors influencing Gini and it is difficult to ascertain a threshold.

**Business As Usual (BAU):** Eligible base is 100,000 credit card accounts. 30,000 accounts are randomly selected for a personal loan cross-sell offer. Uniform pricing with DM followed by TM and average campaign response rate of 4%, resulting in 1200 responders.
**Strategy 1:** Budget constraint, mail file of 30,000 accounts and uniform pricing. Target population is based on deciles up to maximum KS. Response rate increase can be as high as 100% (optimistic scenario) due to focussed targeting (Table 7.42).
**Strategy 2:** No budget constraint, offer made to all eligible. Lift in response rate can be up to 40%(optimistic scenario) resulting from differential pricing (based on price elasticity) and contact strategy (Table 7.43). This is compared to a BAU offer to all 100,000 at uniform pricing.
**Strategy 3:** Target population is based on expected campaign profitability (benefit). This can be determined by calculating the expected profitability by decile (Fig. 7.18).

**Table 7.42** Implementation Strategy 1

| Target Group | Response Rate | % of Eligible Base | Number of Cards | Pricing | Contact Strategy | Expected Response Rate (Period of Offer) | Expected Number of Responders/ Incremental Over BAU |
|---|---|---|---|---|---|---|---|
| Deciles 1, 2, 3 | High | 30% | 30,000 | Uniform pricing | DM followed by TM for all; Prioritisation of TM by score | 8% | 2400/1200 |

**Table 7.43** Implementation Strategy 2

| Target Group | Response Rate | % of Eligible Base | Number of Cards | Pricing Differential Interest Rate | Contact Strategy | Expected Response Rate (Period of Offer) | Expected Number of Responders/ Incremental Over BAU |
|---|---|---|---|---|---|---|---|
| Deciles 1, 2, 3 | High | 30% | 30,000 | Highest | DM followed by TM | 5.6% | 5600/1600 |
| Deciles 4, 5, 6, 7 | Medium | 40% | 40,000 | Medium | DM followed by TM for 4/5; TM for 6 and 7; Prioritisation of TM by score. | | |
| Deciles 8, 9, 10 | Low | 30% | 30,000 | Lowest | Prioritisation of TM by score | | |

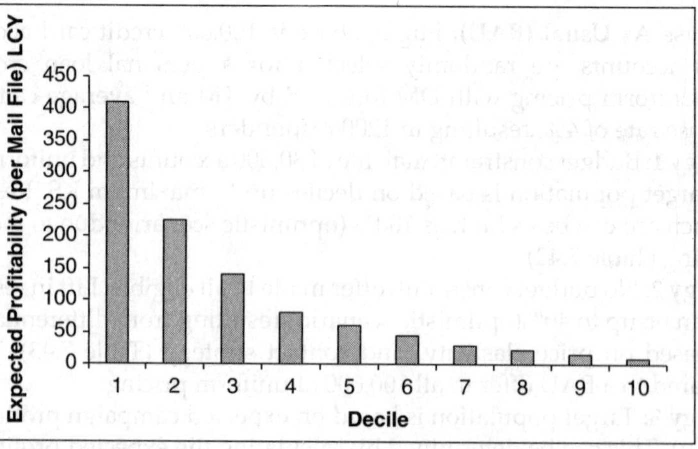

**Figure 7.18** Implementation Strategy 3

*Pricing Strategy* Pricing strategy based on expected P&L or NPV by price point can be the next improvisation of a model-based strategy. For this exercise, price sensitivity can be modelled by building separate price-specific response models (or one base model with adjustment for price elasticities). This is done post data collection from one or several rounds of price testing and readers can refer to the example of decision analysis (under multiproduct models) of the "Cross-Sell" chapter for more information.

*Conclusions* Direct marketing response models and cross-sell models to predict response propensity (using logistic regression) have become the norm, name it any industry. Further, response probability can be effectively used for pricing as well as contact strategy. A further refinement of implementation strategy would be to separate new to offer and past offer eligible segments, for both pricing and contact strategies. For a multiproduct cross-sell strategy, response propensity for different products can be modelled using multinomial logit, for the priortisation of offers by target segment.

### 7.4.3.9 Example II—Multinomial Logit—Motor Claims Fraud Model

*Objective* Insurance fraud is multi-faceted and the purpose of this example is to predict fraud based on different possibilities of fraud—whether the beneficiary is the insured or third party. The rationale is that the probability of fraud may differ for each type of fraud; factors affecting each type of fraud may be different; different types of fraud may yield different benefits to the individual. For example, it is generally more challenging to detect fraud for third party benefit and the pay-out received is lower as compared to fraudulent payment for personal benefit. The underlying model for fraudulent behaviour of an individual is based on expected utility. This example is "Adapted from *Insurance: Mathematics and Economics*, Volume 24, Issue 1-2, Artis et al., *Modelling Different Types of Automobile Insurance Fraud Behaviour in the Spanish Market*, Pages 67–81, Copyright (1999), with permission from Elsevier".

*Data* Sample of car damages from accidents that occurred from 1993 to 1996 for a Spanish insurance company. Dependent variable is FRAUD.

FRAUD = 1 if fraud for self-benefit (insured wants to obtain benefit for himself/herself)
FRAUD = 2 if fraud for third party benefit (insured is trying to benefit a third person, usually another driver)
FRAUD = 0 otherwise (LEGITIMATE)

*Fraud is observed if insurer has no doubt about the existence of fraud, and although no legal prosecution has taken place, the insured finally admits to fraud.*

FRAUD Rate = 38% defined as the percentage of total claims filed which are detected as fraud during the mentioned period (Table 7.44)

*Do note that the mentioned fraud rate represents a data set that was over sampled for FRAUD = 1/2 to obtain a good representation of the event for modelling purposes.*

*Expected Utility Model* The multinomial logit model is used to estimate probabilities of the two types of fraud and the underlying expected utility model is stated as follows.

$$E\,(U\,(F_r)) = (1 - p_r)\,U_r + p_r\,U\,(P) \qquad r = 1, 2$$

$E$ = Operator for expected value
$E(U(F_1))$ = Expected utility of fraud for self-benefit
$E(U(F_2))$ = Expected utility of fraud for third party

**Table 7.44** Fraud Statistics

| Fraud | Number of Claims | Number of Claims/ Total Claims |
|---|---|---|
| Legitimate | 846 | 62.3% |
| Fraud for own benefit | 247 | 18.2% |
| Fraud for third party | 264 | 19.4% |
| Total | 1357 | |

*Source:* Derived using data from Artis et al. (1999).

$p_r$ = Probability of detecting each type of fraud
$U_r$ = Utility of the fraudulent payout
$U(P)$ = Disutility associated with the amount of punishment

For model estimation, independent variables are the following:

- Number of files associated with the claim (NFILES)
- Insured does not accept fault for the accident = 1; otherwise = 0 (FAULT)
- Accident reported to police =1; otherwise = 0 (POLICE)
- Existence of witness = 1; otherwise = 0 (WITNESS)
- Accident occurred in a non-urban area = 1; otherwise = 0 (NONURBAN)
- Number of previous claims of the insured (RECORDS)
- Number of years since vehicle fabrication (VEHAGE)

*Methodology*

- Multinomial discrete choice model is deployed. An alternate model was also attempted using nested logit. However, the results of the multinomial logit from their study are discussed for this example.
- Maximum likelihood estimation with correction for choice-based sampling (to correct for the over-sampling of fraud cases). This was done using weights in the estimation procedure.

*Model Results* Model results for both types of fraud are shown in Tables 7.45 and 7.46.

- An expected result is the positive sign of the RECORDS coefficient. The insured who has had accidents becomes aware of the claim process.
- If the accident is reported to the police (POLICE), probability of fraud is lower, ceteris paribus

**Table 7.45** Fraud for Self-benefit Model

| Variable | Coefficient Estimate | P Value (t-test) | Impact |
|---|---|---|---|
| Constant | 15.57 | 0.00 | |
| Nfiles | −17.11 | 0.00 | − |
| Fault | 1.65 | 0.00 | + |
| Police | −1.66 | 0.00 | − |
| Witness | −11.56 | 0.00 | − |
| Nonurban | 1.15 | 0.01 | + |
| Records | 0.22 | 0.00 | + |

**Table 7.46** Fraud for Third Party Benefit Model

| Variable | Coefficient Estimate | P Value (t-test) | Impact |
|---|---|---|---|
| Constant | 5.63 | 0.00 | |
| Nfiles | – 5.97 | 0.00 | – |
| Fault | – 0.85 | 0.00 | – |
| Police | –1.42 | 0.00 | – |
| Witness | 3.94 | 0.00 | + |
| Nonurban | 0.10 | 0.83 | + |
| Records | 0.23 | 0.00 | + |

Restricted log-likelihood = –915.70; Log-likelihood function= –486.03;
Chi-square = 859.34; Significance level = 0.00
*Source (Table 7.45 & 7.46)*: Adapted from *Insurance: Mathematics and Economics*, Volume 24, Issue 1-2, Artis et al., "Modelling Different Types of Automobile Insurance Fraud Behaviour in the Spanish Market", Pages 67–81, Copyright (1999), with permission from Elsevier.

- Accidents in non-urban areas (NONURBAN) are associated with a higher probability of fraud for self-benefit model. The variable is statistically insignificant in the other model.
- Differences in results observed across both types of fraud are noted:
  - Variable FAULT has opposite signs across models. For self-benefit fraud, probability of cheating the company is higher if the insured does not accept blame. This is not the case for third party benefit fraud.
  - The presence of witness (WITNESS) at the accident site increases the probability (measured by odds) of fraud for third party benefit but decreases the probability of fraud for self-benefit.

*Model Evaluation* While readers should refer to the model evaluation section for a comprehensive review, measures related to this specific model are discussed briefly.

- All coefficient estimates are significant at the 1% level with the exception of one variable
- Most goodness-of-fit statistics reported are satisfactory with a significant likelihood ratio, resulting in the rejection of the null hypothesis that the coefficients of the two estimated equations are equal to zero
- Classification table for model predictive accuracy based on predetermined cut-off of estimated probability is shown in Table 7.47
  - Correct classification rate = 76.3 % [(766 + 179 + 90)/1357]
  - The percentage of legitimate claims being correctly classified is 90.5% [766/846]

**Table 7.47** Classification Table/Confusion Matrix

| | Predicted Type | | | |
|---|---|---|---|---|
| | Legitimate | Fraudulent: Self-benefit | Fraudulent: Third Party | Total |
| **Observed type** | | | | |
| Legitimate | **766** | 56 | 24 | 846 |
| Fraudulent: Self-benefit | 50 | **179** | 18 | 247 |
| Fraudulent: Third party | 123 | 51 | **90** | 264 |
| Total | 939 | 286 | 132 | 1357 |

*Source:* Artis (1999).

  - The percentage of all frauds being correctly classified as fraud irrespective of type of fraud is 66.1% [179 + 18 + 51 + 90/(247 + 264)]
  - The percentage of fraud-self benefit claims being correctly classified is 72.5% [179/247]
  - The percentage of fraud-third-party benefit claims being correctly classified is 34.1% [90/264]
- The classification rate for fraud for third party benefit is low. Authors state that this may be due to the challenges in predicting this kind of behaviour
- The assumption of independence of irrelevant alternatives (IIA) was also tested by estimating the parameters with one choice set removed. Conclusion is that IIA assumption is maintained and the odds ratio of fraud for self-benefit to no fraud remained the same, when the alternative of fraud for third-party benefit was removed.

*Implementation Strategy* Insurance fraud is a significant and costly problem for insurance companies, and one of the many challenges that insurers face is the high cost of detecting fraud. Therefore, an objective framework is required that can be used to help narrow and red flag the possible number of suspicious cases (to be investigated for fraud). Attention is given to claims with relatively high probabilities of fraud. Expected benefits are an increase in the number of fraud cases detected and an improved hit rate of genuine fraud cases. Referral of claims for investigation for fraud can be prioritised based on expected cost of a claim in relation to the cost of the accident.

### *Expected Cost of Claim*

$$E(c) = (1 - q)\,[p_2 M] + (1 - q)\,[(1 - p_2)\,c_2] + q\,[(1 - p_1)\,M] + q\,[p_1\,(c_1 + M)]$$

= Expected cost (*fraud claim classified as no fraud*) + Expected cost (*fraud claim classified as fraud*) + Expected cost (*legitimate claim classified as legitimate*) + Expected cost (*legitimate claim classified as fraud*)

Substituting the values in Table 7.48 into the $E(c)$ equation,

$$E(c) = M\,[1.0095 - .6044\,(1 - q)]$$

The insurance company can determine the cases for referral based on the fraud score. Table 7.49 shows that expected cost of claim increases with decreasing likelihood of fraud. This also explains the fall in the proportion of referrals for investigation by decile as shown in Fig. 7.19.

*Conclusions* The multinomial framework can be extended to analyse different types of fraud such as opportunistic and professional fraud. This model was developed by the same authors in their study published in 2002 and uses more comprehensive variables such as characteristics of the

**Table 7.48** Definitions for Expected Cost of Claim

| Notation | Definition | Values | Notation | Definition | Values |
|---|---|---|---|---|---|
| $E(c)$ | Expected cost of claim | | | | |
| $q$ | Probability of no fraud | | $1-q$ | Probability of committing fraud | |
| $p_1$ | Probability of legitimate claim classified as fraud | 9.5% | $1-p_1$ | Probability of legitimate claim classified as legitimate | 90.5% |
| $p_2$ | Probability of fraud claim classified as no fraud | 33.9% | $1-p_2$ | Probability of fraud claim classified as fraud | 66.1% |
| $M$ | Accident cost | | | | |
| $c_1 + M$ | Expected cost of a legitimate claim classified as fraud | $0.1M + M$ ($c_1 = .1M$) | $M$ | Expected cost of legitimate claim classified as legitimate | |
| $M$ | Expected cost of fraud claim classified as legitimate | | $c_2$ | Expected cost of fraud claim classified as fraud | 0.1M |

*Source:* Derived using information from Artis et al. (1999).

**Table 7.49** Propensity of Fraud and Expected Cost of Claim

| Decile | Predicted Propensity of Committing Fraud | Expected Cost of Claim |
| --- | --- | --- |
| 1 | 50% | .70M |
| 2 | 16% | .91M |
| 9 | 2% | M |

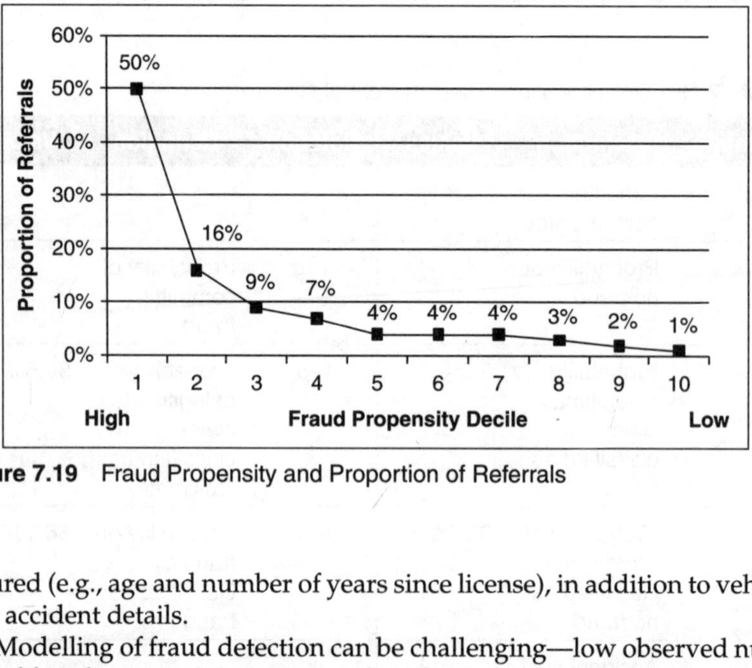


**Figure 7.19** Fraud Propensity and Proportion of Referrals

insured (e.g., age and number of years since license), in addition to vehicle and accident details.

Modelling of fraud detection can be challenging—low observed number of fraud cases; minimising misclassification rate; and the appearance of new types of fraud. Some of the other data-related challenges are disparate data sources. Files that contain information regarding accident details are often stored in physical files, thereby limiting the ability to build a customer one view linking up demographic, policy and accident information.

Various other non-model-based techniques are available for fraud detection. Business rule-based decision systems are defined on specific patterns of activity; text mining of claims process based on text-based information (adjuster notes, emails, claimant interviews); voice stress analysis to identify stress levels in claimant interviews. Moreover, the application of artificial neural networks (ANN) has proven to be an effective algorithm for "rare event" modelling of this kind and for discovering new types of fraud.

## 7.4.4 Survival Analysis

### 7.4.4.1 Introduction

Survival or hazard rate models are most suitable estimation methods when the outcome variable of interest is duration ("time until an event occurs"). The event may be customer attrition, customer bankruptcy, repurchase and failure of a machine. Corresponding duration is customer lifetime, time to bankruptcy, inter-purchase time, and machine durability. Also known as duration models, they not only provide the probability of occurrence of the event at different time periods (when), but also estimates of duration (how long). One of the important advantages of survival analysis is that it can effectively incorporate incomplete observations of time arising from censoring.

The origin of survival analysis dates back to mortality tables of centuries ago. It gained importance during WWII, motivated by the interest in reliability (failure time) of military equipment[13]. With rising consumer demand for safer and reliable products, adaptation to private manufacturing followed soon. Medical research also embraced it quickly for the analysis of clinical trials, to examine the effect of a specific treatment on patient (*subject/observation*) longevity (*duration*) through follow-up until death (*event*). The advantage of survival analysis is that it can handle data-related nuances of medical intervention studies such as delayed patient entry; early withdrawal (quit participating, move far away to follow, or death due to an unrelated event); and not experiencing the event of death before the end of the observation period. This is in contrast to the standard practice of withdrawing the patient from the trial under these circumstances. In the area of financial services, survival analysis has been aptly used for developing risk scores, predicting credit card attrition, mortgage prepayment, and premium persistency. For revenue management, modelling price response functions through the estimation of a car's duration in the market until it has been sold; forecasting length of stay in a hotel; and evaluating how many seats "survive" as empty in a given time period (for casino games) are some relevant applications. Economists rely heavily on survival models to study unemployment spells and related benefit claims. A highly recommended book on this subject is by Hosmer and Lemeshow. A good portion of Sections 7.4.4.3 to 7.4.4.7 is from "*Applied Survival Analysis*, Hosmer and Lemeshow, Copyright (1999), John Wiley & Sons, Inc., Adapted with permission of John Wiley & Sons, Inc.".

### 7.4.4.2 Applications

Table 7.50 gives examples of industry related applications in the area of survival analysis.

---

[13] Smith and Smith, "Survival Analysis and the Application of Cox's Proportional Hazards" *Modelling Using SAS*, SUGI.

**Table 7.50** Applications of Survival Models

| Applications | Industry | Description | References |
|---|---|---|---|
| Cross-Sell | General | Purchase and timing probabilities for choosing more than 2 products. | Kumar et al.; Reinartz (2006) |
| | Financial Services/Insurance | Impact of sociodemographic and economic variables on the probability of purchasing financial products (insurance and savings products) for UK. Survival model to identify factors determining probability of purchase/repurchase and for forecasting time till next purchase. | Tang et al. ( 2007); Salazar et al. (2007) |
| Credit Scoring | Financial Services—Risk | First application to credit scoring; significant improvements in credit-granting decisions. | Narain (1992) |
| | | Survival model competitive with logistic regression for predicting first year default but not the case for predicting second year default. | Benasik, Crook and Thomas (1999) |
| | | Applies concept of competing risks—early prepayment and default. Survival and logistic regression give similar results for both first and second year default models. | Stepanova and Thomas (2002) |
| | | Across Belgium, Germany, and Netherlands—pooled (national) and individual (generic). Similar predictive performance between survival models and logistic. | Andreeva (2005) |
| | | Macroeconomic variables as time varying covariates. Performance improvement of survival (with macro variables) as compared to logistic regression. | Bellotti and Crook (2009) |
| Attrition/ Lapsation | Financial Services/Insurance | Attrition model for financial services based on survival model and time varying covariates using longitudinal data. Evaluates impact of factors (e.g., demographic, policy) on survival time for Singapore market. | Poel and Lariviere (2004); Loi et al. |
| | Telecom | Customer lifetime value through the estimation of survival curves. | Lu (SUGI 120-28) |

### 7.4.4.3 Basic Concepts

*Censored Data* Censored observation is one whose value is incomplete due to random factors for each subject. *Right censoring,* which is more commonly experienced, occurs when the observation period[14] ends before the event is observed or subject terminates before the outcome of interest is observed. Some examples of *right censoring* are as follows: patient is alive at the end of the clinical study (event is death); customer does not default on loan payment or prepay during the observation period (event is default/prepayment); customer moves out of town or dies. Since the incomplete nature of the observation occurs at the right end of the time dimension, observation is termed *right censored. Left censored* observation is one where the event has already occurred before the start of the observation period. Figure 7.20 is a graphical representation of censoring.

*Survival Function* Survival function $S(t)$ specifies the probability that survival time (duration) is at least "$t$". A practical application of survival analysis would give the answer to a question such as: What is the probability that a customer will stay for least "X" days at hotel Y? Duration is the length of stay.

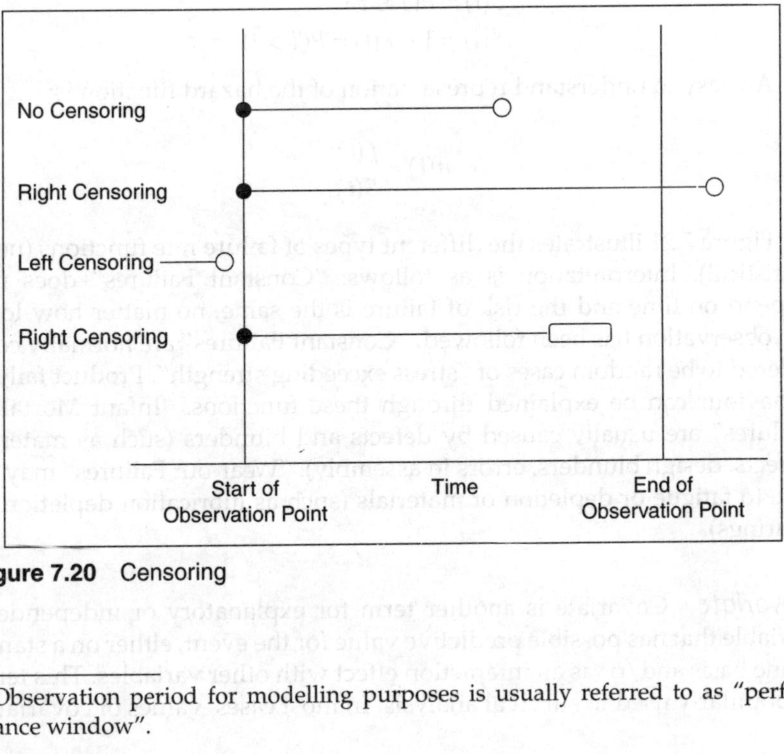


**Figure 7.20** Censoring

[14] Observation period for modelling purposes is usually referred to as "performance window".

*Hazard Function* Hazard is the risk of failure in an interval after time "$t$" conditional on the observation having survived until time "$t$". Hazard rate at time "$t$" specifies the probability of failure during "$t$" and "$t + \Delta t$", given that it has not occurred earlier. Also, termed as failure rate, it is a conditional probability as it applies only to that subset of the sample that has survived up to a particular time. An example of a related query that the hazard function is expected to answer is: What is the probability that the customer will attrite in the next 2 months given that he/she is a current customer? The failure is the event of attrition.

$T$ = Survival time
$t$ = Realisation of $T$
$f(t)$ = Probability density function of survival time = Probability of survival at "$t$"
$F(t)$ = Cumulative distribution function of survival time = Probability that survival time is less than or equal to "$t$".
$S(t)$ = Survival function = Probability that survival time is at least "$t$".
$h(t)$ = Hazard rate
$P$ = Probability

The survival function can be derived from the cumulative distribution function:

$$F(t) = P(T \leq t)$$
$$S(t) = 1 - F(t) = P(T > t)$$

An easy to understand representation of the hazard function is:

$$h(t) = \frac{f(t)}{S(t)}$$

Figure 7.21 illustrates the different types of failure rate functions (non-statistical). Interpretation is as follows: "Constant Failures" does not depend on time and the risk of failure is the same, no matter how long the observation has been followed. "Constant Failures" are normally considered to be random cases of "stress exceeding strength". Product failure behaviour can be explained through these functions. "Infant Mortality Failures" are usually caused by defects and blunders (such as material defects, design blunders, errors in assembly). "Wear-out Failures" may be due to fatigue or depletion of materials (such as lubrication depletion in bearings).

*Covariate* Covariate is another term for explanatory or independent variable that has possible predictive value for the event, either on a stand-alone basis and/or as an interaction effect with other variables. This term is popularly used in survival analysis. In most cases, values of covariates

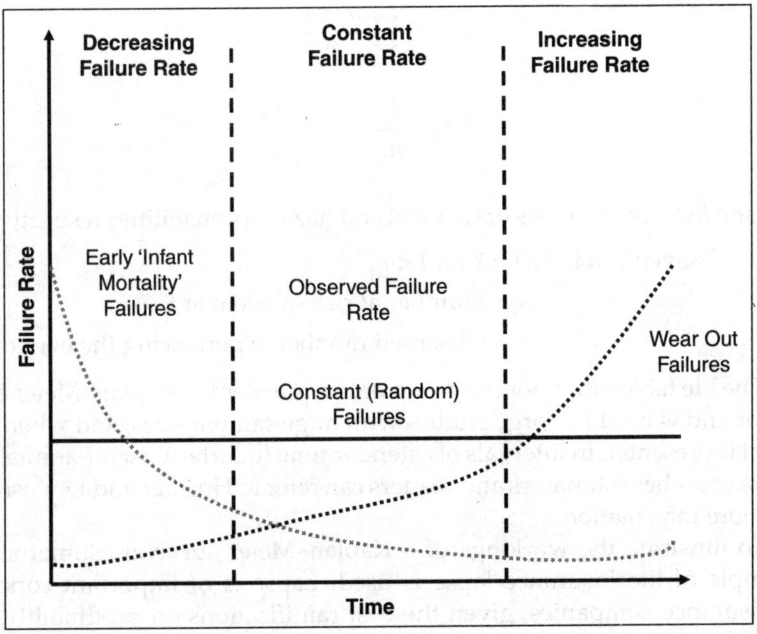


**Figure 7.21** Failure Rate Functions

are recorded at the start time of the observation period, and these values are assumed not to change with time. However, some of these covariates are expected to change over time e.g., age, income, occupation. Time-varying covariates are those whose values vary over time and survival/hazard function may depend on the most current value or lagged value of the covariate, recorded prior to occurrence of the event. For such time-varying variables, the assumption in survival analysis is that coefficients are time invariant. Time-varying covariates can be accommodated as predictors in the class of survival models giving them a competing benefit over standard regression procedures. The examples following later will cover time-varying covariates.

### 7.4.4.4 Non-parametric Estimators of Survival and Hazard Functions

Also called the product limit estimator, the Kaplan–Meier estimator is derived through a step-wise procedure, and is used to calculate the survival function for survival time measured on continuous time scale. It includes information from all observations available (censored and uncensored), and uses individual values to calculate the probabilities. It is a product of conditional survival probabilities at each time period and is viewed as a product of proportions, under the assumption that censoring is independent of survival time.

$$\hat{S}(t) = \prod_{t_{(i)} \le t} \frac{n_i - d_i}{n_i}$$

$$\hat{h}(t) = \frac{d_i}{n_i}$$

$\hat{S}(t)$ and $\hat{h}(t)$ are estimates of survival and hazard probabilities respectively.

Convention is $\hat{S}(t) = 1$ for $t < t_{(1)}$

$n_i$ = Number at risk of event at $t_i$

$d_i$ = Observed number experiencing the event at $t_i$

The life table estimator is a group data equivalent of Kaplan–Meier estimator and is used for large studies with huge sample sizes, and when the event is presented in intervals of calendar time (quarterly/semi-annually). There are other estimators and readers can refer to Hosmer and Lemeshow for more information.

To illustrate the workings of a Kaplan–Meier survival estimator, an example of life insurance lapse is used. Lapse is of important concern to insurance companies, given the cost ramifications on profitability. As a reminder for readers, the concept of survival and hazard rate function was introduced in the usage and retention management chapters. A lapsed policy refers to a policy which has been terminated (no longer in force) due to non-payment of premium by the stipulated period. Policy is censored if it is terminated due to reasons such as death of policyholder or maturity of the policy (before the end of the observation period). Table 7.51 shows the calculations for deriving the estimated survival and hazard rate functions using the Kaplan–Meier estimator for a life insurance portfolio. For this example, the assumptions are that the portfolio comprises mainly of annual premium policies with an average policy term of 15 years and no reinstatement is allowed. Figure 7.22 is a graphical representation of the Kaplan–Meier survival function.

### *Comments on Survival Function for Insurance*

- Downward slope of the survival curve suggests that higher the duration of the policy, lower the survival probability. The probability that the policy will survive at least 1 year is 69.3% and drops to 45.2% for at least 3 years. Only about a quarter of the starting policies survive the average term of 15 years.
- Hazard rate is the conditional probability of lapse, and can be interpreted as the probability of first lapse in this example. 30.7% of policyholders are not likely to pay first renewal premium. Of the policyholders who survived two years (paid their first renewal), 20.8% are not likely to pay their second renewal. Hazard rate is at its highest at first renewal and is an expected finding.

**Table 7.51** Kaplan–Meier Estimator of Survival Function for Insurance

| Time–Year of Policy | Number of Policies at Risk of Lapse at Beginning of Year (t) | Number of Policies Lapsed | Censored | Conditional Probability of Lapse Hazard Rate | Conditional Survival Rate (1 – Hazard Rate) | Cumulative Survival Rate | Probability of Lapse |
|---|---|---|---|---|---|---|---|
| (t) | $n(t) = n(t-1) - d(t-1) - c(t-1)$ | d(t) | c(t) | $h(t) = d(t)/n(t)$ | $1 - h(t)$ | $S(t) = S(t-1)*[1 - h(t)]$ | $f(t) = h(t)*S(t)$ |
| <1 | 15102 | 0 | 1 | 0.000 | 1.000 | 1.000 | 0.000 |
| $1 \le t < 2$ | 15101 | 4643 | 1 | 0.307 | 0.693 | 0.693 | 0.213 |
| $2 \le t < 3$ | 10457 | 2171 | 2 | 0.208 | 0.792 | 0.549 | 0.114 |
| $3 \le t < 4$ | 8284 | 1455 | 0 | 0.176 | 0.824 | 0.452 | 0.079 |
| $4 \le t < 5$ | 6829 | 787 | 1 | 0.115 | 0.885 | 0.400 | 0.046 |
| $5 \le t < 6$ | 6041 | 489 | 0 | 0.081 | 0.919 | 0.368 | 0.030 |
| $6 \le t < 7$ | 5552 | 397 | 3 | 0.072 | 0.928 | 0.342 | 0.024 |
| $7 \le t < 8$ | 5152 | 380 | 2 | 0.074 | 0.926 | 0.316 | 0.023 |
| $8 \le t < 9$ | 4770 | 256 | 0 | 0.054 | 0.946 | 0.299 | 0.016 |
| $9 \le t < 10$ | 4514 | 162 | 2 | 0.036 | 0.964 | 0.289 | 0.010 |
| $10 \le t < 11$ | 4350 | 128 | 0 | 0.029 | 0.971 | 0.280 | 0.008 |
| $11 \le t < 12$ | 4222 | 116 | 1 | 0.027 | 0.973 | 0.272 | 0.007 |
| $12 \le t < 13$ | 4105 | 75 | 1 | 0.018 | 0.982 | 0.267 | 0.005 |
| $13 \le t < 14$ | 4029 | 51 | 2 | 0.013 | 0.987 | 0.264 | 0.003 |
| $14 \le t < 15$ | 3976 | 44 | 0 | 0.011 | 0.989 | 0.261 | 0.003 |
| $15 \le t < 16$ | 3932 | 37 | 0 | 0.009 | 0.991 | 0.259 | 0.002 |

*Note*: Calculations are estimates.

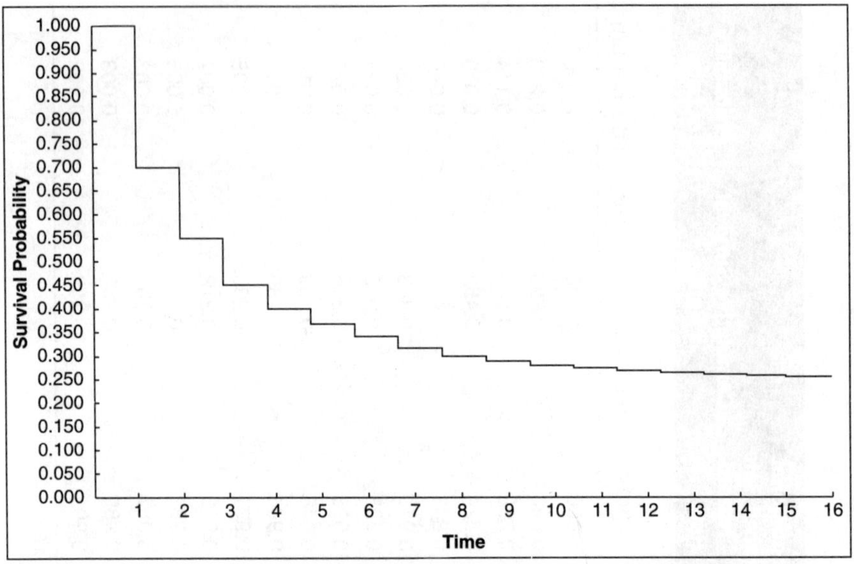


**Figure 7.22** Kaplan-Meier Survival Function

### 7.4.4.5 Consequences of Using Linear Regression

If one tries to use linear regression, it can lead to:

- Downward bias in the estimate of survival time as the regression model is estimated based on only uncensored data(for whom full customer duration has been observed). This bias is further amplified if the number of censored observations is high, relative to non-censored.
- Standard statistics such as mean, median, standard deviation fall short as precise estimators of the parameters of survival time distribution, if both uncensored and censored observations are included in the data sample for estimation. Henceforth, the mean for survival time has to be interpreted as "at least as large".
- Due to left or right skewed distributions of survival time, the normality assumptions of linear regression model are not maintained. This may lead to negative estimates of survival time for observations with short survival time (survival time can take only positive values).

### 7.4.4.6 Survival and Hazard Rate Regression Models

*Semi-Parametric Regression Model—Cox Proportional Hazards Model (PH Model)* Proportional hazard model (Cox, 1972) is a semi-parametric regression model popularly used to evaluate the comparative survival experience of different groups (relative risk), and to understand the impact of covariates on survival time. One of the major advantages is that there is no need to specify the full distributional form of the survival and hazard functions for fitting the model. Therefore, it lends itself very satisfactorily to a situation when underlying distribution of the survival curve is not well discerned. The examples will demonstrate the practicality of this approach in the subsequent section.

Hazard function $h(t, x, \beta) = h_0(t) \times \gamma(x, b)$
If $\gamma(x, \beta) = e^{x\beta}$
Hazard function $h(t, x, \beta) = h_0(t) \times e^{x\beta}$
Survival Function $S(t, x, \beta) = [S_0(t)]^{e^{x\beta}}$

Hazard Ratio $HR(t, x, \beta) = e^{\beta(x_1 - x_2)}$

*$h_0(t)$ and $S_0(t)$ are the baseline hazard and survival functions*
*$\gamma(x, \beta)$ is a function of covariates*

$\beta$=Coefficient (parameter) to be estimated (the model has no intercept term)

$x$ = Single covariate which takes the value $x_1$ for observation 1 and $x_2$ for observation 2; or it can be interpreted as taking different values for the same observation (subject).

- *Hazard function* is multiplicative model between a function of baseline hazard function [$h_0(t)$] and function of covariates [$\gamma(x, \beta)$]. The baseline hazard function $h_0(t)$ is the relationship of the hazard rate with survival time, and the exponential function explains the relationship with covariates alone.
- The *baseline survival function* can be interpreted as the survival curve of a hypothetical "completely average" observation, for which each covariate value is equal to the average value of that covariate for the entire set of observations in the study
- *Hazard ratio* is the ratio of hazard functions and is interpreted as a "relative risk" type of ratio. *Hazard ratio* does not depend on survival time and the term *proportional hazards* is linked to this observation. According to Hosmer and Lemeshow, the *hazard ratio* has comparable relevance to the odds ratio concept of logistic regression. The major difference is that hazard ratio is a comparative measure of survival experience over the entire time period (any time during the study as it is time invariant), while the odds ratio is typically evaluated as a comparative measure of event occurrence only at the endpoint of the study. The examples will show case the relevance of the hazard ratio with respect to the interpretation of model coefficients.
- Partial likelihood procedures are employed for parameter estimation using the likelihood function. It is important to note that baseline hazard and survival function are not estimated as they are not specified and therefore, have to be calculated separately using a separate likelihood approach, by using the calculated parameter estimates.

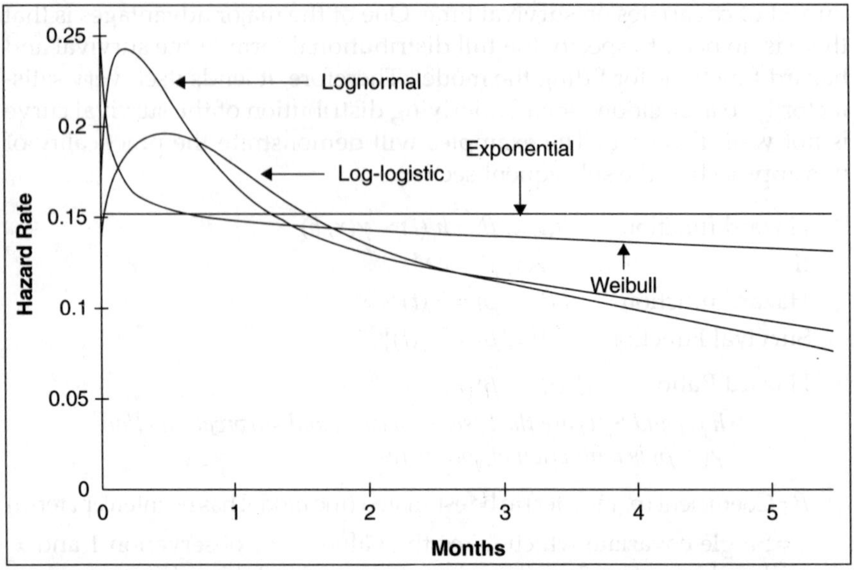


**Figure 7.23** Hazard Functions

*Parametric Regression Models* For parametric models, baseline survival function and covariate effects are parameterised and the focus will be on a class of models called "accelerated failure time" models. Also called AFT models[15], the effect of a covariate is said to "accelerate" survival time. For these type of models, the effect of the covariate is multiplicative on the time scale. Exponential, Weibull and log-logistic are AFT models[16]. The different statistical specifications of the hazard function are shown in Fig. 7.23. It is useful to calculate and plot the hazard function estimates based on sample data as a guide to the choice of the parametric form for modelling purposes.

**Exponential Model**

Hazard function $h(t,x,\beta) = e^{-(\beta_0+\beta_1 x)}$

Survival Function $S(t,x,\beta) = \exp[(-t \times e^{-(\beta_0+\beta_1 x)})]$

Hazard Ratio $HR(t,x,\beta) = e^{-\beta_1(x_1-x_2)}$

**Weibull Model**

Hazard function $h(t,x,\beta) = \dfrac{pt^{p-1}}{[\exp(\beta_0+\beta_1 x)]^p}$

[15] Survival models that can be linearised by taking logs are called accelerated failure time models.

[16] Exponential is a special case of Weibull for shape parameter equal to 1.

Survival Function $S(t,x,\beta) = \exp\{-t^p [e^{-p(\beta_0+\beta_1 x)}]\}$

*where p = shape parameter*

- The *exponential* model is an accelerated failure time model that has proportional hazards. Hazard function for exponential models is constant in survival time (memory less property), which is inferred from the fact that time does not enter the expression for hazard function[17]. This implies that probability of experiencing the event does not depend on how long the subject/observation has survived.
- For log-logistic, hazard rate increases initially and then decreases

### 7.4.4.7 Estimation Method

Maximum likelihood is used for estimation. For a sample of *n* independent observations for $i = 1, 2, \ldots n$, the likelihood function $l(\beta)$ is a product of expressions of non-censored and censored observations. To obtain full maximum likelihood estimator of $\beta$, the log-likelihood function $L(\beta)$ is maximised with respect to $\beta$ by taking the derivatives of $L(\beta)$ with respect to $\beta$, setting the equations to zero, and solving for $\beta$.

$$l(\beta) = \prod_{i=1}^{n} [f(t_i, \beta, x_i)]^{1-c_i} \times \{[S(t_i, \beta, x_i)]^{c_i}\}$$

$f(t_i, x, \beta)$ = *Probability of experiencing event of interest at time t units for non-censored observations*

$S(t_i, \beta, /x_i)$ = *Probabilityofsurivingatleast t timeunitsfor consored observations*

$c_i = 1 =$ *censored*

*Assumptions*

- Time is a continuous variable
- Censoring is independent of values of survival time and covariates
- Reasons for observing a censored observation are unrelated to the event

### 7.4.4.8 Model Evaluation

Model evaluation follows a similar process as logistic regression. Readers should refer to the model evaluation section for logistic regression (Section 7.5). For the proportional hazard model, the assumption of a constant hazard ratio, (with respect to time) needs to be validated. Readers are advised to consult the book by Hosmer and Lemeshow for further details.

---

[17] The quantity $exp(\beta_1)$ is called the acceleration factor.

### 7.4.4.9 Strengths and Challenges

- Provides probability of the occurrence of the event at different points of time that can be used to make inferences on "when the event is likely to happen"
- Estimates of survival time are useful for calculating important customer metrics such as CLV
- Ability to include time-varying covariates brings in the dynamic impact of predictor variables on the event of interest
- Framework adeptly accommodates censored data
- To derive meaningful results from using survival analysis, there should be good variation in the data for survival time
- Careful scrutiny of the data is required in order to decide which variant to apply among semi-parametric and parametric models
- Significant amount of data preparation is required to re-align the data from calendar to duration time, termed as tenurisation of data
- Survival analysis does not necessarily have an edge over binary outcome type of models such as logistic regression, when the sole objective is to determine probability of the occurrence of the event and hazard function is almost constant with respect to time

### 7.4.4.10 Example—Customer Attrition Model

*Objective* The objective is to develop an attrition model. The advantages of using survival models for predicting attrition as compared to the popular logistic regression model are:

- The impact of macro level variables can be directly factored in. These are important determinants of attrition behaviour.
- The factor of "time" of survival models is important for the analysis of attrition. Recent behaviour/events (triggers) prior to the event of attrition have an influential role to play in explaining attrition. This effect is captured by the inclusion of time-varying covariates. Attrition rates vary by time (MOB) and this trend can be modelled through an appropriate hazard rate function specification that is a function of time.
- Customer duration required for CLV estimates can be directly calculated from the estimates of survival time
- Censoring effect is taken care of in the modelling procedure

This example is "Adapted from *European Journal of Operational Research*, Volume 157, Issue 1, Van den Poel and Lariviere, *Customer Attrition Analysis for Financial Services using Proportional Hazard Models*, Pages 196–217, Copyright (2004), with permission from Elsevier". The model was developed for a European financial services company based on a random sample of longitudinal data of bank customers. Different categories of predictors are used (customer demographics, customer behaviour, and macroenvironment predictors) to explain "customer" attrition behaviour (in contrast to account level). A static model with no time varying covariates was also attempted for comparison purposes.

### *Data*

- Performance window: 77 years
- Number of customers: 47,157
- If customer has experienced churn over a 77-year period then CHURN = 1; Else CHURN = 0
- Churn rate (based on CHURN) = 47%
- Censored = 1 if customer does not churn during the 77 years
- Exclusions: Customers who died during the observation window

Customer is observed from the start to the end of the relationship by exploiting the longitudinal aspect of data available. Henceforth, both the dependent variable and covariates move with time.Time-varying predictors take on different values with customer duration. No explicit mention is made in the paper relating to how customer attrition initiated by the bank (involuntary closure due to high risk/loss) is treated.

### *Methodology*

- Cox proportional hazard model with time-varying covariates was used
- Additional issues given time-varying covariates:
  - According the authors, with time-varying covariates, the ratio of hazards (HR) may not remain constant over time. However, authors validate the assumption of proportionality satisfactorily.
  - Multicollinearity is amplified in the presence of time varying covariates (due to common correlation with time). Certain cut-offs were used for inter-correlations to decide whether to introduce new covariates into the model. Correlation coefficient of 0.40 was used as the cut-off after attempting several levels of cut-off.
- Some of the important covariates in the model are mentioned in Table 7.52

*Model Results* Although many covariates of the hazard model were significant, the results are confined to a few important variables in the model, that were statistically significant (Table 7.53).

- Customer behavioural covariates—total number of products and inter-purchase time were significant
  - An additional product held by the customer lowers switching probability substantially by 99.9% [(0.001-1)*100]
  - Probability of attrition is higher by 4.7% for an additional unit of inter-purchase time
  - These results illustrate the fact that regular and timely cross-sell activities are beneficial for increasing retention rate

**Table 7.52** Covariates for Attrition Model

| Class | Covariate | Time Varying | Comments | Expected Relationship to Attrition |
|---|---|---|---|---|
| Customer behaviour | Product specific ownership | Y | 7 product specific ownership dummy variables | No a-priori expectation |
| | Total product ownership | Y | Total number of products over time | Negative |
| | Inter-purchase time | Y | Average time elapsed between two purchases. Takes on new value every time a customer buys a new product | Positive |
| | Home and phone banking | Y | Dummy which can change over time | Negative |
| Customer demographics | Age | Y | Age of customer | No a-priori expectation |
| | Gender | N | Dummy with Male = 1; Female = 0 | No a-priori expectation |
| | Level of education | N | Range from 1-7 with 7 being the highest | No significant relationship |
| | Social status and potential (Geo-demographic data) | N | Elite/high/medium/low status coded as individual dummy variables. At neighbourhood level. | No impact |
| Macroenvironment | Prosperity | Y | Purchasing power measured by "GNP per capita" measured every year over the entire lifetime of customer | Significant impact |
| | Merger | Y | Takes on value of 1 from the moment customer experienced the merger | Positive |

*Source:* Adapted from *European Journal of Operational Research*, Volume 157, Issue 1, Van den Poel and Lariviere, "Customer Attrition Analysis for Financial Services Using Proportional Hazard Models", Pages 196–217, Copyright (2004), with permission from Elsevier.

**Table 7.53** Attrition Model

| Variable | $\hat{\beta}$ (Estimate) | Exp ($\hat{\beta}$) Hazard Ratio |
|---|---|---|
| Total product ownership | −6.856 | 0.001 |
| Inter-purchase time | 0.048 | 1.047 |
| Age | −0.022 | 0.978 |
| Gender | 0.879 | 2.408 |
| Educational level | −0.085 | 0.918 |
| Elite Social Status | −0.498 | 0.608 |
| Merger | −0.235 | 0.791 |
| Prosperity Index | 0.008 | 1.008 |

*Source:* Adapted from *European Journal of Operational Research*, Volume 157, Issue 1, Van den Poel and Lariviere, "Customer Attrition Analysis for Financial Services Using Proportional Hazard Models", Pages 196–217, Copyright (2004), with permission from Elsevier.

- Demographic covariates—age, gender, educational level and social status influence customer duration
    - For every additional year of age, probability of churn reduces by 2.2%. For two additional years, the probability decreases by 4.4%
    - Men are 2.4 times more likely to leave than a female customer
    - More educated customers are at lower probability of attrition
- Macroenvironmental—Customers who experienced a merger event are 20% more likely to stay than those who did not. Higher churn rates are associated with a wealthier neighbourhood.
- Score can be approximated as $e^{\beta x}$ (as the baseline hazard is a function of time only and is the same for all customers)
- Many of the covariates became insignificant in the static version of the model (in the absence of time-varying covariates)

### 7.4.4.11 Example—Credit Risk Scoring

The development and advancement of credit scoring has played an important role in the growth of retail lending. These scores include application scores to assess the likelihood of credit default/loss of a prospect (applicant); behaviour scores to gauge the future credit worthiness of a current customer; fraud and collection/recovery scores. The practice is to classify customers into "GOOD" and "BAD" depending on repayment performance over a specified time period. Binary outcome or choice models such as logistic regression has been the most popular technique for developing consumer credit risk models. However, in recent times, headway has been made on using survival analysis to model credit behaviour as it can answer the dual questions of "if a borrower will default" and "when". Some of the advantages of using survival models over standard procedures such as logistic regression[18] are the following:

- Timing of default is explicitly addressed and incorporated
    - In a retail credit scenario, it has been observed that timing of first default (when "time" is months on book) has a significant bearing on future customer default-write-off behaviour and the health of the portfolio (assuming the absence of an economy-related stress environment and no/low application fraud rate)
    - It is possible to forecast default levels as a function of time through the hazard function. Given the credit cycle of a portfolio by months on book, survival models can mimic the loan default and loss process. Parametric AFT models allow changing hazard rates across time periods, resulting in a different risk ranking of customers across time periods.
- Macroeconomic variables that affect credit risk cannot be readily incorporated in a logistic regression framework. Additionally, time-varying macro level indicators facilitate stress testing under different macroeconomic scenarios.
- Expected profitability of a prospect/applicant can be calculated with estimates of expected duration (one of the inputs)

To this effect, two good studies relating to the application of survival models for risk scoring are worth mentioning. Survival analysis for the development of an application score by Andreeva titled *European Generic Scoring Models using Survival Analysis,* evaluates both semi-parametric(PH) and parametric (AFT) models for the estimation of default risk for credit card applicants. The models are developed for three European countries (Belgium, Netherlands and Germany). A comparison of these models is made with the industry standard of a logistic regression model. Further, predictive performance of country-specific models is compared to a combined generic model. The author concludes that predictive accuracy across the different survival models[19] (semi-parametric and parametric) is similar to logistic regression. This may be attributed to the lack of a distinct time pattern of the hazard functions after 6 months (Fig. 7.24). For parametric versions, log-normal and log-logistic were some of the models that were attempted[20]. The performance

[18] In logistic regression, a customer that is not delinquent during a specified time period is classified "GOOD". In survival models, customer is classified "GOOD SO FAR".

[19] For PH model, score is taken as $e^{\beta x}$. For parametric, the score is interpreted as the probability of surviving a specified time period using the survival function.

[20] The distribution of the hazard rate functions of Fig. 7.24 should be compared to the statistical distribution specifications of Fig. 7.23, for the justification of the choice of log-normal and log-logistic distributions.

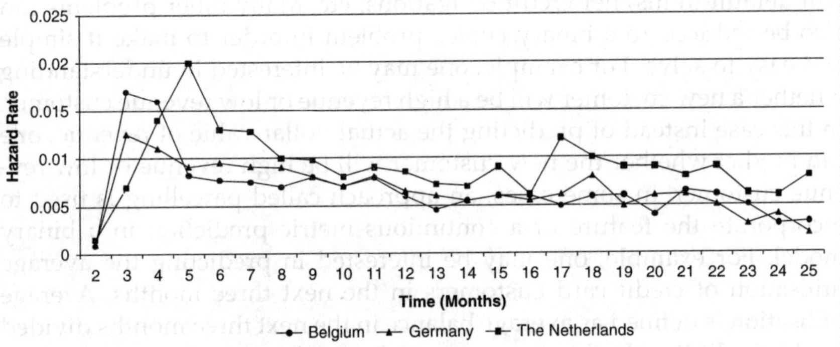


*Source:* Reprinted by permission from Macmillan Publishers Ltd: *Journal of the Operational Research Society*, Volume 57, Issue 10, Andreeva, "European Generic Scoring Models using Survival Analysis", Pages 1180–1187, Copyright (2005).

**Figure 7.24** Hazard Functions by Country

of generic model (combined) and national model (country specific models) were also similar.

The hazard function by country (Fig. 7.24) could be interpreted as "pseudo" vintage delinquency graphs (delinquency based on the definition of "BAD"), that risk managers are familiar with. Do note that a customer who defaults during a certain time period is taken out of the sample for subsequent calculations of hazard rate for the next time period (unlike the case of standard delinquency curves).

Bellotti and Crook develop an application score (credit card) with macroeconomic variables for a UK bank. The study was published as *Credit Scoring with Macroeconomic Variables Using Survival Analysis*. Macro level time-varying covariates are used to test the hypothesis that probability of default is affected by economic conditions over time. Application form related variables are also used in the model. Proportional hazards model is deployed and a relative comparison is made to logistic regression. Macroeconomic variables used at the time of default are interest rate, earnings, FTSE index, unemployment index, UK production index, housing price index, and consumer confidence index. All these variables are statistically significant in the model. Proportional hazards model with macro variables outperforms its counterpart version without macro variables and logistic regression, in terms of predictive performance.

## 7.5 Evaluating a Logistic Regression Model

### *7.5.1 Importance of Binary Choice Models*

Many business problems can be considered as a case of predicting a binary outcome. For example, one is interested in predicting whether a prospect will respond to a marketing campaign, whether a new customer will default in his/her credit obligations, etc. Many other problems can also be reduced to a binary choice problem in order to make it simple and easy to solve. For example, one may be interested in understanding whether a new customer will be a high revenue or low revenue customer. In this case instead of predicting the actual dollar value of revenue, one can predict whether the new customer will be high revenue or low revenue customer. In some cases, an approach called parcelling is used to incorporate the feature of a continuous metric prediction in a binary model. For example, one may be interested in predicting the average utilisation of credit card customers in the next three months. Average utilisation is defined as average balance in the next three months divided by the credit line. In this case every customer has an average utilisation between 0 and 100%, which is the metric of interest. In this case a parcelling approach can be used to convert this to a binary choice problem. A customer with average utilisation of 30% can be considered as the combination of a customer with zero utilisation (with weight 0.7) and a customer with 100% utilisation (with weight 0.3). As per this design, the predicted probability can be considered as a proxy of the expected percentage utilisation.

### *7.5.2 Techniques for Predicting Binary Choice*

A variety of analytical techniques can be used for modelling binary choice. Some of the common regression based techniques include probit regression, logistic regression and discriminant analysis. The next set of common techniques for modelling binary choice involves tree-based techniques such as CHAID (Chi-square Automatic Interaction Detector), CART (Classification and Regression Trees), etc. Other techniques used for modelling binary choice are neural network, support vector machine and ensemble methodologies such as Random Forest, Stochastic Gradient Boosting. Out of these common techniques, logistic regression has been the most widely used technique for predicting binary choice. The popularity of logistic regression stems from its easy to understand and intuitive results. The logistic regression uses a simple linear relationship between the predictors and the log of odds of the outcome. This linear relationship is easy to understand and has an intuitive appeal to most business users. The linear relationship also makes it easy for the user to interpret the results of the logistic regression and to ascertain whether the results make "business sense". The current section outlines how a business user can evaluate a logistic regression model to ascertain if the model that has been built by the analyst is "good enough". Usually the explanatory power, discriminatory power and predictive power of the model are analysed to evaluate the model. The second part of the section outlines how an existing logistic regression model should be evaluated so as to ascertain if the model is "still good enough".

### 7.5.3 Evaluating a Logistic Regression

A logistic regression model needs to be evaluated in terms of its explanatory power, discriminatory power and predictive power. Compared to linear regression models, described earlier in the chapter, discriminatory power is an additional evaluation criteria for a binary choice model. Discriminatory power of a logistic regression (or any other binary choice model) involves its ability of discriminating between the two types of outcomes. For example, if a logistic regression is built for predicting response to a marketing campaign then the discriminatory power refers to the ability of the model in separating responders and non-responders. Similarly, for a risk model, discrimination refers to the model's ability in separating non delinquent (good) and delinquent (bad) accounts. Several measures are used for evaluating the discriminatory power of a logistic regression. The most common metrics for measuring the discriminatory power of the model include Rank Ordering, KS (Kolmogorov Smirnov Statistic), Trade-off Curve, Capture rate ROC, Gini Coefficient, and Divergence. Assessment of the explanatory power of the model involve, analysing the predictors used in the model, in terms of their predictive power and their appropriateness of use in the model. Assessing the predictive power or accuracy of the model involve analysing the difference between the actual and predicted outcome. Measures like Sensitivity, Specificity, Hosmer Lemeshow Test, Kullback Leibler Test, and Score to Log Odds Comparison are used for measuring the predictive power of the model.

#### 7.5.3.1 Explanatory Power of the Model—Evaluating Model Parameters

Before evaluating the performance of a logistic regression model, it is important to evaluate the characteristics or predictor variables that have been used in the model. First, the characteristics need to be tested from a statistical perspective and then from a business and implementation perspective. For evaluating the statistical significance of the characteristics, one most commonly uses the significance and the Wald Chi square measures.

While determining the coefficient of each characteristic, the estimation algorithm also provides the standard error of the estimate. The coefficient and the standard error are used to test the following null hypothesis:

- **Null hypothesis (H0):** The estimated value of the coefficient is equal to zero
- **Alternate hypothesis (HA):** The estimated value of the coefficient is not equal to zero

The estimated value of the coefficient is divided by the standard error to obtain the t-statistic. Next the t-statistic is compared with the standard t-distribution to test if the computed value of the t-statistic is significantly different from zero. The square of the t-statistic is used to calculate the Wald statistic. As is known from standard statistical results, the square of the t-distribution follows a Chi square distribution. Hence, the Wald statistic follows a Chi square distribution. A higher value of the t-statistic or the Wald Chi square statistic suggests that the estimated coefficient is significantly different from zero, that is to say the variable or the characteristic is important. A low value of the Wald Chi square statistic suggests that the variable may not be a good choice. From a statistical perspective, a value of t-statistic between +2 and –2 (which comes from approximately 95% confidence) signifies that the coefficient of a variable is not significantly different from zero. A t-statistic between +2 and –2 will result in a Wald Chi statistic of less than 4. A t-statistic can also be converted to a significance or "p-value" by using the standard t-table. A highly positive or negative value of the t-statistic means a lower p-value. A low p-value indicates that the variable coefficient is significantly different from zero. In most cases, variables with a p-value of less than 0.001 are considered significant for inclusion in the model. A p-value less than 0.001 is sometimes considered as a stringent measure for including a variable in the model, sometimes a more flexible standard of p-value less than 0.01 is also considered appropriate, based on the data and the problem at hand.

However, in reality any variable with a Wald Chi Square Statistic of less than 10 should be properly investigated. At this point, it needs to be kept in mind that these limits are subject to the specific data set and business problem in question. The limits will also vary widely based on the specific data being used for model development.

Another point worth keeping in mind is the notion of importance of a variable in a logistic model. A very high Wald Chi square does not necessarily indicate that a predictor is more important, it only indicates that the estimated coefficient of the predictor is significantly different from zero. Along with Wald Chi, one should use other measures such as the standardised coefficients, change in performance by the exclusion of a predictor (sometimes modellers use change in KS or Gini caused by the exclusion or inclusion of an additional variable as a measure), etc., to ascertain relative importance of each characteristic.

The Likelihood Ratio Test is sometimes used to test the effect of an additional variable or for testing the joint effect of all the predictors is the model. The Likelihood Ratio Test is used to compare the fit of two models, one being the base model, and the other being a model with additional predictors. The Likelihood Ratio Test indicates, whether the model with additional predictors, fit the data better than the base model. The algorithm used for estimating the coefficients in a logistic regression uses a measure called Log Likelihood. It attempts to maximise this measure. For example, consider a model with 6 predictors. Then a set of 4 additional predictors are introduced into the model. The difference between the log likelihood of the two models follows a Chi square distribution with degree of freedom equal to 4. If the difference in log likelihood is significantly different from zero then one can conclude that at least one of these four additional predictors is providing an incremental value to the model.

Furthermore, it is important to note that sometime one needs to estimate the coefficients across multiple samples and ensure that the coefficients are significant across multiple samples. One also should keep an eye on the signs of the coefficient across multiple samples and any change in sign should indicate a grave concern that needs to be investigated. Table 7.54 illustrates the same. The predictor variables marked in grey needs to be further investigated.

Each predictor variable needs to be analysed from a business perspective as well. For example, consider a model that is expected to predict the propensity of credit card customers to respond to a cross-sell offer for personal loan. In this model, one would expect utilisation of credit card to have a positive sign, that is customers who have higher utilisation are more in need of credit and hence, are more likely to respond to a personal loan offer. But in the model if utilisation takes an opposite sign then that should be a reason of further investigation. There may be data errors or other business drivers that are working behind the scenes and need to be understood. Similarly, some of the predictors may be available in the sample used for building the model but may not be available in the operational system used for executing the model. For example, in the earlier case, there may be credit card customers who have a deposit account with the bank and their deposit balance is a good predictor as to whether they will respond to a personal loan offer. Customers having high deposit balance do not need money and hence, would most likely not respond to a personal loan offer. But it may so happen that the front-end system used for implementing the model will not be able to access the deposit data. Hence, though the deposit information serves as a good predictive characteristic, yet it cannot be used in the model.

**Table 7.54** Comparison of Coefficient Significance

| | Development Sample | | Validation Sample 1 | | Validation Sample 2 | |
|---|---|---|---|---|---|---|
| Predictors | Estimated Coefficient | Wald Chi | Estimated Coefficient | Wald Chi | Estimated Coefficient | Wald Chi |
| Intercept | 7.672 | 123.415 | 8.218 | 76.552 | 7.830 | 123.161 |
| Var1 | – 0.237 | 68.253 | – 0.188 | 2.357 | 0.678 | 2.593 |
| Var2 | 3.684 | 127.637 | 4.350 | 66.352 | 4.220 | 43.762 |
| Var3 | 10.537 | 22.234 | 11.140 | 6.771 | – 10.379 | 29.329 |
| Var4 | 0.013 | 658.226 | 0.018 | 403.771 | 0.027 | 663.496 |
| Var5 | – 0.381 | 768.231 | – 0.360 | 410.813 | – 0.890 | 93.743 |
| Var6 | 176.287 | 44.816 | 177.087 | 14.080 | 176.696 | 33.296 |
| Var7 | 1724.276 | 138.116 | 1724.886 | 30.576 | 1724.579 | 58.531 |
| Var8 | – 2.482 | 88.269 | – 2.416 | 54.369 | – 2.845 | 67.707 |

### 7.5.3.2 Measures of Discriminatory Power

*Rank Ordering* The most important property of any logistic regression (or any other binary choice model) is its ability of rank ordering the two types of outcomes. A logistic regression model can be used to predict the probability of a prospect responding to a marketing campaign. If the model produces a score of 300 to 1000, with higher score indicating higher probability of response, then the odds of a prospect responding should increase continuously with the increase in the score. Conversely odds of a prospect not responding should increase continuously with decrease in score. The example in Table 7.55 illustrates the rank ordering property of the logistic model. It needs to be noted, that this example will be used throughout this section and the next section for illustrating various aspects of evaluating a logistic regression model.

**Table 7.55** Rank Ordering

| Case 1 No Break in Rank Ordering | | | | | |
|---|---|---|---|---|---|
| | | | Total | Odds | Response Rate |
| Score Range | Number of Responders | Number of Non-responders | Responder + Non-responder | Non-responder/ Responder | Responder/ Total |
| 1000–832 | 507 | 11564 | 12071 | 23 | 4.20% |
| 831–820 | 187 | 11895 | 12082 | 64 | 1.55% |
| 819–792 | 131 | 11958 | 12089 | 91 | 1.08% |
| 791–783 | 84 | 11946 | 12030 | 142 | 0.70% |
| 782–760 | 69 | 12015 | 12084 | 174 | 0.57% |
| 759–723 | 57 | 11971 | 12028 | 210 | 0.47% |
| 722–682 | 45 | 12031 | 12076 | 267 | 0.37% |
| 681–610 | 39 | 12022 | 12061 | 308 | 0.32% |
| 609–550 | 31 | 11989 | 12020 | 387 | 0.26% |
| 549–300 | 30 | 11977 | 12007 | 399 | 0.25% |
| **Case 2 Break in Rank Ordering** | | | | | |
| 1000–832 | 507 | 11564 | 12071 | 23 | 4.20% |
| 831–820 | 187 | 11895 | 12082 | 64 | 1.55% |
| 819–792 | 131 | 11958 | 12089 | 91 | 1.08% |
| 791–783 | 84 | 11946 | 12030 | 142 | 0.70% |
| 782–760 | 69 | 12015 | 12084 | 174 | 0.57% |
| 759–723 | 57 | 11971 | 12028 | 210 | 0.47% |
| 722–682 | 62 | 12031 | 12076 | 194 | 0.51% |
| 681–610 | 39 | 12022 | 12061 | 308 | 0.32% |
| 609–550 | 31 | 11989 | 12020 | 387 | 0.26% |
| 549–300 | 30 | 11977 | 12007 | 399 | 0.25% |

In the ideal case, the rank ordering should hold for each score point. However, in reality no model will rank order at every score point. Hence, the total population is divided into 10 or 20 equal groups based on the score and the rank ordering is tested for these groups. In case the population is divided into larger number of groups, then there is higher chance of observing a break in rank ordering. For testing the rank ordering effectiveness, it is important to note that each of the groups should have equal number of observations. For Case 1 in Table 7.55, the non-responder to responder odds increases continuously and hence, the probability of response also decreases continuously. Therefore, it can be said that an evaluation of the rank ordering based on 10 groups does not show any rank order break. However, in Case 2, we observe a rank order break for the 722–682 score range. As discussed earlier, rank ordering is the most important property of any binary choice model. Any model that has multiple rank order breaks is not a "good enough" model. However, it needs to be noted that sometimes one may have very low number of one of the types of cases (for example, very low number of responders or very low number of delinquent accounts). In those cases because of the low numbers the model may have multiple rank order breaks. In addition one must keep in mind that each model is used for driving a specific business decision. Hence, if the rank order breaks occur after the score which represent the decision point, then the problem of rank order breaking is less severe. To illustrate the point if one considers Case 2 in Table 7.55, then one will see a rank order break at the score range of 722–682. However, if the business manager wants to target only prospects who have more than 1% chance of responding then no prospect with score lower than 791 will be targeted. Hence, in this case, the rank order break will not impact the efficacy of the model. In conclusion, it needs to be noted that in some cases one may have a small sample size or a small number of responders (or bads). In such cases it may be prudent to look at the rank ordering on the basis of 4 or 5 equal groups based on the score, rather than using 10 or 20 groups, which is the usual practice. In addition, any model needs to be evaluated within the context of its intended use.

*Kolmogorov Smirnov Statistic (KS)* Once a model is able to rank order the two types of outcomes, it is important to judge the power of the model in separating or discriminating between the two types of outcomes. The Kolmogorov Smirnov Statistic (KS) is one of the most popular measures used for evaluating the separation power of a binary choice model. The KS statistic measures the maximum distance between the cumulative distributions of the two types of outcomes. For example, if a logistic model is built for predicting response then the KS measures the maximum distance between the cumulative distribution of responders and non-responders across the entire score range. Table 7.56 illustrates the KS statistic. It needs to be noted that the same response model that was used for discussing rank ordering, has been used in this illustration as well.

**Table 7.56** KS Statistic

| | | | Total | Percentage of Responders | Percentage of Non-responders | | | |
|---|---|---|---|---|---|---|---|---|
| A | B | C | D | E | F | G | H | I |
| Score Range | Number of Responders | Number of Non-responders | Responders + Non-responders | Number of responders/ Total Responders | Number of Non-responders/ Total Non-responders | Cumulative Percentage of Responders | Cumulative Percentage of Non-responders | Cumulative Percentage of Responders— Cumulative Percentage of Non-responders |
| 1000–832 | 507 | 11564 | 12071 | 43% | 9.69% | 42.97% | 9.69% | 33.28% |
| 831–820 | 187 | 11895 | 12082 | 16% | 9.96% | 58.81% | 19.65% | 39.16% |
| 819–792 | 131 | 11958 | 12089 | 11% | 10.02% | 69.92% | 29.67% | 40.24% |
| 791–783 | 84 | 11946 | 12030 | 7% | 10.01% | 77.03% | 39.68% | 37.36% |
| 782–760 | 69 | 12015 | 12084 | 6% | 10.07% | 82.88% | 49.74% | 33.14% |
| 759–723 | 57 | 11971 | 12028 | 5% | 10.03% | 87.71% | 59.77% | 27.94% |
| 722–682 | 45 | 12031 | 12076 | 4% | 10.08% | 91.53% | 69.85% | 21.67% |
| 681–610 | 39 | 12022 | 12061 | 3% | 10.07% | 94.83% | 79.92% | 14.91% |
| 609–550 | 31 | 11989 | 12020 | 3% | 10.04% | 97.46% | 89.97% | 7.49% |
| 549–300 | 30 | 11977 | 12007 | 3% | 10.03% | 100.00% | 100.00% | 0.00% |

In Table 7.56, Column G represents the cumulative distribution of responders and is calculated by the number of responders upto that particular score range divided by the total number of responders. For example, with regards to the score range 819–792 the cumulative percentage of responders is calculated as (507 + 187 + 131) divided by the total number of responders that is 1180. Column H represents the cumulative distribution of non-responders. Column I represents the difference between the cumulative distributions, and the maximum value of this difference (in this case 40.24%) is referred to as the KS statistic. It is important to note that a higher KS value suggests better discrimination power. However, the exact value of the KS statistic depends on the problem at hand and it is difficult to have a standard KS measure across different types of data and problem situations.

It is important to note that along with the value of the KS, the score point where one achieves the maximum separation is also an important measure. For instance, in the example (Table 7.56), the KS of 40.24% occurs at the score band 819–792, it can be assumed that the KS occurs at the mid-point of this score band, that is at the score of 806. In this case, if the business strategy is such that all prospects above the score of 806 are targeted then the model would produce the best results. But if the strategy is to target any one with the score upto 682, then one should look at the difference in the cumulative distribution of responders and non-responders at this point, and it can be seen that the cumulative difference in this case is only 21.67%. Hence, the model is much less effective if the score of 682 is decided as the cut-off point.

*Trade-off Curve and Capture* Figure 7.25 represents a trade-off curve. The X-axis represents the percentage of non-responders and the Y-axis represents the percentage of responders. The diagonal line or the random decision line represents the case where the model is not able to discriminate between the two outcomes at all.

In the current example, selecting a point where 59% of the responders are captured, one will end up targeting 20% of the non-responders also. Similarly selecting a point, where 83% of responders are captured, one will end up targeting 50% of the non-responders. Instead of using the model, if one randomly selects prospects then one will find that selecting a point where 50% of responders are captured will entail targeting 50% non-responders. This is represented by the diagonal line in Fig 7.25.

*Lift Chart or Gains Chart* The gains chart or the lift chart is a diagrammatic representation similar to the trade-off curve. In case of lift chart, the X-axis represents the per cent of the population (instead of the percentage of the non-responders in the trade-off curve). From the gains chart, one can calculate the lift or the capture rate of the model. The diagram in Fig. 7.26 represents the gains chart.

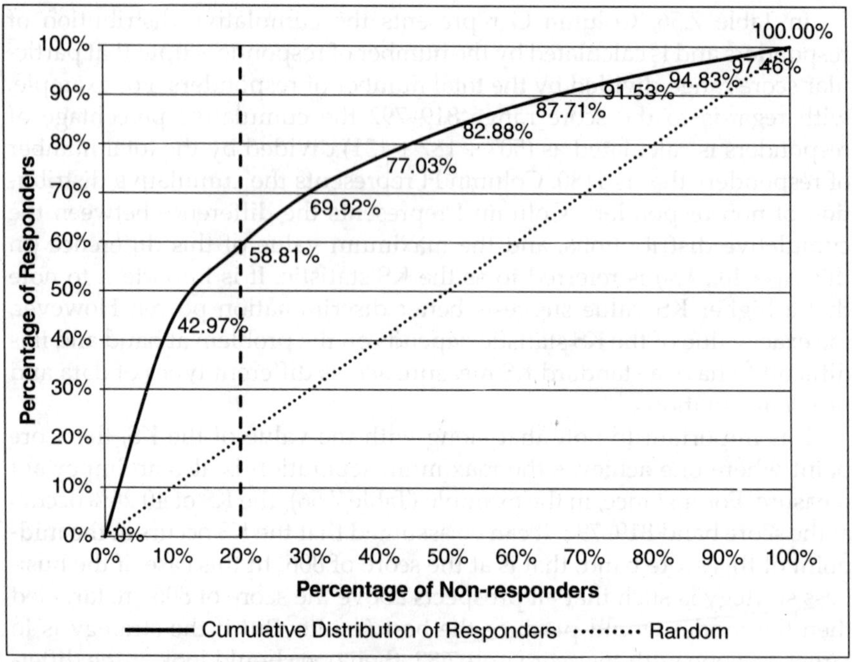


**Figure 7.25** Trade-off Curve and Capture

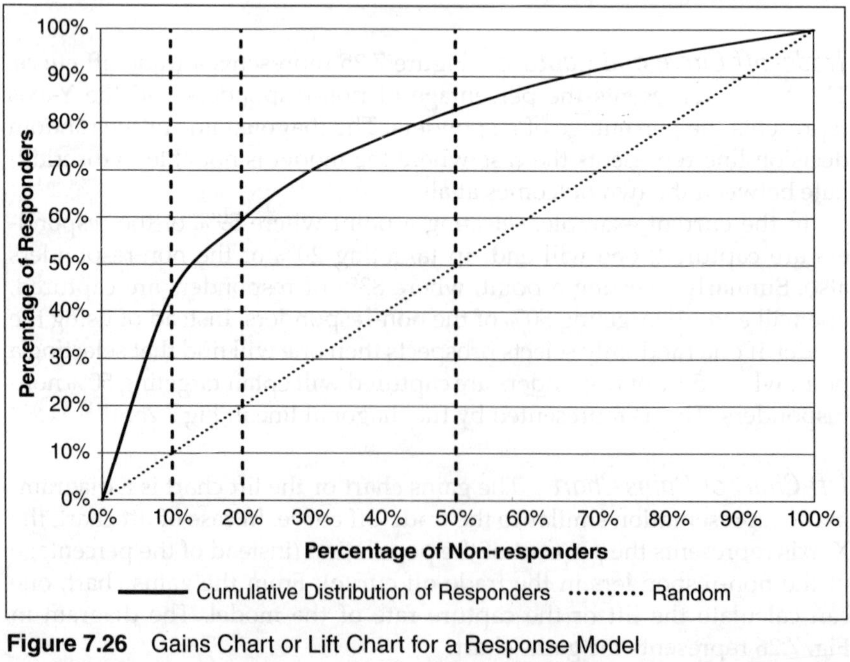


**Figure 7.26** Gains Chart or Lift Chart for a Response Model

The gains chart or lift chart looks very similar to the trade-off curve in cases where the percentage of the outcome of interest (response rate in this case) is very low. The diagram suggests that the top 10% of the population is able to capture 43% of the responders; this is referred to as the capture rate of the model. In this case the overall response rate is 0.98% and the response rate in the top decile is 4.2%. The ratio of the response rate of the top decile and the overall response rate is taken as the lift factor of the model.

However, in cases where the percentage of the outcome of interest is much higher, the trade-off curve and the lift curve have different shapes, typical examples are collection models. Collection models are built for accounts that have not paid their dues for one month, two months, etc. A relatively larger portion of these customers actually never end up paying and thus turn bad. As for example, if one considers the set of accounts that have not paid their dues for two months, one will expect a large portion (say 25%) of accounts not to pay any amount in the next 3 months. These accounts are labelled as "Bad". Accounts which make at least some payment in the next 3 months are termed as "Good". The lift curve and the trade-off curve are depicted in Figs. 7.27 and 7.28, respectively. If one compares the lift curve (or gains chart) of a response model as depicted in Fig. 7.26, with the lift curve for a collection model as depicted in Fig. 7.27, one will find that the line representing cumulative non-responders is absent in the first case. While one will see a line representing both cumulative goods and bads in the second case. The reason for this difference is that fact that the percentage of non-responders is very high in the first case (almost 99%). Hence, the line representing cumulative non-responders is almost same as the random line. However, in the second case, as there are 25% bads and 75% goods in

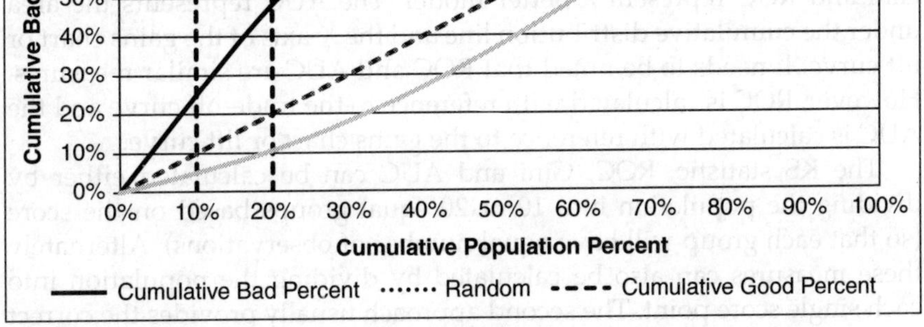


**Figure 7.27** Lift Curve for a Collection Score

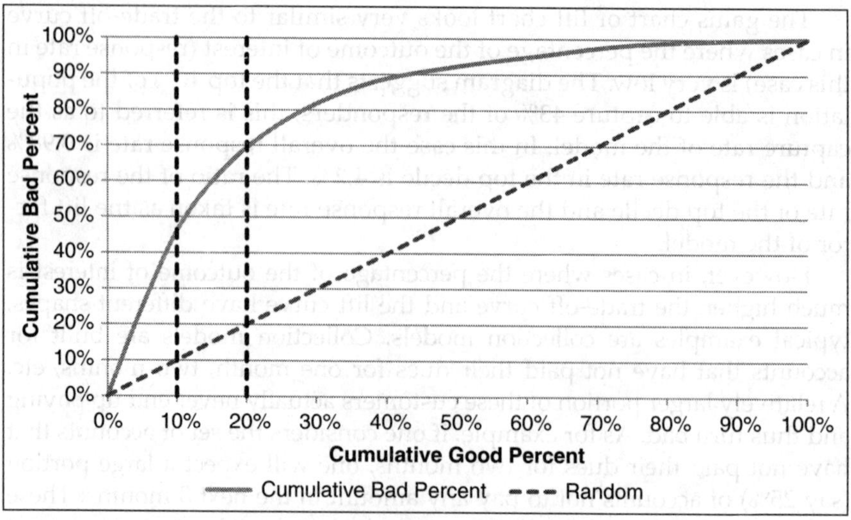


**Figure 7.28** Trade-off Curve for a Collection Score

the total population therefore the line representing cumulative "Good" is quite different from the random line. In fact, in this case one needs to look at both the capture rate of "Bad" and "Good" accounts in order to ascertain the efficacy of the model. From the lift curve it can be seen that the bottom 10% of the population would capture 25% of the bad accounts.

*ROC and Gini Coefficient* The ROC (receiver operating characteristics) measures the area under the trade-off curve and the X-axis. The Gini coefficient measures the area under the trade-off curve and the diagonal random line. The area between the trade-off curve and the X-axis can be calculated by using the trapezoidal rule as illustrated in Fig. 7.29. For calculating the area under the curve, the entire area is divided into one triangle and then a set of 9 trapeziums. The area of the first triangle is calculated as 0.5 * Base * Height. The base is 10% and the height is 42.97%. Similarly the area of the trapeziums are calculated as 0.5 * Sum of parallel sides * Height. The Gini coefficient is calculated as 2 * ROC-1. A higher Gini and ROC represent a better model. The AUC represents the area under the cumulative distribution line and the X-axis of the gains chart or lift curve. It needs to be noted that ROC and AUC are similar measures. However, ROC is calculated with reference to the trade-off curve and the AUC is calculated with reference to the gains chart or lift curve.

The KS statistic, ROC, Gini and AUC can be calculated either by dividing the population into 10 or 20 equal groups based on the score (so that each group will have equal number of observations). Alternately these measures can also be calculated by dividing the population into each single score point. The second approach usually provides the correct estimate of these measure but such estimates may vary when compared

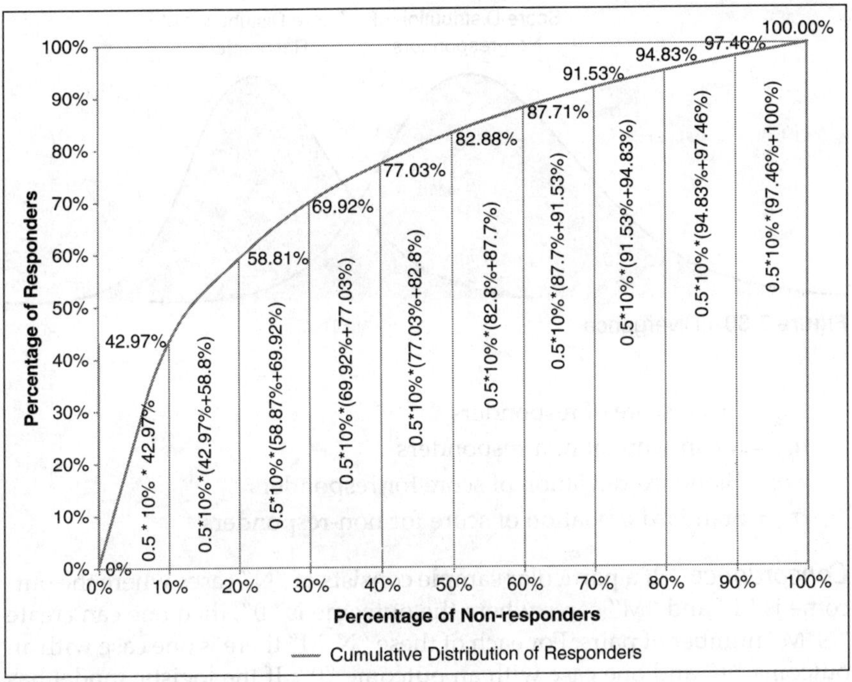


**Figure 7.29** ROC and Gini

across multiple samples. The statistic measured by dividing the population into 10 or 20 equal groups may be more stable across samples. However, the earlier conclusion may vary depending on the data and the actual problem at hand. It is difficult to ascertain the absolute value of KS or Gini, that can be considered as good, this is because these measures vary with the data and the problem at hand. However, in most cases a KS of 20% and a Gini of 30% is considered a floor. In case the KS or Gini of a model is lower than this threshold it is difficult to categorise the model as a good model. But to reiterate, it must be borne in mind that these are judgemental measures and in certain cases, based on the nature of the problem and the data, a KS or Gini lower than these thresholds may be acceptable and even be considered a good model.

*Divergence* Divergence measures the distance between the score distribution of the two types of outcomes. The further the score distribution of the two types of outcomes, the better is the model. Figure 7.30 illustrates the concept of divergence. The further apart the distributions are, the better is the model. Divergence is calculated as:

$$\frac{(\mu_R - \mu_{NR})^2}{\frac{1}{2}(\sigma_R^2 + \sigma_{NR}^2)}$$

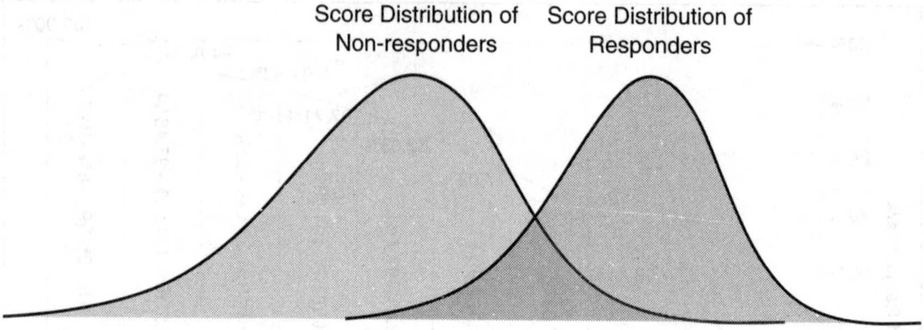


**Figure 7.30** Divergence

$\mu_R$ = Mean score of responders
$\mu_{NR}$ = Mean score of non-responders
$\sigma_R$ = Standard deviation of score for responders
$\sigma_{NR}$ = Standard deviation of score for non-responders

*Concordance* If a particular sample consists of "N" cases where the outcome is "1" and "M" cases where the outcome is "0", then one can create "N*M" number of pairs. For each of these "N*M" there is one case with an outcome "1" and one case with an outcome "0". If the logistic model has been developed to predict "1" then the probability of the case where the outcome is "1" should be higher than the probability of the case with an outcome "0". If this happens, then the pair is categorised as a concordant pair, and in case the predicted probability of the "0" case is higher than the predicted probability of the "1" case then it is categorised as a discordant pair. And if the two probabilities are equal, it is categorised as a tied pair. Concordance is calculated as the number of concordant pairs out of the total number of pairs. The Somer's D statistic is calculated as:

Somer's D = (Number of Concordant Pairs – Number of Discordant Pairs)/Total Number of Pairs

### 7.5.3.3 Measures of Predictive Power

*Miss-classification, Sensitivity and Specificity* Closely related to the trade-off curve is the concept of miss-classification. In the example in Table 7.58 if one assumes that all prospects with score above 783 are going to respond then one will have the following miss-classification as shown in Table 7.57. The miss-classification matrix is also referred to as confusion matrix. The miss-classification can be used as a measure of model accuracy as well.

It can be seen that the trade-off curve can be used to determine the sensitivity and specificity at each score band; Table 7.58 depicts the calculation of sensitivity and specificity for each score band used in the trade-off curve.

**Table 7.57** Miss-classification Table

| | Actual Responder | Actual Non-responder | Sensitivity | Specificity |
|---|---|---|---|---|
| Score greater than or equal to 783—Predicted responder | 909—Model says they will respond and in reality they respond | 47,363—Model says they will respond and in reality they do not respond—Type-1 error | 77% = 909/(909 + 271) | 60% = 72005/(72005 + 47363) |
| Score less than 783—Predicted non-responders | 271—Model says they will not respond and in reality they respond—Type-2 error | 72,005—Model says they will not respond and in reality they do not respond | | |

The sensitivity and specificity measures are critical in estimating the financial benefit of the model and the operating point which will yield the maximum financial benefit. For instance, with reference to the example used for illustrating rank ordering and KS, stated earlier, there are 120,548 customers in the eligible base, who are scored using the model. Out of these 120,548 customers who are targated; 1,180 customers respond to the offer; whereas 119,368 do not respond. Say it takes $5 to target each customer and the company makes $700 of revenue from each customer who responds to the offer. Table 7.59 depicts the profitability calculation for each score band.

As the example suggests, the net profit is maximum for the score range 791–783 and hence, all customers with score greater than 783 should be targeted.

Though profit maximisation is often used for determining the cut-off point yet sometime alternate strategies are also adopted. For example, in this case one may have a budget of $300,000 for the campaign. Hence, one can only target 60,000 customers ($300,000/$5). This will imply that one can target the top 60,000 customers only, which in turn will mean targeting till the 782–760 score band only. Alternately one may have a strategy of getting at least 1,000 responders. In that case one needs to target till the 759–723 score band.

*Hosmer Lemeshow Test* For the purpose of the HL test, the population is divided into 10 groups based on the score, such that each group has equal number of total observations. The actual and expected number of observations of a particular type of outcome within each of these is compared to create a Chi square statistic. The example in Table 7.60 illustrates the same.

A higher value of the HL statistic suggests a bigger difference between actual and predicted.

**Table 7.58** Sensitivity and Specificity Calculation for Each Score Band in the Trade-off Curve

| Score Range | Number of Responders | Number of Non-responders | Total | Percentage of Responders | Percentage of Non-responders | Cumulative Percentage of Responders | Cumulative Percentage of Non-responders | KS | Sensitivity | Specificity 1— |
|---|---|---|---|---|---|---|---|---|---|---|
| | | | Responder + Non-responder | Number of Responders/ Total Responders | Number of Non-responders/ Total Non-responders | | | Cumulative Percentage of Responders— Cumulative Percentage of Non-responders | Cumulative Number of Responders/ Total Number of Responders | (Cumulative Number of Non responders/ Total Number of Non responders) |
| 1000-832 | 507 | 11564 | 12071 | 43% | 9.69% | 42.97% | 9.69% | 33.28% | 42.97% | 90.31% |
| 831-820 | 187 | 11895 | 12082 | 16% | 9.96% | 58.81% | 19.65% | 39.16% | 58.81% | 80.35% |
| 819-792 | 131 | 11958 | 12089 | 11% | 10.02% | 69.92% | 29.67% | 40.24% | 69.92% | 70.33% |
| 791-783 | 84 | 11946 | 12030 | 7% | 10.01% | 77.03% | 39.68% | 37.36% | 77.03% | 60.32% |
| 782-760 | 69 | 12015 | 12084 | 6% | 10.07% | 82.88% | 49.74% | 33.14% | 82.88% | 50.26% |
| 759-723 | 57 | 11971 | 12028 | 5% | 10.03% | 87.71% | 59.77% | 27.94% | 87.71% | 40.23% |
| 722-682 | 45 | 12031 | 12076 | 4% | 10.08% | 91.53% | 69.85% | 21.67% | 91.53% | 30.15% |
| 681-610 | 39 | 12022 | 12061 | 3% | 10.07% | 94.83% | 79.92% | 14.91% | 94.83% | 20.08% |
| 609-550 | 31 | 12263 | 12294 | 3% | 10.04% | 97.46% | 89.97% | 7.49% | 97.46% | 9.80% |
| 549-300 | 30 | 11703 | 11733 | 3% | 10.03% | 100.00% | 100.00% | 0.00% | 100.00% | 0.00% |

**Table 7.59** Determining the Operating Point Based on Sensitivity and Specificity

| Score Range | Number of Responders | Number of Non-responders | Total: Responder + Non-responder | Sensitivity | Specificity | Revenue = Sensitivity* Total Number of Responders* Revenue per Responder | Targeting Cost = (1 – Specificity)* Total Number of Non-responders* Cost of Targeting | Net Profit = Revenue – Cost | |
|---|---|---|---|---|---|---|---|---|---|
| 1000–832 | 507 | 11564 | 12071 | 42.97% | 90.31% | 354,900 | 57,820 | 297,080 | Target group |
| 831–820 | 187 | 11895 | 12082 | 58.81% | 80.35% | 485,800 | 117,295 | 368,505 | Target group |
| 819–792 | 131 | 11958 | 12089 | 69.92% | 70.33% | 577,500 | 177,085 | 400,415 | Target group |
| 791–783 | 90 | 11946 | 12030 | 77.54% | 60.32% | 640,500 | 236,815 | 403,685 | Target group |
| 782–760 | 63 | 12015 | 12084 | 82.88% | 50.26% | 684,600 | 296,890 | 387,710 | |
| 759–723 | 57 | 11971 | 12028 | 87.71% | 40.23% | 724,500 | 356,745 | 367,755 | |
| 722–682 | 45 | 12031 | 12076 | 91.53% | 30.15% | 756,000 | 416,900 | 339,100 | |
| 681–610 | 39 | 12022 | 12061 | 94.83% | 20.08% | 783,300 | 477,010 | 306,290 | |
| 609–550 | 31 | 12263 | 12294 | 97.46% | 9.80% | 805,000 | 536,955 | 268,045 | |
| 549–300 | 30 | 11703 | 11733 | 100.00% | 0.00% | 826,000 | 594,100 | 231,900 | |

*Note:* In this table the cost of targeting represents the cost of targeting the non-responders only (false positives). With regards to the responders, the revenue generated far outweighs the cost of targeting. Hence, the cost of targeting the responders is not considered a major cost item in determining the cut-off score.

**Table 7.60** Hosmer Lemeshow Test

| Score Range | Expected Probability of Response | Total Number of Observations | Expected Number of Responders (Total Number of Observations* Expected Probability of Response) | Number of Responders | Number of Non-responders | Actual Responders – Expected Responders | [(Actual Responders –{ Expected Responders)$^2$]/ Expected Responders |
|---|---|---|---|---|---|---|---|
| 1000–832 | 4.30% | 12071 | 519 | 507 | 11564 | –12.053 | 0.280 |
| 831–820 | 2.10% | 12082 | 254 | 187 | 11895 | –66.722 | 17.546 |
| 819–792 | 0.80% | 12089 | 97 | 131 | 11958 | 34.288 | 12.156 |
| 791–783 | 0.70% | 12030 | 84 | 84 | 11946 | –0.21 | 0.001 |
| 782–760 | 0.73% | 12084 | 88 | 69 | 12015 | –19.2132 | 4.185 |
| 759–723 | 0.60% | 12028 | 72 | 57 | 11971 | –15.168 | 3.188 |
| 722–682 | 0.51% | 12076 | 62 | 45 | 12031 | –16.5876 | 4.468 |
| 681–610 | 0.46% | 12061 | 55 | 39 | 12022 | –16.4806 | 4.896 |
| 609–550 | 0.20% | 12020 | 24 | 31 | 11989 | 6.96 | 2.015 |
| 549–300 | 0.11% | 12007 | 13 | 30 | 11977 | 16.7923 | 21.350 |
| | Sum of [(Actual Responders – Expected Responders)$^2$]/Expected Responders Across All Groups | | | | | | 70.084 |

*Kullback Leibler Test* The Kullback Leibler test uses entropy measure to find the difference between actual and predicted the KL divergence measure is calculated as:

[(Expected number of responders/Total number of expected responders)] * [(Ln(Expected number of responders/Total number of expected responders) – Ln(Actual number of responders/Total number of actual responders)]

Lower the KL measure, better is the fit between actual and predicted. Table 7.61 illustrates the same.

*Log Odds Tracking* The logistic regression uses a linear relationship between log odds and the predictor variables. Hence, an intuitive way of tracking the logistic model involves tracking the relationship between the model result and the observed log odds pattern. The result of most logistic regression models are calibrated to a specific odds scheme. An odds scheme is represented by an anchor point and specific points to double odds. For example, a score may range from 300 to 800 and have a good to bad odds of 10 to 1 at 500 doubling every 20 points. This means that at a score of 500 one can expect 10 good consumers to every one bad consumer; i.e., the probability of default for a consumer with a score of 500 is one over 11. At a score of 520 the odds of good to bad is expected to be 20 to 1 as the score has a point to double odds of 20 (i.e., the odds double every 20 points) and the probability of default is 1 over 21. Similarly, at a score of 480 the good to bad odds is expected to be 5 to 1 and hence, a probability of default of 1 over 6. As it can be easily seen from the example, a change of 20 score points results in doubling of the odds. Hence, the ln(odds) or log odds change by ln(2). Hence, for every one score point the ln(odds) change by ln(2)/20. The following example illustrates this further:

- **Anchor score:** Anchor (e.g., an anchor score of 500)
- **Odds at anchor:** Odds at anchor (the good to bad odds at the anchor score)
- **Point to double odds:** PDO
- Then at any score "S" the natural logarithm of odds will be ln(O1) = ((S-Anchor)*ln(2)/PDO) + ln(Odds at Anchor)
- Hence, the odds at score "S" will be Odds1 = exp(O1)
- Hence, the probability of bad at score "S" is given by 1/(1 + Odds1)

The graph in Fig. 7.31 illustrates the above. The expected log odds is calculated as per the following scheme. Points to double odds: 40. The odd at a score of 600 is 10 to one.

The closer the actual log odds are to the expected linear score to log odds line, the higher is the accuracy of the model.

**Table 7.61** Kullback Leibler Test

| Score Range | Expected Probability | Total Number of Observations | Expected Number of Responders | Actual Number of Responders | Expected Number of Responders/ Expected Total Number of Responders | Ln (Expected Number of Responders/ Expected Total Number of Responders) | Ln (Actual Number of Responders/ Actual Total Number of Responders) | KL Measure |
|---|---|---|---|---|---|---|---|---|
| 1000–832 | 4.30% | 12071 | 519 | 507 | 40.9% | –0.894 | –0.845 | –0.020 |
| 831–820 | 2.10% | 12082 | 254 | 187 | 20.0% | –1.609 | –1.842 | 0.047 |
| 819–792 | 0.80% | 12089 | 97 | 131 | 7.6% | –2.574 | –2.198 | –0.029 |
| 791–783 | 0.70% | 12030 | 84 | 84 | 6.6% | –2.712 | –2.642 | –0.005 |
| 782–760 | 0.73% | 12084 | 88 | 69 | 7.0% | –2.666 | –2.839 | 0.012 |
| 759–723 | 0.60% | 12028 | 72 | 57 | 5.7% | –2.867 | –3.030 | 0.009 |
| 722–682 | 0.51% | 12076 | 62 | 45 | 4.9% | –3.025 | –3.267 | 0.012 |
| 681–610 | 0.46% | 12061 | 55 | 39 | 4.4% | –3.129 | –3.410 | 0.012 |
| 609–550 | 0.20% | 12020 | 24 | 31 | 1.9% | –3.966 | –3.639 | –0.006 |
| 549–300 | 0.11% | 12007 | 13 | 30 | 1.0% | –4.565 | –3.672 | –0.009 |
| | | | 1268 | 1180 | | | KL Divergence Measure | 0.023 |

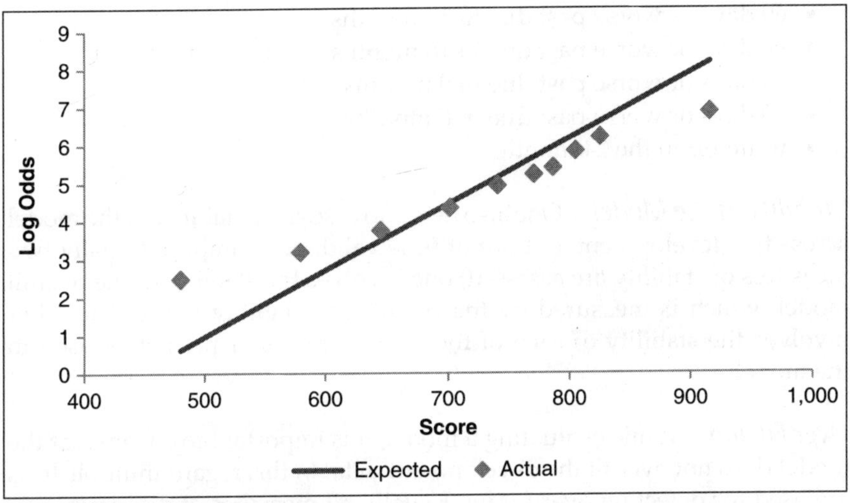


**Figure 7.31** Log Odds Tracking

### 7.5.3.4 Validation

The measures of discrimination and accuracy described previously need to be measured not only on the sample used for model development but also on a validation sample. Usually a random sub-sample of the available model development sample is kept aside for an in-time validation. This is used to ensure that the model does not over-fit the development sample. The measures of discrimination should have very little difference between the development and in-time validation sample. In addition an out of time validation sample is used to validate the model. An out-of-time validation sample relates to a different time frame from the one used for model development. For example, if campaigns conducted during the months of January, May, September and December have been used for building a response model, then the campaigns during months such as March, June and October can be used for an out of time validation sample. Various approaches can be used for selecting the development and out of time validation samples based on the business scenario involved.

In addition the model needs to be validated on various key sub-segments that are of interest. For example, a model which predicts the probability of a credit card customer responding to a cross-sell offer for personal loan, needs to be evaluated for sub segments such as revolvers, transactors, high spenders and the like. In addition, when the model is built, it is built with one specific rule for defining good and bad. However, the effectiveness of the score for predicting various alternate types of bads and goods also needs to be assessed. For example, a particular model may have used a 90 day or more past due, within a 12 month period as bad. However, one also needs to assess the effectiveness of the model in predicting alternate events such as:

- 60 days or worse past due in 12 months
- 90 days or worse past due in 18 months
- 30 days or worse past due in 9 months
- 30 days or worse past due in 6 months
- write-off in the 24 months

*Stability of the Model* One also needs to assess the stability of the model across the development and out of time validation samples. Usually two measures of stability are assessed; one involves the stability of the overall model, which is measured by the population stability index. The other involves the stability of each of the characteristics or predictors used in the model.

*Over Fitting* While evaluating a model, it is important to ensure that the model does not over fit the development data. In this regard multiple tests are used for detecting over fitting. Usually all measures of discrimination such as KS, Gini, ROC are measured in multiple random validation samples and the results should not be very different from the development sample. Usually a difference of more than 3% in KS or Gini will indicate an over fitting. However the exact difference may vary based on the data and the problem at hand. Similarly the coefficients of the predictor variables need to be estimated and any significant change in coefficient value or significant change in the Wald Chi square statistic will indicate over fitting. In cases, where it is not feasible to hold a random sample for in-time validation, one can use the bootstrap technique for validation. A bootstrap validation involves, drawing repeated samples from the same data set and validating the model and the parameter estimates on each of these random samples. If the estimates across multiple bootstrap runs do not vary significantly, then one can assume that the model is not over fitting the data. A detailed discussion on bootstrap methodology is beyond the scope of this chapter, the interested reader can refer standard text books for details.

*Population Stability* Population stability compares the percentage of population at each score band between the development and out of time validation sample. The Population Stability Index (PSI) is calculated as:

$$(\%\ \textit{of population in development} - \%\ \textit{of population in validation})$$
$$*\ \ln(\%\ \textit{of population in development}) - \ln(\%\ \textit{of population in validation})$$

A PSI value of less than 0.1 suggests a stable model and a PSI value of more than 0.25 suggests that there have been major changes between the development and validation sample. There can be multiple factors such as changes in targeting strategy, changes in customer profile, etc., which may affect stability. In some cases (if sufficient justification exists), a model which has high PSI but is able to discriminate the two outcomes might be acceptable. Table 7.62 outlines how PSI is calculated.

**Table 7.62** Population Stability

| Score Range | Percentage of Development Population | Percentage of Validation Population | PSI |
|---|---|---|---|
| 1000–832 | 9.5% | 7.9% | 0.003 |
| 831–820 | 9.8% | 8.4% | 0.002 |
| 819–792 | 9.9% | 9.2% | 0.001 |
| 791–783 | 9.9% | 9.2% | 0.001 |
| 782–760 | 9.9% | 10.1% | 0.000 |
| 759–723 | 9.9% | 10.1% | 0.000 |
| 722–682 | 10.0% | 10.4% | 0.000 |
| 681–610 | 10.1% | 10.5% | 0.000 |
| 609–550 | 10.3% | 11.3% | 0.001 |
| 549–300 | 10.7% | 12.9% | 0.004 |
| | | Population Stability | 0.012 |

*Characteristic Stability* The characteristics stability analysis aims to find out how the distribution of the population has changed across various levels of the characteristic. It also aims to measure the change in the predictive nature of the characteristic. Table 7.63 outlines the results of a characteristics stability analysis. Assume that the characteristic average credit card utilisation in the past six months is used as a predictor in a model that predicts probability of a credit card customer responding to a personal loan cross-sell offer. With an increase in credit card utilisation the chances of responding increase. The weight of evidence for a particular utilisation band is calculated as follows:

ln(Number of responders/Total responders) – ln(Number of non-responders/Total non-responders)

And the information value of a particular utilisation band is calculated as:

((Number of responders/Total responders) – (Number of non-responders/Total non-responders)) * Weight of evidence

One needs to calculate the population stability index for the characteristic and also the change in the predictive pattern. For example, in this case, the utilisation band 0%–15% shows the lowest weight of evidence, which translates to least response rate during development. However, in the out of time validation sample the next group 16%–37% shows the lowest weight of evidence. In this case the modeller should go back and combine these two groups in the model so that the predictive pattern is consistent across development and validation.

**Table 7.63** Characteristic Stability

| | | Development | | | | | | Out of Time Validation | | | | | | |
|---|---|---|---|---|---|---|---|---|---|---|---|---|---|---|
| Range of Utilisation | Score Point Assigned | Number of Responders Responderd | Number of Non-responders | Weight of Evidence | Information Value | Odds | Percentage of Population | Number of Responders | Number of Non-responders | Weight of Evidence | Information Value | Odds | Percentage of Population | PSI for the Characteristics |
| 0% – 15% | 10 | 12 | 27731 | –1.623 | 0.129 | 2311 | 10% | 32 | 17731 | –0.195 | 0.003 | 554 | 6% | 0.014 |
| 16% – 37% | 23 | 58 | 108333 | –1.411 | 0.411 | 1868 | 38% | 26 | 115362 | –2.276 | 0.870 | 4437 | 42% | 0.004 |
| 37% – 47% | 37 | 74 | 112857 | –1.208 | 0.340 | 1525 | 40% | 88 | 102762 | –0.941 | 0.230 | 1168 | 37% | 0.001 |
| 48% – 54% | 44 | 82 | 19070 | 0.673 | 0.044 | 233 | 7% | 56 | 19070 | 0.291 | 0.004 | 341 | 7% | 0.000 |
| 55% – 75% | 56 | 134 | 7882 | 2.047 | 0.387 | 59 | 3% | 276 | 8882 | 2.651 | 0.996 | 32 | 3% | 0.001 |
| > 76% | 65 | 257 | 5319 | 3.092 | 1.229 | 21 | 3% | 198 | 10319 | 2.168 | 0.554 | 52 | 4% | 0.003 |
| | | | | IV in Development | 2.540 | | | | | IV in Validation | 2.658 | | | 0.022 |

### 7.5.3.5 Managing and Monitoring a Model

Once a model is built and is adopted for business use, it is important to have a plan of monitoring the model regularly, so that any change in model performance can be tracked and suitable remedial actions taken. It is important to note that usually most models have a shelf life of two to three years. However, the life of a model depends upon changes in business policy, economic environment, product configuration, etc. For ongoing evaluation a model is tested for discriminatory power, accuracy and stability. The measures of discrimination such as KS, Gini, etc., are compared to the corresponding statistic during development so as to identify any changes in discriminatory power. For evaluating stability measures, the current sample is compared to the development time sample.

At this point it is important to note that while developing the model one identifies the relevant observation and performance periods. The observation window (observation period) refers to the time from which one selects the predictor characteristics, and the performance period refers to the period from which one selects the outcomes. A detailed discussion on selecting the observation and performance period is beyond the scope of this section. However, a few examples have been listed in the following.

- **Response model:** Predictive characteristics are created for a period of six or twelve month, before the campaign date for existing customers. For new customers, predictive characteristics are picked up as of the campaign month. Performance period is one to three months after the campaign date. However, if the offer takes some time to reach the prospect, which is typically the case when direct mailers are used, then the performance period should be adjusted accordingly. Usually multiple campaigns across the calendar year are used so as to eliminate effects of seasonality. In addition, past campaigns which involved a very different offer or product proposition are usually not used. The performance definition is usually response to the campaign. But in many cases it is worth excluding responders, who have attritied within a short time, or have not used the product at all.
- **Attrition model:** Predictive characteristics are created for a period of six or twelve months before the date of interest. Performance period is usually six to twelve months after the date of interest, it also depends on the length of the contract period. The performance definition is usually account closure, decrease in balance beyond a threshold, decrease in activity beyond a threshold, etc. Usually multiple snapshot dates are used to create the modelling sample. For example, a snapshot of the portfolio as on January, April, October, and December might be used for creating the modelling sample. Six or twelve months of prior information is used for each of these snapshots to create the predictive characteristics.

- **Revenue model:** Predictive characteristics are created for a period of 6 or 12 months before the date of interest. Performance period is usually 12 to 24 months after the date of interest. The performance is usually defined as revenue above a threshold. For revenue prediction on new customers, all customers acquired over a period of time is usually used as the model development sample. For example, one may use all customers acquired during 2011. For January 2011 acquisition a performance period from February 2011 to February 2012 is used. For February 2011 acquisitions, a performance period from March 2011 to March 2012 is used, and so on.
- **Risk models for ascertaining risk profile of new applicants:** Observation window is as of the time of application, though a longer credit bureau history is also used for calculating the credit bureau predictive characteristics. Performance period ranges from 12 to 24 months. However, sometime a rolling performance window is used, which results in a longer performance window for accounts acquired earlier and a shorter window for recently acquired accounts. The performance definition is usually ever 60 days or more past due, 90 days or more past due, 120 days or more past due in the performance period. But usually 60 or 90 or more past due days is mostly used.
- **Risk models for ascertaining risk profile for existing customers:** Predictive characteristics are created for a period of 6 or 12 months before the date of interest. Performance period is usually six to twelve months post. The performance definition is usually ever 60 days or more past due, 90 days or more past due, 120 days or more past due or write-off in the performance period. Similar to attrition models multiple snapshots over the year can be used for creating the development sample.
- **Models for collections:** Collection models are used for predicting payment behaviour of already delinquent accounts. Usually separate models are built for customers who have not paid for 30, 60, or 90 days. Predictive characteristics are created for a period of six or twelve month before the date of interest. A shorter performance period of one to three months is usually used. The performance definitions are usually the customer becoming current, or the customer paying more than a threshold or the customer not deteriorating, etc.

*Front-end and Back-end Validation Reports* For a model that uses a longer performance period of six, twelve or twenty four months, one has to wait for that much time after implementing the model, in order to evaluate the real discriminatory power of the model. However, for a response model that uses a three month performance window one can get an idea of the discriminatory power of the model, three months after implementation. For models that have longer performance periods, some of the reports such as Population Stability report and Characteristic stability reports can be obtained immediately after implementing the model. These reports are termed as front-end reports. The reports on the discriminatory power of the model with complete performance are termed as the back-end reports. Reports indicating possible changes in the predictive pattern of in-model characteristics and reports of change in information value of in-model characteristics are also part of back-end reports. Figure 7.32 depicts the development time frame and validation time frame for a revenue model for existing customers. For a model that uses a short performance period like a response model, one can have both the front-end and back-end reports within first few months of implementation. However, for a model that uses a longer performance window (6, 12, 18 or 24 months), one needs to wait till the end of the performance period to obtain the back-end reports. Though, in some cases, a back-end report using a shorter performance period can be used as a proxy.

### *Key Validation Reports*

**Population Stability** Population stability is a font end report that can be analysed immediately after implementing the model. The population stability assessment for on-going validation of the model is similar to the population stability assessment for validation as discussed earlier in the section. A PSI value of less than 0.1 suggests a stable model and a PSI value of more than 0.25 suggests that there has been major changes between the development and current sample.

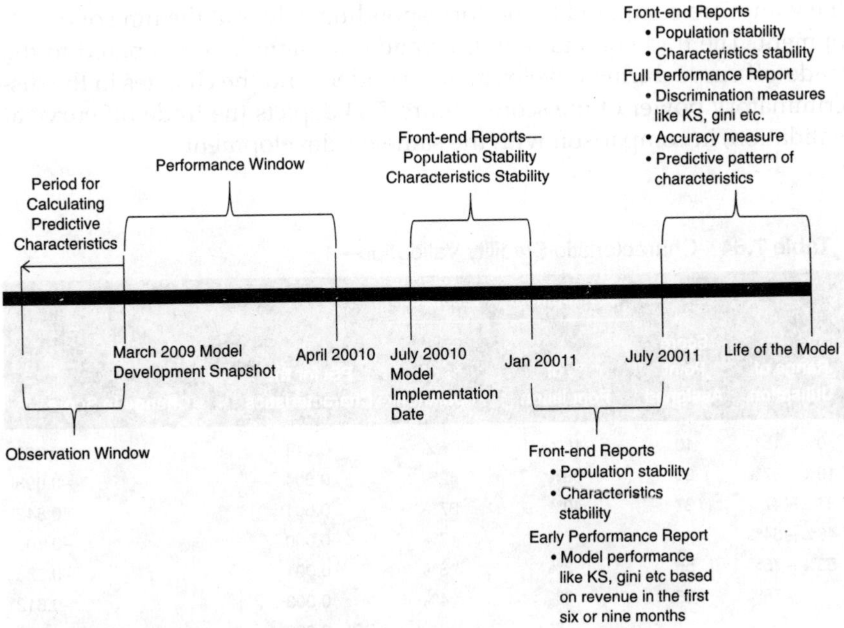


**Figure 7.32** Validation Reports

**Characteristic Stability** Characteristic stability is also a font end report that can be analysed immediately after implementing the model. The example of the utilisation characteristic discussed earlier in model validation is used in Table 7.64 to illustrate characteristic stability during model validation.

Along with the population stability at the characteristic level it is also important to determine the change in score because of the change in the population distribution of the characteristic. The change in score is calculated as (% of population in development – % of population is validation)* score point assigned. The previous example relates to the case when the characteristic is grouped into specific attribute bands and the grouped characteristic is used in the model. In case the characteristic is used as a continuous variable the change in score is calculated slightly differently and is depicted in Table 7.65. In this case the characteristic is divided into groups (mostly 5 or 10) such that each group has almost equal percentage of the development population. As per the example, in Table 7.65, utilisation has been used as a continuous variable in the model. And utilisation had been assigned a weight of 37, during model development. For the purpose of validation, the population is divided into 10 groups based on utilisation, so that each group has approximately 10% population in the development sample. Next, the percentage of population in the validation sample for these 10 groups is used to monitor the stability of the characteristics.

*Change in Discriminatory Power* Measures of discrimination such as KS, Gini, Divergence, etc., are calculated for the validation sample and the values are compared to the corresponding values at the time of development. The trade-off curve in the validation sample is compared to the trade-off curve during development to understand the changes in the discriminatory power of the score. Figure 7.33 depicts the trade-off curve at validation, in comparison with the same for development.

**Table 7.64** Characteristic Stability Validation—1

| | | Development | Validation | | |
|---|---|---|---|---|---|
| Range of Utilisation | Score Point Assigned | % of Populaiton | % of Populaiton | PSI for the Characteristics | Change in Score |
| 0% – 15% | 10 | 10% | 6% | 0.014 | 0.329 |
| 16% – 37% | 23 | 38% | 42% | 0.004 | –0.893 |
| 37% – 47% | 37 | 40% | 37% | 0.001 | 0.842 |
| 48% – 54% | 44 | 7% | 7% | 0.000 | –0.100 |
| 55% – 75% | 56 | 3% | 3% | 0.001 | –0.288 |
| > 76% | 65 | 3% | 4% | 0.003 | –0.612 |
| | | | | PSI 0.022 | Change in Score –0.722 |

**Table 7.65** Characteristic Stability Validation—2

| | | | | Development | Validation | | |
|---|---|---|---|---|---|---|---|
| Range of Utilisation | Average Utilisation | Score Point Assigned to the Characteristic | Average Score Point | % of Population | % of Population | PSI for the Characteristics | Change in Score |
| 0% – 8% | 4.20% | | 1.554 | 10.00% | 9.900% | 0.000 | 0.002 |
| 9% – 15% | 7.12% | | 2.6344 | 9.23% | 12% | 0.006 | – 0.067 |
| 16% – 25% | 19.60% | | 7.252 | 10.12% | 9% | 0.001 | 0.072 |
| 26% – 30% | 28.20% | | 10.434 | 11.10% | 14% | 0.006 | – 0.281 |
| 31% – 36% | 33.41% | | 12.3617 | 10.66% | 14% | 0.011 | – 0.451 |
| 37% – 40% | 38.20% | 37 | 14.134 | 10.44% | 10% | 0.000 | 0.014 |
| 40% – 44% | 42.70% | | 15.799 | 9.68% | 9% | 0.000 | 0.063 |
| 45% – 48% | 46.10% | | 17.057 | 10.20% | 10% | 0.000 | 0.039 |
| 48% – 52% | 50.28% | | 18.6036 | 9.21% | 9% | 0.000 | 0.0428 |
| > 52% | 58.33% | | 21.5821 | 9.68% | 2% | 0.121 | 1.657 |
| | | | | | | 0.145 | 1.090 |

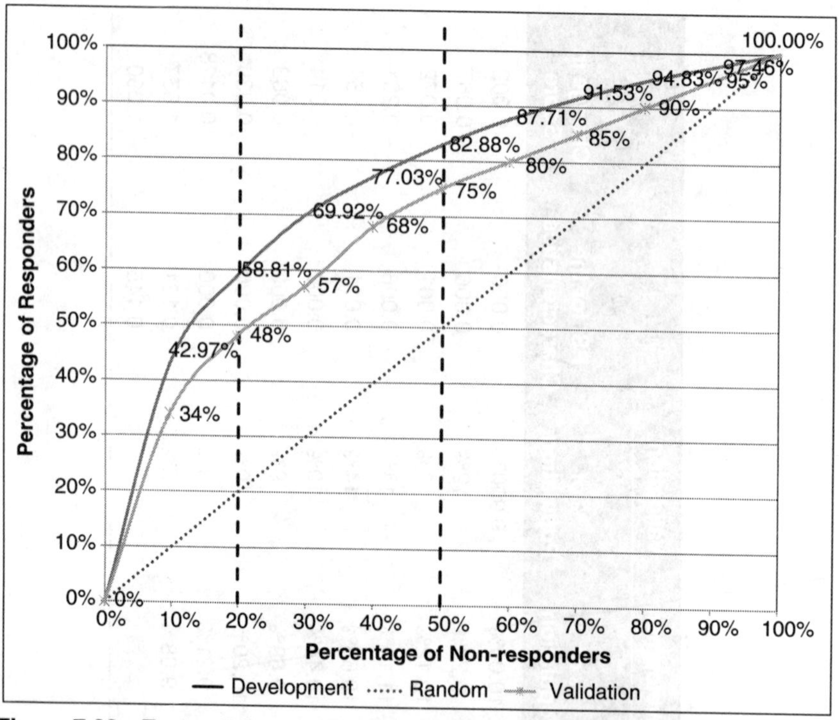


**Figure 7.33** Trade-off Curve—Development and Validation

The comparison of the trade-off curve suggests that in the development sample, selecting a point where 59% of the responders are captured, one would end up targeting 20% of the non-responders also. But in the validation sample selecting a point where 48% of the responders are captured, one will end up targeting 20% of the non-responders also. Hence, it can be seen that the model performance has gone down.

It needs to be noted that tracking of KS, Gini, Divergence and trade-off curve can only be performed after the completion of the entire performance period.

*Change in Characteristic Predictive Pattern* An analysis of the predictive pattern of the characteristic is compared across development and validation samples to identify any change in the predictive pattern of the characteristic. Table 7.66 refers to the analysis of the change in predictive pattern of the characteristic.

It can be seen that though the information value of the characteristic has remained unchanged yet the predictive pattern has changed as shown in the highlighted rows. Hence, this characteristic is not performing as well in the validation as compared to development. One needs to assess the stability (PSI at the characteristic level) and changes in the predictive pattern to evaluate the characteristic in validation.

**Table 7.66 Characteristic Stability – Development and Validation**

| | | Development | | | | | | | Validation | | | | | | |
|---|---|---|---|---|---|---|---|---|---|---|---|---|---|---|
| Range of Utilisation | Score Point Assigned | Number of Responders | Number of Non-responders | Weight of Evidence | Information Value | Odds | % of Population | Number of Responders | Number of Non-responders | Weight of Evidence | Information Value | Odds | % of Population | PSI for the Characteristics |
| 0% – 15% | 10 | 12 | 27731 | –1.623 | 0.129 | 2311 | 10% | 32 | 17731 | – 0.195 | 0.003 | 554 | 6% | 0.014 |
| 16% – 37% | 23 | 58 | 108333 | –1.411 | 0.411 | 1868 | 38% | 26 | 115362 | – 2.276 | 0.870 | 4437 | 42% | 0.004 |
| 37% – 47% | 37 | 74 | 112857 | –1.208 | 0.340 | 1525 | 40% | 88 | 102762 | – 0.941 | 0.230 | 1168 | 37% | 0.001 |
| 48% –54% | 44 | 82 | 19070 | 0.673 | 0.044 | 233 | 7% | 56 | 19070 | 0.291 | 0.004 | 341 | 7% | 0.000 |
| 55% – 75% | 56 | 134 | 7882 | 2.047 | 0.387 | 59 | 3% | 276 | 8882 | 2.651 | 0.996 | 32 | 3% | 0.001 |
| > 76% | 65 | 257 | 5319 | 3.092 | 1.229 | 21 | 3% | 198 | 10319 | 2.168 | 0.554 | 52 | 4% | 0.003 |
| | | | | IV in Development | 2.540 | | | | | IV in Validation | 2.658 | | PSI | 0.022 |

*Predictive Power Model Accuracy* For ascertaining the predictive accuracy of the model, the score to log odds relationship during model development is compared to the score to log odds relationship during validation. Figure 7.34 and Fig. 7.35 depicts two cases of change in score to log odds relationship.

In the first case, the new score to log odds line is almost parallel to the development line. Hence, the current points to double odds (PDO) during validation is expected to be very close to the one seen in development. In

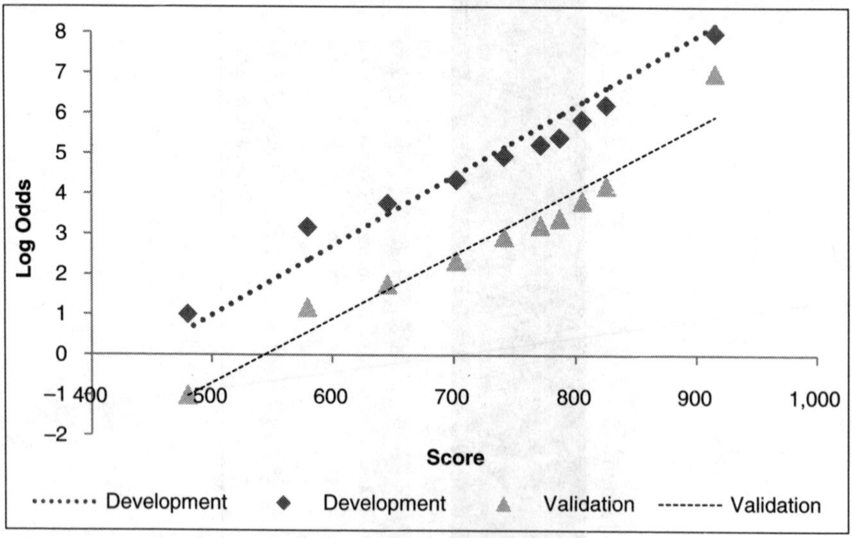


**Figure 7.34** Accuracy—Development and Validation 1

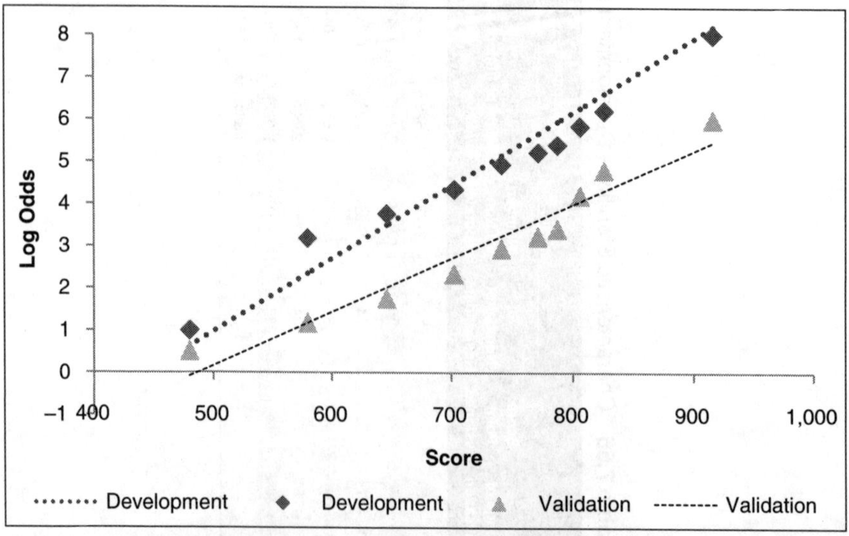


**Figure 7.35** Accuracy—Development and Validation 2

the second case, however, the score to log odds line have flattened, which means that the PDO has changed. The new PDO can be calculated as ln(2) divided by the slope of the score to log odds line. In this case the development PDO was 40, whereas the current PDO has increased to 54. An increase in the PDO suggests a decrease in the predictive power of the score. A parallel shift in the score to log odds line represent an overall change in the response rate and the score can be easily adjusted to take care of such a shift.

### 7.5.3.6 Model Management

A model needs to be tracked at a quarterly or annual basis to identify any degradation in model performance. In case degradation is observed there can be four possible remedial actions that can be undertaken.

*Option—1*: If the score to log odds relationship changes but the discrimination measures such as KS, Gini and Divergence remain unchanged, then the model can be re-calibrated. This implies the predictors and the weights associated with them remain unchanged, and only a linear transformation is used on the score so that the new score to log odds relationship is closer to the one observed during development.

*Option—2*: If the model's discriminatory power changes but none of the characteristics used in the model show a big change in their predictive pattern, then the model can be re-estimated, whereby the characteristic remains unchanged but the weights are changed.

*Option—3*: A further refinement of the re-estimation approach can be adopted where some of the predictive characteristics show change in their predictive pattern. In the new approach, the bins (the way each characteristic is grouped) are also changed.

*Option—4*: If none of these alternatives provide an acceptable solution, then the model needs to be redeveloped.

EIGHT

# Analytics Ecosystem

## 8.1 Introduction

Almost every industry has witnessed an exponential increase in the volume of data and the velocity of change in data, facilitated by a tremendous increase in computation power. Simultaneously, with globalisation and increased competition, most companies have witnessed significant margin pressures. These concurrent phenomena have propelled most companies to explore ways and means of generating insights and predictions from their internal and external data. The potency of using data for driving competitive advantage has become so well recognised that most companies have started viewing data as an information asset rather than as a by-product of business processes. To this end, analysis of data and creation of data-driven strategies have become an integral part of the overall management philosophy. Enormous amount of work both in industry and academia has focused on tools, techniques and methodologies of generating insights, prediction and strategies through analysis of data and the name analytics has become a "catch all" nomenclature for the entire set of activities which focuses on generating business value out of data. Some companies have started to view analytics as a business function in itself much like marketing, finance, information technology or operations. While others believe that analytics is embedded in every function, and every function needs to use the tools and techniques of analytics so as to deliver incremental business value. However, irrespective of the structure that a particular company embraces with respect to analytics, it is critical for organisations to realise that analytics is not a standalone discipline. It needs an ecosystem to survive and deliver incremental business value. This fact becomes even more important because analytics is a much more recent addition to the list of disciplines that are critical to the organisation's success.

The current chapter focuses on the key elements of the ecosystem that are critical for the successful implementation of analytics-driven strategies, particularly within the marketing context. If one starts to list down the elements of the analytics ecosystem, data comes up as the first natural choice. Data is the most important building block for analytics; without data, analytics just cannot exist. However, data that resides in the various operational systems in the organisation are rarely suitable as raw material for analytics, particularly because, most data residing in the operational system lacks sufficient history and is not connected to data from other operational systems. Data needs to be aggregated, summarised and stored for a sufficiently long time window, only then can analytics make use of it. Data warehouses and data marts act as the platform for aggregating, summarising and storing data and hence, act as the single source of input for analytics to work on.

Analytics in the marketing context becomes most relevant only when the organisation is able to have a uniform view of the customer and all business processes are centred round a uniform understanding of the customer. For example, in consumer financial services industry, if a particular customer is a high-value customer for one business then all other businesses need to have that information in their systems while servicing requests of the particular customer. A customer-centric strategy has long been recommended as the optimal strategy for cross-sell, up-sell and customer retention. A customer-centric strategy and customer-centric data forms an important facilitator for reaping maximum benefit out of analytics in the marketing context.

If one considers the interaction of customers with a business organisation then there are essentially two components of the interaction. The first is the business process that is responsible for the interaction and the second is the channel or the mode of the interaction. Customer relationship management (CRM) aims to integrate all business processes and channels around the customer so that every business process and every channel shares the same view as the customer. Customer relationship management systems have been around for quite some time and they form an important building block for harnessing analytics both from an implementation and strategic development perspective.

Very closely related to CRM are the tools for implementing and tracking marketing campaigns. In most cases, the end results of an analytics strategy involve targeting a set of customers or prospects with a certain offer, and a marketing campaign is designed for the purpose.

Hence, it is very critical for an organisation to have a platform for implementing and tracking marketing campaigns. Sometime such platforms are part of the CRM system. But along with the technological capabilities for executing marketing campaigns, it is very important to forecast the profit that the company expects to make out of each campaign and to track the same post implementation. For example, every campaign will have a set of costs associated with them and some short- and long-term revenue implications. It is important to forecast these metrics and arrive at an overall measure of profitability. This calls for robust business processes around campaign implementation and tracking, along with the relevant technology platforms.

Analytics also involves use of quantitative tools for analysing data and for making predictions using past data. With the availability of tremendous computation powers, it is possible to run a lot of complex algorithms on vast amounts of data at high speed and low costs. However, the analyst needs software that can enable him or her to run most of these complex algorithms, often in a black box mode. Thus, various analytical softwares form another key element of the analytics ecosystem. In many companies, the data warehouse/data marts, the analytical software and the servers on which they run are referred to as, analytical infrastructure.

The last element of the analytics ecosystem involves the organisation culture, philosophy and structure. It has been seen that a culture of data-driven decision making needs to be driven by the top management in order to make analytics a success in any organisation.

The first part of this chapter is dedicated to the discussion of data warehouse and data marts from an analytics point of view. The second part discusses CRM systems in brief. The third part is dedicated to the discussion on campaign management (including implementation and tracking), this is followed by a brief discussion on common analytical software tools.

## 8.2 Data Warehouse and Data Marts

Data forms the basic raw material for any sort of analysis starting from simple reports to complex prediction and pattern recognition algorithms. As per William Inmon, one of the key thinkers in the area of data warehousing, there are two major types of data in an organisation—operational data and derived data. Operational data is detailed data that is stored in the operational systems and is used for running the day-to-day operations of the company (transaction processing). The most important characteristic of operational data is that it is application oriented; this implies that data elements that are relevant only for particular processing are present in an operational system. So if one starts analysing operational data contained in a particular application, then one finds that the operational data is not sufficient for the purpose of analysis. Other data elements which are not part of the operational data of a particular application needs to be added to make the analysis meaningful. Moreover, operational data is also stored for a limited period and hence, it is difficult to use operational data, for any analysis that looks into history.

Derived data, on the other hand, is created mostly for the purpose of analysis and reporting and is rarely used for day-to-day transaction processing. As opposed to operational data, derived data is not application-oriented but is subject-oriented; this means that derived data is created around a particular subject, like customer, product or channel. To create derived data, operational data from multiple systems need to be collated, summarised and stored over time.

The purpose of operational data and derived data is so different that it is mostly not possible to have them in the same application. While

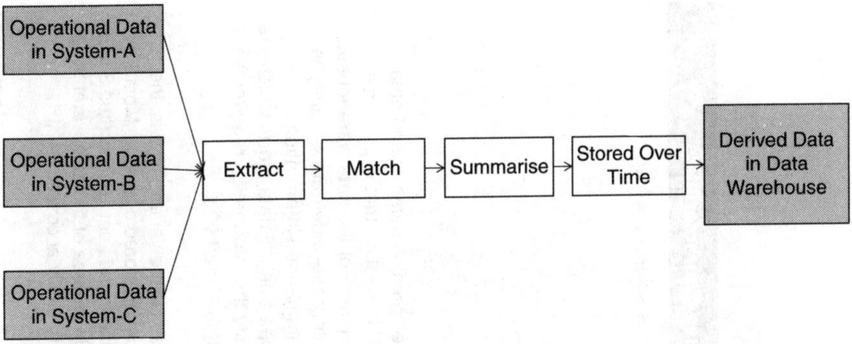


**Figure 8.1** Updating the Data Warehouse

operational data stays in the operational systems which are used for running the day-to-day transaction processing, derived data stays in a separate system mostly called data warehouse or data marts. Figure 8.1 depicts the conversion of operational data into derived data.

To understand data warehouses from an analytical standpoint it is important to delve into the differences between operational data and derived data because many of the characteristics of the data warehouse stems from these basic differences. Table 8.1 has been compiled from various works of William Inmon and Ralph Kimball, two of the leading thinkers on the area of data warehousing.

## 8.2.1 Summarisation of Data in a Data Warehouse

Operational data is extracted from multiple systems, cleaned, matched and summarised around a particular subject before being stored as derived data in the data warehouse. Some of the common summarisation methodologies involve calculating cumulative summarisation or rolling summarisation. For example, a credit card data warehouse will have derived data elements like total count of purchases till date and total amount of all purchases made till date. These are examples of cumulative data whereby new information gets added on top of old information. On the other hand, derived data like count or amount of purchase made in the last one year is a rolling summary. In case of rolling summary, the old information is over written by new information.

Another common summarisation involves creation of a profile record. As an example for credit card, there might be a P&L table which gets populated at the end of each billing cycle. The P&L table contains one record for each customer. The record consist of all the revenue and cost items pertaining to a single customer like volume of sales, interchange income, interest income, fee income, cost of funds. Each of these items are calculated based on specific summarisation rules. For example, all sales transactions made by the customer in that billing cycle are summed up to obtain the total sales. After calculating each of these items, a profile record is created for the customer; that is, one record is created for one customer.

**Table 8.1** Characteristics of Operational Data and Derived Data

| Data Characteristics | Operational Data | Derived Data | Data Warehouse Characteristics |
|---|---|---|---|
| Application orientation of operational data compared to subject orientation of derived data | Operational data is created around the transaction processing need of a particular application. Only data elements needed to fulfil the transaction are present. | Derived data is created around all the dimensions that are needed in defining the subject completely.<br>For example, to define a customer one needs elements of his/her transaction, demographics, service requests, etc. which might be part of different operational data. | Data warehouse is subject oriented. |
| Level of granularity | Operational data contains all types of information needed for transaction processing. | Derived data is always stored in a summarised form, and pieces of information which are considered unnecessary from a reporting or analytics perspective are not retained. | Data warehouse contains summarised data. The level of summarisation that is performed reflects the granularity of the data warehouse. Typically, the enterprise-wide data warehouse contains less summarised information compared to departmental data marts which are intended to satisfy the information requirements of a particular department only. |
| Time horizon | Operational data is stored in operational systems for a limited period of time. | Derived data is stored for a longer period of time so that it is possible to have a historical view of the data rather than a one-time snapshot view. | A data warehouse is time variant. That is, the same data element is stored over time. Most often, data relating to the latest period (last 3 to 5 years) is stored in an area of the data warehouse which can be very easily accessed. |

(*Continued*)

**Table 8.1** Characteristics of Operational Data and Derived Data (*Continued*)

| Data Characteristics | Operational Data | Derived Data | Data Warehouse Characteristics |
|---|---|---|---|
| | | | Slightly older data (5 to 10 years old) is stored in near line storage areas. Most often access to the near line storage involves the loading of a drive. Hence, the access to the near line storage has a higher response time but once access is created, the time required to fetch information is very low.<br>Very old data is often archived and stored in magnetic tapes and access to such data may involve taking help from the technology team. Consequently, accessing archived data is quite time and resource consuming. |
| Level of integration | Mostly all operational data that is required for processing a transaction resides in the same system and hence, access to multiple systems is limited. | Derived data, on the other hand, needs to be integrated across multiple operational systems. | A data warehouse is an integrated information storehouse where data from multiple systems are extracted, cleaned, matched and summarised before storage. Typically, software tools known as ETL (extract transform load) tools are used for this purpose. |
| Volatility | Operational data is volatile in nature, that is, the data gets updated quite frequently. | Derived data should have minimum volatility to be of any use for analysis. | Data warehouse data has to be less volatile. The changes in operational data should be captured either in the time dimension or as changes in the context of the data. |

(*Continued*)

**Table 8.1** Characteristics of Operational Data and Derived Data (*Continued*)

| Data Characteristics | Operational Data | Derived Data | Data Warehouse Characteristics |
|---|---|---|---|
| Context | The context is not very important for the usage of operational data. | Context is of critical importance for derived data to be of any use | Data warehouse data has two components: the first is the data itself and the second is the context. Any change in the context needs to be recorded in order to make sense of data stored in the data warehouse.<br>For example, a consumer durable company may have hundreds of products and it may be grouping products based on category for example TV, music players, laptops, washing machines refrigerators, etc. And each product will have an ID where the first letter stands for the category. In case, there is a change in marketing strategy and consequently, the company aims to group products by customer segments, for example, all products catering to the high-end segment are categorized together. Then the first letter of the ID will change.<br>The data warehouse should not only store the product ID for each customer over time but should also store the meaning of each ID and the change in context. Change in context, refers to the change in product IDs due to the above mentioned change in business strategy. |

(*Continued*)

**Table 8.1** Characteristics of Operational Data and Derived Data (*Continued*)

| Data Characteristics | Operational Data | Derived Data | Data Warehouse Characteristics |
|---|---|---|---|
| Data access | Access pattern is uniform and fixed for operational data. | Access pattern of derived data is quite unpredictable | The quantum and types of data accessed may be very irregular. Some data element may be accessed very infrequently, whereas others may be accessed once in a while. After the data warehouse has been in existence for some time the access pattern could be studied and capture of unnecessary data may be stopped. Or the data warehouse could be tuned to facilitate faster access of data elements which are more in demand. In addition, new summarisation can be added or some data may be made more granular based on observed access pattern.<br>Hence, the data warehouse is more evolutionary in nature as compared to an operational system. |
| Data update | Operational data is always updated in real time either by customer, supplier, a business process owner or other application programme. | Derived data update is never real time. Update of derived data happens in response to certain triggers or as per user requirement (e.g., monthly or end of day update) | The data is loaded into the data warehouse either at a regular time interval (end of day, end of month, end of billing cycle, etc.) or in response to certain triggers like a sale being completed or a claim being closed or a customer being written off, etc.<br>Because of the above phenomena, the data warehouse data is never completely in sync with the operational data. The gap between data warehouse data and operational data is often termed as the wrinkle of time. |

(*Continued*)

**Table 8.1** Characteristics of Operational Data and Derived Data (*Continued*)

| Data Characteristics | Operational Data | Derived Data | Data Warehouse Characteristics |
|---|---|---|---|
| Usage | Operational data is mostly used in business processes and hence, the usage of the data remains mostly unchanged. Changes in the usage of operational data occur only when there is a significant change in the business process. | Derived data, on the other hand, is used for the purpose of reporting, analysis or prediction. It is not known in advance how or which data element will be used for this purpose. Out of the three usages mentioned earlier, reporting is possibly the most structured. Once the content and frequency of a report is established the data usage pattern is fixed over time. However, for analysis and prediction, the usage pattern is entirely ad-hoc. | Data warehouse serves the business analysis and business intelligence community, and hence, needs to have a flexible architecture to enable large amount of ad-hoc queries. |
| Design | Operational data must serve the most important aspect of being able to be accessed and changed very easily and the response times for the same must be very low. If the above conditions are not satisfied, business process would suffer. | Response time is of much lesser importance for derived data. Derived data, on the other hand, must be able to withstand various types of queries. It is also likely that some of those queries may not be designed in the most optimal manner. That is to say derived data must be analyst friendly. | Data warehouse design must address the dual objective of making the data warehouse analyst friendly and making it robust so as to handle huge amount of data over long periods of time. The multi-dimensional model addresses the first requirement very effectively while the relational model addresses the second one more effectively. A separate section of this chapter provides a brief overview of the approaches. |

## 8.2.2 Data Warehouse Design: The Relational Model and the Multi-dimensional Model

From a technical perspective, a data warehouse is a database that stores historically summarised information at a subject level. The methodology of the design of the database is obviously a key determinant of the success of data warehousing. There are two primary approaches for designing the data warehouse: one of the approaches is a relational design and the other is a multi-dimensional design. The relational design approach was propounded by William Inmon, while the multi-dimensional approach was propounded by Ralph Kimball. The current section provides a brief overview of the two approaches without getting into the technical details. The contents of this section have been compiled from the works of Inmon and Kimball on data warehouse design.

- **Relational model**
  - *How the data is stored:* The relational model of data warehouse design involves storing very small amounts of data in a particular table in the data warehouse and multiple tables being linked with a set of identifiers or keys. Data in a relational design model is stored in the normalised form, which means that the data is divided into a large number of small tables and then a relationship is defined between these tables. Most operational databases are designed using this design model.
  - *Key advantage:* This model makes it easy to update the data in the warehouse and to add new tables with additional information. It also makes the warehouse quite flexible in design so that a new report or data request could be easily added to the set of existing reports.
  - *Key disadvantage:* However, the relational model is not very user friendly and access to the data of interest may be quite difficult and cumbersome.
- **Multi-dimensional model**
  - *How the data is stored:* To tide over the problem of difficulty of access, the multi-dimensional model has been created specifically to suit the need of the business intelligence or reporting professional. The multi-dimensional design framework creates two types of tables in the data warehouse: the first are fact tables which contains the actual information and the second are a set of dimension tables which consist of the contextual information. For example, a fact table might have information on sales including the dollar and unit volume of sale, store ID, sales region, product ID, etc. A dimension table will have the list of store IDs, the list of item IDs, etc. The fact table contains more volatile data, whereas

the dimension table consists of information which changes far less frequently.

- *Key advantage:* This structure of storing data has an intuitive appeal for the analytical community. Most analytical reports consist of a set of metrics which are grouped by specific categories. For example, if total annual sales and annual sales per sales person are metrics of importance, then one would like to know the sales by region, division, store, etc. As is apparent from the multi-dimensional design, the metric of interest (which is most often a continuous value like sales, profit, cost, etc.) is stored in the fact table. The grouping information is stored as dimensions which could be used to divide the summary of the fact table by various groups.
- *Key disadvantage:* The storing of data warehouse data in this form makes update of the data warehouse information more difficult. It also may involve the storage of the same data in multiple tables thus making it less efficient.

Figure 8.2 illustrates the difference between the two approaches using a simple example of an elementary data mart for savings (checking) and fixed deposit products. As it is apparent from Fig. 8.2, the multi-dimensional model is easily amenable for creating any reports on income earned and costs incurred. It would be very easy to create reports like total interest cost by account type, customer type, etc. One could think of the fact table information as the content of the body of a pivot table and the dimension table information as page fields. However, in order to query the relational model, one has to join a few tables to get all the desired information to construct the above report. Actually one has to join the account table, customer table, savings table, fixed deposit table and the fees table to get to the information needed for this one report. And of course, the complexities increase with a large real-life data warehouse. The advantages of the relational model is however less apparent in this kind of simple example. If one considers an example of creating another report around account activity where one would like to see information on number of check deposits, number of check withdrawal, most recent fixed deposit date, number of auto shifts from savings to fixed, etc., then it is not possible to build this new report using the tables in the current multi-dimensional design. However, it is feasible by using the current set of tables in the relational design. In case of the multi-dimensional design another set of fact tables around activity needs to be created to service the new request.

As can be seen from this example, in a real-world multi-dimensional warehouse, there will be multiple fact tables and dimension tables. A single dimension table could be linked to multiple fact tables (however, fact tables are rarely linked to one another). This kind of design of multiple

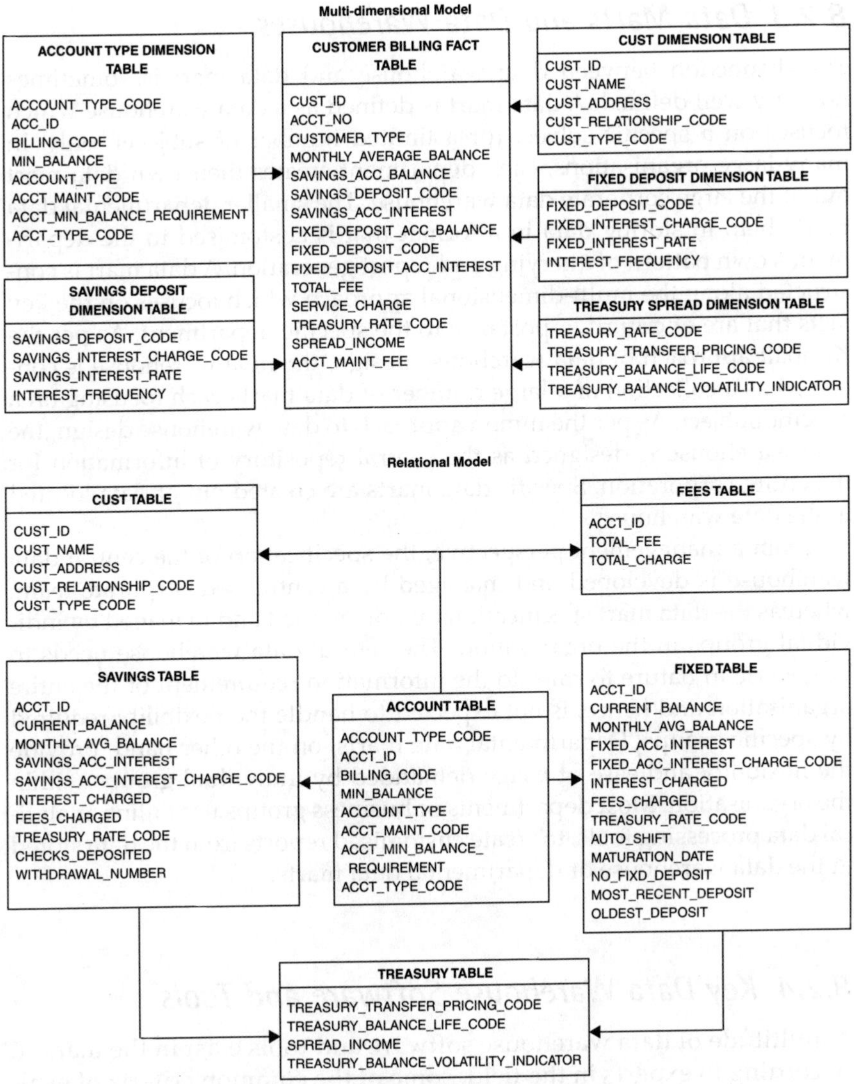


**Figure 8.2** The Relational and Multi-dimensional Models

fact tables sharing a single dimensional table is referred to as the snow flake design.

With this background, it is important to define a data warehouse. As per Inmon, a data warehouse is defined as *"A subject-oriented, integrated, time-variant and non-volatile collection of data in support of management's decision making process"*; and as per Kimball, it is defined as *"A copy of transaction data, specifically structured for query and analysis"*.

### 8.2.3 Data Marts and Data Warehouses

The distinction between data warehouse and data mart is sometimes not very well defined. A data mart is defined as a data warehouse which focuses on a specific subject (or a limited number of subjects) only. In many large organisations, each department creates their own data mart out of the large corporate data warehouse. The smaller departmental data marts help in storing data in a format that is customised to the department's own pattern of querying and report generation. A data mart is constructed along the multi-dimensional approach which focuses on the key facts that are of critical importance to the specific department. As per the Kimball approach of data warehouse design, the data warehouse is conceived as a collection of a large number of data marts each focusing on a specific subject. As per the Inmon approach to data warehouse design, the data warehouse is designed as the central repository of information for the entire corporation. Specific data marts are created out of data located in the data warehouse.

From a management perspective, the specification of the central data warehouse is developed and managed by a centralised corporate team, whereas the data mart specifications are developed and managed by individual groups in the organisation. The central data warehouse needs to be generic in nature to cater to the information requirement of the entire organisation and hence, is not expected to handle the flexibility required by specific groups. Departmental data marts, on the other hand, provide the flexibility and ease of usage demanded by individual groups within the organisation. Most departments or business groups use online analytical data processing tools, to create customised reports from the data stored in the data warehouse or departmental data marts.

### 8.2.4 Key Data Warehouse Software and Tools

A multitude of data warehouse software and tools exist in the market. According to experts in the field, some of the common criteria of evaluating data warehouse software include scalability, optimisation of load processes, ease of query execution, optimisation of query structure, ability of managing structured analytical data, ease of integration with multiple systems, and many more. The common data warehouse softwares include IBM InfoSphere Balanced Warehouse, SAP NetWeaver, Teradata data warehouse, Microsoft SQL server, Oracle Optimised warehouse & Oracle 11g, Sybase Analytic Appliance & IQ 12.7 and Netezza Performance Server 1000 Series Data Warehousing Appliance 4.5. A detailed discussion of software tools is beyond the scope of the current book.

### 8.2.5 Online Analytical Processing

Online analytical processing (OLAP) is a set of methodologies that allows fast and flexible views of summarised data across various dimensions. For example, if the summarised data of interest is sales, then one would like to summarise sales along multiple dimensions like region, division, products, etc. OLAP technologies allow for the creation of cubes which consist of the metric of interest along all relevant dimensions. If one relates to the multi-dimensional model described earlier, the metric of interest in the OLAP cube is the content of the fact table and the dimensions of the cube are the contents of the dimension table. Using the multi-dimensional example in the earlier part of this section, a simple example of an OLAP cube is shown in Fig. 8.3.

As per OLAP methodologies, a set of cubes which are needed for most reporting purposes are constructed and refreshed regularly (every month or week). Any combinations of the dimensions that are desired are created by dragging and dropping the values from the dimensions. Once the cube is created, the combination of dimensions is mostly left to the business users. The key capabilities that are critical for most OLAP applications include:

- Basic calculation on the result set (like percentage, averages over time, etc.)
- Pivot results (ability of looking at the metric of interest along multiple dimensions or combination of various dimensions)

Dimensions

- Length of Relationship—Less than 1 Year, 1–2 Years, 2–5 Years, more than 5 Years
- Product—Savings Account, Current Account, Business Account
- Customer Type—High Net Worth, High Potential, Value Customer
- Geography—Tier-1 City, Tier-2 City, Others

| Metric | Values |
|---|---|
| Number of customers | 326,541 |
| Average quarterly balance | 7,256,394,102 |
| Average monthly balance | 8,161,266,447 |
| Number of fixed deposits | 117,554 |
| Fixed deposit balance | 11,822,129,549 |
| Interest income | 979,352,0 |
| Fee income | 391,849,2 |
| Servicing cost | 816,353 |

**Figure 8.3** A Simplified (Online Analytical Possessing) OLAP Cube

- Drill down analysis capability
- Column and row calculation on pivot results like percentage of total
- Sorting
- Formatting (e.g., highlight any value that is above and below a threshold, highlight any value that is higher or lower than last period)
- Creating graphs and charts
- Creating summary documents
- Flexibility of user for changing dimensions with ease

Some of the common OLAP tools include QlikView, Brio, Cognos, MicroStrategy, Spotfire, SAS OLAP Cube, InformationBuilder, etc. It needs to be noted that this is a fast-changing area and new products and product features are being introduced regularly by a number of established and new software companies.

### 8.2.6 Extract Transform Load (ETL): A Brief Overview

As discussed earlier, a data warehouse needs to aggregate data from multiple source systems. The aggregation of data entails systems and processes that would extract data from various source systems, clean the data, aggregate the data and deliver the data to the data warehouse. These systems are referred to as extract transform and load (ETL) systems. Data in the operational systems tends to be very volatile, that is, it changes all the time. Hence, one important question that needs to be addressed is when will the ETL systems extract the data from various source systems? Most extractions are either time triggered, that is, they happen at a pre-specified time (end of day, end of month, etc.) or are event triggered, that is, they happen in response to a particular event (booking a new customer, disbursement of a claim, etc.). In many cases, the ETL system only updates data that has changed from the last time the update had happened, this makes the process of extracting and loading the data much faster and less error prone. The major activities performed by an ETL system involve:

- **Extracting:** Extracting routines perform the actual extraction and also capture changes in the source systems so as to map changes to the data warehouse.
- **Cleaning and conforming:** Cleaning and conforming routines perform data cleaning, de duplication and summarisation operations, they also fire triggers in cases where data errors are identified. Cleaning and conforming routines also create logs of data audit and error events.
- **Delivering:** Delivering routines update the data in the data warehouse and represent the last phase of activates in the ETL process.

## 8.3 Types of Data

In order to make the best use of data, it is not only important to understand what the data element implies but it is equally important to understand the types of data and how the data can be structured for analytical purposes.

The two basic types of data are qualitative data and quantitative data. Common examples of qualitative data include product type, customer type, sales region, customer zip, etc. Qualitative data can either be nominal, like product type where there is no ordering between the categories or ordinal where there is a natural ordering between the categories. If one considers a qualitative data element like customer value which has three categories, high, medium and low, then there is a natural ordering between these categories. Sometimes ordinal qualitative data is further classified based on whether it can be represented in a ratio scale. For example, if there are five customer category based on profitability, category 1 being least profitable and category 5 being most profitable, and if the difference in profitability between category 1 and category 2 is same as the difference in profitability between category 2 & 3, 3 & 4, and so on, then it is referred to as an ordinal qualitative data that can be measured on a ratio scale. In most reports and OLAP cubes, qualitative data is normally used for filtering various metrics by category; alternately speaking, it represents the dimensions in a multi-dimension OLAP cube. For example, one may be interested in understanding total sales by customer type (e.g, individual vs. SME) or sales region. However, in some cases, qualitative data do form part of the metric that is of interest, for example, one may be interested in understanding the percentage of customers in the high-value category. In all cases where the qualitative data is the metric of interest, it is usually measured as percentage.

Quantitative data is measured as a continuous metric and can always be expressed in the ratio scale. Quantitative data is either numerical continuous where it can take any value from a range, or it is numerical discrete where it can take only certain specific values. A data element like number of months the customer has been on books or number of products the customer has purchased are examples of numerical discrete data. In most cases, numerical data is part of the fact tables in a multi-dimensional structure.

Data needs to be arranged and structured for most analysis. Typically data is structured in any of the following categories:

- **Cross section data:** Cross sectional data refers to a snapshot view of the data. For example, if one considers all open accounts as of a particular month and wants to analyse their sales by various dimensions like geography, customer type, etc., then one needs to obtain a snapshot of all customers as of that month and no historical information is needed beyond this particular snapshot view.

- **Time series data:** Time series data refers to a view of data elements over time. Time series data looks at a set of metrics over time, for example total sales in the portfolio, total profit, etc. However, in a time series view of a metrics, one does not necessarily look at the same set of customers or accounts over time. For example, when one studies total sales over the last five years, then there could be customers who have closed their relationship and new customers who have come in. Time series data looks at the overall metrics and not metrics for specific customers over history. Most macroeconomic data like GDP growth, interest rate, inflation, etc., are good examples of time series observation of data wherein one is looking at the aggregate metrics for the economy as a whole.
- **Panel data or cohort data:** Panel data or cohort data is essentially a combination of cross section data and time series data. It looks at metrics from a specific set of customers (referred to as cohort) over a period of time. Hence, if one adds a time dimension to cross section data, one will end up with cohort or panel data. When one observes a cohort of customers over a period of time, then there will be customers who will drop out from the cohort over time. Hence, in many cases all metrics in the cohort data is measured at a per account or per customer level as of the particular month and also as of the beginning month. Table 8.2 provides an example.
- **Unstructured data:** The data types described above are stored in a structured format, that is, they consists of rows and columns where each row represents a record and each column represents a particular field. Each of these fields can be a number, a string of characters (including space) or a date or can be missing. Each of these fields in the structured data has the same meaning and data type across all the rows. Most importantly each row consists of the same number of fields though some or all of the fields might be missing for some of the rows. Unstructured data, on the other hand, does not follow a predefined structure. Common examples of unstructured data are text and voice data. For example, data on emails written by customers to the service department can be a good example of unstructured data. Each email will vary in size from a few words to a few pages. One needs to convert the unstructured data into usable structured data for further analysis. A common methodology of converting unstructured data involves parsing each word in the unstructured data and then getting rid of punctuations, connecting words and the like. The parsing process then identifies key words that are important for any analysis. In this case, words like "unhappy", "frustrated", "bad", "unavailable", "slow", "unfriendly" will indicate that the customer

**Table 8.2** Example of Cohort Data (Accounts Acquired in January are Tracked for the Next 9 Months)

| | Example of Cohort (Panel Data) | | | | | | | | |
|---|---|---|---|---|---|---|---|---|---|
| | Jan | Feb | Mar | Apr | May | Jun | Jul | Aug | Sep |
| Number of accounts | 1020 | 1020 | 1020 | 1020 | 1020 | 1020 | 1020 | 1020 | 1020 |
| Number of open accounts | 1020 | 1020 | 998 | 980 | 978 | 970 | 967 | 960 | 950 |
| Number of closed accounts | 0 | 0 | 22 | 40 | 42 | 50 | 53 | 60 | 70 |
| Average balance (based divided by number of accounts) | $1,200 | $1,235 | $1,176 | $1,187 | $1,200 | $1,159 | $1,230 | $1,151 | $1,065 |
| Average balance (based divided by number of beginning accounts) | $1,200 | $1,235 | $1,151 | $1,140 | $1,150 | $1,102 | $1,166 | $1,083 | $992 |

email had a negative feedback about the service. Whereas words like "happy", "satisfied", "fast" will suggest a positive experience. These key words can be used to categorise customer emails into positive and negative and then one can go into other data sources to identify the reason for the feedback.

## 8.4 Data Quality

Data has quality if it satisfies the requirements of its intended use. It lacks quality to the extent that it does not satisfy the requirement. The same data element may be of high quality for a particular purpose and may be of very poor quality for some other purposes.

For example, consider two data elements "months since most recent bank card delinquency" and "number of credit cards with utilisation greater than 50%" in the credit bureau data repository of a particular bank. Initially, these data elements were used to judge the credit worthiness of current credit card customers for line increase. The data "months since most recent bank card delinquency" had valid values from –999 to 60, where –999 represent customers who had never been delinquent on bank cards. The next value after –999 was "1" which meant the customer had a credit card delinquency last month, the maximum value 60 represented customers who had a delinquency five years back.

The data element "number of credit cards with utilisation greater than 50%" had values from 0 to 20, where "0" represented no credit cards with utilisation greater than 50%.

The bank used to target customers who had never been delinquent on a credit card (months since most recent bank card delinquency = –999) and had at least one but not more than three credit cards with utilisation more than 50% (1 ≤ number of credit cards with utilisation greater than 50%" = < 3). These customers represented the optimal risk return trade-off for the bank. Now the bank wants to utilise these two data fields for the following additional purposes:

- **Use these data elements to extend credit card offers to student loan customers:** The bank has a small student loan portfolio and it aims to offer a student credit card to student loan customers who do not have a credit card with another bank. While looking at these data elements, the analyst realises that in case of both the data elements ("months since most recent bank card delinquency" and "number of credit cards with utilisation greater than 50%") "–1" represented a valid value which meant that the customer had no credit cards. But as the data elements were used for existing credit card customers this value did not exist for 99.99% of the records. Hence, in the summarisation logic, it was combined with –999 for the data element "months since most recent bank card delinquency". And it was combined with "0" for the data element "number of credit cards with utilisation greater than 50%". Due to the summarisation logic, it has become impossible to identify customers with no credit cards from either of the data elements. Hence, it can be seen that the data elements have very good quality for the purpose of credit line increase on existing customers. But the same data elements become ineffective when one tries to use them for other purposes.

- **Use of this data elements to put in place a pre-delinquent collection strategy:** In normal situations, the bank had a collection strategy in place which focused on customers who were delinquent. However, with worsening credit scenario across the credit card industry, the bank wants to be more proactive about the collection process and envisages calling risky pre-delinquent customers, so as to ensure that they pay on time. The bank wants to specifically target customers who are not delinquent with the bank but has already defaulted on credit card debt, with some other bank. Upon closer investigation of the data field "months since most recent delinquency" the bank finds that the data field is updated once every quarter because that has been the frequency of rolling out the previous line increase campaigns. However, a four month update is very late for using this data field for pre-emptive collection calling.

From the above example it can be clearly seen that the same data may be of high quality for a particular use and may be of poor quality for some other use.

Data must be accurate, timely, relevant, complete, understood and trusted for being of good quality. Creation of derived data from operational data often involve aggregation of data, putting data in a different data structure compared to the source, and adding time period information to the data. Some of these processes may create new errors in the data. In addition, when one looks at the aggregated data, the original data gets lost and hence, it is difficult to trace back errors to the original data. Effect of a wrong value of a data may be smaller in the original transaction processing system but the effect propagates through aggregation. In some cases, a perfectly valid value of a data element in the transaction processing systems may generate an absolutely erroneous value in the data warehouse. For example, in a credit card transaction system some card types may not have any pre-set spending limit and hence, the credit limit may be blank. However, the same field may be used for creating a derived data element called credit limit utilisation, which is credit card balance divided by the credit limit. This operation will return a null value for cards with no pre-set spending limit.

Missing values are another key element of data quality. Very often a data element with high amount of missing values is categorised as poor quality data. However, in many cases, missing values may not be an error in the data field and may represent a perfectly valid business situation.

For example, if one considers the database of all corporate accounts of a bank, a data element like "number of unfavourable judgements" may be having a lot of missing values. A missing value may represent lack of any suit filed against the company. In many cases, analysts tend to assign a zero value to the cases where the field is missing. However, one must be extremely careful about such imputations because in this case, a zero value of this field may represent cases where there were suits filed against the company but all the suits resulted in a favourable judgement. This is a typical case of combining true zeroes with missing information which may significantly reduce the quality of the data element. Hence, in many cases it is advisable to replace the missing with a null value.

Effective metadata management is an important element of ensuring data quality. Correct and up-to-date metadata is an important first step in ensuring that the logic used for creating the derived data in the data warehouse is properly maintained and regularly updated. The logic for assignment of special values should always be made part of the metadata so that any user will be careful while using those special values of the data. Many companies have implemented data quality management programmes, where each department identifies a dedicated resource for monitoring the data elements relevant for all users of the department. The data steward also works closely with the IT organisation for obtaining the correct data definition and for undertaking data quality projects.

Any data quality initiatives consist of two key parts—the first is the detection of data quality issues and the second is the correction of the same. Identification of data quality issues can be performed using structural analysis, value correlation or aggregation analysis.

### *8.4.1 Methods for Identifying Data Quality Issues*

Various authors and data quality experts have propounded multiple approaches for identification of data quality issues. Jack Olsen provides a good summary of some of the key approaches in his work on data quality. The approaches described in this section have been partially adopted from his work *Data Quality: The Accuracy Dimension*.

Structural analysis looks at the data element for uniqueness, consecutiveness or references between data elements. For example, a field like customer ID must be unique. Each account ID must have a valid customer ID and two different customer IDs can share the same account ID only if the account type is linked (or joint) account. Figure 8.4 illustrates the above structure.

Value correlation is another common methodology for detecting data quality issues. Value correlation involves creating rules using one or more data fields and then checking values against those rules. For example, consider the rule on credit card interest depicted in Fig. 8.5.

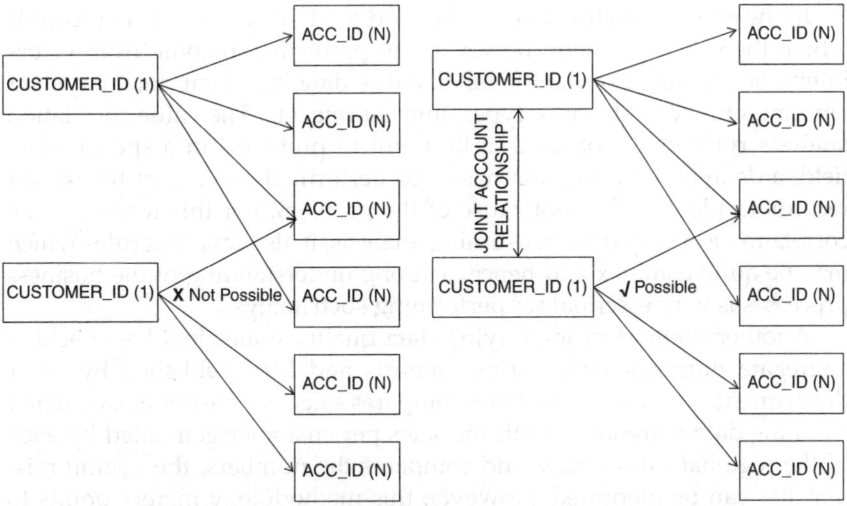


**Figure 8.4** Identifying Data Quality Issues Through Structural Analysis

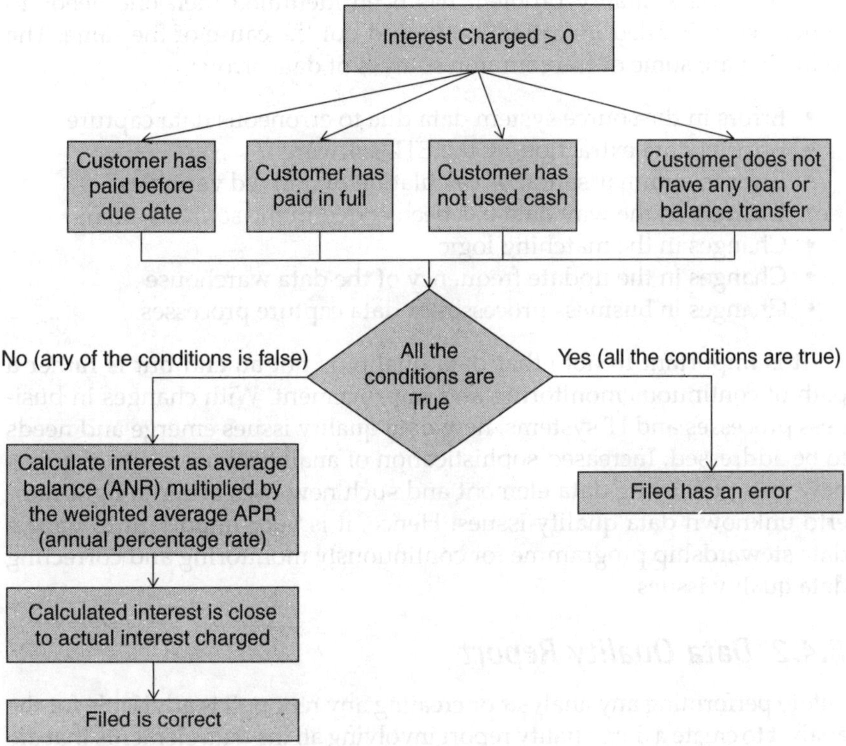


**Figure 8.5** Identifying Data Quality Through Value Correlation Analysis

In the above case, this rule can be used to identify a handful of records where there is a problem; however, the problem can come from errors in one or a number of data fields like due date, payment date, payment amount, number of balance types, interest rate, etc. The value correlation analysis rules does not necessarily point to problems in a specific data field, a detailed investigation has to be performed on each of the wrong records to identify the root cause of the problem. For this reason, value correlation is a very time-consuming analysis, it also involves rules which may be quite complex and hence, a strong understanding of the business processes is very essential for performing such analysis.

Another method of identifying data quality issues involve checking aggregate numbers with various reports and MIS published by other departments. For example, if one compares sales per customer calculated from the data warehouse with the sales per customer generated by each of the regional sales offices and compares the numbers, the overall mismatches can be identified. However, this methodology merely points to the existence of a data quality issue. A detailed structural analysis or value correlation analysis has to be performed to unearth the real problem. However, in some cases all data elements may not be present in the data warehouse for calculating the desired MIS.

Once a data quality problem has been identified then one needs to undertake a detailed investigation to find out the cause of the same. The following are some of the common sources of data errors:

- Errors in the source system data due to erroneous data capture
- Error in data extraction by the ETL software
- Error in summarisation or calculation of derived variables
- Changes in the way data has been coded in the source system
- Changes in the matching logic
- Changes in the update frequency of the data warehouse
- Changes in business processes or data capture processes

It is important to note that data quality is not an end but is rather a path of continuous monitoring and improvement. With changes in business processes and IT systems, new data quality issues emerge and needs to be addressed. Increased sophistication of analytical users also requires new uses of existing data element and such new uses bring to light hitherto unknown data quality issues. Hence, it is very important to have a data stewardship programme for continuously monitoring and correcting data quality issues.

### *8.4.2 Data Quality Report*

Before performing any analysis or creating any report, it is advisable for the analyst to create a data quality report involving all the data elements that are relevant for the analysis. The data quality report consists of the following:

- Number of records and number of unique records for all fields which are used as identifiers (e.g., customer ID, product ID, account number)
- Numeration of the mean, median, maximum and minimum values for each numeric field
- Frequency of the categories that are present in each categorical field
- The number of missing values and special values for each field
- Some of the key MIS (metric) needs to be produced by using one or more of the data elements such that these can be checked with other reports in order to ascertain the correctness of the data
- Value correlation analysis results. Various value correlation rules need to be created and evaluated. Each failed rule needs to be further investigated to identify the root cause of the problem.

The data quality report is an important first step for determining the usability of data for the particular reporting or analytic purpose at hand.

### *8.4.3 Metadata Management*

Metadata refers to the information about the data that is necessary for making use of the data. Metadata management determines the usability of the data. A properly updated and detailed metadata makes a data element more useful. As the data warehouse data is used by analysts across multiple departments, it is very critical to have uniform definitions of variables.

The exact matching and summarisation methodology should be part of the metadata so that analysts know how exactly a data warehouse data element is created. This helps analysts to make the best use of the data element. For example, a telecom data warehouse may have a field named total minutes of usage; this variable can be calculated at the end of month or at the end of the billing cycle. This information, as to which period is used for calculating the summary data, is very critical for using the data in the right manner.

Another key aspect of metadata management involves documenting proper definition of missing values, default values and special values. It is important to note that the quality of a data element in the data warehouse is equally affected by the actual content of the data and the information about the data. In many cases, poor metadata may make a data element of poor quality even if the contents of the data element are absolutely perfect.

## 8.5 Key Report and MIS Types: Marketing MIS Overview

The data warehouse data is used for building reports and as inputs to various analytical models. The usages of data for analytical purposes have been covered in great detail in this book. This part of the current section is devoted to a brief discussion of the various common reports and MIS types that are commonly used across organisations, particularly from a marketing context. The genesis of marketing metrics mostly lies in the endeavour of marketing professionals to quantify the financial impact of the various marketing activities. However, only profitability metrics provide a limited window into the effectiveness of the marketing organisation and hence, a more holistic approach is needed to construct a complete array of metrics to measure and evaluate various aspects of the marketing function. Various researchers in the marketing area have propounded frameworks for combining marketing metrics. Lehmann and Reibstein have proposed a synthesis of these frameworks in their book titled *Marketing Metrics and Financial Performance*. The framework proposed by Lehmann and Reibstein, looks into the marketing activity as a process, wherein certain marketing actions like advertising, discounts, etc., are undertaken for deriving certain financial performances like revenue growth, profitability growth. These financial performances in turn are aimed at creating value for the shareholder, which can be measured by metrics like return on equity, risk adjusted return on capital, etc. The most important aspect of the framework involves the linkage of marketing actions with financial performance and financial value. A structuring of the metrics helps top management in identifying the right marketing action that can be harnessed to drive the desired financial performance. A brief description of the framework has been outlined in Fig. 8.6.

Metrics around marketing activity and marketing spending are designed to monitor the amount of activity which is being undertaken for achieving the desired financial results. If one considers the entire marketing activity as a single process whose outcome is a desired financial result, then these metrics are a way to gauge the quality and quantity of input that is fed into the process. The marketing process can be thought of as

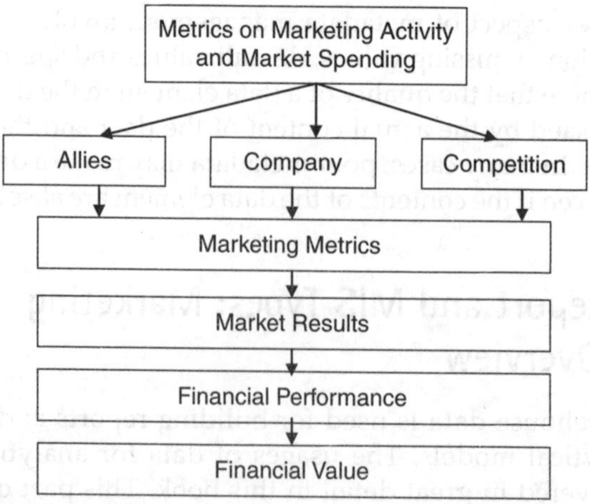


**Figure 8.6** Overview of Marketing Metrics

an engine that will take these inputs and convert them to financial results. It is important to note that the results of marketing activity is not only driven by the marketing activity of the company but is also influenced by the marketing activity of its allies (like channel partners) and competitors. A few examples of metrics around marketing activity include:

- Advertising spend across various media
- Number of direct mails sent for solicitation of new customers (particularly for credit cards and telecom)
- Number of retail outlets, branches, distributors, direct sales agents, telecallers
- Spend and number of point of sales display
- Channel support costs (promotion, commission to sales agents)
- Pricing metrics like interest charged for various types of loans and balances, price at various SKU levels, interest rates offered on various types of deposits, rate plan metrics for telecom, etc

The second level of metrics in the framework aims at investigating the efficiency of the linkage of the marketing activity to customer level metrics. Key examples of customer level metrics include brand awareness, brand perception, customer satisfaction, etc. These metrics are the primary results of the marketing actions and influence customer decision making. Unlike other metrics, these metrics can rarely be calculated from data contained in the operational systems, and one has to rely mostly on customer surveys to obtain these types of metrics. As conducting and tracking customer surveys is a less frequent activity in some industries, these metrics sometimes receive less importance compared to metrics that track observable customer behaviour like sales, attrition, etc. Some of the key metrics of this type are:

- Aided brand recall and unaided brand recall measured from market surveys
- Customer satisfaction measured using customer satisfaction surveys, Net Promoter Score
- Loyalty (measures like the net promoter score propounded by Bain consulting is a good measure that is tracked to access if the customer is willing to recommend the products of the company)
- Number of inbound calls

The third level metrics around results are the set of marketing metrics that are tracked and monitored most closely in every industry. These can be described as the direct measurable impact of the marketing activity. Most of these metrics can also be easily calculated from data in the data warehouse. In fact, most of the reports that are generated out of the data warehouse mostly revolve around these metrics. In specific industries, a few metrics are used as common language for monitoring marketing performance which directly correlates to financial revenue. Some of the metrics of this type are:

- Sales (unit and dollar)
- Revenue measures like average revenue per user (ARPU), a commonly used metric for telecom, premium income for insurance, customer net revenue
- Net receivable (a common metric for all lending products) or outstanding balance
- Outstanding balance (for all deposit business)
- Asset under management (for all investment and insurance businesses)
- Response rate (for direct mailing campaigns)
- Dollar value of loans disbursed, balance transferred

The last two levels of metrics link marketing actions to the ultimate financial goals in terms of profitability and return measures like business income, earnings before interest and taxes, return on total assets, and return on equity.

Metrics are mostly used either for tracking performance, that is, for an evaluative purpose or for finding out root cause for certain problems, that is, for diagnostic purpose. Key usage of metrics includes:

- **Trend analysis and detection of change:** For this purpose, the metrics need to be tracked over time. Any change in data structure or context is extremely critical to filter out changes that are a result of changes in data capture rather than actual changes in business.
- **Measurement and tracking:** Metrics are also used by various levels of management for monitoring the health of the organisation. A dash board approach is mostly used to display key metrics. For an executive, specific colour coding is used to provide a visual representation of problem areas. Key to measurement and tracking is the usage of metrics for drill down analysis.
  - If a specific metric is beyond the expected value, then a set of metrics which contribute in calculating the metric in question are evaluated to drill down so as to identify the root cause of the problem. The supply chain operations reference model (SCOR model) is a very effective framework for calculating metrics relating to the supply chain. It allows for decomposition of a high level metric into various components which help the supply chain manager to drill down and identify the root cause of the problem. As per the SCOR model, a set of lower level metrics are used for calculating metrics at the next higher level. A hierarchy of metrics is defined in such a way that a problem in a particular metric can be tracked to a set of lower level metric that contribute to the higher level metric.
  - Competitive analysis is another key usage of metrics.

Metrics form an important part of management decision making. They are used regularly by top management for monitoring the effectiveness of various strategies and for making changes, if required.

### *8.5.1 MIS and Metrics Framework: An Example of Supply Chain Operations Reference (SCOR) Model*

To illustrate the usage of metrics for analysing business problems the SCOR model has been used as a case study. The reason for using this example as a case study is due to the fact that this model proposed by the Supply Chain Council (SCC) provides a very good approach of drilling down a hierarchy of metrics for identifying the actual business problem.

The (SCOR) is the product of the SCC, an independent, not-for-profit organisation which focuses on improving supply chain management practices across organisations. The SCOR model provides a framework that links business processes and metrics into a unified structure to support better monitoring, control and improvement of all activities related to supply chain management.

The SCOR framework consists of three key elements:

1. **Supply chain processes:** The SCOR framework provides a set of processes that can be used to map the entire supply chain across businesses. These processes extend from the supplier's supplier (the starting node of the supply chain) to the customer's customer (the terminal node of the supply chain)
2. **Supply chain attributes:** Supply chain performance attributes which are important to benchmark a supply chain
3. **Metrics:** Metrics to measure the performance attributes

#### 8.5.1.1 Supply Chain Processes

The SCOR framework identifies five key processes which cover the entire supply chain: plan, source, make, deliver and return, and these processes represent the entire supply chain. Figure 8.7 from the SCC document represents the overview of the process framework.

The definition of the above processes are customised for three sets of supply chain scenarios, namely, made to stock, made to order, engineer to order and retail. Made to stock refers to industries where the product is not made with reference to a customer order but is stocked in anticipation to a customer order; fast moving consumer goods is a typical example. Made to order represents industries where the product is built in response to a particular customer order, typical case in point are industries like aircraft where the aircraft is made only after a customer order is received. Another example is the famous Dell supply chain where the assembly of a desktop

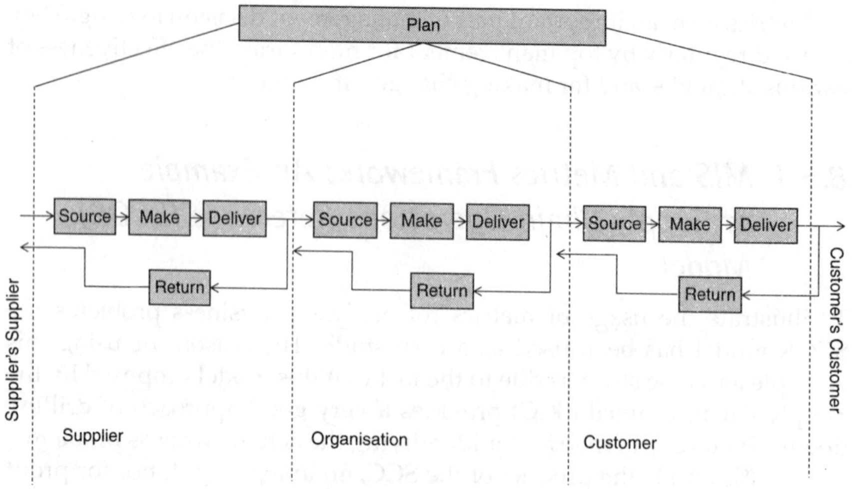


**Figure 8.7** Overview of the SCOR Framework

or a laptop is performed only after an order is received from the customer. Engineer to order scenarios represent industries where the entire specification of the product is designed with reference to a customer order, typical examples are industries like ship building, specialised equipment manufacturing, etc. Retail businesses are in many cases a subset of the made to stock supply chains and represent industries like retail where the manufacturing of the product is not part of the supply chain. The SCOR model defines four levels of these processes: the first is a strategic level where the overall targets are set for the supply chain, the second level involves the configuration of the supply chain whereby the structure of the supply chain is decided. Level three represents the detailed definition of each and every process in the supply chain. The forth level depicts the management processes for managing each of the detailed processes identified in level three.

### 8.5.1.2 Supply Chain Attributes

To effectively benchmark and monitor the performance of the supply chain, the SCOR model identifies five key attributes: reliability, responsiveness, agility, costs, and assets.

- **Reliability:** The reliability attribute addresses the ability to perform tasks as expected. Reliability focuses on the predictability of the outcome of a supply chain process. It measures the accuracy of the processes. Typical metrics for the reliability attribute include: on-time delivery of the right quantity, the right quality, etc.

- **Responsiveness:** Defines the speed with which a supply chain process is performed. Typical measures of responsiveness include cycle time metrics.
- **Agility:** The agility attribute describes the ability to respond to external changes like non-forecasted increases or decreases in demand, suppliers or partners going out of business, natural disasters, labour issues, etc. The KPIs include flexibility and adaptability.
- **Costs:** The cost attribute describes the cost of operating the process. It includes labour costs, material costs, transportation costs, etc. Cost of goods sold and costs of operating the supply chain are key costs metrics.
- **Assets:** The asset management efficiency attribute describes the ability to efficiently utilise assets. Asset management strategies in a supply chain include inventory reduction and in-sourcing vs. outsourcing. Example of key asset management metrics are inventory days of supply and capacity utilisation.

### 8.5.1.3 Metrics

Metrics are used to measure the above attributes and in turn to judge the performance of the supply chain processes. SCOR metrics are diagnostic metrics. SCOR recognises three levels of pre-defined metrics:

Level 1 metrics are indicators of the overall health of the supply chain. These are also known as strategic metrics or key performance indicators (KPI). Monitoring of these metrics allows for establishing objectives and strategic priorities.

Level 2 metrics serve as diagnostic for level 1 metrics and level 3 metrics in turn are diagnostic for level 2 metrics. The analysis of performance on the basis of metrics from level 1 through 3 is referred to as decomposition. Decomposition helps identify the processes that need to be changed in order to achieve the target performance level of the level 1 attribute in question. Most metrics in the SCOR framework are hierarchical, just as the process elements are hierarchical. Higher level metrics are created from lower level metrics.

Figure 8.8 represents a typical set of SCOR metrics with the objective of illustrating the use of metrics for drill down and problem diagnostic.

Each of the level 1 metric is composed of a set of level 2 metrics. The contribution or weight of each level 2 metric in determining the level 1 metric is determined either by pre-determined business rules or by expert judgement. The relative benchmark of each level 2 metric also varies with the type of the metric. In Fig. 8.9 the high and the low demarcation in the level 2 metrics suggest the relative benchmark for each of the level 2 metrics. As an example, the level 1 metric perfect order fulfilment is composed of the following level 2 metrics:

- Percentage orders delivered in full
- Delivery performances to customer committed date

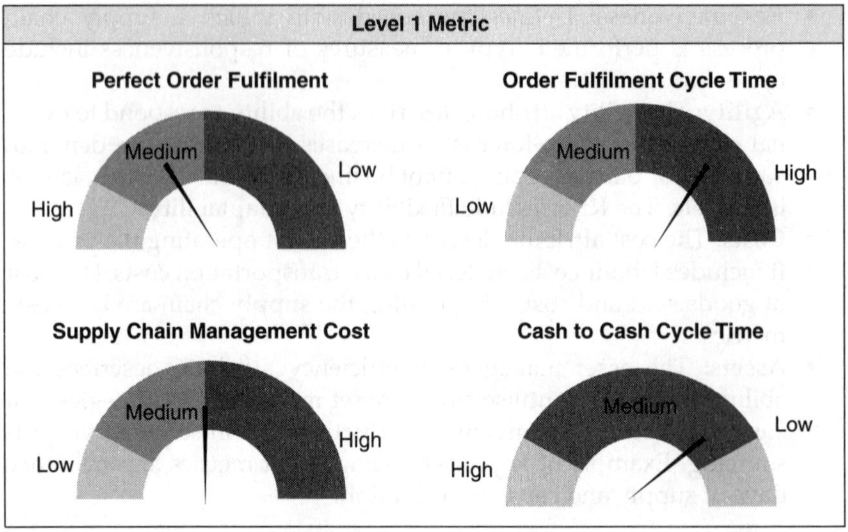


**Figure 8.8** Sample Level-1 SCOR Metrics

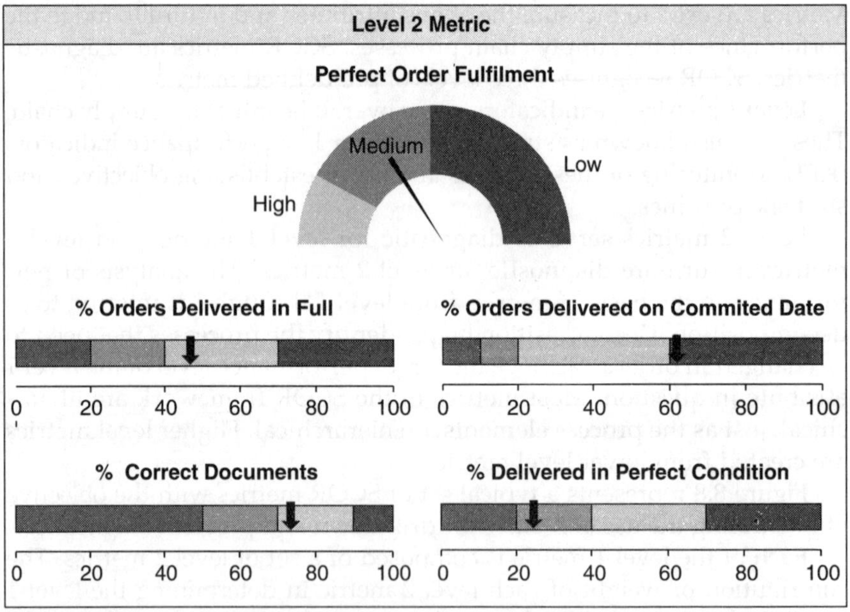


**Figure 8.9** Sample Level-2 SCOR Metrics

- Documentation accuracy
- Percentage orders delivered/installed in perfect condition

Level 2 metrics are decomposed to obtain a set of level 3 metrics. Level 3 metrics are also further decomposed by various dimensions like product type, sales region, customer type, etc. This allows for problem detection and analysis. Figure 8.10 depicts a sample drill down. Level 3 metrics are also plotted across time to obtain a view of changes in performance over time, such changes can be mapped back to find out the root cause of the problem. For example, a breakdown in a plant or introduction of new staff members may be responsible for the problem. In this case, it can be seen that a less than expected performance in percentage order fulfilment is driven by two major factors. The first is a drop in accurate shipment for product "C" and the second is the drop in invoice accuracy for product "C". These two aspects clearly suggest that some changes in the dispatch processes for product "C" must be responsible for the drop in performance.

The interested reader can refer to the SCC website for a complete set of SCOR metrics.

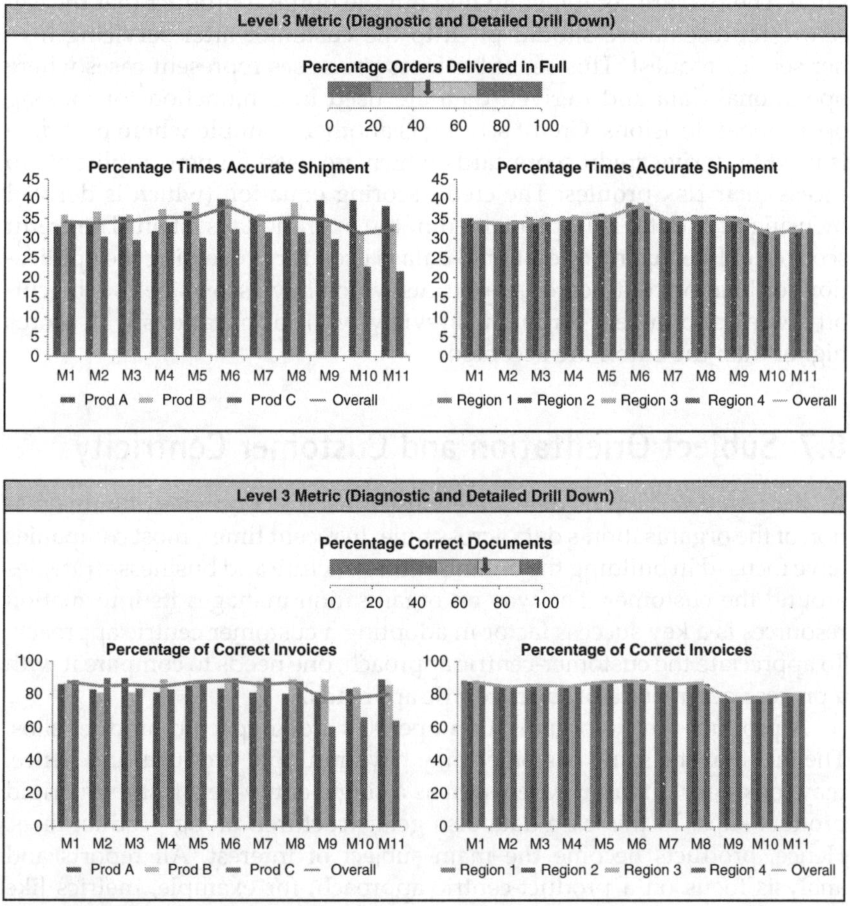


**Figure 8.10** Sample Level-3 SCOR Metrics

## 8.6 Real-time Decision Making: Combined Usage of Operational Data and Derived Data

A key distinction between operational data and derived data is that the operational data is mostly used for transaction processing, while data in the data warehouse is mostly used for reporting and analysis. However, with the increased use of predictive analytics for driving business decision making, the above paradigm is witnessing a significant change. In many cases, derived data is used to drive decisions which are implemented in processing various transactions. Analytical strategies and predictive models based on derived data are increasingly being used for making transaction processing decisions. For example, if a customer calls in to the call centre, a set of models and rules are applied on his/her past transaction and demographic data to evaluate the probability of the customer purchasing another product and the expected revenue from the same. The two are combined to find out the optimal product that the call centre representative should pitch to the customer after servicing his/her service request. This set of business processes represent cases where operational data and derived data are used in conjunction for making operational decisions. Credit scoring is another example where past data is used to derive credit score cards which are used on new applicants to access their risk profiles. The credit scoring equation (which is derived by using past data) is implemented in the operational system. The credit score calculated using operational data is used for processing the application for loan or credit card. Applicants which have scores below the cutoff are rejected or sent for manual review, while applications with scores higher than the cutoff are accepted.

## 8.7 Subject Orientation and Customer Centricity

As discussed earlier, the data warehouse is a subject-oriented summarisation of the organisation's data across time. In recent times, most companies have focused in building the organisation structure and business strategies around the customer. The way an organisation manages its information resources is a key success factor in adopting a customer centric approach. To appreciate the customer-centric approach, one needs to compare it with a process-centric or a product-centric approach.

A product-centric organisation operates along specific product silos. The fact that the same customer may have multiple products and hence, may look very different when seen as a single entity gets lost in the rigid product silos. In this case data also gets structured along product lines. Hence, products become the main subject of interest. All reports and analysis focus on a product-centric approach; for example, metrics like profitability, servicing costs, customer value are calculated and forecasted at the product level. For instance, in a bank with multiple product lines like credit cards, mortgage, savings and investment, etc. if account profitability is considered along product lines only, then a credit card customer who has low balance and never revolves on his credit card would be tagged as low profitability customer. However, the fact that the same customer may have a mortgage or an investment account with a very high balance gets neglected. This results in the customer receiving below average service when he or she calls to the credit card call centre or receives a collection call if he or she is out of the country and forgets a payment. The end result is customer dissatisfaction and possible attrition. In case of a product centric organization, key performance indicators and performance benchmark for managers also get organised around product-centric drivers like product profitability, servicing costs, etc. This results in management focus along narrow product-centric metrics.

Similar to a product-centric approach, the process-centric approach is also aimed at structuring the organisation construct around processes like sales, servicing, customer management, collection, etc. Similar to the product-centric approach, the process-centric approach also focuses on optimising the key processes which may result in a sub-optimal return for the firm as a whole. The chapters on "Cross-Sell" and "Retention Management" discussed the importance of the customer centric approach for cross-sell and retention.

The need for a customer-centric approach is well understood by all managers. However, in many cases it is the limitation of the data systems which presents tremendous hurdles in implementing a customer-centric strategy. The data warehouse is a key enabler in providing what is usually called a "360 degree customer view". The 360 degree customer view is the first building block of implementing any customer-centric strategy. Hence, the customer is the most important subject for designing any data warehouse and for creating all reports and analytical framework that aims at utilising data from the warehouse. Closely related to the customer centric concept, is the concept of Customer Lifetime Value (CLV). Customer Lifetime Value refers to the present value of all future profits obtained from a customer over the life of his/her relationship with the firm. This concept is also sometimes referred to as CLTV. Many researchers like Ang and Taylor, in their work titled *Managing Customer Profitability Using Portfolio Matricies* have used customer tenure and gross margin for estimating customer value. It needs to be noted that, in case of a multiproduct company, one needs to take into account gross margin across products for estimating customer value. Customer lifetime value is more difficult to estimate, because one needs to predict future profits and probability of attrition for calculating customer lifetime value. While estimating future profits, it is critical not only to estimate profits expected from the current set of product that the customer is holding, but also to estimate cross-sell opportunities and profits arising out of the same. A customer centric approach is critical for arriving at the right measure for customer lifetime value.

## 8.8 Customer Relationship Management (CRM)

The idea of customer centricity was introduced by Theodore Levitt in the 1960. He suggested that the purpose of every business is to create and keep customers satisfied and hence, every business process is part of the integrated effort by the business to create and satisfy customers. The idea of understanding the customer, servicing them and creating a long-term relationship with them is quite old. However, building and sustaining a lasting relationship with a large customer base (often running into millions) is a tough challenge. Companies need to put in place the right business processes, the right technology platforms, the right data management strategy and the right analytics to create a long-term relationship with a large customer base. To build long-term relationship with the customer, every part of the business needs to have the same understanding of every customer and need to have an integrated interface with every customer. Today most companies have millions of customers who use multiple channels to interact with the company; creating and managing relationship in such a scenario is a gigantic task. Customer Relationship Management (CRM) encompasses the strategy, process, tools, and technologies, which help companies implement a customer-centric business strategy.

The term customer relationship management was formally introduced by Berry in 1983, though other researchers had identified the importance of long-term relationship earlier, particularly in the context of business-to-business marketing. An attempt to define CRM brings into fore the many perspectives that researchers and practitioners use to describe relationship marketing. Jagdish Seth and Atul Parvatiyar have provided a comprehensive summary of the various perspectives used for defining CRM. Table 8.3 provides a summary of the key perspectives described in their work titled *Customer Relationship Management: Emerging Practice, Process, and Discipline.*

It is apparent from the above set of perspectives that it is difficult to have a one size fit all definition of CRM. In many cases, different departments within an organisation have different definitions for CRM. Information technology may look at CRM more from a system implementation perspective, sales and service may view it more from a channel integration perspective, while marketing may look at CRM more a for long-term customer relationship development perspective. Hence, it would be wiser to bear in mind that CRM means all the above aspects (and may be even more). The current section will focus on the reasons why companies are increasingly looking at CRM and then attempt to develop a framework for CRM. The next few sections provide an overview of CRM, beginning with an outline of the drivers, which have propelled companies in adopting CRM as a strategy for enhancing profitability. This is followed by a section wherein various perspectives of CRM have also been presented starting with the strategic decision making perspective and followed by the functional and technology perspectives. In the concluding section, a brief overview of common CRM tools have been provided.

**Table 8.3** Overview of Key CRM Perspectives

| Key Perspective | Definition |
|---|---|
| Database marketing | Database marketing represents the promotional aspects of marketing using customer information. It centres on identifying customers or prospects for various marketing campaigns using in-house information or information sourced from outside. |
| Customer retention and loyalty | The customer retention approach to CRM focuses on using a variety of after marketing tactics that lead to customer bonding or staying in touch with the customer after a sale is made. This is expected to create a longer relationship with the customer. As shown in a number of leading studies, acquiring new customers is costlier than retaining existing ones. Hence, the retention perspective of CRM tries to underscore the importance of building a relationship with the customer to drive customer retention and hence, higher returns for the firm. The emergence of the service sector as a key economic driver has helped in propelling the importance of this perspective as these industries tend to have a longer term relationship with the customer. Service industries like banking and telecom are also characterised by heavily loaded up front customer acquisition costs and returns over the customer lifetime. Hence, a shorter customer lifetime means a much reduced profitability for these industries |
| Building customised one-to-one relationship | The perspective of one-to-one marketing focuses on the direct interaction between the producer and the buyer that existed in the pre-industrial revolution era. Such a direct one-to-one relationship allowed the producer to customise his offerings to the exact need of each customer. Today the one-to-one relationship management perspective refers to the application of information technology to focus on individual or one-to-one relationships with customers that integrate database knowledge with a long-term customer retention and growth strategy. The emergence of the web as an interactive channel of communication between the company and the buyer has enabled a slew of customisation initiatives like Dell's website allowing customers to configure their computers. Recently many credit card and telecom players have started offering the flexibility of designing a credit card or a telecom plan by the end customer |

(*Continued*)

**Table 8.3** Overview of Key CRM Perspectives (*Continued*)

| Key Perspective | Definition |
|---|---|
| Harnessing customer centricity for enhancing quality of customer relationship | Another key perspective that is very often talked about in relation to CRM is customer centricity. All marketing activities of the company should be directed towards establishing and enriching relationship with the customer. This perspective is more important for the service industry where the final product (that is service) is produced and consumed at the same instant and hence, relationship is the key driver of satisfaction. |
| Long-term relationship development for driving the firm's success | The importance of developing long-term relationship with the customer has been most widely recognised by the business to business marketing companies. This perspective focuses on building co-operative and collaborative relationship with a long-term orientation rather than short-term transactional orientation. This approach also highlights the need to focus on long-term metrics for measuring marketing success rather than relying on short-term metrics for defining success. Long-term metrics like customer loyalty, attrition rate are more critical for measuring the health of customer relationship. |
| Customer selectivity | The customer selectivity perspective focuses on the fact that not all customers are equally profitable. The company therefore must be selective in tailoring its programme and marketing efforts by segmenting and selecting appropriate customers for individual marketing programmes. However, the objective of a company is not really to prune its customer base but to identify the programmes and methods that would be the most profitable for each customer segment. |
| Business process and information technology | The business process and IT perspective of CRM is the one which is most commonly encountered in the practitioner community. CRM implies the integration of all operational systems in such a way that they share the same view of the customer. This implies that data from all operational systems needs to be integrated and all operational systems should have the same view of the customer. The corporate data warehouse is an important piece in this integration. It works as a backbone that collects data from all operational system and creates a single customer view which is shared by all systems across the organization. This is a typical case where operational systems need to use data warehouse derived data for transaction processing. However this approach presents a challenge because derived data always suffer from wrinkle of time and a customer who has just updated a phone number in a particular system will not see the updated phone number if he or she accesses a second system within the time needed for updating the data warehouse. Hence, CRM also calls for significant integration effort between operational systems as well. |

### 8.8.1 *Drivers of CRM*

Several changes in the business landscape over the past several years have propelled companies to look at CRM as a way of remaining profitable and for getting ahead of competition. The growth of the service industry and focus on customer service has been a major driver for CRM adoption across industries. Service quality has become a major factor in enhancing customer satisfaction. Companies have realized the importance of CRM for providing better and customized services. In addition, the increase in the number of channels used for selling and servicing have made it important for companies to integrate their processes and provide an uniform customer view across all channels. CRM has become extremely critical for integrating multiple channels and providing an uniform customer experience across all channels. Systems selling and a focus on total quality management have been important drivers for companies in the B2B markets to adopt CRM.

### 8.8.2 *CRM as a Set of Strategic Decision-making Processes*

In many cases, the technology and business process focus robs the attention from the strategic focus that is critical for the success of CRM initiatives. Sheth and Parvatiyar in their works titled *Customer Relationship Management: Emerging Practice, Process, and Discipline* and *Relationship Marketing in Consumer Markets: Antecedents and Consequences* have highlighted a set of strategic decision making that are involved in building, implementing and improving the CRM framework in an organisation. Figure 8.11 mostly adopted from their work depict the set of strategic decisions that define the CRM process.

The first set of strategic decisions involve decisions around relationship formation; typically a firm needs to ask itself why it needs a relationship marketing framework and with whom? As discussed earlier, the customer selectivity perspective is an important dimension for relationship marketing. The firm needs to identify key customer segments. The relationship strategy may differ across each of these segments.

For example, an affluent high-end smartphone user will be treated very differently by a mobile operator as compared to a predominantly SMS and voice call user. The other important aspect of relationship formation involves identification of the overall objective of creating a relationship marketing programme. The overall objective can be two fold, one involves an enhancement of marketing efficiency and the other involves enhancing marketing effectiveness. Lowering marketing costs, enhancing operational efficiency and reducing customer churn are typical examples of ways of enhancing marketing efficiency. Offering personalised services, anticipating customer needs in advance, enhancing customer loyalty, and creating

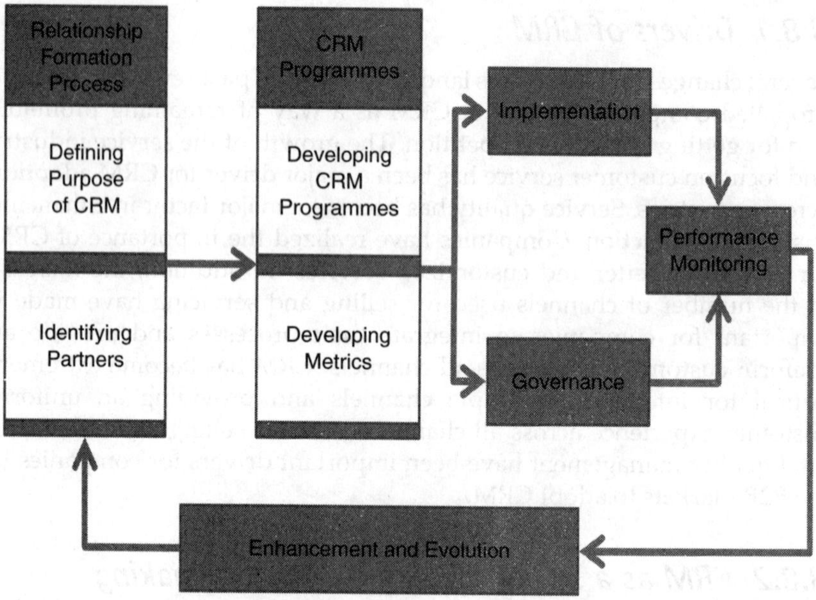


**Figure 8.11** CRM as a Strategic Decision Making Process

new products or markets are typical measures of marketing effectiveness. The objective of a relationship marketing programme is both enhancement of effectiveness and efficiency of the marketing processes; however, the details of the same needs to be worked out carefully to come up with metrics that should be created for measuring and monitoring the CRM process. Also the objectives can be quite different for specific customer segments. The objectives can be more around efficiency for the value seeking customer while it is likely to be more around effectiveness for the relatively lower volume of high end segment.

The next set of strategic decisions involve developing a set of programmes that will help the firm achieve the marketing objectives. The firm needs to test these programmes by rolling out test campaigns. The cycle of "Programme Identification—Testing—Learning—Rolling Out" should be a continuous process. Closely linked with programme development is the requirement for identifying the set of metrics that may be used to measure and track each programme.

The other strategic decisions involve decisions around implementation, governance and monitoring processes. The implementation process is more of a technology and business process re-engineering decision that will help in implementing the set of CRM programmes identified. The set of governance processes involve decisions around organisation structure, incentive structure and the key performance indicators (KPIs) that needs to be put in place for ensuring the success of the CRM programme.

The last two stages involve a roadmap for monitoring the relationship marketing process and for creation of a plan for the evolution of the CRM process. Like most other initiatives that aim at changing the way an organisation functions, CRM is also best suited for a phased approach rather than a big bang implementation approach. The evolution roadmap helps in creating a long-term plan of evolving the firm's relationship marketing strategy over time.

## 8.8.3 CRM as a Set of Functions

Many researchers have also adopted a functional view of CRM because it essentially involves various functions (or functional groups) that must work in conjunction to make it a success. One of the key works in this area is by Joseph Chan, in his work titled *Toward a Unified View of Customer Relationship Management* he presents an interesting functional view of CRM. Figure 8.12 depicts the same.

The functional approach identifies a set of key functions that are important for creating, managing and sustaining relationship marketing. Joseph Chan has categorised them into operational, conceptual, analytical, technical, and enterprise information CRM functions.

At the heart of the CRM framework sits the functions that creates the CRM strategy, this function can be looked upon as the conceptual CRM function that builds the whole conceptual framework around

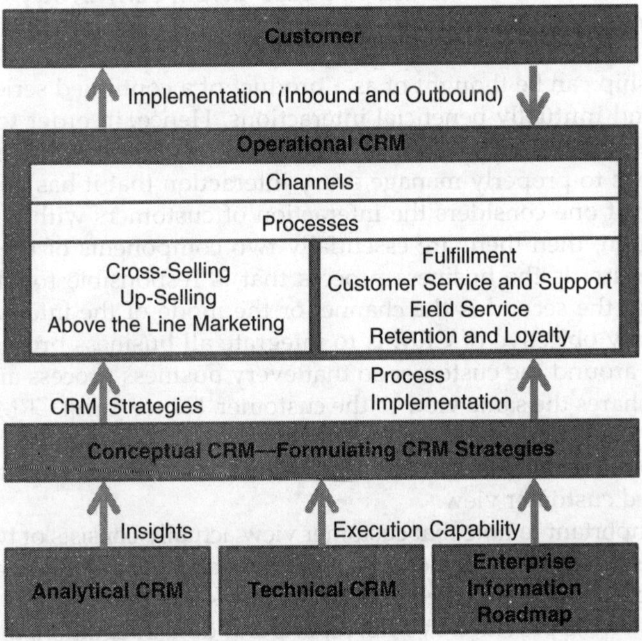


**Figure 8.12** CRM as a Set of Functions

CRM. The conceptual CRM function is responsible for setting up the overall objectives for the CRM function, for identifying the customer segments and the relationship marketing programmes for each segment, the metrics for measurement and finally a plan for implementation, governance, and future evolution. Operational CRM can be thought of as the function that implements the strategies devised by the conceptual CRM function.

The analytical CRM, technical CRM and the information CRM are the building blocks that are necessary for devising and implementing the CRM strategy. The analytical CRM function provides the analytical insights necessary for CRM strategy development. Most common analytical insights involve segmentation of the customer base, prediction of response and profitability for marketing campaigns, creation of an objective measure of customer value, prediction of chance of attrition, etc. The technical CRM provides the technology infrastructure for implementing CRM processes. Technical CRM provides a unified platform for sales, service, campaign implementation, and customer service. A key requirement for CRM is the unified customer view and a customer-centric information architecture that allows each operational unit to share the same customer view and also allows them to have knowledge of past customer interactions in other units. The enterprise information architecture aims at feeding the CRM engine with the raw material of data which is possibly the starting point of any CRM implementation.

### *8.8.4 CRM as a Business Process and Technology Implementation Initiative*

Relationship can be thought of as a product of a continued series of satisfying and mutually beneficial interactions. Hence, in order to build a sustained and mutually beneficial relationship with its customers, a company needs to properly manage every interaction that it has with every customer. If one considers the interaction of customers with a business organisation, then there are essentially two components of the interaction. The first is the business process that is responsible for the interaction and the second is the channel or the mode of the interaction. So the primary objective of CRM is to integrate all business processes and channels around the customer so that every business process and every channel shares the same view of the customer. Hence, most CRM focuses on these three important aspects: business processes that interact with the customer, channels that are used to interact with the customer, and the unified customer view.

It is important to note that customer view actually consists of two parts: the first is what the customer looks like now and the second is based on how the customer is expected to behave or look like in the future. The first of these views is provided by MIS, reports and data integration; the second is provided by predictive tools that attempts to forecast future customer behaviour like response to a campaign, chance of attrition, etc. Figure 8.13 provides a view of the CRM components, taking into account the common features of CRM presented by consultants and technology vendors like Accenture, Oracle, Diamond Consulting, Forrester, Gartner.

### 8.8.5 CRM Software Overview

The CRM software market is quite diverse and complex because of the multiple perspectives that one can use for evaluating a CRM solution. A brief overview of the key players has been provided based on Forrester research publication (*The Forrester Wave™: CRM Suites for Large Organisations*, Q2 2010 by William Band).

*Oracle Siebel CRM and SAP CRM* Siebel is one of the most comprehensive and widely used CRM software which was bought over by Oracle Corporation sometime back. SAP's CRM along with Siebel offers all comprehensive functionalities across every CRM module (marketing, order management, contact centre management, sales force management, partner management, customer service and analytics). However, both of these have relatively longer implementation time frame and are mostly installed in the premise and not as Software as a Service (SaaS). Both of these tools now provide rapid implementation methodologies and easier integration with other applications to tide over the long installation time and higher total cost of ownership.

*CDC Pivotal, Microsoft Dynamics, Oracle CRM on Demand, RightNow, and Salesforce.com* These set of tools are mostly available in the SaaS mode, which makes it easier and less costly to implement. These tools do not have the extensive set of features that are present in a tool like Siebel or SAP CRM; however, they tend to specialise in certain aspects of the complete suite of CRM functionalities. Salsforce.com, for example, is very well known for sales force automation. Similarly Microsoft Dynamics is very well known for its customer service module. Forrester research in its report notes that "Although these players are not full-featured across the board, they are gaining the acceptance by both large and mid sized organisations looking for fast time-to-value and flexible solutions".

*Oracle EBS CRM and Oracle PeopleSoft CRM* These products are of interest to companies which use the PeopleSoft system or the Oracle EBS suite for enterprise resource planning (ERP) applications because they offer easy integration. According to Forrester research "Both products offer strong capabilities across the broad footprint of most CRM functionalities, including marketing, sales, service, field service, and partner channel management, but they remain less robust for customer data management and eCommerce".

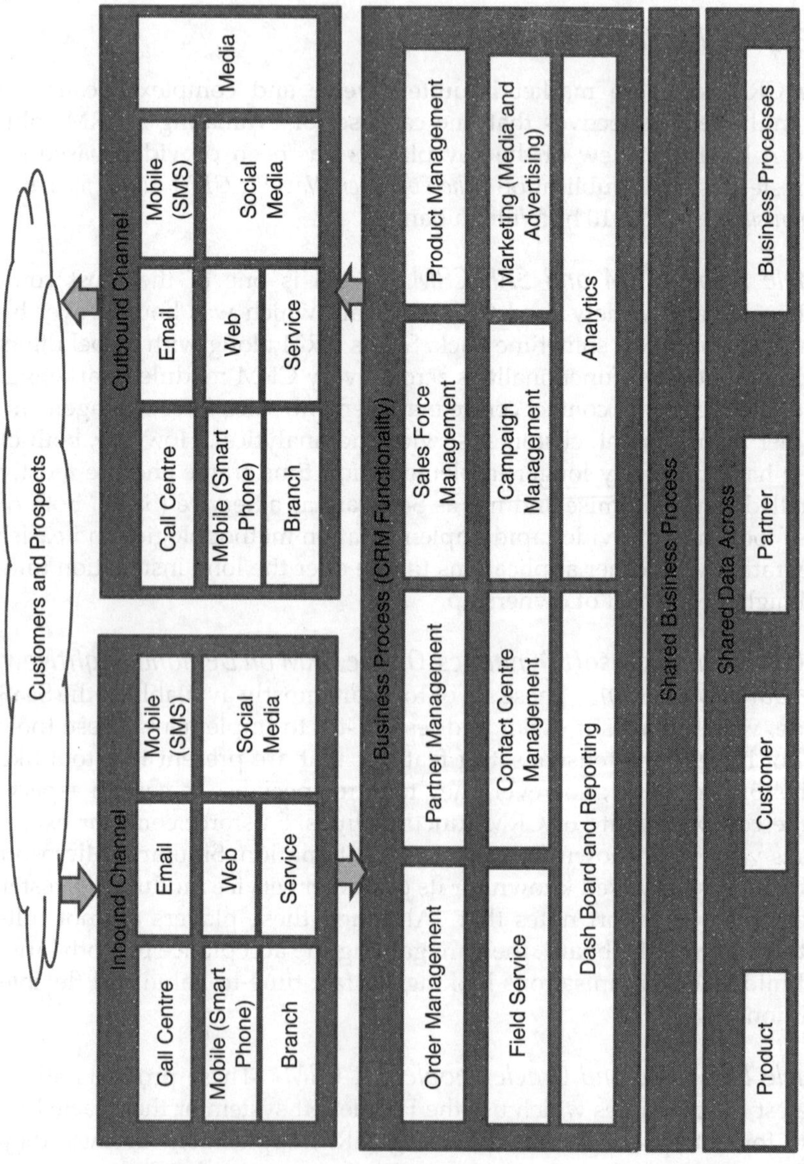


**Figure 8.13** Technology and Implementation Perspective of CRM

*Chordiant Software, Pegasystems and Sword Ciboodle* These tools offer extensive business process management capabilities and can support unique and highly customised process flows. Hence, they approach CRM from a business process management. Pegasystems has recently acquired Chordiant.

*FrontRange Solutions, Maximiser Software, NetSuite, SageCRM, Sage SalesLogix and SugarCRM* These companies provide CRM solutions mostly for mid- and small-sized enterprises. They are relatively less costly and provide limited functionalities.

*TIBCO* TIBCO has traditionally been a middle ware provider, which helped in integrating data across multiple operational systems. Recently TIBCO has started moving into the CRM space, it has recently acquired Spotfire which has strong CRM capabilities. It has also acquired Loyalty Lab which specialises in loyalty management.

## 8.9 Campaign Management

In most cases, the end result of any analytical marketing strategy involves a campaign, which target a certain set of customers with a specific offer so as to elicit certain behaviour. Hence, a proper framework for implementing and managing marketing campaigns is essential for the success of any analytical strategy. As discussed earlier, most CRM software and tools have a dedicated campaign management module. Specific software tools dedicated solely to campaign management are also used by certain companies. Irrespective of the tool that is used, it is necessary to have a set of robust business process for testing, implementing and tracking campaigns.

### *8.9.1 Types of Campaign*

Marketing campaigns can be classified along various dimensions. The first and most common dimension involves how the campaign attempts to reach its desired audience. From this perspective campaigns can be classified as above the line (ATL) and below the line (BTL) campaigns.

#### 8.9.1.1 Above the Line Campaigns

The communication in an above the line campaign is not targeted specifically to any set of customers but is exposed to a wider audience (both customers and non-customers). For example, an advertisement in a newspaper, television or billboard is not directed at a specific set of customers. An above the line campaign is mostly used in cases where the offer or the marketing proposition is not specifically customised to a set of target customers or prospects.

Above the line campaigns mostly aim at influencing a wider range of customers and prospects. The aims of an above the line campaign is not only to drive communication about a specific offer but also to create awareness and interest about the brand in general. Hence, an above the line campaign may yield secondary benefits of enhancing awareness and interest about the brand, along with the primary aim of communicating the specific offer. However, the biggest limitation of above the line campaigns are the lack of customisation of the offer which results in a "one size fit all" offer and the lack of the ability of choosing specific customers or prospects who should be targeted for the offer. However, in some cases, it is possible to create an above the line campaign, which is targeted to a specific customer segment. For instance, many companies create above the line campaigns targeting heavy users with discounts, special offers or superior services. This has the twin benefit of communicating the offer to all heavy users and creating a desire and call to action for other users to become heavy users so that they can enjoy superior services or higher discounts. However, one has to keep in mind that the level of customisation of the offer in above the line campaigns is quite limited. As an example if a company wishes to offer a 5% discount for a specific set of customers and a 20% discount for another set of customers then communicating such an offer through above the line campaigns is quite difficult. The second limitation of an above the line campaign involves the lack of specific targeting. Hence, in order to ensure that all intended prospects or customers have received the message, it is required to over communicate which involves higher costs. Irrespective of these limitations, above the line campaigns remain one of the most important ways of reaching out to customers and prospects particularly for industries like consumer packaged goods, where the offer and product propositions are not highly customised.

Though the roll out and implementation of an above the line campaign is relatively simpler, yet testing and measuring the impact of these campaigns pose very difficult challenges. The difficulty in measuring the benefits of an above the line campaign stems from two basic problems: the first is the difficulty of creating a treatment (test) vs. control group and the second is the difficulty of measuring the secondary effects of the campaign. The section on test vs. control measurement, in the current chapter discusses methodologies of creating proxy control groups for measuring the impact of above the line campaigns.

#### 8.9.1.2 Below the Line Campaigns

As opposed to above the line, below the line campaigns involve targeting specific customers or prospects through channels like direct mailers, telemarketing, emails. As the communication is directed to specific customers or prospects, it is possible to customise the offer for each recipient and it is also possible to exclude certain sets of customers from the offer. Below the line campaigns could either be **outbound** or **inbound**. An outbound below the line campaign is more common and involves the company reaching out to specific customers or prospects. Inbound campaigns involve reaching to customers when they contact the company either for a service request or for resolving a query.

In case of below the line campaigns, it is possible to control who receives the offer communication. Hence, the limitations of above the line campaigns around measuring and testing are not applicable for below the line campaigns. However, below the line campaigns are not able to create brand awareness, interest and desire which above the line campaigns can. Hence, most companies use a judicious mix of above the line and below the line campaigns to optimise the effect on revenue and profitability. It is also important to note that above the line campaigns also positively impact the results of below the line campaigns. For example, if a customer watches an advertisement on television and then receives a direct mailer from a company, then the effect may be higher compared to a direct mailer alone. Hence, it is important to come up with measures that take into account the holistic effect of all marketing activities including all above the line and below the line campaigns. This section will focus more on below the line campaign.

## 8.9.2 Campaign Management Framework

Designing and executing a below the line campaign involves a large number of decisions on the part of marketers and operations managers. In order to ensure the success of a campaign, it is important to align analytical, marketing, operations and technology functions so that they work in tandem to deliver the final campaign results. Figure 8.14 presents a broad overview of a generic campaign management framework for below the line campaigns. The framework (with some minor modifications) is applicable to above the line campaigns as well. The framework (depicted in Fig. 8.14) is not a "one-size-fits-all" campaign management solution but attempts to put together the various perspectives that need to be considered to ensure success of a campaign.

The next part of this section will provide an outline of each of the major steps involved in designing and executing a successful campaign.

### 8.9.2.1 Defining Campaign Objective

The first step in conceptualising a marketing campaign involves identification of the objective of the campaign. The objective of a campaign can be to acquire new customers, increase usage from existing customers, reactivate dormant customers, prevent customer churn, win back lost customers, cross-sell more products to existing customers, up-sell or upgrade existing customers. Before planning a campaign, the marketer needs to identify the overall objective of the campaign and if possible put a hard metric around the objective. For example, the objective of an

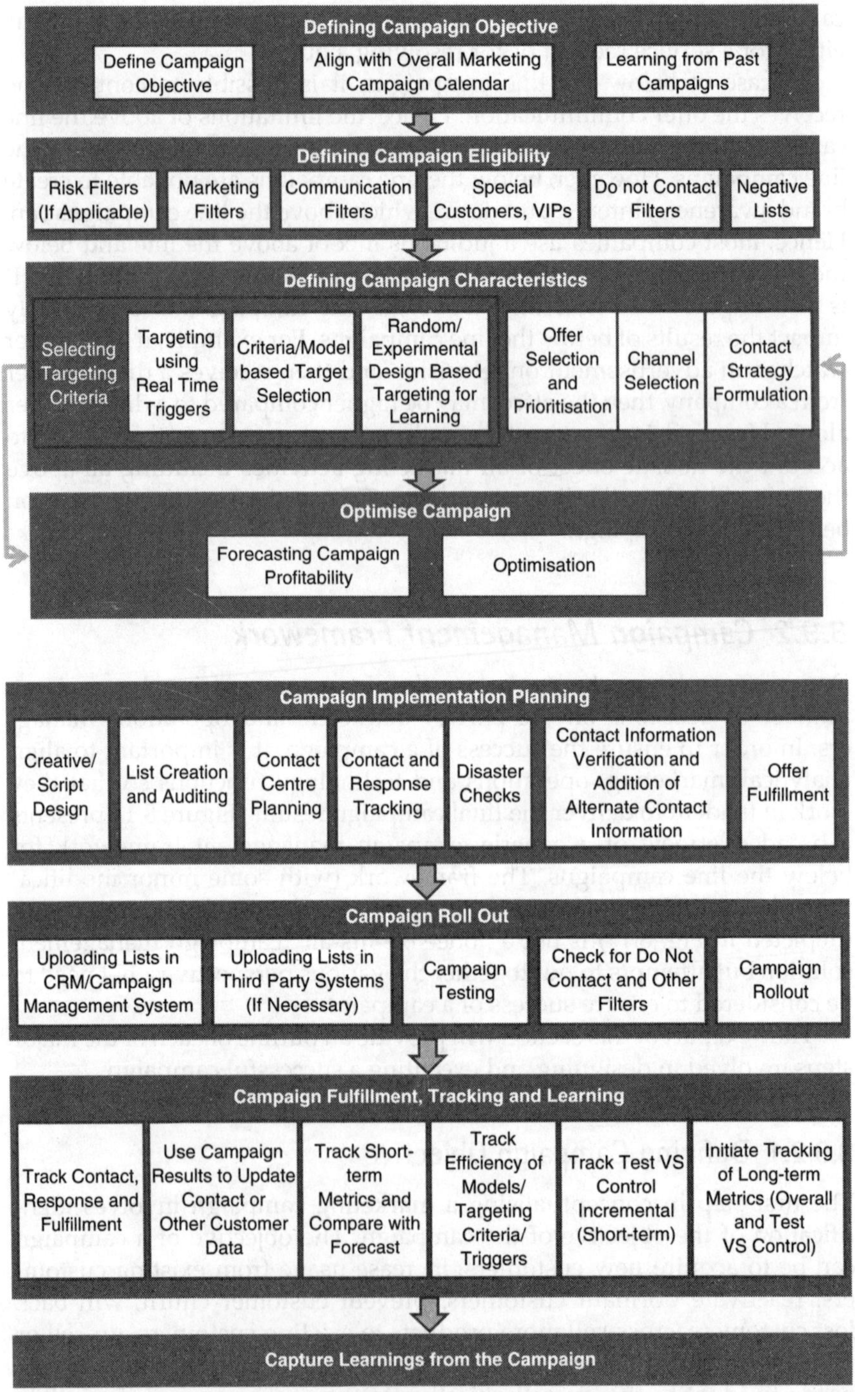


**Figure 8.14** Campaign Management Framework

acquisition campaign can be as simple as "adding at least 10,000 new customers" or the objective of an activation campaign can be to "reactivate at least 10% of all current inactive customers" or the objective of a churn management campaign can be to "reduce voluntary churn by 5% in the next six months". When one looks at these objectives, a natural question arises as to how much of the final result can be attributed to the campaign and how much is the result of natural changes in the business strategy or competition? To elaborate this point further, one can find that at the end of six months of monthly churn management campaigns, the churn rate has indeed gone down and one may be tempted to attribute the success to the churn management campaign that has been running. However, it may well have been the case that a low-cost competitor has gone out of business and that has reduced the options available to customers. Hence, the company would have still seen lesser churn even without the campaign being in place. A test vs. control measurement is frequently used to answer such questions. Some of these issues around measuring the impact of the campaign will be taken up in the sub-section on campaign tracking.

Another aspect of designing a campaign involves alignment of the campaign with the overall marketing calendar. The marketing organisation in any company will have an integrated communication plan for the year that will include all above the line and below the line campaigns. It is important that every out bound or in bound campaign is aligned to the overall communication plan in terms of timing, offer and message. For example, a telecom company may be running above the line campaigns promoting a rate plan which involves very low per minute call rates. At the same time, the company may be running a campaign for increasing usage from the existing customers and the campaign for increasing usage may be promoting an offer with a call rate higher than the call rate promoted in the above the line campaign. This kind of contradiction creates a negative impact in the mind of the customer. It is also important to pace the frequency of marketing campaigns for a particular customer in such a way that customers do not get irritated by the bombardment of too many campaigns.

It is important to have a common archive of past campaign results so that the same can be used in determining the characteristics of future campaigns. Past campaign results are very valuable in designing targeting rules, offer and channel preferences so as to reach out to the right customer, with the right offer through the right channel. In many cases, it is important to test certain offers and campaigns so that it is possible to develop learning from the test result which can be used for designing future campaigns. In such cases, a test plan based on design of experiments needs to be put in place so as to test a wide variety of scenarios which will produce enough learnings to be utilised in designing future campaigns. The section on usage of design of experiments will discuss this in greater detail.

### 8.9.2.2 Defining Campaign Eligibility

The first step in designing a campaign involves defining the customers or prospects that are eligible for the campaign. As shown in Fig. 8.14, the following key filters are used to identify customers or prospects that should "not" be part of the campaign.

- **Risk filters:** In case of products like loans, credit cards, post-paid mobile/fixed telecom services, etc., it is important to judge the risk profile of the customer or the prospect before making an offer. Hence, some of the risky customers are excluded from many marketing campaigns. Risk filters are mostly designed by the risk management department, and are provided as a set of exclusion rules for the marketing department.
- **Marketing filters:** In addition to the risk filters, many campaigns may have a set of filters to exclude customers who may not be the right customers for the campaign. For example, many campaigns may exclude customers who have not been active for a long time. It is important to note that the difference between marketing filters and targeting rules may be quite blurred in many cases. Many of the marketing filters can be applied as targeting rules as well. However, the difference between marketing filters and targeting rules is that if a customer who is supposed to be filtered out by the marketing filter receives the offer, then it will have some negative impact in terms of customer perception; however, if a customer who is not selected by the targeting rule receives the offer, then there will be no undesirable effect.
- **Communication filters:** With increased intensity of competition, customers tend to receive a large number of marketing offers from various companies through multiple channels. These multitudes of offers tend to cause customer fatigue and irritation. Hence, it is important to limit the offers that go out from the company to a customer. Most companies create a rule limiting the frequency of various types of communication. The interval between various types of communications is decided in a way, so as to limit customer fatigue arising out of multiple communications from the same company. The grid in Table 8.4 is an example; it shows the limit in number of days between various types of campaigns. It is important that all communications must be included in the communication grid so as to have a unified view of all communications going out of the company.
- **Special customers:** Many campaigns exclude special customers, VIPs
- **Do not contact list:** Most countries have some legislation around customers opting out of marketing campaigns; while executing campaigns companies need to ensure that all customers who have opted out of marketing communications are excluded. In addition,

**Table 8.4** Sample Communication Grid

| | Limit Rules for Contact Frequency | Prior History | | | | | | | | | | | | | | | | |
|---|---|---|---|---|---|---|---|---|---|---|---|---|---|---|---|---|---|---|
| | | Cross-Sell Direct Mail | Cross-Sell Telecall | Cross-Sell Email | Usage Mail | Usage Telecall | Usage Email | Usage SMS alert | Anti Attrition Call | Anti Attrition Direct Mail | Anti Attrition Telecall | Inbound Service Call | Inbound Call for Service | Inbound Call Fee Reversal (Reversed) | Inbound Call Fee Reversal (Not Reversed) | Reminder Call for Not Paying Bill on Time | Welcome Call | Birthday Mailer |
| Current Campaign | Cross-Sell Direct Mial | 60 | 90 | 30 | 30 | 30 | 30 | 30 | 10 | 10 | 10 | 10 | 0 | 0 | 90 | 90 | 30 | 0 |
| | Cross-Sell Telecall | 30 | 90 | 30 | 30 | 30 | 30 | 30 | 10 | 10 | 10 | 10 | 0 | 0 | 90 | 90 | 30 | 0 |
| | Cross-Sell Email | 30 | 30 | 30 | 30 | 30 | 30 | 30 | 10 | 10 | 10 | 10 | 0 | 0 | 90 | 90 | 30 | 0 |
| | Usage Mail | 30 | 30 | 30 | 60 | 90 | 30 | 10 | 10 | 10 | 10 | 10 | 0 | 0 | 90 | 90 | 30 | 0 |
| | Usage Telecall | 30 | 30 | 30 | 60 | 90 | 30 | 10 | 10 | 10 | 10 | 10 | 0 | 0 | 90 | 90 | 30 | 0 |
| | Usage Email | 30 | 30 | 30 | 60 | 90 | 30 | 10 | 10 | 10 | 10 | 10 | 0 | 0 | 90 | 90 | 30 | 0 |
| | Usage SMS Alert | 30 | 30 | 30 | 60 | 90 | 30 | 10 | 10 | 10 | 10 | 10 | 0 | 0 | 90 | 90 | 30 | 0 |
| | Anti Attrition Call | 10 | 10 | 10 | 10 | 10 | 10 | 10 | 10 | 10 | 10 | 10 | 0 | 0 | 90 | 90 | 30 | 0 |
| | Anti Attrition Direct Mail | 10 | 10 | 10 | 10 | 10 | 10 | 10 | 10 | 10 | 10 | 10 | 0 | 0 | 90 | 90 | 30 | 0 |

some filters like excluding deceased customers, customers who have recently reported that they are out of the country, customers who have some disputes with the company are also applied.

- **Negative lists:** Negative lists are very similar to the risk-related exclusions but are of more universal nature. Common negative lists include fraud and bankruptcy.

### 8.9.2.3 Defining Campaign Characteristics

A below the line campaign can be characterised by the following major characteristics:

- The customers who will be contacted as part of the campaign
- The offer that will be made to the above set of customers; it needs to be noted that within the same campaign, the marketer may decide to have different set of offers for different set of customers
- The channel or channels that will be used to contact the above set of customers
- The contact strategy that will be used to contact the selected set of customers. For example, some customers might be sent direct mailers, others might be sent a direct mailer followed by a phone call, still others might be contacted by email. The contact strategy aims at optimising the response of the campaign and the cost involved in contacting each customer.

Multiple approaches are used by marketers for selecting the right set of customers for a campaign. These approaches vary in terms of the analytical sophistication used in determining the probability or chance of the customer responding to the offer. The first approach involves random targeting which implies that no criteria is used to sub-select a group that has a relatively higher chance of responding to the offer. The random targeting obviously is the most ineffective way of selecting customers for the campaign. However, in some cases when the product or the offer is an entirely new one, random targeting can be the only tool to generate some insights into the profile of customers who are likely to respond to the offer. Random targeting is also used to generate test results which are subsequently used for building sophisticated analytical models that will help in determining customers who are most likely to respond. In this regard, every direct marketing organisation must allocate a test budget, whereby a random (or stratified random), set of customers are targeted so as to generate test results (also sometime called test reads). The test results are used for building new models and analytical strategies. Many organisations use design of experiments to ensure that the tests cover all the different segments, offer types, and price points.

Judgmental selection of customers for the campaign is another common approach for selecting customers for a campaign. In cases where no past data exists, judgmental selection based on the insight or "gut feeling" of the marketer is a viable alternative. Experiences based on campaigns involving similar products or offers can also be utilised for the same.

Most marketers use some form of statistical models for selecting customers with a higher propensity of responding to the offer. All these statistical models are based on the premise that past data on similar campaigns can be used to predict which customers will respond to such offers in the future. Hence, the test results discussed earlier assume key importance. In order to predict which customer is more likely to respond, it is important to have past data, where similar types of customers have been targeted with similar offers in the past.

Various statistical techniques are used for determining the likelihood of response. The most common techniques involve tree building algorithm like CHAID, CART or binary logistic regression. The results of these are used to rank order customers on the basis of their probability of response. This allows the marketer to select a set of customers who have a higher likelihood of responding to the offer. In many cases, more advanced statistical techniques like neural networks, stochastic gradient boosting, random forest are also used for selecting customers with a higher likelihood of response. At this point, it is important to note that in cases where the company has been using a statistical technique for selecting customers for their campaigns, it is important to perform some random tests at periodic intervals so that new data could be generated to build new statistical models. This is important because usage of these models imply that the company never targets all types of customer profiles. Only a select set of customer profiles get targeted again and again. Hence, the data obtained from such targeting is biased and does not represent the complete population, on which the model is used in the first place to select the set of customers. Figure 8.15 illustrates the problem.

In many cases, companies also use real-time triggers instead of statistical models to select the set of customers who, are most likely to respond. The difference between a statistical model based targeting and a trigger based targeting is essentially the fact that a statistical model uses a number of customer characteristics to come up with a likelihood of response, while a trigger uses only one attribute (or a very limited set of attributes) to zero down on customers who are most likely to respond. In the case of a trigger, the power of the single attribute comes from the fact that it is identified in real time, and as soon as a customer hits a trigger the offer is made to the customer. Hence, the recency factor plays a major role in the efficacy of trigger-based selection. Interested readers can refer to the chapters on cross-sell and retention management for further details on usage of triggers.

As an example, a bank which targets current account customers for selling investment products may use a statistical model based on customer behaviour for the past 12 months. This model is used to select customers at the beginning of every month. The selected customers are sent direct mailer or are called for selling investment products.

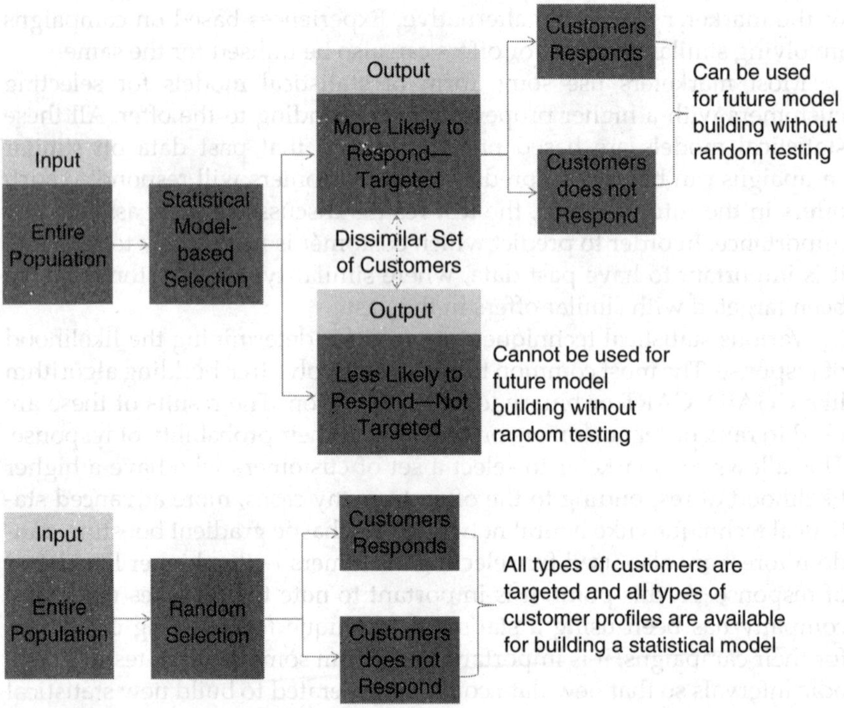


**Figure 8.15** Generating Test Data for Building Targeting Models and Rules

On the other hand, the bank may also use a trigger that runs at the end of every business day and picks up customers who have deposited a large amount of money in their current account on that day. These customers are called the following day with an offer for an investment product. The trigger-based campaign may produce better results, as the customer is targeted at the right time when he or she has the money to invest.

Many companies are realising the advantage of triggers which enable them to target the customer at the right time. However, statistical models use multiple dimensions to determine the propensity of response and this advantage has to be sacrificed if a trigger-based approach is used. Hence, many companies have started to deploy statistical models in a real-time environment which allows them to harness the dual power of triggers and multi-dimensional statistical models.

The next important characteristics of a campaign involves selection of the right offer and the right channel for the selected set of customers. It is important to note that a company might have large number of variations in its offers, in terms of price and other features. Generally, the more attractive an offer, the more the likelihood of customers responding to the offer. However, a more lucrative offer also means lower margins for the company. Hence, most companies use various scenarios to arrive at the optimal offer that would yield the best combination of response and profitability. Similar to offer selection, channel selection involves optimisation of response rate and cost. Generally, telecalling yields higher response rate compared to direct mailer but is costlier. Similarly, sending two direct mailers might yield higher response rate compared to a single direct mailer but involves higher cost. It needs to be noted that certain customers may have preference for a particular channel. For example, a younger customer profile may be more open to an Internet and email channel as compared to an older customer profile. Based on past data, it is possible to identify the channel preference of the customer and allocate customers to specific channels based on their preferences.

### 8.9.2.4 Balancing Multiple Campaign Objectives

As already discussed, designing a campaign involves optimising a number of criteria like how many customers to target, which offer to give to each customer and which channel to use. In order to optimise the campaign it is important to define a set of success criteria which needs to be maximised and a set of constraints which needs to be satisfied. The success criteria can either be short-term metrics like response rate of the campaign, sales volume, etc. or can be relatively longer term metrics like profitability or revenue in the next one or two years. In either case, the marketer needs to have a model to predict the desired metric based on campaign parameters like offer characteristics, channel used, type of customer targeted, etc. In some cases, it is also important to measure the effects of the campaign on customer profitability when compared to a control group. A control group is defined as a group of customers who are identical to the customers who are part of the campaign but are not made the offer. It is important to note that a comparison with a control group is possibly the best way of measuring the incremental value of the campaign. The following example will illustrate the dynamics of measuring and balancing multiple objectives of a campaign. The reader can refer to Chapter 2, "Usage Management" and Chapter 3, "Cross-Sell" for further examples on campaign optimization.

Consider a campaign for cross selling personal loan to credit card customers. This example is taken because it illustrates the fact that a number of dimensions need to be considered while trying to optimise a marketing campaign. In many cases, the possible dimensions involved can be far less and hence, the situation much simpler; however, it is important for the marketer to keep in mind that there can be a lot of drivers other than response rate which are important in ascertaining the success of the campaign. The factors involved in determining the success of this campaign are as follows:

- **Short-term factors**
  - Response rate and conversion rate of the campaign
  - Ticket size of the loans taken by customers who respond

- **Long-term factors**
  - The loan repayment behaviour of customers who take the loan (some of the customers take the loan but do not pay after some time and become delinquent)
  - The change in behaviour on the credit card after taking the loan
    - *Change in the monthly sales made using the card:* After accepting the loan offer, the customer may reduce credit card usage
    - *Change in the revolving behaviour on the credit card:* After taking the loan, the customer may be paying back more of their credit card balances thereby there will be less interest income from credit card
    - *Change in repayment behaviour:* The customer may not be able to manage the increased debt burden, arising out of the new loan. Hence, the customer, may end up defaulting on his/her credit obligations, on both the card and the loan.
    - *Change in attrition behaviour:* After accepting the loan offer, the customer's likelihood of attrition may decrease as he/she becomes more engaged with the product.

From the above discussion, it becomes apparent that a true evaluation of a campaign can only be performed if one uses a longer term view. Mostly metrics around customer level profitability is used as the preferred metric for evaluating the long-term success of a campaign. The time frame for measuring customer level profitability, post-campaign, should be long enough to allow all the changes in customer behaviour to take effect. But, on the other hand, a longer time frame makes predictions inaccurate and it also involve changes in factors extraneous to the campaign, which may have an impact on the outcome. Hence, a judicious view needs to be taken in determining the metrics and the time frame for optimising and evaluating a campaign.

Another important point of consideration is the fact that it is also important to look at short-term metrics like response rate or sales volume generated by the campaign. These short-term metrics are easier to evaluate as they can be observed immediately after the execution of the campaign, and in many cases the long-term metrics are influenced to a large extent by these short-term metrics. A successful campaign must balance both short- and long-term metrics.

At this point, it is apparent that a tool for forecasting long- to medium-term profitability is needed to forecast the profitability of the campaign. Most companies use forecasted profit and loss (P&L) to analyse the cost and revenue drivers and arrive at an expected profitability for the campaign. A separate section in this chapter is dedicated to building a forecasted P&L. Based on the forecasted profitability of the campaign, one needs to make a decision, on whether to implement or not to implement a given campaign.

It is important to note that while measuring long-term impact of a campaign and comparing it with control, one should be aware of the noise that can get into the data. Post implementation of the campaign of interest, other campaigns or marketing programmes may target the same set of customers who are part of the present campaign. This can introduce changes in customer behaviour and consequently noise in the data. Similarly, customers in the control group also may end up being targeted by other offers which may change their behaviour as well. To avoid the change in behaviour of the control group, some companies create a universal control group that is never targeted for any marketing programme. The control group for each campaign is selected out of the universal control group.

### 8.9.2.5 Implementation Planning, Roll Out and Fulfilment

Post conceptualising, the next critical step involves executing the campaign. The following are some of the key considerations that a marketer has to consider:

- **Design the creative or the script of the campaign:** Campaigns are communicated to customers through a mailer or through a telephone call. Hence, it is important to pay lot of attention to the creative design of the mailer or the script of the telephone call. In many cases, marketers do experiment with various types of creative designs and try to find the right design. Similarly, the calling script must be designed to take care of all possible response and questions that the customer might ask during the telephone call.
- The final list of customers to be targeted needs to be carefully audited to ensure correctness
- Once a campaign is designed, it is important to take care of all avenues that the customer might use to respond to the campaign. At the same time, all contact centres must be made aware of the campaign, even if they are not the channel for the customer to respond. For example, a company might have to run a campaign through email, whereby customers are requested to click a link to respond to the offer. However, some customers may call up the call centre and ask details of the offer. Hence, the call centre needs to be updated about the campaign. In case the call centre is the channel for the customer to respond back, then appropriate capacity planning and training needs to be imparted, so that an interested customer does not face any hurdle in responding to the campaign.
- **Audits and checks:** Extensive audit and checks need to be built in so as to ensure that the process flow of the campaign does not face any bottleneck. For example, if a direct mailer is used, then some of the known addresses need to be included to ensure that the mailer arrives properly. In case a toll free number is used in the mailer, then it needs to be ensured that sufficient band width is added so to minimize wait time for incoming calls.

- Customers who have registered in the do not contact category, must be removed from the campaign list. In some cases, a customer may have registered for "do not contact" for a phone channel but not for email or mailers. These nuances need to be taken care of while finalizing the customer list.
- In many cases, the contact information of the customer may not be updated in all databases that the company has. In such a case, all possible contact information from all databases needs to be collated and the most recent one needs to be used.
- In most cases, the campaigns are executed by third party vendors. Hence, appropriate checks around information security needs to be in place.

*Tracking* Tracking a campaign is of critical importance to estimate the success of the campaign and also to learn from the campaign so as to improve the design of future campaigns. A few aspects of tracking are important: the first is the tracking of short-term metrics like response rate, sales. Tracking of short-term metrics is relatively straight forward. However, in some cases the company may be running the same campaign month over month and the same customer may be part of more than one campaign, in which case it is difficult to ascertain the campaign to which the customer has responded. Usually, it is assumed that the customer responds to the most recent campaign. In some cases, a time window is fixed and any response within that time window is attributed to the campaign and response outside that window is not considered a valid response to the campaign.

The second aspect involves the use of control groups for tracking the incremental effect of the campaign. It needs to be noted that the campaign and the test group are chosen in such a way that they are identical at the time of the campaign; however, after the campaign both of these groups may be treated with other subsequent offers which may alter their behaviour. Hence, many companies use a universal control group which does not receive any offer at all. The universal control group is not given any sort of offer and the control group for any campaign is chosen out of the universal control group.

A related aspect revolves around the limitations that arises if the marketer wants to know how the customers who respond to the campaign behave incremental to a control group. Measuring this impact is very difficult as the control group is designed in such a way that it looks like the customers who are part of the campaign. However, customers who respond to the campaign are a subset of this whole population and the control group will be very different from this sub-set. At the beginning of the campaign it is impossible to know who will respond and hence, a control group which is like the responders cannot be designed before the campaign is rolled out. In this case, after the campaign has been executed a sub-group is selected from the control group which looks exactly like the customers who have responded, and the behaviour of this group is compared to the responders.

*Learning from a Campaign* It is important to learn continuously from each campaign to create models, segmentation and rules that will allow targeting the right customer with the right offer through the right channel, so as to generate the maximum profitability. As discussed earlier, it is important to experiment with various campaign designs so as to generate new learnings which will help in creating targeting frameworks that work best. In this regard, tracking and learning from a campaign are quite intertwined.

### 8.9.3 Channels for Managing Customer Interactions

As mentioned in the CRM section, companies utilise multiple inbound and outbound channels for interacting with customers. The usage of some of these channels for acquisition has been described in Chapter 1, "Acquisition"; the chapter also outlines the measurement of campaign response cost, based on the cost dynamics of a particular channel.

As already stated, channels can be broadly classified into inbound and outbound channels. Inbound channels are used by customers and prospects to contact the company. When a customer makes a call to the call centre or visits a branch, sales office or a website they are interested in resolving a problem they are facing, or obtaining information, they need. Sometimes the issue that the customer is facing may present an opportunity for cross-sell or enhancing usage. At other times, once the immediate issue is resolved and the customer is happy, the call centre agent or the branch personnel attempts to cross-sell, up-sell or position various usage-based offers to the customers. The usage of inbound communication for cross selling or for positioning usage offers is termed inbound sales leveraging. In cases where the company has multiple products it creates a customised product palate for each customer. Each product in the palate is ordered based on the customer's propensity to take the product and the expected revenue that is generated from the product. When a customer calls in, then the call is sometimes directed to specialised call centre agents who are most capable at selling the product, for which the customer has the highest propensity of responding. Chapter 3 "Cross-Sell" outlines in detail the next best product and optimising offer based on propensity and expected revenue. In many cases where the customer calls for account closure, the call is directed to specialised retention experts, who can view the best offers for the customers given his profile and position a offer that seems most appropriate for the customer. Chapter 4 "Retention Management" discusses the workflow for managing retention process.

The branch or sales office represents one of the most effective inbound channels, particularly for handling high value or premium customers. However, this is also the highest cost channel. Hence, one needs to carefully plan the location of the branch or sales office so as to cater to the largest possible audience. Chapter 1, "Acquisition" discusses on the methodology of using geographical information systems for location planning.

ATMs and interactive voice response systems also represent low-cost automated inbound channels. Due to the absence of any human interaction, these are less effective means of cross selling or positioning usage offers compared to call centre or branches. Yet these channels also present the most eligible offers to the customers based on an optimisation of response and revenue. Increasingly, many companies are also adopting online chat as a channel. Table 8.5 provides the list of analysis on inbound channel that are commonly used.

As opposed to inbound channels, outbound channels involve company initiated interaction with the customer. Very often an outbound channel is used for targeting customers for acquisition, cross-sell or usage offers. The usage of these channels for acquisition has been discussed in Chapter 1, "Acquisition". Two aspects of an outbound channel are of utmost importance for designing campaigns. These aspects are the cost for targeting each customer and the expected response rate. Usually direct sales agents have highest cost and response rates, followed by outbound calling, direct mail and email. The return on investment (ROI) for each campaign is governed to a large extent by the cost and response dynamics of the channels used. Response and costs are the most used parameters for determining the effectiveness of a channel. But one also needs to look at the quality of the leads that are generated by these channels. In many cases, a channel may have high response rates but a relatively lower percentage of the responders finally take up the offer (conversion) or many of the responders who do take up the offer tend to attrite within a short time. Hence, some of these long-term metrics need to be considered while evaluating a channel. Based on a 2012 report of the Direct Marketing Association (DMA), it is found that for the United States "email is more cost-effective than direct mail or telemarketing. The report found email had the highest ROI, at $28.50, compared the $7 for direct mail". The study also notes that direct mail provides an average response rate of 1.28%, while email provides a response of 0.03% and telecalling provides a response of 8.21% for the US market. The report also notes that display ad and paid Internet search provides a response rate of 0.04% and 0.22%, respectively.

One important aspect with regards to channel management involves creating a customer-centric view across all channels so that the customer is offered a uniform message and service quality across channels. A high value customer must be treated with differentiated service irrespective of the channel used for the interaction.

**Table 8.5** Overview of Channel Analytics

| Channel | Analysis Type | Analysis Description | Key Business Benefits | Data Required |
|---|---|---|---|---|
| Branch | Heat map analysis | "Heat Map" analysis to check customer/prospect density around major hubs | Branch/ATM location planning | Existing ATM/channel location information, ATM/channel transactional data, customer demographics, exclusion/Inclusion information (policy based), GIS system |
| | "Weighting" analysis | Analysis of ATM/channel usage by using competitor/third party information to check whether customer density/usage is "over-represented" or "under-represented" | Beneficial in understanding usage patterns of other bank customers on bank ATMs in particular geographic region and segment | Existing ATM/channel location information, ATM/channel transactional data, customer demographics, third party information, exclusion/inclusion information (policy based) |
| ATM, IVR, Web | "Vault" cash optimisation | Determining the optimal vault cash for Branch/ATM | Inventory management reducing costs and customer dissatisfaction | ATM/channel transaction data |
| | ATM maintenance costs analysis | Reports covering maintenance activities at ATM on the below parameters:<br>• Uptime/Downtime<br>• Time per transaction, timeouts, response time, failures<br>• Approval/Denial of transaction, response<br>• Transactions per second/minute (TPS/TPM) | Reports will cover the maintenance and servicing of channel. Evaluation by costs to serve | ATM/channel transaction data, ATM/channel maintenance information |
| | ATM, IVR offer palate optimisation | Optimal set of top one or two offers that would be presented to the customer at the ATM or through the IVR | Cross-sell and usage enhancement | Customer behaviour and demographic data, past ATM/IVR access data |

(*Continued*)

**Table 8.5** Overview of Channel Analytics (*Continued*)

| Channel | Analysis Type | Analysis Description | Key Business Benefits | Data Required |
|---|---|---|---|---|
| | Channel migration strategies | Develop a strategy to identify which customers are more likely to migrate, from a specific channel (expensive) to the ATM/cheaper channel | Reduces the cost to serve a customer, which in terms leads to customer profitability | ATM/channel transaction data, ATM/channel costs information, Customer demographics, Customer profitability information |
| | Optimal offer positioning on the website | Optimal positioning of different types of data in the website | Optimal conversion and interest generation when the customer visits the website | Customer behaviour data, click stream data to understand click pattern |
| | Campaign management | Designing and tracking of specific marketing campaigns running on different channels | Maximise ROI of campaigns, efficient usage of ATM/channel | ATM/channel transactions, customer demography, promotional information, campaign metrics/tracking information |
| Inbound call centre | Optimal call routing | Identify the optimal set of agents best suited for handling the particular customer segment, so as to offer differentiated services | Superior service to high value customers | Customer transaction and demographic data |
| | Palate optimisation | Optimise the offer palate for each customer based on propensity of response and expected revenue | Better call sales leveraging | Customer transaction and demographic data |
| | Optimal retention offer design | Identify the best retention offer for various customer segments | Higher retention offer | Customer transaction and demographic data |
| | Call volume forecasting and resource planning | Forecast call volume and optimal staffing need for the inbound call centre | Better service quality | Past incoming calling pattern and the changes in marketing strategy that could trigger increase in incoming calls |

## 8.10 The Profit and Loss (P&L) Tool for Understanding Campaign Profitability

Measuring and forecasting profitability at a customer level or a customer segment level is an important decision-making criterion for managing and measuring marketing campaigns. The current section focuses on the approach of creating P&L tools which should help marketers in taking key decisions. P&L analysis is a very critical analytical tool as it is used for making critical decisions like:

- Whether to implement a particular campaign
- Whether to extend a particular offer to a given customer segment
- Which customer segment or products to prioritize

Conceptually, the development of a P&L tool involve understanding the revenue and cost elements and then identifying how each of these elements can be calculated at a customer or customer segment level. This approach is very similar to the activity based costing approach used by cost accountants. As per the activity-based costing approach, each cost element in the company can be attributed and distributed to each and every process or function. This approach is extended to calculate revenue and cost components which form part of the P&L account. The overall approach for forecasting the P&L drivers involve the following steps:

- Dividing each revenue and cost component into sub-components
- Identifying the revenue and cost drivers for each sub-component
- Forecasting each sub component based on a top-down or bottom-up approach

Figure 8.16 illustrates the above approach for building a P&L tool.

### *8.10.1 Revenue and Cost Components*

Each revenue and cost component is broken down into a set of sub-components; a sub-component refers to the most granular level for which costs and revenues are forecasted. For example, in case of mobile telecom P&L, the revenue from outgoing calls consists of sub-components like:

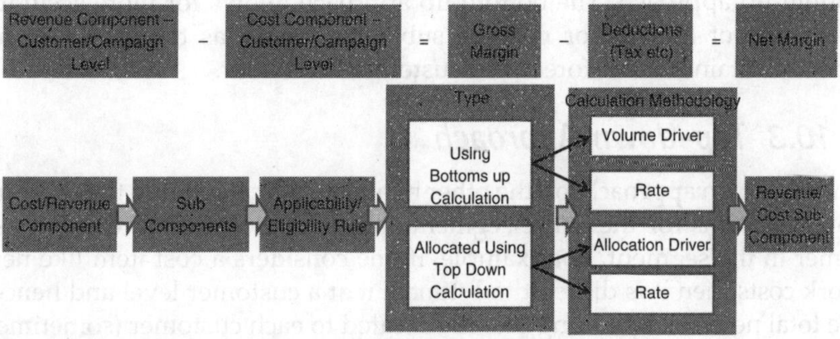


**Figure 8.16** Overview of P&L Forecasting Methodology

- Revenue from calls made to a number within the network
- Revenue from calls made to a number outside the network
  - Revenue from calls made to mobile numbers outside the network, but within the same telecom circle
  - Revenue from calls made to fixed line numbers outside the network, but within the same telecom circle
  - Revenue from calls made to mobile numbers outside the network, but in a different telecom circle
  - Revenue from calls made to fixed line numbers outside the network, but within the same telecom circle
- Revenue from international calls

Similarly, cost components also consist of various sub-components. For example, for a telecom company the network operation expense consists of several sub-components like

- Backhaul lease
- Maintenance and rental costs
- Energy costs
- Personnel expenses
- Other costs

### *8.10.2 Bottom-up Approach*

As per the bottom-up approach, the revenue or cost sub-component is forecasted at a customer level and then aggregated for the entire segment. For example, if one considers the revenue sub-component roaming charges for a mobile telecom P&L, then one can estimate the minutes of roaming usage at a customer level (based on past data) and then multiply the same with roaming charges to get the revenue sub-component at a customer level. Similarly for a credit card P&L, if one considers interchange revenue, then one may estimate the dollar value of sales at a customer level and then multiply the same with the fixed interchange rate to obtain interchange revenue at a customer level. Once the revenue sub-component is forecasted at a customer level, the same can be summed up to obtain the total at a segment level. Usually revenue and cost sub-components that can be attributed directly to customer behaviour are estimated using the bottom-up approach. The bottom-up approach allows for more accurate prediction of the cost or revenue sub-components, as the same can be directly obtained from forecasted customer behaviour.

### *8.10.3 Top-down Approach*

The top down approach, on the other hand, entails calculating the revenue and cost items for the entire segment and then allocating it to each customer in the segment. For example, if one considers a cost item like network costs then it is difficult to estimate it at a customer level and hence, the total network operating cost is allocated to each customer (sometimes an equal allocation is performed for each customer, at other times it is allocated based on forecasted minutes of usage). Usually most cost components like technology and operating costs are calculated using the top-down approach.

### 8.10.4 Identifying the Revenue or Cost Driver

Figure 8.16 illustrates the two methodologies for calculating revenue and cost sub-components. For both the top down and the bottom up methodology, one needs to know the volume driver and the rate or price. The volume driver is multiplied by the rate or price to determine the revenue or cost component. In most cases, the volume driver is predicted based on customer type and expected customer behaviour. However, the rate or the price in most cases is assumed to be a constant for the particular segment or campaign group. The following section illustrates the P&L for credit card, telecom, and bank deposits. The illustration provides the revenue and cost line items, the volume and rate driver associated with each and the methodology of calculating the line item. It needs to be noted that the exact items and the calculation methodology may vary across companies and situations.

### 8.10.5 Understanding P&L Dynamics

At an overall level, the gross profit (profit before tax and other deduction) is calculated by subtracting the total cost from total revenue. Net profit is calculated as gross margin minus deductions. The P&L for key segments within a given business will have very different drivers. For example, if one considers pre-paid vs. post-paid mobile connections, then one will find the following characteristics customers, which are very different for post-paid and pre-paid customers:

- Limited usage of value added services for pre-paid services
- Absence of rental charges for pre-paid customers
- Significant periods of inactivity for pre-paid customers
- Credit loss for post-paid customers emanating from customers who do not honour their payment obligations

Similarly for credit cards the revenue and cost drivers for transactors (who pay their full due within the specified time frame) and revolver (those who make partial payments) are very different. Some of the key differences are:

- There is no interest revenue for transactors, the most important revenue item for transactor is the interchange income that the credit card company earns on sales made by these customers
- For revolvers, interest income forms the most important revenue driver

### 8.10.6 P&L for Credit Cards

For credit cards, revenue is mostly driven by interest income from customers who do not pay in full, and interchange income is generated as part of the fees paid by merchants when customers use their credit cards for purchase and various types of fees like late payment fee, foreign transaction fee, and cash advance fee. The key cost elements are the cost of funds which the credit card issuers incur to fund the credit free purchase and the credit loss which is incurred when customers do not pay their dues at all.

The most common credit card offers are as follows:

- Balance transfer offer where a credit card company offers a lower rate for customers to transfer their balances from another credit card
- Sales offers where various incentives like higher reward points or gifts are offered for usage of the credit card in making certain types of purchases
- Loan on the credit card line where a fixed instalment loan is offered in lieu of the credit limit offered in the credit card
- Conversion of high value purchases into fixed instalment loans

A balance transfer and a loan on the credit card line may increase the interest income from customers who respond to the offer; however, the interest rate on these new balances (either from balance transfer or from loans) is lower than the normal credit card interest rate. A balance transfer offer has a promotional period associated with it which implies that the lower balance transfer interest is applicable for a limited period like six months or one year, after that the remaining balance is charged at the normal (higher) interest rate. Hence, the amount of balance that remains unpaid after the specified promotional period is an important driver of the profitability of the balance transfer offer. Usually customers who accept the balance transfer or the loan offer decrease the purchase on their credit cards because some of their credit limit gets blocked by the loan or the transferred balance. Hence, in most cases these offers also cause a decrease in the interchange income. Balance transfer is an important revenue component mostly in the United States and UK markets, whereas in the Asian markets loan on the cards line is a much bigger programme and consequently the revenue from loan on cards is much bigger than balance transfer in Asian markets. Actually the relative contribution between balance transfer and loan on cards would be almost the other way around in Asian markets.

Sales offers mostly aim to increase the interchange income. However, sales offers also aim at increasing the total balance and subsequently some of the customers will not be able to pay the full amount due and hence, would increase the interest income as well. However, the increase in interest income is a second order effect of the sales offer.

It is important to keep in mind that all offers may cause an increase in credit loss because each offer tends to increase the minimum payment requirement of the customer and the customer may not have the adequate capacity to handle the increased payment requirement.

Table 8.6 illustrates the revenue and cost drivers for a credit card P&L.

It needs to be noted that interest on purchase balances is only charged for customers who either do not pay in full or pay after the due date. But interest on balance transfer and loans are charged to all customers who have

**Table 8.6** Profit and Loss Drivers for Credit Card

| Profit and Loss Drivers for Credit Card | | | | | | |
|---|---|---|---|---|---|---|
| | Component | Sub Component | Sub Component Type | Volume Driver | Rate | Calculation Methodology |
| Revenue | Interest | Interest on purchase balance which is at normal rate | Bottom up | Purchase, payment | Annual percentage rate on normal balances | (Purchase – Payment) * Rate |
| | | Interest on balance transfer balances | Bottom up | Balance, payment | Annual percentage rate offered for balance transfer offer | (Balances transferred – Balance paid off) * Rate |
| | | Interest on purchase balance which is at a lower rate | Bottom up | Balance at lower rate | Annual percentage rate on promotions | (Balance outstanding) * Rate |
| | | Interest on loans offered on credit card lines | Bottom up | Ticket size of the loan | Annual percentage rate offered on loans | (Balance outstanding) * Rate |
| | | Interest on cash withdrawal | Bottom up | Cash withdrawal, payment | Annual percentage rate on cash | (Cash withdrawal – Payment) * Rate |
| | | Interest on balances which have been converted to low rate fixed payment | Bottom up | Balance | Annual percentage rate offered for conversion | (Balance outstanding) * Rate |
| | Interchange | Interchange | Bottom up | Sales | Interchange rate offered by MasterCard/Visa/Amex etc | Sales * Interchange rate |

(*Continued*)

**Table 8.6** Profit and Loss Drivers for Credit Card (*Continued*)

| | Profit and Loss Drivers for Credit Card | | | | | |
|---|---|---|---|---|---|---|
| | Component | Sub Component | Sub Component Type | Volume Driver | Rate | Calculation Methodology |
| Revenue | Fees | Late fee | Bottom up | Number of times late, balance when customer had paid late | Late fee is charged as a fixed amount based on balance or as a percentage of balance subject to a floor.<br>For example,<br>• Balance less then $100 then late fee is $10<br>• Balance between $100 and $500 late fee is $30<br>• Balance above $500 late fee is $50<br>Or<br>• Balance less than $500 late fee is $20<br>• Balance above $500 late fee is 1% of balance (sometime subject to a cap and floor) | Incidence * Fee per incidence |
| | | Annual fee | Bottom up | Number of accounts approaching anniversary | Fixed annual fee based on product type (some times there is a waiver of annual fee if the customer makes more than a threshold amount of purchase) | Incidence * Fee per incidence |

(*Continued*)

**Table 8.6** Profit and Loss Drivers for Credit Card (*Continued*)

| | Profit and Loss Drivers for Credit Card | | | | | |
|---|---|---|---|---|---|---|
| | **Component** | **Sub Component** | **Sub Component Type** | **Volume Driver** | **Rate** | **Calculation Methodology** |
| Revenue | | Cash advance fee | Bottom up | Number of times cash advance taken, cash advance amount | As a percentage of cash withdrawal amount subject to a floor | Transferred amount * Fee |
| | | Balance transfer fee | Bottom up | Number of times balance transfer availed, balance transfer amount | As a percentage of balance transferred subject to a floor | Withdrawal amount * Fee |
| | | Over limit fee | Bottom up | Number of times over limit | Fixed fee | Incidence * Fee per incidence |
| | | Service fees | Bottom up | Number of service requests | Average fee per request | Incidence * Fee per incidence |
| | Cross-sell revenue | Cross-sell fee | Top down | Average cross-sell rate of other products like insurance | Average fee per cross sell | Number of accounts * Average cross-sell rate * Average cross-sell fee |

(*Continued*)

**Table 8.6** Profit and Loss Drivers for Credit Card (*Continued*)

| | Profit and Loss Drivers for Credit Card | | | | | |
|---|---|---|---|---|---|---|
| | **Component** | **Sub Component** | **Sub Component Type** | **Volume Driver** | **Rate** | **Calculation Methodology** |
| Cost | Cost of funds—all cost of fund rates are provided by treasury as part of the transfer pricing | Cost of funds on purchase balance which is at normal rate | Bottom up | Purchase, payment | Cost of funds rate on normal balances | (Purchase – Payment) * Cost of funds rate |
| | | Cost of funds on balance transfer balances | Bottom up | Balance transferred, payment | Cost of funds rate offered for balance transfer offer | (Balances transferred – Balance paid off) * Cost of funds rate |
| | | Cost of funds on purchase balance which is at a lower rate | Bottom up | Balance at lower rate | Cost of funds rate on promotions | (Balance outstanding) * Cost of funds rate |
| | | Cost of funds on loans offered on credit card lines | Bottom up | Ticket size of the loan | Cost of funds rate offered on loans | (Balance outstanding) * Cost of funds rate |
| | | Cost of funds on cash withdrawal | Bottom up | Cash withdrawal, payment | Cost of funds rate on cash | (Cash withdrawal – Payment) * Cost of funds rate |
| | | Interest on balances which have been converted to low rate fixed payment | Bottom up | Balance | Cost of funds rate offered for conversion | (Balance outstanding) * Cost of funds rate |
| | Reward cost | Reward cost | Volume driver is bottom up rate is top down | Purchase sale | Cost per reward point based on estimated burn rate | Purchase sale * estimated reward cost |
| | Cost of credit loss | Gross credit loss – Recovery = Net credit loss | Bottom up | Total outstanding balance | Loss rate and recovery rate | (Loss rate * Balance) – Recovery |

(*Continued*)

**Table 8.6** Profit and Loss Drivers for Credit Card (*Continued*)

| | Profit and Loss Drivers for Credit Card | | | | | |
|---|---|---|---|---|---|---|
| | **Component** | **Sub Component** | **Sub Component Type** | **Volume Driver** | **Rate** | **Calculation Methodology** |
| Cost | Cost of fraud loss | Fraud loss | Top down | Total outstanding balance | Fraud loss rate on the overall portfolio | Fraud loss rate * Balance |
| | Marketing costs | Marketing costs for acquisition | Top down | None | Total marketing costs distributed among all accounts, sometimes marketing costs are allocated based on specific customer segment. | |
| | | Marketing costs for managing existing customers | Top down | None | Total marketing costs distributed among all accounts, sometimes marketing costs are allocated based on specific customer segment. | |
| | Operating costs (including servicing costs) | Operating costs | Top down | None | Total marketing costs distributed among all accounts | |
| | Reserve and provisioning | Reserve and provisioning | Top down | Total balance | Expected loss rate | Expected loss rate * Total balance * Adjustment factor provided by finance |
| | Capital costs | Capital allocation charges | Top down | Total balance | Unexpected loss rate | Capital allocation as per capital adequacy (Basel) regulation |

taken up a balance transfer or a loan. Similarly, interest on cash advance is also charged to all customers who use their credit card to withdraw cash. Interchange fee refers to the fee that is paid to the credit card company net of the amount deducted by the network like Visa or Mastercard.

The key metrics that are used for measuring the credit card P&L (along with the calculation methodology) are as follows:

- **Customer net revenue (CNR):** Total revenue at a customer level net of cost of funds and reward costs

$$\text{CNR} = \text{Revenue} - \text{Cost of funds} - \text{Reward cost}$$

- **Net interest margin (NIM):** Interest revenue net of cost of fund as a percentage of total balance

$$\text{NIM} = (\text{Interest Income} - \text{Cost of funds})/\text{Balance}$$

- **Net credit margin (NCM):** Interest revenue net of cost of fund and cost of credit loss as a percentage of total balance

$$\text{NCM} = (\text{Interest Income} - \text{Cost of funds} - \text{Cost of credit loss})/\text{Balance}$$

- **Effective interest rate (EIR):** Interest revenue as a percentage of total balance

$$\text{EIR} = \text{Interest Income}/\text{Total Balance}$$

- **Business income:** Total revenue net of all costs (cost of funds, reward cost, cost of credit loss and operating costs) other than provisioning and capital costs
- **Earnings before interest and taxes (EBIT):** Business income net of provisioning and capital costs

Customer net revenue, loss rate and net credit margin are the most critical metrics used by credit card companies. All three metrics are mostly measured as a percentage of the total outstanding, though customer net revenue and net credit margin are sometimes measured in dollars as well. Figure 8.17 illustrates the relative contribution of various revenue and cost items for credit cards.

### *8.10.7 P&L for Liability (Deposit) Account*

For a bank, the products like savings and checking account represents liability accounts. The main revenue driver for a liability account is the balance revenue which is earned by the bank on deposits. The treasury pays a spread on deposits obtained by the bank and this spread is the main income on liability account, for a bank. Similarly, the most important cost item for a liability account is the interest paid out to customers. The interest paid to customers represents the price of the deposit. Higher the interest paid out to customers, more deposits will flow in but higher will be the costs.

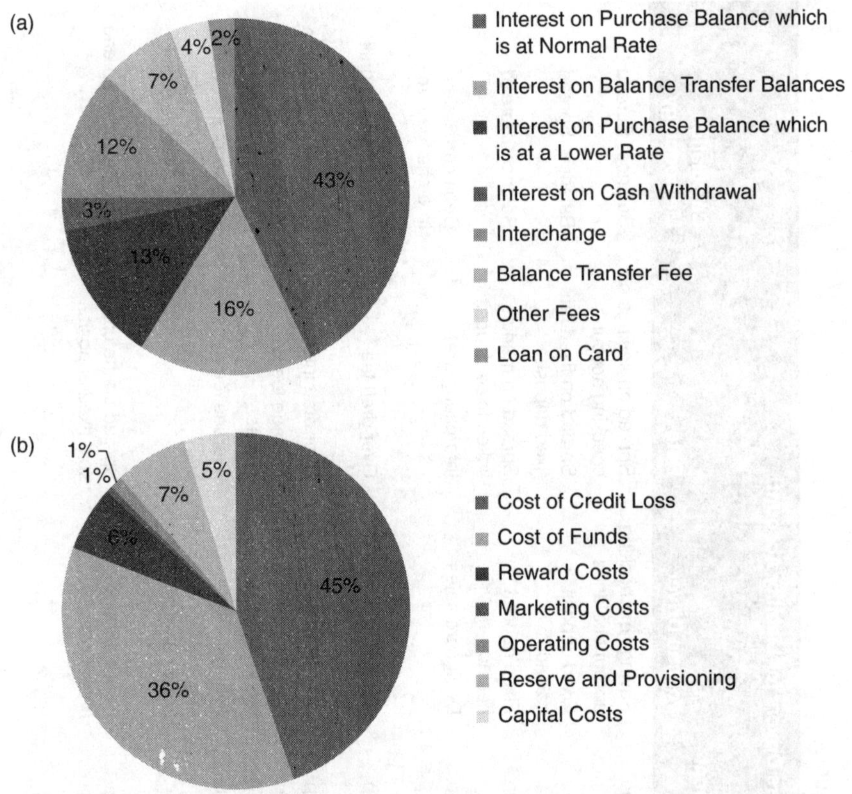


**Figure 8.17** (a) Relative Revenue Contribution—Credit Card and (b) Relative Cost Contribution—Credit Card

For liability customers, the most important offers are cross-sell offers aimed at selling more liability products or other asset products (e.g., loans, credit card) to liability customers. Hence, the revenue from such cross-sell is an important driver of the profitability of the liability account. Table 8.7 illustrates the revenue and cost drivers for a liability account P&L. It is important to note that the fee revenue consists of various types of fees including fees for service requests like cancelling an already issued check, penalty fees for not maintaining minimum balance, fees for extra statements, etc.

The key metrics that are used for measuring the P&L (along with the calculation methodology) are as follows:

- **Customer net revenue (CNR):** Total revenue at a customer level net of cost of funds and reward costs

CNR = Revenue – Interest cost – Cost of funds for overdraft – Reward costs

**Table 8.7** Profit and Loss Drivers for Liability (Deposit) Accounts

| | Profit and Loss Drivers for Liability Account | | | | | |
|---|---|---|---|---|---|---|
| | Component | Sub Component | Sub Component Type | Volume Driver | Rate | Calculation Methodology |
| Revenue | Balance revenue | Balance revenue on savings or checking account | Bottom up | Savings or checking account balance | Spread on savings or checking account | Balance* Spread |
| | | Balance revenue on fixed deposits with fixed interest rate | Bottom up | Fixed deposit balance | Spread on fixed rate fixed deposit | Balance* Spread |
| | | Balance revenue on fixed deposits with market linked interest rate | Bottom up | Fixed deposit balance | Spread on market linked fixed deposit | Balance* Spread |
| | Interchange from debit card usage | Debit card usage | Bottom up | Debit card sales | Interchange rate | Debit card sales* Interchange rate |
| | Overdraft charges | Over draft fees | Bottom up | Number of over draft accounts | Over draft fee | Number of accounts* Over draft fee |
| | | Over draft interest charges | Bottom up | Over draft balance | Over draft interest rate | Balance* Interest rate |
| | Fees | Service fees | Bottom up | Number of service requests | Average fee per request | Incidence* Fee per incidence |
| | Cross-sell revenue | Cross-sell fee | Top down | Average cross-sell rate of other products like insurance | Average fee per cross sell | Number of accounts* Average cross sell rate* Average cross sell fee |
| | | Cross-sell revenue from cross-sell of other liability product for example, cross-sell of fixed deposit, wealth management etc | Top down/ Bottom up | New balances brought in | Spread on the cross-sold fixed deposit | New Balance* Spread |

(*Continued*)

**Table 8.7** Profit and Loss Drivers for Liability (Deposit) Accounts (*Continued*)

| | Profit and Loss Drivers for Liability Account | | | | | |
|---|---|---|---|---|---|---|
| | **Component** | **Sub Component** | **Sub Component Type** | **Volume Driver** | **Rate** | **Calculation Methodology** |
| Cost | Interest paid out on deposit balances | Interest paid out on deposit balances | Bottom up | Balance | Interest rate paid to customers | Balance* Interest rate |
| | Cost of funds for over draft | Cost of funds for over draft | Bottom up | Balance | Cost of funds rate offered for conversion | (Balance outstanding)* Cost of funds rate |
| | Reward costs | Reward cost for debit card usage | Volume driver is bottom up rate is top down | Purchase sale | Cost per reward point based on estimated burn rate | Purchase sale* estimated reward cost |
| | | Other reward costs | Bottom up | Incidence of other rewards | Average reward cost | Incidence* Average reward cost |
| | Marketing costs | Marketing costs for acquisition | Bottom up | None | Total marketing costs distributed among all accounts | |
| | | Marketing costs for managing existing customers | Top down | None | Total marketing costs distributed among all accounts | |
| | Operating costs (including servicing costs) | Operating costs | Top down | None | Total marketing costs distributed among all accounts | |

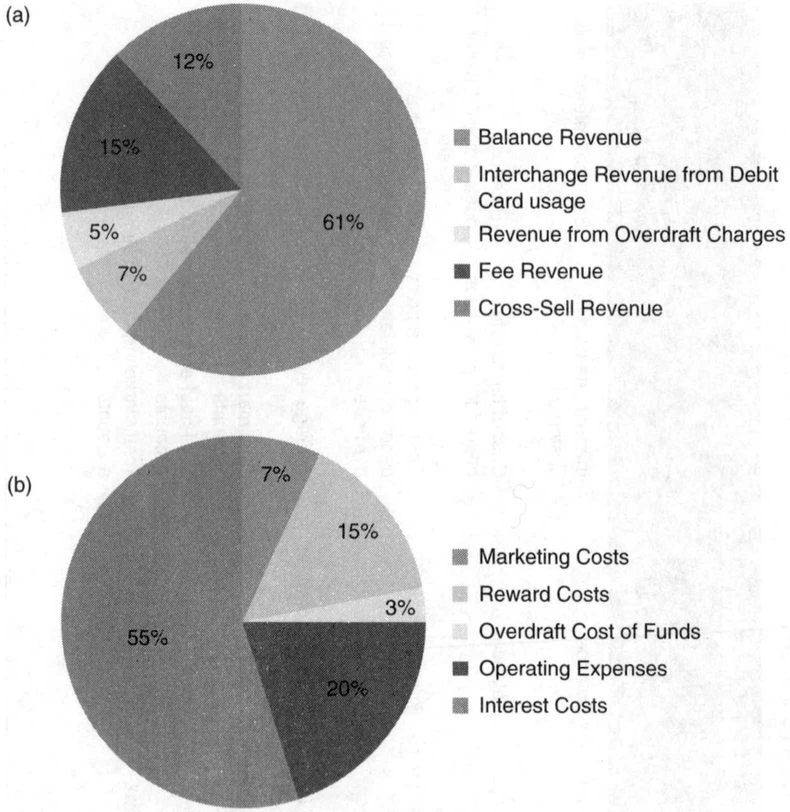


**Figure 8.18** (a) Relative Revenue Contribution—Liability Account and (b) Relative Cost Contribution—Liability Account

- **Effective spread:** Balance revenue net of interest cost as a percentage of total balance
- **Earnings before interest and tax (EBIT):** Total revenue net of total costs

Figure 8.18 illustrates the relative contribution of various revenue and cost items.

### *8.10.8 P&L for Mobile Telecom*

For a mobile telecom company the key revenue items include

- Usage revenue generated from the basic telephone services which is measured by the minutes of usage
- Revenue from usage of value added services
- Revenue generated from rental and other fixed fees

Most mobile operators closely monitor overage which is essentially the usage beyond the limits of the current pre-paid or post-paid plan subscribed by the customers. Overage is important for three key aspects: one, it provides higher revenue per minutes of usage because the per minute charges are higher when customers cross the limits prescribed in the plan. Second, overage also represent an opportunity of selling usage offers to the customer. For example, once a pre-paid customer crosses the limit of the allotted minutes, companies can cross-sell a post-paid offer thereby turning the short-term pre-paid customer to a long-term post-paid customer. Overage can also be analyzed for understanding customer needs and offering a rate plan that is more suited to the need of the customer, this in turn reduces the risk of churn and helps in creating long-term relationship.

Key offer types for telecom companies include cross-sell offers for value added services like data services, video calls, games and download, etc. and rate plan migration offers. Cross-sell offers ensure a newer revenue stream from customers in terms of usage of the new service and can sometimes be combined with an activation or usage fee. Value added services also enhance customer engagement and reduces the risk of churn. Understanding the impact of rate plan migration offers is more complex. The primary purpose of rate plan migration offers is to reduce the risk of churn by increasing usage. Rate plan migration may reduce the overage for customers thereby reducing some of the usage-based revenue as the customer is less likely to go over the new limit for the particular service. For detailed discussions on rate plans, the interested reader can refer to Chapter 2, "Usage Management".

Table 8.8 illustrates the revenue and cost drivers for a mobile telecom P&L. The key metrics that are used for measuring the P&L (along with the calculation methodology) are as follows:

- **Average revenue per user (ARPU):** Revenue per subscriber for a specific type of service

  ARPU = Total revenue/Average number of subscriber for the period

- **Cash cost per user (CCPU):** Cost of service and operations per user

  CCPU = All costs other than bad debt costs/Average number of subscriber for the period

- **Average margin per user (AMPU):** Gross profit per subscriber

  AMPU = (Total revenue – Total costs)/Average number of subscriber for the period

- **Average profit per user (APPU):** Net profit per subscriber

  APPU = (Total revenue – Total costs – Depreciation and other charges)/Average number of subscriber for the period

**Table 8.8** Profit and Loss Drivers for Mobile Telephony

| | Profit and Loss Drivers for Mobile Telephony | | | | | |
|---|---|---|---|---|---|---|
| | Component | Sub Component | Sub Component Type | Volume Driver | Rate | Calculation Methodology |
| Revenue | Non-recurring revenue | Connection fees | Bottom up | Number of new connection | Fee | Number of new connection * Fee |
| | | SIM sales revenue | Bottom up | Number of new connection | Fee | Number of new connection * Fee |
| | | Revenue from initial deposit amount for post-paid connection | Volume driver bottom up rate is determined top down | Number of new connection | Allocated rate | Number of new connection * Allocated rate |
| | Recurring non-usage based revenue | Usage of services | Bottom up | Number of subscribers using the service | Fee | Number of subscribers * Fee |
| | | Activation of services | Bottom up | Number of subscribers using the service | Fee | Number of subscribers * Fee |
| | | Other fees (like late payment fee) | Bottom up | Incidence of fee | Fee | Incidence of fee * Fee |
| | Usage revenue | Voice call to mobiles in the same telecom circle | Bottom up | Minutes of usage | Per minute usage charge | Minutes of usage * usage charge |
| | | Voice calls to mobiles in a different telecom circle | Bottom up | Minutes of usage | Per minute usage charge | Minutes of usage * usage charge |
| | | Voice calls to fixed line in the same telecom circle | Bottom up | Minutes of usage | Per minute usage charge | Minutes of usage * usage charge |
| | | Voice calls to fixed line in a different telecom circle | Bottom up | Minutes of usage | Per minute usage charge | Minutes of usage * usage charge |

(*Continued*)

**Table 8.8** Profit and Loss Drivers for Mobile Telephony (*Continued*)

| Profit and Loss Drivers for Mobile Telephony | | | | | |
|---|---|---|---|---|---|
| **Component** | **Sub Component** | **Sub Component Type** | **Volume Driver** | **Rate** | **Calculation Methodology** |
| Revenue | Voice calls to international numbers | Bottom up | Minutes of usage | Per minute usage charge | Minutes of usage * usage charge |
| | Video calls | Bottom up | Minutes of usage | Per minute usage charge | Minutes of usage * usage charge |
| | Data usage—SMS | Bottom up | Volume of SMS | Per SMS charge | Number of SMS * usage charge |
| | Data usage—email | Bottom up | Minutes of usage | Per minute usage charge | Minutes of usage * usage charge |
| | Data usage—internet access | Bottom up | Minutes of usage | Per minute usage charge | Minutes of usage * usage charge |
| | Usage of value added services—ring tone | Bottom up | Volume of download | Per download charge | Number of downloads * per download charge |
| | Usage of value added services—information update | Bottom up | Minutes of usage | Per minute usage charge | Minutes of usage * usage charge |
| | Usage of value added services—entertainment | Bottom up | Volume of download | Per download charge | Number of down load * per download charge |
| | Usage of value added services—games | Bottom up | Volume of download | Per download charge | Number of download * per download charge |
| | Usage of value added services—others | Bottom up | Volume of download | Per download charge/ Minutes of usage | Number of download * per download charge Minutes of usage* usage charge |

(*Continued*)

**Table 8.8** Profit and Loss Drivers for Mobile Telephony (*Continued*)

| | Profit and Loss Drivers for Mobile Telephony | | | | | |
|---|---|---|---|---|---|---|
| | Component | Sub Component | Sub Component Type | Volume Driver | Rate | |
| Cost | Network operational expenses | Backhaul lease | Top down | None | Total operating costs distributed among all subscribers | |
| | | Electricity | Top down | None | Total operating costs distributed among all subscribers | |
| | | Real estate | Top down | None | Total operating costs distributed among all subscribers | |
| | | Others | Top down | None | Total operating costs distributed among all subscribers | |
| | Interconnect charges | Interconnect charges | Top down | None | Total operating costs distributed among all | |
| | Marketing costs | Marketing costs for acquisition—handset costs/ subsidies | Bottom up | Number and type of new connection | Actual cost incurred | Number of new connections * Average cost |
| | | Marketing costs for acquisition—dealer commission | Top down | None | Total marketing costs distributed among all subscribers | |
| | | Marketing costs for managing existing customers | Top down | None | Total marketing costs distributed among all subscribers | |
| | Other operating costs (including servicing costs) | Operating costs (including servicing costs) | Top down | None | Total operating costs distributed among all subscribers | |
| | Cost of bad debt | | Top down | None | Average loss rate | Out standing balance * Average loss rate |

- **Minutes of usage (MOU):** Minutes of usage per subscriber for a particular type of service

  MOU = Total usage/average number of subscriber for the period

- **Average revenue per minute (ARPM):** Average revenue per minute of usage for a particular type of service

  ARPM = Total revenue/Total minutes of usage

- **Cost per gross addition (CPGA):** Cost to acquire a new customer calculated as the average cost of acquiring one additional new customer. CPGA is calculated as all costs for acquisition divided by the number of subscribers acquired in a specific period.
- In addition to the financial metric discussed above, churn rate and net subscriber addition are important aspects which drive the financial performance of a telecom company.

Average revenue per user (ARPU) and minutes of usage (MOU) are the most well-known metrics in the telecom business; however, metrics around margin are becoming more popular as they provide a holistic picture of both costs and revenues. Figure 8.19 illustrates the relative contribution of various revenue and cost items.

It needs to be noted that in emerging markets the contribution of data revenue is significantly lower than voice revenue.

### *8.10.9 P&L Forecasting*

In order to measure and evaluate a campaign, it is necessary to forecast the revenue and cost components so as to obtain a measure of future profitability. Forecasting campaign profitability is critical as it used for making multiple strategic decisions, including:

- Decision on whether to roll out the campaign based on forecasted revenue and profit
- Deciding the offer and price for the overall campaign and for key customer segments
- Identify key revenue and cost drivers for a campaign and track the same post implementation
- Correlate the key revenue and cost drivers with customer behaviour
- Identify the expected break even period for the campaign
- Identify the risks that may reduce campaign profitability, once the campaign has been implemented

As discussed earlier, the forecast is based on a projection of the volume driver of each of the revenue and cost components. The rate is mostly assumed to be fixed. The forecast of the volume driver is based on past campaigns and an adjustment is applied based on the offer, macroeconomic environment, and competitive dynamics. There are two

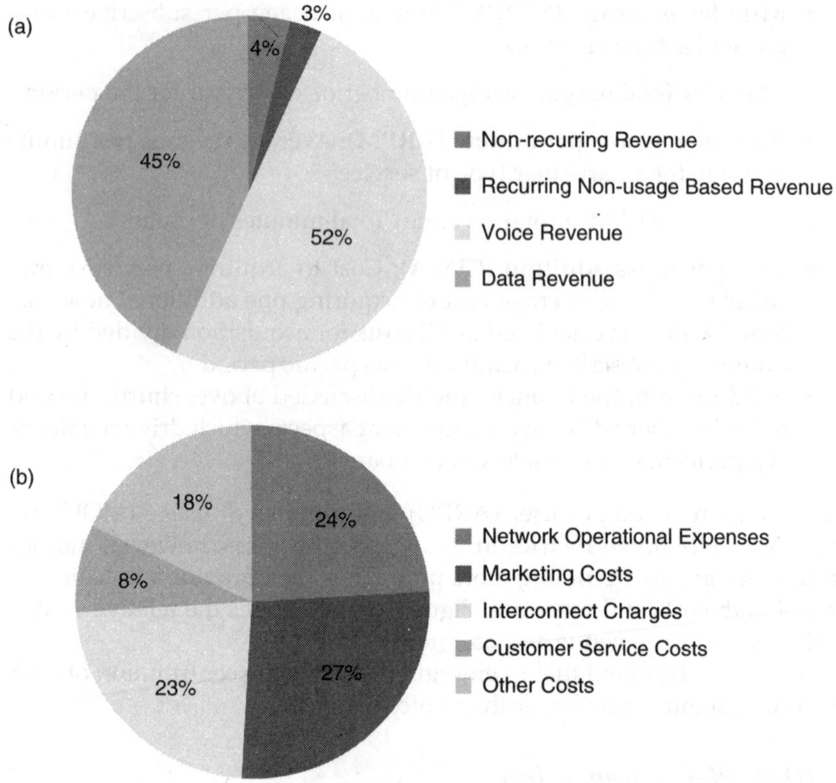


*Source:* Capgemini study.

**Figure 8.19** (a) Relative Revenue Contribution—Mobile Telecom and (b) Relavive Cost Contribution—Mobile Telephone

important adjustment factors: the first is level adjustment which is used to shift the forecast curve up or down but parallel to itself, the other is a shape adjustment which is used to change the shape of the forecast curve. The following example will illustrate these adjustments.

### 8.10.9.1 Campaign

Consider a campaign for cross-sell of credit card to existing liability (deposit) account customers. Based on earlier campaigns the balances of the credit cards follow a certain pattern. However, for an offer which promises a higher reward on the card, it is expected that the balances will be higher overall compared to the baseline pattern (parallel shift). However, for an offer which promises a better rate for the first six months, the balances will be higher initially but lower in the later months (change in shape). The idea is illustrated in Fig. 8.20. The above methodology is used for forecasting each revenue and cost driver. Once a revenue or cost driver

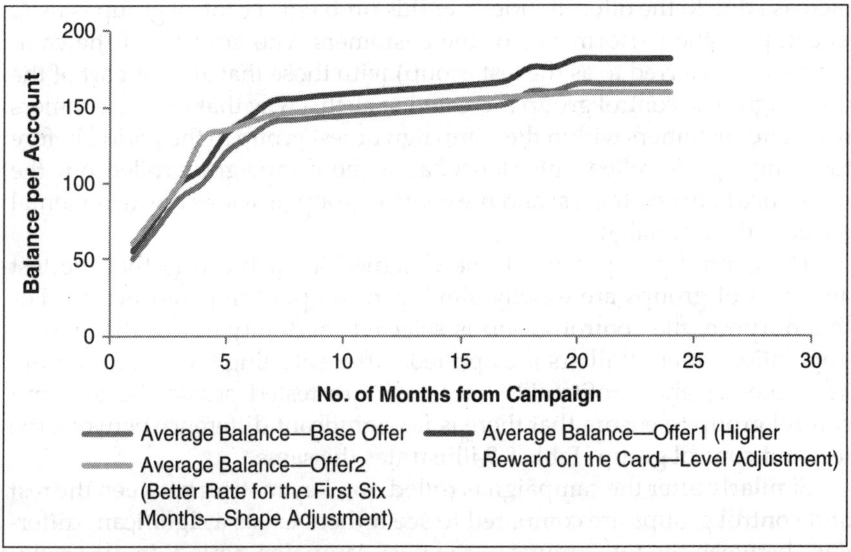


**Figure 8.20** Shape and Level Adjustment of a Revenue Driver

has been forecasted, the corresponding revenue or cost component can be calculated by multiplying the driver with the applicable rate (as described in Section 8.10). It needs to be noted that the forecast methodology described above needs to be applied at the level of a revenue or cost driver as the same can only be related to expected customer behavior.

The profitability of the campaign is forecasted using the forecast for each revenue and cost components. The forecasts are tracked over time so as to fine tune the base line results for all future campaigns.

## 8.11 Use of Test vs. Control as a Measurement Technique

In order to know the effect of a campaign, it is important to measure the change in key revenue and profitability metrics for customers who, have been targeted as part of the campaign. One possible way of measuring the effect is to find the change in key metrics before and after the campaign. This is called pre vs. post analysis where the effect of the campaign is measured on the customers who are part of the campaign only. The pre vs. post analysis provides information about the effect of the campaign, but does not provide information on what would have happened if the campaign was not carried out at all. For example, if one considers a campaign where bonus reward points are awarded to credit card customers for shopping above a particular threshold during the Christmas shopping time, then one will off-course observe an increase in sales before and after the campaign. However, it is difficult to say if the increase would have naturally occurred because of the festive shopping season or was the increase due to the offer. To tide over this problem, a control group is used to compare the performance of the customers who are part of the campaign (also referred to as the test group) with those that are not part of the campaign. The control group is created in such a way that these customers resemble customers within the campaign or test group in the period before the campaign is rolled out. Hence, after the campaign is rolled out the difference between the test and the control group provides the incremental effect of the campaign.

The control group needs to be designed in such a way that the test and control groups are exactly similar in the pre-campaign period. For this purpose, the control group is selected randomly out of the eligible population, after all filters are applied. After selecting the control group, key revenue and profitability measures are tested across the test and control group to ensure that there is no significant difference between the test and control group. Table 8.9 illustrates the same.

Similarly after the campaign is rolled out, key metrics between the test and control groups are compared to see if there exists a significant difference between the two groups in the post-campaign period. In case a significant difference exists, only then can it be concluded that the campaign has created an incremental effect. Otherwise any change in key metrics

**Table 8.9** Test vs. Control Measurement

| Metric | Test (Size 75,000 Accounts) | Control (Size 5,000 Accounts) |
|---|---|---|
| Size | 75000 | 5000 |
| Minutes of usage (monthly)—average | 685 | 701 |
| Minutes of usage(monthly)—standard deviation | 22 | 27 |

| Objective | Evaluate If Test is Similar to Control Before the Campaign is Rolled Out |
|---|---|
| Test | Null Hypothesis: Average in test = Average in control |
| Success criteria | Fail to reject null hypothesis |
| Pooled standard deviation | 22.345 |
| Difference in mean | –16 |
| Test statistic | –0.716 |
| Decision criteria | If the test statistic is between +0.96 to –0.96 then we can say that test and control are similar (the limit of +/–0.96 is obtained from the Z-table based on 95% confidence) |

**Table 8.10** Test vs. Control Measurement

| Metric | Test (Size 75,000 Accounts) | Control (Size 5,000 Accounts) |
|---|---|---|
| Size | 75000 | 5000 |
| Minutes of usage(monthly)—Average | 720 | 690 |
| Minutes of usage(monthly)—Standard Deviation | 31 | 26 |
| **Objective** | **Evaluate if minutes of usage in test is higher compared to control after the campaign is rolled out** | |
| Test | Null Hypothesis: Average in test = Average in control | |
| Success criteria | Reject null hypothesis | |
| Pooled standard deviation | 30.711 | |
| Difference in mean | 30 | |
| Test statistic | 0.976 | |
| Decision criteria | If the test statistic is more than +0.96 then we can say that the test has higher minutes of usage than control (assuming a 95% confidence) | |

cannot be attributed to the campaign. Table 8.10 illustrates the test vs. control comparison in the post-campaign period.

Some companies use a universal control group which is not part of any campaign or customer management activity. For each campaign, the eligible population, which is part of the universal control group is kept aside as the control group for the particular campaign. However, a possible limitation of this approach can be that in some cases, the eligible group can have very few customers from the universal control group. In that case, the control group may become too small.

In some cases, designing the control group can be more difficult, the following two examples illustrate the same:

1. **Example-1: Above the line campaign:** For a case where a campaign in a restaurant offers a 10% discount to customers who use a particular credit card, it is impossible to know which customers will see the offer. In such a case, it is difficult to select a control group beforehand. Only after the campaign is over and some customers have responded to the offer it is possible to know who all responded to the campaign and then it is important to quantify the incremental effect of this offer. In this case, it is required to carve out a control group out of the overall population in such a way that the control group resembles the responder population.

2. **Example-2: Control group which looks like customers who respond to the offer:** If one considers any direct marketing offer then a very small percentage of customers respond to the offer. The control group which is designed before the roll out of the offer looks exactly like the overall population which was targeted in the campaign. But the group which responded to the offer is a small biased sub-sample of the population which was targeted. Now if one wants to quantify the effects of the campaign on responders only, then one needs to carve out a subset of the control group in such a way that the subset resembles the responder population, in the pre-campaign period. The overall control group which resembles the overall campaign (test) population is not suitable for this purpose.

In both the examples, it is necessary to carve out a control group from the overall population (in the first case) or from the bigger control group (in the second case) which resembles (has similar profile in the pre-campaign period) the population of interest. A stratified sampling technique or a nearest neighbour technique is used for this purpose. The following example illustrates the stratified sampling technique for creating a desired control group.

If one considers two dimensions on which the control group needs to be similar to the test group and the two dimensions have three levels each, namely, high, medium and low, then the distribution of the test group is first checked along these two dimensions (depicted in Table 8.11).

The control group must also have the same distribution along these two dimensions. If one wants to have a control group of size 1000 then the distribution of the control group should be as depicted in Table 8.12.

The group High-High consists of 5% of the test population, consequently it is expected that 5% of the control group (5% of 1,000), should also belong to this group. The desired control group population in each of the groups (High-Medium, Medium-Medium etc.) can be determined

**Table 8.11** Creating a Control Group—Analysing the Test Group Composition

| Dimension-1 | Dimension-2 | Proportion of Test |
|---|---|---|
| H | H | 5% |
| H | M | 7% |
| H | L | 20% |
| M | H | 23% |
| M | M | 12% |
| M | L | 5% |
| L | H | 7% |
| L | M | 9% |
| L | L | 12% |

**Table 8.12** Creating a Control Group—Identifying the Required Size of the Control Group*

| Dimension-1 | Dimension-2 | Desired Control Size | Actual Control Size | Actual Control Proportion | Proportion |
|---|---|---|---|---|---|
| H | H | 50 | 500 | 25% | 0.10 |
| H | M | 70 | 200 | 10% | 0.35 |
| H | L | 200 | 300 | 15% | 0.67 |
| M | H | 230 | 200 | 10% | 1.15 |
| M | M | 120 | 100 | 5% | 1.20 |
| M | L | 50 | 100 | 5% | 0.50 |
| L | H | 70 | 100 | 5% | 0.70 |
| L | M | 90 | 200 | 10% | 0.45 |
| L | L | 120 | 300 | 15% | 0.40 |

*A control group cannot be carved out if the required proportion of any group is greater than 1.

similarly. Now if one looks at the Medium-High and Medium-Medium group then one would find that the required number of customers in these two groups are more than the available number of customers and hence, this is clearly not possible to create these groups out of the existing control group population. So given the size of the current overall control group, it is not possible to carve out a desired control group of 1000. Hence, one has to be satisfied with a smaller control group size. If one wants to create a control group of size 800 then all the proportions are less than 1 and hence, it is feasible to create a control group of size 800. To illustrate further, in the test population the group "High-High" consists of 5% of the population. Hence in the control group also this group should consist of 5% of the control group population. Given that the desired control group size is now 800 (as it was not possible to create a control group of size 1000), the control group should have 40 (5% of 800) customers in this group. However, the control group actually has 500 customers in this group. Hence, out of 500 customers one needs to choose 40 customers at random, these 40 randomly chosen customers would be included in the newly created (carved out) control group. The exercise is repeated for other groups (e.g., "High-Medium", "Medium-Medium" etc.) to carve out a new control group, which has the same distribution as the test group, along the two key dimensions of interest (Table 8.13 illustrates the same).

The above observation illustrates the limitation of approaches of creating control groups, if there are multiple dimensions along which the test and control group needs to be identical, then one may run into a sample size issue where one will not be able to find enough observations in each group.

**Table 8.13** Creating a Control Group*

| Dimension-1 | Dimension-2 | Desired Control Size | Actual Control Size | Actual Control Proportion | Proportion |
|---|---|---|---|---|---|
| H | H | 40 | 500 | 25% | 0.08 |
| H | M | 56 | 200 | 10% | 0.28 |
| H | L | 160 | 300 | 15% | 0.53 |
| M | H | 184 | 200 | 10% | 0.92 |
| M | M | 96 | 100 | 5% | 0.96 |
| M | L | 40 | 100 | 5% | 0.40 |
| L | H | 56 | 100 | 5% | 0.56 |
| L | M | 72 | 200 | 10% | 0.36 |
| L | L | 96 | 300 | 15% | 0.32 |

*A control group can only be carved out if the required proportion in each group is less than 1.

### 8.11.1 Pre vs. Post Analysis

In cases where it is impossible to have a control group, one needs to perform a pre vs. post analysis on the campaign group itself for understanding the effect of the campaign. Though a pre vs. post analysis does not provide the real impact of the campaign, yet in the absence of a control group, it is the best possible alternative. Similar to the test vs. control analysis described earlier, one can perform a hypothesis, the null hypothesis being that the pre and post metrics are equal. Sometimes one might use a percentage difference between pre and post as a measure as well. This assumes importance when the campaign needs to be compared with agreed benchmarks. For example, a campaign might promise a 5% lift in minutes of usage (MOU). In this case, one can calculate Percentage lift = (MOU Pre – MOU Post)/MOU Pre and the lift needs to be compared to the benchmark set prior to the campaign. In the ideal case, if a control group did exist then, one should not only see the lift but also examine the incremental lift (Lift in test – Lift in control).

## 8.12 Design of Experiments for Testing

Marketers often need to test the impact of a wide range of targeting, advertising, promotion, pricing and product options so as to find out the optimal combination of factors or features. For this purpose, most companies set aside a testing budget that will allow them to test and learn. However, it is never possible to test all combinations of every marketing parameter. Hence, marketers often build a testing framework, which helps them in identifying the critical few learnings that they want to derive out of the limited test budget they have. In many cases, the concept of design of experiments is widely used in building the testing framework. A design of experiments approach helps in limiting the number of tests that need to be conducted, to generate all the required learnings.

To illustrate the use of experimental design, one could consider the pricing of balance transfer offers for credit cards. Balance transfers are offered to customers who are willing to transfer balance from some other credit card to the credit card of the particular issuer. The balance transfer offer promises to offer a lower rate (also called promotional rate) on the transferred balance for a specific period of time, after the specified time, whatever balance is left is charged at the normal interest rate which is higher than the promotional rate. The balance transfer offer is communicated to existing credit card customers through various channels like direct mailers, telecalling, email, etc. Most often the customer is also able to see the offer once he or she logs in to the Internet site of the credit card issuer. The pricing of a balance transfer includes the following components:

- The interest rate offered to the balance that is transferred (this interest rate is lower than the normal interest rate charged on the credit card).
- The period for which the lower interest will be applicable.
- The upfront fee that is charged at the time of balance transfer (mostly this fee is charged as a percentage of the amount that is transferred).
- The maximum amount that can be transferred. Sometimes customers are allowed to transfer as much amount as is allowed by their available credit limit. However, in some cases, the credit card issuer imposes a cap on the amount that can be transferred.

In order to ascertain the price elasticity along all these components of pricing, it is critical to conduct experiments where all possible combination of the above are offered to customers in a particular segment and the effect is measured on the response rate (i.e., the number of customers who respond to the offer) and the quantum of balances transferred by customers who respond to the offer. For a hypothetical example the following combinations may be considered.

- Promotional interest rate: 6.99%, 9.99% and 12.99%
- Duration of the promotional rate: 9 months, 12 months
- Balance transfer fee: 1% of transferred amount, 3% of transferred amount
- Cap on maximum amount that can be transferred: no cap, cap of $5,000

Table 8.14 depicts the total combinations. The cells marked in grey are the ones which take a value of zero for that particular combination. For example, C1 involves:

- Promotional interest rate of 6.99%, duration of 9 months, transfer fee of 1% and no cap on transfer.

There are three promotional interest rates, two types of durations, two types of transfer fees and two offer types (with cap and no cap). Hence, there will be 3 * 2 * 2 * 2 combinations that one can have. Marketers have

**Table 8.14** Design of Experiments—List of all Possible Combinations for the Sample Balance Transfer Offer

| | Interest Rate | | | Duration | | Transfer Fee | | Cap on Transfer | |
|---|---|---|---|---|---|---|---|---|---|
| Combination | r1 = 6.99% | r2 = 9.99% | r3 = 12.99% | d1 = 12 Months | d2 = 9 Months | f1 = 1% Fee | f2 = 3% Fee | c1 = No Cap | c2 = cap of $5,000 |
| C4 | 1 | | | 1 | | | 1 | | 1 |
| C8 | 1 | | | | 1 | | 1 | | 1 |
| C12 | | 1 | | 1 | | | 1 | | 1 |
| C16 | | 1 | | | 1 | | 1 | | 1 |
| C20 | | | 1 | 1 | | | 1 | | 1 |
| C24 | | | 1 | | 1 | | 1 | | 1 |
| C2 | 1 | | | 1 | | 1 | | | 1 |
| C6 | 1 | | | | 1 | 1 | | | 1 |
| C10 | | 1 | | 1 | | 1 | | | 1 |
| C14 | | 1 | | | 1 | 1 | | | 1 |
| C18 | | | 1 | 1 | | 1 | | | 1 |
| C22 | | | 1 | | 1 | 1 | | | 1 |
| C3 | 1 | | | 1 | | | 1 | 1 | |
| C7 | 1 | | | | 1 | | 1 | 1 | |
| C11 | | 1 | | 1 | | | 1 | 1 | |
| C15 | | 1 | | | 1 | | 1 | 1 | |
| C19 | | | 1 | 1 | | | 1 | 1 | |
| C23 | | | 1 | | 1 | | 1 | 1 | |
| C1 | 1 | | | 1 | | 1 | | 1 | |
| C5 | 1 | | | | 1 | 1 | | 1 | |
| C9 | | 1 | | 1 | | 1 | | 1 | |
| C13 | | 1 | | | 1 | 1 | | 1 | |
| C17 | | | 1 | 1 | | 1 | | 1 | |
| C21 | | | 1 | | 1 | 1 | | 1 | |

used concepts of design of experiments to limit the number of combinations (out of the set of all possible combinations) that needs to be tested to make meaningful inferences. In understanding how design of experiments can help one in limiting the number of combinations that need to be tested, one needs to understand the effects of each attribute separately and the effect of these attributes acting in tandem (conjoint effect).

### *8.12.1 Design of Experiments Without Interaction Effects*

If one assumes no interaction effect between the factors, then the response function can be written as:

$$\text{Ln}(p/1 - p) = \alpha + \beta 1(\text{Interest rate r1}) + \beta 2(\text{Interest rate r2}) + \beta 3(\text{Duration d1}) + \beta 4(\text{Fee f1}) + \beta 5(\text{Cap c1})$$

In this expression, "p" represents the probability of response (and hence, response rate) $\beta$ represent the effect of each factor and each attribute. Based on past experience, it has been found that response can be predicted by using a logistic function.

The variables interest rate r1, interest rate r2, duration d1, fee f1, presence of a cap on amount transferred c1, are all binary variables and take the value of 1 when that particular attribute is present and "0" otherwise. The function for each offer combination is depicted in Table 8.15.

From Table 8.15 it can be see that if one tests combination C4 ($\ln(p4/(1 - p4)) = \alpha + \beta 1 + \beta 3$ ) and C23 ($\ln(p23/(1 - p23)) = \alpha + \beta 5$) then one can easily estimate the response rate for combination C3 ($\ln(p3/(1 - p3)) = \alpha + \beta 1 + \beta 3 + \beta 5$). The combinations C4, C23 and C3 represent the following combinations:

- **C4:** Interest rate of 6.99% (r1 = 1), duration of 12 months (d1 = 1), fee of 3% (f1 = 0), cap of $5,000 on the transferred balances (c1 = 0)
- **C23:** Interest rate of 12.99% (r1 = 0, r2 = 0), duration of 9 months (d1 = 0), fee of 3% (f1 = 0), no cap on the transferred balance (c1 = 1)
- **C3:** Interest rate of 6.99% (r1 = 1), duration of 12 months (d1 = 1), fee of 3% (f1 = 0), no cap on the transferred balance (c1 = 1)

It can be seen that:

$$\ln(p4/(1 - p4)) + \ln(p23/(1 - p23)) = \ln(p3/(1 - p3))$$

This feature is the key benefit of a properly designed experiment or test. By performing a limited number of tests it is possible to infer the results of some of the combinations which have not been tested. The importance of this result lies in the fact that marketers always have a limited budget for testing and hence, it is always crucial to identify the limited number of tests that needs to be performed to derive maximum amount of learning. From the above example one can clearly identify the following limited set of experiments, which can provide all the learnings that are required to assess the effect of any combination of the above factors:

**Table 8.15** Design of Experiments—List of all Possible Combinations for the Sample Balance Transfer Offer Along with the Response Equation for Each

| | Interest Rate | | | Duration | | Transfer Fee | | Cap on Transfer | | |
|---|---|---|---|---|---|---|---|---|---|---|
| Combination | r 1 = 6.99% | r2 = 9.99% | r3 = 12.99% | d1 = 12 Months | d2 = 9 Months | f1 = 1% Fee | f2 = 3% Fee | c1 = No Cap | c2 = Cap of $5,000 | Response Equation |
| C4 | 1 | | | 1 | | | 1 | | 1 | $\ln(p/(1-p)) = \alpha + \beta 1 + \beta 3$ |
| C8 | 1 | | | | 1 | | 1 | | 1 | $\ln(p/(1-p)) = \alpha + \beta 1$ |
| C12 | | 1 | | 1 | | | 1 | | 1 | $\ln(p/(1-p)) = \alpha + \beta 2 + \beta 3$ |
| C16 | | 1 | | | 1 | | 1 | | 1 | $\ln(p/(1-p)) = \alpha + \beta 2$ |
| C20 | | | 1 | 1 | | | 1 | | 1 | $\ln(p/(1-p)) = \alpha + \beta 3$ |
| C24 | | | 1 | | 1 | | 1 | | 1 | $\ln(p/(1-p)) = \alpha$ |
| C2 | 1 | | | 1 | | 1 | | | 1 | $\ln(p/(1-p)) = \alpha + \beta 1 + \beta 3 + \beta 4$ |
| C6 | 1 | | | | 1 | 1 | | | 1 | $\ln(p/(1-p)) = \alpha + \beta 1 + \beta 4$ |
| C10 | | 1 | | 1 | | 1 | | | 1 | $\ln(p/(1-p)) = \alpha + \beta 2 + \beta 3 + \beta 4$ |
| C14 | | 1 | | | 1 | 1 | | | 1 | $\ln(p/(1-p)) = \alpha + \beta 2 + \beta 4$ |
| C18 | | | 1 | 1 | | 1 | | | 1 | $\ln(p/(1-p)) = \alpha + \beta 3 + \beta 4$ |
| C22 | | | 1 | | 1 | 1 | | | 1 | $\ln(p/(1-p)) = \alpha + \beta 4$ |
| C3 | 1 | | | 1 | | | 1 | 1 | | $\ln(p/(1-p)) = \alpha + \beta 1 + \beta 3 + \beta 5$ |
| C7 | 1 | | | | 1 | | 1 | 1 | | $\ln(p/(1-p)) = \alpha + \beta 1 + \beta 5$ |
| C11 | | 1 | | 1 | | | 1 | 1 | | $\ln(p/(1-p)) = \alpha + \beta 2 + \beta 3 + \beta 5$ |
| C15 | | 1 | | | 1 | | 1 | 1 | | $\ln(p/(1-p)) = \alpha + \beta 2 + \beta 5$ |
| C19 | | | 1 | 1 | | | 1 | 1 | | $\ln(p/(1-p)) = \alpha + \beta 3 + \beta 5$ |
| C23 | | | 1 | | 1 | | 1 | 1 | | $\ln(p/(1-p)) = \alpha + \beta 5$ |
| C1 | 1 | | | 1 | | 1 | | 1 | | $\ln(p/(1-p)) = \alpha + \beta 1 + \beta 3 + \beta 4 + \beta 5$ |
| C5 | 1 | | | | 1 | 1 | | 1 | | $\ln(p/(1-p)) = \alpha + \beta 1 + \beta 4 + \beta 5$ |
| C9 | | 1 | | 1 | | 1 | | 1 | | $\ln(p/(1-p)) = \alpha + \beta 2 + \beta 3 + \beta 4 + \beta 5$ |
| C13 | | 1 | | | 1 | 1 | | 1 | | $\ln(p/(1-p)) = \alpha + \beta 2 + \beta 4 + \beta 5$ |
| C17 | | | 1 | 1 | | 1 | | 1 | | $\ln(p/(1-p)) = \alpha + \beta 3 + \beta 4 + \beta 5$ |
| C21 | | | 1 | | 1 | 1 | | 1 | | $\ln(p/(1-p)) = \alpha + \beta 4 + \beta 5$ |

- From the results of experiment C24 one will be able to ascertain the value of $\alpha$
- From the results of C4 and C8, one can obtain the value of $\beta 3$
- If one plugs in the value of a and $\beta 3$ in the results of C4, one can obtain the value of $\beta 1$
- Now if one has the results of experiment C12, then one can plug in the values of a and $\beta 3$ to obtain $\beta 2$
- If one has the result of C10 one could use the values of a, $\beta 2$ and $\beta 3$ to obtain $\beta 4$
- The value of $\beta 5$ can be obtained by plugging in the value of $\beta 2$ into the result of experiment C15.

Hence, if one has the results of experiments C4, C8, C12, C14, C10, and C15, then one can arrive at the results for all the other combinations.

## 8.12.2 Design of Experiments With Interaction Effect

One could easily infer that the combination of a lower promotional interest rate and higher duration would incentivise customers to respond more as compared to each of these factors individually. That means the interaction between interest and duration needs to be taken into account. Hence, the response function would take the following form:

$$\begin{aligned}\text{Ln}(p/1-p) = {} & \alpha + \beta 1(\text{Interest rate r1}) + \beta 2(\text{Interest rate r2}) + \\ & \beta 3(\text{Duration d1}) + \beta 4(\text{Fee f1}) + \beta 5(\text{Cap c1}) + \\ & \beta_{10}(\text{Interest rate r1* Duration d1})\end{aligned}$$

[it needs to be noted that $\beta_{10}$ represents the effect due to interaction].

Similarly, if other two-way interactions are considered, the response function will take the following form:

$$\begin{aligned}\text{Ln}(p/1-p) = {} & \alpha + \beta 1(\text{Interest rate r1}) + \beta 2(\text{Interest rate r2}) + \\ & \beta 3(\text{Duration d1}) + \beta 4(\text{Fee f1}) + \beta 5(\text{Cap c1}) + \beta_{10} \\ & (\text{Interest rate r1* Duration d1}) + \beta_{11}(\text{Interest rate r1 * } \\ & \text{Fee f1}) + \beta_{12}(\text{Interest rate r1* Cap c1}) + \beta_{13}(\text{Duration d1*} \\ & \text{Fee f1}) + \beta_{14}(\text{Duration d1* Cap c1}) + \beta_{15}(\text{Fee f1* Cap c1})\end{aligned}$$

If three-way interactions are considered the response function will take the following form:

$$\begin{aligned}\text{Ln}(p/1-p) = {} & \alpha + \beta 1(\text{Interest rate r1}) + \beta 2(\text{Interest rate r2}) + \\ & \beta 3(\text{Duration d1}) + \beta 4(\text{Fee f1}) + \beta 5(\text{Cap c1}) + \beta_{10} \\ & (\text{Interest rate r1* Duration d1}) + \beta_{11}(\text{Interest rate r1 * Fee} \\ & \text{f1}) + \beta_{12}(\text{Interest rate r1* Cap c1}) + \beta_{13}(\text{Duration d1* Fee} \\ & \text{f1}) + \beta_{14}(\text{Duration d1* Cap c1}) + \beta_{15}(\text{Fee f1 * Cap c1}) + \\ & \beta_{100}(\text{Interest rate r1* Duration d1* Fee f1}) + \beta_{101}(\text{Interest} \\ & \text{rate r1* Duration d1* Cap c1}) + \beta_{102}(\text{Duration d1* Cap c1} \\ & \text{* Fee f1}) + \beta_{103}(\text{Interest rate r1* Cap c1 * Fee f1})\end{aligned}$$

As it can be easily seen, it is difficult to limit the number of experiments or tests that need to be conducted if there are significant interactions. To generate the maximum learning from any test programme, it is best to adopt a full factorial test design whereby all the possible combinations are tested; however, because of cost constraints, a partial factorial design, where a limited set of factors are tested is very often used to test the vital few combinations and infer the results of the untested combinations. Table 8.16 illustrates how a limited set of experiments can be used to compute all the required test results.

**Table 8.16** Finding the Minimum Number of Experiments that Need to be Conducted

| Combination | Response Equation |
|---|---|
| C4 | $\ln(p/(1-p)) = \alpha + \beta1 + \beta3$ |
| C8 | $\ln(p/(1-p)) = \alpha + \beta1$ |
| C12 | $\ln(p/(1-p)) = \alpha + \beta2 + \beta3$ |
| C16 | $\ln(p/(1-p)) = \alpha + \beta2$ |
| C20 | $\ln(p/(1-p)) = \alpha + \beta3$ |
| C24 | $\ln(p/(1-p)) = \alpha$ |
| C2 | $\ln(p/(1-p)) = \alpha + \beta1 + \beta3 + \beta4$ |
| C6 | $\ln(p/(1-p)) = \alpha + \beta1 + \beta4$ |
| C10 | $\ln(p/(1-p)) = \alpha + \beta2 + \beta3 + \beta4$ |
| C14 | $\ln(p/(1-p)) = \alpha + \beta2 + \beta4$ |
| C18 | $\ln(p/(1-p)) = \alpha + \beta3 + \beta4$ |
| C22 | $\ln(p/(1-p)) = \alpha + \beta4$ |
| C3 | $\ln(p/(1-p)) = \alpha + \beta1 + \beta3 + \beta5$ |
| C7 | $\ln(p/(1-p)) = \alpha + \beta1 + \beta5$ |
| C11 | $\ln(p/(1-p)) = \alpha + \beta2 + \beta3 + \beta5$ |
| C15 | $\ln(p/(1-p)) = \alpha + \beta2 + \beta5$ |
| C19 | $\ln(p/(1-p)) = \alpha + \beta3 + \beta5$ |
| C23 | $\ln(p/(1-p)) = \alpha + p5$ |
| C1 | $\ln(p/(1-p)) = \alpha + \beta1 + \beta3 + \beta4 + \beta5$ |
| C5 | $\ln(p/(1-p)) = \alpha + \beta1 + \beta4 + \beta5$ |
| C9 | $\ln(p/(1-p)) = \alpha + \beta2 + \beta3 + \beta4 + \beta5$ |
| C13 | $\ln(p/(1-p)) = \alpha + \beta2 + \beta4 + \beta5$ |
| C17 | $\ln (p/(1-p)) = \alpha + \beta3 + \beta4 + \beta5$ |
| C21 | $\ln (p/(1-p)) = \alpha + \beta4 + \beta5$ |

## 8.13 Analytical Tools

Analytical tools and softwares form another important component of the analytics ecosystem. Analysts use a variety of tools to manipulate data and apply various quantitative techniques on data to generate insights and predictions. The current section aims at discussing some of the commonly used analytical tools. As already pointed out, all analytical tools have two key purposes: the first involves manipulation of data and the second involves application of various algorithms to the data. With regards to manipulation of data, SAS is possibly the most flexible and scalable tool available commercially. For application of quantitative algorithms a host of commercial tools are available, though SAS is still the dominant tool used by the analytical community.

Before listing down the common commercial tools which are frequently used by the analytical community it is important to understand the key algorithms, or quantitative techniques that are most frequently used. Based on surveys conducted by KDnuggets and other surveys (like *Surveying the Field: Current Data Mining Applications, Analytic Tools, and Practical Challenges* by Karl Rexer, PhD; Paul Gearan; & Heather N. Allen, PhD) the most commonly used analytical techniques include:

- Decision trees (mostly CHAID and CART)
- Regression
- Cluster analysis
- Neural nets
- Association rules
- Factor analysis
- Time-series
- Bayesian
- Support vector machines (SVM)
- Boosting algorithms
- Rule induction
- Survival analysis
- Genetic algorithms
- Link analysis

These techniques have been listed in order of frequency of usage (as per study by KDnuggets and others). The most frequently used techniques have been listed in the top of the list. One important aspect that needs to be noted is that optimisation techniques and operations research techniques like linear programming, integer programming, etc. have not been considered in the list. These techniques, most often used in supply chain management, logistics, transportation and airlines, could have been there in the list after regression or cluster analysis. The reason for their omission is because they are possibly not considered pure data mining techniques. Hence, optimization routines are not part of most data mining software tools. Though, some tools like SAS provides a SAS operations research package which provides these functionalities. However, most operations research techniques are part of independent software tools.

These techniques and algorithms are used for various types of analysis and one particular analysis may include a combination of many of these algorithms. And every analysis will have a data manipulation component built into it. As per the survey conducted by Karl Rexer, Paul Gearan and Heather N. Allen, the factors that influence the choice of software tools include:

- Dependability/stability of software
- Ability to handle very large data sets
- Data manipulation capabilities
- Quality of output/ease of interpretation
- Ability to automate repetitive tasks
- Speed
- Availability of specific analytic technique of interest
- Variety of available algorithms
- Ease of applying scoring models to other datasets
- Ease of use
- Cost of software
- Ability to modify algorithm options to fine tune analysis
- Experience/familiarity
- Enables mining within one's database
- Quality of manuals/documentation
- Ability to write own code
- Quality of the graphical user interface
- Compatibility with other software
- Enables batch processing
- Quality of graphics
- Compatibility with colleagues/peers
- The software is widely used/well-regarded

The common analytical software tools offer these features in varying proportions. Some of the tools like SAS score very highly on data manipulation and scalability while others like Angoss Knowledge Seeker and Knowledge Studio score very high on the quality of their graphical user interface and the robustness of some of the algorithms. Before embarking on a brief description of the common tools, it is important to list down the common software tools used by the analytical community. However, it is important to note that in many cases a particular analytical team may use more than one of these tools at the same time. For example, it is commonly observed that a team uses SAS for data manipulation and most analysis particularly regression but uses Angoss Knowledge seeker for decision trees and R or S Plus for some seldomly used techniques like link analysis, association rules mining, etc. Another important point to note is the fact that the area of analytics and data mining is a fast evolving area and new tools are being added almost every quarter. Each tool has its own key merits and sometimes a particular tool may be very popular with a particular analytical group but may not be very widely used. This section aims at listing the current frequently used analytical software tools. Today the most frequently used analytical software tools include:

- SAS and SAS enterprise miner
- SPSS and Clementine
- Angoss Knowledge Seeker and Knowledge Studio
- R and S-Plus
- Salford Systems CART, MARS, RandomForest and TreeNet
- KXEN
- Other free tools like Weka
- Statistica
- Fair Isaac Model Builder
- Xeno
- C5.0

The rest of the section provides an overview of these tools from an analytical user's perspective. It is very important to note that most of these tools are getting enhanced every day and the software vendors are coming up with new techniques and newer ways of looking at analysis. Hence, some of the limitations of each tool discussed here may not be relevant.

Many analytical teams use SAS as the default software tool and other tools to complement SAS. Though SAS is primarily a code and programme-driven software, the SAS enterprise miner has a graphical user interface that helps an analyst to have a visual description of the analytical process. However, some of the other tools provide better visual representation of data and analysis results. In certain cases, some of the newer algorithms like stochastic gradient boosting, random forest, etc. are not available in SAS, which makes it important to explore other tools which provide these newer algorithms.

SPSS and Clementine have recently been bought over by IBM. The SPSS family offers very good graphical user interface to the analyst and can be mastered quickly. However, SPSS is less effective in automating the analytical process. Being mostly graphical user interface-driven, it is difficult to automate repetitive analytical tasks using the SPSS platform. This is important not only from a process automation perspective but also from an analysis perspective because when an analyst is running any algorithm he or she will run the same algorithm multiple times to find out the optimal set of predictor variables. This process becomes very tedious without a flexible automation environment.

Angoss tools are very popular for running decision trees using the CHAID algorithm. The strongest feature of Angoss Knowledge Seeker and Knowledge Studio is the visual representation of data. These tools also offer a feature called strategy trees wherein multiple objectives can be optimised in a single decision tree. For example, one may want to build a decision tree that optimises response rate to an offer at the first stage and profitability of the offer at the second stage. A strategy tree is a very good tool for such purposes. Angoss Knowledge Studio also offers other algorithms like regression, clustering and neural network.

R and S-Plus have developed out of the open source space and offers a wide variety of algorithms, some of the algorithms which are new and seldom used can only be found as a R or S-Plus package. Being open source these tools offer the flexibility of adding the latest available algorithms into their list very quickly as they don't have to go through the licensing cycle of a typical commercial software. Secondly, due to the open source environment, a lot of innovation and new thinking gets embedded in the new R and S-plus packages. However, the biggest limitation of these tools is their data handling and data manipulation capability. Many commercial organisations, particularly organisations providing financial services are less open to using a open source tool within their IT environment. This makes these tools less attractive.

Salford systems CART, MARS, RandomForest and TreeNet offer excellent cutting edge algorithms particularly for solving classification type problems. These represent niche tools which are extremely good in a few critical algorithms and can be used along with an existing wide tool like SAS or SPSS for performing specialised analysis.

KXEN offers very good capability around support vector machine (SVM) and is a widely used tool for classification problems, particularly in cases where the event rate is very low. FICO's model builder and InfoCentricity's Xeno are software tools particularly for building risk score cards. These tools have automated many of the important elements like binning which are critical for building risk score cards. The above discussion of the common tools is not a comprehensive discussion, and analytical teams need to have an evaluation strategy to identify the correct tools that best suit their need.

# Bibliography


**Chapter 1**

Applied Geographic Solutions. "The Mosaic Handbook." http://www.appliedgeographic.com/.

D&B Global Trade Program. http://www.dnb.com/global-trade/dnb-global-trade-program.html.

Environment Health and Safety Online-The U.S. Standard Industrial Classification (SIC) "Introduction to Naics-The U.S. Standard Industrial Classification (Sic)": United States Department of Labour, 2012.

Government of India Census Data. "Houselisting and Housing Census Data - 2011." Government of India, 2011.

Huff, D. and McCallum, B. "Calibrating the Huff Model Using ArcGIS Business Analyst." An ESRI ® White Paper, 2008.

Hughes, A. "The Loyalty Effect: A New Look at Lifetime Value." Data Base Marketing Institute, 2009.

Lewis, M. "Customer Acquisition Promotions and Customer Asset Value." *Journal of Marketing Research*, 43, no. 2 (2006): 195–203.

Lix, T., Berger, P. and Magliozzi, T. "New Customer Acquisition: Prospecting Models and the Use of Commercially Available External Data." *Journal of Direct Marketing*, 9, no. 4 (2006): 8–18.

Mangold, W. and Faulds, D. "Social Media: The New Hybrid Element of the marketing mix.

Nakanishi, M. and Cooper, L. "Parameter Estimation for a Multiplicative Competitive Interaction Model: Least Squares Approach." *Journal of Marketing Research* 11, no. 3 (1974): 303–11.

Nakanishi, M. and Cooper, L. "Technical Note—Simplified Estimation Procedures for MCI Models." *Marketing Science* 1, no. 3 (1982): 314–22.

Nash, E. *Direct Marketing - Strategy, Planning, Execution*: McGraw-Hill, 1999.

PAYDEX[R]: Business Definition. http://mycredit.dnb.com/glossaries/paydex/.

Pick, J. "Geographic Information Systems in Business." Idea Group Publishing, 2005.

Promotion Mix. "*Business Horizons*", 52 (2009): 357–65.

Punj, G. and Stewart, D. "Cluster Analysis in Marketing Research: Review and Suggestions for Application." *Journal of Marketing Research*, 20, no. 2 (1983): 134–48.

Smith, S. and Morrison, P. "Small-Area and Business Demography." In *Handbook of Population*, Springer, 2005.

Tetrad Computer Applications Inc. "Canadian Demographics." http://www.tetrad.com/demographics/canada/environics/.

Villanueva, J., Yoo, S. and Hanssens, D. "The Impact of Marketing-Induced Versus Word-of-Mouth Customer Acquisition on Customer Equity Growth." *Journal of Marketing Research*, 45, no. 1 (2007): 48–59.

Webber, R. "Designing Geodemographic Classifications to Meet Contemporary Business Needs." *Interactive Marketing* 5, no. 3 (2004): 219–37.

**Chapter 2**

Aasael, H. *Consumer Behaviour and Marketing Action*. Fourth ed. Boston, MA: PWS-Kent, 1992.

Alexander, W. and Grimshaw, S. "Dynamic Delinquency Movement Matrix Forecasting." Unpublished.

Benavent, C., Crie, D. and Meyer-Waarden, L. "Analysis of the Efficiency of Retailer Loyalty Programs - Empirical Investigation Based Upon Store Scanner Data." In The 3rd AFM French-German Conference, 2000.

Berman, B. "Developing an Effective Customer Loyalty Program." *California Management Review* 49, no. 1 (2006): 143–48.

Bierman, H. and Hausman, W. "The Credit Granting Decision." *Management Science* 16, no. 8 (1970): B519–B32.

Blattberg, R., Briesch, R. and Fox, E. "How Promotions Work." *Marketing Science* 14, no. 3 Supplement (1995): G122–G32.

Blattberg, R., Kim, B. and Neslin, S. *Database Marketing*. First ed, International Series in Quantitative Marketing. New York, NY: Springer, 2008.

Blattberg, R. and Neslin, S. "Sales Promotion: The Long and the Short of It" *Marketing Letters* 1, no. 1 (1989): 81–97.

Blattberg, R. and Neslin, S. "Sales Promotion Models." In *Handbooks in Operations Research and Management Science, Volume-Marketing*, edited by J. Eliashberg and G. Lilien, 553–609. Amsterdam: North-Holland, 1993.

Boland, D., Morrison, D. and O'Neill, S. "The Future of CRM in the Airline Industry." 1–17: IBM Institute for Business Value, 2002.

Buckinx, W., Verstraeten, G. and Van den Poel, D. "Predicting Customer Loyalty Using the Internal Transactional Database." *Expert System with Application* 32 (2005): 125–34.

Chatfield, C. *The Analysis of Time Series: An Introduction*. Sixth ed. New York: Chapman and Hall/CRC Texts in Statistical Science, 2009.

Chin, A. "Impact of Frequent Flyer Programs on the Demand for Air Travel." *Journal of Air Transportation* 7, no. 2 (2002): 53–86.

Cigliano, J., Georgiadis, M., Pleasance, D. and Whalley, S. "The Power of Loyalty." McKinsey on Retail, Fourth of a Series on Growth in Retail, 2000.

Dick, A. and Basu, K. "Customer Loyalty: Toward an Integrated Conceptual Framework." *Journal of The Academy of Marketing Science* 22, no. 2 (1994): 99–113.

Dolnicar, S., Grabler, K., Grun, B. and Kulnig, A. "Key Drivers of Airline Loyalty." *Tourism Management* 32, no. 5 (2011): 1020–26.

Dowling, G. and Uncles, M. "Do Customer Loyalty Programmes Really Work?" *Sloan Management Review* Summer (1997): 71–82.

FICO. "How Are Credit Line Decreases Impacting Consumer Credit Risk?" In *Insights, FICO*, 2009.

Gerpott, T., Wolfgang, R. and Schindler, A. "Customer Retention, Loyalty and Satisfaction in the German Mobile Cellular Telecommunications Market." *Telecommunications Policy* 25, no. 4 (2001): 249–69.

Goehring, B., Janardhan, A. and Boyce, M. "Committed Customers or Captives?" In *Travel and Transportation*: IBM Global Business Services, IBM Institute for Business Value, 2008.

Gross, D. and Souleles, N. "Do Interest Rates and Liqudity Constraints Matter for Consumer Behaviour? Evidence from Credit Card Data." *The Quarterly Journal of Economics* 117, no. 1 (2002): 149–85.

Hallowell, R. "The Relationships of Customer Satisfaction, Customer Loyalty and Profitability: An Empirical Study." *International Journal of Service Industry Management* 7, no. 4 (1996): 27–42.

Jones, T. and Sasser, W. "Why Satisfied Customers Defect?" *Harvard Business Review* 73, no. 6 (November - December 1995): 88–99.

Kim, H. and Yoon, C. "Determinants of Subscriber Churn and Customer Loyalty in the Korean Mobile Telephony Market." *Telecommunications Policy* 28, no. 9–10 (2004): 751–65.

Lewis, M."The Influence of Loyalty Programs and Short-Term Promotions on Customer Retention." *Journal of Marketing Research* 43, no. 3 (2004): 281–92.

Magi, A. "Share of Wallet in Retailing: The Effects of Customer Satisfaction, Loyalty Cards and Shopper Characteristics." *Journal of Retailing* 79, no. 2 (2003): 97–106.

McGoldrick, P. and Andrew, E. "Consumer Misbehaviour: Promiscuity or Loyalty in Grocery Shopping." *Journal of Retailing and Consumer Services* 4, no. 2 (1997): 73–81.

McKinsey. "Getting More from Prepaid Mobile Services." *McKinsey Quarterly* (February 2008).

McKinsey. "Loyalty: Is It Really Working for You?" *Chief Marketing & Sales Officer Forum* (December 2011).

Meyer-Waarden, L. "Effects of Gratifications on Loyalty Program Utilities." Paper presented at the Proceedings of EMAC conference, Athens, 2006.

Meyer-Waarden, L. "The Effects of Loyalty Programs on Customer Lifetime Duration and Share of Wallet." *Journal of Retailing* 83, no. 2 (2007): 223–36.

Meyer-Waarden, L. and Benavent, C. "The Impact of Loyalty Programmes on Repeat Purchase Behaviour." *Journal of Marketing Management* 22, no. 1–2 (2006.): 61–88.

Meyer-Waarden, L. and Benavent, C. "Rewards That Reward." *Wall Street Journal*, Sep 17, 2008.

Neslin, S., Henderson, C. and Quelch, J. "Consumer Promotions and the Acceleration of Product Purchases." *Marketing Science* 4, no. 2 (May 1985): 147–65.

O'Brien, L. and Jones, C. "Do Rewards Really Create Loyalty." *Harvard Business Review* May (1995): 75–82.

O'Malley, L. "Can Loyalty Schemes Really Build Loyalty?" *Marketing Intelligence and Planning* 16, no. 1 (1998): 47–55.

Raju, J. "The Effect of Price Promotions on Variability in Product Category Sales." *Marketing Science* 11, no. 3 (1992): 207–20.

Reinartz, W. "Customer Lifetime Analysis: An Integrated Empirical Framework for Measurement and Explanation." Doctoral Dissertation, University of Houston, 1999.

Reinartz, W. "Understanding Customer Loyalty Programs." In *Retailing in the 21st Century, Current and Future Trends*, edited by Murali Mantrala and Manfred Krafft, 361–79. Berlin, Heidelberg: Springer Verlag, 2006.

Reinartz, W. and Kumar, V. "The Mismanagement of Customer Loyalty." *Harvard Business Review* 80, no. 7 (2002): 63–79.

Sharp, B. and Sharp, A. "Loyalty Programs and Their Impact on Repeat-Purchase Loyalty Pattterns." *International Journal of Research in Marketing* 14, no. 5 (1997): 473–86.

Soman, D. and Cheema, A. "The Effect of Credit on Spending Decisions: The Role of the Credit Limit and Credibility." *Marketing Science* 21, no. 1 (2002): 32–53.

Trench, M., Pederson, S., Lau, E., Ma, L., Wang, H. and Nair, S. "Managing Credit Lines and Prices for Bank One Credit Cards." *Interfaces* 33, no. 5 (2003): 4–21.

Watterson, A., Hornick, S. and Lalsare, R. "The New Economics of Customer Loyalty Programs." *The Journal of Professional Pricing* First Quarter (2008): 22–27.

Watterson, A., Hornick, S. and Lalsare, R. "The New Economics of Loyalty Programs." Oliver Wyman.

Weatherford, L. and Kimes, S. "A Comparsion of Forecasting Methods for Hotel Revenue Management." *International Journal of Forecasting* 19, no. 3 (2003): 401–15.

Whyte, R. "Frequent Flyer Programmes: Is It a Relationship, or Do the Schemes Create Spurious Loyalty?" *Journal of Targeting, Measurement and Analysis for Marketing* 12, no. 3 (2004): 269–80.

Winters, P. "Forecasting Sales by Exponentially Weighted Moving Average." *Management Science* 6, no. 3 (1960): 324–42.

Zeithaml, V., Berry, L. and Parasuraman, A. "The Behavioural Consequences of Service Quality." *The Journal of Marketing* 60, no. 2 (1996): 31–46.

**Chapter 3**

"A Conflict of Interest." *The Economist*, Oct 14, 2010.

"A Rich and Poor Strategy for Mexico." Retailer Banker International, http://www.vrl-financial-news.com/retail-banking/retail-banker-intl/issues/rbi-2009/rbi607/a-rich-and-poor-strategy-for-m.aspx.

Accenture. "Banking 2012: Revenue Growth and Innovation.", 2011.

Aksin, O. and Harker, P. "To Sell or Not to Sell." *Journal of Service Research* 2, no. 1 (1999): 19–33.

Amadeus. "Qantas Cross-Sell Case Study."

Ballenger, T. "Crossing the Balance Sheet." *White Paper* (2006), http://www.kendalltodd.com/downloads//crossingbalancesheet.pdf.

"Bank of America and Merrill Lynch: Moynihands Full." *The Economist*, April 14, 2010.

"Bankinter Tops Global Cross-Selling League." Banking and Payments ASIA, http://www.vrl-financial-news.com/bpa/banking--payments-asia/issues/bpa-2009/bpa3/bankinter-tops-global-cross-se.aspx.

Berry, M. and Linoff, G. *Data Mining Techniques*. Second ed. Indianapolis: Wiley, 2004.

"Call Centers Said to Miss Chances for Cross-Sales." (Feb 11, 2009), http://www.americanbanker.com/issues/173_28/-343724-1.html.

Celent. "Bancassurance in the Asia-Pacific Region: Replacing the Agency Distribution Model." Celent 2010.

Cohen, M. "Exploiting Response Models - Optimizing Cross-Sell and Up-Sell Opportunities in Banking." *Information Systems* 29, no. 4 (2004): 327–41.

"Core Matters." *The American Banker* (July 2010), http://www.americanbanker.com/magazine/120_7/core-matters-1021267-1.html.

Credit Union Journal. "Walmart Heats up Financial Competition." (June 20, 2011), http://www.cujournal.com/issues/15_25/walmart-heats-up-financial-competition-1009081-1.html.

Diakova, E. "*Electronic Alternatives and Direct Mail Marketing*." Pitney Bowes, 2005.

Forrester. "Case Study: BBVA's Tú Cuentas Shows What Next-Generation Online Banking Will Look Like." Forrester Research Inc, 2009.

Forrester. "Cross-Sell Your Way to Profit": A Forrester Consulting Thought Leadership Paper Commissioned by Amadeus Jan 2011.

Forrester. "Driving Sales through the Branch Network." Forrester Research Inc, Nov, 2005.

Forrester. "How Did Wells Fargo Boost Online Sales?" Forrester Research Inc, 2005.

Hallowell, R. "The Relationship of Customer Satisfaction, Customer Loyalty, and Profitability: An Empirical Study." *International Journal of Service Industry Management* 7, no. 4 (1996): 27–42.

"HDFC Transforms Customer Experience at the ATM with ACI Worldwide." ACI Payment Systems, http://www.aciworldwide.com/en/What-we-know/Case-studies/HDFC-transforming-customer-experience-at-the-ATM-with-ACI-Worldwide.aspx.

Herrmann, A., Huber, F. and Coulter, R. "Product and Service Bundling Decisions and Their Effects on Purchase Intention." *Pricing Strategy and Practice* 5, no. 3 (1997): 99–107.

"In Tribute to Wells, Banks Try the Hard Sell." *The Wall Street Journal*, Feb 28, 2011.

Kamakura, W., Ramaswami, S. and Srivastava, R. "Applying Latent Trait Analysis in the Evaluation of Prospects for Cross - Selling of Financial Services." *International Journal of Research in Marketing* 8, no. 4 (1991): 329–49.

King, B. "Consumer Lending Cross-Sell and Product Bundling." *Benchmark Consulting International* (2006), http://www.benchmarkinternational.com/Articles/Consumer%20Lending%20Cross-Sell%20and%20Product%20Bundling.pdf.

Knott, A., Hayes, A. and Neslin, S. "Next-Product-to-Buy Models for Cross-Selling Applications." *Journal of Interactive Marketing* 16, no. 3 (2002): 59–75.

Kumar, V., George, M. and Pancras, J. "Cross-Buying in Retailing: Drivers and Consequences." *Journal of Retailing* 84, no. 1 (2008): 15–27.

Kumar V., Venkatesan, R. and Reinartz, W. "Knowing What to Sell, When and to Whom." *Harvard Business Review* (March 2006).

Lepro, S. and Sposito, S. "Wal-Mart Heats up Financial Competition." *Credit Union Journal* 15, no. 23 (June 20, 2011).

Linden, G., Smith, B. and York, J."Amazon.Com Recommendations: Item-to-Item Collaborative Filtering." *Internet Computing, IEEE,* 7, no. 1 (2003): 76–80.

Mankila, M. "Application of Price Bundling Strategies in Retail Banking in Europe." In *FE-reports*: Göteborg University. School of Business, Economics and Law, 2001.

McKinsey. "Back to the Future: Rediscovering Relationship Banking." *Financial Services Practice, The Future of Retail Banking*, Nov 2010.

McKinsey. "Bundling Europe's Broadband." *Web Exclusive* (February 2005).

McKinsey. "Refocusing the Sales Force to Cross-Sell." *McKinsey Quarterly* (Dec 2007).

McKinsey. "Using Call Centres to Boost Revenue." *McKinsey Quarterly* (May 2006).

PricewaterhouseCoopers. "Getting to Know You: Building a Customer-Centric Business Model for Retail Banks." Financial Services Institute (FSI) April 2011.

Prinzie, A. and Poel, D. "Investigating Purchasing Patterns for Financial Services Using Markov, MTF and MTDg Models." *European Journal of Operational Research* 170, no. 3 (2006): 710–34.

"Rise in M&A Work Lucrative to Big Law Firms." *Washington Post*, July 18, 2011.

"Santander Extends Zero Account to Take on Rivals." *London Evening Standard*, March 1, 2010.

Schafer J., Konstan, J. and Reidl, J. "E-Commerce Recommendation Applications." *Data Mining and Knowledge Discovery* 5 (2001): 115–53.

Stremersch, S. and Tellis, G. "Strategic Bundling of Products and Prices: A New Synthesis for Marketing." *Journal of Marketing* 66, no. 1 (2002): 55–72.

Sundarajan, R. et al. "Marketing Optimization in Retail Banking." *Interfaces* 41, no. 5 (2011): 485–505.

"The 2011 Telecommunications Industry Review: An Anthology of Market Facts and Forecasts." The Insight Research Corporation, 2011.

"Triple-Play Subscriptions to Quadruple." Digital TV Research, http://www.broadbandtvnews.com/2011/07/18/triple-play-subscriptions-to-quadruple/.

"United We Find." *The Economist*, March 2005.

Verhoes, P., Frances, P. and Hoekstra, J. "The Impact of Satisfaction and Payment Equity on Cross-Buying: A Dynamic Model for Multi-Service Provider." *Journal of Retailing* 77, no. 3 (2001): 359–28.

Villanueva, J. and Hanssens, D. "Customer Equity: Measurement, Management and Research Opportunities." *Foundations and Trends in Marketing* 1, no. 1 (2007).

Vindevogel, B., Poel, V. and Weets, G. "Why Promotion Strategies Based on Market Basket Analysis Do Not Work." Ghent University, October 2004.

"Wal-Mart Undeterred." *American Banker* (Sep 1, 2010), http://www.americanbanker.com/magazine/120_9/wal-mart-gets-serious-1023966-1.html.

"World Demographic Trends, Report of the Secretary-General." United Nations Economic and Social Council, Dec 2004.

Yang, T. and Lai, H. "Comparison of Product Bundling Strategies on Different Online Shopping Behaviors." *Electronic Commerce Research and Applications*, no. 5 (2006): 4.

**Chapter 4**

Accenture, Institute for High Performance Business. "Reducing the Risk of Customer Defection." March 2008.

Agarwal, S., Chomsisengphet, S., Liu, S. and Souleles, N. "Benefits of Relationship Banking: Evidence from Consumer Credit Markets." FRB of Chicago Working Paper, No. 2010–05, May 2009.

Au, T., Shaomin, L. and Ma, G. "Applying and Evaluating Models to Predict Customer Attrition Using Data Mining Techniques." *Journal of Comparative International Management* 6, no. 1 (2003).

BankTechnologyNews. "What's the ROI of Mobile Banking?" http://www.americanbanker.com/bulletins/–1037534–1.html.

BCG. "Leveraging Consumer Insight in Insurance." The Boston Consulting Group (BCG), February 2010.

Blattberg, R. and Deighton, J. "Manage Marketing by the Customer Equity Test." *Harvard Business Review* 74, no. 4 (July-August 1996): 136–44.

Blattberg, R., Kim, B. and Neslin, S. *Database Marketing*. First ed, International Series in Quantitative Marketing. New York, NY: Springer, 2008.

Buckinx, W. and Poel, V. "Customer Base Analysis: Partial Defection of Behaviourally Loyal Clients in a Non-Contractual FMCG Retail Setting." *European Journal of Operations Research* 164, no. 1 (2005): 252–68.

CommsMEA. "Customer Acquisition." (2011), http://www.commsmea.com/11306-customer-acquisition/.

Coyles, S. and Gokey, T. "Customer Retention is Not Enough." *Journal of Consumer Marketing* 22, no. 2 (2005): 101–05.

Dawkins, P. and Reichheld, F. "Customer Retention as a Competitive Weapon." *Directors and Boards* 14 (Summer 1990): 42–47.

DNA. "Portability Launch Spurs War for Post-Paid Users." http://www.dnaindia.com/money/report_portability-launch-spurs-war-for-post-paid-users_1496764.

Dua, J. "Persistency is the Name of the Game." *Business Standard*, March 22, 2012.

E&Y. "Private Insurers Need Upside Down Biz Model to Survive." *Business Standard* Sep 19, 2010.

Eling, M. and Kiesenbauer, D. "What Policy Features Determine Life Insurance Lapse? An Analysis of the German Market." In *Working Paper on Risk Management and Insurance*: Institute of Insurance Economics, University of St. Gallen, 2011.

Ferreira, J., Vellasco, M., Pacheco, M. and Barbosa, C. "Data Mining Techniques on the Evaluation of Wireless Churn" Paper presented at the European Symposium on Artificial Neural Networks, Bruges (Belgium), 28–30 April 2004.

Fitzgerald, K. "As Card Use Slows Retention Strategies Gain Importance." *American Banker* 176, no. 95 (June 21, 2011): 7–7.

Fitzgerald, K. "Capital One Card for Affluent Offer Deals and Strings." *American Banker* 176, no. F333 (August 26, 2011): 5–5.

Forrester. "Optimizing Customer Retention Programs." Forrester, 2008.

Gerpott, T., Rams, W. and Schindler, A. "Customer Retention, Loyalty, and Satisfaction in the German Mobile Cellular Telecommunications Market." *Telecommunications Policy* 25, no. 4 (2001): 249–69.

Gupta, S., Lehmann, D. and Stuart, J. "Valuing Customers." *Journal of Marketing Research* 41, no. 1 (2004): 7–18.

Hakim, S. "Autonomous and Financial Mortgage Prepayment." *Journal of Real Estate Research* 13, no. 1 (1997): 1–16.

Hommer, M. and Krause, A. "Profiting from Prepaid Phone Customers." *McKinsey Quarterly*, no. 2 (2004): 12–14.

Hu, X. "A Data Mining Approach for Retail Bank Customer Attrition Analysis." *Applied Intelligence* 22, no. 1 (2005): 47–60.

Hung, S., Yen, D. and Wang, H. "Applying Data Mining to Telecom Churn Management." *Expert Systems with Applications* 31 (2006): 515–24.

IRDA. "Lapsation and Its Impact on Indian Life Insurance Industry (2002–2007)." 2008.

IRDA. "Lapsation in Life Insurance." *IRDA Journal* VI, no. 8 (August 2008).

Iyengar, R., Jedidi, K., Essegaier, S. and Danaher, P. "The Impact of Tariff Structure on Customer Retention, Usage and Profitability of Access Services." *Journal of Marketing Science* 30, no. 5 (2011): 820–36.

Jacada. "Insurance Providers: Improving Customer Retention through the Contact Center." *Jacada White Paper*, 2008.

Jones, T. and Sasser, E. "Why Satisfied Customers Defect." *Harvard Business Review* 73, no. 6 (November-December 1995): 88–99.

Kamakura, W. et al. "Choice Models and Customer Relationship Management." *Marketing Letters* 16, no. 3/4 (2005): 279–91.

Keaveney, S. "Customer Switching Behaviour in Service Industries: An Exploratory Study." *Journal of Marketing* 59, no. 2 (1995): 71–82.

Kiesenbauer, D. "Main Determinants of Lapse in the German Life Insurance Industry." *North American Actuarial Journal* 16, no. 1 (2012): 52–73.

Kim, C. "Modeling Surrender and Lapse Rates with Economic Variables." *North American Actuarial Journal* 9, no. 4 (2005).

Kim, H. and Yoon, C. "Determinants of Subscriber Churn and Customer Loyalty in the Korean Mobile Telephony Market." *Telecommunications Policy* 28, no. 9–10 (2004): 751–65.

Lemmens, A. and Croux, C. "Bagging and Boosting Classification Trees to Predict Churn." *Journal of Marketing Research* 43, no. 2 (2006): 276–86.

Loi, L., Yuan, W. and Heong, R. "A New Approach to Analyzing Persistency of Insurance Policy." Unpublished.

Loveman, G. "Creating Actionable Business Intelligence to Drive Customer Loyalty and Profitability." In *Balanced Scorecard Collaborative*. The Drake Hotel, Chicago, May 1–19, 2006.

McKinsey. "Limiting Churn in Insurance" *The McKinsey Quarterly*, Web exclusive (2004), https://www.mckinseyquarterly.com/Limiting_churn_in_insurance_1546.

Mint. "A Persistent Customer is Good for Life Insurers." http://www.livemint.com/2010/05/05211038/A–8216persistent8217–cus.html.

Moroney, D. "Credit Card Attrition: Causes and Countermeasures." Tower Group, April 2003.

Neslin, S., Gupta, S., Kamakura, W., Lu, J. and Mason, C. "Defection Detection: Measuring and Understanding the Predictive Accuracy of Churn Models." *Journal of Marketing Research* 43, no. 2 (2006): 204–11.

Nie, G., Rowe, W., Zhang, L., Tian, Y. and Shi, Y. "Credit Card Churn Forecasting by Logistic Regression and Decision Tree." *Expert Systems with Applications* 38, no. 12 (2011): 15273–85.

O'Reilly, radar. "T-Mobile Challenges Churn with Data." http://radar.oreilly.com/2011/08/t-mobile-challenges-churn-with.html.

Owczarczuk, M. "Churn Models for Prepaid Customers in the Cellular Telecommunication Industry Using Large Data Marts." *Expert Systems with Applications* 37 (2010): 4710–12.

Pfeifer, P. "The Optimal Ratio of Acquisition and Retention Costs." *Journal of Targeting, Measurement and Analysis for Marketing* 13, no. 2 (2005): 179–88.

Pilecki, M. "Customer Retention is a Process, Not an Event." Forrester, 2007.

PricewaterhouseCoopers. "Are They Worth It? Managing the Value of Customers in the U.K. Financial Services Market." London, 2002.

PricewaterhouseCoopers. "Customer Retention in the Consumer Finance Industry." 2007.

Reichheld, F. "Loyalty and the Renaissance of Marketing." *Marketing Management* 2, no. 4 (1994): 10–22.

Reichheld, F. *The Loyalty Effect*. First ed. Boston, Massachusetts: Harvard Business School Press, 1996.

Rosenfeld, A. "A Fresh Approach to Assessing Consumer Impacts of AT&T/T-Mobile Merger." M+R Strategic Services, 2011.

Solon. "Bundling Wins: The Case for Cable + Mobile Integration." *Solon Telecoms White Paper* (2011), http://www.solonstrategy.com/uploads/tx_soloncm003/Solon_White_Paper_Telecoms_-_Bundling_Wins.pdf.

Van den Poel, D. and Lariviere, B. "Customer Attrition Analysis for Financial Analysis Using Proportional Hazard Models." *European Journal of Operations Research* 157, no. 1 (2004): 196–217.

Verbeke, W., Dejaeger, K., Hur, J., Baesens, B. and Martens, D. "New Insights into Churn Prediction in the Telecommunication Sector: A Profit Driven Data Mining Approach." *European Journal of Operations Research* 218, no. 1 (2012): 211–29.

WDS. "Industry Briefing Mobile Churn" (2011), http://www.wds.co/enlightened/churn/WDS_Churn_2011.pdf.

"Winning the Customer Churn Battle in the Wireless Industry." *Insights*, no. 1 (2001), http://www.boozallen.com/media/file/Winning.pdf.

Wong, K. "Using Cox Regression to Model Customer Time to Churn in the Wireless Telecommunications Industry." *Journal of Targeting, Measurement and Analysis for Marketing* 19 (2011): 37–43.

**Chapter 5**

Anand, K. and Aron, R. "Group Buying on the Web: A Comparison of Price-Discovery Mechanisms." *Management Science* 49, no. 11 (2003): 1546–62.

Blattberg, R. and Neslin, S. "Sales Promotion: The Long and the Short of It." *Marketing Letters* 1, no. 1 (1989): 81–97.

Blattberg, R., Briesch, R. and Fox, E. "How Promotions Work." *Marketing Science* 14, no. 3 (1995): 122–32.

Brian, K., Arie, J., Mark, M. and Thomas, L. "Dynamic Pricing Tariffs for DTE's Residential Electricity Customers." University of Michigan, 2010.

Chapman, R. "Assessing the Profitability of Retailer Couponing with a Low-Cost Field Experiment." *Journal of Retailing* 62, no. 1 (1986): 19–39.

Cross, R. and Dixit, A. "Customer-Centric Pricing: The Surprising Secret for Profitability." *Business Horizons* 48, no. 6 (2005): 483–91.

Edelman, B., Jaffe, S. and Kominers, S. "To Groupon or Not to Groupon: The Profitability of Deep Discounts." In *Harvard Business School (bedelman@hbs.edu) - Working paper*, 2011.

Faruqui, A. and George, S. "Quantifying Customer Response to Dynamic Pricing." *The Electricity Journal* 18, no. 4 (2005): 53–63.

Faruqui, A., Hledik, R., Newell, S. and Pfeifenberger, H. "The Power of 5 Percent." *The Electricity Journal* 20, no. 8 (2007): 68–77.

Harmon, R., Raffo, D. and Faulk, S. "Value-Based Pricing For New Software Products: Strategy Insights for Developers." http://citeseerx.ist.psu.edu/viewdoc/download?doi=10.1.1.135.8014&rep=rep1&type=pdf

Marriott. "The Power of Marriott® International." http://www.marriott.com/Multimedia/PDF/Hotel_Development/PowerofMarriott_brochureEMEA.pdf.

Netessine, S. and Shumsky, R. "Introduction to the Theory and Practice of Yield Management." *INFORMS Transcations on Education* 3, no. 1: 34–44.

Smith, B., Leimkuhler, J. and Darrow, R. "Yield Management at American Airlines." *Interfaces* 22, no. 1 (1992): 8–31.

Smith, G. and Nagle, T. "How Much are Your Customers Willing to Pay?" *Marketing Research* 14, no. 4 (2002): 20–25.

Talluri, K. and Ryzin, G. *The Theory and Practice of Revenue Management*: Springer.

**Chapter 6**

Chakravarti, R. and Chea, B. "The Evolution of Credit Bureaus in Asia-Pacific." 2005.

Ferretti, F. "A Historical Primer on Consumer Credit Reporting Systems - A Lesson for EU Policy Makers?" *International Journal of Communications Law and Policy* no. 12 (2008): 92–119.

Hunt, R. A Century of Consumer Reporting in America. http://www.philadelphiafed.org/research-and-data/publications/working-papers/2005/wp05-13.pdf.

Jappellia, T. and Pagano, M. "Information Sharing, Lending and Defaults: Cross-Country Evidence." *Journal of Banking & Finance* 26, no. 10 (2002): 2017–45.

Jentzsch, N. and Rientra, A. "Information Sharing and Its Implications for Consumer Credit Markets: United States Vs. Europe." European University Institute Workshop "The Economics of Consumer Credit: European Experience and Lessons from the U.S.," 2003.

Padilla, A. and Pagano, M. "Sharing Default Information as a Borrower Discipline Device." *European Economic Review* 44, no. 10 (2000): 1951–80.

Pagano, M. and Jappelli, T. "Information Sharing in Credit Markets." *The Journal of Finance* 48, no. 5 (1993): 1693–718.

Rothemund, M. and Gerhardt, M. "The European Credit Information Landscape. An Analysis of a Survey of Credit Bureaus in Europe." Centre for European Policy Studies (Brussels). ECRI Research Reports, 2011.

Wu, P. and Guszcza, J. "Does Credit Score Really Explain Insurance Losses? Multivariate Analysis from a Data Mining Point of View." 113–38: Casualty Actuarial Society Forum Casualty Actuarial Society - Arlington, Virginia, 2003.

**Chapter 7**

Anderson, R. *The Credit Scoring Toolkit*. First ed. New York: Oxford University Press 2007.

Anderson, T. and Sclove, S. *The Statistical Analysis of Data*. Second ed. Palo Alto: The Scientific Press, 1986.

Andreeva, G. "European Generic Scoring Models Using Survival Analysis." *The Journal of the Operational Research Society* 57, no. 10 (2005): 1180–87.

Artis, M., Ayuso, M. and Guillen, M. "Detection of Automobile Insurance Fraud with Discrete Choice Models and Misclassified Claims." *The Journal of Risk and Insurance* 69, no. 3 (2002): 325–40.

Artis, M., Ayuso, M. and Guillen, M. "Modelling Different Types of Automobile Insurance Fraud Behaviour in the Spanish Market." *Insurance: Mathematics and Economics* 24, no. 1–2 (1999): 67–81.

Bellotti, T. and Crook, J. "Credit Scoring with Macroeconomic Variables Using Survival Analysis." *Journal of the Operational Research Society* 60, no. 12 (2009): 1699–707.

Benasik, J., Crook, J. and Thomas, L. "Not If But When Will Borrowers Default." *Journal of the Operational Research Society* 50, no. 12 (1999): 1185–90.

Berry, M. and Linoff, G. *Data Mining Techniques*. Second ed. Indianapolis, Indiana: Wiley, 2004.

Blattberg, R., Kim, B. and Neslin, S. *Database Marketing*. First ed, International Series in Quantitative Marketing. New York, NY: Springer, 2008.

Blattberg, R. and Neslin, S. "Sales Promotion Models." In *Handbooks in Operations Research and Management Science, Volume - Marketing*, edited by J. Eliashberg and G. Lilien, 553–609. Amsterdam: North-Holland, 1993.

Boer, L., Labro, E. and Morlacchi, P. "A Review of Methods Supporting Supplier Selection." *European Journal of Purchasing and Supply Management* 7, no. 2 (2001): 75–89.

Breiman, L., Friedman, J., Olshen, R. and Stone, C. *Classification and Regression Trees*. Belmont, CA: Wadsworth, 1984.

Chapman, R. "Assessing the Profitability of Retailer Couponing with a Low-Cost Field Experiment." *Journal of Retailing* 62, no. 1 (1986): 19–40.

Chung, K., Oh, S., Kim, S. and Han, S. "Three Representative Marketing Segmentation Methodologies for Hotel Guest Room Customers." *Tourism Management* 25 (2004): 429–41.

Dunteman, G. *Principal Components Analysis*. First ed, Quantititive Applications in the Social Sciences: Sage, 1989.

Fair Isaac. "A Discussion of Data Analysis, Prediction and Decision Techniques." *A Fair Isaac White Paper* (May 2003).

Greene, W. *Econometric Analysis* Third ed. Upper Saddle River, New Jersey: Prentice Hall, 1993.

Gujarati, D. *Basic Econometrics*. Fourth ed: McGraw-Hill, 2003.

Hosmer, D. and Lemeshow, S. *Applied Survival Analysis* First ed: John Wiley and Sons, 1999.

Hotelling, H. "Analysis of a Complex of Statistical Variables into Principal Components." *Journal of Educational Pyschology* 24, no. 6 (1933): 417–41.

Jain, A., Murty, M. and Flynn, P. "Data Clustering: A Review." *ACM Computing Surveys* 31, no. 3 (1999): 264–323.

Joliffe, T. *Principal Component Analysis*. First ed. New York: Springer-Verlag, 1986.

Kennedy, P. *A Guide to Econometrics*. Third ed. Cambridge, Massachusetts: The MIT Press, 1992.

Ketchen, D. and Shook, C. "The Application of Cluster Analysis in Strategic Management Research: An Analysis and Critique." *Strategic Management Journal* 17, no. 6 (1996): 441–58.

Kumar, M. and Patel, N. "Using Clustering to Improve Sales Forecasts in Retail Merchandizing." *Annals of Operations Research* 174, no. 1 (2010): 33–46.

Kumar V., Venkatesan, R. and Reinartz, W. "Knowing What to Sell, When and to Whom." *Harvard Business Review* (March 2006).

Leone, R. and Srinivasan, S. "Coupon Face Value: Its Impact on Coupon Redemptions, Brand Sales, and Brand Profitability." *Journal of Retailing* 72, no. 3 (1996): 273–89.

Loi, L., Yuan, W. and Heong, R. "A New Approach to Analyzing Persistency of Insurance Policy." Nanyang Business School, Nanyang Technological University, Singapore.

Lu, J. "Modelling Customer Life Time Value Using Survival Analysis - An Application to the Telecommunications Industry." SUGI Paper 120–28, SAS.

Maimon O. and Rokach, L. "Introduction to Supervised Methods." In *Data Mining and Knowledge Discovery Handbook*, edited by Maimon and Rokach, 149–64: Springer, 2005.

Malhotra, N. *Marketing Research*. Second ed. Upper Saddle River, New Jersey: Prentice Hall, 1996.

McCarty, J. and Hastak, M. "Segmentation Approaches in Data Mining: A Comparison of RFM, Chaid and Logistic Regression." *Journal of Business Research* 60, no. 6 (2007): 656–62.

Moore, M. and Carpenter, J. "A Decision Tree Approach to Modeling the Private Label Consumer." *Marketing Intelligence and Planning* 28, no. 1 (2010): 59–69.

Moutinho, L. and Hutcheson, G., ed. *The Sage Dictionary of Quantitative Management Research*: Sage, 2011.

Murthy, S. "Automatic Construction of Decision Trees from Data: A Multi-Disciplinary Survey." *Data Mining and Knowledge Discovery* 2, no. 4 (1998): 345–89.

Narain, B. "Survival Analysis and the Credit Granting Decision." In *Credit Scoring and Credit Control*, edited by L. Thomas, J. Crook and B. Edelman, 109–21. Oxford, UK: OUP, 1992.

Neter, J., Kutner, M., Nachtsheim, C. and Wasserman, W. *Applied Linear Statistical Models*. Fourth ed: Irwin, 1996.

Pearson, K. "On Lines and Planes of Closest Fit to Systems of Points in Space." *Philosophical Magazine* 2 no. 6 (1901): 559–72.

Petroni, A. and Braglia, M. "Vendor Selection Using Principal Component Analysis." *Journal of Supply Chain Management* 36, no. 2 (2006): 63–69.

Raju, J. "The Effect of Price Promotions on Variability in Product Category Sales." *Marketing Science* 11, no. 3 (1992): 207–20.

Rao, C.R. "Principal Component and Factor Analysis." 1–20: Center for Multivariate Analysis, Penn State University, July 1996.

Saaty, T.L. "Decision Making with the Analytic Hierarchy Process." *International Journal of Services Sciences* 1, no. 1 (2008): 83–98.

Saaty, T.L. "How to Make a Decision: The Analytic Hierarchy Process." *European Journal of Operational Research* 48 (1990): 9–26.

Salazar, M., Harrison, T. and Ansell, J. "An Approach for the Identification of Cross-Sell and Up-Sell Opportunities Using a Financial Services Customer Database." *Journal of Financial Services Marketing* 12, no. 2 (2007): 115–31.

Schultz, D. and Block, M. "How U.S. Consumers View in-Store Promotions." *Journal of Business Research* 64, no. 1 (2011): 51–54.

Smith, T. and Smith, B. "Survival Analysis and the Application of Cox's Proportional Hazard Modelling Using SAS." SUGI Paper 244–26, SAS.

Srinivasan, V. and Kim, Y. "Credit Granting: A Comparative Analysis of Classification Procedures." *The Journal of Finance* 42, no. 3 (1987): 665–81.

Stepanova, M. and Thomas, L. "Survival Analysis Methods for Personal Loan Data." *Operations Research* 50, no. 2 (2002): 277–89.

Tang, L., Thomas, L., Thomas, S. and Bozzetto, J. "It's the Economy Stupid: Modelling Financial Product Purchases." *International Journal of Bank Marketing* 25, no. 1 (2007): 22–38.

Vaidya, O. and Kumar, S. "Analytic Hierarchy Process: An Overview of Applications." *European Journal of Operational Research* 169, no. 1 (2006): 1–29.

Van den Poel, D. and Lariviere, B. "Customer Attrition Analysis for Financial Analysis Using Proportional Hazard Models." *European Journal of Operations Research* 157, no. 1 (2004): 196–217.

Xevelonakis, E. "Developing Retention Strategies Based on Customer Profitability in Telecommunications: An Empirical Study." *Database Marketing and Customer Strategy Management* 12, no. 3 (2005): 226–42.

Yurdakul, M. and Tansel, Y. "AHP Approach in the Credit Evaluation of the Manufacturing Firms in Turkey." *International Journal of Production Economics* 88, no. 3 (2004): 269–89.

## Chapter 8

Band, W. "The Forrester Wave™: CRM Suites for Large Organizations, Q2 2010." Forrester Research, 2010.

Band, W. "The Forrester Wave™: CRM Suites for Midsized Organizations, Q2 2010." Forrester Research, 2010.

Berry, L., Shostack, G. and Upha, G. "Emerging Perspectives in Service Marketing." *American Marketing Association* 2 (1983): 25–28.

Chan, J. "Toward a Unified View of Customer Relationship Management." *Journal of American Academy of Business, Cambridge* 6, no. 1 (2005): 32–38.

Inmon, W. *Building the Data Warehouse*: Wiley Publishing Inc, 2011.

Kimball, R. *The Data Warehouse Toolkit: The Complete Guide to Dimensional Modeling*: Wiley Publishing Inc, 2010.

Lehmann, D. and Reibstein, D. *Marketing Metrics and Financial Performance*: Marketing Science Institute, 2006.

Olson, J. *Data Quality: The Accuracy Dimension*, Morgan Kaufmannthe Series in Data Management Systems: Morgan Kaufmann, 2003.

Panda, T. "Creating Customer Life Time Value through Effective Crm in Financial Services Industry." *Journal of Services Research* 2, no. 2 (2003): 158–71.

Parvatiyar, A. and Seth, J. "Customer Relationship Management: Emerging Practice, Process, and Discipline." *Journal of Economic and Social Research* 3, no. 2 (2001): 1–34.

Rexer, K., Gearan, P. and Allen, H. "Surveying the Field: Current Data Mining Applications, Analytic Tools and Practical Challenges." Rexer Analytics - Data Miner Survey Summary Report, 2007.

Seth, J. and Parvatiyar, A. "Relationship Marketing in Consumer Markets: Antecedents and Consequences." *Journal of the Academy of Marketing Science* 23, no. 4 (1995): 255–71.

Supply Chain Council (SCC). "SCOR Model." http://supply-chain.org/scor.

# Glossary

**Account** Refers to a single account of a product held by a customer e.g., a single checking or savings account belonging to product "deposits".

**Adverse Selection** Occurs when a product or service is selected by only a certain group of people who offer a lower than average return for the company. It results because of information asymmetries and difficulties in selecting customers.

**Algorithm** A specific set of logical procedures for solving a problem, usually with the requirement that the procedure terminates at some point. Specific algorithms sometimes also go by the name of method or technique.

**Amortisation** An accounting practice whereby expenses or charges are accounted for over the life of the asset rather than at the time they are incurred. By amortising an asset or liability, the value of the item is reduced gradually over time by some periodic amount (i.e., via installment payments).

**ANR (Average Net Receivables)** Average receivables over a period of time (usually a month). Approximately, ANR can be calculated as {Net accounts receivables (current month) + Net accounts receivables (prior month)} ÷ 2. For a credit card and loan portfolio, it is commonly measured as outstanding balances averaged over a period of time.

**Application Score** Score is used to evaluate the credit quality of prospects at the time of application; to forecast chances of the applicant becoming delinquent on credit obligations, if granted credit.

**Approval Rate** Percentage of responders that are approved for an offer. Calculated as number of responders approved divided by number of responders.

**APR (Annual Percentage Rate)** Annualised interest rate charged on a loan or credit card. This includes the cost of funds and the risk premium associated with lending.

**ARIMA (Autoregressive Integrated Moving Average) Model** Analysis of time series data which involves model identifi cation, estimation, diagnostic checking, and forecasting. The ARIMA model is represented by ARIMA (*p,d,q*); (*p*) represents the order of autoregression, (*d*) for differencing and (*q*) for moving average in the models.

**ARPM (Average Revenue per Minute)** Average revenue per minute of usage for a particular type of service, commonly used in the telecom sector.

ARPM = Total revenue/Total minutes of usage

ARPM = Total revenue/Total minutes of usage.

**ARPU (Average Revenue per User)** Revenue per subscriber for a specific type of service, commonly used in the telecom sector.

ARPU = Total revenue/Average number of subscribers for the period.

**Artificial Neural Networks (ANN)** Data mining technique that attempts to mimic human cognitive processes. *Source:* Anderson (2007).

**Association Rule** To look for frequent patterns that establish a typical directed concurrence of two frequent set of items. *Source:* Moutinho and Hutcheson (2011).

**Attribute** A variable or characteristic. In the case of a credit risk scorecard, the values of a variable or characteristic are usually referred to as attributes of the variable or characteristic.

**Bad Debt Costs** Equal to Gross Credit Loss (GCL).
**Balance Active** Positive balance in an account of a customer.
**Balance/Outstanding Balance** The amount of funds in a checking/savings account. The total amount of money owed to an institution such as bank, credit card company, or utility company. The account balance will always be the net amount after factoring in all debits and credits. Good and Bad Balance is balance on a non-loss and loss incurring account respectively.
**Balance Transfer** Balance transfer for credit card is the act of moving debt from one credit card to another, assuming that the newer card has better terms and rates.
**Bancassurance** Distribution channel whereby third party insurance is sold by banks to their customers.
**Bayesian Inference** Method of inference in which Bayes' rule is used to update the probability estimate as additional evidence is learned.
**Behaviour Score** A score calculated on existing customers to predict the chances of a specific event (e.g., delinquency) on credit obligations; used primarily for customer management actions.
**Bill Pay** Service of online payment of bills offered to customers.
**Binary Choice Model** Discrete choice model with choice of only two alternatives. The model can be estimated using regression analysis such as logistic or probit regression.
**Binomial Distribution** Distribution showing the probability of a given number of successes in a two-outcome trial. The underlying assumptions of the binomial distribution are that there is only one outcome for each trial, that each trial has the same probability of success, and that each trial is mutually exclusive. For example, flipping a coin would create a binomial distribution.
**Boosting Algorithms** Boosting is a general method for improving the accuracy of a learning algorithm. A boosting algorithm is one which can convert a "weak" learning algorithm (with accuracy just slightly better than random guess) into one with high accuracy.
**Bullwhip Effect** Can be explained as an occurrence detected by the supply chain where orders sent to the manufacturer and supplier create larger variance than the sales to the end customer.
**Bundling** Sale of two or more separate products in one package. Separate products defined as such if separate markets exist for each of the products, thereby giving consumers the choice to buy products with or without a bundle. *Source:* Stremersch and Tellis (2002).
**Business Income** Total revenue net of all costs (cost of funds, reward cost, cost of credit loss and operating costs) other than provisioning and capital costs.
**Buyer's Remorse** Buyer's remorse is a sense of regret after making a purchase, which prompts early closure of the account by the customer; or the lack of visible engagement, often seen within the first three to six months of account opening.
**Calibration** Calibration refers to the process of mathematical transformation of a score in such a way that the transformed score exhibits a particular relationship with respect to log odds.
**Campaign** A specific set of marketing activities designed to promote a particular product or service. A campaign which is directed only to a specific set of prospects or customers is referred to as Below The Line Campaign. Whereas a campaign which is not targeted specifically to any set of customers but is exposed to a wider audience (both customers and non-customers), is termed Above The Line Campaign.
**Cannibalisation** Trade-off in which sales of a new product or service decrease sales/ revenue from existing products or services.

**CART (Classification and Regression Trees)** Segmentation method for deriving classification/decision tree, developed by Breiman et al. (1984).
**Cash Sales** Value of cash withdrawals on a credit card.
**Categorical Variable** Variable has two or more categories, but there is no intrinsic ordering to the categories. For example, gender.
**Ceiling Price** The maximum price allowed for a product or service. The ceiling may be established by market conditions or a government requirement.
**CHAID (Chi-square Automatic Interaction Detector)** Segmentation method for building classification/ decision tree based on chi-square statistic to identify optimal splits.
**Charge Card** A card that charges no interest but requires the cardholder to pay total bill amount in full. No pre-set credit limit.
**Chi-square Statistic** Statistic used for testing significant differences between observed and expected values. *Source:* Anderson (2007).
**Classification/Decision Tree** Rule-based data exploratory method for discrimination, classification, generalisation, and prediction. Discrimination is the process of deriving classification rules from samples of classified observations. Classification is applying the rules to new observations of unknown class. Generalisation is uncovering a mapping from independent to dependent variables that is useful for prediction of the dependent variable.
**Cluster Analysis** Multivariate technique whose primary purpose is to segment observations/customers based on the characteristics they possess. Groups are based on the concept of distance (proximity). *Source:* Moutinho and Hutcheson (2011).
**CNR (Customer Net Revenue)** Total revenue at a customer level net of cost of funds and reward costs. This measure can also be calculated at an account level.
**Cohort** A group of customers who share a common characteristic or experience within a defined period.
**Collaborative Filtering** A recommender system that uses the known preferences of a group of users to make recommendations or predictions of the unknown preferences for other users.
**Collateral** Property or other assets that a borrower offers a lender for a secured loan.
**Collection Score** The probability of recovery of the outstanding balance for those accounts in collections; used for improving collections efficiency.
**Concordance** In case of a logistic regression, a pair of observations with different observed responses is said to be concordant if the observation with the lower ordered response value (outcome = 0) has a lower predicted mean score than the observation with the higher ordered response value (outcome = 1). Concordance refers to the percentage of all possible pairs that are concordant.
**Confusion Matrix** Is a visualization tool, which contains information about actual and predicted for a discrete choice model. It is used to evaluate the performance (predictive power) of a model.
**Contact Rate** Percentage of mail file customers that are contacted.
**Continuous Variable** Numeric variable that can have an infinite number of possible values and differences between values have meaning. Example is income. *Source:* Anderson (2007).
**Control/Champion** Group of customers who are identical to the customers that are part of the campaign but are not made the offer (made to the test group) for the particular campaign. The control group however may receive other offers. In some cases a company adopts the strategy of creating a universal control group, one that will not receive any marketing offer at all (hold out).
**Conversion Rate** Percentage of responders (leads) who have taken up or accepted the offer.

**Cost per Contact** Cost of a below the line marketing campaign divided by the number of customers or prospects contacted as part of the campaign.

**Cost per Mail File** In case of a direct mail marketing campaign, the cost per mail file refers to the total cost of the campaign divided by the number of customers or prospects in the target set.

**Cost per Response** Cost of a below the line marketing campaign divided by the number of responders to the campaign.

**Credit Bureau** Repository of credit information for the entire economy; all credit grantors by regulation must submit information about their borrowers to the credit bureau.

**Credit Characteristics** Credit characteristics are set of variables which summarises the credit information that is available for a consumer at the credit bureau.

**Credit Criteria** Risk based criteria to evaluate eligibility of a customer for product/service offer. In addition, marketing exclusions are also applied for evaluating eligibility.

**Credit Limit/Line** Maximum amount of credit that a lender will extend to a debtor on a particular credit product.

**Credit Loss** Equal to Net Credit Loss (NCL). Amount loss rate is credit loss expressed as a percentage of average net receivables. Account loss rate is the number of accounts in write-off status expressed as a percentage of total open accounts.

**Credit Score (also called Bureau Score)** A credit score predicts specific future credit behaviour over a certain time frame, e.g., delinquency. Is solely based on credit bureau information; used for both customer acquisition and customer management decisions.

**Cross-Sell/Up-Sell** A customer management strategy, which involves selling multiple products or services offered by a single provider to a new or existing customer. Up-sell is a strategy which involves selling higher valued products or services to an existing customer.

**Cross-sell Ratio** Average number of products held by a customer or household.

**Cross Section Data** Refers to a snapshot view of the data.

**CSR** Customer Service Representative.

**Cumulative Distribution Function (CDF)** Also called the distribution function, it describes the probability that a variable X takes on a value less than or equal to a number x.

**Customer Centric** An approach whereby strategy, processes, and data are centered on the customer so that every part of the organization shares a common view of the customer.

**Customer Level** Refers to all accounts held by a customer at either a product level (e.g., checking and savings account) or across all products (e.g., deposits, personal loan and mortgage). It is usually defined at a product/service provider level.

**Customer Lifetime Value (CLV)** Present value of all future profits obtained from a customer over the life of his/her relationship with the firm. Readers can consult Blattberg et al. *Database Marketing* for details on specification/formulae.

**Customer Relationship Marketing (CRM)** Refers to the strategy, process, and technology that are used to create a lasting, one-to-one profitable relationship with customers and prospects.

**Customer Replacement Cost** One definition is the number of new customers required to replace an existing customer.

**Customized Pricing** Refers to the practice of segmenting the customer base and charging a different price (or sometimes a different pricing structure) for each segment.

**Data Warehouse and Data Mart** A subject-oriented, integrated, time-variant, and non-volatile collection of data in support of management's decision making process. A data mart is defined as a data warehouse which focuses on a specific subject (or a limited number of subjects) only.
**Debt Restructuring** A method used by companies with outstanding debt obligations to alter the terms of the debt agreements in order to achieve some advantage.
**Debt Service Ratio (DSR)** It is a measure of debt burden. An estimate of the ratio of debt payments to disposable personal income. Debt payments consist of the estimated required payments on outstanding mortgage and other consumer debt.
**Decision Analysis** A logical and systematic method to address a wide variety of problems involving decision making in an uncertain environment.
**Default** Failure to honour financial commitments.
**Delinquent** Unpaid or overdue debt. 30 refers to 30 days past due (DPD), 30+ refers to 30 and more days past due, 60 refers to 60 days past due etc. The definition of variable "BAD" is commonly based on delinquency status.
**Dependent Variable** Variable explained by changes in one or more independent variables. Also referred to as response, target or outcome variable. *Source:* Anderson *The Credit Scoring Toolkit.*
**Depreciation Costs** An expense item set up to express the diminishing life expectancy and value of an item.
**Design of Experiments** Structured and organised way of conducting and analysing controlled tests to evaluate the factors that are affecting a response variable.
**Discrete Choice Model** Describes decision maker's choices among a set of alternatives.
**Discrete Variable** Variable that has a countable number of distinct possible values, e.g., number of times delinquent.
**DPD** Days past due.
**Dynamic Pricing** The strategy of charging a different price to different customers based on their characteristics.
**Dynamic Programming** An optimisation approach that transforms a complex problem into a sequence of simpler problems; essential characteristic is the multistage nature of the optimisation procedure.
**EAD (Exposure at Default)** An estimate of the amount outstanding (drawn amounts plus likely future drawdowns of yet undrawn lines) in case the borrower defaults.
**EBIT (Earnings before Interest and Tax)** Business income net of provisioning and capital costs.
**Econometrics** Social science in which the tools of economic theory, mathematics, and statistical inference are applied to the analysis of economic phenomena. *Source:* Gujarati (2003).
**Economies of Scale** Reduction in cost per unit resulting from increased production, realized through operational efficiencies.
**Effective Interest Rate (EIR)** Interest revenue as a percentage of total balance.
**EMI (Equal Monthly Installment)** A fixed payment amount made by a borrower to a lender at a specified date each calendar month. Equated monthly installments are used to pay off both interest and principal each month, so that the loan is paid off in full over a specified number of years.
**Endogenous Variable** A factor in a causal model or a causal system whose value is determined by the states of other variables in the system.
**Estimate** Particular numerical value obtained by the estimator.

**Estimator** Rule or formula or method for estimating the population parameter from a given sample.
**Exogenous Variable** A factor in a causal model or causal system whose value is independent from the states of other variables in the system, i.e., it is a factor whose value is determined by factors or variables outside the causal system under study.
**Exponential Smoothing** General class of forecasting procedures that rely on simple updating equations to calculate forecasts. *Source:* Chatfield (2009).
**Extract Transform Loan (ETL)** Systems and processes that extract data from various source systems, clean the data, aggregate the data, and deliver the data to the data warehouse.
**F-statistic** Statistic to test whether two population variances are equal; to determine if a group of variables are jointly significant (statistically) in a regression model.
**Fuzzy Matching** Method that provides an improved ability to process word-based matching queries to find matching phrases or sentences.
**Gains Chart/Table** Visual aid for representing model performance (discriminatory power). Specifically, the ability of a model to separate the event (bad) and non-event (good).
**Game Theory** Formal study of decision making where several players must make choices that potentially affect the interests of other players.
**GCL (Gross Credit Loss)** Outstanding principal in write-off status.
**Generalized Linear Models (GLM)** Class of regression models that allows the generalisation of the linear regression approach to accommodate many types of dependent variables by specification of the link function.
**Genetic Algorithms** Class of robust and efficient search techniques based on the concept of adaptation in natural organisms. *Source:* Blattberg et al. (2008).
**Geo-Demographic Segmentation** Based on identifying demographically similar small geographical areas (zip code, election ward, parish, etc.). The basic theory behind geo-demographic segmentation rests in the old adage that "birds of a feather flock together".
**Geographic Information System (GIS)** System designed to capture, store, manipulate, analyse, manage, and present all types of geographical data.
**Gini Coefficient** A measure of separation usually used to assess income disparities; used to assess the discriminatory power of a binary choice model.
**Gross Margin** For non-financial industries gross margin is defined as the difference between revenue and the cost of goods sold as a percent of revenue. In financial services industries, gross margin is defined as total revenue (interest and fees) net of cost of funds and cost of credit loss, expressed as percentage of total revenue.
**Hazard Rate** Hazard rate at time "t" specifies the probability of the event or failure during "t" and "t+$\Delta$t", given that it has not occurred earlier.
**Highest Line (credit card)** The highest credit limit on competition credit cards; can also refer to the highest line on competition non credit card products.
**Hill Climbing Method** Local improvement procedure for nonlinear programming problems. Starts with an initial trial solution and at each iteration searches in the neighbourhood of the current trial solution to find a better trial solution. Process continues until no improved solution can be found in the neighbourhood of the current trial solution.
**Hurdle Rate** The required rate of return in a discounted cash flow analysis, above which an investment makes sense and below which it does not.
**Independent Variable** Refer to exogenous variable.

**Information Asymmetry** Differences in the quantity and quality of available information to parties involved in a transaction.

**Inquiries (credit bureau)** Records created in the credit bureau when a lender looks at a consumer's credit information. Credit inquiries are either "hard inquiries," as when a lender views a consumer's credit report in connection with an application for credit, or "soft inquiries" when a consumer's credit is checked for most other reasons. A soft inquiry does not have any impact on credit quality or credit scores.

**Installment Loan** A loan repaid with interest in equal periodic payments.

**Interaction Effect** The simultaneous effect of two or more independent variables on a dependent variable.

**Interchange Revenue** Revenue earned from purchase sales on credit/debit card.

**Internal/External** With reference to the book, internal refers to information relating to products offered by the firm. External refers to information on competitor products.

**Interval Scale** A scale or measurement such that the distance between any two adjacent units of measurement (or "intervals") is the same. However, interval scales do not have a "true zero" point. Therefore, statements about the ratio of values in an interval scale cannot be made. Examples are temperature scales and standardized tests.

**Key Performance Indicators (KPIs)** A set of metrics that are used to gauge the performance of a particular process or business.

**KS Statistic** Kolmogorov-Smirnov statistic is a measure of discriminatory power of a binary choice model. The KS statistic measures the maximum distance between the cumulative distributions of the two types of outcomes.

**Lapse** Non-payment of renewal premium in the case of insurance.

**LGD (Loss Given Default)** The percentage of exposure the bank might lose in case the borrower defaults. These losses are usually shown as a percentage of EAD, and depend, amongst others, on the type and amount of collateral as well as the type of borrower and the expected proceeds from the work-out of the assets.

**Lifecycle** Life cycle of the customer is defined as the different stages of the relationship between the firm and the customer. The customer life cycle starts with the acquisition of new customers followed by strategies of enhancing value of existing customers through usage enhancement and cross sell. It is also important, that customers do not end or reduce the depth of their relationship with the firm and hence managing attrition is yet another important aspect of customer life cycle management.

**Lifestage** A stage or phase in life-such as being single, independent and working, being a parent of young children, or being an 'empty nester' (those whose children have recently left home).

**Likelihood Ratio Test** Test statistic used to determine whether overall model fit is improved by relaxing one or more restrictions; usually used to test whether individual coefficients or linear combinations of coefficients are equal to specific values.

**Line** Refer to credit limit/credit line; Line utilisation is defined as total outstanding balance divided by credit limit. Bad utilisation is line utilisation on a loss incurring account.

**Linear Regression** Regression of a linear (i.e., straight-line) relationship between the dependent variable and independent variables, usually under the assumption of normally distributed errors.

**Link Analysis** Set of techniques for exploring associations among large number of objects of different types (including organizations, people and transactions).

**Loan on Card** An installment loan which is granted on the basis of the available credit limit of a credit card. These loans usually carry a lower interest rate compared to the rate charged on credit card balances.

**Logistic Regression** Regression method for a binary discrete choice model; to calculate the probability that one of the two possible binary outcomes will occur.

**Look-alike** To reflect a look-alike profile of a customer in relation to the event of interest, e.g., responder profile.

**Mail File** File consisting of customers selected for product offers which is further segregated into test and control groups.

**Margin-based Pricing** A pricing strategy which aims at setting price in such a way so as to deliver a minimum profit margin.

**Marginal Cost** Change in total costs resulting from a one unit change in output.

**Mark Down** Mark down refers to the discount that is offered on the base price, particularly for style goods like apparels.

**Market Basket Analysis (MBA)** A technique based on association rules that identifies frequently purchased baskets of goods and advocates different combinations of products to bundle.

**Marketing Efficiency** Lowering marketing costs, enhancing operational efficiency, and reducing customer churn are typical examples.

**Marketing Mix** Set of controllable marketing tools that a company uses to create a desired response in the targeted market. Set of these tools is generally referred to as the 4P's of marketing-Product, Price, Promotion and Place.

**Markov Chain** A stochastic process in which the probability of which state the customer moves to next depends only on the state he/she is in at present.

**Meta Data** Refers to information about data contained in a particular system or data warehouse. Meta data consists of data field definition, the meaning of special values, percentage of missing values, update frequency, calculation logic, and other details.

**MIS (Management Information Systems)** Provides information that organizations require to manage themselves efficiently and effectively, e.g., reports.

**MOB (Months on Book)** Number of months since account/customer has been with the product/service provider.

**Moral Hazard** The risk that the presence of a contract will affect the behaviour of one or more parties. The classic example is in the insurance industry, where coverage against a loss might increase the risk-taking behaviour of the insured.

**MOU (Minutes of Usage)** Minutes of usage per subscriber for a particular type of service. MOU = Total usage/average number of subscribers for the period.

**Multicollinearity** Statistical phenomenon in which two or more predictor variables in a multiple regression model are highly correlated.

**Multivariate** Referring to two or more variables. Bivariate refers to two variables.

**NCL (Net Credit Loss)** Gross credit loss (GCL) net of recoveries; often expressed as a percentage of average net receivables.

**NCM (Net Credit Margin)** Interest revenue net of cost of funds and cost of credit loss; often expressed as a percentage of average net receivables.

**Nearest Neighbour Technique** Simple but effective method of classification that identifies the category of unknown data point on the basis of its nearest neighbour whose class is already known. This is widely used in pattern recognition, text categorisation, object and event recognition.

**NIM (Net Interest Margin)** Interest revenue net of cost of funds; often expressed as a percentage of average net receivables.

**Nominal Scale** Scale of measurement used for discrete categorization. Does not require the use of numeric values or ordered ranking of categories by class. It simply requires unique identifiers to label each distinct category. Categories are mutually exclusive and collectively exhaustive. Example is region.

**NPV (Net Present Value )** Discounted value of future cash flows over a specified time frame.

**NRV (Net Relationship Value)** Monetary value of all relationships of a customer with a product/service provider.

**Null Hypothesis** In statistical inference, it is actually the hypothesis which is tested. It is often presented as being the nullification of the researcher's hypothesis.

**Numerical Continuous Variable** Quantitative variable that can take any value from a range.

**Numerical Discrete Variable** Quantitative variable that can take only certain specific values e.g., number of products purchased by a customer.

**Odds** Odds in favour of the event is defined as the ratio of the probability that the event will occur to the probability that it will not.

**Off-us** External information.

**On-us** Internal information.

**Online Analytic Processing (OLAP)** Online Analytical Processing (OLAP) is a set of methodologies that allows fast and flexible views of summarised data across various dimensions.

**Open to Buy** Available credit limit defined as credit limit minus outstanding balance on credit card.

**Optimisation** Technique to maximise or minimise an objective function without violating resource constraints.

**Ordered Variable** Measure of a variable that can be put into order, without being quantified and can be compared with equality and with greater than or less than. Example is classroom grades.

**Ordinal Scale** Measurement scale for relative ranking. Indicates a logical hierarchy and provides information on whether measurement varies in degree, but does not specifically quantify the magnitude between successive ranks. Example is socio-economic classification (SEC-A, SEC-B etc.).

**Ordinary Least Squares (OLS)** Regression method for estimating the unknown parameters in a linear regression model.

**Outlier** A data point that is distinctly separate from the rest of the data; an observation that is numerically distant from the rest of the data.

**Outranking Method** An alternative for solving complex choice problems with multiple criteria and multiple participants. Outranking indicates the degree of dominance of one alternative over another.

**Overage** Usage beyond the limits of the current pre- or post-paid plan subscribed by the customer.

**P&L** Profit and Loss. P&L statement lists all the revenue and cost items for a particular company, business, product line or portfolio.

**P-value** Probability of obtaining a test statistic, at least as extreme as the one that was actually observed, assuming that the null hypothesis is true. The smaller the p-value, the stronger is the evidence against the null hypothesis.

**Panel Data** Refers to observations over multiple time periods for the same firms or individuals.

**Parametric** Approach that requires assumptions relating to the statistical distribution of the underlying data.

**Parsimonious Model** Simple model in the sense it relies on relatively few assumptions and prevents the researcher from manipulating the model so that it over-fits the available data. Over-fit model is one that works well in a given situation but fails to make accurate out-of-sample predictions.

**Pattern Recognition** Pattern recognition can be defined as the categorisation of input data into identifiable classes via the extraction of significant features or attributes of the data. The field of pattern recognition employs a large variety of techniques including regression, clustering, genetic algorithms, principal component analysis, classification trees, and neural networks.

**Payment Ratio/Pay Ratio** The ratio of payment to total bill amount.

**Pivot Table** A dynamic table that facilitates interpretation of data in different ways. Pivot table reports are particularly useful for narrowing down a large data set or analyse relationships between data.

**Poisson Regression** Regression method used to model count data and assumes the response variable to have a Poisson distribution.

**Pre-approve** To approve before the usual procedures or formalities have taken place.

**Predictive Model** A statistical model to predict future behaviour. A model is a representation and a statistical model is one that is derived using statistical theory and methods.

**Predictor Variable** Independent variable used for predicting the dependent variable. Also termed as explanatory variable or regressor.

**Preferred Line (credit card)** Credit limit associated with the highest balance on competition credit cards. Can also refer to the same on competition non credit card products.

**Prepayment** Payment made by the borrower over and above the scheduled payment. If the additional payment pays off the entire balance, it is termed as "prepayment in full"; otherwise, it is a "partial prepayment".

**Prescreen** The process of pre-selecting a set of prospects or customers before making an offer. Usually the pre-screening is performed to exclude risky customers from a marketing campaign.

**Price Discrimination** Price discrimination refers to the strategy of charging different prices based on the customer's willingness to pay.

**Price Elasticity** A measure of the responsiveness of the quantity of a good to a change in its price.

**Prime** Good credit history.

**Principal Components Analysis/Factor Analysis** Principal component analysis attempts to analyse the structure in a data set, in order to define uncorrelated components that capture the variation in the data. Factor analysis defines factors that capture the variation in the data; assumes that relationships between variables are due to the effects of underlying factors and the observed correlations are the results of variables sharing common causes. *Source:* Moutinho and Hutcheson (2011).

**Probability Density Function (PDF)** Describes the probability that a variable X takes on a value equal to a number x. For a continuous distribution, it is defined as the derivative of the cumulative distribution function.

**Probit Model** Binary choice regression model with normality assumption.

**Product Centric** An approach whereby strategy, processes, and data are centered around the product.

**Promotion (price promotion)** Short term price reductions which are mostly used for consumer packaged goods. Promotions are mostly of three types: trade promotions, retail promotions, and consumer promotions (direct discounts to consumer).

**Prospect** A potential customer.
**Provision** A provision is an amount set aside for the probable but uncertain economic obligations of a firm.
**Public Record** In the credit bureau, it refers to information pertaining to law suits, legal notice, repossessions, and others which are obtained from public records like court, police, etc. Usually presence of public records is considered to be derogatory information.
**Purchase/Retail Sales** Value of purchase/retail transactions on a credit card.
**Qualitative Data** Information which does not present itself in numerical form and is descriptive. For example, gender, socio-economic status or religious preferences.
**Quantitative Data** Information that can be measured on a numerical scale. For example scores on achievement tests, number of hours of study, or weight.
**Random Forests** A collection of CART like trees following specific rules for tree growing, tree combination and self testing; data visualization for high dimensional data; anomaly, outlier and error detection; analysis of small sample data; explicit missing value imputation; and generation of strong (accurate) predictive models.
**Rank Ordering** Extent to which a predictive model can effectively rank observations by some measure. *Source:* Anderson (2007).
**Ratio Scale** Scale of measurement that consists not only of equidistant points but also has a meaningful zero point. The most sophisticated of scales as it incorporates all the characteristics of nominal, ordinal and interval scales. For example in the case of outstanding balance, if account-1 has a balance of $1,000 and account-2 has a balance of $2,000, then one can say that account-2 has twice the balance of account-1. In addition, one can also say that at an *absolute* scale account-2 has an outstanding of $2,000.
**Recommender Systems** An interactive intelligent system developed to give recommendations, which match customers' preferences.
**Redemption Rate** The percentage of distributed coupons, rebates or reward points that are used (redeemed) by consumers.
**Reference Price** Price level that the buyer has in mind for the particular product.
**Regression** Formal expression of a statistical relation between a single dependent (outcome or target) variable, and one or more independent (explanatory or predictor) variables.
**Reinstatement** Revival of a lapsed policy in the case of insurance.
**Relationship Based Pricing** A pricing strategy of offering a favorable price based on relationship/relationship value of the customer e.g., loyalty pricing based on customer tenure.
**Reservation Price** The highest price a buyer is willing to pay for goods or a service; or the lowest price at which a seller is willing to sell a good or service.
**Reserve** Reserve or loss reserve refers to the expected amount of loss that an insurer or lender is expected to incur over a specified time. Usually the loss reserve is included as a cost item in the profit and loss statement.
**Responder** A customer who has expressed interest in the offer. Also termed as lead generated by the campaign.
**Response Model** Statistical model that predicts the propensity to respond to an offer. Response score is the outcome.
**Response Rate** Response rate is calculated as number of responders (leads) divided by number of customers/prospects targeted.
**Revenue Management** Refer to Yield Management.
**Revenue Score** Score is used to predict the potential revenue of an account/customer over a specific time frame.

**Revolver** If a credit card customer pays less than the total bill amount.
**Revolve Rate/Ratio** Outstanding balance of all revolvers divided by the total outstanding balance.
**Revolving Balance** Outstanding balance which revolves or earns a finance charge. The total balance that is due from revolvers is also referred to as revolving balance.
**RFM** Recency, Frequency, and Monetary Value.
**Risk-based Pricing** The alignment of pricing of a credit product with borrower's credit risk.
**ROE (Return on Equity)** The amount of net income returned as a percentage of shareholders equity. Measure of how much profit a company generates with the money shareholders have invested.
ROE = Net Income/Shareholder's Equity.
**ROI (Return on Investment)** A performance measure used to evaluate the efficiency of an investment.
ROI = (Gain from Investment-Cost of Investment)/Cost of Investment.
**ROTA (Return on Total Assets)** A ratio that measures a company's earnings before interest and taxes (EBIT) against its total net assets. The ratio is considered an indicator of how effectively a company is using its assets to generate earnings before contractual obligations must be paid.
ROTA= EBIT/Total Net Assets.
**Rule Induction** Area of machine learning in which formal rules are extracted from a set of observations.
**Sales Active/Spend Active(credit card)** If purchase/retail sale or cash sale on a credit card. Sales activation rate is defined as the percentage of open credit card accounts that are sales active.
**Sample Selectivity** A type of bias caused by choosing non-random data for statistical analysis.
**Scale** Besides being described as either categorical or numerical, variables are labelled according to scale. Refer to interval, nominal, ordinal, and ratio scale.
**Score** A number that represents propensity, quality or performance.
**Scorecard** Regression model used as part of a rating process. *Source:* Anderson (2007)
**Secured Loan** A loan which is backed by collateral belonging to the borrower, in order to decrease risk for the lender.
**Securitisation** A pooled group of financial assets that together create a new security, which is then marketed and sold to investors.
**Self-activation** Account activation by the customer without any programme intervention by the product/service provider.
**Self-selection** Situation in which individuals select themselves into a group resulting in a biased sample.
**Sensitivity Analysis** Analysis to determine how different values of an independent variable will impact a particular dependent variable under a given set of assumptions.
**Share of Wallet (SOW)/Wallet Share** A marketing term referring to the amount of customer spend/balance that a business captures (by the products and services that it offers) in relation to its competitors.
**SKU (Stock Keeping Unit)** A distinct item, such as a product or service that is offered for sale. It embodies all attributes associated with the item which distinguishes it from all other items. For a product, these attributes include, but are not limited to, manufacturer, product description, material, size, color, packaging, and warranty terms.
**SME** Small and medium enterprise.

**Standard Error** The standard deviation of the sampling distribution of a statistic.
**Statement Active** If an account statement is going out to the customer.
**Statistical Significance/ Hypothesis testing** Procedure by which sample results are used to verify the truth or falsity of a hypothesis. Purpose is to make inferences about a population parameter, by analysing differences between observed sample statistics and the results one expects to obtain if some underlying assumption is true.
**Stochastic** Pertaining to a process involving a randomly determined sequence of observations, each of which is considered as a sample of one observation from a probability distribution.
**Stochastic Gradient Boosting** An iterative algorithm that combines simple classification rules with "mediocre" performance in terms of misclassification error rate to produce a highly accurate classification rule. Provides an enhancement, which incorporates a random mechanism at each boosting step showing an improvement in performance and speed in generating the ensemble.
**Stratified Random Sample** A method of sampling that involves the division of a population into smaller groups known as strata. The strata are formed based on members' shared attributes or characteristics. A random sample from each stratum is taken in a number proportional to the stratum's size when compared to the population. These subsets of the strata are then pooled to form a random sample.
**Straw-man Analysis** Data analysis to create profile of an ideal customer based on customer/other attributes.
**Sub-prime** With poor or very little credit history.
**Super-prime** Customer with excellent credit history. Often considered the best customer from a credit risk perspective.
**Supervised Learning** Methods that attempt to discover the relationship between the predictor (independent) variables and the target (dependent) variable.
**Support Vector Machines (SVM)** A classification and regression algorithm that uses machine learning theory to maximize predictive accuracy without overfitting the data. Uses an optional nonlinear transformation of the training data, followed by the search for regression equations in the transformed data to separate the classes (for categorical targets) or fit the target (for continuous targets).
**Survival Analysis/Model** Regression method for modelling dependent variable "time until an event".
**t-statistic** Statistic used for testing hypotheses about the mean of a small sample drawn from a normally distributed population when the population standard deviation is unknown.
**Target Variable** Refer to Dependent Variable.
**Test/Challenger** Group of customers who are tested for a particular treatment.
**Text Mining** Process of deriving meaningful information from text data such as email messages, web pages.
**Time Series Data** Sequence of observations ordered by time parameter. Time series may be measured continuously or discretely.
**Top-up Loan** A loan taken from a financial institution with whom the customer already has a loan. It is an extra loan that a lender allows for an existing customer that tops up an existing loan to a higher level.
**Trade (credit bureau)** Entry by a credit grantor to a consumer's credit history maintained by a credit reporting agency. A trade (or trade line) describes the consumer's account status and activity. Trade line information includes names of companies where the applicant has accounts, dates accounts were opened, credit limits, types of accounts, balances owed, and payment histories.

**Transactor** If a credit card customer pays the total bill amount.
**Trigger** Signal of event /change in customer behaviour.
**Type I/Type II Error** Prediction of a positive result that is incorrect (false positive); Prediction of a negative result that is incorrect (false negative). *Source:* Anderson (2007).
**Univariate** Referring to a single variable.
**Unsecured Loan** A loan that is issued and supported only by the borrower's credit-worthiness, rather than by a type of collateral.
**Unstructured Data** Usually refers to information that doesn't reside in a traditional row-column format. Unstructured data files often include text and multimedia content. Examples include e-mail messages, chat transcripts, word processing documents, videos, photos, audio files, presentations, webpages and similar data sources.
**Unsupervised Learning** Exploratory data analysis without a target (dependent) variable.
**Utilisation** Refer to Line Utilisation.
**Value at Risk** One of the most widespread models in use in most of risk management departments across the financial industry. Value-at-Risk (or VaR) calculates the worst expected loss over a given horizon at a given confidence level under normal market conditions. VaR estimates can be calculated for various types of risk: market, credit, operational, etc.
**Value Correlation Analysis** Refers to the methodology of identifying data quality issues through analysis of relationships between different data fields.
**Vintage** Refers to the month and year the account/customer was acquired.
**Wald Statistic** Wald statistic is a chi-square statistic calculated for variables in a regression model (e.g., logistic and survival model) to determine whether a variable should be removed based on significance testing.
**Write-off** Non-performing asset status on a credit product; amount of debt that is unlikely to be unrecoverable.
**Yield** Yield refers to the effective interest earnings on an asset portfolio divided by average net receivables. For a credit card portfolio, yield is defined as the annual percentage rate (APR) multiplied by the revolve rate.
**Yield Management** Process of allocating the right capacity or unit to the right customer at the right price and at the right time so as to maximise revenue or yield.

# Index

# About the Authors

**Sandhya Kuruganti** is a senior analytics leader with more than 18 years of experience in the financial services domain. As a management consultant, she currently advises companies in India in adopting data driven analytical strategies across various business functions.

Sandhya has been one of the evangelists who had pioneered the usage of decision sciences for analytics led business strategies within the Indian banking industry. In her previous roles she has held diverse leadership positions. As Senior Vice President, she was responsible for nurturing and leading the business analytics function for Citibank India and the analytics centre of excellence for Citibank Asia Pacific. Sandhya was at the forefront of Citibank's strategic drive for implementing analytical decision making across markets in Asia Pacific. She started her journey in analytics with American Express, New York where she was part of the risk management group.

Sandhya's thought leadership in developing advanced analytical solutions for customer life cycle management has been a key success factor for corporates that have leveraged her expertise in successfully embedding analytics in their business practices.

Sandhya holds a Masters degree in Economics from the Delhi School of Economics, India and a Doctorate in Economics from Rutgers University, US.

**Hindol Basu** has more than 12 years of experience in the area of risk and marketing analytics, mostly in the financial services industry. He currently heads the analytics consulting practice for FICO India. In this role he is responsible for analytical solution conceptualization, development and implementation for financial services companies in the Asia Pacific region. He had held leadership roles at Citibank where he was responsible for managing risk modelling for the US market.

Hindol possesses deep analytical expertise in the areas of price management, development of risk and marketing models, and credit bureau analytics. He was responsible for building the initial set of credit bureau solutions for the Indian credit bureau. Outside of the financial services industry, Hindol has also worked in the travel and entertainment, manufacturing and logistics industry.

Hindol holds a Bachelor degree in Engineering from the Indian Institute of Technology, Kharagpur and an MBA from the Indian Institute of Management, Bangalore.